Autobiography

John Cowper Powys

Books by John Cowper Powys

ALL OR NOTHING
ATLANTIS
THE BRAZEN HEAD
A GLASTONBURY ROMANCE
HOMER AND THE AETHER
THE INMATES
IN SPITE OF
LETTERS TO LOUIS WILKINSON, 1935–1956
LUCIFER
MAIDEN CASTLE
THE MEANING OF CULTURE
MORWYN
OWEN GLENDOWER
THE PLEASURES OF LITERATURE
PORIUS
RABELAIS
SELECTED POEMS
UP AND OUT
VISIONS AND REVISIONS
WEYMOUTH SANDS

John Cowper Powys
AUTOBIOGRAPHY

Introduction by
J. B. PRIESTLEY

A Note on Writing the Autobiography by
R. L. BLACKMORE

COLGATE UNIVERSITY PRESS

First published in Great Britain in 1934
First published in the United States by the Colgate University Press in 1968
Introduction © J.B. Priestly, 1967
This edition published by the Colgate University Press in 1994

Library of Congress Catalog Card Number: 68-11703
ISBN 0-912568-17-8

DEDICATED TO
MARY COWPER POWYS

Contents

Introduction

THE first sixty years of John Cowper Powys's life are described in this autobiography. To say anything about them here would be like turning on a tap before introducing people to Niagara Falls. But after he had finished this book he had still thirty more years to live, so a few facts here may be welcome. In 1934, having finished his autobiography, he left America—for the last time—and after a short stay in Dorset he settled in North Wales, first in Corwen and afterwards in Blaenau Ffestiniog. He died in June 1963 in his 91st year. During this last period, living very simply and economically, he still wrote copiously just as he still went out walking with a stout stick. And anybody who wishes to meet him in his old age should read *The Letters of John Cowper Powys to Louis Wilkinson: 1935–1956*, in which his vitality triumphantly sparkles and crackles and he seems to exist in a blazing Indian Summer.

Writers rarely pay tributes to publishers and their literary advisers. But this is what I shall do here. Admirers of John Cowper Powys are deeply indebted to Mr. Malcolm Elwin, the literary adviser, and to Messrs. Macdonald, the publishers. Without their enterprise and enthusiasm, Powys's later works might never have reached print. And our debt does not end there. What is more important still, this same publishing house is now offering us admirable reprints of earlier works, in some instances, where there had been cuts in the original issues, now restored to their author's proper text. It is to this enterprise, this enthusiasm, this recognition of Powys's stature, we owe this new edition of his great *Autobiography*.

A small group of us—not, however, taking any concerted action—had for years grasped every opportunity to declare in print or on the lecture platform that in John Cowper Powys we had a major writer, an original, a genius, who was being quite shockingly undervalued, often completely neglected. (And by the same Eng. Lit. critics who never stopped praising D. H. Lawrence, especially for his courageous and subtle appreciation of sexual relationships, in which, to my mind, he is inferior to Powys.) Though he lived to be 90, this lonely giant was never given any official recognition of his genius, his extraordinary contribution to contemporary English Literature. No Nobel Prize, no Order of Merit, came his way. He is not even given a British Council booklet to himself, but has to share the miserable 40 pages with his brothers, Theodore and Llewelyn, and indeed receives less attention and praise than the former. But while Theodore (T.F.) Powys is an original, he is a small original. John Cowper Powys is a great original. And now more and more readers are beginning to realise this.

For the past ten years or so we have suffered from an avalanche of autobiographies and memoirs by important public personages. (And not always their own unaided work.) These heavy volumes have offered us at least a glimpse of historic events and long lists, neatly indexed, of famous names. But though they have commanded so much space in the Sunday newspapers and the bookshops, I think it is doubtful if anybody except historians will ever read them again. And no autobiography could be further removed from them than Powys's life-story. It pays no attention to historic events. It contains no index of famous names. It is free from any suspicion of self-importance and portentousness. Its author is astonishingly frank about himself, confessing to all manner of aberrations and absurdities. And it is a book that can be read, with pleasure and profit, over and over again. It is in fact one of the greatest autobiographies in the English language. Even if Powys had never written any novels—and at least one of them, *A Glastonbury Romance,* is a masterpiece—this one book alone would have proved him to be a writer of genius.

Like all copious and large and broadly-based writers, what Van Wyck Brooks called *primary writers*, Powys is not without faults, weaknesses, absurdities. This is only to be expected. He is a great sprawling author, not a fastidious *petit maître*. After years of lecture platforms, both in Britain and later in America, where his deeply imaginative sympathy with the authors he most admired, his astonishing eloquence and sheer histrionic power together almost hypnotised his audiences, now and again in his writing he cannot help returning to an oratorical platform manner. He is too rhapsodical for cold print. The actor-lecturer in him ousts the author. Again, while more often than not he can capture and express the most subtle fleeting impressions, the merest wisps of feeling, there are times when he seems to be forcing himself and missing the mark, just indulging himself in fine writing. Again, in this autobiography, while he describes his friends both warmly and with notable insight, now and again we feel he goes on too long about them. ("And well I know him—bless him!" cried the lady who had been boring Lamb at dinner by her account of a friend. "Well, I don't," said Lamb. "But damn him—at a hazard!") Finally, there are a good many short passages here when, writing about himself, he is rather embarrassingly *arch*. It is as if the feminine side of him—and he has one, of course, like most men of genius— suddenly insists on revealing itself. I am making a distinction here between the feminine *side* and the feminine *depths*, without which a man could not be so triumphantly creative. But the feminine *side* is always inferior in its femininity : hence the kind of archness that all sensible women now avoid, just as they avoid the ultra-effeminate "camp" speech affected by a certain type of homosexual.

Such faults, however, are no more than occasional blemishes in a text of extraordinary richness, subtlety, power. Its secret, which may be discovered in his fiction too but is more obvious here, is this. Powys joins together two extremes while ignoring almost everything that lies between them. What is dropped out is the whole world, familiar to most of us, of business, politics, money-making and getting on, social life and fashion, everything we might say that finds its way into newspapers. It has gone; Powys has shrugged it away. (And here, I may add, as a man who has been sharply concerned with this world both in life and writing, I find its absence—for once—immensely refreshing.) He makes it plain, when describing himself as a young man, that he had "not the remotest interest" in his career, was entirely without ambition.

> . . . What is called ambition had no room or time to sprout. Ambitious people are forced—as one learns from reading their lives—to cut down rigidly upon their contemplative tendencies, to harden themselves *against* their momentary sensations. I *lived* for sensations; and have always, in my deepest heart regarded such a life as the only adequate return we can make to Nature for giving us birth!

We are here about as far from that busy world and its rat-races as we can go. But one odd and ironical fact is worth mentioning. It is notorious that the keenest rat-racers often suffer from stomach ulcers. Yet it was precisely such ulcers that plagued and tortured Powys during all his lecturing years, and he gives us some appalling accounts of his suffering.

What he says above about living "for sensations" helps me to explain what I meant when I declared that Powys joins together two extremes. At one end is his constant observation of minute details—moss on an old wall, a patch of lichen on a rock—of the natural scene, through which his greatest pleasure was to walk for hours and hours. At the other end or extreme is what is happening, during such walks, in the recesses of his inner world, only explored by people of his particular temperament. It is here that he discovers these "sensations", which have a peculiar magical effect just because they are associated with the mysterious depths of the inner world. This explains too his mania—which he describes at length and with unusual frankness—for staring at the ankles and knees of girls on Brighton beach or at the pantomime, his peculiar lust of the eye for sylph-like shapes, quite removed from ordinary male desire. He was enchanted by the magic of his own unconscious. He was under the spell of one of its archetypes, the anima.

If this brings us, as it does, to Jungian depth psychology, I shall make no apology. After all, Powys tells us himself that he vastly preferred Jung to Freud. Moreover, his peculiar temperament and outlook are far more easily explained in Jungian terms than in any others known to me. If curious readers will consult Jung's *Psychological Types*, they will discover in his general description of types one that he calls *The Introverted Sensation Type*. After they have made some allowance for what must be rough-and-ready in all such classification—for we are all too complicated to be neatly pigeonholed—they will find a great deal of John Cowper Powys in this particular type. Unfortunately I have space here only for one short quotation from Jung. Of the Introverted Sensation Type he notes among other things:

> Above all, his development estranges him from the reality of the object, handing him over to his subjective perceptions, which orientate his consciousness in accordance with an archaic reality, although his deficiency in comparative judgment keeps him wholly unaware of this fact. Actually he moves in a mythological world, where men, animals, railways, houses, rivers, and mountains appear partly as benevolent deities and partly as malevolent demons. . . .

And I am ready to maintain that much of this book seems at once strange and fascinating to us just because it exists in this peculiar atmosphere.

There is, of course, more to Powys than this. He was, after all, a well-educated man with strong intellectual interests and abilities. He was also rather more shrewd in worldly matters—as, for example, earning a living and paying his way—than he makes himself out to be. His account of himself as a zany, clown, idiot or innocent, is deliberately overdone. His literary achievement proves him to have been capable of unusual feats of concentration, creative zest, memory. (Thus it is extraordinary that this autobiography, recording so many minute details of his early life, could be written years afterwards in America.) Yet we might reasonably declare that the essence of him, what shapes and colours his temperament, can be found in this Introverted Sensation Type. Now it is plain from what he tells us more than once that he felt himself to be an oddity, just as most of his family and friends did. But what makes him an oddity—and a very valuable one too—is not that he belongs to this particular type but that, belonging to it, he has also his superb gift of expression. This gives him a unique value.

We can put it shortly like this. Most people who write well do not belong to this type. And most people who belong to this type cannot write at all. They have no wish to communicate the vague news from their inner worlds, their strange "sensations". They are men who prefer out-of-the-way places, odd solitary jobs, roaming the world on their own; they are the hermits, the close-mouthed wanderers, the inarticulate tramps. Most of them, I fear, will never read John Cowper Powys, and yet over and over again he is expressing what they have often thought and felt. We can say this of him then. He brings eloquent and often subtle expression to a type that has known very few spokesmen. And to the rest of us, belonging to very different types, he explains, with a wealth of illustration and meaning, these other people, solitary and brooding, we have never understood. And this alone justifies attributing to him and his work a unique value.

However, just because he is so deeply introverted, we can approach him from another direction. (As I did in an essay for the special Powys number of the *Literary Quarterly*, an essay reprinted later in *The Moments and other pieces*.) Because modern civilisation is so dangerously one-sided, so little concerned with man's inner world, so over-extraverted, our arts and artists, trying desperately to restore a balance, have become more and more introverted. Fashionable critical opinion has assumed for years now that all serious writers are introverts, writers who are extraverts being no more than entertainers. But writers need more than the admiration of a small *élite*. They cannot help wanting to be widely understood and appreciated, so all too often they have felt frustrated and rejected. Thus they have largely offered us a literature of darkness and despair. The unhappy introvert is a familiar figure in twentieth-century writing. Now John Cowper Powys is as deeply introverted, as passionately concerned with his own inner world, as any of the others, but instead of being an unhappy man he is a happy one. He had every reason not to be. Travelling for years from one lecture platform to another; not always knowing where the next engagement would come from; often in agony from his ulcers; living on bread-and-milk and weak tea; unable to find a time and place in which to write the books that were beginning to stir in his imagination; he ought to have been one of the most miserable of the literary introverts. But it is clear from this autobiography, though in it he spares us nothing, from spewing in the gutter to the maniac depths of his voyeurism, that in spite of all (and he came to write a book called *In Spite Of*) Crazy Jack Powys was a happy man. He enjoyed among other things this very craziness. ("Just as I saved myself from my worst suffering at Sherborne by pretending to be mad, it is possible to save yourself, *the other way round*, by pretending to be sane", as he tells us here.) In point of fact, though wilfully eccentric, Powys was always a good deal saner than most men, who cannot live their own lives as he always did. And as the happy introvert, he is again a great original.

Powys's younger brother, Llewelyn, himself an excellent writer, had an enormous admiration for the first half or so of the *Autobiography* but disliked the latter part of it, which he felt lacked the deep sincerity of the earlier chapters. There is some truth in this criticism. From where the American section begins, Powys is less concerned to describe exactly how things were with him, to deal sincerely with his past, than he is to give us a dazzling performance as his wilful eccentric self. But what might ruin a personal record for a brother does not necessarily spoil a book for a reader. And it seems to me that what we lose on the swings here, we gain on the roundabouts. The later chapters may be more of a self-indulgent showing-off performance, the lecture-platform manner may arrive too often, there may be too much deliberate heightening of prejudices and whims and fancies, but even so it is magnificent literary entertainment. Having brought us so far along the road, Powys can afford to dance a jig or two. Moreover, he offers us a great deal more than entertainment. The sudden sharp insights and the flashes of wisdom are there.

For example, they can be discovered all over the place in his account of America. And this, to my mind—and I am well acquainted with the American scene—is one of the most rewarding sections of his chronicle. He seems to me to *understand* America as few other non-American writers have ever done. What he likes and what he dislikes may seem equally surprising. His view of America and the Americans is entirely his own. I have marked scores of passages for possible quotation but must be content with this brief one, which does, however, give us both America and John Cowper Powys:

> American men are tragic without knowing they are tragic. They are tragic, by reason of the desolate thinness and forlorn narrowness of their sensual and mystical contacts. Mysticism and sensuality are the things that most of all redeem life. Let the workers march to triumph, singing the International. But when you *have* marched, when you *have* reorganised society, when you *have* given the people bread and the circus, the question comes, *what next?* It is then that we want to commune with angels and demons; it is then that we want to worship the elements; it is then that we want to return to the imaginative and poetic life that Science has for so long been destroying.

And that was written thirty-odd years ago, long before the affluent society began to discover great holes in its fabric and heard the songs and cries of rebellious youth.

Both before and after the *Autobiography* Powys wrote

books directly advocating the outlook and style of life he had long adopted himself. They are worth reading but he seems to me a far better advocate of his basic type and the life of introverted sensation in this long rich account of his life, in which, making use of an astounding memory, he recaptures the finest shades of feeling while at the same time creating out of himself a gigantic half-comic character— a clown, as he often calls himself, but a wise clown, a huge younger brother of Feste or Lear's Fool. And now I propose a test, chiefly as an excuse to bring in one of my favourite quotations from this book or indeed from any book. After describing an old friend here, Powys continues: "He combined scepticism of everything with credulity about everything; and I am convinced this is the true Shakespearean way wherewith to take life." If this seems sheer nonsense to you, reader (and it isn't), then stop here, read no more. But if it begins to have a glimmering of sense (and it has lots), then read on and on. You will have a wonderful time.

J. B. Priestley

Writing the Autobiography

MIDSUMMER of 1933 was intensely dry and hot in Columbia County, one hundred miles north of New York City, where John Cowper Powys had been living and writing for the four years since retiring from the American lecture circuit. The stream just beyond the unpaved country road in front of his small white clapboard cottage was but a dry-cracked bed of clay and gravel, with sporadic pools where trapped fish swam; each morning Powys netted minnows from shallow places that threatened to dry up completely, and carried them to deeper pools. The game warden from the village of Philmont came to investigate rumours of trout poaching, and stayed to watch the sixty-year-old, long-haired author trudge down the hard creek bed with a few fingerlings in his pail—a Noah seeking water. Afternoon heat had driven him from the low attic-room where he usually wrote, but Powys was a persevering writer, as his letters to his sister Marian so often reveal:

> Yesterday Saturday (St. Mary Magdalene's) I posted *Weymouth Sands* off, insured for $100, to the Inner Sanctum [Simon and Schuster]. This stir about *A Glastonbury Romance* in England will make them more ready to accept it I hope without any cuts! D.V. D.V. D.V. I've now got to write a new preface for Cape's English edition of *Solitude* which he is bringing out this fall. . . . When I have finished this preface and caught up with a whole Drawer full of letters needing answers, I am going to seriously consider my next work, though this extreme heat is enough to melt one's brains and I had got jumpy, irritable, and very highly *pitched* over that hard piece of work finishing *Weymouth*. I am meditating what ought to be an exciting book

to write, namely a sort of original mental *autobiography* not an *ordinary* autobiography but a very queer one *such as has never been writ before*! I have many thrilling notions for it and wonderful tricks and devices by means of which I shall not only avoid hurting feelings whether of the dead or living but steer clear of *any risk* of such a thing; *and yet* catch the salient and *curious* points in my own mental and moral and spiritual pilgrimage . . . Our brook is dry and this rescuing of fish is a burden, not only when I'm doing it, but on conscience when I'm not.

Nine days later, on July 31, a letter to his sister at her Devonshire Lace Shop in New York City (Marion Powys Grey later became Consultant on Lace to the New York Metropolitan Museum) tells of "the heat yesterday—the worst we have had," and reports that he is still "pondering on my next book which is going to be (I think) some fantastic kind of a mad and never thought of before type of Autobiography— totally different from all the Autobiographies in Existence."

Then the heat wave broke, and on August 14th, 1933, he wrote:

Marian Dearest,

I see there's a letter from you but I shall write this all the same ere I open it *after tea*—before wh hour I never (with rigid ordinance and routine) touch "my mail."

I am back again in my Attic. I can hear scarcely a sound to disturb me! A car passes—is gone—the crows call—the rain falls—the katydids make their noise, even while it is raining and at night—and I have decided that tomorrow I shall begin on the Feast of the Assumption of the Virgin my new Book— which is my Autobiography. This book will be written on a very singular method. It will *contain No Women at all*—not even my Mother. It is thus very appropriate that I begin it on the day of the *Assumption* of the Mother of God!

Nor will it deal very much with Men either or with boys and of such of them as I mention they will only be pleased by what I shall say. Thus neither the Living nor the Dead will be disturbed or fretted or in the remotest degree hurt by John's Autobiography! No—no mention of any women and damned little of any men. It will not have very much about myself— except in so far as my experiences sensations ideas feelings over-tones, sins, vices, weaknesses, manias, recoveries, books, places, pictures, scenes, surroundings lend themselves to a sort of Faustian Pilgrimage of the Soul—or a sort of Goethean Pilgrim's Progress towards the City of God! So it will be somewhat unique among autobiographies—and extremely different from Rousseau's Confessions! It will be amusing however to read and not stilted and tiresomely ideal—you do not need to fear that. It will be a sort of *Prose Faust*—if I may use so grandiose a comparison and I may to *you* who know my humble pride and proud humility thro' and thro'.

Nine months and one week later, John Cowper Powys delivered the *Autobiography* to his publishers. The 1250-page holograph—owned now by Colgate University, a gift from Norman H. Strouse—shows legible ink handwriting that seems to belie the manuscript's bulk and the speed of its composition. But even in the final weeks before his return to Britain—weeks when he was busy arranging passage, selling his Phudd Bottom cottage, and writing the last section—he was meticulous about revisions, as the average of forty words deleted on each page shows. "Well I am slowly revising and very *carefully* (so you may be satisfied) these chapters of my Autobiography that I keep writing at such amazing lightning speed." And another letter tells Marian, "fear thee not. I am revising it word by word—after each chapter. I take as long revising as I do writing so it won't be full of ! ! ! ! ! as was *Visions and Revisions*." Powys cancelled phrases and paragraphs with a heavy circular stroke that makes retrieval of his first thoughts an eye-pulling task, but, as anyone who has read more than a few pages into this "frankest of autobiographies" must suspect, he concealed no attitudes, softened no opinions. Most changes are stylistic or structural—finding a sturdier phrase or transferring an incident to a later section. Only on rare occasions did Powys forget that there were to be *No Women at all*—"the only reticence" that he had predetermined in the Dedication: early in Chapter Two he began to write of his "father's mother," then replaced those words with "our aged relative."

His last American letter to his sister carries a May 23rd, 1934, postmark:

Dearest Marian,

Such shocks and changes! The Berengaria's sailing was *cancelled* suddenly! Had she sprung a Leak? Now we are going on the Westernland starting, I think in the afternoon, on the 1st of June. A Friday but can't be helped. *Absit Omen!* . . . I'll come in late on Monday and stay *that* night with Arnold [Shaw]; then on Tuesday go to Bank, office, etc etc: etc etc! and come out to you in the country on Tuesday afternoon and stay with you there till Thursday and come in to town with you on Thursday morning—so we'll have the whole of 2 nights together and all Wednesday out there! . . . We have been having a *distracted* time—One night Phyllis didn't go to bed at all [Phyllis Playter was typing the manuscript] and I sat up—even I—till one working to get my Book done. I shall take it to them on Tuesday!

The letter sent to Marian Powys Grey on June 11th, after arriving in his homeland, shows a heavily underscored date line—*Monday Morning*—and carries this closing line: "I heard the Cuckoo from the ship from the shore at the mouth of Southampton water." He relaxed during the summer— "months of comparative idleness such as I have not had for years and years!"—but by the time the *Autobiography* came out in London during the week of his sixty-second birthday— October 8th—his letters to Marian disclose that John Cowper Powys was thinking about the outlines of *Maiden Castle* and starting to write *The Art of Happiness*.

1967   R. L. Blackmore

Autobiography

John Cowper Powys

Chapter One

Shirley

THE part of Derbyshire which centres round the Peak is like the boss of a shield. Dovedale must be included in the circumference of this Omphalos of England; and with some largess of extension, like the elaborate margin of a Homeric shield, the little pastoral villages around the country-town of Ashbourne might be regarded as coming into this formidable circle.

Swift and furious are the waters of the Dove; and rough and wild are the rocks and shallows, the rapids and the falls over which its rain-swollen torrents run. The steep and very often cavernous precipices that mount up on both sides of this swift stream, a stream that might be compared to a falcon in dove's feathers, arrive at a greater measure of the tremendous and the awe-inspiring than the comparatively confined limits of this particular stretch of scenery might at first glance have seemed to imply.

At any rate to the eyes of a small child the rocky valley of the Dove was nothing short of a *Tremendum Mysterium*. One of my earliest memories was the dim feeling of *immensity* produced by that grassy hill—to my mind now, for I have not seen it for more than fifty years, resembling a conical tumulus —which rose, and I presume rises still, in the neighbourhood of Dovedale. How magically sagacious is childhood in its power of arriving at boundless effects through insignificant means! For though this eminence—and its name was Mount Cloud—can certainly have been no towering Alp it will always remain to me synonymous with sublimity. Many aspects of children's days are silly enough; but how often the whole course of our subsequent history becomes an attempt to regain this sorcery, this power of finding the infinitely great in the materially small!

Since the overwhelmingly larger number of the things that come back to me from those early years are shameful, destructive, and grotesque, I am inclined to make the utmost of the one solitary constructive activity I can remember, which was a passion for erecting, at the edge of the shrubbery by the drive, numerous replicas of "Mount Cloud," composed of damp earth-mould covered over with moss.

It is a criminal blunder of our maturer years that we so tamely, and without frantic and habitual struggles to retain it, allow *the ecstasy of the unbounded* to slip away out of our lives. Another idolatrous fetish that became a medium for an oceanic in-pouring of this "unbounded" and has left an even greater dent in my mind than the construction of all those microcosmic "Mount Clouds" was a wooden axe made for me by my father out of the trunk of an ancient laurel-bush. Well do I remember the cutting of those laurels from which this enchanter's weapon fell into my hands. I had been absorbed all the morning in the most wicked pleasure then known to me, although not the wickedest *possible* to me, of transferring tadpoles from the pond in the field to the puddles left by the rain at the side of the drive. Now my father always followed, in all moral and casuistical problems, certain primitive rules that had descended to him from *his* father: such as, for instance, when you took birds' eggs out of a nest, to add to your collection, *always to leave two;* or when you caught a fish with a hook never to let it remain flapping and gasping on the bank, but always *to put it out of its misery.*

But that an offspring of his should derive God knows what perverse satisfaction from taking the inhabitants—luckily tadpoles were all the little boy could catch—of a dark, cool, deep pond and placing them in shallow puddles, was something so outside his experience that he had no mandate on the matter. It was therefore the merest coincidence that by noon that day, when he had so strewn the paths of the little spinney at the end of the garden with cloven laurel-boughs that a sweet savour of aromatic wood, in this cruel hewing and wounding, was carried across the lawn, my father should have been moved by a natural desire that his son should behold these deeds of devastation and glory in his begetter's skill and strength.

Thus the tall figure of the Vicar of Shirley, in black trousers and grey flannel shirt-sleeves, might have been seen that day dragging his protesting son away from his puddle-colonies and conveying him by force to his own devastated spinney. Oh, how hard it is to live in Arcadia and not meddle with *some* species or other of autochthonous aboriginals! But aye! that axe of laurel, whose blade and handle were both of the same sweet-smelling wood, and from whose whole entity emanated such a glamour of fairy-story enchantment, that long after, when I was a boy with catapult, butterfly-net and fishing-rod, it often used to come over me that I had lost—for ever and for ever lost—a mystery that would have guarded me all my days. To get back that laurel-axe from that garden spinney at Shirley would now be to get back the full magic power of that timeless fetish-worship by the strength of which the quaintest, most ordinary object—a tree-stump, a pile of stones, a pool by the roadside, an ancient chimney-stack—can become an Ark of the Covenant, evocative of the music of the spheres!

The country immediately round Shirley was pastoral and undulating, not wild or terrific like that Vale of the Dove. At the same time it was as far removed from any influence of town or city as if it had been "among the furthest Hebrides." The little village of Shirley was reached by a narrow lane leading due East, if I am not mistaken, out of the broad highway that ran between Ashbourne and Derby, and it lay, so I have always imagined, just about the point where Charles Stuart's army of picturesque rebels turned back to Scotland, back to their lamentable defeat at Culloden, in place of advancing boldly upon London.

Between the Derby Road and the Vicarage drive-gate, for our house was the first human dwelling reached by this lane, grew a tall pine-tree, one of the sort which my father was in the habit of teaching us to call "Scotch Firs." Near this tree, which offered an appropriate objective to many a nursery walk, was a small stile, leading by a short-cut across the fields to the historic highway, as it swept on, where the Highlanders had relucted to follow it, towards the valley-built town of Ashbourne.

Our house itself, as I recall it now, was a square whitish-yellow building surrounded by shrubberies and closely-mown grass. It was comfortable, rather than pretentious, but in the light of later acquired feelings about such contrasts, it was an absurdly big place to house a man in, even a man who was the father, as he became before we left, of five children—considering that the village, of which he was the parish priest, never in his time exceeded two hundred souls.

Since I was born here, and lived here till I was seven, it is singular that I have absolutely no recollection of the parish church. As far as my memory goes my father might have been a tall, powerful man in black clothes who did nothing but trim laurel-bushes, traverse hills, valleys, woods, lanes, spinneys, copses, at an incredible speed, and tell my two brothers and me, as we sat beside him after tea on the dining-room sofa, an interminable story about two mythic personages called Giant Grumble and Fairy Sprightly. All I can remember now of this never-completed tale was that its villain, the devil of the piece, was always a scientific pedant, called by the narrator "*the Professor*," whose sinister activities required all the arts of both Giant and Fairy to circumvent and neutralize.

But although my father's labours as a parish priest and indeed every image connected with the little grey church in the midst of the village about half a mile away have been completely obliterated by time, the lineaments of the man himself come back to me as vividly from that early time as they do from all the later periods of my life. Enormous emotional and magnetic explosiveness, held rigidly under an almost military control, was the most characteristic thing that emanated from Charles Francis Powys. Born at Stalbridge Rectory in Dorset he had imbibed from his Wessex childhood certain West Country words and intonations which he would occasionally make use of, not so much in moments of excitement as upon occasions when solemn or poetical issues were involved. The greatness of my father as a personality was first manifested to me not as a priest, not even as a trimmer of laurels, but as the possessor of boots *with enormously thick soles*. If I could capture now the real significance of the soles of my father's boots I should be master of one of the great clues to the secret of the cosmos. Was it purely a matter of the wonder of contrasted size—the difference between the thickness of *my* boots and those of my father—that so enraptured me? No, there was something else! Those great boot-soles as I saw them in a row in a little back room near the kitchen must, I really believe, have become significant to me, in that mysterious way in which all through my life certain inanimate objects have become significant, by gathering into themselves that element in life that might be called *inscrutable ecstasy*.

Even when I think of my father's boot-soles in *these* days, when I am nearly thirty years older than *he* was then, I am conscious of some wonderful secret of happiness. This secret I have clutched at again and again, but always just missed it. Is it some very ancient magical formula that revives in me? Is it some subconscious awareness of all the Derbyshire mud and Derbyshire moss and grass and rubble that those thick soles had trodden upon? No! The stimulus that my imagination drew from my father's boot-soles, the thrill of psychic release and mysterious joy that I experience even now when I think of them in a certain way, have nothing in the least to do with what the man stepped on as he walked over hill and dale. They have to do, these feelings, with that under-tide of life-reaction which by degrees reveals, to a mind that learns to watch for its revelations, a secret of awareness which cannot be overrated. The fact that they *were* boot-soles, and their *raison d'être* the pressure of the earth under the legs of a man of my father's volcanic intensity of earth-feeling, is doubtless a significant symbol, but it by no means explains this singular childish emotion nor the yet more mysterious sense of something "far more deeply interfused" which still tantalizes me in regard to it.

My earliest impulses of a morbid or anti-social kind must belong to my third year of life upon this freak-bearing planet. I recollect very clearly the panic I felt when, playing the role of a hangman with the great bell-rope—I suppose it originally was used to summon people from garden or stable—that hung in the passage at the top of the stairs, I remarked that my brother Littleton's face had suddenly assumed a swollen and purple aspect. My screams brought assistance quickly enough and no doubt I was soundly slapped; but it is the terror of *having gone too far in a life-and-death game* that remained in my mind. The punishment left no memory.

My father must have been totally devoid of the least trace of sadism—that aberration of which I was doomed as I grew older to become so fatally familiar—for the only way he ever punished us, me and my two brothers, was by suddenly and without a second's warning, giving us one single rather violent box on the ear, the kind of blow that the Dorset labourers in his own childhood would have described as "a clip over the ear-hole."

That there is a vast chaotic element in life must be admitted, and that one of the most powerful among the Immortals who preside over our fortunes is the great Goddess Chance cannot be denied, but there is also a curious pressure among the experiences that befall us, experiences that our character moulds in their occasion, which, for all this play of Chance, has an underlying tendency, a verifiable direction, a motion, a drive, through all the twists and turns of accident, towards some implied fulfilment in accordance with some deeply-involved entelechy.

In the light of what I am now at sixty, taking this ambiguous "what I am" as an entirely subjective vision—for who with all his efforts can see himself objectively—such a destined direction, steered by the interior life-urge in its moulding of circumstance, takes the form of a half-conscious self-creation. And what shape, as I regard myself now, myself and what I have come to call my life-illusion, does this character-destiny assume? Unless all my self-analysis is superficial it assumes the shape of a compound, less self-contradictory than it used to be, but not even yet entirely harmonized, of five rather discordant elements. I will name them in the order in which, at the present moment, I feel them to be more or less dominant. They resolve themselves into—a desire to enjoy the Cosmos, a desire to appease my Conscience, a desire to play the part of a Magician, a desire to play the part of a Helper, and finally a desire to satisfy my Viciousness.

Now it is clear that among the other four only the Magician-wish really lent itself, and that not altogether, to an enjoyment, half-mystical and half-sensual, of this bewildering Universe. For by degrees I discovered that the *kind* of enjoyment of life I wanted was what might be called an *imaginative sensuality*, a sensuality that required for its satisfaction a fluctuating margin of vague memory, of memory that, as I was dimly aware of it, seemed to recede, if I may say so, into the human lives that went before me, lives that had experienced the same feelings I was experiencing, only in an unrealizable past. Now it will be clear, I think, that the desire to be a Magician, that is to say to exercise a certain supernatural control over my destiny and that of others, did not completely coincide with the pure, unadulterated enjoyment of sensuous feelings surrounded by an aura of obscure memories. Sometimes it coincided with the cult of such feelings; but sometimes, especially in hard times, it derived an independent pleasure of its own from a certain attitude of formidable and stoical endurance. And if the rôle of a Magician—with its implication of personal pride—did not always harmonize with the imaginative sensuality that was my dominant urge, the remaining elements fell often into disturbing conflict with it.

Conscience for instance! I cannot remember a time when Conscience was not a trouble to me, ordering me to do what I didn't want to do and to refrain from doing what I wanted to do. In fact it may be said at once that the grand struggle of my life has been between my Conscience and my impulse to live a life made up solely and entirely of sensual-mystical sensations.

I indicate my desire to play the part of a Helper as something distinct from Conscience, not only because it has often happened that this desire has conflicted with the more humdrum mandates of Conscience, but because it would undoubtedly have been strongly operative in me—by reason of those imaginative nerves which compel us to identify our own feelings with those of an alien existence, human or otherwise —even had I no Conscience at all.

Clearest of all, I fancy, to understand is the difficulty I have had in harmonizing my Viciousness with a life of sensuous contemplation. It is unfortunately evident enough that any sort of Viciousness, by the mere fact of its insatiable exclusiveness and savage intensity, militates against any subtler, more continuous, more comprehensive form of happiness.

Without any question, from earliest childhood up to the present hour, my dominant vice has been the most dangerous of all vices. I refer to Sadism. I cannot remember a time—so early did this tendency show itself—when sadistic thoughts and images did not disturb and intoxicate me. One of my picture-books, when I could not have been more than three years old, contained a picture of an eagle seizing upon a lamb; and from the age of three, that is to say from the year 1875— for I was born in 1872—till about the year 1922, when I was fifty, this deadly vice transported and obsessed me. As a boy and as a young man it had greediness for its rival, and much longer than that it had a more normal, though never altogether normal, attraction to young women as its companion-vice; but it was not till I was fifty, and that date remains very clear in my mind, that I entirely overcame it. By "overcoming" it I mean never allowing myself to derive pleasure even for a moment in those sadistic thoughts which were my bosom-houris, the attendants at my pillow, for nearly half a century!

For the last ten years my Conscience—finding no doubt the temptation more within its power to resist—has been so rigid with me that it has compelled me even to skip those passages in modern books, and they are many, which play upon the sadistic nerve. I doubt if there is any reader of books in England or America with a more infallible wand than I for detecting the various degrees of sadism in a writer. I could name authors who deliberately indulge themselves in it—and I can catch the precise quiver of the evil nerve as they do so —whereas in Dostoievsky to whom it was obviously a temptation but who, as obviously, completely conquered it, every single trace of it in his books—not excluding "Stavrogin's Confession," deleted from *The Possessed*—has been sublimated and purified by the power of the spirit.

Whatever tricks I may play with my Conscience in other matters, in this matter—just because it *is* my dominant temptation—I am as honest as the most exacting and super-subtle casuist. I am *more* than moral in my avoidance of the thing. Even the faintest projection of sadistic pleasure in reading or in writing—not to speak of thinking—is nipped, and nipped rigidly in the bud. In fact it is nipped in its embryo protoplasm, much earlier than any bud! My Conscience in this particular has indeed become so powerful that it has habituated my consciousness to act automatically, until all sadistic situations —that is to say where the practise of cruelty has any "ricochet" of voluptuousness—are mentally expurgated, so to speak, in advance! This does not—any more than with Dostoievsky— mean that I am not "allowed" to write of sadists. What I am not "allowed," is to write of sadists in such a way as to give to myself, *and to other sadists* this ambiguous thrill.

There is not one flicker, for instance, of this ambiguous thrill to be derived from *A Glastonbury Romance;* and yet in this book I describe in detail the pathology of a well-nigh hopeless sadist. But I achieve this—and with infinite care— without once striking the sensitive responsive chord. So inflexible is my Conscience in this matter that I would ten thousand times sooner spoil the "art" of a book by keeping this deadly shiver out of it altogether than run the risk of providing fuel for this sinister flame. In this point I am in complete agreement—and I think Dostoievsky would be too —with the old ladies of the lending-libraries who think that certain modern books come straight from the Devil. The old ladies are not in error. That *is* precisely whence they come! But except for Dante—where I *do* detect it—how few of the really great writers have the remotest trace of it! None in Homer, in Aristophanes, in Aeschylus, Sophocles, Euripides. None in Rabelais, in Montaigne, in Shakespeare, in Cervantes, in Goethe. But the truth of the matter is the general public can be fed with this sweet poison, and enjoy it too, without having

c

the remotest idea as to the devil's-dam-dugs from which the sweetness comes.

One curious and interesting thing about my moral history is this, that throughout all the fifty years I gave myself up to the pleasure of sadistic thoughts I was intermittently struggling against perfectly legitimate and perfectly commendable sensuality. Since I grew to be fifty I have totally emancipated myself from the unfortunate notion that sensual pleasure *as such*, or sex pleasure *as such*, is wrong and I think that if in my youth I had had more completely free love affairs this peculiar viciousness would have had far less influence over me. I don't say it would not have always been a tendency of mine, for it is quite clearly an inalienable fatality of my nature, but I have always found that by far the best alleviation of my kind of cerebral sadism was to absorb myself in more normal sensuality.

It is therefore a curious thing that while my Conscience—in this matter I think in complete error—forced me to struggle against all sex-pleasure as essentially evil, I was constantly indulging in sadistic thoughts; whereas, when I stopped allowing myself the least flicker of a sadistic thought, I became convinced that every kind of sensual thrill that did not imply cruelty was wholly and entirely justifiable. And that is where I stand to-day. It is not that I ever practised—no! not in the smallest degree—the sadistic actions that I was always thinking about and telling myself stories about. I shall have occasion presently to confess in detail practically every one of my sadistic acts; for they all occurred in my boyhood and they could all be counted on the fingers of my two hands, possibly on those of one hand. No, it is in my thoughts that I have devoured—to dark ecstasy after dark ecstasy—this sweet, abominable Dead-Sea fruit.

"But to whom does that do any harm?"

I will tell you, my cynical friend. You may, if you please, be as uncompromising a believer in destruction and futility as you like, you must nevertheless admit that from any intense and concentrated cult continued night after night and year after year with intense absorption over a long period of time there must emanate magnetic vibrations of some sort permeating the surrounding air and leaving an evil impress that only gradually dies away. Thoughts, as Paracelsus taught, when they are visualized and brooded on for a long while, *tend to become entities.*

A person with a severe Conscience like mine, and a mind like mine, far too sceptical to be fooled by the dogmas of modern science, naturally relucts at the idea of creating elementals of cruelty and letting them loose on the air.

It is strange to me that I should have lived at Shirley till I was seven, and yet can retain so few recollections of my life during that time. I remember there was some sort of a summer-house in the garden in our day and I recall how once I made a hell-broth in a rusty iron cauldron in this secluded place, mixing in among other ingredients—none of which were as sinister as those mentioned in Macbeth—a little of the urine of both of us. If the most disgusting thing I ever did, or the most resembling the arts of Black Magic, was to mingle my urine in a cauldron with that of my brother Littleton, I have not incurred any very heavy retribution from "the spirits that tend on mortal thoughts"; but it is evident to me that though pushed on to break the routine of decency by mixing my urine with my brother's I had a reaction against the whole episode; for as it comes back to me now I am conscious of a sort of queer puckering in my mouth and a movement of saliva from one part of it to another which is a sign of a faint "rising of the gorge."

Our uncle Littleton, my father's elder brother who was a captain in the army, came to stay with us at Shirley, a dignified, bearded man, with a square forehead. Our notion was that being a soldier he was necessarily braver than other men— braver for instance than Heber Dale, the postman, who was a hydrocephalic dwarf, braver even than "Stephen," the gardener, who with my father's help cut and carried the heavy Derbyshire hay in the glebe-field. I recollect well the vicious pleasure I got when seated on his knee in the evening, he permitted me to pound his bearded face with my fists to test the courage of this officer of the Queen.

No, I can remember nothing of the church at the foot of

the hill; but of the narrow lane between high hedges leading down to the church I recall to this day, and it is one of my vividest memories, the exultation that poured through me like quicksilver, when walking once a little ahead of the perambulator, which carried my brother Littleton, I turned to the nurse-maid who was pushing it and announced triumphantly that I was "the Lord of Hosts." A still earlier articulate speech of mine, uttered before I experienced what it felt like to be "the Lord of Hosts," fell from my lips in our day-nursery, as I sat in my high chair with my brother opposite me and Theodore—the baby then—on the nurse's lap, had to do with the respective sizes of two crumbs of bread to which I called the attention of the world, indicating that the large crumb was myself and the smaller one Littleton. Thus did the Principle of Relativity present itself to my intelligence.

It can, however, be well believed by any reader who can divine what opposite pole of emotion awaited the swing of a pendulum that could tilt as high as mine did that day in the lane, what an abyss of humiliating terror such an infant was challenging. Most children, as Dickens is always reminding us, are liable to appalling secret terrors. My whole life—yes! up to this very day, when in my hiding-place in the New York hills I recall these things!—has been one long struggle with Fear, self-created fantastical Fear. The shape which this Fear took in those Shirley days was one that has recurred, humorously enough, since I have lived in America, though from the age of seven to the age of fifty I have pretty well escaped it. I mean fear of the police. We had been taken to a private lake in the middle of Osmaston Park, a grand estate which was at that time passing into new hands; and after our picnic in this secluded spot I had flung into the water a considerable-sized dead branch! Oh! how that unfortunate branch—no more really than an old rotten stick—came to torture my mind! One of the grown-up persons of our small picnic party uttered, as foolish grown-up people will, the senseless remark that Johnny had better look out. The police would have him for throwing things into the pretty lake! Alas, poor Johnny! He not only "looked out," but he looked round, night after night, after night, from his cot opposite Littleton's cot, thinking to himself:

"They'll come for me. They'll come and take me away."

And such is, as always, the nature of Fear—that Proteus of a million masks—that not a word durst Johnny breathe of all this to a living mortal. Does any "immortal" ear ever listen to the heart's cry, to the wordless heart's-pulse cry, of the human soul cherishing in its bosom a Fear it must not reveal? It requires faith to believe it! Certainly when Bishop Ken's beautiful evening hymn . . . "Keep me, O keep me, King of Kings, beneath Thine own almighty wings" . . . was recited over my pillowed head, it brought only a temporary relief from that dark unrevealed, unspoken terror.

Well! Such is the nature of mortal life upon earth. Few of us but have, hidden away deep down in our nerves, some secret Fear which we are not "allowed" to speak of, even to our dearest. I suppose there *have* been cures by these ambiguous and dangerous psychoanalytical methods; but for myself I am inclined to think that it is better "to leave well," though it is not exactly well, "alone." It is certainly alone we are, and must ever be in the last resort; and it seems to me that it is the wisest and safest course to carry our "madness," our hidden Fear, about with us, and allow it to change, as it will, its outward form according to the age we have reached. The great thing is to have faith in our power of forgetting, faith in that magical reservoir of Lethe which we all cherish in our being at a deeper level even than our torment. If anyone asked me what is the most precious gift that Nature has given us, I—worshipper of Memory—would reply; "the art of forgetting!"

When I now look back over my life I would certainly never say that my childhood, from birth to seven years, was a happy one. If it was, I certainly do not remember it as being so, and if that accursed stick, flung into that water, was the first shape that this Fear-Proteus took it must be remembered that the divine art of forgetting takes long to develop. May it be developed completely before I drink the cold, all-obliterating forgetfulness of the grave!

One thing those seven years at Shirley did. They bound my life with the life of my brother Littleton in so fast a knot that death alone—and perhaps not even that—can ever loosen it. Oh, my old, old friend, whose hair at this late day is so much whiter than your despotic Johnny's, how have I ever managed to withstand the buffets of Time and Chance since Fate swept us so far from each other? Far in space but not in heart or understanding! For though I no longer strangle you with bell-ropes, or hang you by your belt out of windows, that childish urine that we mingled in our youthful witches' cauldron has mixed more than the chemistry of natures.

When I summon up my rather scanty memories of my Derbyshire birthplace, it comes over me as a singular thing what a difference there is between the more superficial alarms of life. Some of these, as I now think of them, carry a delicious shiver, a sweet imaginative tremor with them. But others, though equally external to the deeper motions of my soul, seem steeped in a bitter, harsh, acrid, evil juice.

There was a pond near Shirley, in some farmer's field, that we used to hear tales about, and that several times I was taken to gaze upon from the bank and wonder at. Once—and the priceless holy terror of that occasion is with me still—I beheld a great circle of ripples rise and expand in the centre of those mud-obscured depths. For months afterwards I kept working myself into self-hugging paroxysms of sweet dismay over that circle of mysterious ripples. It must have been some kind of a fish—probably a perch—but that circle of ripples grew and grew, until to my infant imagination, fed by a desperate desire for disturbing marvels, they became a manifestation of some huge pike, of preternatural dimensions, that had lived there in solitary grandeur for half a century!

My earliest impressions of my father never changed: nor did he change. He was a man who derived more thrilling pleasure—a deep, massive, volcanic pleasure—from little natural things than anyone I have ever known. My father's personal pride was stupendous, but it was nourished upon a simplicity that was equally majestic. As I think of him now it seems to me that he was more childlike than any of his eleven children. And we were all childlike to an unparalleled degree; and have ever remained so! Yes, it is clear to me now —and how well his children came to understand him!—that he used to derive a proud, emotional glory from the simple fact of being able to walk at all, with long steady strides, over the face of the round earth. But this touching pride of his, rising up from the atavistic depths of his broad *homo sapiens* chest, gleaming from beneath his corrugated brows, making his long shaven upper lip quiver and protrude, causing him to rub his bony hands together in silent ecstasies, always culminated when in his walks he found a rare flower or caught sight of a rare bird or butterfly. He was in no sense a scientific naturalist, you must understand. Few and far between were the botanical or entomological names he knew; but he was able to give the common English name, and I dare say it was often some primitive Dorset nickname, to these specimens of Derbyshire life, while Littleton and I watched with wonder how he came back with his discovery from the bottom of a ditch or the top of a bank. Seldom did he return home from his walks without a small bunch of wild-flowers in his hand; but his grand pride was his collection of birds' eggs, a really formidable collection, the remnants of which, sadly diminished by accidents in moving-vans, my brother Llewelyn still retains in his Dorset cottage. How proudly he used to talk—they were among some of his happiest moments—about his dangerous climbs, up trees, up walls of ruined castles, up sea-cliffs, down the sides of quarries, among precipitous rocks. Stories, too, of great rowing adventures, he would relate with flashing eyes, for he was an unwearied oarsman; and long before I had seen anything of the Weymouth coast except the wet and dry sand by the bathing machines, all the well-known sea-marks there, Redcliff Bay, the White Nose, Sandsfoot Castle, were imprinted on my imagination through a mythological haze of enchanted wonder.

For our life at Shirley was varied by yearly visits, by way of Derby and Bristol, to Brunswick Terrace at Weymouth, from whose sands and sea-banks he was always increasing his collection of shells. How few visitors to seaside resorts make any attempt to know the names of the shells that strew our stormy shores! But my father's volcanic pride, sustained by an inaccessible reticence, communicated to his offspring from their earliest years an abysmal contempt for worldly frivolity as compared with a certain grave, majestic, simple passion for natural history. But even this passion, the moment it took a more recondite *scientific* form became to him in a curious way absurd and ridiculous! It began to border upon the foolishness of that imaginary *bête noir* of his, "the Professor" who was always the villain in his never-ended fairy story.

He was followed as a matter of fact, in his position as Vicar of Shirley, when we left in my seventh year, by Mr. Linton, a nephew of his by marriage, who was a scientific botanist; but whenever science entered the field of his amateur natural history my father retreated into volcanic depths of contempt. The truth was, his interest in Nature was part of his passionate—but totally subjective—romance of life. Never have I known, and never shall know, a man with a more childlike sense of the incredible romance of his own existence upon earth. In this he was Homeric rather than Biblical. Every person of his life, every place he had ever lived in, took on for him the importance of something tremendous and mythological! His pride and his egoism in this ultimate matter were absolute. He had only to link up any human being, any place, with the experiences of his own life, and that person and that place assumed a curious fairy-like quality, *beyond normal reality*.

The man's force of character was so deep, so formidable, so majestic—and incidentally so restrained—that in a thousand little things which touched his life he was *liable* to burst out with an intensity of emotion that was terrifying. That he did not more often "burst out"—it is the only way such a mountainous explosion can be characterized—was due to his really astounding self-control. Never once—no! not once—have I known him to indulge in physical violence. He never struck us when he was angry. That boxing of our ears—which he gave up when we left Shirley—was done "for our good," quite judicially, and in cold blood. I doubt if Theodore can recall it. Probably Littleton can. But I am not sure even of that.

Our periodic journeys from Shirley to Weymouth were, as may be imagined, great events for me. And yet such a bad memory have I—the result, I fancy, of my imaginative sensuality which at once devoured and forgot!—that I can recall very little of these momentous excursions. The *colour* of the railway engines was one thing that transported me with excitement. That the Great Northern engines should be green, and the Great Western engines a different shade of green; that the Midland engines should be of a muddy purplish tint, so it seems to me now, while the Great Eastern engines were black —these things thrilled me through and through. And again with the railway stations! The *length* of the station at Bristol, for instance, was a phenomenon that fascinated me. But it was in the actual movement of these trains that the particular thing obsessed my mind that has returned to me since *sans cesse* in travelling, and never without giving me the same curious and complicated sensation. I refer to the manner in which if you fix your eyes on the telegraph wires that accompany the railway-line you will notice them rising and rising and rising—till they are brought down with a jerk by the next telegraph-post. Wires mounting up and being jerked down, only to mount up again! And with the jerk that brought them down there occurred—I record the exact nature of my sensation—a curious kind of whirring sound like the throwing of a spear, combined with a humming and drumming in my ears, as if the spear had transfixed me. Was it the monotony and simplicity of our life at home that filled these rising and falling telegraph-wires with some ineffable secret? Or was it that the mere movement up, up, up, up—and then *down*, with a vertiginous shriek—was in some subtle way so significant of the whole secret of life that it cried aloud to some kindred, tragic, and perhaps equally resigned rhythm in my human pulses?

I think the thoughts and prejudices of our family have been profoundly influenced by what they ate and drank in childhood. My father never touched alcohol except as a priest at the altar, and he ate only the smallest quantities of meat and fish. He never even—to our astonishment as we grew into boyhood

—had more than one egg at a meal! His chief food was bread and butter, varied by bread and treacle, for he never mingled these luxuries, or by bread and Dundee marmalade. His sole drink except water, which he did not enjoy, was tea. All eleven of us, while I was at Cambridge, and all ten of us to-day are still regarded by our friends as peasant-like and even cattle-like, in the delight with which we willingly devour slice after slice of thick-cut bread, enriched by jam, honey, or marmalade. The aged relative, to whose house at the end of Brunswick Terrace we used to go when those Posts of Destiny between Derby and Weymouth had fulfilled their appointed toll of dragged down wires, was in the habit of relating that the first infant lips that came to greet her from Shirley did so in the unexpected and not very polite fashion by uttering the imperious words: "Make tea!" Such was certainly not the refreshment indicated in Rabelais as proper for philosophical travellers; but no Pantagruelist has ever got a richer ecstasy, even from drinking of that Sibylline Fount which uttered the word "Trinc," than we have got, as a family, from drinking tea.

But Penn House, Brunswick Terrace, brings back to me many sensations besides tea-drinking. The bow windows of the drawing-room opened straight on the Esplanade—which was very narrow just there—and on the pebbled bank of the sea, across whose surface to the West you saw Portland, and to the East the White Nose and St. Alban's Head, but it was not these grander features of the view that I remember from those early visits. It was the contents of a curious room that you entered through folding doors from the drawing-room. This room might have been a studied and carefully selected exhibit of Early Victorian bric-a-brac, and its peculiar smell—where no lively tea-drinking disturbed the wistful Sylphs who hover over mother-of-pearl boxes and inlaid lacquer-work trays— that pathetic and beautiful smell of old fragrant carved wood —was wont to mingle with the smells of seaweed and fish and sun-warmed pebbles that came in through those large bow windows. This little room was really an ante-room; but it was an ante-room that was behind, instead of in front of, the room to which it was attached.

In those early visits to Brunswick Terrace it was a considerable event to be taken as far as the "dry" sand, where the donkey-stand was, and it was a gala-day to be allowed to play in the "wet" sand, out by the bathing-machines. For it must be understood—such is the variety of marine phenomena at Weymouth—that the seashore opposite Brunswick Terrace was entirely composed of shelving banks of pebbles, and it was here, because the water grew so quickly deep, that the fishermen drew in their nets and it was here—beyond "the red post" that later made such an impression on my brother Llewelyn's mind—that men were allowed to bathe without bathing-clothes.

It must have been in one of these visits, when I was five and Littleton four, that my father first took us across the ferry near the mouth of the old harbour. I cannot describe to you, and you would find it difficult to believe it if you had not seen it, the primordial pride—like a Neanderthal parent guiding his progeny along untraversed shores—with which my father would help us down the slippery stone steps covered with green slime into the rocking boat below! The whole occasion was an exciting one, for you had to select your ferryman from quite a number of boat-owners, and I can remember well the peculiar sense of somewhat ambiguous power I derived, in begging my father to choose *this* one and reject that one. Aye! but how he would expatiate on the art of "feathering" when we had ascended the steps on the Nothe shore and were sufficiently out of distance of the boatman! I can see him now in his long black coat, sitting by Littleton's side, with the massive gold seals hanging from his watch-chain and a little streak of green slime on his sleeve. When he was happy and at peace he had a peculiarly strong resemblance to one of the larger carnivores; a resemblance that was not only due to the squareness of his face but to his low forehead and his long, quivering upper lip.

I expect before I was seven he had conveyed me by boat—himself using a pair of skulls without assistance—as far as Redcliff Bay; and without doubt before we left Derbyshire he had taken Littleton and me across the ferry, round the Nothe

Fort, as far as Sandsfoot Castle. Here in the rock pools he made us acquainted with sea anemones.

"They are very sensitive creatures, Johnny," he would say, as at the approach of my hand their tendrils closed up.

He would show us cowry-shells too, holding them with exquisite care in one of his broad palms and saying with intense pride: "My brother tells me they use cowries as money in India." It was one of my father's Homeric peculiarities—those grave ritualistic ways of his that did so much to enhance for us the whole dignity of life—never to say "Uncle Littleton," when he spoke to us of the Captain, but always, with a respect in which awe seemed to swallow up familiarity, "*my brother.*"

Oh, how can I describe the peculiar smell that used to intoxicate my childish senses, unconsciously at first, but gradually quite consciously, when after any sort of an outing the inner door of Penn House porch was opened—the outer door, blistered by long hours of morning sunshine was never closed—of the interior of the little passage that was then revealed to us! Whether it smelt like that all the year round I cannot say; but the dominant element in it, though mingled with a vague sense of curios, larger than cowry-shells, brought home in his furloughs by "my brother" from India, was undoubtedly our own buckets and spades that stood there together with trailing riband-seaweeds hanging from the wall. To my childish senses there was a constant interpenetration between the whole seashore and the interior of this house; the spray and the foam and the jelly-fish and the starfish floating in and floating out all the while, and carrying my consciousness backwards and forwards with them between objects of art from India and the enchanted sands beyond the donkey-stand.

But we had other relatives to visit, during my seven years at Shirley, who lived in a very different part of the country from Weymouth. My maternal grandfather was at that time the Rector of Yaxham in Norfolk; and upon my simple and sensuous, if not passionate nature, another and very different landscape imprinted itself. In this country, lying almost at sea-level, and where nothing but poplars and alders and willows obstruct the rising and sinking of the sun, I remember at an age when my stature made it hard for me to see over the tops of the ears of full-grown wheat-fields, being transported with delight in a road near the railway-line by the feeling of absolute and unbounded power I got from grasping a stick by the middle so that the two ends protruded in front and at back pretending to be one of those Great Eastern Railway engines that in their black colour interested me so profoundly, after the green Great Western ones.

Many men when they come to be sixty can, I take it, recall the pleasure they derived from playing trains. Can they recall as I do, with the most vivid clearness, the precise *feelings* that accounted for the pleasure they got? I mean the sense that Johnny Powys, staying with his grandfather at Yaxham, was really occupied with some transaction of a vaguely grandiose character that placed him in a position where others watched him, clung to him, depended on him, awaited his will, submitted to his caprices, and wondered at his wayward and mysterious purpose.

Of all mortal creatures one of the most desirable and enviable is the eft, or water-lizard, or newt, especially the black-backed orange-bellied newt; and I know that the intense ecstasy I derived from "playing trains" on that road near the Yaxham railway bridge, was balanced by the miserable disappointment I had when I found that the village pond at Yaxham—a pond in the meadows not far from the Norwich and East Dereham Railway—contained no newts, contained at the time I fished in it not even a tadpole. Theodore must have been three years old, Littleton four, and myself five at the epoch of our later visits to Yaxham. For I remember it was for the benefit of, but not in concurrence *with*, these younger ones, that I transformed myself, by a subjective metempsychosis, into a black locomotive; and in my rage when my net brought up from that muddy water nothing but a peculiar species of large water-snail—I can see the things now! They were in their right world at the bottom of a pond; but as a substitute for an orange-bellied newt, floating, floating, its feet outstretched, as it sinks voluptuously down, without a movement of its tail, they were decidedly unappealing—I cannot recall that my feeling was comprehended by my fellow-infants.

I have already named as one of my dominant life characteristics a desire to be a magician. But along with this desire appears a much less commendable one, a desire to be recognized as the possessor of noble sentiments! A pitiable example of this latter tendency, which I am afraid must be sternly differentiated from a desire to feel noble sentiments, occurred when the news reached us, while we were staying at Yaxham, of the sudden death from cholera, of my father's brother Littleton, the soldier, whose face I had so perversely enjoyed striking with my fists. I can remember the exact look of the rain, making little pyramids of water as it fell in the puddles by the side of the avenue that led to my grandfather's house, while my heart expanded with pride while I explained to my relatives how impossible it was for either Littleton aged four, or Theodore aged three, to feel this event in the manner in which I felt it.

But to return to our life at Shirley. Here too, as at Penn House, there was an ante-room connected with the drawing-room, but this ante-room had to be traversed before the drawing-room could be entered. Rooms in a house where a child spends its infancy take sometimes their lasting character from the most curious accidents. This ante-room at Shirley remains in my mind to-day as a place of execution! I had overheard my father retail aloud from his reading of *The Standard*, the conservative daily paper by which he regulated his very simple political ideas, an account of the execution of some unlucky member of our uncle's military profession. With a lurid interest I had followed every detail of this tragedy: how the unfortunate man had been compelled to dig his own grave into which he finally fell backwards under the bullets of the firing-squad. On this occasion both Littleton and Theodore were dragooned by their elder brother into assisting at a court martial in the ante-room. Who it was who fired the volley, who it was who fell into the grave I have forgotten; but among all the games we must have played together in those days the only one I can remember with any distinctness was this of "the Traitor's Execution" carried through with such realistic verisimilitude in that colourless apartment.

The life-long detestation of what is called "Society"—the ingrained anti-social tendency in me—was clearly manifested on one occasion at Shirley which even now gives me a little shiver of revolt when I recall it. It was, if I am not mistaken, when some of our kin from Norfolk were staying with us, that I was taken, Littleton and Theodore being too young to participate in such an event, to a large garden party at Osmaston Park. I fancy this must have been one of the first entertainments given by new owners of this old estate and I dare say there was an atmosphere of new-fangled ways about it all, very different from what we would have found in the domain, for instance, of old Mr. Okeover of Okeover, another squire of the neighbourhood, whose ancestors without a break went back to Saxon times.

We were all assembled in the pleasant June weather on the sloping lawns of the big house, and the scene must have assumed that particular look of an English Fête Champêtre so dear to Henry James, when some brisk fantastical pedant—an embodiment no doubt of all the qualities of my father's detested "Professor"—skipped up to us with the request for a party of children to hunt about for some rare specimens of feathered grasses, then in their hey-day of flowering, which he was anxious—or made out he was—to add to his "Herborium." Our hosts insisted that little Johnny Powys—sulky, miserable, rebellious, distracted—should join this accursed botanical fashionable search-party; and I now recall the helpless misanthropy with which I made my lugubrious way through those feathery growths, too cowardly to leave my companions in a desperate retreat, but resolute not to pick a single grass blade in the interests of science.

Precisely the same sort of situation arose long after—on what was called "Flower Sunday" at Sherborne School, when all the boys in their tall silk hats were sent forth in gregarious charity to pick flowers for a hospital—and Powys Major once again neither joined in, nor heroically absconded.

How often in my life there have come such moments when

I have turned away in sullen apathy from the tribal activity into which I have been flung! I can recall the feelings so well with which at such times I have hunted round in my recalcitrant mind for a fellow-Ishmael, or Ishmaeless, and found none. I can remember once ever so much later—when we lived at Montacute—feeling aggrieved with every member of our large family—and walking alone up the lane, beyond Mr. Marsh's farm, in the direction of Thorn Cross, searching for this unknown fellow-outcast.

I never found out the trick of reading to myself till after we had left Shirley, when I was seven years old. This I know for a certainty; though seven seems a very late epoch in a person's life for such a momentous discovery. But as a family we were all extremely slow in mental development and such achievements as we subsequently arrived at were the achievements of invincible childishness prolonged into mature days. Yes, I know for a certainty that when we left Shirley, in my seventh year, I had not yet learnt the trick of *reading to myself*. Let me anticipate a little to make this point clear. It was just after we were settled in Rothesay House, Dorchester, that I spent the whole of one very wet afternoon reading to myself in my father's study. My father was absent, visiting the poor in this ancient town, for he had become curate then to Mr. Knipe of St. Peter's Church; and seated in his high-backed arm-chair—I forget which of us possesses that chair now, but it was the object against which we all used to kneel by his side in preparation for every important crisis in our lives—I read with intense, prolonged, and spell-bound absorption *Alice Through the Looking Glass*. Equally with *Alice in Wonderland* which must have been read aloud to me, this book was at once completely metamorphosed to the purposes of the Powys family. We treated the facetious, the jocular aspects of it *as if they did not exist*. We took the literal words of it; and solemnly proceeded to render them grave, serious, realistic, and mythological! And as I did this with the creations of this fantastical-brained mathematician *I did it with the whole of life*.

As I have insisted from the start, my dominant life-illusion was that I was, or at least would eventually be, a magician;

and what is a magician if not one who converts God's "reality" into his own "reality," God's world into his own world, and God's nature into his own nature?

But what impression, if any, had I received of the magic of *literature* before we left Derbyshire for Wessex? I will tell you; for this is as clearly remembered by me as was that first occasion at Rothesay House when I read *Alice Through the Looking Glass*. It happened in the dining-room at Shirley, where often, instead of in the drawing-room, we used to gather round the mahogany table after tea. The whereabouts of this table at the present hour I believe I *do* know. I think it has crossed the East African jungle from Mobasa to Nunyuki, and now occupies the sheepman's house of my youngest brother Willy. It was at this table, then, under the lamp, and I fancy it was in winter, for the great green curtains with red-embroidered tassels covered the windows, that my father read to Littleton and me—Theodore being asleep in his crib upstairs—a warlike poem called "The Passage of the Rhine." He chose this poem, for reasons of his own, out of a big illustrated quarto we had of Aytoun's *Scottish Cavaliers*. The German river was crossed on that occasion by exiled Highlanders, in the service— I suppose, of the King of France. Whether he read any of the much more thrilling poems in that volume I cannot say, such as "Dundee" and "Flodden," but the important point—at least to me—is that I received my first impression of the enchantment of literature in connection with exiles, and with exiles whose own cause seemed irretrievably lost.

It was however the illustrations of Aytoun's book that influenced me most. Take it all in all, no book—no, not any!— has had an effect upon me equal to this one. Aytoun's verses did a lot, but the illustrator of this grand edition did much more, to turn me once and for all into an obstinate, incurable romanticist. Nor did the influence of this book stop there. It was not towards any merely *vague* romantic world that it set my heart groping and fumbling. Aytoun's *Scottish Cavaliers* stirred up, down deep in the central pit of my stomach where the umbilical cord must have been, that peculiar Celtic emotion —Matthew Arnold describes it beautifully, nor is it important

D

whether he describes it correctly—which, like the spirit of Wales itself, is always returning, like water seeking its level, to its own proud, evasive, ingrown, interior being.

My father's eyes used to burn with a fire that was at once secretive and blazing, like the fire in the eyes of long discrowned king, when he told us how we were descended from the ancient Welsh Princes of Powysland. From an old Welsh family long ago established in the town of Ludlow in Shropshire in what were formerly called the Welsh "Marches" we undoubtedly did—Princes or no Princes—as the genealogies put it, "deduce our lineage"; and I am inclined to think that there has seldom been a mortal soul—certainly no modern one —more obstinately Cymric than my own. I am quite prepared to admit that the Cymric tribes were not the aboriginals of Wales. But whatever they were, even though they made use of legends and traditions belonging to the conquered, who in *their* turn probably made use of the yet earlier legends of the men who carried out of Wales the "foreign" stones wherewith to build Stonehenge, they seem to have been, to use Jung's phrase, the most "introverted" of all races. Possibly the men before them in that remote and mountainous principality were "introverts" too! Probably the oldest wisdom in Wales was that wisest and most ancient of all human wisdom; namely that it is within the power of the will and the imagination to destroy and recreate the world. Yes, it was perhaps more the illustrations of this particular edition that stirred up this old Welsh temper in me than the verses themselves; and yet I soon came to know one of these verses, "The Burial of Dundee" so literally by heart that the emotion it contains, mingling with what I inherited from my father of secret, furtive, reticent pride, and mingling with the general "aura" of these romantic illustrations, has affected deeper than I could possibly make you believe, the actual feelings I have when I catch sight of certain rocks and stones and trees and rivers and wooded hills.

It was at this same dining-room table one winter evening that Littleton and Theodore and I were shown a very queer book—but I am certain that they have both forgotten it— which takes its place for me side by side with that laurel-wood axe in its supernatural importance. *People do not understand how imaginative a child's life is.* When we grow up we ourselves forget. So it comes about that whole symbolic worlds, full of the strangest marvels, vanish into an annihilation so deep that it is hard to conceive it. This book in appearance was as big as a folio but it was a new book and not an old one, and it was as thin as a wraith. It was a real book, some kind of an illustrated fairy-story—in fact it is conceivable that it was one of the more fantastic of Shakespeare's fairy-plays. Even as I write I see it under the lamp on that bare mahogany table—and, mark you, reader! I have never, as well be the case again and again in this present work, breathed a word to a living soul about this incident—but it had that same effect on me that the laurel-axe had. It seemed to be something more than ordinary, *natural* enjoyment! It was as though in that wooden axe and in this enormous book, so large, and at the same time *so thin and frail* that I feel now as if it had only a paper binding. I touched some incredible secret of happiness; some of the sort of happiness that elementals know, or beings who are exempt from the infirmities of human flesh.

Where children have the grand advantage over grown-up people is in their freedom from the weight of authority and tradition. They are forced to behave properly at meals and lessons and never to make themselves a nuisance; but in their play-time, which is of course the bulk of their time, the majority of children, even *only* children, are left to invent their own "games" as they are called. Now this use of the word "games" for the great purposes of children's life is extremely misleading. Older boys and girls play games of course; and as they play them they accept them as games; and the younger children are often cajoled or bullied into learning the arbitrary rules of these pastimes. But the passionately intense *inner life* of children, that imaginative existence which is to them the whole purpose and vital interest of their days *is not a game.* It seems a game to the grown-up people around them. But so far from envying the grown-up reality of these older person's life, or admiring it, or thinking how to imitate, children have a permanent underlying contempt for it as lacking in the one thing important.

This one thing important is *magic*. Children are unable to explain this! They do not know what the word means. I confess I am not perfectly clear about that myself. But whatever it is, it implies two things. It implies the feeling of a living power over matter and over nature. And it implies a great gap in space, a pure clear void in this whole system of things, where absolutely new reactions to life rise, like fairy bubbles, and go floating off into the unknown! It implies a lot else besides. But the great point is that the most thrilling moments of happiness with a child are *secret and magical* and come from *a level of reality* which is completely different from the level of reality of grown-up people. Children do not play ordinary conventional games unless they are encouraged to do so by the older boys and girls. Children's "games," strictly speaking, are not games at all. They are the child's inmost reality! They are the child's life-illusion. They turn back to them with a sigh of relief from the impertinent intrusive activities of grown-up people.

The truth is, children are not half-men and half-women, or half-boys and half-girls. They are a race *sui generis*. They are a race of beings to themselves. And it is in the power of this curious race of beings to plunge into the secret of life more deeply than all other mortals. More deeply? Ah! The whole problem of the blunder of our Western civilization is implicit here; for it concerns the nature of what we call reality.

Real reality is entirely of the mind. It is partly good and partly evil. But it holds the *lower reality*—that mere plastic agglomeration of matter and material force—in subjection. It creates and it destroys this *lower reality* at its wilful and arbitrary pleasure. This is why it is only vulgar and ill-bred people who give their children expensive toys. To a real child *anything* will serve as a toy. Cheap toys do no harm; and they give these unique beings incalculable pleasure. But it is always their old toys, however cheap, that children cling to. Why? Because they are no longer simply *toys*. They have become the mediums, the bridges, the ladders, the trap-doors, the magic carpets, by which they enter the kingdom of heaven; enter, in other words, the rainbow-land of their own imagination!

Fumbling about, as my imperfect memory is doing now, among the scanty impressions of those Shirley days I ask myself what dominant urges of my after-life can be traced as far back as this and what cannot. The desire to be a magician is there without any question! When I was suddenly transported with rapture in that little lane going down the hill to the village, as I stumbled along the muddy ruts in front of Littleton's perambulator, pretending to be "The Lord of Hosts," it was a desire for some obscure magical power that inspired me.

What I cannot find in my memory, do all I can to find it, is the faintest evidence of that conscious embracing of Nature with a psychic-sensuous ecstasy in which I came to experience later my deepest sense of the purpose of life. I am convinced that many people looking back on their childhood before the age of seven can recall moments in which they cried aloud with entrancement: "Oh, I am so happy! Oh, I am so happy!" simply and solely from their conscious awareness of what Wordsworth calls "the pleasure which there is in life itself."

Such moments I can remember well in other places and later in my life. For instance at Penn House in Weymouth, when I must have been about fifteen an ecstasy came to me, morning after morning, as I saw the sun glittering on the sea. The glitter of the sun upon water has since that time become one of my recurrent symbols of the enchantment with which the self can fling itself upon the not-self in a spasm of mystical sensuality. But not a single one of such moments can I remember at Shirley Vicarage! I will tell you the nearest approach to such a thing that I can recall; but I regard this memory as entirely different from those glimpses of the sun on Weymouth Bay because it was not accompanied by any conscious awareness of its relation to the happiness of life, an awareness that *could* be disentangled, if you cared to make the distinction, from the particular phenomenon that called it up at the moment. The experience I am now thinking about might be called a purely æsthetic one, though it had to do with Nature.

We always had prayers at eight in the morning, and breakfast afterwards; and on winter mornings, although if I am not in error our dining-room looked East, my father had to read the Bible by candlelight. One morning, between prayers and breakfast, I recollect perfectly well being thrilled by seeing the sky assume a greenish tint. I must have seen many a red sky during that winter and during earlier winters—for I take it that I was six when this occurred—but I had never seen this peculiar tinge of green covering the whole expanse of the Eastern sky, and it made a tremendous impression on me. I suppose the near approach of the cottage loaf of brown bread and the enormous pat of butter from which my father loved to dole out every helping we had, enhanced my pleasure in this green sky, but as I think of it now it was the marvellousness of the sky being *green* that made such an impression upon me. It is certain that I have retained, ever since that day, a curious lust for that green colour in the sky, and a delight in it that has remained what I am inclined to call a purely æsthetic pleasure. Other effects of sunrise or sunset—for instance the more usual one of bars of massy gold, or of blood-red streaks against a watery-gold background—have often filled me with that vague spiritual nostalgia which seems one of our universal human feelings; but the feeling that a *green sky* gives me is quite different. It has no mysticism of any sort about it. The surprise of there being a green colour at all up there in the sky seems to preclude mystical emotions; and with me at any rate that peculiar green tint is so intensely, so physically satisfying that like the cottage loaf and the home-made butter, it is complete in itself and has no margin for afterthoughts.

There was another natural phenomenon at Shirley that made an indelible impression on my mind, but, like the green sky, an æsthetic rather than a mystical one, and that was a widely spreading Pirus Japonica that clambered up the front of the house. This oddly enough is the only garden flower I can recall from those days; and I never see a specimen of this beautiful shrub without thinking of my infancy. It too, I think, like the unusual sky, has something about it that surprises the mind. A person does not—at least I did not—expect a fruit-tree to bear blossoms so extremely red! The only wild-flower that I can remember at Shirley—except when cowslips were made into "cowslip-tea" or into a "cowslip-ball"—had an effect upon me, *and still has*, totally different from the green sky or the red fruit-blossoms. I am speaking of cuckoo flowers. It comes over me now as I think of these unequalled growths and summon back the tall dewy grasses in the midst of which their lavender-coloured, light-blowing petals waved, that they are by far the most poetical of all our English wild plants. Yes, from the very earliest dawn of my consciousness of Nature I think of cuckoo flowers as fleeting and fitful, appearing shyly for a while, when the grasses, mosses, fern-fronds, are still full of new, fresh sap, fading all too soon, but while they last always growing where the dews are heaviest and where the streams are over-brimming their banks. Born of chilly dawns in wild wet places cuckoo flowers are the coldest, chastest, least luxurious, most hyperborean, most pale, most Gothic, most Ophelia-like of all our island flowers. Once and once only have I fancied I've caught sight of some of these "cold maids" in my adopted America. It was once when I was "on the road" with Padraic Colum, and he too thought that what we saw were cuckoo flowers—but I don't know! I doubt it; and with the malicious home-sickness of the psalmist in Babylon I am tempted to wish that they grew nowhere else than in our grey rainy England.

I think it must have been the tone with which my father always spoke of cuckoo flowers, rather than anything he said in praise of them, that made these pale growths the very epitome of romantic poetry for me. He must have spoken of his native Stour and how they grew by its banks in such a tone that, as a dog understands things by the inflexion of the voice, so I must have understood that there was a fleeting magic about those particular flowers that made all others—those richly blue wild forget-me-nots, for instance, that grew by the banks of the Dove—seem arrogant and even fashionable! Pride, pride, pride! Yes, it was by a thousand slight touches, and sideway thrusts, and casual hints, and inarticulate indirections, that my father, in the manner of an exiled wolf or imprisoned fox, would indicate *the absolute inferiority*—a thing to be felt and known rather than argued about—of Derbyshire ways, scenery, people, customs, dialect, flora and fauna, to those of his native Wessex.

It was this fierce, inarticulate, irrational loyalty *to his own*, to all the old things, the old ways, the old people, the old battle-cries, the old causes, the old customs, that my father had the power of communicating to me without direct speech of any kind. A savage intensity of emotion, rising up perhaps —who can tell?—from some submerged level of Cymric *pride in defeat* that flowed down to him, from "battles long ago," through all the numberless generations wherein his ancestors had mingled with the invader, would be often stirred up over some little negligible occasion, some occasion ridiculously slight in itself, but in connection with which it was possible to pit the old, the artless, the quiet, the natural, the dignified against the showy, the artificial, the luxurious, the scientific, the modern!

In all matters connected with domestic economy, in all matters connected with domestic furniture, in all matters connected with the management of his garden, just as much as with regard to religion and morality, my father's strongest word of reprobation was "new-fangled," his strongest word of praise "old-fashioned." His egoism as I have hinted projected itself over its own past with such imaginative tenacity that without his making the least effort to do so he endowed everything in the least connected with the old Dorsetshire ways, with a superiority so infallible that to challenge it was to betray yourself as vulgar and new-fangled.

It must, I presume, have become known to my father at a very early epoch of my Shirley life that I was in the habit night by night of making my little cot shake with the feverish intensity of my infantile eroticism. I recollect well that I would be asked every morning if I had been "doing that"; and as I was then —as, judging from some reactions to my writings I am still —gravely and most solemnly honest in such little matters, I always answered with pathetic truthfulness; and since it invariably happened that I *had* "done that" I was accordingly punished, and had the fever of my childish viciousness cooled, by having ice-cold water poured over me. So strong was my tenuency to premature perversity however, that when the night came the discomforting thought of this ice-cold water to be endured in the morning was as nothing to the dark, secret immediate satisfaction of my forbidden indulgence. And these intense orgies that—in my excited mind—shook not only my guilty bed, but all the pillars of my whole small cosmos, were without exception free from every sort of sensuality except pure sadism! Sadistic imaginations, and these alone, from my first awakenings of consciousness till I must have been about seventeen were able really to excite my abnormal eroticism.

I can well remember when we were driving one day into Ashbourne—my father had a tall dog-cart in those days and he would drive into the cobbled court-yard of the "Saracen's Head" with the gravest punctiliousness and order I-don't-know-what for his horse's comfort before he went out to do his business in the town—as we passed a little stuccoed cottage —ah! how long a memory our vices have!—that stood alone on the left hand of the great hill that goes down into Ashbourne, I caught sight of an old woman through the window holding a young woman—as it seemed to me—by the throat. The young woman's head was leaning back in a position that looked extremely unnatural, and the blood rushed to *my* head —but my father drove on, and the vision left this world. But though leaving this world it was not annihilated. On the contrary it transferred itself to that invisible "Book of Perdition" the nightly turning of whose pages condemned me, though without their self-imposed impulse of penitence, to the freezing cure for such temptations welcomed by the ancient Saints of the Thebaid.

Yes, below all the great systems of philosophic thought, behind all the great systems of mystical redemption, stir these ultimate personal reactions to the terrible urge of sex. It has been a wonder to me in later life, as I have listened to the wholesale attacks upon normal sex-delight made by puritan fanatics and to the wholesale defence of such pleasures made by sweet-natured sun-born pagans like my brother Llewelyn, how little, aye! how little, either of these indignant crusaders realize the maniacal intensity of the force they are quarrelling about. To my brother Llewelyn the word "sex" seems always to mean lovely poetic dalliance with warm-blooded friendly wenches under hay-smelling hedges. To the puritan it seems to mean a hatred of bare limbs, flushed cheeks, shining eyes and dancing feet. But to my less normal moon-struck nature it means a desperate insane obsession, completely abstracted from the poetry of the elements and having no connection at all with the æsthetic beauty of bare limbs, bright eyes, warm breasts and floating hair.

My own subjective definition of the power of sex would always be *vice*, that is to say an abstract impersonal sterile lust, entirely divorced from what is called "love" and selecting the objects of its desire without regard for either beauty or mental sympathy. Nothing has ever seemed to me so irrelevant as the championship of sex as something under the godlike auspices of earth and sun, a beautiful creative force full of life and joy. To me it has—until by infinite cunning I have steered it, purged it, sublimated it, narrowed it, concentrated it, diffused it—been always a world of intense absorption, a world of maniacal exclusiveness, of delirious exaction, of insane pursuit, a world existing parallel to the ordinary world of normal human activity, a world into which, when once you enter, and graze like a mad Nebuchadnezzar upon its fatal grass, the ordinary world appears completely dull, "stale, flat and unprofitable," without lustre and without purpose.

There have been occasions—I can recall two such out of my American travels, one as I walked along a squalid interminable slum-street in Cleveland, and one as I sat eating buttered toast in a dingy little café in Scranton, Pennsylvania —when I have emerged through my demonic postern-gate into the world of normal reality and normal solidity to find this natural home of the human senses a place of intoxicating sweetness and charm. What I felt on those two occasions I have never forgotten. It was a unique feeling, a new birth! It was like that escape from "The Will to Live" described by Schopenhauer. Every desolate roof and forlorn mud-patch along that Cleveland road was radiant with a beckoning enchantment, every gleam on the sordid counter of that little tea-shop was a ladder leading to paradise. I had turned from my dead-sea with its apples of ashes and those terrible mirages in the unreal sands back to the sweet securities of the homely chemistry of de-sorcerized matter!

Llewelyn himself tells us how shocked he was by those symbols of pure lust on the sinister brick-red walls of the scoriac streets of ancient Pompeii; and you have only to enter one of the little Byzantine churches in the Rome we know to-day to realize what a rainy dew of cuckoo flower freshness must have fallen upon the jaded sexuality of the ancient world when—just as I did in that long street in Cleveland—it turned away from the slavery—*not* of the flesh, for had not the Word been made flesh?—but of the remorseless, unmitigated erotic nerve.

The word "sensuality" covers a great deal. I have now come myself to use it for a certain sort of *concentrated sensuousness* penetrated by something more intense, more ecstatic, than is usually associated with what we call by that name. But it has been by the path of a deliberate and concentrated sensuality that I have at last found a working substitute in our natural world for that terrible *other world* of purely vicious—and with me always sadistic—mirages of fatal obsession. Where the fantastical puritans make their mistake is in their abuse of these harmless words "carnal," "fleshly," "sensual," and all that these represent. It isn't the senses that lead us astray, it is the one terrible nerve. It isn't the general amorous instincts that are at fault, it is the one solitary sex-nerve, isolated from the rest of life, and projecting a demonic insatiable fever of its own, *a land of fever*, whose purlieus and borders are the ghastliest of all "Terres Gastées." This isolated sex-nerve in each of us resembles my own heretical and I dare say unphilosophical and illogical conception of the first cause. Its energy can be used to create and sustain a world, or it can be used to blight and destroy a world.

Human personality has other possibilities of cruelty. Brutality, violence, exploitation, oppression, insensitive thoughtlessness and anger and malice are not I suppose necessarily sadistic. Sometimes I seem to suspect that there may be found in all these evils a faint sadistic tincture; but I certainly do encounter plenty of malicious, brutal and cruel people whom it is very difficult to accuse of sadism. In fact much of the cruelty in the world appears to me to spring from mere thoughtlessness and a lack of imagination; whereas sadism is, in its inherent nature, aware, and imaginatively aware, of what it is doing.

Looking back over my life at Shirley then—those first seven years of my existence as a *homo sapiens*—I am struck, as I recall that remote past, by the complete absence of any memories implying either sensuality or sensuousness. These enchanted gateways into the mystery of life, these paradisic embracings of the elements which have done so much to mould my later days seem absolutely non-existent in those childish years. I cannot recall—I who later was so obsessed by greediness—one single instance of a thrilling moment produced by food of any kind. I cannot recall—I who have made such awareness into a religious cult—one single instance of ecstatic enjoyment of life for its own sake!

As far as my memories of these seven years at Shirley are concerned my whole psychic-sensual response to Nature appears a deliberate intellectual achievement, something *into which I have willed myself*, knowing it to be the true Tao, or Path of Deepest Wisdom. And yet I do not feel as if the little Johnny Powys of those seven years was not completely realized by me now and remembered by me now. He is clearly there, that little boy! I can see him; I can feel him; *I am he.* And yet he is so startlingly different, in so many ways, from what I am now! But I know him—oh, I know him so well in the things where this little "Johnny," and the later "Jack" too, fuse themselves with the still later "John"!

Forgive me, reader, if once more I enumerate the particular experiences in those days that I share at this very moment, as I write this, lying on my couch at the window in "Up-state" New York. As I write this I am certainly that same Johnny-Jack-John who could be made to shiver and shake by the sight of a girl with her head thrown back, if that scene were brooded upon in connection with sadistic thoughts. I am certainly the same Johnny-Jack-John who can stare entranced at a green sunset or hunt for cuckoo flowers in tall wet grass. I am, oh most certainly! the same who has to struggle day by day, week by week, year by year, to forget, to annihilate by forgetting, the presence of this or that not-to-be-revealed fear. I am the same, too, as that little boy who cried aloud to the Universe in Shirley Lane that he was "The Lord of Hosts."

But there the likeness ends! With the little Johnny who wanted to mingle his urine with his brother's urine, I, John, feel as though I had nothing in common. From the "Johnny" who takes tadpoles from ponds to put them into puddles I have become the not less meddling but less murderous "John" who takes fish from shallow pools to put them into deep pools. Although I no longer try to hang my brother Littleton, or "strangle him with my fingers long and lean," or even—as I did at the "Powys Major" epoch of our life—want to roll him in a ditch, or run him down a steep hill into iron railings, I *do* sometimes feel an inclination, as I did one afternoon, when we were together only four years ago, on the road to Harrod's Mill at Northwold, to dig my horny, antiquated chin into him, and burst out into a totally uncalled for Defence of Immorality!

There is one tragic thing about all these childish memories that I note however. If John has the advantage over Johnny in the matter of behaviour to tadpoles, Johnny has the advantage over John—and over Jack and "Powys Major" too!—in the matter of the laurel-bough axe. I still know what fetish worship is. I have a fetish worship to this day, for instance, for all three of my walking-sticks, and though I have never actually put them at the window, in my travels, so that they could share my view of the world, I do catch myself treating them as if they were demi-semi-animate. I also know what it is to be transported into a Seventh Heaven of rapture by the sight of some particular inanimate object or of some peculiar grouping of inanimate objects. I can recall a tattered purplish-bound volume of Euclid that gave me one of the most intense transports of my life. I can recall the sudden sight of my pipe —for I smoked pipes in my early days—lying upon the *Poetical*

Works of Wordsworth. I can recall a certain fir-tree bough that always seemed to me, as I watched it from the dressing-room window which was my Montacute bedroom, to be floating upon an emanation of its own soul, which hovered like a blue vapour about it in those quiet autumn evenings, as I washed my hands with Pear's soap before going down to tea.

Such things and many similar to them I can recall throughout my life. But I can recall nothing approaching the emotion I experienced over that axe of laurel which my father cut for me in the Shirley shrubbery. And it hovers in the air when I think of it—not like Macbeth's weapon of blood—but like some magical Excalibur, brought arbitrarily from some world of enchantment and carried arbitrarily away again, out of my sight for ever. It is not merely my rapturous delight in this laurel axe that I recall. I recall the nature of that delight. In fact—mad though it may sound to say so—I feel the same *kind of delight* when even now, I think of that axe as I did when my father cut it and trimmed it with his knife! It may have been connected with those romantic illustrations of Aytoun. But it may—as Wordsworth hints of similar feelings in his "Intimations of Immortality"—represent something much deeper and more tremendous. The point about it that seems to me tragic—as it really did to Wordsworth, though he made the best of it in his sturdy stoical manner—is the fact that these ecstasies occur at rarer and rarer intervals as we get older. But after all this mystical advantage of childhood over manhood—of every Johnny over every John—is more than compensated for.

I, for one, would sooner have almost any continuous seven years of my life, perhaps even—grim though those were—the seven years, from ten to seventeen, of my time at school—than have my early childhood over again. I would never say I had a happy childhood. And, in this matter, nothing in heaven or earth—not even if my father had been God, or had been able to walk from Mount Cloud to Osmaston Park in Seven-League Boots—could have reassured me.

"The mind, the mind, Master Shallow!"

I should under all conceivable circumstances, being the

person I am, have suffered from Fear. It might not have been Fear because of a stick thrown into a pond; but Fear of some sort it would have been; and a magician not yet seven is able to call up but few protecting spirits from "the vasty deep."

It is all a great mystery, this passage from being a helpless neurotic Johnny to being a crafty neurotic John; but I sometimes feel as I survey my turbulent life that a human soul resembles a fountain whose native spring is choked up by every kind of rubble and constantly invaded by a tidal estuary from the salt sea. Not until the fountain has banked itself up with great stones against this dead-sea invasion, not until it has pushed the sticks and leaves and gravel and roots and funguses and mud and cattle dung out of its way, can it draw upon the deep granite wells of its predestined flow. To look back to that Shirley childhood of mine is to look back to a convulsed mudpool of Chaos. In the midst of that Chaos a wavering human soul is gradually taking shape, gathering to itself curious and conflicting signs and symbols and tokens of what its blind urge is driving it towards. From the beginning madness and fear beset us, vice enthrals us, humiliation benumbs us, pride intoxicates us. It may be hard to be a man; it is much harder to be a child; and if the Lord said: "Of theirs is the Kingdom of Heaven," he must have said it of a childhood that one child at any rate has completely forgotten!

Chapter Two

Weymouth and Dorchester

IT was not only to thoughts of things that without any malicious puritanism must really be called "wicked," that I used, when left alone in my darkened bedroom in my eighth year, to close my eyes. I had found out a wonderful trick in connection with this shutting of eyes, which at a touch, and quite an innocent one this time, transported me into Elysium. I used to press my knuckles against my closed eyelids and in that manner stare entranced into the Void. And lo and behold! The Void presently gave birth to a lovely kaleidoscope of incredible patterns and colours! It is Keats who somewhere talks of the "spangly" gloom thus evoked; but my visions of these rainbow spirits, when to-day I take off my spectacles and try to call them up, do not come as they were wont to do.

In those days, however, they were much more than "spangly." It was like some pre-cosmic panorama, imprinted on the aboriginal retina of chaos, of all the Iris-tints, of all the butterfly stains and tints and dyes, of the "dome of coloured glass" of the unborn world. It is not only that I've lost the trick of conjuring up out of squeezed eyelids a colour-orgy. I have no longer any wish to do it! Isn't it a queer thing how the main urge of a person's inmost being changes? I lack the least desire now to behold the dance of those Euclidian Rainbows! And yet, just as I did then, I live for sensation. It is strange! I suppose I have some sort of æsthetic conscience now which censors my sensations and insists that I should only make a cult of such among them as, as have got—how shall I put it?—a poetical and elemental value.

But it certainly becomes clearer and clearer to me as I

ponder over these early years of my life that there is some secret, and a secret far more valuable than the revelation of that impersonal-personal Eternal Being which came to Proust, to be found in the feelings of a young boy as to the nature of the Universe. This queer expression, "having an ecstasy," what does it really mean? What are the ingredients that compose them, the atmosphere out of which such ecstasies arise? The following is my own analysis of these precious moments. I think they always come, just as everything living does, *out of duality*, out of the energizing of opposite poles of existence, poles of substance, poles of being, poles of electricity, if you prefer that scientific word. I think these moments of ecstasy are apt to come when, as you contemplate some particular scene or object, you suddenly recall some *other* deep cause of satisfaction in your life, but a cause totally independent of the one you are now regarding *and not in the same plane of feeling*.

For instance, I am looking at a patch of moss on a greenish marbly rock and I am aware of a deep sensual pleasure. But there suddenly comes into my mind the thought of a coal fire and of the light of candles, and of a chess-board, with the men all arranged for the game, and of old leather-bound Homeric Lexicon. Now either for a game of chess or for the looking out of Greek words the mind has to be active, whereas in drinking up the deliciousness of this dark wet green surface of stone, matted with moss, the mind is in a state of concentrated passivity. And my idea is that it is the sudden impact of the thought of pleasurable activity upon a mind concentrated upon pleasurable passivity that brings that tingling up-flow of exultation which is named "ecstasy." Had the mind in contemplating this dark rain-dripping surface and these emerald-green spores been led away to think of the earth mould of a damp flower-bed strewn with rain-wet petals, there would almost certainly have been no increase in the sensual pleasure already being enjoyed. If however the mind had summoned up a spade or a fork left sticking in the border of this flower-bed it is very possible that an ecstasy of the same sort as that called up by the image of the chess-board or by the image of the Homeric Lexicon would have resulted.

It is in fact *contrast*, contrast first and last, that plays the major part in what we call ecstasy; and this appears natural enough to a person who has come to hold as I have that the First Cause Itself is of a dualistic nature.

Well! I must hurry on now to the end of our Shirley life. This was brought about by a rapidly conceived and rapidly executed move to Dorset. My father seems to have felt, after his only brother's death, that it behoved him to reside within call of that bow-windowed house in Weymouth where our aged relative lived. So he accepted—a rather unworldly move in a young priest's life—the subordinate position of a small-town curate, after having enjoyed for seven years the sweets of an authority that was practically despotic; for there was no squire in Shirley Village. My father became then the hard-worked curate of the Rector of St. Peter's, the chief parish church, though there were others in the place, of the old Roman town of Dorchester.

With a characteristic gesture, just as when shopping in Ashbourne he had always bought good solid and surprisingly large objects, he now took, on some sort of a lease, an enor-mously large dwelling in an extensive garden, quite heedless of the fact that the house was still being built and the garden still being dug. This was Rothesay House, the birth-place of three more of his eleven children. It was, I think, one of the Mayors of Casterbridge, the excellent Mr. Gregory, who let Rothesay House to my father; and Mr. Knipe, the elderly rector, used to point out to his amazed friends this brick-and-mortar castle arising so near the South Walk for the lodging of a curate. Poor Mr. Knipe! He must have felt sometimes that it was his destiny—good, easy man—to be the clerical superior to a veritable "Giant Grumble" whose dis-turbing pretensions were only matched by his astounding and disconcerting simplicity!

While the Mayor of Casterbridge was building us this surprising house in Dorchester, we lodged in no very grand manner in Weymouth, in a lodging to the rear of Brunswick Terrace.

It was at this time that our aged relative in Penn House

gave me an infinitesimal cedarwood cabinet of tiny black and gilt drawers and with a paradisic smell. This little object contained only five drawers and was really of dolls' house proportions, but it became a fetish of mine and it makes me feel a little sad now to think how completely it has disappeared. There ought to be a "Fairy Sprightly" whose chief purpose in life is to guard from neglect and destruction the inanimate things into which human souls have been flung! There were pieces of my soul—and some of these pieces sold to the Devil too!—in every drawer of this little black and gold object. I kept in it a picture of the second little girl I ever seriously thought about. I am compelled in strict veracity to say "the second"; but the first only manifested herself like a figure in an artificial Pastoral-Picture while I sat with Littleton near my grandfather's fish-pond at Northwold. We were like a couple of childish Machiavels then, talking about fish-hooks and fish-kettles and artificial flies, but touching lightly too upon the love of women.

Littleton in this, as in all else, far more *efficient* than I was, had already made a little girl-friend; and it was my rôle in these talks by the fish-pond to try to *think up* another one that would do for me! I can well remember—for it was not till some twenty years later that I linked any idea of women with my sadistic vice—the vague, vague, *vague* sense of something remotely desirable about long silky hair and a soft form. Nor was this "second" lady-love of mine much more than a proud little statue, upon whom to hang these vague, vague, vague sentiments which in those days were totally unconnected with "the brutish sting" of my vice. Once and once only when this "second" young girl was sitting on my knee, did I experience in connection with her anything approaching to a sensual feeling; and by this time I was an undergraduate at Cambridge.

But it was always a characteristic of mine—for I was not only a born actor, as they say, but what might be named an impassioned "metamorphosist"—to bring to bear upon these vague, vague, vague attractions an overwhelming and most literally *creative* imagination. Fetish worshipper as I was, magician as I conceived myself to be, indurated romanticist as I have proved first and last, it was my delight to pretend to be "in love" and then to buttress up this pretence with a concentrated mythological will-power that was really terrific and abnormal.

I suppose, if the truth were confessed, I got ten times more pleasure from sealing up this young woman's countenance—I can see it now *as it looked in that little picture*—in about twenty paper wrappings, all carefully fastened with sealing-wax, than I ever got from converse with its original! No girl's face has ever been wrapped up—whether living or dead—in so many cerements, and only on very ritualistic occasions did I so much as open this sacred drawer and contemplate the outside wrapping!

In another drawer of this cabinet I preserved certain scriptures of my own, very ambiguous, although extremely decent writings, dealing with various never-to-be-indulged caresses; caresses whose object was no woman, caresses that were far beyond the power of achievement by such a cowardly pilgarlick as I was, between the sun and moon!

It was a wonderful day for me when once walking with my teacher—who loved Littleton and detested Johnny—along the hot Weymouth pavement in front of that noble row of eighteenth-century houses called Belvedere, and I recollect exactly how I felt at that moment, I experienced the first conscious "ecstasy" of my life, at any rate the first conscious ecstasy that I can remember. And, mark you, this ecstasy came to me under quite unpromising conditions. I was not a *persona grata* with my teacher. I wanted—*that* goes without saying—to be down by the sea, digging in the wet sand, not advancing rapidly along Belvedere towards St. Thomas' Street. But as I walked I skipped for joy, like the "little hills" in the Psalms of David. Such a flood of happiness raced through me that I did not scruple to invite the confidence of my teacher. No shame had I, nor any scruple. I whistled every consideration of a sense of fitness to the winds. My teacher was Littleton's friend but not mine; therefore my enemy! Such was my psychology. And oh, what voluptuous joy—so it seems to me now, but I may be exaggerating—to cry out shamelessly to my enemy just those very aspects of my feelings which would most of all excite contempt! Then it was that I put my ecstasy into a riddle, as I dare say the Sphynx did in *her* childhood, and I bade my teacher guess why I felt so happy. My teacher of course—and what a priggish, incalculable, unlovable little boy I must have seemed!—murmured some reply that indicated complete indifference to whether I was happy or not. But, as Blake says, "damn" braces while "bless" only relaxes; and this rebuff, though I still can recall it, by no means stopped my mouth; and I proceeded to explain, and my feelings must have been overpowering, for I recall the very spot where I expressed them, that I was happy, first because I was, at the moment, "good," and second because I hoped that it would shortly occur to my aged relative to present me with *another* black and gold cabinet, twice as large as the one I possessed!

This other cabinet I never did receive; but the original one remained in my possession, its sacred drawers packed with the proud and furtive secrets of my under-life for five years at least after I was happily married. I think it was on the occasion of my son's birth that I buried its contents in other than Wessex soil, and my impression is that the precious cabinet itself fell to pieces. Oh, little secret chest-of-drawers, companion of a restless heart's revolt against all that *was*, in the strength of all that *was not*, where are you now? Has the passing of half a century left not at least one tiny broken fragment of you, lying even yet perhaps—oh I know not where!—but keeping a trace, a savour, a lingering, clinging, ghostly revenant-breath, where you lie, of the bitter sweetness that was a boy's whole fancy-world?

How many forms of stress, of strain, of tension there are in life that have no relation at all to a person's main life-purpose! It sometimes seems as if we all move for years—sometimes for half a lifetime—through a perfectly meaningless chaos of irrelevant events, events that gather themselves together like bubbles on a stream—only they obstruct our boat more than any bubbles could—and then vanish into absolute nothingness! Man seems more subject to this tossing welter of irrelevance than anything else in Nature. What could be more beautifully *fatal* in the movement of its significant destiny than the life of a cow or the life of a tree? The truth is we each of us have to *invent* our own destiny out of the confusion and pell-mell around us, and it is because we are so long in deciding what destiny to invent that so many completely meaningless, insignificant, irrelevant episodes follow one another in our life, unconnected with any general "stream of tendency," springing from nothing, returning to nothing. Chance, not destiny, rules us, swirling the litter and the debris into endless insignificant patterns that form and re-form, only to dissolve even as we gaze at them.

But it is not merely the person who has been lucky enough to find some main purpose for his earthly days that these silly, little, empty occurrences jolt, shake, prod and infuriate. They hurt us and tease us with their meaninglessness, long ere we have found any sort of *raison d'être* for our days equal to what chewing the cud is for a cow or being rained upon for a tree. Who in looking back over their early life can escape being put to shame and utterly confounded by the things that occurred, things for which you feel later nothing but a slowly fading disgust accompanied by a sort of gaping curiosity and base inquisitiveness, and a low, morbid, egotistical interest, a staring bestial interest that it was to you yourself and not another that they happened, an interest comparable to that with which infants contemplate their own excrement.

It is this element of self-love, in totally irrelevant happenings, that accounts for the indescribable tediousness of so many autobiographies and, to speak the honest truth, of so much human conversation. What excites our more intelligent interest *is a story*, that is to say the struggle of a soul, conscious or half conscious, with the obstacles that hinder its living growth, that obstruct the lilt of its pulse and joggle to left or right its integral continuity. The only interest in events, devoid of the negative significance of being obstacles in our path, is a symbolic one. It *is* possible for detached and isolated and even very unpleasant events to be pathetically significant symbols in the course of a life; but it is claiming too much to suppose that everything that happens to us is *intended* to be part of our particular story by an omnipotent artist. Interest, drama, meaning, purpose are qualities given to events by the individual mind. We are ourselves the gods who create the values of our life—what is essential, what is symbolic—and it is left to chance to provide the occasions for the application of these meanings and purposes.

How totally without meaning, for instance, unless along with other vices I have the destiny of a miser in my bones, is the vivid memory I have of watching, with perhaps unworthy pride and awe, my Norfolk grandfather, when he visited us on Dorset coast, take out of his trouser pockets a handful of half-crowns, florins, shillings, sixpences and threepenny bits! My father kept his money in a leather purse, as I myself have always done, doubtless esteeming it, as I still do, a sort of rapscallion insult to the preciousness of metals carrying our sovereign's head upon them, to be rattled about against your groin, along, it may well be, with nuts and string and tobacco and dice and pocket-fluff. This can hardly have been my first acquaintance with money, but it was certainly the first time I can remember feeling an inflation of pride in being related to a man who kept several half-crowns in his trouser pocket. So profoundly did that handful of silver affect me that it threw such a memory search-light over all that surrounded it that I can recall minutely the whole occasion.

It was on the deck of the first British man-of-war—the fleet was always coming into Portland Harbour—to be built with a turret for its guns. To me who retained such an exalted memory of the stupendous length of that noble steamship, the *Great Eastern*, as we had seen it from the windows of Penn House, this round, squat gun-turret was completely unimpressive. My miser-like interest in all that shining silver, emerging from a pocket actually related to me, is indeed the only cause of my recalling the *Thunderer*. Nor was my father, I am sure, one bit more impressed by all this scientific armament than I was. It was the work of professors, this great new Engine of Destruction, and it certainly was "new-fangled"; whereas the turf-covered bastions of the Nothe fortress which had been familiar to him from boyhood—alas! the noble old fort, together ¦with the red coats who paraded its defences, must be totally superannuated now!—had a kind of sacred Battle of Trafalgar dignity.

Long before we actually moved into that grand new house, being built for us by the mayor, my father had begun almost daily excursions to Dorchester. Indeed, I suppose his laborious curate's work was in full swing before we left that lodging behind Brunswick Terrace.

I must now record an episode which left an indelible impression on my mind. Encouraged by the example of my father who would frequently walk the eight miles to Rothesay House from Penn House, across the Downs, Littleton and I —we must have been respectively nine and eight when we made this resolve; for it was before we went to school, and he was only just nine then—decided to undertake this enterprise. We skirted Lodmoor and ascended the Downs to the west of the famous White Horse, passing, I take it, the small hill hamlet which is the scene of Hardy's *Trumpet Major*. We advanced sturdily enough till we were about half-way up the main ascent of the high, grassy, tumulus-crowned ridge, and then quite suddenly my heart and strength failed me and I sat down on the sunburnt, thyme-scented grass, and hopelessly indifferent to the familiar butterflies, "Marble Whites" and "Clifton Blues," that fluttered round, gave myself up to despair. We had gone so far that to return seemed as impossible as to advance, and that kind of "whoreson lethargy" that attends on mortal weakness, when heart and legs collapse together, reduced me to brutish inertness. It was then that Littleton showed "the rock from which he had been hewn and the pit from which he had been dug" by doing what anyone would have supposed absolutely impossible. He took the collapsed "Johnny" upon his small unconquerable back and actually staggered under this burden *up* the remaining portion of the ascent!

Thus it came to pass that my first crossing of the South Downs was not upon my own feet but upon the feet of my younger brother. Aye! how often in my subsequent life, when my spirit has failed me and my bones have melted within me have I cried out for this strong aid; nor ever cried in vain, until three thousand miles of salt-water came to roll between us! Littleton's physical courage and endurance were always putting me to shame in those days.

I remember how my father loved to take us both, our weariness of the way forgotten as we followed the adventures of that unwearied Giant and Fairy, past Lodmoor Hut, past the coastguard cottages, to the little beach where Preston brook ran, and I suppose still runs, into the sea. There was one place here where a spirited boy could just succeed in jumping over this small stream; and this feat Littleton invariably accomplished. As invariably, and without one single redeeming exception, I used to make frantic and desperate runs to the challenging spot, but always pulled up at the last second, fearful of the leap into the air.

At such times both Littleton and my father, whose "rapport" in such matters was as deep as it was silent, received my discomfiture with grave indulgence, sorry for me but feeling that the honour of the family had been sufficiently upheld without my aid. It was curious how early in our life that singular relation was established between Littleton and me which lasted on until I went to Cambridge. The essence of this relation was that while in all practical, physical, and worldly situations Littleton surpassed me, defended me, championed me, in things of pure fantasy I retained my primogenital prerogative. I say in things of the fantasy rather than of the mind; for in many mental achievements, especially where scholarship was concerned, he was always ahead of me. Indeed I have never known any man more thoroughly conversant with the groundwork of Greek and Latin than he eventually became.

When we quarrelled—need I tell you?—it was always my fault. I had a devilish love of teasing! Indeed, I often recall the prophetic voice that said to me once:

"One day, Johnny, it will be *you* who will be teased."

But that day did not arrive till long afterwards; not indeed until Destiny had put the ocean between Littleton and my serpent's tongue. But in those days I even had the presumption —limb of Satan that I was!—to want to tease my father! It was a little later that I did this, but I always *wanted* to do it, just as I always wanted to tease my younger brothers and sisters. But it was a little later in our life that in the drawing-room at Montacute—knowing perfectly well how it would annoy him —I expatiated at exhaustive length upon the *Seven Principles of Man*, as interpreted by Annie Besant. I went on till he lifted up his head from his netting—he used to make our lawn tennis nets then—and burst out, trembling with fury:

"She is a Demon . . . John . . . a Demon! *The woman is a Demon!*"

Well, I must have teased Littleton into some similar paroxysm of anger that got him into serious trouble, for I recall very well how one day—seized with bitter remorse—I decided to do something for him that would counterbalance this piece of cruelty. Littleton collected fossils and butterflies; while it fell to my rôle to collect birds' eggs; for it was of course unthinkable that a son of my father should collect nothing. No doubt it was for precisely this reason that Theodore, always so terrifyingly original, did actually collect nothing. Perhaps it was from this Nothing he collected that there emerged later his extraordinary works of genius!

It was long before we left Dorchester that I reached a quite peculiar understanding with Theodore, an understanding of a totally different kind from any I have ever had with Littleton, and one that may be said to have consisted in a fantastical "rapport" between our most extreme and least communicable personal peculiarities. At this time of our living in Weymouth lodgings all I can recall of the future hermit of East Chaldon was his tendency—not to fall asleep as one might have expected of so young a child during family prayers —*but to faint*, and fainting slide down upon the floor! This was the beginning of a long series of not always very considerate compulsions, into which the little Theodore—like a unicorn in a lion's den—was dragged here and there by my father and me. With Littleton his relations were of a peculiar and special nature, consisting of a hand-to-mouth exchange of an especial kind of badinage quaintly charged with all the little humorous details of their daily life. But Littleton never tried to force him—as my father and I were prone to do—to enter paths that were outside his grooves and against the grain. My father's tyrannies were confined however to dragging him for great walks, longer than his strength could endure, whereas I used to find in his imagination a quick response to some of my most devilish games and some of my most scandalous experiments. But oh dear! how well I can see little Theodore, white in the face and with great forlorn eyes like an over-driven animal, as he was dragged along some dusty road where the very flies joined forces to persecute him!

But to return to my remorse over getting Littleton into trouble. Some startling and spectacular deed I felt must be done, and done at once, which would overwhelm him with amazement at my penitence. Brooding upon this, and full of the deepest contrition, I set off alone—we had from a very early age been allowed the most incredible liberty—to a spot somewhere beyond the coastguard cottages, where I had noted on a previous occasion an enormous stone fossil. It was a colossal ammonite, embedded I think, though I may be mistaken in this, in a geological substance known, or at least known to my father, as "Blue Lias." For all his contempt for science, and his preference for traditional pastoral lore, he was wont to utter such proud phrases as:

"I am glad you have noticed that formation, my boy. It is Blue Lias," or "Here is something, Johnny, that is worth seeing, a piece of Kimmeridge Clay!"

He would say this just as he would say "The Cormorant is the greediest of all birds," or "My brother once stared into a tiger's eyes till he put the brute out of countenance."

Every phenomenon he referred to, whether animate or inanimate, became a sacrosanct thing, a privileged object like those objects in fairy-tales that travellers carried to work magic with. I think it materially increased his appreciation of any landscape he was traversing when he could gravely refer to "Purbeck Marble," or say, "Do 'ee see, me boy, how uneven the 'Rock Formation' is, in those cliffs over there? Such a peculiar strata"—he would use the word as if it were a feminine singular word, but use it with so much authority and weight that as with a great many expressions he used, like the syllable "goss," for instance, in place of "gorze," his repeated misnomer finally became an organic entity with far more substance in it than most dictionary words could claim. Well, my great ammonite was embedded in the cliff's edge, whatever the cliff may have been made of, and this small repentant Prester John was soon occupied in gouging it out with his fingers. But the grand act of penance, for it was twice as large as a human skull, was to go staggering under the weight of this terrific fossil all the way home. Past Lodmoor Hut I had to go, past the clipped evergreen hedges of Victoria Gardens, and along that sandy pavement beneath the pebbly wall that enclosed the garden of the turreted stucco house where the great Doctor Smith lived, who attended upon the invalids of Brunswick Terrace with a deportment that combined the Divine with the Physician. I forget exactly how Littleton received my offering; but I know that all the years his collection was preserved at Rothesay House this penitential ammonite could be seen. Did it go to Montacute and after staying there for thirty years come back to Weymouth when my father returned to his own again?

One of the ghastliest of the lesser pities of life is the way so many precious symbolic objects disappear forever. Such forlorn Inanimates have no Limbo to go to, no kindly funeral-blazes. They remain the same as they have always been; but they are cast out upon the world's rubbish-heap; and no Redeemer can ever come that shall restore *them* to honour. Blessed shall the man or the woman be in the Day of Judgment who has rescued even one of these castaways and saved it from the Scavenger's Cart!

The grand delight of those months in lodging at Weymouth —and this delight returned every time we visited the place afterwards—was digging with a wooden spade in the wet sand near the sea's edge. Oh, how deep a pleasure, oh, how quivering and trembling a pleasure it was to watch the salt-water flow into an estuary that you yourself had prepared for it! What a commentary it is upon the ways of mortal life that such a proverbially vain thing, such an ultimate example of useless activity, as digging in sea-sand should be attended with such ravishing transports of happiness, while upon the useful and the enduring work of our hands, performed in labour and sorrow, we can scarcely bear so much as to look! But that incredible sensation when the sea at last really rushes in and our sandbanks grow paler and whiter, as the long ripples reach them; till they begin to yield and to sink and to flatten out, and their edges are overpoweringly smoothed away and rounded off and silted into indistinction; and the sand we have piled up comes sliding down, sinking, sinking, sinking; till finally there is nothing left but the smooth sea-floor, just as it has been for a thousand years—what can describe the mystery of it? It is a sensation wherein the depths of some profound cosmic consciousness are shared by us. Creation, destruction . . . destruction, creation. . . . It is the ecstatic in-breathing and out-breathing of Brahma! I certainly feel, looking back on my life, that few pleasures I have known have excelled digging with a wooden spade in wet sand. The permeating presence of sun and sea, the complete isolation and delicious solitariness of the pursuit, if you are of an unsociable turn of mind, the immediate response to your human effort of such a vast force as the incoming tide—think of a child of seven choosing the direction, like a little deity, that an estuary of the great moon-drawn antagonist of the whole earth should take, *this* way rather than *that* way!—these things, combined with the heavenly absence of nurse or governess, make up an "ensemble" of beatitude rarely experienced, I fear, on this planetary globe. I cannot believe that I was still—at seven and eight and nine —totally unconscious of what has now come to be my most obstinate cult, I mean the conscious drinking up of all the various sense-impressions which the Self receives as it embraces the Not-Self; but I confess, much as it annoys me to do so, and much as it spoils what might be called *the logic of temperamental destiny* in my life, that I haven't one scrap, one faintest flicker of memory about any such feeling!

"Isn't it sad," as the Chinese Sage Kwang-Tze always exclaims, in his whimsical-wistful way, that wicked, vicious, troubling memories remain so much more vivid than good, satisfying, soothing memories? To confess the truth, though I well recall the diffused pleasure of these long days on the wet sand, I cannot remember—no! not sharply or vividly—any one single occasion when I was thus so happy! But with abominable clarity can I recall how once, during the annual Weymouth Regatta, when we were watching the yachts racing across the bay, I saw a middle-aged man in one boat—the spectator's boats were all crowded close together—tormenting with the most devilish malignity, a youth in another boat who was beside himself with impotent fury. Being "a tease" myself, the scene had a morbid interest for me; but it frightened me a good deal too. It comes back to me now as a grim vignette from the worst passions of the Inferno; and I think it gave me a pretty ghastly inkling of the *infiniteness* of evil. It burnt itself anyway into the most sensitized portion of my nerves.

Another unpleasant memory returns to me of this epoch; but this one has to do with our first few nights in Rothesay House. The windows of my room—I always had a room to myself then, and on the wall of this room, both at Dorchester and at Montacute, I used to have a small, oval, coloured print of the Duke of Wellington, which for some queer reason gave me extreme satisfaction—opened on the South Walk whose tall, thick, horse chestnut-trees were visible across our newly-laid-out garden. Dorchester, as Hardy, whose own house was only half a mile across the fields to the East of the East Walk, explains in the *Mayor of Casterbridge*, is singularly like an ancient city in its freedom from suburbs. It had been a walled town in the Roman times, some of the Roman masonry serving this purpose even yet, as it has done for nigh two thousand years, but these umbrageous avenues of thick horse chestnuts had come, since the Napoleonic Wars, to take the place of walls. I can remember with the utmost distinctness seeing the aged William Barnes, Thomas Hardy's ancient friend, whose statue now stands, and a fine one it is, outside St. Peter's Church, walking slowly down the South Walk under these chestnut-trees, dressed, in the style of a hundred years ago, in knee-breeches, black stockings, and silver-buckled shoes. But it was no aged poet I beheld on this occasion as I tried to go to sleep in my room through the long, slow-fading midsummer twilight—

but a fantastic procession of phantoms, who moved like mechanical images up and down the South Walk! Were they the ghosts of the old French prisoners who originally planted these noble trees? No! they were just the ordinary passers-by; but by some mirage-like trick of distance they presented themselves to my startled eyes as ghosts, and not only ghosts, but ghosts who had the power of automaton-like progression, without a movement of legs or feet!

I have always been one to expect, and to accept, marvels and wonders, as part of what might be called the natural "chaoticism" of the world. To be a Pluralist rather than a Monist, is as much of an instinct with me as it is to every East Indian to be obsessed by Unity. The world was then—*and is so still* for in this matter my reason has only defended my instinct—an incalculable welter of criss-cross forces, each one of which has its own particular measure of consciousness or demi-semi-quaver consciousness. I am thus less liable to supernatural shocks than people whose minds are less credulous than mine, or if you will, for it comes to the same thing, less sceptical than mine as to all that they call scientific truth. If I actually did behold a ghost or a phantom, or some inexplicable phenomenon of magical origin, I should undoubtedly be bothered, and up to a certain point startled, as I was by the sight of these images in the South Walk, but I should not be paralysed or panic-stricken, because I should not be profoundly *surprised*. Every living organism—it is the fatality of our identity—has its own peculiar universe, not quite like any other—and my world remains a world under the sway of inscrutable mystery. In plain speech I still feel wholly convinced that the cause of every natural phenomenon is personal—the exertion of energy by a conscious, or at any rate a half-conscious *will*.

It is for this reason that no arguments anyone can use are able to convince me that the First Cause is not responsible for the pain of the world. The First Cause is for ever pleading its cause with me by contending that without free will no happiness is possible, and that free will *once given*, pain becomes inevitable; but my reply to Its argument seems to me a conclusive one:

"Who made free will to be fatally inseparable from pain?" and if It retorts: "The Nature of Things, my child," I should merely repeat: "Who made the Nature of Things to be like that?"

My own feeling is—it may be a rooted insanity but I do not think so—that the only profoundly philosophical way of taking life is a threefold act of the intellect. First to accept our sense impressions of the world as the world's true reality, against all electronic reduction. Secondly, to accept what interiorly we feel of our consciousness and will as our deepest hint as to what causes the nature of this reality to be as it is. Thirdly, to force ourselves to enjoy in a particular way this self-made universe that we are for ever destroying and recreating.

It was during my eighth and ninth years of human experience that we found ourselves fully established in Rothesay House, Dorchester, just south of the South Walk. In my own memory these particular two years, after I had ceased to be a child, but had not yet gone to school, are the most important, most significant, and certainly most happy of my whole life. In pure happiness I consider these years to be rivalled by only two epochs in my whole life; the first of these consisting of several intermittent fragments of flawless felicity, namely, my visits to Northwold in Norfolk; and the second consisting of my quite recent retreat, after giving up lecturing, to the peaceful seclusion of these New York hills. I won't say I cannot imagine greater happiness than I experience now, or than I experienced at the age of eight and nine, but, taking my life as a whole, these three epochs, are the happiest periods I have so far known and the ones for which I shall utter my "Vixi!" when I come to die.

While I am dealing with this subject why should I not indicate in the same clear terms what I consider the most *unhappy* epochs in my life? Without doubt I should say the three years between the ages of fourteen and seventeen and the particular year of grace, it was 1917 I think, when I was forty-five. The first three unhappy years came upon me when I left the Preparatory School at Sherborne and entered the Big

School there, and this other unhappy year came to me before my second Major Operation, and culminated during the summer months; when, having let my city room to Padraic Colum I roamed these Eastern States like a veritable lost soul seeking rest and finding none.

Yes, my eighth and ninth years, when we were settled at Dorchester and before I went to school were years of extraordinary and exultant satisfaction. And yet I have no memory —and that I have none makes me feel a disappointed anger with this fortunate era—of experiencing that Wordsworthian "Pleasure which there is in Life itself," which is now my dominant cult. The absence of even the faintest, obscurest, vaguest memory of that kind makes me almost feel as if when the Johnny of those days turned into the Jack of the later time, some completely different spirit had entered into me; and this is a feeling extremely distasteful to me!

Littleton and I used to go to a small private Dame's School, situated near the Great Western station, to reach which we daily made our way along that portion of the South Walk which continues beyond the thoroughfare where South Street ends and the Weymouth Road begins. This continuation of South Walk is a very secluded place and few people frequent it. The general stream of human movement flowing down South Street follows a parallel approach to the Great Western Station or makes its way across the open square to the Weymouth Road. But no human movement enters the precincts of this continuation of South Walk. It is one of the most secluded spots in the town. Its umbrageous solitude is protected even from children's perambulators by certain ancient and venerable posts. Against these posts lovers can lean by day and by night in a peace which is rarely interrupted, and once having pushed your way through them you breathe that peculiar atmosphere of mellow security, as gracious in winter as in summer, where the exclusion of wheeled vehicles and the sense of old paths, old walls, old trees, old grass, evokes a feeling of collegiate if not of monastic retirement. Along this avenue of undisturbed seclusion we used to observe, making her way to *her* school, a grave, self-possessed little girl.

F

The repeated sight of this small dignified figure—I can recall nothing of her but her composure and her demure preoccupation with her own affairs—must have roused the very devil in me. It has all receded now into hopeless obscurity; but I can remember how disappointed and aggrieved I was when weary of these encounters with such an odious little boy, as I must have seemed to her, she took a different road to her school or went to a different school. Were my persecutions confined to making faces, or did I attempt to utter challenging words? I cannot remember. My impression is that I attempted to interest Littleton in this secret obliquity but quite in vain. Littleton himself at that time had struck up a dumb, romantic friendship with one of the little choir-boys in St. Peter's Church, to whom he would discreetly refer as "the brown-coated choir-boy"; but the difference between us was made clear enough, in the fact that while his interest was tender, sentimental, and very personal, mine was perverse, unsympathetic, and totally impersonal.

Oh, what a number of queer memories come back as I think of those chestnut walks of Dorchester! It was in this same secluded South Walk that we used often to overtake a fellow pupil at our own Dame's School, whose father was none other than the Governor of the County Prison. This little boy was always escorted by a nurse-maid, and, as it happened, by a nurse-maid of Spanish origin. What must my imp of darkness put into my head to do but to start a long persecution—I dare say to revenge myself for the disappearance of the little girl—of this unfortunate foreign servant! Littleton I am afraid was dragged willy-nilly into this roguery; and we used to hide behind the chestnut-trees and rush out like a pair of unconscionable "gamins" shouting in our shrill young voices: "Spanish maiden! Spanish maiden! Spanish maiden!" My behaviour on this occasion *did* lead—for this harmless pair were unable to change either their route or their destination —to discovery and disgrace. For the "Spanish maiden" complained to her mistress, the Governor's lady, and Master Johnny—though he did not go to prison—was put to bitter shame and something like public ignominy.

But it would not be only stories of misconduct that those great chestnut-trees, if they could murmur like the oaks of Dodona, would relate. Once I was caught—and here I am sure I was in the right and my accuser unjust—red-handed in the act of throwing flint stones with all my might at the heads of a group of town boys. It was the august personality of Mr. B.——, the High Street haberdasher, whose beard reached to his navel—who came down on me on this occasion, making a great todo, I recall, of my being the son of the curate. Sharp and enduring is a boy's memory of injustice; and I hasten to assure *you* at any rate, impartial reader, that I had been protecting our own "maiden"—not a Spanish one, but a fellow subject from Berkshire—against the insults of the rabble.

But if the South Walk, leading to our daily lessons, was linked up with ambiguous and questionable doings, the East Walk, on the Fordington side of Dorchester, can have rarely witnessed greater human happiness than ours was, as, with our butterfly-nets transmuted into fishing-nets and with watering cans to hold our captures, we took our way to those felicitous water meadows—veritable Elysian fields, though vulgarly named Stinsford Ditches—where we caught the minnows wherewith we stocked our aquarium.

This aquarium was an intense and unique pleasure to me. I think it satisfied in some profound manner my desire to be God, or at least *a* god, and there is undoubtedly something about watching the movements of these restless beings, as they swim in and out of the stones and weeds from which you have *created their world*, that gives you a mysterious feeling of excitement. Yes, it is as if you "possessed" in the way I fancy the First Cause must possess *his* aquarium, these darting, silvery, rose-tinged aboriginals of our human organism. My satisfaction lay very much in the thought of what a complicated world of hills and forests and glades and gorges I had made for these fish, and how large and infinite it must seem to them—while to me it was so small, and every plant and pebble so carefully chosen! My conscience in these matters has grown very touchy within the last forty years. How could I endure for a moment not taking back a sick minnow to those Stinsford

Brooks as soon as it began to go round and round at the top
of the water, gasping with piteous little gasps at our thinner
air, as if in its extremity it would fain change its element?

The more I ponder upon my memories of my early life the
more I am convinced of two things. *First* that there are abysses
of Being and Reality totally outside this astronomical "pinfold,"
in which, as Milton says, we are "confined and pestered."
Second, that all the great urges of our spirit come nearest to the
secret of the Universe when they enjoy Nature with the detachment of a Pilgrim rather than analyse her with the curiosity
of a Scientist.

But what is forever escaping me as I look back on these
days is what might be called my normal mood. I cannot recall
any average, ordinary, commonplace, humdrum mood, whether
cheerful or the reverse, to which I awaked every day and upon
which I relapsed from my moments of unnatural excitement.
What I feel now is that *all* my moments were moments of
unnatural excitement! In fact I feel almost tempted to go a
step further and to maintain that the whole conception of the
normal, the average, the commonplace, is due to a specific
mental disease. To call a thing "commonplace" becomes
therefore just the same as if you confided to your friend the
fact that you felt sick or insane. I believe the most unphilosophical, irreligious and immoral word in the English language
is the word "commonplace."

If there was ever a saying of any sage that pierced to the
heart of things it was that word of Jesus that we must become
as children to enter heaven; and when St. Paul says we must
"cast away childish things" I believe he is speaking of those
annoying conventionalities, those teasing, bullying silly social
fashions which boys and girls indulge in as they grow older.
For what does it mean to become "as children"? It means that
to be what is called "bored"—by anything but the society of
these young people who so worried St. Paul—is *henceforth
impossible*. Children are never bored; because the state of
boredom is so appalling to them that they scent its approach
afar off, and either run away, or fall into a tragic fit of blind
despair.

Green gravel, sea-sand castles, submarine forests in an aquarium, blue beads strung on a string, toy pistols in a lathe-and-plaster roof, the stalks of artichokes used as spears—from one point of view all these things are childs' play; but from another point of view they are the sublime and mystical "Gleichnis" of our whole Faustian Quest.

No words can describe what I am now trying to approach —hovering around it and about it but perpetually prohibited from seizing it by that troublesome law of Nature which makes it impossible to express a living truth except by suggestion and indirection. All I can do is to indicate, by one clumsy analogy after another, the gap, the lacuna, the niche in our daily psychology where this mystery dwells like an unseen picture in a magic crystal. And there is an emanation from the thing's presence, which is as disturbing to our human consciousness as the presence of the black poodle was to Faust, and as corrosive to worldly ambition too, as a secret chest of sea-sunk treasure might be to a fisherman. The hatred it excites among clever people is like the fury of flame-touched adders; for it is a revelation of the Eternal totally unknown to mathematics and logic. If at nine years old I felt it to be something "whose course," as Scott says of Arthur's Wain, "doth roll in utter darkness round the pole," it is to me now as I fumble towards it far less definable than 'any polar darkness.

But whatever it is it endows the sands of the sea and the grasses of the field with an enchanted light, and it reveals this world as a place where lobworms and newts have souls, and where the Inanimate has a disturbing porousness and transparency.

In one thing I know well the neurotic John of sixty is identical with the neurotic Johnny of nine, and that is in being born, so to speak, *fresh every day*. I certainly woke up every morning with a tremendous life energy pulsing through me and with a feeling that I could *flow through* every material object I looked at in a rapture of identification. I think—though confound it all! this is just what I do not remember!—that I expected daily to come upon some magical object, made of earth or of sea-sand or of moss, like that laid upon the top of my miniature Mount Cloud, which would immediately thrust into the world of grown-up people's reality a wedge of *my* reality, so that it would be forced to come to terms with it! I am convinced that I *knew*, without question or doubt, that my world—the world in which I was a magician—was a great deal more than mere pretending.

I wish I could communicate in intelligible speech what I really felt myself to be—I will not say what I really was—in those days at Rothesay House. I believe I can recall exact inner feeling on many separate highly-pitched occasions. What I cannot reproduce in my mind are my less agitated, less excited, less troubled moments. But perhaps there were no such moments! Perhaps, except when I was asleep, I lived such a nervous, strung-up life that my only relapses were changes from one kind of tension to another. I believe I *am* able, in a manner that I fancy must be rare among men or women of sixty, to feel the actual, identical feelings that I used to have at particular moments in those days. I certainly lived in a constant repetition of gestures of extreme psychic intensity. My head was always full of some fantastical transaction that broke up the normal world.

I touch here upon what is to me one of the profoundest philosophical mysteries: I mean the power of the individual mind to create its own world, not in complete independence of what is called "the objective world," but in a steadily growing independence of the attitude of other minds *towards* this world. For what people call the objective world is really a most fluid, flexible, malleable thing. It is like the wine of the Priestess Bacbuc in *Rabelais*. It tastes differently; it *is* a different cosmos, to every man, woman, and child. To analyse this "objective world" is all very well, as long as you don't forget that the power to rebuild it by emphasis and rejection is synonymous with your being alive.

It must have been in my ninth year that I established—like a young Mussolini—what I called the "Volentiā Army." This organization played an overwhelming part in my life at that time; and, such was my hypnotic energy, I forced it upon every one of my fellow pupils at that Dame's School near the Great

Western Station. What led me to the use of the word "Volen-tiā" I don't know, but I know it had to be pronounced "Volentiā," the final "a" like the syllable "aye." Oh! with what an incredible sense of importance, as the enchanted chief of an occult revolutionary régime, I used to sit in the lathe-and-plaster "roof-room"—it was not really a "room" at all—that the workmen employed by Mayor Gregory had left half-boarded under the slates of Rothesay House! I dragged—I presume with Littleton's help—a little table up there, and on this table I placed two lit candles—it is extraordinary what amount of licence I was allowed in these enterprises!—and there I sat, in exultant state, feeling like a re-incarnation of Owen Glendower, a toy pistol, loaded with real explosive "caps" *in both hands*, and the ferocious scowl of a dealer-out of life and death on my misanthropic countenance, while our noble, imaginative, high-spirited, sympathetic, much-enduring, but totally un-Spanish "maiden" from Berkshire would be brought as a captive before me.

It must have been about this time—before this enchanted ninth year of my life passed into its fatal tenth—that Theodore, then aged six, began to play a more prominent part in my life. My impression is that while Littleton always regarded the activities of the "Volentiā Army" with certain shrewd reserva-tions the small Theodore gave himself wholly up to them. But even that could not have been altogether the case, because I recall that somewhere, in one of the very immature shrub-beries of our newly laid-out garden, beneath a curious pink blossoming bush that bore seeds which *popped* when a person touched them, Theodore established, entirely for himself, a solitary retreat—a kind of infantile "Beth-Car"—to which he gave the name of "Bushes' Home." And just as the "Volentiā Army" had to draw in its horns and vanish when it found Littleton seated at the dining-room table, drawing ships, so it never dared to intrude upon the sacred precincts of Theodore's "Bushes' Home."

But it must never be supposed that my "Volentiā Army" was a mere game of robbers, or pirates. I surrounded it on every side by the *mythological!* It was really a sort of secret

Rosicrucian, or Thaumaturgic society, of which I—a young Prester John—was the head.

Now there was at that time a newly made road that led southward across the South Western Railway towards the high downs, and upon the surface of this road, during the early period of its construction, had been sprinkled gravel of a very peculiar kind—gravel such as I have never seen before or since. It was as a matter of fact of an intermittent *green*. Now green is a colour that has always come to me with a pleasurable shock; especially when it has come—so to speak —in the wrong place! That green sky during prayers at Shirley was an example of this; but for a road to be green struck me as more curious than for the sky to be green.

"Green gravel, green gravel, the grass is so green!
The fairest young lady that ever was seen!"

But this particular "green gravel" led me, while our un-wearied Berkshire friend pushed the big perambulator over all impediments, to things that were much more exciting than any "young lady." For this new road under the railway, leaving Fordington at the point where you go North towards Mr. Hardy's house, ended in a field-path across Fordington Great Field that led to the top of the Downs. These Downs were surmounted, as Mr. Hardy himself pointed out to me long afterwards, by no less than fifty tumuli above old dead chieftains' graves. At the spot towards which this path ascended there were several of these tumuli—high grassy mounds exactly like those that bore the bonfires on their summits in the first chapter of the *Return of the Native*.

By this time my longing' to possess supernatural powers had become a perfectly conscious and clearly articulated thing; and now on the strength of it I set to work, bit by bit, fragment by fragment, to invent a mythology! I did this with a thorough-ness that showed I had not forgotten my father's interminable fairy-story; only this was not a "story." This was a way of life. Most of my mythology I have forgotten now, but I can remember the names of certain terrific beings that lived in those pre-historic mounds and what I used to call them. I used to call them "Dromonds." And in addition to the "Dromonds" I called into existence a whole tribe of extremely powerful but rather dwarfish men, called "Escrawaldons," whose rôle was to be the official enemies, in my History of the World, of the "Volentiā Army." The "Volentiā Army" became in fact a sort of multiple Logos, standing midway between the visible and the invisible. In its realistic aspect it entered constantly into my daily life whereas in its ideal aspect it became part of an imaginary history that had no counterpart in reality. In this connection I still can feel the exact and identical thrill which I set to work, with several half-penny note-books before me, to compose a language for the "Volentiā Army."

The satisfaction I got came, I suppose, from arbitrarily inventing words that other people—presumably—would subsequently have to use. Indeed the pleasure I derived from all this must have been more akin to the sense of power in an Arch-Medicine-Man, or a Super-High-Priest, who invents a ritual for subsequent generations to follow than to anything merely scholarly. Indeed, I am sure it had nothing of the feeling of scholarship in it, any more than my mania to-day for looking out words in a Homeric Lexicon has to do with scholarship. It is the magic significance of words and the proud feeling of dealing with secrets known to very few that pleases me so much to-day. And I think this is the kind of thing I felt when I created the Volentiā syllables destined to perplex the wits of future generations of Escrawaldons. I think too that words, the magic of words, is a deep and occult part of the mystery of life. Gibberish—the inventing of nonsense—is an irrepressible tendency of mine, and to me it is never comic or facetious or amusing. It is more tragic, more grave, more religious than intelligibility is! What is in my mind about this baffles me and escapes me, but I feel that I am on the track here of something possessed of a curious importance. The giant Nimrod, on the road to the Ninth Circle of Dante's Inferno, utters tremendous and most awe-inspiring gibberish: "Rafel mai amech Zabi almi!"—and this is no doubt the reason why, though I am far too unscholarly to understand a single word of it, I get such extraordinary pleasure from reading aloud *A Work in Progress* by James Joyce.

A totally different pleasure, however, from inventing a language, was the pleasure I got from hearing Scott's *Ivanhoe* read aloud in the evenings, and soon afterwards, in the same year of grace, *The Talisman*. These romances, and indeed the whole of Scott's works, of which I must have read all except *Count Robert of Paris*, were in those days, and remain now, by far the most powerful literary influence of my life. That massive solidity, that slow-moving convincingness, that leisurely, friendly, whimsical humour, that Homeric nobility, that cheerful endurance of the buffets of fate, was even capable of doing something to counteract the natural weakness, waywardness, cowardice, morbidity, selfishness, of my furtive and evasive character. And this impassioned reading of Scott encouraged me—though recalling the fate of Norna of the Fitful Head it perhaps ought not to have done so—in my living a life that was almost purely a life of playing at magic. Why not? What I feel now, and with what seems to me to be my very deepest intellect, is that any imaginative illusion by which a person half lives, any mythology in which a person half believes, is truer, "in the only sense in which truth matters," than the most authenticated scientific facts.

But *what was I after* in this rebelliously individualistic ninth year of my life, the last year of real liberty I had till I went to Cambridge? I can tell you exactly—oh! to a nicety what I was after. For in every important essential—with the single exception of my cult of the senses—my nature is the same now as it was then. What I wanted was that kind of romantic struggle with things and people, things and people always yielding as I advanced, *but not too easily*, a struggle which takes place in an ideal region, hewn out of reality and constantly touching but never quite identified with reality, such as might be most conveniently described by the expression, *a Quest*.

The kind of "Quest," however, that I wanted was not a simple one. To satisfy me it had to take place in a world that was at once the real world and yet a world of marvels. Thus it might perhaps be best defined as a Magical Quest, a Quest undertaken by a young neophite in magic. The end or purpose of the Quest was not definable; *was not even considered.* It was enough that it went on and on. But though indefinable, there was Something ahead of me, Something rich and strange, Something mysteriously satisfying, a sort of Beatific Vision, composed of a synthesis not so much of sensations as of exultant emotions. Our aquarium, given to us I think by that maternal grandfather in Norfolk whose pocketful of loose silver had so impressed me on the deck of H.M.S. *Thunderer*, was in a curious way an integral part of this Magic Quest, for these inquisitive minnows exploring the miniature submarine forest we prepared for them were so many darting and fluttering projections of myself swimming through a world of dim under-water marvels!

That new road to Fordington Great Field, sprinkled with green gravel—could this gravel have been broken fragments of *fire-touched flint?*—leading to those tumuli on the ridge, that we always spoke of as "The Humps," was only one among many paths along which I pursued this Quest. Another one was a field-path leading out of the Weymouth Road before you came to the hamlet of Monkton, where was a big fallen willow-tree. Whatever may have been the vague, rich, dim Vision at the end of this Faustian Quest of mine, it was certainly approached by a variety of circuitous ways! This great fallen willow was perhaps of all these ways the one that had the most mysterious charm. We always spoke of it as the "Herringstone Tree," but what kind of a place Herringstone was, to this day I have not the least idea. It was the tree that led me on; and I shrewdly suspect that tree held something, in its moss-grown, massive, fallen branches, that brought back the enchanted laurel-axe of the Shirley shrubbery.

My Quest took one rather quaint and even in a sense, when you try to envisage an odd-looking, untidy, surreptitious little boy, in muddy knickerbockers and navy-blue jersey, putting on an expression that he believed as ethereal and Ariel-like, rather pathetic form. Our aged Penn House relative had given me a small musical box, no bigger than a half-penny bun; and with this in my possession, turning the handle with one hand while I held it, as I supposed, in an airy feminine manner in the other, I used to hurry on tiptoe from room to room of Rothesay House, I will not say "pretending to be," for my transformations were more than pretence, but *being* for the nonce, a supernatural agent.

I wish I could recall the half-indulgent, half-scared expression with which Littleton, at the dining-room table, industriously drawing ships, for he was loth to rouse Johnny's irrational anger, and yet found it difficult to see the despotic Head of the "Volentiā Army" in the light of a butterfly-winged Ariel, must have turned to greet my perambulating tinkle of sweet sound.

It must have been at the beginning of my tenth year—that year that saw Littleton and myself deposited in the Preparatory School at Sherborne—that I composed my first poem. I find it impossible to remember whether this, or a fragment of a prose romance entitled, *The Knight of the Festoon* was my earliest literary inspiration, but I cannot resist transcribing the verses, which were written after we had all been for a visit to Corfe Castle. . . .

> "At Corfe Castle when the light
> Has vanished and the shades of night
> Steal o'er the ruins grey
> There is a dungeon from light of day
> Where now a grisly Spectre holds his sway.
> Among the shadowy ruins groping creeps he
> And when he hears a fearful shriek up leaps he
> And sees another Spectre of the night
> A Bogy that surpasses him in height.
> Then there commences such a fearful fray
> As was ne'er seen by the broad light of day.
> Then morning breaks and both dissolve in air
> And nothing's left but the old castle fair!"

I am so little of an artist—real artists willingly return to their past works, over every detail of which they are ready to pore, just as they have laboured over them to the full extent of their power—that when I have once finished, for I am afraid I cannot use the word "completed" any work, I never want to hear of it, to see it, or even to think of it again. These verses therefore must be considered, from this point of view, the sole work of art, which I have produced from ten years old to sixty: for from the moment of writing them I knew them by heart, and it was indeed on the strength of reciting them, in the wildest and most terrifying manner, when I was fifteen years old, and in the Big School, that I proved my claim *to be out of my mind*, a claim that got me placed at night in the housekeeper's room, which was the escape, from a certain cruel bully that I above all desired.

My nightly orgies of sadistic imagination were never for long intermitted; but it was only in this strictly cerebral and extremely impersonal manner that I was ever cruel unless you can call my pleasure in teasing by this name. The occasions upon which I have actually *practised* sadism, or even tried to practise it, I shall confess in the fullest detail as my story continues. At this age I can only recall one episode that might be so interpreted, but even this returned to me now—though this may be self-delusive—as done for some other motive. But I *do* remember killing a collection of live beetles which I kept in a box by pouring boiling water over them; but this, I recollect, was quite unaccompanied, either in the anticipation, or in the performance, by any emotion except those of shame and disgust.

I remember so well one day, when Littleton was not with me, meeting a girl, a little older than I was, who had been to our house; meeting her in fact in the narrow alley at the west end of the South Walk, where the public gardens now begin, and actually telling her about my nightly orgies and about the particular images that I called up to cause myself these inebriating sensations. But this young person disappointed me. What I told her seemed evidently in no way startling to her nor in the least degree engaging or provocative. She was neither shocked nor excited. To my bewildered surprise, my revelations of the intoxicating sweetness of my wicked paradise seemed negligible, nay! *even dull*, to this sophisticated feminine intelligence. It must be remembered that except for being rude to the Spanish maiden and that little person of the South Walk with her demure look and her straight hair, whose self-possession so excited my maliciousness, girls were not girls to me at all—they were only quiet ineffective boys—until I was nearly of an age to go to Cambridge.

It may be that my teasing was always due rather to maliciousness than to sadism. Some of it certainly was. And what a strange thing, when you come to think of it, such malice is. It is not, I am quite sure of that, the same as sadism; and I wish I could analyse it! I *ought* to be able to; for I believe there has never lived a human being so addicted to it as I am. Is it perhaps connected with that tickling irritation, that itching sweetness of fidgety tantalization, we feel sometimes in the presence of personalities who are what is called "cute"? Let me narrow down the possible objects of *my* particular kind of malice; which, I admit, may easily turn out to be *sui generis*. Strong, fierce, formidable people never excite this feeling in me. Very wicked people never excite it in me. Extremely ugly, deformed, crippled people never arouse it. I was on the point of saying that grave, dull, conceited people never do; but I remember a pale, red-haired, neatly-dressed boy at the Preparatory School, whom I used to force to the ground by a turn of my wrists—my wrists have always been as strong as a murderer's—who could not in any conceivable way, either in the spirit or in the flesh, have been called "cute." There *was* a boy, on the contrary in the same school against whom I behaved abominably: it is one of my very worst actions; and *he* might, with certain reservations, have been called "cute"; but the other could have but excited my malice, if that *is* the word for it, only by his annoying neatness, tidiness, primness —for he was otherwise at the extreme opposite pole from anything seductive.

What then is the true nature of this feeling that I am in the habit of calling my "maliciousness"? My friends laugh at me when I use this word. *They* think of me as touchingly artless, harmless, well-meaning! I think that what it really and truly is, is misanthropy. I think it is an *anti-man grimace*, a desire to

escape being surrounded by men and women. That this is a
true analysis of the feeling is borne out by the fact that towards
extremely wicked, extremely formidable, extremely ugly,
extremely intellectual, extremely degraded persons, I never experience this sensation. These are already super-human or sub-
human; but I suppose the demureness and composure of that
South Walk girl and the primness and neatness and self-satisfaction of this Westbury House boy may be regarded as
essentially "human-too-human." Yes, the more I think of it
the more I feel that it is the absence of strength and formidableness combined with a certain unruffled self-importance that
excites this devilishness in me. The feeling differs completely
from sadism in the fact that all my malice wants to do is to
disturb, or see disturbed, the equilibrium of these worthy
people in some rough or violent manner. Sadism is something
entirely different from this.

I must not forget another of these magic "apercus," these
glimpses into that enchanted land, towards which, without
knowing where I was going, I directed my boyish pilgrimage.
This was a visit we paid to Ventnor and Shanklin in the Isle of
Wight. That we ever went to these places I know was due to
the fact that some old servant of my father's youth was living
there as a pensioner. His faithfulness to his personal past, his
heightening of it till it resembled one of those poetical autobiographies that the Homeric heroes delight to indulge in
before they slay each other or exchange arms, was, as I have
hinted, one of his most marked characteristics.

But in the sands along this island shore could be discovered
in those days certain small, hard crystals, called Isle of Wight
diamonds. These diamonds were to be purchased in the shops;
but it was a great hobby among the visitors at that time to
collect them for themselves and become amateur misers. This
hunting for crystals—or whatever they may have been—in the
sea-drenched shingle, which was just there neither ordinary
pebblestones nor yet sand, was an intense and rapturous
pleasure to me. To sit on a sea-beach forever and collect Isle
of Wight diamonds seemed to me all that any heart could wish.
I, at any rate, required no more. Curse it! What is it that we

all lose as we get older? It is something in life itself. Yes, it is *in* life; but it is a much deeper thing—no! not exactly deeper; I mean it is of a more precious substance—than what we think of as "life" as we grow older. Now I am inclined to think that to a quite unusual extent I have retained to my sixtieth year the attitude of my early boyhood; and such being the case I am tempted to hold the view that the more obstinately I exploit this childishness and take my stand on this childishness the wiser—if the less human—my mature life will be.

It was while bathing at Ventnor out of a bathing-machine that I had my first experience of being what they call "ducked," in other words having my head thrust forcibly under water. This "ducking" was one of the things I disliked most at school, and I record here and now that older people bathing with children are greatly to be blamed for resorting to this practice. Let them scoop up the water, if they must, in their own hands and drench their children's heads, but this "ducking" business should be stopped. It is an abominable shock to be ducked, not only to our nerves, but to our personal self-respect. Whether from exposure to the sun as I hunted for "diamonds" or whether from this accursed "ducking," it was in the Isle of Wight that I had an attack of something uncommonly like an epileptic fit. Of this fact I have all my life been extremely proud, having discovered in my reading that such fits have been, throughout history, the peculiar "sacred sickness" of persons endowed with messages from the gods.

Returning to our Dorchester life, which must altogether have lasted about seven years, I want to set on record the passionate delight I used to take in stringing together small coloured beads upon cotton thread and making them into rings and bracelets. I can now recall the exquisite pleasure I got in choosing particular colours for this craft. Colour has always played a part in my life about twenty times greater than form. Perhaps Blake was right when he uttered the words that my friend John William Williams, the Roman Catholic apologist, used to repeat with such prelatical austerity:

"He who does not prefer Form to Colour is a Coward!"

Certainly the art of painting has ever been far more

important to me than the art of sculpture, towards which, along with music and every sort of bric-a-brac, I have been, following my father's indurated limitations, obstinately cold. I can see now with incredible vividness certain particular ones among these little beads—dark bottle-blue ones coming back to me with the clearest delight. *Colour!* What a thing to have appeared at all under the sun! To anyone who like myself is not only a coward but a confirmed sensualist, this phenomenon of colour is like a vast number of entrancingly delicious fragrances *grown visible*. No it is more than that. It is like a human body with which you are infatuated. It is at any rate something you touch, taste, feel, and embrace with your whole soul. It is something *you sink into* and enjoy like the revelation of an erotic Fourth Dimension. It was at Shirley in my very earliest infancy that I used to press my knuckles against my closed eyelids and watch with intense delight the marvellous kaleidoscope of colours which then formed and re-formed before me. And I never see pansies without remembering how once I was shown a collection of them—I would protest indignantly *now* against such a proceeding—pressed under a glass frame, as if they formed the contents of a framed picture.

One definite purpose I have in view in the calling up of all these memories is the confirmation and defence of certain habits of thought and feeling—I would almost say a philosophy of life—which is largely the deliberate and shameless adaptation to mature experience of the dominant instincts of childishness. But I must not let myself dodge—for the sake of giving my life the sort of fulfilled entelechy for which one's maturer life-illusion clamours—those disturbing eruptions of pure wanton mischief, those explosions of caprice, wherein the aboriginal chaos revenges itself upon our rational gravity.

One of my greatest joys was to pour mustard and water down the holes of lobworms. What an interest it had for me to observe these indignant earth dwellers, great lubberly sons of darkness, come sprawling into the daylight, thinking doubtless that the end of the world had come since the sky rained brimstone. Another absorbing pleasure was the making of man-traps. We had an aged gardener then, called Mr. Curme, whose laborious life had bent him double, "head and feet," as Wordsworth says, "coming together in life's pilgrimage." I used to inveigle Littleton and Theodore into helping me dig deep holes in the earth where the artichokes grew, those English artichokes that resemble pinkish-white bulbs, and whose tall stalks used to supply the "Volentiā Army" with some of its deadliest weapons. These holes we covered with sticks, then with rhubarb leaves and lastly with earth mould. I am glad to report that I cannot recall Mr. Curme falling into these holes; but I expect this was because in our eagerness to see them in action we deliberately plunged into them ourselves.

Those were days when, as the eldest of the family, my primogenital despotism exercised unruffled sway. Littleton's natural gifts for athletic sports were, I can assure you, not allowed the ghost of a chance to develop under my dictatorship. His only revolt always took the same form, that of settling himself down at the dining-room table to the quiet task of drawing ships. Theodore, to my tyrannical satisfaction, showed no inclination to draw ships. There was something bizarre, even then, in *his* nature, which lent itself, when I could decoy him out of his "Bushes' Home" to my most erratic undertakings. Yes, orthodox games were as alien to me in those days as they are now. I can remember well the sensation of shivering uneasiness, like a gipsy child peering at soldiers drilling, with which I watched our cousins, who were then at Winchester, playing with a football.

To sum up my experiences of this terrestial incarnation during these three years from seven to ten, I felt working in me a passionate desire to exercise a very especial kind of power, a power that was above everything else secret and anti-social. In the pursuit of this power I was distracted by obscure and mysterious fits of inexplicable delight in certain wonders and marvels—like those blue beads and that green gravel and those Isle of Wight "diamonds" and those pansy petals under glass, and the glimmering movements of the minnows in our aquarium. But I can well recall waking up one morning in my room looking out on the South Walk and thinking to myself

that I must and would bring into my real life those fancies
about being a magician, like Merlin or at least like Norna of
the Fitful Head which were for ever hovering in my brain.
Causing lobworms to come out of their underworld did not
satisfy me. I wanted to call up demons. Digging holes for Mr.
Curme to fall into did not satisfy me. I wanted to entrap
"Dromonds" and to overwhelm "Escrawaldons." To be the
General of the "Volentiā Army" was in the ordinary day's
work: I still had obscure intimations of what it felt like to be a
ruler over invisible angels. My desires were certainly disconnected and irreconcilable. My sadistic thoughts were totally
unconnected with my yearning for supernatural power; so also
was a tendency to greediness which I now began to develop
especially with regard to raspberry vinegar and Huntley and
Palmer's oaten biscuits.

I have already mentioned how I used to listen with entranced absorption to the reading of the *Waverley Novels* and
how these books encouraged my dominant obsession. But
better even than these were Scott's romantic poems. How I
used to repeat to myself under those overarching chestnuts,
as I lay in wait to leap out upon the "Spanish Maiden":

> "Glimmering faint and distant far
> Shimmers thro' mist each planet-star!
> Well may I read their high decree!"

And I have no doubt that the description of Michael Scott,
holding in his dead hands in Melrose Abbey his Book of
Magic, was one of the influences that effected my whole earthly
vision of human and inhuman possibility.

Night by night as I took off my clothes I must have felt
like one moving down the aisle of a darkened cathedral, under
the torn emblazoned banners of the world's oldest superstitions. But once snugly in bed, Oh how I would give wild
rein to my wicked thoughts! There were many times however
when the Arch-Devil Fear, that enemy of mankind, not
nowadays taking the shape of a stick floating in a lake, but
taking *some form*, you may be sure, totally incommensurate
with the enormity of its abominable menace, would make me

shudder. And it was then that I would seek assuagement in the sweetly solemn stanzas of Bishop Ken's Evening Hymn, that hymn of hymns for the soothing of human nerves. But not unfrequently it would come to pass that even this gentle "Glory to Thee, my God, this night"—would fail of its purpose. It might serve to quell the hot fevers of unsanctified thought, but it proved totally ineffectual in driving away Fear. And so I used to have recourse to a less literary incantation. No, it was not to the majestic Michael Scott in his unhallowed cerements, that the little Johnny, in his white night-shirt, cried aloud when Fear glared at him. None others than Messrs. Moody and Sankey—I must confess it—were in those days my Ministers of Grace and my final defence; and hugging my thin knees to my thinner chest, crouching in fact in the very posture in which people were still finding the buried bones of the great Legionaries who guarded Dorchester from the Barbarians, I would forget sadism and minnows and lobworms and green gravel and traps for Mr. Curme and the terrible death of the wicked Front-de-Bœuf, and whisper hurriedly into the stormy Wessex night:

"Safe in the arms of Jesus, safe on His tender breast!"

Chapter Three

Prep. School

INDELIBLY is it branded on my mind the day when my father took Littleton and me to Sherborne and left us at the Preparatory School. How well we subsequently came to know that journey from Dorchester to Sherborne! Leaving the Great Western Station the train emerges from a tunnel near the barracks and passes between "Pummery," an ancient encampment, and the flat water-meadows in which stands the Elizabethan house belonging to the Banks family. Many a time had we been taken by our Berkshire maiden down the West Walk, under the remains of the Roman wall, past the barracks' gate, to these open slopes of "Pummery." Five years ago, leaving my companion at the "Antelope," I slipped off to renew with these turfy ramparts an acquaintance interrupted then for more than forty years, and I found the place completely unchanged.

With what thoughts did little Johnny and little Littleton, sitting opposite their broad-shouldered progenitor, gaze at that familiar spot as the train increased its speed? Into the Great World they were now plunging, plunging indeed—as everyone knows who knows anything of school life—into stresses and tensions, shocks and endurances, the like of which, unless they went to war or became penniless outcasts, they would never again have to experience till the day of their death.

Passing Frampton, Maiden Newton, Evershot and Yetminster we reached Yeovil Pen Mill, and there we had to change our train. There are three stations in this busy town on the borders of Dorset and Somerset; and changing again at what is called the Town Station it was not till we reached Yeovil Junction that we were able to establish ourselves in the South-

Western express that runs from Plymouth to London; where the first stop we were to make would be at Sherborne. Close to the noble tower of Bradford Abbas Church the train would gather speed, and following the banks of the muddy Yeo would not utter its shrill whistle again till it ran parallel with the Big School cricket-field; parallel too with a certain row of dingy cottages, whose long line of pensive chimneys any wretched boy, trying in vain to enjoy cricket, might distract himself by counting, till the Day of Judgment saved him for ever from compulsory games.

Characteristically enough my father was all impatience to escape the social amenities offered to the parent of two new boys, and you may be sure his sons shared this feeling. So, having deposited our luggage in the care of the school matron, and having been shown by Mr. Blake himself the dormitory we were to share with three other boys, my father hurriedly carried us off for one of his dearly-loved walks. You can believe I shall never forget this walk! All the rest of my time at school I remembered it. I would take that same pleasant field-path across the stately Sherborne Park simply because it was here he came with us that day.

Since the manor was snatched from Sir Walter Raleigh by King James this unrivalled house and park, with the ruins of the older castle, has remained in the hands of the Digbys, another famous Elizabethan family. Not a park in England, no! not even that charming one at Montacute, do I know so well, or admire so much, as this one at Sherborne! Even in my unhappiest years at the Big School I admired it and though it is not free of shameful memories it is I think a proof of the kindly obliterating power of Nature that happy recollections of it, of its sweeping vistas, its beds of deep bracken, its oaks reverting back to the days when the King murdered Raleigh, are what have finally come to possess my mind.

I cannot remember, I fortunately have forgotten, the actual moment when we saw that tall dignified figure take leave of us and depart for his train; but I *can* remember my sensations in the evening as one by one the other new boys entered the schoolroom and we all gathered round the fire. Our Preparatory School terms opened on Tuesdays, just as those of the Regular School did, but I seem to recall that the new boys were established in the house before their initiated colleagues returned. It *may* be therefore that the new boys arrived on Monday. There was a little boy called Mansel—one of the nicest, and, as I now see him in retrospect, one of the best-bred of us all—who came I think from Ireland, though Mansel is a Dorsetshire name—and what must I do, in my nervous volubility and eager impertinence, but begin trying to "tease" this child, after my accustomed manner, by pressing him with challenging questions as to whether he was a *Fenian*, a word that in my father's newspaper was synonymous with the Devil. I cannot recollect the sequel of this silly waggery, but my impression is that Mansel, without resorting to fisticuffs, made a complete fool of me. I should not have recalled the incident at all or the words of a thoughtless remark made by me at the age of ten, if it had not been the cause of a hot blush. How strange it is that what bites most deeply into our consciousness and lasts the longest in memory should be neither great pleasure nor great pain—but simply *shame*, some intolerable hurt to our self-respect! I wish I could, for the sake of pressing home this point, recall how Mansel *did* retort when, on my first night in the Great World I tried to tease an Irishman in the same heavy-handed way I had teased the Spanish maiden; for I expect it would have taken its place at the head of that list of cheek-burning rebuffs which no waters of Lethe will ever wash out.

But well-merited reproofs for ill-placed jests, however long they may last in a boy's mind, do not *at the moment*, rival the terrible force with which physical persecution hits him. When Mr. W. H. Blake showed my father the bedroom we would occupy he told him we should be under the care of a steady, quiet, reliable boy, called W——. Now I fully believe that W—— *was* a steady and reliable boy in relation to obeying the rules which were hung up in each dormitory, such as: "No talking after 'Lights Out'," but I am compelled to believe he shared with me the vice of deriving a lively sensual emotion from being the cause of certain kinds of suffering. Of course there are—there must be—people who inflict sufferings on others without any of these sensual stirrings; but I must confess my own feeling is that these virtuous dispensers of punishment are very few, and that most people who deal in it, unless they are in a wholesome fit of fury, find in so doing their own somewhat questionable account.

How well I remember waking up in the grey dawn on our first morning in the Prep., and staring at Littleton's calm sleep in wonder, till at last, under my stare, his eyes opened too, and then, oh! what great, round, *slow* tears I saw rolling down his manful cheeks! Littleton's bed and mine were side by side; while W——'s bed was just opposite mine, on the other side of the room. W—— did, I confess, display in one respect what most authorities would have regarded as praiseworthy "reliability"; for when in the hushed hours of the night there came the smallest movement from my bed that could be interpreted as "sinful" he would send one of his heavy slippers flying at my head. It was indeed a perfect case of that irony of moral blame referred to so bitterly by the mad king in the play:

> "Thou rascal beadle, hold thy bloody hand!
> Why dost thou lash that whore? Strip thine own back;
> Thou hotly lust'st to use her in that kind
> For which thou whipp'st her."

It was with more than one instrument of torture that W—— exercised his ambiguous authority. But however hard I try I cannot recall his countenance with any clearness. I know he had a high forehead like that of a bishop or a statesman; but his expression was not ingratiating. It was indeed singularly sullen. Speaking of torture, I confess I did at a later time in the Prep. *play* at being a Grand Inquisitor and get the same sort of pleasure from it as I got when with a toy pistol in each hand I ruled my robber-band in the roof-room at home; but I have no recollection of *really* hurting anyone at such games.

The Preparatory School at that time occupied a house which as far as I know, still stands in that same spot. It fronts a street leading from the almshouses to the school cricket-field; but its back premises open upon that broad and cheerful approach to the abbey from the railway station that runs in front of the Digby Hotel. Opposite the hotel are now the town's public gardens; but when we went to "Westbury House," as it was called, there was a pleasant smooth meadow with railings round it where these gardens are now.

Yes, the first letter I ever received from my father must have been addressed to Westbury House. He had a morbidly careful hand—the hand of a person so inherently averse to writing and so reticent in what he wrote, that he would form each separate letter by a separate act of his conscious intelligence! But though my father's hand was neat and firm and clear, it suggested in some way that, as he held his well-trimmed quill pen between his thumb and his first and second fingers, it was *from his thumb* rather than from his fingers that the dominant pressure came. My own thumbs resemble my father's, which were I think as characteristic of the man as anything about him, being very thin and very flat and very broad and very spatulate. But I when I form *my* letters—alas! not with a quill-pen—must, I fancy, exert the chief pressure with my index finger. At any rate the kind of arrogance with which I used to scrawl in my school books: "Powys Ma, Westbury House, Sherborne, Dorset, England, Europe, the Eastern Hemisphere, the World," seemed to draw its nervous energy from a totally different zodiacal sign from any in my father's horoscope. But aye! how familiar that handwriting of his has become to us all! It has a look like the smooth roots of a beech or like the smell of Herb-Robert. How well we knew the sort of way it imprinted his whole character on each reticent page! He would write his sermons in black ink on paper of a blue colour, as he stood at a standing-desk in his study, and then before taking them into the church he would put them into a binding of black velvet, suitable, as he thought, to the dignity and decorum of Divine Service according to the rites of the Established Church. Were I to expect now any letter from my father I should be prepared to feel towards it the sort of feeling I would have towards the Sign-Manuals of old unsophisticated warrior kings.

My father had given me a football to take to school and well do I remember how on our very first afternoon in the Preparatory playing-ground, which in those far-off days was a field behind the music-and-science departments, this football of mine came to its end. As the General of the "Volentiā Army" and the inventor of magic formulae for controlling "Dromonds" I had no conception of the etiquette of football. I was an individualist, though somewhat of a dictatorial one, and I fancied that in giving this football to *me* rather than to anyone else my father dedicated it to my private enjoyment. I hugged it as I carried it. And as I walked gravely along the road—now so familiar!—past the abbey, past the little postern-entrance to the school, past the entrance to the fives courts and the bath, past the entrance to the gymnasium—I left a thrill of elation. With a bold step corresponding to what I was carrying I followed the crowd of little boys, led by Mr. Hawkins, the usher, and as I went I hugged my football. No doubt Littleton, even then, could have told me that a football is not an indivi-dualistic toy to be enjoyed in solitude, but he was running along with the rest, for he could not *always* be taking care of his elder brother. Thus, with my football in my arms I entered the Preparatory playing-field. The sequel I need hardly relate. In the first place the ball was not the right kind of a ball. It was round; but a Rugby ball, like the earth, is not round. It was a ball; but it was not a Rugby ball. Indeed, for all I know, it may have been that perverse and heretical object, an Associa-tion ball. But whatever it was when it entered that field in Powys Ma's arms when it came out it was a crumpled-up, indistinct mass of shapeless bladderlessness. It was no longer any kind of ball. It had been kicked, and so would Powys Ma have been kicked had he interfered, from one to another of the biggest boys in the Prep., till it had no more air left in it or leather left on it. Such was the ignoble end of my father's careful purchase at Mr. Pouncey's, the saddler's in South Street. He had bird-nested so much in the past when he was himself at school at Kennilworth that he thought a Rugby ball was as like an Association ball as one heron's egg is like another.

W. H. Blake, our head master, was a tall, powerful man, a

great fisherman and a fellow of a formidable and unyielding, but very gentlemanly personality. We were all afraid of him, and he unbent very little; but he had a certain "penchant" for literature and I remember once he set us as a task the writing of an essay called, in imitation of the French classic with that name, "A Voyage round my Chamber." My first public literary triumph was my response to this with a rambling description of our own drawing-room; and I remember his praise of my allusion to the sharp edges of my father's arm-chair in that room, against which, I averred, we often painfully collided in our more violent games. What occurs to me in connection with this is the difficulty that I have always found in avoiding, when I have a pen in my hand, a certain facile obviousness, an obviousness which springs from thinking of what would be the nice, friendly, unctuous, appropriate, human thing to say, rather than what had the teeth-marks of reality in it.

But Blake very soon made me the "librarian" of the little Prep. library, which was kept behind glass doors—and I dare say now, after fifty years, is still kept there—in the large play-room. Showing me these books and listening with a good deal of indulgence to my extremely priggish strictures upon some of them, he asked me what I thought of Charlotte Yonge's *Little Duke* and commended me warmly—and it was my first triumph as a critic—when I expressed my admiration for this work.

We used to receive on every Saturday afternoon what was called an "allowance," fourpence for the older boys and three-pence for the younger, and with this in our pockets we would hurry off as soon as possible, for we had full liberty to walk where we liked, to the little bake-shop and sweet-shop kept by the Tuffin family, which was snugly ensconced amid mellow old buildings of Ham Hill stone just opposite the armorial entrance to the school house. A savage greed for sweetmeats quickly became now one of the most important things in my life. It became a vice. It grew so intense—I had almost said so passionate—as to supersede in considerable measure my erotic musings. There does seem to be something in greed as a vice that can mitigate sexual self-indulgence. But as I grew older and the violence of my erotic obsession increased, this lust for sweetmeats completely lost its hold upon me. I remember well, however, what form its final out-cropping took; nothing less, in fact, than a passion for plum-cake when I first went to Corpus! I had, oddly enough, an economic mania in those days, almost amounting to miserliness, though its origin was to please my father. This was certainly a queer tendency in a young collegian and one by no means appreciated by friends. Thus this passion for plum-cake, and it is not a very gracious memory, was confined to devouring it at the expense of others. I never even bought it on those rare occasions when I gave what I regarded as a festive entertainment. After those days, when together with my erotic instincts my tendency to ulcers gave me trouble, plum-cake vanished from among my temptations. I am at the present time, though poetically fastidious in my diet, as free from greediness as a hunting dog.

What I used to like best at Tuffin's was Cadbury's chocolate-cream, which I would buy in great bars, and sucking off the chocolate in a disgusting manner keep the cream till the last. I had a furious fondness too for a sweetmeat called apricot paté, which was always enclosed in silver paper, and for a delicacy known as raspberry "noyau" which was wrapped in a gauzy edible film. In regard to these precious condiments, into the mastication of which I flung the solemn intensity of my sensual nature, I was selfish to a revolting pitch. It was an unthinkable wrench to part with the least morsel of them. Indeed, I cannot recall, in those Prep. days, one single occasion when I gave away so much as a bite of apricot paté, or so much as a lick of raspberry "noyau."

It must be understood that the Prep. customs were modelled —and I think it was an excellent thing—upon those of the Big School itself, and on half-holidays, of which there were more than one in the week in addition to the splendid freedom of the long Sunday afternoons, we were often let off the compulsory games and allowed to wander about the country at our will. In all this Mr. Blake was a very wise head master; indeed in the matter of letting us off games he went a good deal further than most of the authorities in the Big School.

It was not long before I found out, and on Sundays I used to enjoy this pleasure with Littleton, certain steep banks—more than mere banks they were; indeed, I might describe them as precipices, overgrown with brushwood—that rose on either side of a narrow road at the top of what were called "The Slopes," a road which bore the amiable appellation of Lovers' Lane. So steep were these overgrown banks hanging precipitously above Lovers' Lane, that it was for me an enterprise of quite lively interest to climb along the edge of them near the top, where you were entirely hidden from the path below and were driven to cling tight, as you made your way along, to various protruding roots and emergent sapling-trunks that grew in the slippery clay.

Deep in my nature—inherited directly from my father—was a longing to escape from organized society and find a temporary home for myself, a private, secret domain of my own, where no one could intrude, where it was indeed almost impossible for anyone to intrude! This instinct—and I like to fancy it was an atavism going back to the times when our Welsh ancestors hid themselves in their mountain fastnesses—was composed of two kindred impulses, one to escape into the wilds, and the other to make a home of your own, a lair, a retreat, an embattled fortress, into which you could retire and defy society.

My dominant desire during the whole of my school life—whether in the Prep. or in the Big School—was to lead a double existence, and while just "getting by" in the School Dimension, to find my real happiness in a secret subjective Dimension where I was "monarch of all I surveyed." Littleton was only moderately captivated by these proceedings. They would have suited Theodore much better. But the whole question of the deep and complicated pleasure I got from these overgrown banks above Lovers' Lane is an obscure and subtle one. Some would say it had to do with that deep-rooted longing in human hearts to return to the security of the maternal womb, but I think it was more closely allied with a desire to substitute a secret reality of my own for the reality created by humanity. A longing for a lair, for a cave, for a fortress, for any hidden

domain, which cannot be disturbed, is still deep in my nature,
It is doubtless for this reason that I have always wanted to
live in narrow quarters, a *little* house in the country or in a
single room in the city, and that I have a positive detestation
of large houses. The feeling of being safe and snug in a hidden
retreat, while the world passes by outside and cannot reach
you, is very dear to me. I have always loved that passage in
Scott's poem about the hunted stag:

> "There, close-couched, while thickets shed
> Cold dews and wild flowers on his head,
> He heard the baffled dogs in vain
> Rave through the hollow pass amain
> Chiding the rocks. . . ."

As soon as Littleton and I had escaped the "steady" and
"reliable" W——, and were happily dormitoried with boys of
our own age, I invented the childish and singular pastime of
creeping down under the bedclothes to the very bottom of our
beds. Such was the hypnotic power I possessed of extending
the domination of my manias that if Mr. Blake had entered our
room after "lights out" he might on occasion have found the
whole six of us entirely concealed from view, as we turned our
bedclothes into rabbit-burrows; but what does seem odd is
that even now, as I approach my sixty-first birthday, I can
exactly reproduce the mystic ecstasy with which I thus bur-
rowed—as some would say—in search of pre-natal concealment, but certainly to escape the real world. While I am upon
the subject of hypnotizing others with my manias I cannot help
recalling how towards the close of my life at the Prep. I actually
persuaded all the bigger boys to form themselves into two
hostile bands and play-act a sham battle, a battle full of am-
buscades, hiding-places, fortresses, retreats, and circuitous
flanking movements, among certain old quarries that border
what is called the Bristol Road.

I like to think that it was with a successful escape from the
conventionalities of school-life that I brought to a close my
time at the Prep., just as it was with my famous oration at
Wildman's supper table that I ended my much less happy life

at the Big School. For I must put on record that thanks to the excellent liberty granted us by W. H. Blake I was often extremely happy at the Preparatory. Some of this happiness was doubtless due to a more complete escape from the real world than could be found above Lovers' Lane or among those quarries on the Bristol Road. I refer to books. Hour by hour I used to sit at the table in the Prep. play-room reading Jules Verne. What I liked far best in this lively author were the stories relating to "Captain Nemo," beginning with "Twenty Thousand Leagues under the Sea." In that incredible *Nautilus*—and it has never interested me in the least to know how far modern inventions have succeeded in imitating the imagination of this fine author—I got a full measure of the sensation of being snug and safe and secluded and unapproachable. Where, as a matter of fact, could anyone be better hidden than at the bottom of the deep sea? And so seated at that table in the play-room, with the library to which I had the key opposite me, I read indiscriminately! The first book of European celebrity I enjoyed, however, apart from Scott, was *The Three Musketeers*, and this was not in our library. It was lent to me by my closest Prep. friend, a little boy of grave literary tastes, whom later I used to name by the feminine name "Tetine." *The Three Musketeers* was one of the first books out of which I derived the least morsel of fuel for my wicked imagination but I do not think I cared for it in other respects very much. Swashbucklers and toss-pots have never allured me.

As I say, my chief preoccupation at school—whether in the Prep. or the Big School—was to live *as if I were at home and not at school;* and in this, considering the difficulties I encountered, I was really wonderfully successful. I think that we all tend to overrate the power of the world; I mean of the hard, brutal, practical element in social life. As a matter of fact before a very little audacity and a very little mother-wit the power of the world crumples up. I found one magical way of retaining the identity of my life for which I shall be grateful to the end of my days. This was offered me by the admirable custom which obtained equally in the Prep. and in the school of devoting Sunday afternoons to long country walks. Littleton and I, for in this matter so clannish were we that it would never have entered our heads to spend these precious afternoons apart from each other, used to wander to every point of the compass till for miles round we knew that countryside with the knowledge of poachers or gamekeepers. North, south, east and west we used to go until it came about that to this day I know the lanes and fields for miles round Sherborne better than I know the landscape of any other terrestial spot. Our favourite direction in the final issue was to what we used to call "The Trent Lanes." These were really a very singular phenomenon in that part of the country where Dorset and Somerset touched. They were quite a network of narrow grassy lanes between high hedges separating the Yeovil Road from the little village of Trent. It was from a woody eminence above this village that we used to be able to see the tree-topped summit of Montacute Hill, and this fact when Montacute became our home was enough in itself to draw our footsteps here. There was a "bottomless" pond between Trent Village and the park-like slope where the lanes converged, and this particular region possessed enchanted vistas for my imagination.

Oh how I can to-day smell the damp earthy smell of the cold clay mixed with rotting apples into which our feet would sink in those leafy purlieus of that "bottomless" pond! Oh how I can feel the rainy wind drive through those orchard hedges in the autumn equinox! I used to get angry with Littleton when it rained in those days and threaten to "beat him like a dog." He was a great one for telling the weather-signs; but his predictions did not always come true.

We were very hungry on these occasions; but the few apples and blackberries we got hold of satisfied much more than our physical craving. They made us forget—at least they made *me* forget—that we were at school at all. I can well remember when nibbling at the sweet-bitter outer rind of the hips and haws how disagreeable it was when those little straw-coloured filaments inside got into your throat! I can well remember a particular treasure-trove of cider apples that we found on the grass by the edge of a lane not far from Marston

Magna. Sherborne is really in a wonderful position as far as the romantic and fruit-bearing valleys of Wessex are concerned. On one hand it has the Blackmore Vale, and on the other the beginning of the Great Somerset Plain that very soon becomes the fen-lands of Sedgemoor.

Another of our favourite walks was to the Corton Down, at the end of which is no less a place than the original site of the walls and towers of Camelot. This is unquestionably vouched for by the fact that the word Camel is used in those parts both for a stream and for the hamlets built along the stream; while at the foot of Cadbury Camp above Queen's Camel there is to this day a spring called Arthur's Well. We were always assured by local antiquaries that Arthur and his Knights were playing chess in the heart of Cadbury Hill until the Day of Judgment.

It was pathetic to see how our walks invariably showed a tendency to direct themselves towards that quarter of the horizon where our home was; and this resulted, before we left Dorchester, in our selecting the park, and the Long Burton Road, and the Honeycomb Woods, rather than Cadbury Camp or the Trent lanes for our walks. Beyond the Honeycomb Woods we discovered, not far from the roadside, some small ponds of singularly unmuddied water in which there used to live a number of orange-bellied newts. These ponds were holy places to me. Here I really could forget school. They reminded me of our aquarium. On the way to these ponds above Honeycomb Woods there were, as soon as you had crossed the railway and the "Bog Stream," some extremely pleasant meadow-lands with a right-of-way footpath leading through them. In a thick-set hedge near this path grew—and I hope grows still—a magnificent oak-tree. It was a tree worthy of the Druids, though not, I suppose, to be compared with its venerable brethren in the park. Into the branches of this refuge Littleton and I used to climb. Indeed, we made of this tree a kind of medieval keep in which we could hide in security, untroubled by the battle-cries of any "Escrawaldons."

My readings in Jules Verne soon launched me upon an enterprise that was full of intense excitement—namely the

H

concealment of "Treasure," and the composition of an elaborate clue to its hiding-place in the form of a cryptogram. In such undertakings and indeed in many others of a less childish character, I was forever being fooled—and so it is still—by my own blunderings when it came to practical details. There is a curse upon my hands! My hands, powerful though they would be in strangling an assailant, fail me hopelessly when anything requiring skill is required. It was in the drawing of the maps for the clue to my hidden treasure—which consisted, I have no doubt, of several weeks' "allowance"—that I got so fooled; and in the end I was ignominiously compelled to accompany the searchers. But, as happens in the poppied oblivions of life, all these misadventures fell away at last like troublesome vapours from the landscape of my mind; and for the rest of my school days—yes! until I was in the Sixth Form of the Big School—all these fields on the way to the Honeycomb Woods remained transformed by the mystic light emanating from these three-penny bits hid in a tree-stump.

As I grew older and passed my eleventh and twelfth birthdays the bullying I suffered in the daytime—though Littleton and I, thanks to our escape from "Old Reliable" were free from it at night—increased rather than diminished. I can see now the countenances, but I must not put the "evil eye" upon men who may now be grandfathers, of B—— and of H—— and of a robust young devil whom I will not even name by an initial letter, as they looked when they were repeating their well-aimed blows—technically entitled "poops"—upon a portion of the arm they were twisting. I can recall the unsympathetic appearance too of the French window at Westbury, leading into the yard where once these gentlemen—for I cannot think of them as boys of thirteen or fourteen—directed very vigorously towards my nose the most excruciating prods with the end of an old billiard-cue.

When I think of these things my one regret is that I had not the spirit to burst into a frenzy of anger and hit out fast and loose. If I had *always* fought, even if I had been badly mauled once or twice, all would have been well! As it was, all this contemptible submission left my own evil tendencies "unbled," so to say, of their bad humours. Indeed, I became by degrees, on the strength of my murderous wrists something of a bully myself; but I am afraid a very mean one. I became a solemn bully, a bully who was totally devoid of the frolicsome humour of converting a human nose into a billiard-ball.

I remember with shame, and it is the one solitary instance of my life when I *practised* my sadistic tendency upon a human being, how I engineered, with a cunning only equalled by its infernal cowardice, an ambush for a little red-faced boy whose tears at a touch were wont to gush from his eyes and pour down his rosy cheeks as if he had been the Cupid of a fountain. Cowardly devil as I was, I put into the head of some rough-handed idiot that this child had "cheeked" him, and then proceeded to look on with the most sinister feelings while this unamiable Roderigo, skipping out from behind a door, slapped the little boy in the face. The Erinnyes for once did not prove oblivious of this dastardly behaviour; but I doubt whether, when a few years later Powys Ma. found himself standing in unspeakable misery and shame, his hands tied behind his back, in a public road, opposite a row of workmen's cottages, calling upon "the Slopes" to cover him and upon the abbey tower to fall on him, he remembered the smarting cheeks of that fountain-Cupid.

Of all spots on the surface of the terraqueous globe I suppose the great school bath, one of the largest bathing-places in England, built of solid stone and cement, is the one most vividly engraved on my mind. Aye! what I did go through in this magnificent swimming-pool! W. H. Blake and his usher endeavoured to teach us all the swim by dangling us at the end of a cord, like miserable little fishes at the end of a line, from a solid wooden bridge which crossed this enormous volume of greenish-grey water where it was about six feet deep. We must often have appeared more like newts than fishes for we often used our arms, not to swim, but to cling frantically to the cord at the end of which we dangled. Littleton learned to swim in this peculiar manner almost at once; and before he had left the Prep. he had won what was called his "Doubles" which meant that he had swum up and down the whole enormous

length of the bath some nine times. We wore bathing-drawers
of distinguishing dyes to denote how near to the "Deep End"
we were allowed to go. Those who could not swim a stroke
were called "Muds" and were compelled to conceal their
nakedness in drawers of rainbow hue. Such "Muds" however
as reached the minor distinction of being able to jump in
at the deep end and swim to the shallow end were promoted to be "Reds", and thus escaped the penalty of wearing
the school colours round their loins. I think it was at the
very end of my Prep. time that "I got my Reds," and beyond
this I never progressed. The manner in which I taught myself
to swim was a disgrace; and I have only to think of it, among
a thousand other humiliating experiences, to bring down
completely any physical pride I might have left. I held my nose
with one of my hands, and with my face completely under
water struck out with my free arm and my two legs, and thus
acquired by slow degrees a certain trust in the buoying-up
capacity of that Sherborne bath.

"I would never wish a son of mine"—but what am I saying?
For the son I *have* got, when he was ten, *insisted* on going to
Sherborne, holding that the glory of a noble and ancient
tradition outweighs a host of physical discomforts.

But is it not a strange thing, how, if you are an Englishman of the upper-middle class, you suffer the greatest hardships
of your life before you are twelve years old? School in England
—the Public School system—has a hundred times a greater
influence over you than Oxford or Cambridge or any other
University. My own brothers differ greatly between themselves
over this question of the Public School system. Littleton, who
greatly enjoyed it, upholding it steadily, and Llewelyn, who
also enjoyed it, attacking it fiercely. My own attitude is, I
fancy, not very different from the attitude of many ex-soldiers.
I would not like to condemn others to such experiences; but
I am proud, in a sense, to have gone through them myself!

In a certain way I think the cricket-field—for football was
never such an ordeal for me, and after all it only lasted an
hour—was even a worse purgatory than that terrible bathing-
place. Cricket it was impossible to escape—whereas for one

term I did persuade my father to give me a kind of ticket-of-leave off bathing, on general medical grounds; but "O Poppoi!" I have never in my whole life felt such shame as when *with a dry head* I slouched, cringed, crouched and sneaked back alone, during the grand rush to the bath, feeling like a leper, a pariah, an untouchable. But, as I say, in one sense this accursed cricket was worse than the bath. Not worse perhaps than being ducked; but Littleton so often would come with a rush and a dive to my rescue there and *duck the ducker* whereas on this Field of Desolation Littleton was always far away; and not all the protective instinct in the world could lure a successful batsman away from the wicket where he was making his hundred. Besides what could he have done? To make his brother Johnny into a cricketer would have been like making his father into an actor. Oh! those interminable hours when I stood fielding, never being allowed to bowl a single "over" and finally when my innings came round, always out for nothing! I well remember—but this was in the Big School, after I had missed a catch at "long-leg"—saying to myself in bitter degradation and complete misery:

"O Lord take away my life, for I am not worthy to live!"

It is that cricket-field that in all the sharp and bitter moments of life as they come to me now, gives me a sense of wholesome proportion: "At least I am not playing cricket!" I can say to myself and, on the strength of that, become like the much-enduring Ulysses.

How I came to envy the old almshouse men who sometimes used to watch our games! I would even envy the very weeds that I used to find on the outskirts of the level "pitch" when I hurried after a boundary. They at least had escaped the scythe, the mowing-machine, the roller, and all the other appurtenances of a national sport. Yes, for all misfits, and "funny ones" in this world Nature is the only refuge. She may give the tiger his claws and the cobra his poison, but she looks with a very wanton mischievous eye—an irresponsible *Ionian* eye, you might say!—upon all the severe rules and disciplines of "lovely Lacedæmon."

I liked the winters at school better than the summers. In

one of our first winters in the Big School, Wildman's yard was invaded by a mob of town boys armed with snow-balls; and it was a proud moment, and no forlorn desperation, to find myself, on this occasion, shut out, as the chances of battle ebbed and flowed, alone with the enemy! I confess my heart sank a little, when the whole school, including the Sixth Form who had a right to carry canes, set off *en masse* along the Bristol Road in order to toboggan down a particularly steep hill. But the younger among us carried metal trays to slide down upon; and I am still proud of the fact that I got quite definite delight, as I went bumping down this precipice on my belly, with a smaller boy seated on my back, both of us every now and then tossed up into the air as we flew, like the Dolphin and Arion, when they were tossed upon the crests of the slippery waves.

If I had become priggish or arrogant in my ninth year, I certainly had little left of these mental faults after I had been a year at the Big School. I recollect how a boy called B——, one of my worst enemies at Wildman's turned once to Stodger A——, when, as one of the older boys himself, that potentate was supervising our evening preparation.

"Can I speak, Stodger?" he said.

"Yes," that magnate replied, "if you can speak quietly. What is it?"

"Do look Stodger, *do* look! Did you ever see such an ugly mug in all your days, as Powys Ma.'s mug?"

A conceit of my personal appearance had never been a peculiarity of mine. Our earliest teachers in Weymouth and Dorchester always fell in love with Littleton, as who indeed could help doing, and felt an instinctive distrust of me.

"You have a prejudice against me!" I remember crying out once with intense emotion when I was only six or seven; and my general attitude was that all competent, effective people of the world had a prejudice against me. They were certainly in the right of it if they had; for the abysmal misanthropy with which at Dorchester as Johnny and at Sherborne as Moony I regarded the well-constituted persons who derided me was a hell-broth as "thick and slab" as that which I concocted out of our urine in the Shirley garden. I never showed anger and I never forgave. In this I resembled an elephant. But my physical and athletic disabilities at school must have made a dent on my mind from which I shall never recover. I got it thoroughly lodged in my brain that I was an awkward fool, a clumsy fool, a blundering fool, a cowardly fool, an idiotic fool, an impossible fool, a pitiful fool, a graceless fool, a windy fool, a complete fool, an untidy fool, a master fool, an absent-minded fool, a vicious, sneaking, ungainly fool, a greedy-gut fool, an ugly-mug fool, a nondescript fool, a mad fool, an inexplicable fool.

Why, at Wildman's, my unpopularity grew and grew to such a pitch that it ended in what amounted to a Powys Ma. outlawing, a Powys Ma. baiting. They said that I ate my very food, in some gross, sub-human, sub-animal way, chewing it with my front teeth instead of with my grinders! I was not unhappy at the Prep. but I was not liked by the other boys. When my wrists became so strong that it was recorded in my report, "A decided tendency to bully," I remember being cordially and with but single exception universally disliked. Although a bully, as far as my power of putting people on the ground with the strength of my wrists is concerned, I went in deadly fear of several much smaller boys. One of these little demons who was bent on fooling me received one evening a laconic warning from Powys Minor, who signed himself with classic brevity:

"From one who *can* lick you."

Aye! How there comes back to me now one autumn afternoon in that Westbury House yard, when we were all gathered at the big gates that opened on the Station Road. We were waiting to start upon a paper-chase, the two foxes already gone, Mr. Blake and Mr. Hawkins already gone, Mr. Blake's short-legged, long-haired poodle gone, only the unfortunate hounds who had to follow the sprinkled bits of paper over hedges and ditches, left there in their chilly football clothes, till the moment came to set off. Blake, with his inquisitive poodle, had been informed of some particular spot, several miles away, which the boys who acted as the quarry in this chase had arranged to pass; while, from the bags they carried, a thin paper-trail, leading to every thickest hedge, to every deepest pool, to every densest covert that their desperate escape could find, fluttered down upon the ground.

I can recall—and it was doubtless a premonition of those gastric ulcers that afterwards, in our unscientific family, were accepted as an act of God and laconically known as *Jack's pain* —a queer, sickening dead-sea taste in the pit of my stomach, as I stood there shivering, summoning all the endurance I had. How it comes back to me too, the sight of old Blake waiting for us at some remote lane's turning, with his broad shoulders and military moustache, and that ubiquitous little dog at his feet.

"Well, Powys Ma.," he would cry, as panting and breathless I trailed past him, bitterly envying that complacent poodle at his feet, "Well, Powys Ma., no spurt left in you, I see!"

No spurt indeed! It was a wonder that I managed to call up enough of what was known as the "second wind" to get back to that yard before darkness descended on the Blackmore Vale. To walk any distance, and to surmount most obstacles, my father *had* taught me; but never in my life had I seen him run; and this running at such a sustained speed for three or four miles was totally beyond me.

Only once were Littleton or I *caned* by Blake in that little study of his at Westbury. I don't think he had—honest country squire as he really was at heart—the faintest touch of *my* vice. But his pride of domination was tremendous and it made him a terrific disciplinarian. And he had a villainous collection of canes. Any boy who had been caned was wont at night, before "lights out," to hold a sort of court of honour in his dormitory, at which he would proudly display the black and blue stripes, often tinged with blood, that had brought him to heel, bruises that seemed, curiously enough, to redound both to his own glory and the glory of the master! What were we caned for? Both of us, oddly enough, for the same thing. We were caned for introducing caning into art! Since it was not a matter of ships, Littleton probably got the idea from me; and so difficult are the technicalities of perspective that Blake mistook what

were really drops of blood for a Bewick-like insistence upon a
less cruel but a good deal grosser effect of the rod.

It must have been early in the 'eighties when Blake began
building the New Preparatory. This spacious erection arose on
the edge of the open fields towards the Yeovil Road and I can
recall well how one Saturday afternoon, my pockets full of
apricot paté and raspberry "noyau," I imitated Romulus and
Remus by jumping over these embryo walls. It must not be
supposed that I was unable to get *any* normal pleasure from
games. I was not quite as sub-human as that. Indeed, when we
were at Wildman's House in the Big School, a house situated
near the cricket-field—though it is I believe at the present time
some sort of convent—Littleton and I were wont to betake
ourselves in the summer evenings, alone of the whole school,
to the outskirts of this field where we would bowl at each
other with excited interest. Our life-long friend and well-loved
master, the Reverend Mr. King—*eheu! non est qualis erat!*—
actually took this proceeding of ours as a memorable illustration of a proper spirit in such matters. It was an illustration
of an *unconventional* spirit anyway; and as a matter of fact it was
a proof of a contention that I have always upheld, namely that
in this affair of games it is your amateur rather than your
professional who gets the absorbing marrow of the sport.
And, as for football, before I left the Prep., yes! and afterwards
too in the Big School, I used to derive great satisfaction from
an amateurish form of diversion that obtained on the football-
field, to which boys could casually drift in, on their way to or
from any sort of country stroll without having to assume the
orthodox football attire. This custom consisted in kicking the
ball just as your whim dictated—either by the process of
"placing" or of "punting" or of "dropping," when once you
had made it your own; and you made it your own—and the
scrambling for it was always courteous and amiable—by
pursuing it when it fell and "touching it down," or by catching
it before it reached the ground. This harmless and peaceful
sport was entitled "Punt-about," and it was a wonder to see
the subtle mixture of nostalgia for old conditions and pride in
new conditions with which ex-Prep. boys, who had just entered

the Big School, would casually gravitate towards "Punt-about"
with their former cronies.

They would appear with a lethargic, nonchalant air, as if,
though on their way to unintelligible privileges, they might,
just as well as not, look in at the old place for a moment, and
please the kids by a kick or two at their ball! Not that we ever
spoke of our late companions, or of any other Sherborne boys,
as "kids." We would always say "people."

"Do any of you people want some chocolate? Are any of
you people coming to see the match?"

I fancy that not even the Chinese themselves are more
touchy about their personal dignity or more preoccupied with
"saving their face," than are boys at school in relation to one
another. They *have* to be. The whole system inculcates it. I
suppose no human expression is more natural to an Englishman—whether he be a little boy, a big boy, or a master—than
a certain selfconscious complacent satisfaction as he permits
his eyes to follow a cricket-ball or a football that he has projected through the air to a considerable distance. Then,
especially if it is a "boundary" and other people are running
after it, you will see a smile of infinite contentment on his face,
which will quickly change however—as his self-consciousness
returns—into a look that says: "Pshaw! That's nothing. *That's
all in the day's work!*"

The actual change from Westbury House to Acreman
House made no impression of any kind on my mind. Important
event as it must have been to W. H. Blake, it was a bagatelle
to Powys Ma. The only thing that impressed me about this vast
erection—the first of so many new buildings in Sherborne—
was the way we had now to go to reach the school chapel. We
Prep. boys had our own seats there and used to run the gauntlet
on Sundays between rows of quizzical lads who enjoyed
knocking our tall silk hats over our eyes. But to get there from
Acreman House we had to pass some extremely old-fashioned
labouring men's cottages which stood back above the road.
Do you know, I really believe that a great deal of my mania
—for it is no less—for contemplating peaceful human homes,
especially little ones, where unknown personalities are trans-

acting all those simple, domestic, routine affairs that have to
be done under the sun, has one of its origins in the sight of
these little houses.

It was always there at the back of my mind, this incredible
luck of the grown-up persons who were not at school. To
take in the milk in the morning while you observed what the
weather was going to be from the doorstep of your own house,
was not this the height of human felicity? To go in and go out
of natural rooms—not necessarily with as much furniture in
them as I had described in my "Voyage round my Chamber"
but at least free of the desolation of desks and blackboards—
from a garden where the crocuses and cabbages knew nothing
of school etiquette, seemed like coming forth from Malebolge
and "re-beholding the stars." It was in the Lenty meadows
that Theodore and I decided—he was in the Prep. and I was
in the School—as we watched some navvies working on the
line, that it would be far better to be a navvy on the railway
track than be at school.

But it was the women I envied most, for not only were they
not at school, but they did not have to go to war, or to go to
sea, or to go to work anywhere *under discipline*. They did what
they liked. In my idealization of home-life it never occurred to
me that in these very houses there were probably women who
—like Eustacia in *The Return of the Native*—were pining to
listen to the military band at Dorchester or to attend the Pier
Theatre at Weymouth, and to gain those ends would have
worked at any mortal job under any sort of discipline. But the
envy which I felt for the happy women who opened their own
house doors *to take in the milk* did not end with my life at school.
I felt it at college. I even felt it when, as a lecturer in the Brighton girls' schools, I lived a bachelor life over Mr. Pollard's
grocery shop, in the town of Southwick.

Well I can recall on a certain dark autumn afternoon
watching a peaceful delivery of evening milk at the door of a
little house in Rottingdean, on the other side of Brighton; and
this incident has remained in my mind as the living symbol
of a certain deep-rooted nostalgia in me for a life of primitive
routine in a very small house! There is some magical and

mystical secret to be found in this, I feel sure, a secret profoundly subtle, and in no way connected with the crude generalizations of psycho-analysis. Passing these cottages to get to the school chapel we also had to follow a little private alley that led between the north wall of the bath and the head master's garden.

This wall is consecrated to the massive link that binds—and will ever bind—Littleton and me together; for it was over this that I leaned once, when I had the liberty of the sick-house—oh how lucky you were when you were ill in those days!—to hand to him a branch of dogwood with caterpillars on it. I had found these caterpillars down by our favourite oak-tree, and you can see from this episode that natural history collecting was not discouraged at school; but all the same I can now behold with my eyes the kestrel hawk's egg—I can see the brown blotches on the pale ground, like rusty blood-drops on a fungus—which some meddlesome boy broke and which I mended with stamp-stuff, weeping despairing tears. Collecting eggs was a passion that both Littleton and I shared with my father; but when I began collecting postage stamps my father had a very odd look on his face. I think he regarded a philatelist as next door to a professor.

School life made it very difficult for me to pursue my secret mythological ways. It is not easy to be a magician at school. Nor was that tendency to fetish worship, which is so strong a thing in me able to find much scope. Dormitories and schoolrooms and cricket-fields do not lend themselves to the cult of the inanimate. All the same when some revolutionary day-boy dared to introduce—they were soon suppressed by orders from the Big School and some well-bred thief appropriated to himself the whole lot—marbles and tops, those playthings of the streets—into Westbury House, I had an opportunity to cherish at least one inanimate object with primitive veneration. I can well remember a black top I had at that time—they were only very little tops we played with, to be spun with the fingers—and I can see the small entity now and the spirited personality with which I endowed it.

Walking-sticks we were not allowed to carry at school till

we got into the Sixth. I can remember the first stick I ever had as a small child. It was of a reddish colour and had a horn handle. This was when I was nine, I think; for I can remember walking with it to the Roman Amphitheatre at Dorchester feeling like a young Lictor or a young Pro-praetor taking the air. I can remember another important stick in my life, the one I bought when I got at last—Littleton was there, I expect, already—into "The Sixth." This stick had a curious knobby handle, like a club, and was of a sandy yellow tint. Take it all in all, walking-sticks have usurped the same prominence in my life as swords did in the medieval life. I have had my present hickory stick since 1917 while my witch-hazel stick has only been about six years in my possession, being given to me, in Patchin Place, by Mr. Gilman, at the haughty command of the incomparable Miss Rowe. But the most important stick, so far, I ever had—though Llewelyn has given me a serpent stick of marble-wood, that affords me immense satisfaction— was a round-handled oak-stick which I had all the time I was at college. This stick I named "Sacred"; and sacred it indeed was, in the true antique and superstitious sense of that word, being an accomplice of mysteries and an intimate of manias.

I suffered in those days from the well-known mania of always wanting to wash my hands. I used to have to call out to people to open doors for me out of fear lest I should dirty my fingers by touching door-knobs. I may notice in passing that the happier I am and the more my inborn nature has its free fling, the more I tend to indulge in superstitious, animistic rites and ceremonies! I always used to wash the handle of "Sacred" in the puddles in the road when my hand sweated at all, and it is a matter of grave importance to me even now where each of my particular sticks will "like" to stand, while it is awaiting its turn to be taken out. Yes, this animistic superstition of mine has grown much stronger the happier I have grown, and as a wise voice out of the air once said to me:

"Learn from this that it is better not to try to be *too* sane."

I confess, for all my anti-social tendency, I always got an exultant thrill at the school commemoration. Blake used to give us all a button-hole for this occasion from the garden under the high wall at Westbury. Well can I remember my pleasure in receiving a pink rose bud from this formidable man's great fist! Sherborne School commemoration, praying for the souls, so to speak, of all its ancient saints and kings, took my hero-worshipping mind back to St. Aldhelm and King Alfred; took it back to the boy king Edward VI, that prodigy of the Renaissance, took it back to the days when our grandfather—he of the silver coins—came down by coach from Norfolk, and to the days when our Uncle Littleton, dead and buried in India, won glory such as we should never gain, for his rare skylarkings and devilries.

I keep struggling to remember some occasion at the Prep. when my present-day cult of a life of sensation rather than of thought could be said to have originated. But in vain! Hopelessly do I struggle to recall anything in the least resembling what is my chief preoccupation to-day. This inability annoys me. I wonder it does not give me a sort of spiritual vertigo. And yet I feel myself the same person! I *am* the same person. The moment I get out of the control of my own will, the moment my thoughts wander as they please, I become again the Johnny of Rothesay House and the "Moony" of Westbury House. But I always refuse to let them get out of my control, these thoughts which are my life, these thoughts that are me. "They shall march"—as Captain Toby Shandy said to the corporal—"they *shall* march!"

No, in these days I never let my mind wander when I can help it; but the worst of this volitional inner life is that it sets itself to fling, into the sort of annihilation that we feel befalls gnats and midges, the far-away Johnny who used to dig pits for Mr. Curme and the still farther away Powys Ma. who had a passion for apricot paté and a weakness for "punt-about."

Yes, the most teasing discovery I make now as I fumble in the twilight of my memory about these days, is that the only mental unity I can lay hold on, the *string*, so to speak, on which the beads of my impressions are strung, is simply a nervous imaginative ego, driven here and there by temporary manias and obsessions and totally lacking in any inner formula of resistance to life. A young boy cannot be expected to be a philosopher or even a conscious devotee of cosmic sensations, but that I should have been so absorbed in the drama of the moment as to be totally lacking in any moments of thought about life as a whole is a blow to my self-respect to-day.

An opportunity for such a feeling might well have been those fleeting moments when as a "Forward," in Rugby football I waited, bent double and locked closely between the panting forms of my fellows, the signal for the "scrimmage" or the "grovel" to get underway, but I would be guilty of a gross insincerity if I tried to pretend, after all these years, that I made at such moments the least approach to such a mental gesture. I can remember once saying to myself in the thick of this football "grovel" that I was made for reading romances and not for butting like a bull; but out of the whole course of my life I can name only two definite occasions when my present "philosophy of resistance" rose in my consciousness as a clinching necessity, an ultimate standing-at-bay.

The first was nearly thirty years ago when with my son, then a child of three or four, I was staying in my relatives' house in the Close in Norwich. In my wayward restlessness and my longing "for more exciting bread than is made from wheat" I was feeling ungrateful to the calm, rich, settled background of that consecrated enclosure, ungrateful even—as I lay in the most comfortable bed in the world—to the precious memorials of the poet Cowper that surrounded me, such as his dark-blue washing-basin and jug and chamber-pot; until in my graceless rebelliousness I became aware of a queer ultimate release to be got *from lying in a particular position*, a position in which a muscular relaxation in my limbs did actually give me the feeling I am now trying to indicate, the feeling of being a conscious entity, able on the strength of certain private sensations to isolate itself from the pressure of historic humanity. The other occasion was in the rather desolate privy at No. 4, Patchin Place, New York, about eight years ago, when without any reason I can explain, as I was calling upon the spirit of ultimate resistance to tribulation, I was suddenly inspired with the idea of a black-ribbed, brass-handled *chest!* This object I mentally lifted on high; and for several years the image of this black chest became a symbol to me of my residual powers of resistance to the impinging cosmos. The truth is I am so made that my imagination inevitably converts every mental process which is at all important to me into a ritualistic symbol. Such symbols and such conscious image-creating acts of the imaginative reason have become an incalculable help to my secret mental life; and I confess it now seems to me nothing short of amazing that I had the courage—like an unfledged soul in a state of helpless nakedness—to endure all the shocks, all the alarums and excursions, that came to me at that tender age.

Hockey, played with almost any sort of an amateur stick, was a game we used to indulge in in that big new yard at Acreman House; and I recollect I played it again in the yard of Wildman's House in just the same informal manner. These games of hockey were indeed an incredible comfort to me; and in the heat of them I could forget my "ugly mug," my worse than incompetence at cricket, my unhappy way of chewing my food, my dread of being "ducked" and my inability to compose Greek verses.

Meanwhile, that sickening tormentor of the human soul, Fear, Fear the Arch-Demon, was always waiting to make me long to bury myself at the bottom of the sea. I am speaking now of the sort of Fear a person never, or *hardly* ever, reveals; and indeed I am against attempts to reveal it. Better, far better, carry about with you your own torment and sprinkle it with your own sluice-pipe of Lethe water!

We are all mad; and the best thing is to learn to forget our madness. Forget it! Never fight against it. But it must not be supposed that I was uninspired, while at the Prep., by those moods of mysterious emotional exultation that by the indulgence of great creative Nature come at times to all men born. I remember well one night going out under the stars through the new yard of Acreman House to visit the urinal; and as I gazed upward, dazed from reading Bulwer Lytton, at that time a new discovery to me, making a vow to those flickering, glittering points of white light and to the starlit roof of the latrine towards which I was directing my steps, that what I would be, when I grew up, was a poet. The transporting ecstasy that thrilled through me then must have been of an unusual violence, else I could hardly remember it, as I do now, after nearly half a century. It had to do with the stars; and never again have the stars seemed quite so friendly as they did that night! What a special, and what a curious page in a person's life is the history of his relation to those glittering points of white fire that redeem the dizziness of black space. It always strikes me as strange and unnatural when modern writers speak of the stars as "indifferent" or "unsympathetic." They seem to me not the least more indifferent than great mountains, or the stormy sea, or the face of the dark earth herself. On the other hand they never, as they apparently did with Kant, turn my mind to the grandeur of their opposing miracle—the towering moral sense in man.

No, it is not with my conscience that I get these candles of the Infinite under control and fixed in appreciable sconces. It is with my intelligence. Size, distance, boundlessness never worry me much. I regard them as a mathematical trick—almost an illusion—not to be compared with the expansiveness of the mystery of thought, thought which grasps them, encloses them, surmounts them.

But now I must allude to an aspect of my feelings when I was at the Prep. that sprang, and still springs, from one of the deepest currents in my being. I refer to hero-worship. No set of personalities will ever impress me with the grandeur of *homo sapeins*, or with the same awe and reverence as did those great "Shepherds of the People," as Homer would say, the athletic heroes of Sherborne School. How I knew them—every turn and glance of their unique physiognomies, every movement of their incomparable frames! In the chapel on Sundays I would gaze at them with awe as they came in; and when the school played her desperate football matches with outsiders and we all rushed up and down the field, wild with excitement, I became far more intimately acquainted with the old Roman emotion of corporate piety than I have ever been since over any cause.

But beyond even these football matches, in this rousing

I

of my Homeric hero-worship, were the annual school steeple-chases. How I used to recognize and salute each well-known figure, as they came panting, leaping, stumbling, falling, recovering, hurling themselves over hurdles, over thick-set hedges, over dykes and ditches, over walls, fences, and swamps, until they passed finally through the very "Bog-Stream" itself! We all had our special heroes among these champions. Mine —and do you think I have forgotten him?—was *Perch Ma.* I have a vague impression that there was a Perch Mi. too, but *his* lineaments remain obscure to me. Perch Ma. was my Achilles, my swift-footed child of the immortals. And aye! what a pure unalloyed rapture it was when your bones melted within you at the sight of the triumph of your particular darling of the gods! As Goethe so profoundly says—probably when he was putting the worthy Eckermann's carpings in their place—"Love alone renders us able to endure superiority in others!"

I am inclined to think that before I left the Prep. I had already become acquainted with the works of George Mac-Donald. This writer must have found me a morbid savage and left me a moralistic prig. But this man's books, with all their crudities do really possess some special vein of poetic senti-ment, and they did much to thicken out my life-illusion. I cajoled Littleton himself into reading one of them, which was about a lovely young woman called Euphrasia. Most interest-ing it is to me now to note the difference between us in these matters. To the mystical superiorities that made *me* feel—as I said I felt to my unsympathetic teacher that day on the Wey-mouth pavement—so exceptionally "good," Littleton was totally impervious. They ran off his sound nature like water off a duck's back. But when it came to sentiment—from which my "occulted" vice was destined to protect me—Littleton threw up his hands. Oh that sweet, soft, flexible, beguiling "Euphra," how she did bring the tears to his suceptible eyes! He so rarely read a story, that when he *did* read one it dominated him day and night. I can tell you I did not leave him and his Euphra alone. I teased him as he *loved* to be teased on such a topic. But although armoured by my vice against normal sentiment,

I can clearly detect—and I am proud to record it—a subtle instinct in me, even in those Prep. days, for a certain kind of amorous *romance*.

There was a boy I was very fond of then, a grave rather womanish child, who had, in another boy, a friend more purely passionate than I ever was, whether to man or woman. This boy had picked up somewhere the piquant balladish expression, "Tetine and Thomas Bedlam," and had promptly applied it to his friendship with my friend. This phrase enchanted me; and it gave me the most complicated pleasure to tease these two —for the drama of the situation robbed it of all jealous pangs —by repeating like an incantation "Tetine and Thomas Bedlam . . . Tetine and Thomas Bedlam" . . . till they were forced to flee from me in confusion. I seem to find in this "Tetine and Thomas Bedlam" episode thus enjoyed vicariously, the clue to almost everything that I later became. A message eventually reached the Prep. from some boy high up in the Big School, who knew my friend's friend, that Powys Ma. would be wise to keep his mouth shut. I am afraid this is not the only occasion in my life when from "higher up" such a message has reached me.

Chapter Four

Sherborne

LITTLETON and I entered the school together; and just as every detail of our first day at the Prep. is branded on my mind, so is it in this case, save that it is *bitten in* even more deeply.

As in the other case the new boys had to turn up before the rest, and how we were impressed by the grown-up airs and the *light clothes* of the habitués, as they began drifting in on that memorable afternoon! At school of course everyone had to wear modestly dark and quiet clothes; but apparently it was the custom for all the older boys to make their appearance in man's attire, with Norfolk jackets and turned up collars.

Littleton and I, who knew already by sight and reputation the famous figures in Wildman's, became more and more awed as the younger boys, asking us the usual arrogant questions, began revealing terrifying stories of the reckless deeds of these mighty ones. We were shown for instance with bated breath the dandified figure of G.W. whose legend actually included an affair with a factory girl, one of the very girls whom we often saw at work in the small silk-weaving establishment near the bridge over the "Bog-Stream." The mingling of a vague mysterious sweetness with a sense of something startling and shocking that this unrealizable factory girl cast round the tweed-coated figure of G.W. was a queer element to encounter in your first day at school; but another surprise awaited us in the disturbing remoteness, from all our ideas of what a school house-master would be like, of the unique personality of Mr. Wildman.

"Come back," I might cry now, "in the heyday of thy fancy,

life like a fiery column before thee, William Beauchamp Wildman, philologist, antiquary, scholar!"

Mr. Wildman was indeed a remarkable character. He was a bachelor in those days and the inexhaustible and wayward high spirits of his pantagruelian soul had not yet been tempered by responsibility. What a Latinist and Hellenist he was; and what a rare eccentric! His real interests were all intellectual. He was a first rate form-master, but I think he never "cottoned," as the saying is, to being responsible for a houseful of turbulent boys. Not one of us knew how to take him. In many ways, like a true scholar, he was as simple-minded as a child; and then again he would make it quite clear even to the most unfledged intelligence that he was, in regard to religious and moral tradition, emancipated to a degree that bewildered and disturbed. Nor could you ever know how he would behave! When angry he fell into a blind fury; but not into a schoolmaster's fury; into a child's fury. Indeed, considering the really powerful intelligence it put to rout, it was a pathetic fury! I always admired and liked Mr. Wildman; though I never understood him. Few did, I fancy; whether among the boys or the masters. His chief friend and crony was our deaf music-master, Mr. Louis N. Parker, who, with his famous Sherborne Pageant actually inaugurated that form of historic panorama, and who subsequently became a considerable playwright. No, you never could predict how Mr. Wildman would react to any mortal event. This unpredictableness endeared him to all except the stupid and dull; but it was a disconcerting trait in a schoolmaster.

I remember an occasion when he had some ladies with him at our midday meal. And, fool that I was, without thinking what I was doing, I made a pellet of a bit of bread at my side, and flicked it from me with my finger and thumb. As ill luck would have it, this unfortunate missile, cast upon the air, struck, or came near striking, one of Wildman's lady visitors! He was beside himself. It was, I fancy, solely at the intercession of the lady in question—whose magnanimity was only equalled by her beauty—that I was not dragged out of the room and flogged then and there. As it was I received "five hundred lines"; which was an excessive punishment, and meant that I got no fresh air at all for the whole day.

But now for an example of Mr. Wildman's clemency. Years after this—two or three years anyway—when I was in his own form, which was the one just below the Sixth, he suddenly, as we used to say, "put me on"—I mean stood me up to translate. It was a passage in some Greek poet, which I had not, in my unscrupulousness, so much as glanced over. But there was no going back. I simply had to undertake a desperate and miserable struggle, making frantic guesses and appalling blunders, and hoping against hope that some miracle would interfere. Never, to my dying day, shall I forget the feelings I had as I stared at those indecipherable hieroglyphs and plunged from one wild conjecture to another. In the end, after helping me through with it himself, he made me sit down. "Execrable!" he exclaimed; and that is the only occasion in my life when I have heard the word "execrable" uttered whether applied to myself or to anyone else. To me it is—with the word estimable—a combination of syllables that some peculiarity in my gullet makes it impossible to pronounce.

But, passionate scholar as he was, in his rôle as housemaster he just left us alone! His Sixth Form boys too followed his example and left us alone. One of them was H. B., the well-known popular writer. Another, nearer our own age, was the International Mile-Race Champion, the famous W. E. Lutyens. Lutyens was as good and kind as he was great; and it was an honour to have him as a friend.

Our house was all the same a chaotic democracy rather than a constitutional monarchy: and it tended to get more and more into the hands of demagogues and gangsters. As God willed it, one of the new boys of our own time of entry proved himself the worst bully I have ever known. My indignation against this person, whenever I think of him, is so great that if I met him now—both of us over sixty—I would willingly plunge into a physical contest with him. Among the more primitive forms of satisfaction left me at this late day, I cannot imagine many I would like better than to try my strength against this other elderly gentleman, and *to get him down!*

"That," I would say, "is for ——; and *that*"—hitting him again "is for ——" And even after punishing him in that way —so much do I resemble God—I would put him in the lowest circle of Malebolge when I write my Inferno. I offer these sentiments as a modest contribution to what might be called pathological ethics; insisting only that it is not a question of *personal* revenge; since the brute I am thinking about never laid a finger upon *me*.

I was always much better at examinations than at ordinary classes; thus it came about, to our equal astonishment, that I was placed straight away in the Lower Third Form, while Littleton had to start at the very bottom of the school! But I can tell it was quick work for him to overtake me; and during the larger part of our life at Sherborne, Powys Ma. was at least one form below Powys Mi.

Well do I recall the singular individual who was the form-master of the Lower Third at that time, and well do I recall also the skill with which he managed his classes, classes which, in those days, were held in the great central hall of the school. This imposing structure was hung round, and is so still, with awe-inspiring honour lists and it was with his back to one of these that this man sat. His name, if I am not mistaken, was Griffiths; and I rather fancy he may really have been Welsh; for he had a drooping yellow moustache like those in the pictures one sees of the ancient Britons. I liked him. He took the profession of schoolmastering with more than a pinch of salt. He used to announce to us at frequent intervals, "I am the Fountain of Justice"; and the way he uttered this phrase added a sort of puckish unreality to that historic school hall. I am sure some of the learned personages on those portentious honour lists must have looked down with deep suspicion upon this whimsical Celtic teacher thus snugly ensconced in their grave Saxon foundation.

But it must have been in the Upper Third where Littleton overtook me. This form was presided over—I use the word designedly—by the amiable and good-natured ruler of Wilson's House, and I am convinced that for warmth of heart and geniality of temper Mr. Wilson had few rivals in the school.

He was a cricketer too, and a most sociable person. But alas! "Tommy" Wilson, as he was always called by those who loved him, was not born to do justice to the eldest son of C. F. Powys. He allowed himself a certain easy, conventional latitude in the matter of teaching which was fatal to me. In that old monastic classroom of his, reached through the medieval dimness of Norman cloisters, I was contemptuously neglected and rebuffed. Mr. Wilson must have esteemed the art of "Drawing from Still Life" as one of the most important aspects of culture; and with this view I no more agreed then than I do to-day. He made us "take places" as it is called, entirely on the strength of these weekly art lessons; which, I can assure you, were very rowdy and casual affairs. Oxford and Cambridge scholars who had been trained to keep order, tended to fight shy in those days of teaching art. This was in "The 'Eighties," you must understand. But I doubt if anyone, hardly Ruskin himself, could have taught art to the Upper Third at Sherborne. For the truth is that art, beginning it as we were beginning it with "Drawing from Still Life," had none of the weight of the National Ethos of England behind it. Latin and Greek and mathematics breathed, smacked, tasted of this. Even Shakespeare—that irresponsible rebel—was made to attune his "native wood-notes wild" to the Dorian strain.

The "mores" of a public school in those days—and I doubt if things have changed much to-day—were an intensification, within rigid limits, of this National Ethos. And neither these "mores" nor this "ethos," built up upon the heathen Roman tradition, favoured the only sort of "art" that we were likely to be taught. As a matter of fact—I speak not for myself, reader, for I have always been a fish out of water in such things—we at Sherborne did in our own fashion represent Plato's ideal Sparta. The worst bullies were excrescences, ugly ogre-like figures that took advantage of the subtle unwritten laws by which we lived—such for instance as never, *under any conceivable condition*, to appeal to a master—to pursue their ingrained brutality. Yes, serious bullying was an excrescence on the system; and yet in almost every one of the out-houses it existed. And as for the school-house, there flourished in our time there, as the heroic Godfrey Carey himself, enemy of all cruelty, bears me witness from the grave, one of the very worst of these bloodthirsty ogres. The unhappy victim of the particular monster of this species that we had in Wildman's died, if I remember right, of some illness in the holidays and thus escaped; but there must be many boys who lived to be men who carried the pathological marks of such treatment to their graves.

Psycho-pathological science is still in its infancy, and its dogmatizing will, we may hope, grow more subtle as time goes on; but I should like to suggest at this point that some other word, quite different from "sadism," ought to be used for the heavy-handed insensate brutality, thoughtless and stupid, and sometimes malignant, which was characteristic of the worst cases I knew. I am no neophite, as I have confessed, in the appalling psychology of what is called "sadism," which is, of course, an erotic perversion; and it is my profound conviction that the worst cruelties I saw at school were not sadistic at all. They were either thoughtless brutality or they were malignant vindictiveness.

My own experience of life has taught me that when Jesus prayed that His tormentors might be forgiven because they knew not what they did, He prayed for the most wicked and dangerous people in the world. *Not to know* what they do is indeed their sin—and it is the unpardonable sin. These "not-knowing" ones are worse than any devils.

I cannot tell you how I disliked the French language in those days. I dislike it still; but with reservations in favour of Rabelais, Verlaine, Proust. I am afraid, according to the "national ethos" which dominated our Public School system, French ranked with "Drawing from Still Life." Our French lessons, taught us by a master who evidently disliked French almost as much as he disliked boys, were held in a room near the old Prep. cricket-field in the midst of the music and science reservations. They were attended by riots almost as flagrant as those that attended the drawing classes.

But I used myself to forget the annoying French accent and the general misery and indignity of those lessons when I heard the strains of the new school song practised a few doors off. This song thrills me now as much as it did then. I think it must easily be the best of all school songs. It is in Latin, the only suitable language for scholastic patriotism, and it is free from all those puerile references to cricket and football that make other school songs so ineffably silly. It was written by E. M. Young, the head master, a cultured and liberal-minded gentleman who was persecuted by all the bully boys of the place and finally compelled to resign; while the music was composed by Mr. Louis N. Parker. I cannot refrain from quoting the first stanza of it.

> "Olim fuit monachorum,
> Schola nostra sedes,
> Puer regius illorum
> Fecit nos heredes;
> Hoc in posteros amoris
> Grande dedit signum;
> Sonat ergo fundatoris
> Nomen laude dignum!"

And it ended with a chorus of "vivats" to the memory of Edwardus Sextus.

There was at that time in the school-house a boy quite as delicately beautiful as our royal founder himself, and I think it is a credit to my emotion in the presence of such loveliness that merely to be within sight of this boy made me brave as Socrates. You will hardly believe it, reader, when I tell you that this wretched Powys Ma.—with his incredible depths of funk, with his inability to catch the easiest "catch," or to tackle the feeblest "half-back," with his feeling that the gymnasium was a place of grotesque and monstrous engines of torture, and the bath a kind of icy Giudecca—was wont each day, the moment when the Lower School was bathing, to select his place of undressing and drying *next* to this notoriously beautiful person. My delight in this boy's loveliness was so intense that when I stole timorous, nervous, furtive, and yet ardently satyrish glances at him, as having undressed at my side he stood for a moment in his bathing-drawers meditating his plunge into those blue-green waters, I was totally lost to the world. The boy himself was completely oblivious of me. I never in my life spoke to him, though I must have undressed by his side a hundred times. But it was so delicious a paradise to me merely to snatch quick glances at his lovely form that I altogether forgot that such an unpleasant phenomenon as "ducking" existed anywhere on the earth.

It is really extraordinary that the miseries I went through at Sherborne have not made me shrink from that quiet Wessex town as a Spanish Jew might have shrunk from the city of Torquemada. Such however is not at all the case; and as a matter of fact conditions at school have probably changed from what they were then. Once I could not see the straw hat of a Sherborne boy without a sensation as if I were a Helot watching a young Spartan go by! But I have outgrown this feeling; and just as many victims of the war must have settled down peacefully in a landscape, full for them of frightful images, so I would willingly spend my declining years at Sherborne; though I should always glance anxiously at the walls of all the "houses" and utter an invocation on behalf of any little "Johnny," turned into a contemptible "Moony," who might be crying in vain to heaven for a drop of pity as small as a wren's eye.

I think it must have been about the time Littleton and I entered Wildman's that Mr. W. R. Phelips, owner of one of the most spacious Elizabethan houses in the country, appointed my father, as his vicar, to the large and ancient village of Montacute in Somerset. Here my father was still within reach of Brunswick Terrace; for Montacute was only one station away from Yeovil, on the Taunton line, and you could get from Yeovil to Weymouth in an hour. I can well remember walking home with him one evening from a walk to Ham Hill and remarking, as the drive-gate swung behind us with its familiar clatter and final click, how much I admired the umbrageous approach to our new domicile and the curve of the drive beneath Mr. Cole's railings. He was extremely gratified—for his eldest son did not often praise his undertakings—and rubbing his hands together and protruding his upper lip, after his fashion when he suddenly felt happy, he replied with infinite pride:

"I'm very glad, John, my boy, that you appreciate the home I have provided for you!"

I sometimes think that no one who has ever lived has had intenser moments of happiness in life than my father. His personality was so massive, so monumental, that he seemed to have a power of enjoyment, in mere weight and volume, about double that of ordinary human beings. And since his pride and his reserve hindered him from displaying this emotion in public, he hardly ever started down that vicarage drive, to set out upon one of those parochial excursions which were an excuse for the long walks he loved, without at some moment —between front door and drive gate—quickening his steps in this silent ecstasy which was his worship of life. This is really —as my brother Llewelyn has said, and said much more to the purpose than I can—what all his eleven children owe to him: the power of falling into an ungovernable transport, in the midst of the most ordinary doings.

I can so well recall one of my first nights at Montacute; for we went to see a Christmas-tree at Montacute House. Mr. Phelips was always very friendly to me and his personality and peculiarities of manner and speech made a great impression on my mind. Whether he was like a Grand Seigneur of the old times I cannot tell; but he certainly was a very learned and even, to some extent, an eccentric gentleman of the new times. He was the first person I ever heard utter the words "By Jove!" "By Jove," he said, "this tree will soon be in a blaze!" I recollect too how he took us in his carriage, driven by his coachman, Fred Montacute—always a good friend of ours and in later days our gardener—to Brympton House, the home of the Ponsonbys. Stray expressions of this unusual squire remain in my mind as if they were words from royal lips at court.

"We are being chaffed by the populace!" he remarked, as some boys raised a lively shout while our ponderous vehicle —this was before the day of motor-cars—lumbered through "The Borough."

At Brympton, a far less magnificent but not less picturesque edifice than the great Elizabethan house we had started from, they must have kept up Christmas in the most traditional manner for when we finally passed down the entrance hall, on our departure, it was beneath an arch of extended sword-blades! Coming to Montacute from the Roman remains of Dorchester was like plunging into the earth-mould of medieval romance. A portion of the Holy Road itself had once been found on the top of Montacute Hill, and from the high ground above the village could clearly be seen the conical shape of Glastonbury Tor rising over the Sedgemoor marshes. The fief had belonged to the Nevils in ancient times; and there were still Nevils among Mr. Phelips' "populace," tall, stately labouring men, with the gaunt frames and hooked noses of the Bayeaux Tapestry. The richest farm in the place had for its farm-house all that was left of the famous medieval abbey, destroyed by the Tudor king whose courtier the first Phelips was. Of this farm the high-spirited tenants in our time were the Harding family, and many a substantial and hospitable meal did we boys enjoy in that medieval structure. With Montacute House itself, as magnificent as a palace, with Brympton a mile or two away, and with this noble abbey standing behind our church, we were in a position to disregard not only the country houses of the neighbourhood but the country parsons too. These were —it must be confessed—with the redoubtable exception of Mr. Rowland of Stoke-sub-Ham—no very inspiring group of hedge-priests. But into the rich soil of Montacute itself, that history-charged, mystical clay of Somerset, my mythological imagination sank at once like a plummet of privileged lead.

What a life we had, what a rare happy life, in that old rambling Early-Victorian vicarage! To see the eleven of us, for the last three of my father's progeny were born here, grouped round the great mahogany table in the dining-room, was a sight none of us will ever forget. Llewelyn has described it all incomparably in his *Skin for Skin;* but Llewelyn was at this time a very small child, his life-loving heavy-lidded eyes only just beginning to take in that marvel of being conscious upon the earth, about which he has been—shall we say by the Providence he loves to flout?—preserved to make such an unequalled ado! Yes, Llewelyn was a small child then, with a "penchant" for bread—a great deal of bread—soaked in very weak, sweet tea. I teased him once shamefully, in my devilish way, when I discovered among the presents hung on our Christmas-tree in the big, damp, fire-lit room—that was alternately named the servants' hall and the schoolroom—one parcel inscribed in all gravity: "Lulu from Lulu." I remember his figure too, when he was still a very young boy and I was at college, as he looked in at the open drawing-room window, where I was reading, and watched me a long while in intense puzzled earnestness; anxious apparently to learn the secret of such absorption. I can see his face now, and his warm, radiant, little body in its flannel suit, standing upright there, like "the angel that John saw in the Sun."

One of our greatest delights in the winter holidays at Montacute, when the ice would "bear," was to set out for a day's skating excursion. Following our father's example we never fooled with the outer edge of our skates or with any fancy tricks, but just ploughed forward at top speed, as far as the available ice extended! Vagg Pond was one place we would go to, and the floods towards Ilchester another; and since these excursions meant that he would have to give up too much time, my father let us go alone. For pure enjoyment of food—of the simple act of satisfying extreme hunger—I cannot recall any occasions equal to these, when, returning home before or after the family's regular tea, we had a royal banquet all to ourselves!

I have forgotten what book I was so absorbed in, the day when the little Llewelyn, with the hot sun all about him, peeped in upon me with such quizzical wonder; but I well remember how my erotic obsession drove me to search through all the the *Addisonian Spectators* in that drawing-room. I can now see the delicate rosewood of the bureau where these volumes stood, as I hunted feverishly for fuel for the fever that consumed me. I can recall some particular passage now, two or three of them, to which I would turn; but I will let those of my readers who possess these volumes pursue their own quest! Certainly some of the happiest hours of my whole life—and when I think of the tenuous atmosphere of enchanted glamour that suffused them I cannot find it in me to be ashamed—have been occupied in this cult of cerebral eroticism.

Very, very slowly in those days I was learning to get pleasure from the exposed limbs of young women as well as of lovely boys; but, so far, this was confined to their representation in pictures. Descriptions of ordinary amorous scenes I disliked. They left me, and still do, cold and disgusted. And as for the least approach to gross or lewd bawdiness—such things froze, like the touch of ice, the very roots of lechery in me! These were the days of that fantastical publication, known as *Ally Sloper*, and although the comic portions of this periodical were abhorrent to me, I soon found that it contained daintily sketched outlines of the feminine form most perfectly adapted to satisfy my exacting senses. These *Ally Sloper* young ladies I would cut out with trembling hands and carry about with me in my pocket. Is it not strange how moralists forget their own early feelings in such matters, how entrancing, and also how harmless, they were! My own feelings, I know, were touched with a kind of quivering poetry of lust, a soft, melting, ravishing, spring-like tenderness of lust, that was at the extreme opposite pole from all indecency. I can remember exactly how I felt when, during my first visit to London, staying with a most friendly clergyman there who was my father's closest friend at Corpus, I was taken to the Covent Garden Pantomime, and beheld a whole galaxy—so it seemed to y dazzled and swimming eyes—of girl-angels straight from the well-loved section of my egregious periodical.

It was always a surprise to me, and is so still, that people can find it in them to introduce the element of the gross, of the humorous, of the obscene, of the indecent, into any pleasant pandering to our legitimate desire for the satisfaction of the lust of the eye. Panders in this kind are messengers of the gods; and let them remember the sacredness of their mission! Personally I was always very touchy about the backgrounds of my erotic musings. I liked these to be poetical. I liked them to be pure and noble and lovely and of good report; and I here and now utter my strongest protest against these foul-minded moralists who persist in linking up the intense delights of pure lust—"engendering," as Plato says in his *Banquet*, at the mere sight of beautiful forms and shapes—with the obscene, the disgusting, the repulsive.

I like myself always to separate entirely the Rabelaisian element in life—which has its own purgative and cosmic value —from the feelings excited by lovely forms. What I call lust is an intense, ecstatic contemplation of beauty. It is disinterested. It is impersonal. It seeks no advantage beyond to look and to enjoy! What matter if these enchanting figures that I so feverishly cut out and so religiously preserved were torn from the ridiculous and vulgar pages of *Ally Sloper*? Why! I can recall the exact spot, near a grocery shop and opposite a seedman's, where the road from the station widens out at the foot of Sherborne Abbey, where I wished, in that intense way that often makes our wishes come true, that I might have a whole bound volume of *Ally Sloper*, a volume as big as my *Boys' Own Annual*, wherewith to feed my furious fancies! What has always been so annoying to me in my course through life is the tendency that most men have—it is essentially a masculine tendency; for the laughter-loving Aphrodite grows serious when laughter begins to kill desire—to turn lust into comedy! Rabelaisian obscenity may have its place; though I confess I prefer the Rabelaisian dung-hill; but what has always annoyed me is this confounded linking up of humour with lust. When you contemplate a bed of cuckoo flowers, do you go and proceed to spoil it by dragging in something facetious? Why should you feel that it is your manly duty when you are absorbed in delight at the contemplation of a young woman's limbs to be funny about it? I suspect that this linking up of sensuality with the comic has some deep pathological cause. Probably it springs from the normal man's instinct of self-preservation when he finds himself caught out of himself! But where normal men grow humorous, your moralists grow malignant and obscene. Away with them!

"You beastly-looking fellows,
Reason doth plainly tell us,
That we should not
To you allot
Room here, but at the Gallows,
You beastly-looking fellows."

Let it be clearly understood that I am not defending any aspect—even the most apparently harmless—of sadism here! I certainly think it is preferable to read sadistic books and brood over sadistic pictures rather than to *practise* this wickedness in the slightest degree—as I have done at least twice in my life; once over that little fountain-cupid in the Prep., and once by killing worms with a knife in the Northwold garden —but I think it is wrong even to read anything of a sadistic nature, or to think sadistic thoughts; for may there not be invisible "eidola" of such imaginations, which, projected into the air, might affect other minds? But on the contrary I am in favour of reading provocative passages or looking at pictures that excite your erotic feelings. Why not, when the emotion is so deep a part of the original movement of creation?

In one particular, during our holidays at Montacute, I fell back upon my old tyrannical ways; for I hypnotized Littleton and cajoled Theodore into acting some of the tragedies of Shakespeare. The Phelips children were persuaded without difficulty—in spite of their Ponsonby grandfather being Her Majesty's Censor of Plays—to make part of the cast for these performances which indeed brought the squire himself into our schoolroom, where the good man must have gazed with wonder at the ancestral Welsh dragon painted in red and gold above the fire-place. You can believe how it fell to the lot of "Johnny-Moony" to play Hamlet in his own person; and I fancy this whole idea of Shakespeare-acting was an expression of something in my nature that went very deep. Into the moods of Shakespeare, particularly the tragic ones, and among the tragic ones those especially where the feeling is expressed in sardonic gibberish, my whole nature flung itself.

I think that down at the bottom of my being has been concealed from pretty early days a deep distrust and a shrewd

K

suspicion of that solidity of the objective world that most people take for granted. I was always superstitious—at one time I even believed in Hell—but I am pretty sure that the more I became true to my subtler instincts the more I regarded the whole astronomical universe with a certain detachment, regarded it in fact as the mere *material stage* for playing whatever romantic, picturesque, or fantastical rôle a person's life-illusion might arbitrarily select. It has always appealed to me —that legendary last word of Cæsar Augustus:

"Have I not played the Farce well? Put out the lights: ring down the curtain! Plaudite et vale!"

Deep, deep, deep must have sunken into my soul that grandiose acting in the presence of the gods and of Fate, of those classic Greeks and Romans! My mania for the sceptical Shakespeare, who like his own more sceptical master Montaigne, had a passion for these consummate actors, encouraged this predilection in me. Oh, how I revelled in every line of his *Julius Cæsar*; and how startled I was when, in reading Dante, I found Brutus and Cassius thrust down to the bottom of Hell!

At a very early age somebody read to me Church's *Stories from Homer*, and I found out that those more primeval and more elemental heroes were just as addicted to this vision of themselves as acting a spectacular part before gods and men, whether in exultation or desperation, as were the Greeks and Romans of the historical times. Thus I learned at a very early age what a consolation in life it is to enjoy things and to endure things as an actor; that is to say, not *hugger-mugger*, and in brute unconsciousness, but as though in default of any god or even of any fellow mortal, you could play out your part before your own awareness, and be to the end both performer and audience!

Had I *any* happy hours at Sherborne School? A few. It was for example an enchanted pleasure to me, on certain Sunday afternoons, to sit for hours in the school library, a lovely, old, medieval building, with deep window seats that had leather cushions, searching through all manner of ancient and modern volumes, if so be that I might find some paradisic passages of sweet immorality. O books, O book-shops, O libraries, how,

all my long life, have ye, like great Nature herself, fed the
desires and nourished the feelings that the stupid brutality of
a false morality would fain stamp out! No wonder every tyranny
that has ever existed has suppressed, censured and burned books!
For in books, and in books alone, save for the indulgent
solitudes of Nature, can the individual soul disport itself in
sweet security, and laugh at the moral censor. No bullies ever
came near this noble and ancient school library. It was, no
doubt, to perpetuate and eternalize a sanctuary of this very kind,
that the young bookish Tudor—Vivat Rex Edwardus Sextus!
—re-endowed the old monastic institution of St. Aldhelm. In
this mellow retreat I was as much secluded in a fabulous castle
of my own as when I was hidden in the branches of that
Druid oak-tree, or climbing amid the precipitous tree-roots
above Lovers' Lane. The sun might fall in warm slanting rays
through the mullioned windows, or the rain might stream
down the diamonded panes, I was ensconced here in an oasis
of happiness where no enemy could find me, where no barking
dogs could leap at me and where the loud laugh of the tormentor was reduced to silence.

I used to hurry over to a particular shelf, where I had
discovered a volume of the *Plays of Massinger*, inscribe my
name with trembling hand in the great book on the refectory
table, and then shuffle off to find a retired window-seat where
I could be alone. I recollect getting great erotic satisfaction
too from old bound editions of *Punch!* In the pages of the
oldest among these volumes I had discovered certain oval-
faced, delicate-limbed sylphs that the early Victorian artists
used to amuse themselves by tossing with a certain elfin mischief into their marginal spaces. This sylphid type of feminine
loveliness, evasive, aerial, characterless as flowing water, soon
came to be the type that appealed most to my intense, if sterile
desire. I have always had a tenderness for those shadowy beings
known in the history of magic as elementals; and have invariably preferred the society of an Undine to that of a Thais.
It does indeed seem as though Christianity, with all her
spiritual subtilizing of our life, has not yet inspired us with the
wisest and noblest attitude towards these things; else how could

it have been that we boys were in perpetual danger of being birched or expelled for a fault that would have merely amused Socrates, while these accursed bullies went on with their infernal cruelties in complete immunity? But our authorities, like most authorities, were so preoccupied with the suppression of immorality that they never set themselves to stamp out cruelty; while our own boyish public opinion—which would have been the only effective deterrent—remained completely indifferent, only concerned with keeping both bullying and immorality from the knowledge of the masters.

If all the persons who wrote autobiographies would dare to put down the things that in their life have actually caused them their most intense misery, it would be a much greater boon than all these testy justifications of public actions. I am myself tempted to say that what really caused me my greatest sufferings at school was the trouble I had with regard to the simple and natural function of making water. I was nervous —and am still—of doing this in public. In fact when, during the recent war, I had to offer myself for enlistment, what secretly worried me the most was my knowledge of my absurd nervousness in this personal matter. I used to steal out of bed five or six times in our dormitory when the others were going to sleep; and I remember distinctly how it became one of the things I looked forward to at the approach of the holidays that I would be able to urinate happily in private! What a human being *can* survive, and live to tell the tale! No doubt in the Middle Ages many persons went about, quite serenely, with scars of the rack and of other deliberately-inflicted tortures upon their bodies. The powers of recovery from physical and nervous stress which we human beings have is astonishing; but animals, of course, especially wild animals, surpass even our resuscitations in this kind.

Littleton and I used to achieve one glorious triumph over destiny. We actually discovered that it was possible, on certain Sunday afternoons in the Summer Term, *to run home to Montacute* in the afternoon! We achieved this between our regular school dinner which was over before two, and our regular school tea which did not begin till six. Twenty miles

—ten each way—did our nostalgic legs carry us on these occasions, running or walking, as the intervening hills went up or down! How gaily we trotted down Babylon Hill into Yeovil! How sturdily we breasted the final deep grass and muddy paths that led to the edge of Mr. Phelips' Park! And how our hearts beat as we skirted the precincts of that palatial house and crossed Cole's orchard to the railings of the vicarage garden! I recollect that we took care to select the particular Sundays for these exploits that happened to fall in the season of strawberries. Aye! how many a plateful of this fruit, squashed up, after our buccolic fashion, with milk and sugar, did we dispose of, ere the moment arrived for our start on the return run ! I do not remember that we allowed longer time for this retracing of the way, even with Babylon Hill to be stoically *ascended* instead of lightly *descended*, than we allowed for our first run, but I have no recollection of ever being late for our bread and butter tea at Wildman's.

And what books did I solace myself with in these days? Well, my favourite volume of all was at this time La Motte Foucqué's *Theodoric the Icelander;* and I can clearly remember the indescribable transport that this fantastical tale of the Varangian Guard in Constantinople excited in me. But at school I used to devour voraciously, in those days, the works of Harrison Ainsworth. These lurid tales—*Herne the Hunter, The Tower of London, The Lancashire Witches*—I used to enjoy in very small print, in wretched paper editions procured I know not how; but I had a fervent, secretive way of hiding them under my pillow, and then, waking up in the early dawn, I would hold them close to my eyes and read and read, while the sleeping dormitory about me faded, dissolved, and vanished away, and I floated in space with these grotesque and blood-curdling inventions!

In our dormitory on the third floor we kept hearing horrid rumours of the cruelties practised by that devilish brute—I cannot, *even now*, cry "God forgive him!"—in the dormitory on the second floor; and it once occured to some of my worst enemies in *our* room to compel "Powys Ma." to take a certain big sponge belonging to one of them, and descending in his night-shirt to the floor below enter the bully's room and fling this missile at his head! Do you think I have forgotten the sick terror that this command sent shivering through my bones? What *was* I to do? To obey was hell. To disobey was hell. It was then that great creative Nature put it into my inventive skull—why had not the brute's victim, down below there, thought of such an escape?—*to pretend to be mad*. I therefore began—with that fatal sponge in my hand—to dance a Bedlam dance, while I chanted in shrill and piercing tones my childish lines about Corfe Castle. My reputation as a half-witted Loony was by this time so well established, that not one of the dozen boys in our big dormitory questioned my pretence, or doubted for a minute the fact that Powys Ma. had quite lost whatever feeble intelligence he once had; and the result was that somebody fetched the matron and I was transferred for nearly a week to a room by myself. Whether the worthy matron ever whispered a word to Mr. Wildman about one of his boys having gone off his head I do not know. Probably not. At any rate I went on with my school routine exactly the same, and even managed to refrain from reciting "Corfe Castle" in the presence of any of the form-masters. I did, however, renew my escape-dance when confronted by the "Trapeze," or the "Horizontal Bars," in the gymnasium; but, even there, our puzzled sergeant only made me "fall out" until the exercises were over. Save for this command to "fall out" in the "gym," not one of the constituted authorities showed the least sign of being aware that the elder of the Powys brothers had gone mad. Thus it was made evident to my slowly unfolding intellitence that if you have the gall to carry the very weakness for which you have suffered to its fantasticalest extreme you may come out safely on the other side!

It must have been from the age of fourteen to that of nineteen as far as I can work it out, that I remained at Sherborne; and there is no doubt that my school life made a far deeper dent on my imagination than my subsequent brief three years at college. In America, young lads get the external style and stamp of their character from Yale or Harvard or Princeton; but in England it is the school that works this ambiguous magic. Oxford or Cambridge add very little. What is known as "the Oxford manner" is as superficial and unimportant, as far as an Englishman's real character goes, as the few tricks of speech or affectations of tone that he might pick up on the race-course, or on the hunting-field. His "mores," his "ethos," his attitude towards fortune or disaster, has been formed long before he went to the university. It is school that makes him what he is.

I must now relate to you one of the most important moments in my whole life. While still in that unconscionable "Upper Third" presided over by the amiable cricketer, "Tommy" Wilson, I used to have my mathematical lessons in another of those very old monastic chambers; in the classroom, in fact, of Mr. Whitehead. Mr. Whitehead, like nearly all the Sherborne masters in those days, was a dignified middle-aged gentleman who lived his own private life and regarded schoolboys much as a medieval monarch regarded his subjects. Without boys there could be no school, and without a school there could be no schoolmaster! But there were only two masters that I encountered in my experience of Sherborne who shared with their pupils a real living, thrilling interest in the subject they taught, and one of these was Mr. Wildman. Wildman was really an impassioned philologist; and I can recall well a private lesson I had from him once in Greek grammar that turned the very tendons, fibres and bones of that intricate language into things as lovely and provocative as coral or sea-shells.

It may well be that had our Mr. Whitehead exploited mathematics, as his namesake of to-day exploits it, namely as an open sesame to the golden candelabra of an exciting philosophy, he might have endowed the study of Euclid, even for that form, with a different kind of glamour from what it had; but it is of the glamour that it *did* come to have for me that I must now speak. The truth is my mathematical lessons with Mr. Whitehead were an oasis of peace and quiet in my tumultuous life; not because I learnt from him the Platonic secrets of some supra-mundane world into which I could escape from the ramshackle litter of reality, but because his manner of teaching was such that while he preserved perfect order and suppressed all confusion, he demanded less mental effort of his pupils than I should have supposed it was possible for any older person locked up for a couple of hours with a lot of boys to demand, if only out of self-protection. But the wise Mr. Whitehead—as if he had been Laotze himself—demanded nothing; and if there be in mathematics such a thing as *less than nothing*, this would have been the limit of Mr. Whitehead's demands! Thus when we were weary of digging out of the woodwork of the immemorial desks in front of us little tiny slips of inscribed paper—posthumous pellets of ribaldry for posterity—that might have laid buried there for a couple of generations, we used to solace ourselves, as the abbey clock kept striking the quarters and the rain kept beating upon the panes, by falling into long reveries; reveries that concerned matters such as needed no *quod erat demonstrandum* to prove their perfection. Well do I recall the floating, fluctuating, dissolving fantasies all too exquisitely sweet, with which I would open in thought that second drawer of my black-and-gold treasure box and tear open the score of enswathing swaddling-bands that made a mummy of the face of my Love.

We were not yet old enough to have a study—or it may well be that Littleton alone was in the Fifth Form and had a study—when one morning, leaving the day-room to get my books out of my locker, I suddenly remembered it was Tuesday or Thursday. Oh, heavenliest days in the week, how my Sherborne life has touched you with a mystery that makes you transcend all the rest! Tuesday and Thursday; it was Sherborne and not any ancient god that made you holy to me for ever! Yes, it was Sherborne and Mr. Whitehead's lessons. For even as I said to myself: "It is Thursday," and took up my little, worn-to-pieces, plum-coloured edition of Euclid, such a great wave of ecstasy rushed over me that I can recall its subtlest essence even unto this hour. This little, ragged, plum-coloured Euclid—Ailinon! Ailinon! That I should have ever lost that book!—became at that moment, if I may say so without irreverence, a sort of consecrated wafer, into which every lovely sensation I had ever had, had miraculously gathered itself. It is really possible that that moment was the most important of my whole life! We have to live a long time to know what *are* the important moments. We think, at the time, they are the days when we change continents, or hemispheres, or nationalities, or religions, or infatuations, but they do not as a rule turn out to be these great lumbering events. They turn out to be some little, tiny, infinitesimal *sensation*—like Proust's "*Madeleine*" dipped in camomile tea—that reveals to us the clue to our life. And what actually *did* that Euclid, picked up there in that leather-stinking, rotten-apple-reeking lobby, where stood our lockers and play-boxes, reveal to me? It revealed to me something much more precious that that Eternal Being of Proust's, reaching him purely by chance and doing him, when it did reach him, no particular good. This tattered Euclid revealed to me that it is possible, even when the bulk of your days and the larger number of your hours are full of discomfort, to embrace a thousand essences of life. The limbs of the loveliest of women, the flanks of the noblest of hills, the mosses upon the most marbly rocks, the clearest waterfalls, the freshest of ploughed-up fields, the blackest of rooks feeding in the furrows, the whitest dust rising up from the most ancient of classic roads, the gleam of glittering sea-pebbles, the faint music of the dying away of the burdens of old ballads, the taste of newly baked bread, the feel of the mystery of things as you muse over your tea—to enjoy such presences and such essences of life, and to do so in the scope of some negligible fragment of matter, this and nothing less is what I found I could compass under the spell of this little plum-coloured Euclid! Yes, I learnt from this moment in that littered lobby, smelling of acrid leather, sour sweat, and rotten apples, that our deepest pleasure strew behind them—even when at the time they are not consciously enjoyed—leaves of delight that become enchanted with the passing of time, like petals gathered in an ancient *pot pourri*.

And if they are always there in that storehouse, why cannot they be summoned up at will? *And they can!* Proust, with his impersonal Eternal Being, stops short at this point, leaving it all to the accidents of our way. But when I think *now* of that

Euclid something comes back! Not in any thrilling rush does it comes. It comes quietly and *prepense*. But something does actually comes from where that book lies in my mind.

Certainly Mr. Whitehead's classroom, old and dark and like a Norman crypt under the shadow of the abbey's buttresses, was something that redeemed many sorrows in my life at Sherborne. As I have hinted, in all the forms I passed through there was only one other master beside Mr. Wildman whose interest in matters of scholarship and learning communicated to me any answering thrill. This was the Reverend Mr. King, commonly known as "Crusoe." One after another, as we followed each other into his form, which was the Upper Fourth, we Powys brothers came under the influence of this remarkable man and loved him well. Mr. King was friendly to me from the very start! I well remember when the man was ill once, in his bachelor days, how astonished and profoundly touched I was at a roundabout message I received from him, that he would like a visit from me! Nobody else in Sherborne, young or old, had ever expressed a desire to see Powys Ma. when they could have escaped seeing him, and I can behold Mr. King now, with his great grizzled moustache and his weather-beaten North Country features, brooding and humorous and reserved and Wordsworthian, as he talked to me from his bed. "*He was a man*," this Crusoe King, "take him for all in all," and we shall surely never look upon his like again. Of all the masters, it seems to me, Mr. King's love for the school was by far the deepest, and his benefactions, both material and spiritual, far the greatest. He was one of those men who by some massive instinct of their whole being gather up as they go about the world the lasting essences of life and savour them with a calm and constant satisfaction. Mr. King was profoundly English. Old English books he would enjoy and linger over, like an athletic Epicurean; and in the manner of Montaigne he had the wisdom to intersperse certain deliberate hardships among his solid satisfactions thereby to relish these more fully. I remember seeing him at the beginning of the autumn term bathing quite alone in the famous bath; and rumour said he frequently plunged into those chilly waters in the middle of the winter.

The master of the Lower Fifth was at that time the handsome and scholarly James Rhoades, the poetical translator of *Vergil*. Mr. Rhoades always gave me a peculiar thrill of pleasure at the school concerts on the last night of each term, not by anything he did or said, but by his elegant appearance, with his pale, courtly, clean-shaven countenance, and his immaculate evening-dress. But between this distinguished-looking translator of *Vergil* and the Powys brothers there never was any love lost. He was too super-refined for us and too addicted to sarcasm; and he lacked the impulsive heathen earthiness of Mr. Wildman and that Montaignesque zest for life of Mr. King.

How queer they are, these intangible vibrations of attraction and the reverse that arise between human skeletons! One after another, as we went to Sherborne, we made friends with Mr. King; and as for Mr. Wildman, who was still teaching the Upper Fifth when my own son—another Littleton—was in the school, that impetuous Rabelaisian scholar lived to win *his* heart too—the heart of the next generation—in addition to ours!

By the time I was in Mr. King's form Littleton and I had a study of our own. How well I recall choosing our first flowers for our window-box! These were, to my recollection, those blue cornflowers, said to be the favourite flower of the Kaiser; but Littleton is of the opinion that they were dwarf convolvuluses. Certainly I *have* some curious far-off emotion about these latter flowers which would bear him out. It may be believed what a comfort it was to me to have this little private cell—small as it was—alone with Littleton. My father let us have *his* brother Littleton's East Indian low chair; and to make this chair more comfortable we brought away to this academic retreat one of the most heavily embroidered of all our drawing-room cushions! This cushion was bordered with dark-green velvet, if I am not mistaken; and I well recall how, when an overpowering desire to embrace beautiful human limbs seized upon me like a fever, I used to lean desperately against the window-sill and hug this velvet-fringed cushion, in a forlorn spasm of unsatisfied longing. On the wall of our study I hung up my little black and gold chest-of-drawers, into the sacred recesses of which, I need hardly tell you, Littleton was forbidden to gaze. We bought a rubber pipe and a little iron tripod; and with this apparatus, by the aid of a gas jet, we used to heat up Epp's, or Van Houten's, cocoa; and sweeten it with condensed milk out of a tin. Every night as we worked at preparing the next day's lessons we used to enjoy cups of cocoa for our refreshment; and as a rule we had a pot of home-made rhubarb jam to go with it, which we used to spread with a spoon upon Osborne biscuits. Hampers from Montacute would arrive in the rainy autumn term, full of walnuts from the tree in our field and of a variety of apples from our orchard. These edibles with an occasional sponge-cake, we kept in our study, where their sweet fragrance sustained us; and we shared them most scrupulously; not forgetting, when we used to meet the melancholy figure of the little Theodore, who was by this time in the Prep., waiting for us at the end of the lane, where later they built Richmond Villa, to fill our pockets for his benefit.

I recollect perfectly how one night after some quarrel with Littleton, and when, too, I was burning with an erotic fever that none of the treasures in my gold and ebony chest could assuage, I tried to overcome the two most formidable of human passions—anger and desire—by abandonment to the vice of pure gluttony. In that one night I ravenously devoured a whole sponge-cake.

I seem for some deep inborn reason—perhaps connected with the fact that I first saw the light in October—to recall our Sunday walks in the autumn term more vividly than any others. On one particular walk—and Littleton will smile as he reads this passage—we got nearly as far as the top of the high ridge between Sherborne and Dorchester, the ridge that overlooks Cerne where the great Phallic Giant contemplates the valley of the Frome. Here it began to rain. Now I am afraid I was often cruel to Littleton; not always with sadistic pleasure as when I once ran him down "The Slopes" in front of me till we collided—or rather Littleton collided—with the iron rails at the bottom, rendering him breathless and speechless and white-cheeked; but with a kind of arbitrary capriciousness and fantasticalness. It was in this latter mood that I would threaten to "beat him like a dog"—which must have been a phrase picked up in my readings of Harrison Ainsworth—if he allowed it, or God allowed it, *to rain!* Like my father I had an extreme hatred in those days of rain and mud, an unpoetic attitude which I am proud to say I subsequently outgrew; and it was my custom at the beginning of these long walks, where the meadows, the lanes, the copses, the rabbit-holes, the slow-worms, the ploughed fields, the yellow bracken, the stubble, the clamorous rooks, the peewits and yellow-hammers and starlings, all lost their charm for me if my clothes were getting wet, to demand imperatively of Littleton—like some touchy Nebuchadnezzar of his chief astrologer—whether it would rain or not; and then, if he said *not*, and the heavens in their wantonness refuted this prediction, I was accustomed to behave towards him as savages behave towards their medicine-men. Thus, as in the streaming rain Powys Mi. fled from the fury of Powys Ma. down the long hill this side of High Stoy, the elder brother tripped over a grotesque umbrella it was his wont to carry, before he was allowed to carry a stick, and fell heavily on the wet road. If Littleton was treated like a dog when it rained, he was menaced with a wrestling-bout in the ditch if he so much as looked at his brother when that blunderer fell on his face, as he was wont frequently to do when descending a hill; so on this occasion he took to his heels and fairly buggered off; a proceeding which by no means allayed the smart of my indignity and pain. Ailinon! Ailinon! What shameful episodes a person does stumble upon when he retreads the far-off roads of the past!

But I must now indicate to you how that same tendency to passionate and even medieval penitence which made me carry that huge ammonite from the coastguards to our lodging seized me by the hair of my head for this day's cruelty to Littleton; and this time I punished myself—for our autumn hamper had just arrived—by resolving that I would hand it over just as it was to my younger brother. This I did; and to the last refused to touch so much as a slice of a tangerine, or a morsel of a crushed walnut. Yes, Littleton can bear me witness, even unto this day, that I kept my vow to the uttermost.

Oh how we talked about home on these heavenly Sunday walks and how we counted the days to the end of the term! Sometimes we would follow the Yeovil Road till we reached a little spinney—I can see it now—just at the spot where the road to Nether Compton branches off, close to the railings of Squire Gooden's park. Here between two branches, in this small wayside coppice, we were accustomed to place, early in the term, a consecrated stone—the freedom stone—which we were not allowed, by our own felicitous superstition, to do more than glance at till the last Sunday of the term, *when we threw the stone away*. On my soul I think there can be few ancient mythological rituals mentioned in *The Golden Bough* that did not find some sort of representation in our queer fetishistic goings on. Yes, there is no doubt that my happiest times and my most characteristic times too—I mean when I was most my real self—as far as my time at school was concerned, were when I was walking with Littleton all these miles and miles round Sherborne. Deep has that West Dorset countryside sunk into my soul! Nature has conquered in the end and overcome all the miseries I suffered in that place; so that when I go back there, it is only of my walks with Littleton that I think. We would tell ourselves stories of the future when we should be no longer at school, but grown-up and out in an easy, friendly, malleable world. We realized I think clearly enough, at least *I* did, that we were enduring stresses and tensions then, *very then*, far more crucial than anything, save an actual battle-field, that we could possibly encounter in the future.

Well do I recall our conversation one Sunday afternoon as we were walking towards the village of Milborne Port, and I had been contemplating a queer little medieval chapel that stands in a field close to the road. At this time of my life I was beginning to display certain curious debouchings into forms of learning not catered for in a public school. For instance I "took up" Gothic architecture. Someone—very likely at Penn House, or it may have come from Northwold Rectory—pre-

sented me with an illustrated manual of this historic art. My
formidable architectural brother, Albert Reginald, would
certainly peer quizzically at me now under his pulled-down cap
and over his sardonically-held pipe, if he could have heard me
discourse to Littleton on the differences between the Early
English and the Decorated styles, and then again between this
latter and the epoch known as Perpendicular. I certainly had
plenty of opportunity to practise this erudition at Sherborne;
and I now recall how excited I was to discover that particular
kind of zigzag ornament, which so pleased the childish minds
of the Normans, in the abbey porch which I had to pass twice
a day. But on this occasion at Milborne Port—and what a queer
thing it is, these old conversations, that come back to the mind
after forty years, with every emotion revived too that you
experienced at that far-off time—we told ourselves a story as
to how I would be a country curate near some river like the
Wissey at Northwold, and how Littleton would come and visit
me and enjoy the fishing. Well! I did not become a country
curate, or any other kind of curate; and now that I *have* got a
river near me—not the Wissey, but the Agawamuk—three
thousand miles of water are rolling and tossing between us.

Priggishness is, of all human faults, the most pardonable
in a selfconscious boy. I don't feel the least twinge of shame
in recording the gross examples of it that were displayed in
my own life.

My mania for acting Shakespeare in those Montacute
holidays, was but the most overt sign of my inveterate tendency
to be what I like to think of as *a philosophic actor*. My deepest
instinct to this hour justifies this tendency; for what are the
great dramatic philosophies themselves—Plato's, Spinoza's,
Schopenhauer's, Nietzsche's, Spengler's—but the gestures of
the play-acting ego as it gathers up within itself its most
exciting life-illusion, to heighten the intensity of its normal
life-experience? Metaphysical system-making, for which I have
always had a passion, can co-exist, I have found, with the most
fluid, the most far-reaching, the most Pyrrhonean scepticism. I
have never let myself be betrayed by heavy-witted dogmatic
people into turning my instinctive prejudices into rational

convictions. I have always been an actor in ideas—a charlatan if you will—and I am prepared to justify it; for is not Nature herself the nursing mother of all Mimes and Mummers, of all Pierrots, Petrushkas, and Punchinellos? The truth is that the majority of our cautious, objective-minded "truth-seekers" are really unconscious hypocrites of the deepest dye. Rogues too they are. Half their *real* feelings they seek craftily to suppress, in order to present a grave face of stolid common sense to the mad freakishness of real reality.

I can well recall the solemn pleasure I got one evening in our Montacute dining-room, when, playing at bagatelle with my brothers, I kept glancing at Young's *Night Thoughts*. I can see this little leather-bound volume now; and I can recall exactly what it felt like to be the kind of person who, even while he played at bagatelle, must solace his deeper nature with thoughts of eternity.

I was no natural scholar. My dramatic nature relucted at the laboriousness of philological niceties. Well do I remember scurvily dodging our common task in that tiny study, while Littleton and W. E. Lutyens—the great mile runner, now an Anglican priest—turned over the pages of the Greek Lexicon and gave me the translation. At Greek versees too I was anything but a dab. Thus it usually worked out that Littleton had to compose two separate versions in this kind, one for himself and one for his elder brother. Through Mr. King's wisdom and indulgence I was at last permitted to "take up" practical chemistry in place of Greek verse, and aye! what a Faustian pride I had in mixing the elements in these astonishing "retorts," in making celestrial greens and blues out of nothing, and causing golden rains to be precipitated in crystalline water! I spent a sovereign in buying a collection of chemicals at the end of one term; and there in our apple-loft, where my various bottles—"Jack's chemistry"—remained for years, I would play at being an alchemist, gravely mixing this and that, and warning the inquisitive Llewelyn not to meddle with my oil of vitriol. All this while I lacked the faintest rudiments of scientific curiosity. It was only that I liked the sensation of playing with these strange constituents of our planet's flesh and blood. It was the sensation of magic I was after, not scientific knowledge; and, besides, was it not a new way of pressing my knuckles against my eyelids, as I had done at Shirley, and contemplating yet more remarkable greens and blues?

But meanwhile my indurated sadistic vice was always seething in the background of my nerves. I recollect wandering alone on more than one occasion over hill and dale near Sherborne looking for something to tear to pieces. I never revealed, you may be sure, these devilish tendencies to Littleton, who would be at such times intently following the languid course of the Yeo, in the earnest hope of catching a glimpse of the smallest fish's fin amid those muddy waters. Aye! but I can see now the particular expression his eyes would assume under his frowning forehead, as he pushed his way through the purple loosestrife and meadowsweet of those Lenty meadows!

I can only once—and that very obscurely—remember really practising my sadism in those days. Was it only my wicked wish on that occasion? No! I believe I did actually offer up to my raging Demon a whole nestful of unfledged little birds in one of those quarries on the Bristol Road. We had catapults in those years, and it was pure "sportsmanship"—O dastard word!—but at least there *was* no sadism in it, when once, on that same Bristol Road—out there towards Corton Down and Cadbury Camp—I actually succeeded with my catapult in slaughtering a yellow-hammer. I can only hope that that loveliest of the Buntings whose eggs my father had taught us so much to admire, with their mystic hieroglyphs, died without suffering the sharp pang *we* used to suffer, when our backsides felt the leaden shot from the catapults of B—— and of H—— those lively bullies of our early Prep. days!

Colour—different colours—gave me, and give me still, mysterious initiations into the Unknowable. Even the very colours on the ribbons round our straw hats—hats bought at Mr. Lemon's shop in High Street—were symbols to me of so much! Price's house colours were dark blue. I never could do any justice to Mr. Price himself, who was a big terrifying man, and incidentally the grand enemy of that admired head master whose sermons I used so much to enjoy and who was so fine

L

a poet in Latin. A light-blue ribbon, on the other hand, adorned the hats of the boys of Blanch's house.

Providence did not endow me with insight enough to do honour to Mr. Blanch either, who, when long afterwards I was telling him I lived "in Sussex," remarked: "What? All of it?" Mr. Blanch taught mathematics; and it was in his class-room—oh, I can see those unpleasantly new desks!—that I used to shut my eyes, and call up with intense vividness the wet pebbles and the tossing foam of the beach outside Penn House. He was a heavily-bearded man and like other bearded persons I have known seemed immune to any untoward shocks of fate. But "all the same for that," as Homer would say, his end was a tragic one.

Heaven pardon all! You never can tell what sufferings are going on behind another man's spectacles. But it was an important discovery that I made, in Mr. Blanch's well-appointed classroom, that it was possible by a concentrated effort of the will to imagine yourself so vividly in a particular spot that you could touch it with your hand. Does the spirit at such times leave the body? Could a clairvoyant eye have seen a shadowy eidolon of Powys Ma.—pale and tenuous as the cast-off skin of a newt—pursuing its blameless way over the roofs of the abbey, over "The Slopes," over the park, over the Cerne Giant, over Mr. Hardy's house by Fordington, till it reached, like the pitiful thoughts of poor Eustacia on Egdon Heath, the esplanade of its desire. It was this same trick that I was driven to practise during my first major operation in a London nursing-home; but it was a Sussex scene I called up then, not Weymouth beach.

To Weymouth, however, in the flesh I often went, in the holidays of those schooldays. I went into lodgings alone there once, as a convalescent from our Sherborne sick-house. One of the most beautiful boys in the school had been with me in that sick-house—not the young Charmides of those rapt occasions at the bath, but a scarcely less lovely boy—and he, with another companion of a less winning appearance but much more flirtatious, had been sent to a country cottage to recruit, not far from the Coastguards.

I had a passion at that time for collecting seaweeds—*there* indeed were colours to ravish anyone; but alas! their gleaming mysteries faded when you took them out of their native pools. But the truth is I have, ever since that time, linked together the scent of salt-water, the swirl of in-rushing waves among jagged rocks, the upheaving swell of a full tide, not only with crimson seaweeds, but with the greenish-black eyes and foam-white skin of this young invader of my native haunts!

It is interesting to note that my superstitious belief in a flaming Hell for wilful sensualists, which troubled me till I went to college, never prevented me from indulging my attraction to beautiful boys as long as I did not actually embrace them. Indeed, as I never *did* embrace them, save in those scribbled *perdita erotica* which I kept in my treasure-box, I had no anticipation of any final payment for these clinging glances in the bonfire of a jealous deity.

But in my lonely convalescence at Weymouth, for, as Nietzsche says, it is in convalescence that we are especially porous to the magic of life, the green-black eyes of B—— Minor were not my only temptation. Twice in that epoch of my life I actually knelt down on the ground to wrestle with my desire to gaze at young people's beautiful legs. I remember the two precise spots where the knees of the General of the "Volentiä Army" were thus bent before his feudal overlord. One was in Redcliff Bay and one was upon Dartmoor. And I said to myself that it was better not to stare at lovely forms, or to embrace velvet-embroidered cushions or pillows dressed up in my own vests, as long as by such abstinence I escaped being boiled alive like a Lodmoor eel in eternal Hell. It was therefore with knees that trembled and shook—have you, reader, ever experienced that breath-catching feeling?—that I would furtively enter that well-known Weymouth Railway Station and casually glancing—or so I trusted it might seem —at the contents of the bookstall, absent-mindedly possess myself of the Summer Number of *Ally Sloper*, and gravely lay down my penny, as if I had been my father himself buying the *Standard*. But far more romantic, though not, I confess, quite so provocative, as the long legs of the Houris in Sloper's

Paradise, were the illustrations in certain works of Rider Haggard that I found in a bookshop library behind the statue of George III. How little would authors like it if they knew all the reasons for which their books are taken out of libraries! In my longing to immortalize these tiny little vignettes of classical charm, I even went so far as to *trace*, upon a slip of transparent tissue-paper, their divine outlines, and I can well recall the heavenly security and luxurious leisure with which, in my high-ceilinged eighteenth-century front-room, under the large illuminated candalabra, and safe from all interruption, my pencil followed those delicate curves.

My relations with Theodore had grown closer of late, though while we still were at Wildman's, he had been transferred to the Wilkinson School at Aldeburgh, in Suffolk, on the strength of some old family friendship. But so close had I drawn to Theodore by this time—though our link was of a somewhat eccentric nature—that I began a romance about smugglers of which he was the chief. This story was my first real attempt to do what is called "draw character"; and Theodore was my first model. May the devil take me—all the same—if I have not totally forgotten, the one thing I would like *now* to recall, namely what Theodore's comments were when in the dining-room I read this first chapter to him.

But in all the earlier years of my school life the nearest fulfilment of that passionate vow I had made in the Prep. yard, between the stars and the urinal, did not appear in my vapid and extremely imitative verse, but in those of my *letters*— "Jack's descriptive letters" was the satirical name they went by at home—where I discoursed freely and at large, and with all my natural play-action, upon things in general. How well I recall being at Penn House one summer when both Littleton and Theodore were at Northwold. This was the first occasion when "Jack's descriptive letters" were something that I deliberately and with abounding self-confidence poured forth. Did I write them to Littleton or to Theodore? That is a nice point. But from what I have already hinted of the queer fantastical link that now began to be forged between my most original brother and myself, we may *suspect* it was to Theodore.

But I well recall the snobbish pride with which I wrote the grandiose word "Canon" before my Norfolk grandfather's name! Here was a second occasion when this eloquent priest of God, with his hair white and curly as the vision in the Apocalypse, betrayed me into ignoble weakness. What would my father have felt had the Bishop of Bath and Wells made *him* a canon? He would have felt, I think, much as his Giant Grumble would have felt if he had been addressed as Archdeacon Grumble. He would have gone down to the terrace-walk, no doubt, and rubbed his hands in an ecstasy—whether his fifth son were hid in the laurels or his sixth son were even then entering the world—but it would have been merely a moment's childishness. Being written to as a canon by Mr. Phelips would never have given him the thrill that it gave him, on choir-supper nights in the servants' hall, to announce to Charles Childs, and Charlie Blake, and Mr. Pippard, and Mr. Rogers, that he was descended from Roderic Mawr, King of All Wales. Had he announced to them that he was descended from Mohammed Ben Ali, King of All Arabia, Mr. Geard of "The Borough" would have inclined his dignified old head with no less tactful respect.

But I have never beep able to extinguish my snobbish feelings as effectively as my father did, though I am, just as he was, thrilled to the very midriff by the more romantic forms of personal pride. Not one of those old ladies in Cranford could possibly feel her heart beat faster than mine has done when I have had to encounter titled persons. And solely and simply because of their titles; not because of any personal merit in the holders of them. Not that I don't distinguish among these gentry. I can greet a baronet without a tremor; and I have got away without a blush from an encounter with a baron. It is your earls and marquesses who give me these ambiguous feelings. Dukes—though generally regarded as greatest of all—have always had for me a smack of something, not exactly vulgar, but certainly unpoetical. In Shakespeare for instance his earls have always seemed to me much more romantic than his dukes. It is perhaps my historic sense that betrays me; but the word "earl" seems as full of the long embattled history of England as painted church windows or ancient illuminated missals or the Bodleian Library.

My snobbishness has however another side. The great working class, the class-conscious proletariate, is more awe-inspiring to me than any peer of the realm. Nor when it comes to officials and to political magnates am I much less obsequious. The truth is I have never in my life known anyone more troubled, more put about, more generally metagrabolized than I am by encounters with *any* specimens of human beings! I fall at once, in the case of almost all the men I meet into a vein of idiotic obsequiousness and half-crazy flattery. The human eye disturbs me to the depths of my being. I seem aware, much more vividly than others are, of the dangerousness of these bone-cracking wolves in woolly sheeps' clothing, that we see in all our looking-glasses.

I have, Heaven forgive me, a passion for being *liked*—I will not say for being admired, for I am not exacting about that—by every child of Adam I meet! The bottom of it is, I suppose, simply Fear. I must resemble a cowardly dog in my conviction that the most negligible person, any sort of a poor devil, *could* be terribly dangerous. What I expect them to do to me I am sure I don't know, but when I meet their eyes—the eye of a peddler, of an organ-grinder, of a grocer's assistant, of a waiter, of a cab-driver, of the forlornest beggar—I feel as if I could not flatter this ferocious and terrifying being humbly enough, or get away quickly enough! Yes *that* is what it is. It is just *fear*. My life would have been different at every point, not only at school but long afterwards, *now* in fact, if I only had the power to stand up to people and speak out, or strike out, boldly. I am in fact the worst coward in this particular that has ever disgraced the perpendicular form of *homo sapiens*. There were occasions at Wildman's when the least flash of normal pugnacity would have saved me from endless misery. If only I could have got angry! But I couldn't. I have a long memory for insults, but I cannot flare up and hit back! It is this combination of a cold and even deadly analytical judgment with a perfect terror of scenes, contradictions, clashes, man-to-man challenges, that does the harm.

And Destiny has given me my chance to redeem myself again and again. Our dormitory opened upon another one; and one night, when I was at the height of my later unpopularity, the door between us was thrown wide open, and a well-directed boot, while I was quietly perusing *The Lancashire Witches* made it plain to all that here was a challenge for Powys Ma. to be something different from himself. The faintest show of fight would have done the trick. No prolonged fisticuffs would have been necessary. But not a finger had I the gall to raise! I must have excited the sort of disgusted distrust that country boys feel for a grass-snake when they stone it to death. Another time and this was the final catastrophe of the comedy, all my enemies were gathered in a mob outside our study and once more the door was flung open, and with it the door of fate. Did I take advantage even then of this ultimate opportunity? Not a bit of it! And, what is worse, on this particular occasion my cowardice was so hypnotic that it effected even Littleton; so that in all its history that Powys family has never been so betrayed. To strike a good, straight, honest, violent blow, in simple, open self-defence seemed to be impossible to me. And it is so still! Elderly gentlemen of three-score years are not any longer called upon to knock people down; but they *are* called upon, in ordinary decency, not to allow themselves to present the appearance of a circus-freak of sub-humanity. Even the philosophic Chinese—the least belligerent of all mortals—could teach me something. I would anyway learn from them how, as the phrase is, to "save my face." A person who *cannot get angry* except with his nearest and dearest —and only with considerable difficulty then—is a fish out of water in this contentious world. He is a sort of anti-human, a male "Aunt Sally," and it is only a matter of time before even his friends begin to fight shy of him, and to shirk dealing with a fish so queer that if you prick him he doesn't bleed and if you tickle him he doesn't laugh.

It is always easy for me, as I have hinted, to act out to the limit any spiritual gesture that has come to appeal to my particular life-illusion; but my dislike of social facetiousness is no spiritual gesture. The *normal humour* of the human race has always been one of the greatest trials of my life. I have my own humour; and I can assure you that it is very often in full activity when I am standing gravely agape among flying repartees like a Hallowe'en turnip head. But the genial jocosities that are the recognized wit of our lively world chill me to the bone. They fill me with an icy distaste; and I am always at a loss how to respond to them. I look at such times as I feel; a fool, a zany, a bewildered, drivelling, drooling "ambassador from the Moon."

On the other hand Nature has endowed me, as a sort of protective colouring, with a Protean cleverness of my own. Sub-human though I am, I am devilishly shrewd. It is one of my most marked peculiarities. I am a regular Machiavel among idiots. What was it but an infernal cleverness that helped me at the two great crises of my life at Wildman's; once when I pretended to be mad to avoid being made to throw B——'s great sponge at that torturer in the room below.—Would I had had the guts to fly to the rescue of his victim, and get my lean fingers on his bull's throat!—and once, as I shall presently relate, when I was being mobbed by the whole house. My character was forming, rapidly forming, during those years at Sherborne. For one thing clever though I could be at a crisis when I was forced to use my wits, I was too ego-centric, too obstinately committed to my own furtive way of life, too devoted to my sub-human or anti-human sensations, *to want to assert myself*, as a general rule. People who pity me for being "put upon" by self-seekers do not understand me at all. I am a grotesque individual and at times a wretched one, but I am never pitiable; because I have been able, *if I had wanted to*, to escape from almost any imbroglio. But as a rule I did not want to do this, since I was all the while, after my own secretive fashion—"like water seeking its level," as Llewelyn says— getting by hook or by crook the sensations that I required. Thus for all my extreme cowardice I never was a whimperer or self-pitier. I doubt if anyone has ever lived who pities himself less than I do! I always have the rooted conviction that if I am miserable it is my own fault.

Yes, in those letters from Penn House to Northwold,

addressed in such a proud hand to the care of "the Canon"
and I expect written to Theodore, I used my imagination freely
upon the events of each separate day. Each *separate* day! Yes,
great, unjust, careless, indiscriminate Nature has certainly
given me all my life the power of living *afresh* every twenty-four
hours. I retain this, at least, of my forgotten Shirley childhood
that I automatically engender a great wave of Lethe that rolls
over me every night and enables me to wake up every morning
like the Titan Antæus when he touched the sod.

I was extraordinarily happy that time at Penn House. Do
you know I can feel, almost as vividly as I feel this "up-state"
air at this moment, how it was when I came out of my bedroom
at the back of the house, which looked upon St. John's Spire,
and walked slowly, step by step, down the stairs to the
drawing-room, in a perfect ecstasy of delight. Out of the
drawing-room window I then used, in stealthy quietness—for
Penn House was the house of an invalid—to gaze at the
dancing, glittering, dazzling sun-path on the waters of the bay.
Sun upon water, element upon element, and both of them in
radiant spasms of white glory—such phenomena simply rapt
me away in those days, in an indescribable Nirvana. This was
the moment on the stage of my life when the good-evil,
irresponsible Lord of my Destiny uttered the significant words:
"Enter Llewelyn!"

My brother, Bertie, always characteristicaly known as
"A.R.P.," had entered my life-stage before this time. I remember so well being once at Penn House with him, when, with
the most massive and temperamental calm he listened to my
murmurs of erotic frustration as I paced backwards and
forwards from the bow-window to that interior ante-room—I
can smell those spicy East Indian perfumes still, like a *pot-
pourri* of old lotus-leaves—and made no audilbe comment upon
my groans but *looked* a deep, rational faintly sardonic, indulgent
disapproval of his unbalanced elder brother, when he heard
me repeat the word "ennui" over and over again. I had just
discovered this expressive phrase; and I well remember how I
repeated it, tagged with my own translation, "Ennui—Sick-
of-Everything" . . . "Ennui—Sick-of-Everything!" Such were

the words that Uncle Littleton's pearls and tusks and cedar-boxes and tiger-claws and jewelled daggers heard with oriental aloofness from the mouth of the world-weary Johnny. How clear is my memory of that particular day! For, like Schopenhauer's universal man, I now proceeded, on that same grey morning, to lurch spontaneously from the Horn, Boredom, to the Horn, Unsatisfied Desire, of the World-Dilemma imposed on us by the Will to Live.

From the window of the drawing-room it was given me to perceive, at that very moment, a young lady, who in spite of the cloudy weather was meditating a modest advance, at least up to her knees, into that unpromising sea! Do you know this was the first of the *only three occasions*, up to the present hour, when my Saxon-Celtic soul has understood what that confounded French word "ennui" means; and I warrant there is no word at all in that lecherous, critical tongue to describe the Nordic sea-wave of mystical romance and predatory longing that swept over me as I saw that solitary unknown girl! The author of *Undine* would have understood my feeling, just then, better than the author of *Madame Bovary*.

Yes, my brother Bertie—at this time well established in the Prep.—gave me during that epoch my first volume of the poetry of Coleridge. Shelley I had received from the head master as a school prize. Wordsworth—if I mistake not—I had bought for myself. There was one poet I never needed to buy, or to be given; and *that* was Tennyson. Yes, of all volumes of all poets, second to that illustrated Aytoun, the green and Moxon edition of Tennyson's early poems dominated my poetic vision. But Coleridge—that thwarted, baffled, verbose, moribund, fish-cold phantasmalest and maudlin-dismalest of our poets—had never, until then, materialized for me out of his West Country fog.

I took the book—for all the squally gales that were then blowing—to the near-by public gardens. It also, like the Moxon Tennyson, was bound in green and gold. I must say I am still a heretic over our modern chaste, smooth bindings. I share the Early Victorian notion that *the dirt of wear* shows best and looks most mellow upon royal gilt and emblazoned tooling.

But, as I have said, it was at this time that Llewelyn, as an imposing personality, began to impinge on my consciousness. I made a deep dent recently on his physiological life-consciousness when I told him that it was at Penn House that I had held him first in my arms, *before his baby skull had closed*. He alludes to this in one of his books in his unequalled manner; and I can see that it profoundly arrested his attention. If I could have told him that I had heard his first cry—for "When we are born we cry that we are come to this great stage of fools"—he would have bent the familiar brows, so wrinkled *then*, so corrugated *now*, with grave and absorbed interest as to the exact accents of that struggled-for sound uttered in a Rothesay house bedroom. Certainly Llewelyn's humour has proved itself to be more innately indued to the spirit of the earth than any humour I have so far met in my wayfaring. And where was the Chiron who taught him what old honey-dropping trees in our literary forest would best serve the turn of his unique style?

He was still a very little boy when I took him, along with the other younger ones, on an excursion to Portland—I forget if he ever refers to this in his writings—and as we waited for the incoming train that was, with reversed engine, to take us back to Weymouth, we were all pushed by the surging crowd to the platform's edge, and as the train came in Llewelyn was flung down upon the stepping-board of one of the moving compartments and carried along with it as the train slowly drew up. I am sure he changed not a jot of his inquisitive serenity when someone who was sitting in the train lifted him up and lugged him in! He was the first of us to enter that train, as he has been the first of us to follow the long lines of far-away camels that sink into the sands where the winds cover the footprints of Jesus. Nothing that belongs to the fate of man upon the earth is alien to this child of the "South Walk," born, I have no doubt, simultaneously with innumerable little badgers, foxes, hedgehogs, hares, weasels, squirrels, otters, stoats, not to mention billions of rats and mice "and such small deer," who must have all chattered, chattered, clicked, whiffled, lapped, gurgled, yelped, barked, squealed, whined, grunted, gasped, yawned, gabbled, squalled, whickered, wailed, gurked, gibbered, groaned, whistled, screamed, growled, sighed, panted, and squeaked this same thirteenth of August, but who have all gone by now into an oblivion too absolute, as Hardy suggests somewhere, for any mind to grasp. Well! Those other mouths and eyes and ears and paws and pricks, of that far-off birthday, are all turned to dust ages ago; but Master Lulu still licks up his quota of honey, still pulls on his Seven-League Boots, still takes his stick, and having done his business in the backyard sets off to see if the tide is coming in, or going out, and if the swallows have come, or gone.

But to return to those early holidays at Weymouth. Just not to be at school and to have Littleton as my companion was enough for me; and troublesome though I must often have been to this great cricketer and football player, he was always one to be thrilled by the varying sights of land and water, and was indeed, in natural history, as learned as my father and in some things *more* learned. How we loved to row ourselves out beyond the little Weymouth Breakwater! I do not recall however that we ever ventured—as father told us *he* did once, and with his first-born baby on board too—as far as Redcliff Bay. Once we were taken on a day's fishing excursion almost out of sight of land, and well do I remember the dog-fish and jelly-fish that were hauled into that boat; but I remember too that the whole thing was spoilt for me before the end by a frantic desire to urinate. "Water, water everywhere," but Johnny, with bursting bladder, and fixed, staring eyes, was forced to contain! How *can* people have the gall to call their autobiographies the truth about themselves while they make no mention of these things? It presents itself to me as a *sine qua non* of any honest, recital in this kind that it should at least not totally rule out the intimate miseries and reliefs of this diurnal passing of matter through the body.

Two things there are, it seems to me, that make a deeper impression on our whole consciousness and more completely paralyse both our mind and our soul, than any of the more tragic events of our lives. The first is when, for any reason, we have had to put off for an unconscionable time either of our natural evacuations; and the second is when the pride below all pride within us, the self-respect that is the very keel of the vessel, has been hit to the heart by some deliberately poisonous rebuff. The sickening and intolerable suffering of the first has a mental effect that convulses our whole being, and makes us indifferent—like a sort of paralytic stroke—to everything else; while the second makes a person feel, as I felt that day when I missed the catch on the cricket-field, that it would have been better had he never been born. Both these things seem to me worse than any bullying I have ever known, except perhaps the treatment of that little boy in the room below ours at Wildman's.

It was a strange compensation in my dualistic history that during the very years when I was most unhappy at Sherborne I should have been so intensely happy in our visits to Northwold. Never, I dare swear, in any human life has boyhood, in everything it loves best—in everything ours did anyway—been as beautifully catered for, as it was in the case of Littleton and me at Northwold Rectory. Just four years ago, after a lapse of forty years, Littleton and I went back there; and for a whole week were the sole lords of that familiar house, that garden, and that "little river" and were left completely to ourselves! But stirred to the soul though we were by the experience, and unspeakably happy as we were to be together, we mutely and silently knew well that it was doubtful if we should ever come to Northwold again. Over the gulf of those forty years the now white-headed Littleton and the now invalidish Johnny exchanged worldless signals with those two little boys whose whole life in those enchanting purlieus and with those incomparable people had been one scarce broken paradise; and in a sense it was our farewell to those little boys! Back together they receded from this momentary re-incarnation, back hand-in-hand, little Johnny and little Littleton, till they faded into the branches of the cedar on the lawn, into the bushes by the fish-pond, into the poplars along the river, into the alders of Alder Dyke. Shall we ever be able to summon them back again, those little wraiths of the past, as we did during that week? Have they retreated now for ever into an oblivion as deep as if they had been buried, side by side with "The Canon," under that tall flint tower?

Well! at any rate they were not, those two, like Elia's Dream-Children, *always* insubstantial. In their day they bustled about in their small world, lively enough, threw their lines into Dye's Hole, watched the great salmon-trout in Harrod's Mill-pond, found greenfinches nests in the rose-garden with eggs in August, caught pike with their butterfly-nets and butterflies with their caps, saw a breath-taking vision, at least one of them did, of the almost extinct "Large Copper" in the fields by Oxborough Ferry, swung the old Venetian print that hung above their bed till its corners cracked holes in the ceiling, plunged with a submerging splash, at least one of them did, into the round lily-pond among the frightened frogs, devoured green gooseberries, and pink strawberries, got their boat from "little river" into "big river," found plums in unknown trees and dab-chicks where they looked for water-rats, learned to say "Sir" to retired captains, "How is my Joy?" to retiring maidens, carried live perch in fish-kettles and dead dace on withy-twigs, and even stole his handcuffs from the village policeman. Yes, in their day, they were substantial enough and different enough from dream-children; *but where are they now?* The persons we have been are lost rather than fulfilled in what we become, and many who labour for bread in a penurious manhood carry within them the ghosts of children who had cake for the asking.

But—*dum loquimur, fugerit invida ætas*—those days, whether any parcel of them survive or not, were ineffably happy; and it may be that there really is some planetary consciousness in the old earth under our feet that gathers into itself these vibrations of supreme happiness; gathers them up into some precious granary of such feelings, where, if not eternal, they can at least last as long as she herself does.

Epochs were always arising in the lives of Littleton and me when the sturdiness of his character displayed itself in commanding contrast to the weakness of mine. In getting our boat from the "little river" to the "big river," for instance, it was frequently necessary to push it under bridges that were so low that they nearly touched the surface of the water. At these times it always fell to Littleton's lot to remain in the boat. He used to stretch himself out on his back at full length within it, and thus, with its rowlocks and its rudder carefully removed, propel it, by the pressure of his upturned hands against the under-beams of the bridge, till it emerged into the light and into the vision of his elder brother. This elder brother, prone on his face on the top of the bridge had nothing to do but to watch, with excited expectation first the prow, then the basket of provisions, then the scooper for bailing, floating in bilge-water, then the tin of fishing-bait and finally the head of Littleton himself, with an expression of concentrated intensity upon his countenance, his brows puckered, his eyes screwed up, his lips quivering.

About this time, perhaps when I was in the Upper Fourth and dabbling in chemistry to escape Greek verses, I began to grow conscious of a more definite response to different kinds of natural scenery. My father made so much of these differences, implying rather than asseverating the advantages of his native Wessex over all others, that it was natural enough for the varying quality of landscapes to become as important to us as silks to haberdashers, skins to furriers, wines to dotards and cynics. He brought us up to note every undulation, every upland, every spinney, every ridge, every fen and the effect produced upon all these by every variety of season or weather.

My experience even up to the point when I left school for college had been very varied in its scenery. From Derbyshire I had taken nothing but what was purely imaginary; the memory of Mount Cloud as a towering mountain, and of the image of the pond in somebody's meadow as a lake with supernatural fish; but every aspect of the Weymouth coast sunk into my mind with such a transubstantiating magic that it might be said that when I think now of certain things I think *with* St. John's spire and the Nothe, and the old Backwater, and the Harbour Bridge, and the stone groins, and the green pier-posts, and the dead seaweed and the windrow-flotsam, and the stranded star-fish! Yes, it is through the medium of these things that I envisage all the experiences of my life; and so it will be to the end.

Second to the influence of the sea at Weymouth, which,

mind you, was not the open sea of the skimming flights of the cormorant, but the marginal sea of the hoverings of the herring-gull, it is Sherborne scenery that has left the deepest impression on my mind. This Sherborne landscape is on the very border between Dorset and Somerset and combines the pastoral expansiveness of the one with the vaporous umbrageousness of the other. As a matter of fact Blackmore Vale, in the heart of which my father, like Tess of the D'Urbervilles, first saw the light, bears many resemblances to Somerset. His arrival at Montacute must, therefore, have been a very different thing from his Derbyshire exile, for indeed, as he was constantly pointing out to us during his thirty years as a vicar here, you can see the same tower of King Alfred from the uplands above the Dorset Rectory where he was born that you can see from the uplands above the Somerset churchyard where he longed to be, and now is, buried.

My life at Sherborne came to an end, as I have already hinted, in a somewhat dramatic way. There arrived a day, when in some temporary absence of Mr. Wildman, the management of supper and prayers fell to our friend Lutyens, the great runner; a personage who, as is shown by the semi-monastic retirement in which he now lives, has never been one to seek, or even to exert when thrust upon him, what is called worldly authority. It was a Sunday afternoon; and after tea, before setting off to chapel, as Littleton and I amused ourselves in our study, he with his artificial trout-flies, upon which he was composing in the manner of Viscount Grey, a fisherman's manual, and I with *Robinson's History of the Church*, which, as I gravely followed the Great Heresies, was my introduction to philosophy, there were obvious indications of an *emeute* in the passage outside. As Mr. Phelips would have put it, "we were being chaffed by the Populace." Finally our sacred study-door itself was thrown open; and the mob outside, full of both malice and fear began pushing one another in. To my everlasting disgrace—and I still have this panic dread of mobs—I became paralysed with terror. Before a malevolence, which in reality was probably only skin-deep, I became as a dead man. My fear affected Littleton, who opened his grey eyes very wide

and closed his *Manual of Fishing*. It was the moment for me
to have made use of the traditional characteristics of the county
of my birth.

"Derbyshire born, Derbyshire bred,
Strong in the arm, weak in the head!"

One single honest blow with the full force of my bony fist
at the handsome, derisive countenance of D—— Ma. would
have done the trick. But in place of such an air-clearing gesture,
a contemptible scene followed that still makes me, as Rabelais
says, "blush like any black dog," even after four and forty
years. Haverings and hoverings ensued, blows that were no
blows, hits that were no hits, abuse that did not dare to rise to
effective vituperation, combined with a confused barging and
hustling and jostling and threatening. Heavens! the holy
religious women who took possession of Wildman's house at a
later time and turned our studies into cells would have made
a better show of it. But our athletic head of the house, whose
Achillean feet had probably taken him to Melbury Bub and
back that afternoon, intervened at last, and we all drifted off
ignobly enough to prepare for evening chapel.

Up the town we were soon hurrying, past Westbury, past
the abbey porch with its zigzag ornament, past the outside wall
of Mr. Wildman's own classroom, till, entering the school
cloisters by the little postern gate, we ascended the chapel steps.
Here, scattered in our different places, we prepared to worship
the God of our fathers, or to think our own thoughts in peace.
But my mind and my nerves were all in a mad whirl. My
inability to strike a decent blow in self-defence, my inability to
get humanly angry, my inability to come off without shame
from a crisis that only needed a little natural spirit—all of these
things upset me as I had never been upset before. Mechanically
I followed the familiar rubric, made the familiar responses.

"O Lord show thy mercy upon us;
"*And grant us thy salvation.*
"O Lord, save the Queen.
"*And mercifully hear us when we call upon thee.*

"Endue thy ministers with righteousness.
"*And make thy chosen people joyful.*
"Give peace in our time, O Lord.
"*Because there is none other that fighteth for us,*
    but only thou, O God."

And then it came about as the service proceeded that a strange and startling resolution took possession of me, so that the heart within me was stirred to its depths. I was unable to use my Derbyshire fists, why should I not use my Welsh tongue?

"For there is none other that fighteth for us, save
    only——"

Yes, this was what I would do! This very night I would utter to the whole of Wildman's house my accumulated and long-smouldering apologia! The idea burned like a fire within me. I already began forming passionate sentences, rounding off reverberating Ciceronian declamationsl Not for nothing had I composed that Latin thesis—zealously modelled on the great orator's terrific eloquence—that had won the Fifth Form prize. Yes, yes, I would defend myself, justify myself, redeem myself, with my tongue! It is likely enough that Cicero himself would have shunned fisticuffs if Cataline had "gone for him." But I had found my weapon. I was ready.

"Lighten our darkness, we beseech thee, O Lord; and by thy great mercy defend us from all perils and dangers of this night——"

I overtook Lutyens, for all his mile-runner's stride, near, I dare say, those very windows at Westbury House by which we had stood, when my father walked away on our first night in Sherborne. This was to be my last official night in that Saxon school. And before I left why should I not imitate Owen Glendower and "call up spirits from the vasty deep?" Thus my request I made to "Podas okus" Lutyens; and he—bless his swift feet and kind heart!—agreed at once to my astonishing proposition. It was decided between us that as soon as supper was over—a supper consisting entirely of beer and bread and cheese—he was to rise and announce that Powys Ma. "had something to say." I cannot recall how these proceedings struck Littleton. His expressive countenance must have assumed, I think, a look I knew very well, the look it wore when I once recited Tennyson's "Revenge" at an impromptu school concert.

Well, the moment came; and I stood up. The extraordinary, nay! the unique nature of this revolution held all the boys spell-bound. You could have heard, as they say, a pin drop. And then, beginning lamely enough, but quickly catching my cue, I poured forth a flood of tumultuous speech. Out of my foolishness it came, out of my humiliation, out of my inverted pride. It came literally *de profundis*. I had prayed in the chapel: "And take not thy Holy Spirit from us!" but whether the torrent of self-accusations, of self-incriminations, of wild self-mockery, proceeded from the Creator Spiritus, or from the Devil, I cannot tell. I dragged in every single detail they derided me for, I exposed my lacerations, my shames, my idiocies. "Moony" was talking at last out of the madness of the mistress of his horoscope! I referred to the great delapidated umbrella I placed such stock in. I referred to my obscene fashion of chewing my food with my front teeth. I stripped myself naked before them. Taliessin himself could not have prophesied to such a tune when he celebrated the procession of his planetary metamorphoses.

When I sat down there was a moment's dead silence. I did not dare to look at Littleton. But I had not failed. A hullabaloo of applause, puzzled, bewildered, stupefied, confounded, rose up around me. Lutyens whispered something to Littleton before he made the sign for us to kneel down for the accustomed evening Collect. Next morning I was in the sick-room with an attack of my gastric trouble; and it turned out that only once again was I destined to appear in public as a boy at Sherborne School. This was when, driven from my long convalescence at Montacute in Mr. Phelips' great state carriage—he was a governor of the school—I went there on the last day of the term to recite my Prize English Poem. The very morning after that eventful supper at Wildman's, when I made my shame to be my glory, my handsome enemy D—— Ma. brought me—coming shyly into the sick-room—a bunch of violets!

"No cloud," I wrote, in my tame and conventional prize poem, whose subject was "Corinth"—and there certainly was no "Holy Spirit," or any other kind of spirit, about this feeble and uninspired performance—"no cloud," I wrote, "obscures the brightness of the sky."

> "Superbly huge, majestically steep.
> The Citadel looks down with steadfast eye;
> About its base the careless seagulls fly,
> Seeking their rocky homes secure from harm;
> While over sea and land there reigns a deathless calm."

The gods had let me keep my vow, made between the stars and the urinal. I *had* become a poet; but the subject of my poetry had been something different from "Corinth."

Chapter Five

Cambridge

THE summer which I passed between the end of my school life and the beginning of my college life, was largely spent in learning to translate at sight the *Ion* of Euripides, the designated text that year for what is—or was then—known as the "Little-Go." I have never read this play since that summer, in the only way I ever read the classics now, that is to say with a Loeb translation on the opposite page; but the figure of that young neophyte, a sort of Greek Marius the Epicurean, "at his priest-like task of pure ablution" in that quiet temple, has always remained in my mind. I think of that boy's figure now in connection with my son at Oxford; but before my son entered the service of *his* Immortal, I used to think of it in connection with two large bare mahogany tables, the one in the dining-room at Montacute, and the one in the dining-room at Northwold! It must have been in an indulgent concession to a morbid dislike of certain stuffs and fabrics that began to manifest itself in me, that I was thus allowed to spread out my pen and ink and papers and books on these smooth, precious, polished surfaces!

But how devious, how subterranean Nature is, and how crafty and subtle are the impulses of one's own mind in this matter of the getting of wisdom! Yes, the acquisition, little by little, of what subsequently we come to regard as the conjuring trick by which life can be adequately handled, does not arrive by any steady or rational development. It comes by airy, evasive, indirect, intermittent approaches, and then by occasional violent earthquake shocks! It saves us from evil very much as my father's Giant and Fairy used, between them, to save their prétegé's from "the professor."

Wisdom, this miraculous talisman, of which all of us are privileged to steal a modicum before we die, is no rational *quod erat demonstrandum*. On the contrary it is made up of paradoxes and contradictions, of shifts, compromises, transformations, adaptations, adjustments, balancings, calculated blindness, artful avoidances, premeditated foolishnesses, cultivated simplicities! It is made up of the suppressions of curiosity, of the suppressions of cleverness, of narrowings down, diggings in, bankings up, not to speak of a cautious, guarded, tentative, gingerly use of reason.

What do I recall of those moments when I worked at the *Ion* with Lexicon and notes and "Crib" spread out on those two smooth mahogany tables, from one of which I could look forth on our huge *laurestinus*, and on Mr. Cole's meadow, and from the other on my grandfather's drive and the shrubbery where the fish-pond was? I recall nothing! Nothing, that is, but a vague sense of undisturbed well-being and a peace like that of an unruffled sea. I was alone with those calm classical figures each of whom was acting out its own grandiose rôle, with its own dignity in anger, in joy, in sorrow, and all in the presence of Fate and of the immortals. There I was, with my school life over and my college life unknown; but I took no stock, I made no vow, I interpreted, conjectured, resolved, decided nothing. Such is the life of a man! From epoch to epoch we stumble and slide, and it is as if the great goddess, whom in our tongue we call *Chance*, grudged that we should attribute to reason, or will, or religion, or philosophy, or the influence of the stars, or even to Destiny itself, what she regards as her indisputable arbitrary prerogative.

My father himself took me up to Cambridge. I wish I could remember our interviews with the authorities there; for they must have been full of touching subtleties. I am sure they treated my father as Mr. Wildman would in a few years be treating me, and I am sure they treated me as that fiery philologist would in a few years be treating my son! For these Cambridge "dons" were extraordinarily like our Sherborne masters, just as I have a shrewd inkling that the "dons" of to-day must be like the masters of to-day; and how different, in both cases, from what they were in my time! Wherein lieth this difference? Read Charles Lamb's *Essay on the New and Old Schoolmaster*. These things must come in cycles. In my time our authorities were middle-aged men, preoccupied with their own well-established lives, and only impinging on the younger life around them when, as in the case of Mr. Wildman's passion for philology, or Mr. King's delight in literature and amicitia, we shared the same interests.

But it is all different now! Both masters and dons, for good and for evil—for it is hard to imagine that it doesn't "cut both ways"—feel it on their conscience to *influence the lives* of the young persons about them. It is impossible for me to imagine Mr. Fanshawe, or Mr. Charles Moule, still less the Master of Corpus, who at that time was an old gentleman called Dr. Perowne, meddling with my private life, any more than I can imagine Mr. Wildman doing such a thing to me when I was in his House. Just as with Mr. Wildman, what any of us picked up from contact with the exquisite sensitivity of Mr. Moule, or with the robust, humorous country-squire character of Mr. Fanshawe—who used to walk four or five miles, into and out of Cambridge, every day—we could use to our advantage; but otherwise, for good and for evil, these wise and excellent men *let us alone*. Mr. Fanshawe was a connection of my father's by marriage; and Mr. Moule, whenever he went home, went to *his* home and *our* home; for the Moules came from Dorchester, and knew Wessex better than we did; but neither of these very intimate links meant that these reserved Nature-loving scholars felt it incumbent upon them—as long as I obeyed the rules—to meddle with my morals, my taste, my religion, my habits.

What I can very clearly recall of my father's taking me to Corpus were our expeditions to the shops in the town, and the particular type of purchases he made, wherewith to start me in my first experience of housekeeping. They were such objects as seemed to me to bring all Stalbridge Rectory—from which *his* father had taken *him* to Corpus—into my room. And I have no doubt that this yet older gentleman had been himself in his day brought by *his* parent to this college of the generations from yet another rectory!

By the time my son went to Corpus, however, old Dr. Perowne had long been in his grave, and Dr. Pearce, my son's uncle by marriage, was in the lodge; so that there was no necessity for me to carry any further that ancient tradition and no doubt, in consequence, my son's rooms were more æsthetically, they could hardly have been more substantially, furnished, from those kindly Cambridge shops.

The rooms I myself finally succeeded in occupying, though they were entered from the New Court, *looked out* on the Old, and were indeed part and parcel of one of the most romantic relics of medieval scholasticism that I have ever seen. If I had needed a rather priggish study of Gothic architecture to interest me in the old buildings at Sherborne, at Corpus I studied nothing. I hardly realized what I was enjoying as I swam about in this bottomless pond of antiquity. The Corpus Old Court had the look—especially before they removed the ivy, which my father always averred *his* father had planted—of some enchanted ruin in a fairy-like forest of old romance. After they had scraped off the ivy it looked exactly as it must have done in the days when Christopher Marlowe had his rooms there! It was upon a great beam running across the ceiling of my chamber that Llewelyn, years later—well! I suppose exactly a dozen years later—discovered the words: "Pray for the Soul of John Cowper Powys." My soul still looks about her in this mortal world, and Llewelyn, in a manner that would delight Christopher Marlowe, has done doughty work in lambasting such holy gestures, but it gave him a queer feeling all the same to see those words in that place.

It was a notable experience to me when I first "dined in hall." It was wonderful to be eating my meal in so medieval a manner, and as my predecessors before me had done for five hundred years. It was thrilling to glance up at the pictures of the Old Worthies hung round the panelled walls and at the painted windows that "blushed with the blood of kings and queens"; and if my skull allowed certain wild and indeed mad thoughts a temporary lodgment, between those stately courses, it was only as if a few of Mabinogion ravens had flown in and flown out at a primitive feast. I can hear still that hastily mumbled Latin grace; ending up with the words "per Jesum Christum, Dominum Nostrum": and how different this "Jesum Christum" sounded in its secular resonance and with all the turbulent history of the Church behind it, from that "Safe in the arms of Jesus" which I used to mutter into my pillow when the night-nursery candles were blown out!

Over the ancient roofs of the interior of the Old Court there rose a church tower that was older than William the Conqueror, that was in fact that extremely rare thing—as I had already learnt—a *Saxon tower*. I looked at this square erection with infinite interest. The romance of race! Is there anything in existence that is more poignant than that? Well! I suppose the peculiar vibration, the deep "pit-of-the-stomach" feeling, I have about such things comes from my impassioned readings of Sir Walter Scott and from those amazing illustrations of the quarto edition of *Aytoun*, but perhaps it comes, all down the long centuries, from my drop of proud Celtic blood! I had a daily occasion to contemplate this tower; for the Corpus privies were close beneath it. Here it was the custom to leave the door open while you were at stool, and I am afraid that this was one of the customs of my ancestors, along with others of a more religious nature, against which I was driven, by the weakness of my nature, to revolt. I used, timidly at first but afterwards more boldly, to push *to* these doors, so that I could make my evacuations in at least a semi-retirement.

I may have been bold in this matter, but the timorous conservatism of my deepest character has never been better illustrated than by the fact that simply and solely because all my days I had heard my father tell stories of his rowing, and of how he had persuaded *his* father to allow him to "stay up" longer than usual, in order that he might have the satisfaction of rowing in the Corpus *second* boat, I also must needs enter upon this activity. Could anything have revealed better not only my own inherent stupidity but the stupidity of our common human nature? Had I not already suffered miserably enough from compulsory cricket at school, that I should go and put myself under the yoke again? Why the devil didn't I tell these impertinent young men—full of chat about "serving the college"—that those also "served" who only stood and waited? I might have done this and come off triumphantly! For as a matter of fact this was before the days when, both at Sherborne and Corpus, athletics were made a moral duty and indeed were vehemently encouraged by the authorities, to keep our hands out of plackets and our feet out of brothels!

But unfortunately, at Corpus in those days there were three completely separate groups of people. There was the fast set, who, on the whole, gave athletics to the Devil. There was the pietistic evangelical set, some of whom actually preached, to any who would listen, on that rather desolate expanse towards the railway station known as Parker's Piece. And finally, there was the athletic set, divided again among themselves into those who favoured football and those who favoured rowing.

I fell into the hands of the rowing ones. It was a ridiculous thing. What good did I do to the college or anything else? I certainly did not save myself from immorality; for I well recall that it was in the very bloom and flower of the rowing season that I used to go for walks with the most profoundly immoral man in Cambridge, a man whose personality exuded a morbid sensuality that was pathetic. This rather unhappy individual's advances—they were not carried very far—evoked the only occasion in my life when I was erotically excited *without the least accompaniment of pleasure;* an occasion which I resolved should never be repeated, for it was extremely disagreeable to me.

It was during my first year at Cambridge that a vein in my nature that had long been threatening to give me trouble began to assert itself. *I refer to asceticism.* I have got in me a vein of the most obstinate asceticism, that is always ordering me about and curtailing my freedom. I accept its commands with a docility that is slavish! I yield to it as I yield to all my other quite innocent, but sometimes most annoying peculiarities. I yield to it as I certainly have never allowed myself to yield to my sadistic tendencies. Llewelyn has come to believe that this ascetic element in me *is* itself a sort of auto-sadism. Possibly. But for my own part I tend to regard it as a purely *asthetic* peculiarity! Yes, I tend to explain my asceticism as an eccentric form of *astheticism;* and I believe I am not wrong in this solution. The thing had begun before I went to Corpus. I can remember the delight—a kind of rapturous orgy of priggish unction—with which, in one of my walks with Littleton, I think on the road to Long Burton, I gave what amounted to almost a shilling—and think what a shilling's-worth of apricot paté would have been—to a respectable young woman who was drawing water at a well. I rather fancy she thought at first that this ungainly schoolboy was regarding her as a light-of-love. But reassured by my foolish gravity and by the fantastical rigmarole I uttered, she finally came to the correct conclusion, namely, that I was a boy from Sherborne School acting the part of a bestower of alms.

My asceticism at Corpus on the contrary took the form of extreme parsimoniousness. I have always had an incurable itch to be regarded as good and noble, a desire that my convoluted sensuality combined with my extreme timorousness renders difficult of attainment. But my awe of my father was so great that above everything else I wanted to be in his good graces; and I knew that one of the shortest cuts to this end was to live more economically than even he had supposed was possible! Thus, following his own example, for in spite of his powerful frame he was more abstemious in his diet than any man I have ever known—stewed pears and rice pudding being his only temptation to excess—I never had more than one egg for breakfast, and when I made porridge on my fire, and it tasted especially delicious, I would deliberately leave it in the pot for the delectation of the servant who cleaned my room. I have already referred to my passion for plum-cake and the indirect manner in which I gratified it; but I carried my self-persecutions much further than this.

I would choose, for instance, as the companions of my walks, the particular young persons of my acquaintance who were the least esteemed in the college, and who inevitably took the lowest seats; and when, by reason of something hypnotic about my disturbing personality, I *did* make friends with popular people, I fawned upon them and furiously flattered them; not, you must really believe me here, from the remotest desire for social advancement, but solely because a kind of young girl hero-worship concealed itself in my clumsy frame.

Just as with the new boys at Sherborne, the freshmen at Corpus appeared on the scene a day or so before the others; and it was then that I heard the most astonishing rumours about the behaviour of the rowdier members of the fast set, and how they were liable to burst into a newcomer's rooms and throw his possessions out of the window! I had, however, made up my mind long before I came to Corpus that I was not going to endure any repetition of my school experiences. There did exist, I had pondered, weapons of defence that made the weakest and the most cowardly the equal of the strongest and the bravest. In conspiracy with Theodore therefore, who by this time had left the Wilkinson School in Suffolk, and had gone, as a pupil in farming, to a village in that same county, I bought a revolver. Theodore and I used to climb out of the "end room" at Montacute by the aid of a rope, and in addition to this fooling with fire-arms, for which no two youths could have been less adapted, we had by this time launched into the smoking of tobacco. I can remember the fear and excitement I felt as we walked through Stoke Wood in the middle of the night and I can remember the measureless satisfaction with which I felt that we resembled these Dutch pirates in *Guy Mannering*. I longed to hear Theodore say, "Douse the Glim!" and to reply, "Donner and Blitzen!" and as we two demoniac outlaws advanced towards Stoke Church I felt that I could say to the ghost of King Stephen: "I do not set my life at a pin's fee!"

All the while, therefore, that my father was making the sort of purchases in Cambridge for me that *his* father had made for him, I would be fumbling in my coat pocket to make sure that my loaded revolver was still safe. Did it lie between my brand-new pocket-book there, and my last illustration of feminine charms out of *Ally Sloper*? But when those drunken rowdies eventually materialized—and they actually did visit me—I can assure you it was only necessary to cause the mouth

of this formidable weapon, bought at Petter's, ironmonger,
Yeovil, to emerge a brief distance from its hiding-place. And
the result was that not only was my room not gutted, but a
warning was spread through the place that it would be unwise
to attempt any ragging of a freshman who might resort to
fire-arms.

But with what awe I regarded these notorious Third Year
rapscallions, as at the beginning of our chapel services—these
were compulsory then—they lounged in, swollen with
insolence, pale with dissipation, brimming over, in fact, with
what Homer calls "hybris," and with the barest relics of their
undergraduate gowns hanging in weary effrontery from their
drooping shoulders! When I think of my tremulous obeisance
before a set of preposterous asses, as most of these fellows
were—though they were harmless, I can assure you, compared
with the bullies at Sherborne—I wonder to myself if the respect
which most of us feel towards the historic ruffians of our race
is not made of the same stuff. I think there must be some subtle
æsthetic instinct at work here though, else why should we feel
such peculiar annoyance when Mr. Wells, in his famous
history, sets to work to disparage these picturesque cut-
throats?

How one's life does revolve in cycles! How it does keep on
repeating itself! Before my first term was over I had taken
upon myself to invite anyone who liked to turn up to come to
my rooms and listen to a weird prophetic denunciation I had
composed, entitled "Corpus Unveiled." The fast men came to
this in the hope of a sensation, and the anonymous Pariahs,
despised by all, came to this as if to hear the voice of some
Corpus Danton. There was even a sprinkling of athletes;
though why *they* came, heaven alone knows! One pious evangelical, of those who preached on Parker's Piece turned up,
partly because he was a rowing person, and partly because,
being profoundly simple, he anticipated some kind of sermon.
Why was I not more tender to this evangelical piety? I might
at least have refrained from egging on these bully boys to
badger this young oarsman. I can see his simple face now.
But no! I hated his co-religionists too deeply! For a certain

kind of sleek, self-satisfied, *redeemed* look, these men were unequalled. They were not ascetics, let me hasten to assure you. Not one of them! If they did not, like Epistemon at Orleans, play the whore-master, they gulli-gutted most filthily upon the buttered toast that old Mr. Dobs, the most gentlemanly of butlers, provided from the college kitchen.

But where—you will say—thinking of Christopher Marlowe, where were the imaginative, the poetical, the intellectual sons of Corpus? Where were the young Phædruses, the young Mirandolas? Alas! There were none. Not one single one!

I had to beat up out of my own crazy wits, out of a skull that, as you have detected, was like the skull of an hysterical Petrushka, all the poetical idealism that I craved. All manner of inchoate ideas were at that time surging in my brain, and leaping up and down like the fish in Harrod's Mill-pool! I remember well how once walking out of Cambridge on a road that started—I never could master the compass—in the opposite direction from Byron's Pool, along with a brisk, neutral-minded lad whom the great Goddess Chance had made to be of a clay so different from my own that not one single vibration of comprehension could possibly pass between us, I launched out into a metaphysical defence of the Trinity, that comes back to me now as having been a tirade of torrential inspiration—not, I admit, as comprehensive as Sir Thomas Browne's discourse on the Quincunx; but a good deal livelier than anything that Coleridge—that subtle mystogogue—has left behind him on the Number Three. The truth is that first year at Corpus was one grand outpouring of seething, surging, whirling ideas; varied by fits of fawning, wheedling, almost girlish cajoleries as I indulged my admirations and attractions.

I will not say that I got nothing from my vain efforts to become an oarsman; but what I got from my daily walks to where the rowing took place, which is a long way from Corpus, had nothing at all to do with boats. I could not help, as in autumn and in spring, I walked this mile or two, snatching a thousand opportunities to enjoy those fleeting, fluctuating, purely contemplative feelings, which I have now come to regard as the essence of my life. Yes, I am ready to bless that

Cambridge river and the lively custom of boat-racing on it; but only for the indirect and subsidiary benefits I received therefrom. And it has been the same all my life.

By slow degrees it has made itself manifest to me that the purpose of my life was to dodge—when I could get leave of absence from my exacting conscience—all obligations to humanity, and to cultivate certain totally useless, purposeless, unprofitable feelings. These feelings, which to me have come to be precious beyond any power of description, are regarded by many as pathetically colourless and sapless, by others as a kind of wilful insanity, by a few as a damnable affectation! But to most of my acquaintances at Corpus at that time my manias were taken for granted, exactly as was "Jack's pain"; and my long walks alone, or with "chandala" companions, became to these lads the same sort of thing as my habit when at home of bending my body across gates, of rolling on the sympathetic ground, and of persuading the little Llewelyn to use my stomach as a seat.

I think it must have been in these crazy monologues—bearing a certain resemblance to those of Coleridge at his Blue Coat School, only much less erudite—that I first began to develop my gift for pierrot-like oratory, an oratory into which I flung the wild grotesqueries of my being, and at the same time played with ideas; for though I took part in the Corpus Debating Society my formal speeches, like my written poetry, were lame, clumsy and inept. I remember well composing a poem in which the line: "suns and suns of sad and soulless seeming" occurred, and being amazed when someone protested that this was not poetry at all.

My three years at Corpus were years when my sadistic vice remained in complete abeyance. Why this should have been so I have no idea! And not only did that deepest and most congenital vice vanish during that epoch, but my more normal, but not entirely normal mania for pictures of young women with long slender legs, receded too. Was I becoming attracted to men? Not to my knowledge! As I look back on my time at Cambridge it presents itself to me as a period of pure idealism; and I really think it must have been by far the most idealistic epoch of my life. Religion played absolutely no part in it. I might dally fancifully with the metaphysics of the Trinity; but neither the idea of God nor the idea of the figure of Christ had the faintest interest for me. And yet I certainly was, during those three Cambridge years, more moral—in the special sense of being more chaste—than I have ever been before or since. I cannot recall one single lapse from this impeccable virtue!

As a pilgrim and sojourner at Corpus I was indeed a good man, "as all my fathers were"! But I certainly was eccentric. It was with me at Cambridge, just as it was at Sherborne, and just as it is now in New York State. I danced my own dance and sang my own song. My grand object was to get off for lonely walks in the country. All my life I have been like this. I have always regarded my existing domicile, whether it was an institution, or my father's house, or a house of my own, or a hotel in Rome, Washington, Montreal, Florence, or San Diego, as a resting-place from which I could walk *into the country*. It is for this reason that I shall probably never go to Venice again. A city of gondolas is not at all the place for a person of my peculiarities. But Cambridge *was* an ideal place! I could follow those long, straight, flat monotonous roads for miles and miles, north, south, east and west.

What curious thoughts I had, as I followed these unpicturesque unromantic highways and used to see, far off, as I drew homeward, the familiar form of King's Chapel outlined against the sky! My thoughts were not of my particular studies, which very soon assumed an historical bent. Nor were they of my relatives at home. And they certainly were not of the affairs of Her Majesty's Empire. What I am revealing to you now is the deepest and most essential secret of my life. My thoughts were lost in my sensations; and my sensations were of a kind so difficult to describe that I could write a volume upon them and still not really have put them down. But the field-dung upon my boots, the ditch-mud plastered thick, with little bits of dead grass in it, against the turned-up ends of my trousers, the feel of my oak-stick "Sacred" whose every indentation and corrugation and curve and knot and grain I knew as well as

those on my hand, the salty taste of half-dried sweat upon my
lips, the delicious swollenness of my fingers, the sullen sweet
weariness of my legs, the indescribable happiness of my calm,
dazed, lulled, wind-drugged, air-drunk spirit, were all, after
their kind, a sort of thinking, though of *exactly what*, it would
be very hard for me to explain. Did I share at such times the
sub-thoughts, or over-thoughts, that the old earth herself has,
as she turns upon her axis, or that the vast volume of the ocean
has, as his tide gathers along his beaches or draws back
hoarsely into his gulfs?

They were at any rate what might be called sensation-
thoughts. They had to do with the impact of the wind on my
face and with all those vague, obscure half-memories that the
wind can bring with it, full of half-realized impressions from
days far off, days perhaps *so* far-off that they actually belong to
previous reincarnations. As I write these lines now, there comes
back to me—simply from the mechanical obliteration of all
those tiresome rational thoughts and worrying practical
thoughts that spoil one's life—one scene after another from
those lonely roads. Even as I try to seize upon them they dissolve and melt away; but in their vanishing they leave a lovely
residue, a mysterious satisfaction, that seems to well up from
the inner being of old posts, old heaps of stones, old haystacks
thatched with straw. From glimpses of white roads, appearing
and disappearing in the twilight, these feelings spring; from
wayside ditches, desolate ponds, solitary trees, windmills
caught against the sky! What I would like to emphasize just
here is that the pleasure I got from these things of my solitary
walks did not present itself to me as an *æsthetic* pleasure, nor
did it call up in my mind the idea of beauty. What gave me
these sensations seemed to be some mysterious "rapport"
between myself and these things. It was like a sudden recognition of some obscure link, some remote identity, between
myself and these objects. Posts, palings, hedges, heaps of stones
—they were part of my very soul.

But the mere movement of walking, the mere contact with
earth and air and the breath of the free wind as I left the town
behind, always seemed able to engender in me a mood in which

N

the present took to itself a sort of winnowed essence of similar memories from the past and thus became a continuity of half-forgotten feelings that welled up in my consciousness and reduced the future to complete non-existence. I thus became on these lonely walks like one who has found the clue to the obliteration of the future; and although I did not feel as though I touched the Eternal, I certainly felt as though I ceased to want anything or wish for anything that I did not already possess. What I possessed was in fact—if I may put it so—a sort of *half-eternity*, made up of a fusion of past and present, with the future, and all its wants and wishes, totally annihilated.

I had proof enough at Cambridge how unnatural to my real instincts had been that priggish attempt to "take up" Gothic architecture; for I left the place without having so much as even stepped inside some of the most beautiful and famous of the courts, halls, chapels, libraries, gardens that are its glory. But it has been just the same in other towns and cities of old renown. Engaged in the study of history though I was, I had as little of the antiquary in me as I had of the scientist; and if Goethe shocks me in his "Travel Sketches" by the bland imperviousness with which he turns away from so many famous works of art in order to visit botanical gardens, I am afraid I should incur that great man's rebuke by the shameless way in which, when surrounded by historic buildings I invariably sneaked off to find the nearest lane, or towpath, or cattle-drove, where I could be alone with the elements.

Certainly my three years at Cambridge were years of an unbalanced and chaotic idealism. I remember I was constantly formulating in my mind the wildest and most arbitrary rules for my intimate life. In my poetical, or at least what I supposed to be my poetical fastidiousness I relucted at committing these fantastic rules to paper! Rules, do I say? They were formulations of a series of sublime purposes of life. But in my unwillingness to write them down and in my natural tendency to start fresh each day as if I had been newly born, I was sorely put to it to remember what my last rule of life, my last purpose of life, was. It was then I had recourse to the stars. In my egoism I used the stars as a philosophical index. As I have hinted before, I have seldom suffered from Pascal's sublime "frisson" at the spectacle of these glittering punctuations in the enormity of the inscrutable. My tendency has been as with everything else in Nature, to accept them with what Spengler calls the "physiognomic eye"; in other words to wonder at them *in their precise visible appearance*, eliminating from my consciousness all those bewildering astronomical and mathematical calculations with regard to their size and distance, their origin and destination. What has always arrested me are the actual configurations of the stars; so many astounding twists and twirls and spirals up there in the Boundless. And even more than by their actual pattern have I been fascinated by the legendary mythology of the stars, their astrological influences. I accept them, in fact, *at their face value* as the imperishable companions and fatal accomplices of our tragic human drama.

"Many a night," as Tennyson would say, from the edge of that well-kept lawn, forbidden to the feet of undergraduates, that separates the porter's office from the master's lodge, "did I look on Great Orion, sloping slowly to the West."

And as I contemplated all those celestial marks and scrawls, all those illuminated scribbles, so arbitrarily fantastical—here an index, there a codex, here a gloss, there a colophon— I proudly suspended my latest solution of life's riddle on the horns of some Babylonian mystery, or on the heraldic tail of some Zodiacal monster. For I pondered thus:

"Whenever I see yon heavenly curlecue, made upon the shores of Immensity by the walking-stick of the Demiurge, I shall say to myself: 'the object of life is to pursue the True, the Good and the Beautiful': or I shall say to myself: 'the object of life is to evoke the Greatest Happiness of the Greatest Number': or I shall say to myself: 'the object of life is to develop the spirit at the expense of the body': or I shall say to myself: 'the object of life is to find my alter-ego, my eternally-destined True-Love'!"

Thus pondering I would hang my latest ideal gonfalon, torn from the pages of *Hereward the Wake* or *Sartor Resartus*, upon the belt of Orion or round the neck of Cygnus, and then go off perfectly well-satisfied, to visit my private tutor in the snug precincts of Selwyn.

In spite of my violent prejudice against science I did have one scientific friend. His name was Rowland and he was the eldest son of one of our nicest Somersetshire neighbours, the friendly if somewhat cynical Vicar of Stoke-sub-Ham. Rowland belonged to Downing, a foundation for which I soon came to have a special predilection. I savoured so fully those wide expanses of grass that separate its mellow buildings and I relished too something that seemed to me almost pastoral about its architecture. Sidney Rowland was a man who "with Epicurus denied the immortality of the soul" and with Democritus *il mondo a caso pone;* but although such doctrines were as tedious to me as the drawing-class at Sherborne, they interfered little—for was not my latest revelation ready to brandish its oriflamme, the moment the stars came out—with my respect and liking for this most honest infidel. I think it showed that I was at least *honest* myself; or I am sure Sidney Rowland would have bowed me downstairs; for he was not one to be fooled.

Take it all in all there were very few people I knew at Cambridge; and I did not desire to know more. My suspicion of the great world, and of those who ascend to eminence therein, was as powerful then as it is to-day. Ambitious young men were sealed books to me. I could make, as they say, neither head nor tail of such goings on. Deep in every fibre of my being stirred my father's towering and solitary pride, a pride that needed, I can assure you, neither applause from the world, nor a place of authority in the world.

My long apprenticeship at Sherborne, from my tenth to my nineteenth year, had established in my mind once and for all that secret that I had discovered when I was only eight and nine, namely that it is possible to find your life-cult and pursue your life-cult in complete independence of the community in which you have been thrown. Thus at Corpus while I felt a puzzled contempt for ambitious men, I simply did not recognize the existence of society ladies. As my tastes hardened and clarified I found that I derived from the acquaintance of girls-of-the-street and of other equally uneducated and equally easy-going young women, all the idealistic and romantic thrills that I wanted. Not that my commerce—slight and intermittent as it has been—with girls of joy ever satisfied my sensual cravings. It was my moral sense, my spirit, my soul, my æsthetic feelings, my imagination, my longing for romance, my tenderness for ideal femininity that these courageous and kind-hearted wenches fulfilled. And—odd though it may sound —what I especially valued in them was their chastity. But of course any one not a fool could have foreseen that I would find them that! It seems indeed to be a congenital peculiarity of mine that the girls who appeal to me should possess the chastity of whores.

It is I suppose what might be called the Platonic idea of girlhood that attracts me. Certainly my instinctive attitude to women is a mixture of impersonal and extremely fastidious lust with a romantic tenderness. It must have been about the time of my entrance to Corpus that I first cajoled a young woman into my bed. This was not a bed, you may be assured, within those monastic precincts; but it was my own bed, and I antici-pated the moment of sharing it with a feminine shape with heart-beating eagerness. But it was not a success! I found my companion sadly different from those slim sylphs whose pic-tures filled the lower drawer of my treasure-box. Her appear-ance in her long white night-gown, her grave be-ribboned tresses, her stillness and passivity, all this was heaven to me; but my experience suggests either that most women are singularly ignorant of the perversities that Nature loves to strew in her path, or that Providence has fooled them into thinking that the seduction of any close contact with them must be irresistible. But alas! such contact has generally proved in my case only too easy to resist; and yet my bedfellow on this occasion would merely have had to stand once more at the mirror and tie the ribbon round her locks again, to restore that Platonic image of femininity which contact with her destroyed. But such young persons never—or very, very rarely—have the wit to realize this; or am I to suppose—and perhaps this *is* nearer the truth—that the mixture of impersonal idealism and fastidious lust with which I regard them is of all things the most antipathetic to a girl's nature?

My friends at Cambridge, as I have hinted, were very few compared with those of most men of my age. Thomas Henry Lyon, of whose striking personality rumours came to me the minute I set foot in Corpus, soon became, not only the most intimate, but certainly the most beguiling, of these. I wonder if the famous Thomas Henry, whose destiny has caused him to play such a dominant rôle in the lives of so many nervous, eccentric, and imaginative people, can feel himself back into that young Henry Lyon whose unequalled charms held me spellbound? I dare say he can, for his awareness of his own remarkable identity was always exceptionally vivid. His companionship was certainly more eagerly sought and more passionately prized than that of any person of either sex that it has been my lot to meet in my whole life. In after years, when we had become more closely linked together, for Thomas Henry is my son's uncle, we had a way of entangling ourselves in such long, intricate, and I might say furious arguments, that the delicate charm, full of all manner of chivalrous nuances, of our earlier contact was bruised, as these things so often are, by the merciless buffets of the implacable reasoning faculty. Heaven forgive us! We certainly allowed our fantastical opinions, neither of us, I fear, being very Socratic in his logic or even prepared to meet the other a quarter of the way, to bully into quiescence, and finally into exhausted apathy, one of the most promising friendships that ever beat— within those Corpus walls—against life's implacable retiences.

But what a man Thomas Henry Lyon was, and must be still! What sardonic wit illuminated in those days his Voltairean countenance! What flickerings of convoluted emotion crossed and recrossed his Prince-of-the-Church profile! His humour was savage, his gall triumphant, his heart tender, his fancy fertile, his energy insatiable, his contempt for the hypocrisies of the world unbounded. But he was, and probably remains, one of those intransigent despots whose zeal for righteousness is only equalled by their inability to leave the righteous in peace, their passion for truth only equalled by their terrific preference for their own path thereto.

But if he was tyrannical towards me, I was cruel towards him. I remember once going so far as to say—and what a thing to say to a friend!——

"Do you think I would really reveal to you the depths of my heart?"

And I remember once in a lonely spot on his native moor actually *giving him the slip* and returning home alone, for no reason at all except my selfish desire to enjoy my private sensations uninterrupted by human companionship.

At his worst, the brains of Harry Lyon resembled a bitter walnut encased in a steel helmet; whereas, at *my* worst, *my* brains became like a miasmic mist hovering over a churchyard. The difference between us was extraordinary. I think the man is essentially a Norman; but a Norman whose compact skull turned its terrific volition away from tournaments and battles to the lists of art! And it was art *à outrance;* it was art carried to the limit. His artistic manias expressed with ferocious intensity, kept riding, like men-at-arms with sword and spear, into the devious fastnesses of my Welsh imagination. I can recall so clearly an actual spot, on the road from Arundel to Burpham in Sussex, where he could not contain himself at my lack of æsthetic—or indeed any other—"convictions." I remember mumbling and muttering something about my secret life of pure sensation, concentrated upon Nature; but this only added fuel to his Dantesque flame. "Nature!" he would cry; and once more that scoriating artillery, fed with the very brimstone of "creative art" would blaze about my head. But willy-nilly I must have picked up *some* æsthetic standards from the words of this furious crusader. But art-principles seem to be as varied as scientific hypotheses; and I was soon to encounter an almost completely reverse set of æsthetic axioms in the more measured, but hardly less implacable opinions of my own brother Bertie.

But I dare say it helped us both—Harry Lyon and me— thus to batter at each other's heads; helped us, not so much in the direction of modifying our basic assurances as of clarifying them to ourselves. He would announce to his disciples: "Jack Powys is a man without a soul!" and I, in the privacy of my own nondescript circle, would retort: "Harry Lyon has the soul of Saint Augustine!" Peace be unto thee, O strange friend of my youth! When we next meet it will very likely be as doddering, querulous old gentlemen, more anxious about the effect of the weather on our rheumatism than as to how man can, or cannot, scrape through life without putting Rubens above Titian.

But an older friend of mine at Corpus, though I lost touch completely with him after we went into the world, was Constantine Koelle. Koelle was some years, I should say ten years, older, and this naturally led to his becoming a kind of psychological master to me. If my arithmetic is not wrong the dear man must be over seventy to-day. Think of Koelle over seventy! It gives me that weird shock that Proust so incomparably describes in those last two volumes of his masterpiece.

If with Thomas Henry, save at the very start, when his good looks and brilliant humour overawed me, I was on fairly equal terms, with Koelle I gave full vent to that element of almost girlish hero-worship which has so many times since won me a particular kind of favour with powerful people. Looking back on that time now, I confess that the character of this chosen mentor of mine seems a little obscure. This is doubtless due to the fact of the difference in our ages. But I cannot refrain from thinking it must be also due to a certain cautious reticence in my friend. Personally I am one who discourses with shameless freedom to younger people; not to only people ten years but twenty, nay forty years younger than I am! Koelle certainly cannot have been like that! But how good he was to me, how sweet, how tactful, how gracious, how affectionate and considerate! I warrant it added a lot to my prestige in Corpus, and softened the asperity of many harsh judgments about me, that a man of Koelle's knowledge of the world should have made a crony of such a queer one. There was indeed no earthly reason why he *should* unbosom himself to me! How could he know that in the matter of confidences I was deep as the grave? But if I became cruelly reticent towards

Harry Lyon, Koelle became what might be called amiably reticent towards me. As an example of this, it was not till a day or two before we separated forever, that my friend announced to me that he was going to be married. God help me! When *my* time to marry drew near, as it did pretty soon after this, who was there among my circle who did not give me every possible kind of advice. They all spoke up; though they did not all say the same things. But the astute Koelle wisely dodged all this. I suspect that he agreed with Robert Browning in that virile sentiment about keeping one side of your nature—or was it one side of your soul?—hidden from all the world so as to be able to reveal it to the woman of your choice. Personally I am cantankerous and disconcerting in this matter. It gives me a curious pleasure to hold my secrets away from my closest intimates, and then to publish them, as the Scripture says, "from the house-top."

No doubt it was to Koelle that I owed my dip into the work of Browning, that, for exactly three years—when I was twenty, twenty-one and twenty-two—delighted and obsessed me. Then I turned from it in fastidious detestation; and I have never gone back to it! Browning remains in fact the one single *great* author for whom I cherish a venomous and malignant hostility. My feeling is personal, *and physical.* I feel towards him as a woman might feel towards a man who has made unprovoked and unpleasant advances to her. In fact I feel as if in his super-masculinity Browning makes such advances to all his readers. It is this virility of his that I find so objectionable. I am indeed as touchy over what I *divine to be* the physical characteristics of my authors, their nerves, their *kind* of sensuality, the temper of their blood, as I am about similar peculiarities in my friends! If I like a person—be it man, woman or child—I like such an one *physically.* Am I that opprobrious thing a "polymorphous pervert"? Possibly I am. The astute reader is doubtless already on the look-out! But my own deep personal instinct is always warning me that psycho-analytical pigeon-holes must be accepted with extreme caution. Even as far as they go at present these theories by no means cover the field; and we may be sure that another generation will invent a completely new set of ocean-plummets for sounding the heart of our mystery.

Why do I hate Browning so to-day, when I fell so completely under his spell when Koelle brought him to my notice at Corpus? Walt Whitman is equally sensual, equally gross, equally optimistic; and I remain a devoted lover of Walt Whitman! It is queer. But I believe what I have come to fight shy of in Browning is the exact replica of those normal and virile instincts in Koelle himself which led us to drift apart. What Koelle and Browning felt is a vein of emotion that neither resembles my pure satyrish lust, nor my ideal magical romance. It is "human, too human." It is what Browning himself would call, "the way of a man with a woman."

Yes, I expect the real secret of Koelle's drifting, as a girl would say, "out of my life," was what he correctly felt to be my sub-humanity. I made him jumpy. I gave him the sensation that he was listening to the cracking of hyperborean ice forever receding and receding! I made him feel as if he were in danger of being embarrassed by the chilly breath of such a merman-disciple, come inquisitively up to learn of his kindly nuptials from the frozen ooze where they neither marry nor are given in marriage.

One of the links between us was the unsophisticated awe with which I listened to his stories of Anglo-Indian regions, where he had been a planter, almost a Conrad character, before he decided upon being a clergyman. He visited us at Montacute in the days before we both left Corpus; and I remember talking to my father once in the park about him—near the idyllic spot where Mr. Phelips allowed the village cricket-team to practise —and in a vein of boastfulness, anxious to impress my father with my friend's knowledge of the world, I explained how Koelle had steered clear of those amorous relations with black women which was so lively a temptation in those parts. My father remaining silent, I continued my discourse on the various temptations of young men, hinting that there were other "primrose-paths" at a place like Cambridge, for all its lack of dark-skinned Houris, which might lead a person to the everlasting bonfire. The pleasure of boasting about the perils of the world became greater and greater to me at that moment, under those familiar trees, and I was surprised that my father continued silent.

Piqued a little at the small effect of my words, I was led on to indicate that although I had at present encountered few loose women near the gates of Corpus, there had been grave cases of alcoholism of late in his Alma Mater, and that I myself had more than once found the power of our famous college port insidiously attractive. My father continued silent. And under the weight of that silence we advanced gloomily enough along the path by the edge of the Montacute House garden. I was racking my brains for further revelations and was just, like Lot's wife, looking towards the Cities of the Plain, when at last he broke the uncomfortable silence.

"John," he remarked. "I should be glad if you would read the Lessons for me to-morrow morning. It's a real help to me, my boy, during this season of long gospels."

Thus did my father prove to me that he understood some aspects of his eldest son's character.

Another friend, if that is not too intimate a term for our relations, that I made at that time, was none other than the well-known author, G. P. Gooch. If I made dear old Koelle jumpy by my queer ways, the companionship of Gooch, who was attending the historical lectures with me—he was I think at Trinity then—would have given anyone except myself a kind of metaphysical goose-flesh. I am prepared to confess that even my tendency to Boswellian adoration was strained to the uttermost in Gooch's company. He had an astounding brain. His learning was unbelievable and he possessed an indomitable will. He was not a humorist like Johnson or Porson or Bentley, but in his own quiet way he was very formidable. His intellectual nature was keyed up to a pitch that was awe-inspiring. He was entirely devoted to the most recondite historical pursuits. A prodigy of learning, he had the calmest way of mapping out his own future career, which was to be dedicated, as indeed it subsequently was, to the service of humanity and the bettering of his mind. He told me he would be in Parliament. And he *was* in Parliament. He told me—but it was not what he "told" that mattered. It was his *way* of telling things. He had a predilection for darkness. Light hurt his eyes; and he had, quite obviously, to save his eyes. So hour by hour, in those rooms of mine, overlooking the Old Court, he would sit by my side, his hand laid upon *my* hand, discoursing at large on all the most subtle and difficult points in history, in philosphy, in politics, in political science. My Corpus friends were terrified of him, as well they might have been; for he moved in a sphere of intellectual interests that, except in the archives of Archbishop Parker's library, were unknown among us. The man's learning was something monstrous. It shocked and startled like a sea-serpent. There was indeed something about it that was morbid and unnatural.

It certainly betrays the earth-bound proclivity of my own temperament and a certain lack of interest in the *things of the mind* that I did not afterwards follow up Gooch's life's work. I followed up at Cambridge though. In my naiveté I would ask him so many silly questions that he was moved once to remark that my intellectual curiosity resembled that of extremely small children who persist in enquiring whether two bears would be a match for one tiger, or whether, if it came to the scratch, a lion could overcome a rhinoceros. When I think of the woman-like attention, rapt and spellbound, with which I listened to Gooch, it occurs to me that I must have displayed with regard to him that particular kind of self-abasing humility, with which I have so often misled the men I have admired into completely underrating my real mental independence, and, if I may say so without conceit, my real mental qualities.

I have never known what Gooch really thought of me. He was not only very learned; he was also, I gathered, very rich. But in some mysterious way both his learning and his wealth were "dedicated." He might have belonged to that weird Pedagogic Society, in *Wilhelm Meister*, whose activities in-volved the mystical training of ardent but wayward spirits like my own. He *had* a picture of Goethe in his pleasant rooms, opposite the entrance to King's College, and it was to him that I owed my first introduction to those wonderful *Conversations with Eckermann*. I was myself, however, a good deal more like

the sly, though impulsive Boswell, than I was like the worthy
Weimar disciple and I have a notion that Gooch regarded me
towards the close of our brief acquaintanceship as something
between a fraud and a fool.

I don't think he did me justice; but it were unfair to blame
him for this since it had already become a second nature with
me to assume a good deal more pliability and impressionable-
ness than I really possessed. I admired; I listened; I asked
intelligent questions, not always "how many bears could overcome a tiger," but mentally I went my own way; and such
reserves are not calculated to win favour with one's cultural
master.

If Gooch introduced me to Goethe, Koelle not only
quoted Browning to me; he frequently, when smoking his pipe
in his big East Indian lounge-chair, would garnish his allusions
to the ways of the great world by snatches from the alliterative
melodies of Swinburne. It is queer to think that it was not until
I left Cambridge—and this alone indicates the kind of cultural
lacunae which existed in our circle—that I so much as even
heard of Walter Pater, or Henry James, or Thomas Hardy.
Matthew Arnold's poetry must have begun, however, to gather
significance for me at that time and to thrust back Tennyson.

It was during the visits Littleton and I used to pay to
Wyaston House in Oxford, where our Shirley cousins then
lived, that Ralph Shirley began to take an interet in me. *His*
interest took the very best shape possible and I shall always be
grateful to him for it. It first took the form of reciting to me,
in a manner that was itself a revelation of the magic of poetry,
passages from Matthew Arnold, and then, soon after I left
Cambridge, of actually getting published, through his connection with Rider and Company, my own first two volumes
of verse.

Our holiday visits to Oxford—it was on the Isis that I first
learnt to skate—come back very pleasantly to my mind. Cousin
Ralph, then an undergraduate at New College, gave me access
to the University library, and though the books I took from
those weighty shelves were of a simple nature—mostly the
works of Jules Verne—Oxford came to mean for me long

snowy days of reading by warm fires, varied by happy excursions with Littleton on a frozen river. A noble figure of a man Ralph Shirley was, with his spacious forehead, Viking moustache, and pure Saxon eyes—eyes that "melted in love and kindled in war"—but he was the only person I knew, *and remains so still!* to whom the enjoyment of poetry is a kind of physical necessity, like smoking tobacco or drinking tea.

Llewelyn indeed runs him close in this; and so, in his different fashion, does Littleton himself; but Ralph's enjoyment of poetry was a kind of absolute. It was unexclusive, catholic, all-embracing. Homer was not too elemental for him, nor Ernest Dowson too sentimental; but I have a notion that he loved Matthew Arnold best of all.

Thus it was in her more artless moods that the Oxford of the Anatomy of Melancholy and of Marius the Epicurean had her effect upon me. As for her cynicisms and affectations, my Wordsworthian simplicity rendered me immune; and such are the limitations of my sub-human intelligence that I find it hard even at this time of day so much as to know what they mean by the "Oxford manner." I go obstinately forward on my mythological way, protected by my father's spirit, oblivious alike of the sciences of the Cam and of the sophistries of the Isis.

In reading for the Historical Tripos—in which I ultimately obtained a very moderate Second Class—I must confess I was only once really thrilled by any of the university teachers. This was by Professor Seeley, a far-sighted and indeed a rather Goethean person who was certainly a different sort of bird from the sinister antagonist of my father's fairy-tale. Seeley was already failing in health, and I think he died soon after; but I shall never forget—as he gave one particular lecture upon the Athenian view of life—the reverberating unction with which from his seat on the dais, for he was too weak to stand, he uttered the word "Ecclesia."

Take it all in all, the university *as* a university had not the least influence upon my taste, my intelligence, my philosophy or my character! All these things had been created at Shirley, enlarged at Weymouth and Dorchester; and then had been finally branded into me—by harrowing necessity—at

Sherborne. As for Corpus and its authorities—except for my pleasure in walking over to visit the Fanshawes at their country house, the best I can say for them is that they never meddled with me nor I with them. I obeyed their rules, I "kept" my chapels, I passed my examinations, I took my degree. I was studious. I was quiet. No Proctor ever had to pursue me. No Dean ever had to interview me. I slipped into the place, and I slipped out of the place, totally uninfluenced. Corpus leaving me thus intact, and the university, in its larger aspects, barely impinging upon my consciousness, it would be the rough truth to say that *socially*, which is the grand motive—and damned close it is to the worst kind of snobbishness—of most Englishmen's going there at all, I gained little or nothing, from my college life. This was owing to my secretive, backyard ways of conducting myself.

But if I did not gain much from Cambridge I gained all the world from Cambridgeshire! Oh how can I express my deep, my indurated, my passionate, my unforgettable, my *eternal* debt, to that dull, flat, monotonous, tedious, unpicturesque Cambridgeshire landscape? How those roads out of Cambridge —and it seems as if all my most heavenly roads have been out of, rather than into somewhere—come back to my mind now! Those absurd little eminences known as the Gog and Magog hills: that long interminable road that leads to some pastoral churchyard that once claimed precedence of Stoke Poges as the site of the Elegy: that more beguiling, but not *very* beguiling road that led in the Ely direction, past the place where my father's father, when a fellow of Corpus, used to go courting: those meadows towards Grantchester where there is that particular massive and wistful effect about the poplars and willows that always makes me think of Northwold: these are my masters, my fellows, my libraries, my lecture-halls; these are my Gothic shrines! And not only these in their large aspects, but every swamp-pool, every rushy brook, every weedy estuary, every turnip-field, every grey milestone, every desolate haystack became part of my spirit.

I inherited from my father, though with him it was inarticulate, that Wordsworthian reverence and awe, a sort of mystical awe, that totally explodes and disperses all snobbish bourgeois airs of superiority, in the presence of manual labourers. Secretly my father only reverenced three kinds of men in the whole world, workers with their hands and soldiers and sailors! From the bottom of my soul the sort of life that would best suit my life-illusion, that would nearest fulfil the classic *actor's* rôle that hits my humour, would be some primitive labour, requiring no skill, but that had an ancient and poetical tradition behind it. I would have nearly all I wanted if I could link this up with the reading of the old classics and with the writing of new romances! My ideal life would be to do *some* manual work every day and some reading of Homer with a crib and to spend the rest of the time either walking or writing or making love. I do not "cotton" to financiers of any kind; but *small* shopkeepers I hold in high esteem, and I have always found that the small shopkeeper in a village is the nicest and kindest person in the place. The sympathy I feel with labourers in the fields is no mere ideal emotion; it is a profound poetical reverence that goes down to the very bottom of my soul. It is mingled with the very life and stuff of my whole sensuous and imaginative being.

As I walked by myself in that monotonous Cambridge country I used to practise what I practised in my walks at Sherborne, a metamorphosic partaking of—or vicarious participation in—the supposed feelings of lonely persons labouring by land and sea. Of course a weak, cowardly, fastidious degenerate like myself cannot *really* enter into the feelings of a peasant, or a factory hand, or a sailor; and of course I am always unspeakably grateful to the great goddess Chance for having made me lucky enough to be able to earn my living by my voice and by my pen; but I *have* the power, say what you please, of a certain direct man-to-man comprehension and *feeling with* such persons so that although *you* may call me a humbug, these labourers do not. The truth is I have a monkish conscience rather than any bourgeois complacency in the presence of those who work, and I always regard it as much harder to work with your hands than with your brain.

Thus in place of those convictions which Harry Lyon held

so essential, and in place of that "Self-realization for Public Ends," advocated by G. P. Gooch, my own ,secret life of imaginatized and poetized sensations was for ever fumbling to fill itself out and round itself off by a sort of devotional transmigration of soul into the lives of soldiers and sailors and peasants and factory hands.

I hear at this point an indignant murmur in a familiar voice: "Hypocritical Charlatan! Sentimental Humbug! Bastard of Jean-Jacques Rousseau!" Yes; I know what you are saying my good friend. But I could not go on drinking my tea and eating my toast and humming and drumming over these hills, like a caricature of Taliessin, if there were not something in the vast inanimate about me, something between this gleaming hawk-rock and that far-off Arthur's wain, that does not disapprove of my antics, that lends me at least a dumb encouragement as my nature hardens in its destined mould. Heaven forbid however, that as I recall the persons who were kind to me when the mould of my fate was still fluid, I should give the impression of ingratitude. It has never been a fault of mine to allow difference or distance to make me forget what I have been given. From my cousin Ralph, for instance, I learned the inestimable value of that kind of humorous detachment in adversity, when the mind pushes back its burden, which is, I think, one of the greatest gifts of the Saxon race, and one too that does not come very easily to the irritable Celtic temper.

I often find myself recalling, as in their native region, I observe the quaint proceedings of the animals known as woodchucks, how my cousin would suddenly enquire, when I took life too hard: "How much wood, Cousin Jack, does a woodchuck chuck, when a woodchuck would chuck wood?" And then to my angry gravity he would blandly continue: "A woodchuck would chuck all the wood it could chuck if a woodchuck could chuck wood; and a woodchuck *would* chuck wood, if a woodchuck *could* chuck wood!"

Littleton came up to Corpus when I was beginning my second year. He came up with a tremendous athletic reputation, which he increased still further at Cambridge. It must have been this, combined I dare say with his dread of finding me

o

closetted in the dark while I listened to Gooch's discourses on Spinoza, that brought it about that I saw very little of him while we were undergraduates at Cambridge.

I had picked up from Ralph Shirley, who soon became one of the Argonauts of Occultism in London, an interest in theosophical doctrines; and I well remember how once, as Littleton and I were walking together over those forlorn flats that lead to the wider reaches of the Cam, I priggishly reproached him for his absorbing interest in cricket. His pleasure in fishing I had shared too deeply at Northwold for me to have the indecency to drag that in. *That* was always a kind of sacred thing between us. But I remember that I went so far, on this occasion, in my patronizing animadversions upon his prowess at cricket, as even to express a fear that in our next incarnation we should not meet unless he mended his ways; Powys Ma., in this ascent, being likely to be promoted to some spiritual "Five A," while Powys Mi. was still in "Three B."

It was during my first summer vacation, when Littleton had left Sherborne and was preparing to go to the university, that we stayed together in Weymouth. The Penn House days, alas! were already at an end; but we stayed very contentedly in a quaint lodging in the inland part of the town, not very far indeed from the old Backwater, that water-mark, if I may say so, of some of our earliest memories. "Invicta House" was the name of this new abode; and our windows looked out, if I remember correctly, upon a small grassy square. It was the sort of spot, only not so trim or white-washed, that Betsy Trotwood must have lived in, in her Kentish watering-place; and happy indeed was our time together there.

That teasing vein of asceticism which has always plagued me, with its fussy, pharisaic exactions, was particularly active during this "Invicta House" epoch. I can recall, during one of our walks—and as always with these notable occasions when I made a fool of myself I can see the very spot where I made the remark—gravely observing, after half an hour's intense silence, that I thought I might continue to allow myself *one egg* for breakfast. To such a conclusion as this—and there were not a few of them—Littleton would always reply by the same indulgent and not in the least quizzical stare, opening his mouth a little and his large grey-blue eyes a good deal, and wrinkling his forehead. On another occasion—and this I recall was on the hilly side of Lodmoor—we were suddenly arrested by the appearance of an unusually perfect rainbow. "Ah!" I cried, for it was after another of my long silences, "*That* is a good omen for me!" This time Littleton *did* speak, and I can remember to this day the faint, very faint tone of reproach in his patient voice, when he protested that he saw no reason, this being so comprehensive a sign in the heavens, why it should not be a good omen for him too! When I consider how he had come to "Invicta House"—which at its best was no Burdon Hotel— to be put upon by such fantasies, straight from his authoritative position as captain of his "Eleven," if not of his "Fifteen" too, it is wonderful to me to recall his sweetness of temper. It was an extremely wily old tramp, whom I insisted on hauling in to share our tea one day, who did come nigh to being the last straw; but even to him, such was this unusual athlete's good nature, he remained gracious and friendly.

Lutyens, our constant ally, then at Cambridge with me, and now on the point of representing the university on the race track, was tutoring with some people who lived between Chickerel and Wyke Regis, somewhere near the western reaches of Chesil Beach. Him we used to meet, in the late August afternoon, when our day's reading was over, at the old bridge across the Fleet, and I enjoyed these encounters right well— until it entered our swift-footed one's head—a head as immune to misanthropy as it was to ambition—to introduce us to his pupils' relations.

It was about this time that my father, who always conveyed his family to some seaside place on his brief annual holiday, took Littleton and Theodore and me, along with the others, to Barmouth in Wales. I had never been to Wales, and this visit ought to have been a memorable one. A *notable* one, in a sense, it did become; but it by no means returns to my memory with any feeling of pleasure. Littleton and Theodore and I slept in a room suspended, you might almost call it, above Barmouth Estuary, and I can see now the cold and rather terrifying motion of this tidal inlet, as the moonlight brought those waters, swelling them and brimming them till they seemed—as their nocturnal volume gathered and grew—about to flood the actual masonry out of which our window looked.

There had been one point, while Littleton and I were at "Invicta House," when he had really revolted against my psychic overbearingness and egoism. This was on a certain occasion when we were together in a pleasant little coppice, somewhere between Lodmoor and the Dorchester Road. It was a warm day and Littleton laid himself down on the fragrant moss under the trees and prepared to enjoy a summer's afternoon trance. To this timely repose Nature persuaded, the gods were acquiescent, the hour was propitious; but not so the athlete's elder brother. For all my mania for the elements I have the greatest difficulty in making myself sit down in the middle of a walk. A demoniac restlessness urges me forward. I fancy this works upon me much in the manner in which Wordsworth describes his own mood, when he says:

"And his own mind did like a tempest strong
   Come to him thus and drove the weary wight along."

The truth is, it is as a rule only by constant physical movement, even when alone with Nature, that I can escape those self-created, self-torturing incarnations of Fear, which, like that luckless stick thrown into the lake in Derbyshire, rise up from Hell to torment me. But Littleton's mind was like the lake *before the stick was thrown into it;* and it was more than he could endure to be persecuted into walking when he felt like "trancing," He became angry. I also lost my temper; and in that quiet spinney a physical wrestling-bout took place, the conclusion of which was that Littleton, for the first time in our life, proved himself my master. He overthrew me. He even, in a literal sense, sat upon me; and I learned at last the power of those sturdy muscles that had kicked so many goals for Sherborne and had hit so many boundaries.

I was reading Stubbs's *Constitutional History of England* then; and now at Barmouth in that bedroom above those moon-drawn volumes of gathering water I was still reading that laborious account of our complicated liberties. But in Wales I took care to avoid physical contests with a Rugby football captain.

When weary of using the worthy Bishop's researches as jumping-off places for my extremely unhistoric thoughts, I sought in Theodore's companionship the greatest contrast I could find! Theodore was certainly very different from Bishop Stubbs. *His* Magna Carta was shortly to take the form of acquiring, with my father's help, a small farm of his own at Sweffling in Suffolk; and it presented itself to our restless minds, as these fitful lanterns revolved in search of excitement, that it would be behoveful to both of us to practise a little horseback riding. To this end we procured two ponies—the more sagacious Littleton remaining aloof from the whole transaction —and endeavoured to ride into the mountains. I don't think we tried to ascend to the top of Cader Idris; and I seem to remember that we more often dragged our recalcitrant steeds by their bridles than rode on their backs; but it all ended—*that* I do clearly recollect—by my pony falling down a waterfall.

I must have been a grievous trial to my father during that Welsh visit, with all my manias and carryings on. I well remember explaining to him once at considerable length— perhaps it was after my misadventure with the pony—that I detested mountains and that the only scenery in which I felt really happy was the fen-country of Norfolk. I can hear now his accents of grave expostulation:

"It's a pity you came with us then, John, my son!"

But in his massive, reserved fashion he was touchingly indulgent to me. He even endured it in silence when I insisted upon confining my diet, during that holiday, to bread and treacle, on the austere grounds that no one ought to eat what everyone could not get. The fact that his own diet was always far simpler than that of most clerics—I am sure Bishop Stubbs would have scorned his rice puddings—must have made this particular gesture of mine appear peculiarly priggish.

Finally Littleton, Theodore and I were packed off by him— and glad, I dare say, he was to get rid of us!—on a few days' independent excursion to climb to the top of Snowden. This was, I regret to say, anything but an harmonious adventure. Following my usual rigid economy—for, like Judas, I kept the purse—I clashed all the time with Littleton's more generous notions of what was proper on such a trip; while Theodore, whose health was never as robust as ours, not only found the climbing hard and the weather trying, but was barely allowed a sip of brandy to help him along. If it did not come to Littleton's having to carry both his brothers up the last half-mile of our ancestral mountain, it came to something near it; but you can believe it was not Littleton but Theodore and I who decided what the three Powys brothers were to write in the *Climber's Book* which was kept—and for all I know may be kept still—in the hut upon the summit. What we finally did write up there were the lofty but somewhat rung-upon words: "Love Never Dies"; and since, on our return journey, I conspired with the Devil to start Littleton and Theodore actually fighting, it seems hard to believe that no ironic spirit of the mountains I had maligned had dictated these audacious words.

It must have been before I left Cambridge that Theodore really was established in that farm of his at Sweffling. Many a time, later, did I stay with him there, and contemplated with wonder his courage in giving orders to those difficult East-Anglian peasants. I think this courage—fortified though it was by nocturnal readings of the works of Nietzsche, whom he discovered and appreciated long before I did—was not attained without a considerable nervous strain; for it soon became—as Llewelyn, now beginning to watch the proceedings of his grown-up brothers with characteristic sagacity, has not failed to indicate—a sort of symbol of ultimate desolation among us, to think of Theodore, of a windy November afternoon, making his way, like Christian with his forlorn pack, to his weekly purgatory at Saxmundham Market.

It is remarkable that I cannot recall one single, solitary occasion, in all my three years at Corpus, when I indulged in those sadistic thoughts that *alone seem to stir my erotic feelings to their depths*. I do not speak, mark, you, of practising any *actual* sadism; for the few times in my life when I have done this—

such as running Littleton down "The Slopes," such as causing that fountain Cupid in the Prep. to be suddenly smitten, such as cutting worms to pieces in the arbour at Northwold, such as killing those young birds, if I *really* did do so, in the quarries on the Bristol Road—did not give me, *while I did it*, the least pulse-beat of pleasure, nor, in the memory of it, the least quiver of re-awakened temptation. Whereas my wicked thoughts, confined entirely to my own brain, have simply intoxicated me; and I have only to think of certain wicked books in this unspeakable *genre* to feel the liveliest shiverings in the perverted nerve.

I would like to know how deeply a priest would condemn me, if *now*, and for the rest of my mortal days, I hesitated not to indulge myself in such abominable books; and yet, in real life, never hurt a fly? Well, whatever the priest said, I should condemn myself, because to the end of my existence I shall believe that our thoughts are of the utmost importance, and have the power of projecting impalpable *eidola* such as can fatally influence the thoughts of others: yes! and actually start them upon crime.

But why was it that in these years of my life, from nineteen to twenty-one, I was suddenly relieved entirely from my fiendish vice, as if an actual indwelling Devil had gone out of me? Was it the constant contact with young men of my own age? Was it the rumbling thunder of my thaumaturgic obsession with the elements, which, and for the first time, was consciously awakening within me? Or was it that I was beginning to become conscious of the real existence of living young women, as rivals to that fair-skinned, fair-haired little idol, that I had thought of even before I left Sherborne, and who still lived in my black-and-gold cabinet of Eros?

I recollect two frightful shocks that I received at Corpus. One was when one of my fellow collegians informed me with lurid realism of the hemorrhages that women have to suffer from in the revolutions of the moon; and the other was when somebody—Koelle I think it was—told me about vivisection. This latter piece of information, revealing the existence of an abominable crime against the only morality that is worth a fig, a crime committed not only against animals, but against every-thing that is noblest in ourselves, outraged—and continues to outrage—something in my deepest being. No excuse, make it as plausible as you please, justifies vivisection, especially the vivisection of dogs; and that governments are not forced to put a stop to it shows that the cruel curiosity of science is more artful in pulling wool over our eyes than our righteous indigna-tion is passionate in its protest.

Recently there has been founded in New York, at 88, Lexington Avenue, the first Library of Vivisection Investi-gation. This is certainly a move in the right direction.

Another peculiarity that ceased to agitate me while I was at Corpus was my infinite nervousness and selfconsciousness in the presence of other people. At Corpus I lost all fear of people. I said the boldest things. I did the boldest things. And if I made no use of this absence of shyness as a ladder offered to young ambition at least I knew what it was, for three years of my life, to be free from one of my greatest afflictions. What explanation can account for this? Why, for just three brief years, did I lose all my lifelong terror of the human eye? This boldness of mine—or was it insensitiveness or egoistic imper-viousness?—lasted on, though to a diminished degree, after I left the university; lasted on some while, in fact, after I was married.

Not that I was free from Fear—that primordial curse, that blight which I always fancy weighs most heavy upon the eldest born—but I seemed to lose, *pro tem*, my dread of facing people. *But then*, shock by shock, episode by eposode, shiver by shiver, it began coming back, so that at the present time my nervous-ness about going into the City to transact business resembles the nervousness I used to feel as a boy at Montacute when I would pause to collect my thoughts under the kitchen garden wall, in miserable anxiety because I had to go to dinner that night at Montacute House. But, Heaven be praised, when one gets to be over three score, one's dread of facing one's fellow-freaks in the fair is a bit more under the control of the philo-sophy—such as it is—that one has scraped together.

In my hurried sneakings forth into those long, weary,

muddy roads leading out of Cambridge; in my desire—bold as I was in those years!—to escape without meeting anyone I knew, I used to snatch furtive glances at occasional fragments and groupings, under particular weather conditions, of the ancient buildings of the place. But these glances were shy, exclusive, arbitrary, wilful, and were almost always directed to those particular spaces in the old walls where the forces of Nature—rain or moss or lichen, or frost, or sun, or river water—had added something, added the artistry I suppose, of the only artist that I could thoroughly appreciate, to these Early English, Decorated, Tudor, Jacobean, Queen Anne designs!

But the real discovery that I made while I was at Corpus was so important to me as to be alone quite sufficient to explain the vanishing of sadism, and the vanishing with it of so many dreads. For it was while I was there, that I consciously came to realize that mysterious thing, the thing which, after that became the secret within the secret, the essence within the essence, of my whole life.

Gooch used frequently to express to me the spiritual difficulty he had in realizing the Pantheistic Absolute which was the object of Spinoza's singular love. I can see his long white face and curious mouth and unhappy intellectual eyes as he said: "I can't catch the thing, Powys. I can't catch the thing!" and he uttered the words just as if the Absolute were a sort of "Questing Beast" and he was Sir Pallenure. Isn't it Walter Pater, that grave Pyrrhonian monk of God, the man whom these mathematical Cantabs took damned good care to hide away from me, who says somewhere that one curve of a solitary rose-petal is worth the whole of the Spinozistic Absolute? But it was not the flawless, æsthetic beauty of the rose-leaf I was after. No! not that; not *that* at all! Like poor Gooch under his favourite trees by the river-bank, in the wide spaces of King's, I too am sorely put to it; I too am fain to fumble and grope, and to hum and drum for want of words in a most disconcerting manner. How *can* I catch that stir, that rustle, that indrawn sigh, that indescribable *silence* which emanates from the passing of my voyaging soul over all these little, casual chance-groupings of the Inanimate? How can I find the right expression for the feelings that came to me in those days when the wind blew in a certain way as I followed some muddy grass-track along the edge of the Ely Road or the London Road? How can I describe the feeling I got, as if all the scarce-noticed sensations that had come lightly and incidentally to long generations of my ancestors, when they met the rain, or felt the sun, or heard the calling of rooks or the twittering of sparrows, or saw the smoke rising from human hearths, were rushing over me, in a hardly bearable flood of ecstatic happiness, simply because, on that undistinguished road to the railway station, I heard some patient shop assistant mowing his scrap of grass behind a privet-hedge?

I know perfectly well that everybody born into the world has the feelings I am describing, is visited by these indescribable and apparently causeless transports. I am not in the least suggesting that I am peculiar in this. But why, in the Devil's name, then, do we go on making a cult of everything else except these? Why must politics, religion, philosophy, ambition, revolution, reaction, business, pleasure—all be considered intensely important, and these rare magical feelings not to be considered at all?

"Because, my good John," you will answer, "these feelings come of themselves, and go of themselves, and don't leave us any wiser or cleverer or kinder or richer!"

You have said it. It is because they *are* different from these things; it is because they represent something totally beyond these things, that such feelings are so precious! A time will come when these feelings will no longer be the monopoly of women and babies and lovers and saints and mystics and idiots!

When I went up to Corpus it was with the idea of becoming a clergyman. I use the word advisedly; because these, you must remember, were the days when only a few very daring individuals in the English Church had the spirit to think of themselves as "priests" or to call themselves "father." *My* father would have far more easily thought of himself as a mole-catcher than a priest. "I don't like all this 'bowing and scraping'," he used to say; and he made this remark so often and in such a tone of contemptuous disgust, that it finally got lodged in the minds of all his children that the act of genuflection is an act more proper to an ape than to a man. Perhaps it is for this very reason—for it may be dangerous to suppress the human instinct for prostration—that I, his eldest son, am forever "bowing and scraping," and that not always to *his* God either.

But I had proved myself in the holidays at Montacute so good at reading the Lessons and so clever at playing my part in the extremely Evangelical adult school, that it was taken for granted that as the grandson of two clergymen, and the great-grandson of at least two more, I should, as the phrase ran, "enter into Orders." So I began attending classes in Hebrew, a language which I soon discovered to be much more difficult even than my ancestral Welsh; and it shows how very casually and lightly I took the whole subject of the choice of a profession that I cannot even remember how or when I told my father that I had decided against the Church. With his accustomed indulgence he made not the faintest protest; and I went calmly on at Corpus, without the problem of my future career receiving a thought from anyone.

It was, I think in my very last term, just before I took my degree, that one evening I conceived the notion of addressing a letter to the celebrated journalist, W. T. Stead, to ask his advice on what profession to choose. Mr. Phelips, I remembered, had enquired, at one of my recent dinners at Montacute House, whether I had thought of being "Called to the Bar." That our philosophical squire regarded me as a possible Queen's Counsel made this letter to Mr. Stead seem a mere wave of the hand. It was therefore one of the bitter humiliations of my life—one of those humiliations that bite into the very bone of a person's life-illusion—when I received his answer. I had, I think, alluded to the possibility of my doing a little journalistic work, till something of a more weighty character offered itself; and I can tell you that old wainscotted room of mine grew suddenly unreal and queer, shaky and wavering, like Faust's cell when he conjured up the Devil, when I read Mr. Stead's words. My reader will smile— especially if he is an American—and make nothing of it. But it was not nothing to me. Mr. Stead recommended me to study the advice tendered to somebody or something in Mark Twain's "Jumping Frog" Series.

Another shock to something very deep in my personal pride—and I am sure my father would have felt the same; only he would have been too cautious to get caught in such a way —occurred in connection with my encounter with an Italian seller of terra-cotta statuary. Here was something wherein I could satisfy at one and the same time my feverish desire to contemplate young ladies' limbs, and my ideal passion for classic mythology. I bought seven or eight quite large and entirely nude terra-cotta divinities from this astonished tradesman.

It pleased me rather than otherwise, when one of the authorities told me during a visit from the Corpus Mission in London, that these Apollos and Aphrodites might be misunderstood; but it hurt me, like one of those devilish blows on a person's twisted arm that the bullies in the Prep. so delighted in, when one of my own intimates, of whom I was foolish enough to ask *which* of the world-famous Apollos one among these figures was, leered like the father of all goblins and roared out: "Call it Budge-Fudge and have done with it!"

This vulgar explosion was peculiarly disagreeable to me; but I have noticed that there is something about my intense and shameless naiveté that excites an almost sadistic annoyance even in good and sensible people. I fancy this is largely caused by the fact that I have such a power of keeping my own malevolence out of reach, that all that can be seen of me is an ardent, impulsive, unsophisticated, rather foolish enthusiasm; an enthusiasm so subjective that its justification—as in the case of this terra-cotta statuary—is left obscure to any ordinary intelligence.

I received several very unpleasant, and to me quite inexplicable shocks of this kind in those days. In my childishness I was always discounting the average person's sense of humour; while, in my intense desire to be liked—I say *liked*, mind you, not admired—I was continually carrying my impulsive propitiations to an extent that was evidently both distasteful and humiliating. I can recall how, for instance, as I lingered with my friends one evening over our meal, in that Corpus dining-hall under the richly-escutcheoned windows, feeling a wave of spontaneous warmth towards one of the most striking and noble looking of these young men; and in my anxiety lest he should break up this felicitous moment—for he had begun displaying signs of restlessness—I offered to rush off to his rooms and fetch anything on earth that he was in need of. "My tooth-pick!" he cried savagely; but I was already on my feet, and it had to be explained to me by someone else, as if to an idiot totally devoid of all sense of proportion that he was only jesting. On my soul, I was on my feet, ready to fetch that chap's tooth-pick; and it was not with the least thought of playing the saint.

But a far greater shock than this did I receive a little later; and this was in a communication from a much closer friend than the gentleman of the dining-hall. Totally unaware that I was going too far in my devotion, I must have allowed my pen to carry me away in some impulsive piece of flattery that struck my friend as fulsome and unbecoming to us both.

"Don't —— my a——e so 'ard, 'Arry," he wrote, in gross Cockney vein, "it 'urts!"

I fancy some characteristic element of non-human obtuseness showed itself in me in those days, which my Sherborne punishments had been too physical to beat out of me; but which a better knowledge would eventually teach me to conceal. This obtuseness was always rendering me oblivious to what might be called the decencies of established social ritual.

My final departure from Corpus, after I had taken my degree, was a flagrant example of this. I had received an invitation from a pretty person in London to go to the theatre with her—the old Haymarket Theatre I think it was. I was expecting a letter from my father containing money wherewith to pay my college bills, and instead of waiting till this came, what must I do in my impulsive recklessness but give instructions to the college porter to open this letter and disburse its contents. Then giving orders to have my luggage sent after me, I left Corpus forever, and taking the afternoon train to town arrayed in full evening-dress I kept my assignation. It was in the same costume that I appeared next morning, for I had nothing else to wear, at the breakfast-table of an elderly relative in Kensington; not even a relative of my own I fear; a relative in fact of Thomas Henry Lyon. Yes, it was Harry's elderly relative who was destined to pour out tea for this deboshed-looking Petrushka, and to feel, I have little doubt, very much as Littleton felt at "Invicta House" when it was his lot to entertain that lewd old wayfarer.

What wild feelings had been mine the night before! I can clearly remember making a vow to myself, as I clutched "Sacred," my magic stick, between my knees, that one day it would be to see a play of my own that I would thus sit under glittering lights before a tremulous curtain and with a still more tremulous companion! This aspiration has remained unfulfilled.

I wish, however, that I could recall what my father's words were when I reached home. Harry Lyon's clothes could not possibly have fitted me, so how I was attired when I finally emerged from the train at Montacute as a Bachelor of Arts I have no idea. I know I felt, after such a whirl of Balzacian events, as if I had taken my degree in evening-dress.

I ought not to fail to record, before I leave the subject of Cambridge, the exceptional kindness I always received from one of the younger Corpus dons. This was Mr. Pollock. It was Mr. Pollock's admirable method not to interfere with my eccentric ways; but he was the only one of all the authorities who steadily displayed a sympathetic interest in me. Others did kind things on my behalf; but Mr. Pollock was really interested in me and took me seriously and was prepared to listen to me. I can see his heavy, dark ironical countenance now, with the whole head always drooping a little to one side and his eyelids weighed down with all manner of subtle equivocations. He had a deliciously whimsical and evasive smile, a little sad, but full of flickering benevolence; and I always felt in my heart that Mr. Pollock was a rebel, though a somewhat languid one, against the ways of God to Man.

How little we realize at the time the difference between the events in our life that are of importance and those that are completely trivial! The greatest event in my life at Cambridge was a very quiet event, an event totally different from the lively manner in which I made my undignified and ridiculous exit. There was a lad at Corpus whose parent was a local novelist; and one afternoon this son of a writer invited me to tea at their house. I can recall nothing of the event itself beyond a vague impression that the personage I had tea with was of a satiric turn. The important thing was of a much more personal kind. It was indeed a sort of Vision on the Road to Damascus. I remember the exact spot where it took place. Not far from Trumpington Mill—somewhere in the umbrageous purlieus to the rear of the Fitzwilliam Museum—there stands an ancient wall; and as I drifted along to visit my lively satirist, I observed, growing upon this wall, certain patches of grass and green moss and yellow stone-crop. Something about the look of these small growths, secluded there in a place seldom passed, and more seldom noticed, seized upon me and caught me up into a sort of Seventh Heaven.

A few seconds ago, before touching my pen to tell you what kind of Seventh Heaven it was into which, leaning upon the handle of "Sacred," I was transported, I felt all that I have ever felt, of the burden of this extraordinary moment. It certainly penetrated every recess of my being. I would call it a *beyond sensation*, and it lies in my consciousness now, like a sunken ship, full of fathom-deep treasure. But the touch of my pen—and I suppose it will always be so—breaks the spell. I can tell you nothing! It has, however, whatever its fluctuating mystery may be, a power upon me that is like the power of a hidden Mass, celebrated by no human hands. It is impossible for me to describe it! And yet I never see the least patch of lichen, or moss, or grass, in the veinings of an ancient rock but something of the same feeling returns. Not, however, quite the same; for *that* impression, that vision of "Living Bread," that mysterious meeting-point of animate with inanimate, had to do with some secret underlying world of rich magic and strange romance. In fact I actually regarded it as a prophetic idea of the sort of stories that I myself might come to write; stories that should have as their background the indescribable peace and gentleness of the substance we name grass in contact with the substance we name stone.

It was the fact that I was on my way to visit my first novelist that put all this in my head; and it was my reaction from the sort of novelist I expected to encounter, and *did* encounter, that made the event so significant.

Yes, how different is the real fatality of a person's life from the stupid blunders and impulsive idiocies that he outwardly commits! When I rushed off so madly in evening-dress to a London theatre leaving the college porter to pay my bills I sorely outraged the feelings of old Koelle, who had chosen this very day—my last at Corpus—to arrange for me to meet his fiancée; and I learned afterwards that he and Gooch had shaken their heads sadly over my unreliable character.

"A clever man," they said to each other; "but lacking in all moral scruple!"

Ah me! thus began those comical and grotesque misunderstandings of my nature which have sprouted up into monstrous mushrooms all my days! *Clever?* Good God! What is such a thing as that? *Moral scruple?* I am convinced that in the most meticulous and burdensome performances of moral efforts, both "pro" and "con," I was more scrupulous than all the Corpus dons put together! Had old Koelle ever worried the life out of his fiancée by the problem as to whether it was lawful to have more than one egg to his breakfast? No, no! Of course the real matter with me went far deeper than social irresponsibility. As Harry Lyon said—and it is true—I was, and am still, totally unable to understand the meaning of the word "conviction." My knowledge that the practise of vivisection, for example, is a crime against everything that is noblest in our race, is not a conviction, *it is my life.* Goethe cursed Eckermann once for asking him what was the main "idea" in Faust.

Do you suppose," he cried, "that a work into which I've put *my life*, would condescend to so poor a category of living value as a mere idea?"

And I would say the same when people ask me for proof that these miserable dogs suffer.

"With my whole being I *know*," I answer them, "that the vivisecting of dogs is evil!"

That is really how we all know that all evil is evil. You can find reasons to defend anything.

But not only was I without human convictions, I was without a human heart. What Gooch ought to have said, was not, "Powys is unscrupulous." He ought to have said: "That poor, fussy, pharasaic, over-scrupulous Powys is lacking in every natural human feeling." And what Harry Lyon ought to have said, instead of saying, "Jack has no soul," was, "Jack has no heart." To this accusation—in many people's view a far more serious one—I should simply plead guilty; protesting however that there *are* people in the world so queer that they would prefer to live with a person without a heart than with a person without—but let it go! You'll be saying presently that it was not for nothing that my father's ancestors, on the distaff side, came from Geneva.

No, what I carried off from Cambridge was nothing that I got from that ancient university always so much more beautiful to me than Oxford, nor was it anything that I got from my friends, none of them really very intimate except the brilliant Harry, and even from him *I ran away*, nor was it anything I got from books, for I did not read a single volume of the least importance to me all the while I was there, nor was it anything I got from trying to write, for what I wrote was prose like "Corpus Unveiled," or poetry like "Suns and Suns of Sad and Soulless Seeming." What I carried off when, as the phrase runs, "I went down," was—strangely as it may sound in view of my impulsive ardours and my emotional Boswellisms—a most formidable mental power of hiding up my real identity until I could get away alone, and then of pouring forth my whole soul—that soul of which the Voltairean art-priest with whom I had made friends could find no trace —into such inanimate or such lowly-animate things as I could encounter along the most desolate country road. Yes! wherever I go I shall carry with me to the end what I learnt from Cambridgeshire while I was at Cambridge.

P

Chapter Six

Southwick

I HAD not the least idea when I left Cambridge how I was going to earn my living. My father, doing exactly what *his* father had done for him, which was always his deepest test of what was proper and fitting, declared his intention of giving me sixty pounds a year as an allowance. It would have been possible, with this sum, to cross the channel and actually to live for a while in France, learning that language which I had been led to despise at Sherborne, and satisfying my cerebral vices without let or hindrance! Heavens! What would the pictures in *Ally Sloper* have been to the much more provocative incitements that I could thus have obtained? But—true son of my father as I was—it was as inconceivable to me to live on this allowance *without working* as it would have been to become a tramp. It never once crossed the threshold of my consciousness that I might have gone—as I could easily have gone in those days—not only to Paris but, if I cared to do so, to Rome.

Under that same scrupulous conscience, that had forbidden me to order even so much as buttered toast from the college buttery, and that had forced me to leave untouched my nicest achievements in porridge-making as a *bon-bouche* for the two individuals known as "the Bedder" and "the Help"—I can see the pair of 'em now—who no doubt gave it to their cats, I was forced, compelled, driven, dragooned into becoming *financially independent* without a moment's loss of time.

My mind has always had a tendency to be what might be called "a Foreground Mind," that is to say a mind absorbed in the present and totally unconcerned about the future, and this turn of character I had, as you have seen, cultivated to the

top of my bent. Thus—save in pure fantasy, as for example
when I read the stories of Disraeli, for which I soon came to
have a lively "penchant," and imagined myself an eloquent
demagogue, or told myself stories about being a master-writer,
visited in my retreat by other master-writers—I assure you I
never gave one serious thought to my future career. I lived
then, just as I have done ever since, in the particular philosophy
and in the particular sensations which occupied me *at the
moment.*

I still held vaguely to that inspiration of mine in the yard
of the new Prep., between the urinal and the stars, that I
would be a poet, but I never went so far as to conceive of
poetry as a profession. I did compete at the end of my Cambridge time for the University Prize Poem, which that year
was upon the Lake District, but this prize went not to me but
to that clever contemporary of mine, Mr. Masterman. I wish
I could recall a specimen of the patient banality of what I
wrote; for I am sure the brilliant prize-winner never took half
the pains I did.

I went with an unequalled companion to Ullswater—my
father willingly providing the expense to give "dear John"
his opportunity—but a certain tiny little yellow flower, adapted
to rockeries, and triumphantly planted at the end of our terrace
walk, was the best thing I brought back. That and a memory
of those singular prefaces written by Wordsworth, which, for
the print bothered me, my companion read aloud, are all that
remain of this academic tour. Well! not quite all; for I never
see a pink stock—whose smell is perhaps my favourite of all
smells—without thinking of a small plant of this flower that
grew in the garden of the cottage where we stayed. The contrast between the wild, bare, Ullswater mountains and the
sweet security of this heavily scented flower struck deep into
my being.

The memory too of a certain particular kind of shame
comes back to me from that trip, a shame that I have only
quite recently learned the trick of disposing of. I left my companion with the intention of climbing alone to the top of
Helvellyn; but about a mile from the top fear seized me and I

came pelting down like a frightened beast. All the way home, to the shores of the lake where our cottage was, my oak stick, my magic stick "Sacred," seemed to utter speech, as I grasped it by its curved handle. It kept repeating at every step I took "Recreant . . . recreant . . . recreant!" And my impression now is—or my fancy, if you will—that it departed after that and removed itself from me, so that I saw it no more! Whether it vanished in the bosom of some mountain tarn, or whether, as a counter-talisman to that fatal stick in the Shirley lake, it still floats, like the "rod and staff" of the heavenly shepherd, in some fairy limbo of the spirit, I know not. I only know that it was *before* this trip that I can remember propping it up against a privy-wall in Crewkerne, and plodding with it in the twilight, tap, tap, tap, along the Stoke Road. After my *gran rifiuto*, in refusing to carry it to the summit of Helvellyn, "Sacred" disappears.

Like almost all second-class and third-class graduates of our universities at that epoch who found themselves in want of work I hurried up to town, and turned my conscientous but reluctant steps to the famous offices of "Gabbitas and Thring" —what Dickensian names!—who stood, I think near Waterloo Bridge, but I may be wrong about that, as intermediaries between head masters of preparatory schools and their lucky —or unlucky—assistants. I certainly had no thought of becoming an assistant master. Nor had I any thought of becoming a tutor. What *did* I have in my cat-head—for so Padraic Colum says my particular shaped cranium should be named—as a possible job that Gabbitas and Thring might offer me?

Heaven knows! But my guardian angel, or one of my "angels" in that black-and-gold cedar-scented drawer, brought it about that no sooner had Mr. Gabbitas, if he it were, set eyes upon me—did I look like a young Wilhelm Meister?—than he informed me that he had just heard of the sudden death at West Brighton of the German professor who lectured at all the girls' schools there! I could hardly credit my ears. This was something I had never thought of. Girls' school? *Schools* of girls! I saw them like gleaming porpoises; shoals and shoals and shoals of them, waiting for their new professor at West

Brighton. Were all those invisible lovelinesses, that I had so
often told myself stories about, going to incarnate themselves
at this crisis in my life, going to call upon me to lead, guide,
teach, instruct, inspire, encorcerize them?

I thanked Mr. Gabbitas with the gravest discretion—my
pulses beating furiously—and taking a hansom to London
Bridge caught the next train to Brighton. What did I feel as
in the mid-rush of traffic I looked down upon the Thames,
looked towards Southwark where old Gower lies, and where
the Globe Theatre was, and where, maybe, on some wild night
in a garret near the bear garden, an actual mortal hand, with
fingers like my own, made those hurried scrawls upon paper
—black upon white—that are now *King Lear!* Dickens is the
one for describing the emotions of young men setting out on
these reckless quests, with all their lives before them, and he
would certainly have described to a nicety all that I saw and
heard from London Bridge that afternoon. But I am afraid it
would only have been in his uneasy, scimble-scamble, comic-
sketch vein that he would have described the feelings of this
impatient successor of the dead German.

Schools of girls . . . shoals of girls . . . flocks and flurries
of girls . . . what a thing, what an incomprehensible thing for
my destiny to evoke! The very word "girl," especially if pronounced, as some of my relatives pronounced it, not to rhyme
with "pearl," but to rhyme with "there'll," even as you would
say it in the sentence: "there'll be gairls," thrilled me at that
time of my life in a manner impossible to describe. It conveyed
to my mind a sort of fleeting, floating, fluttering fantasy of
femininity, a kind of Platonic essence of sylph-hood, not exactly
virginal sylphid-ness, but the state of being-a-Sylph carried to
such a limit of tenuity as almost to cease to have any of the
ordinary feminine attributes. This incarnation of airy tantalization was all that the word "girl" evoked for me, however
pronounced. It always conveyed the idea to me of an impres-
sionability, under an embrace, so flexible, so yielding, as to
bear a resemblance to that ethereal vaporousness of the
Homeric shades in *Hades*, that could not be felt at all as you
embraced them! Thus the word "girl" almost ceased for me to

have the least connection with the living personalities of real girls. When I saw a real girl I saw a feminine person, almost a feminine man; but these "girls" of my imagination, or rather I ought to say of my desire, could all have stood, thousands of them together, like those jeered-at angels of scholasticism on the narrow apex of my winnowed, purged, and three-times-over-refined fastidiousness.

For the truth is, what I am so intensely attracted to, what I worshipped in those days to a point of idolatrous aberration, are hardly of the feminine sex at all! It is as if I had been born into this world from another planet—certainly not Venus: Saturn possibly!—where there was a different sex altogether from the masculine and feminine that we know. It is of this sex, of this Saturnian sex, that I must think when in the secret chambers of my mind I utter the syllable "girl." I suppose women are more like these elfin sylphs, these fleeting elementals, than most men are; but I am not perfectly sure even about this! The maternal instinct in women, so realistic, so formidable, so wise, so indulgent, is more remote from, and destructive of, the sylph-nature—the nature of these girls who are more girlish than girls—than the spirit of Hercules himself. I think that the inmost flame of my soul, the vital leap of my life-force, must be as fragile and tenuous as it is formidable and fierce; and that it is this brittleness and fineness in this interior flame which makes it flee, as if from cartloads of horned devils, at the faintest approach of any warm maternal lovingness, as if such lovingness would bury it under a thousand bushels, like the scriptural candle.

I cannot believe that a person's sex-emotions exist in some disconnected by-alley of his being without affecting the whole of his nature. My attitude to everything I worship, to the sea, to the mountains, to the earth, to the sun, to the moon, to Homer, to Shakespeare, to Rabelais, to Don Quixote, to lichen growing upon tree-stumps, to moss growing upon stones, to smoke rising from a cottage chimney, must be of this same fine, tenuous intensity; an intensity terribly shy of large, warm, human normality, and always flickering round and about the magic candles of the exceptional.

In my most thrillingly happy moments I feel as if my nature were essentially light, volatile, porous, transparent. I seem to float at such time on waves of a quivering ether, an ether vibrant as the hovering heat-waves over an August cornfield. And it is on such an air-tide of quivering vibrations that I seem to be floating, when for a brief moment, *in any real woman*, I catch some faint resemblance to my sylphid ideal. It is pure impersonal lust; it is lust without the faintest mixture of anything that from the moralist's point of view could be called "redeeming." And yet I am prepared to justify it without scruple or shame! It is my religion, my beatific vision, my rapturous initiation into the mysteries.

But whatever this intense inner life-flame of mine may be in relation to sex, one thing is true of it—as true of it *then*, when for the first time in my life I beheld that East Sussex landscape, as it is true of it *to-day*, as I glance out upon these frozen American hills—namely that it withdraws and recedes with a shrinking of its whole nature from contact with ordinary, normal, natural sex-expression. Any sort of sex-jesting, any kind of bawdy stories are unspeakably revolting to me. They make me doubly sick: sick, as a blasphemous parody upon the magical loveliness of my own secret lusts; and sick, as the monstrous sex-antics of a race of beings as alien to me as hippopotami.

I ought to have mentioned that after my visit to London to stay with the clergyman who took me to my first pantomime —a veritable orgy of sylphs—I stayed there a second time as the guest of a boy I was very fond of, and used constantly to go about with, called Hugh Hill Bell. Hugh Hill Bell was a most humorous and gallant elf, a daring heroic elf, and I adored him, from some very deep ice-crack in my boreal heart. But it was when I was in his company somewhere in town, that we beheld—like Caliban and Ariel peering at the loves of mortal men—a normal pair of infatuated megalopolitans, and I have not yet forgotten the austere distaste with which I turned away.

"*One third-class single to Brighton, if you please!*"

What fatal words these casual ministers of destiny, to

whom we speak through these little apertures in stations, convey to our ears—unwitting, and we unwitting!

What a feather's weight of chance it was that led me to make Sussex—"all of it?" said the jesting Mr. Blanch—my home for thirty years and the birth-place and bringing-up place of my son! Thirty years is a long time. Thirty years is nearly half a normal person's whole life; and it *might* have been Anglesea, or Inverness, or Padstow, or Carlisle, or Caerleon-upon-Usk where that German professor had died and whither Gabbitas and Thring were now packing me off. I think it was ten shillings a lesson I was to receive from each of these schools and I was to give two lessons every week; so this did mean that I was already—if they accepted me—a semi-independent person; and even if my father cut off that sixty pounds a year I would not be quite penniless.

Sussex scenery, as I now looked out on it from my third-class smoking-carriage, was certainly different from any scenery I had ever seen. Those huge Sussex barns whose vast sloping roofs were encrusted with orange-coloured lichen that was as strange to me as were the "orange-tipped" butterflies I saw on the railroad banks, in place of our Dorset "marble-whites," those mellow Sussex cottages where old dark woodwork was so cunningly mixed in with brickwork and flintwork, those Sussex bricks themselves that were so much brighter and gayer than the red bricks of my native Midlands and gave a look to the whole scene so much warmer and sunnier than the Dorset thatch or the Somerset stone, those enormous Sussex wagons, painted blue and scarlet, and of a size so large that they would have astonished a Somerset farmer, the trim, neat, picturesque Sussex villages themselves, where it seemed as though everyone was so much more well-to-do than in the West Country, all these things struck me, sank into me, and abode with me, as to some literary person, who has been reading Sir Thomas Browne and Thomas Hardy, it would be if he suddenly discovered a volume of Water Pater. It was not my country, this warm, mellow, gracious, tender-soiled Sussex, just as they were not my people, these blue-eyed South-Saxons, but there was something about the place that was profoundly English;

more English, in the narrowest sense of that word, than any
other county in the kingdom. Yes, I liked the look of the
scenery more and more as the train made its way through the
hollows of the Sussex Downs, downs so much higher, wider,
steeper, and in every way more formidable than the downs of
my father's Dorset.

"*Lewes! All change for Eastbourne!*"

This particular cry, on this particular platform, how well
I was to know it in later years! It was accompanied by the shrill
voices of the newspaper boys selling Brighton papers, voices
that had a distinct Cockney flavour, for the Sussex dialect has
some ancient affiliation, which I am not enough of a philologist
to analyse, with the manner of speech of England's Metropolis.

Perhaps it is this accessibility of Sussex to London, together
with something at once warmly gay and comfortably home-
like—the "aura," in fact of rose-coloured bricks flecked with
golden lichen—that gives to this picturesque, and reassuring
county its peculiar quality. The great downs themselves, like
huge waves solidified into chalk and turf are never as desolate
as their wide sheep-cropped undulations would lead you to
expect. Something about their wind-swept clumps of beeches,
something about their gorse-patches and beds of thyme and
harebells and milkwort, softens their austerity; and from every
point along their highest ridges you can see the glittering
waters of the English Channel to the south, and to the north
the vaporous blue haze of the great wooded Weald. Steep to
ascend though these Sussex Downs are, the chalk tracks that
lead down from their summits plunge a wayfarer with surprising celerity into the snug and homely villages that nestle in the
hollows beneath them; while even the straggling little seaside
places on their Channel side—between Brighton and Worthing
—Portslade, Southwick, Shoreham, Lancing, have, for all
their rather ramshackle dinginess, a certain friendly and
human look, suggestive of the presence of quaint Dickensian
characters dwelling in those rows of little stucco houses.

Brighton, itself, as I soon discovered, has many old-
fashioned alleys and time-mellowed retreats, snugly protected
and sequestered, and quite as redolent of the regency and of

the whole Georgian era as its more fantastically rococo pavilion. Blustering, free-blowing winds, smelling of the salt sea, and in summer-time whirling up the thick dust in raw, scorching, sun-warmed clouds, give to the dingiest and most squalid quarters of the great sprawling town a certain curiously invigorating character. These heady Brighton winds seem to play the part of a sort of *aerial ale*, of a nature so profoundly English that they cause satisfaction rather than perturbation to the crowds of London visitors who contemplate from the wet pebbles and asphalt parades the redoubtable excursion-boats and excursion-yachts—in my day the latter seemed all called *Skylark*—which vociferating "captains," often in dripping tarpaulin, were for ever pushing out and dragging in. White dust, white glare, white houses, white sea-foam alternated with the rolling bottle-green breakers and with the motley crowds of jostling, lively, good-humoured people, moving from pier-head to pier-head and from brass-band to brass-band, it was all certainly as unlike Weymouth as a famous circus is unlike a rural county fair, and after my semi-monastic life at Cambridge it was as bewildering as it was novel; but I very soon —like a pond-duck among wild ducks—began to find my own account in it, and you can believe that it came eventually to enlarge the narrow boundaries of my furtive obsessions.

The school authorities seemed just a little taken aback by my youthful appearance; but I must have gathered up all that "cleverness" which old Koelle and Gooch had discovered in me, and it was not long before everything was arranged. Then, however, came the grand question—for me—as to where I was to live. I can well recall one day at Montacute, a little before this, when, walking back from Yeovil with Littleton, I discoursed to him at that spot, just beyond the hamlet of Preston, where there grew periwinkles in the hedge, about my future career. This discourse, characteristically enough, limited itself to a resolute vow that however big the town might be where I found a job I would be at pains to obtain a lodging in the country. With my job secure, this is what I now set about doing. So ignorant was I of the exigencies and possible satisfactions of my vague erotic desires that it never entered my simple head to hunt up—as any other young man in my situation would have done—a lodging in Brighton itself. West Brighton—then just beginning to be entitled Hove —was to be the scene of my activities as a lecturer to these heavenly beings, whom I thought of as neither "gurls" nor "gairls," but as entities of a purer element than these ale-tasting Brighton airs; and I decided without delay to walk out westward from the stately West Brighton terraces in search of rural seclusion. I kept so close to the coast however—for the bare inland downs just there looked uninviting and inhospitable—that I found nothing for what seemed miles and miles but rather desolate expanses. Portslade did not attract me—I speak, you must remember, of nearly forty years ago—and I was getting weary of stretches of bare ground, with nothing but gasworks between the road and the sea, when I reached the little town of Southwick.

Here there was a harbour—which pleased me for the same reason that Shakespeare's Fluellen was pleased by the word "Monmouth," for it reminded me of home. It made me think of the Weymouth Harbour. No two harbours could be more different. For this one at Southwick—and oh how hard it was to row against its tide!—had neither ancient wharfs, nor antique houses, nor any old stone bridge. It was simply a terrific volume of salt water, entering at top speed a long narrow backwater between the road and the beach and retreating in its allotted hour as it came in. But Southwick *had* a harbour. It had also a backwater. I therefore decided that Southwick should be my home! There was a high-roofed, rather sorrowful-looking dissenting chapel in the middle of the main street, no very startling thoroughfare, and next door to the chapel was a grocer's shop with a bow window protruding from the upper floor. The name over the shop was "Pollard." In the dust and heat the place smelt of sardines; but I went in, was shown this upper room by Mr. Pollard, and a small bedroom besides, and without delay came to terms. I think I only paid a pound a week for lodging and attendance, which was cheap enough. Whether it included food too I cannot recall, but I had all my meals there. O, so vividly does the view out of that window return to me now . . . the open sea, the harbour, the backwater, a boat-builder's yard and the unimposing little street! Here I speedily settled down and began my lectures at those two schools. They really *were* lectures rather than lessons; although my sylphids wrote essays for me, upon which it was my business to comment.

Thus I began—Johnny—Moony—Jack—John—that career as a lecturer which was not only to outlast my life in both East Sussex and West Sussex, but to outlast too a whole quarter of a century of my life in America. How smoothly, lightly, easily, unthinkingly I slid at that time, not realizing what was happening, into a business, or an "art," if you will, from which, at sixty, helter-skelter, and as impulsively as I went in, I have now at last come out.

But what of those mirages of rare delight, these "linkèd sweetnesses," those laughing and yielding sylphs, who, like a *fata morgana* of pantomimic forms, had led me into my destined career? As I look back at it all now—all those years when I lectured at such schools—I can only recall one solitary maiden in the whole long procession who excited the least stir of erotic emotion in me. She was in a school in Eastbourne, a school I only went to for about a year, nor can I now remember anything about her except that she was fatherless and motherless. God send her grace, the one single Leontion or Ternissa, that I can recall from all those reiterated labours!

The bigger ships, if I recall correctly, and there were quite a number of them, mostly Danish and Swedish and Dutch and Norwegian, used to anchor outside this Southwick Harbour; and it was the affair of Mr. Pollard to race out in a rowing-boat, contending with other grocers, in order to be the first to obtain each ship's business as it anchored. He was a small lively brown-eyed man with a pointed beard and something of a gipsy air. He was a kindly man, and considering that he had me at his mercy he was certainly no cheat. His bills were not exorbitant; and though everything I ate tasted strongly of the shop I was pleasantly ensconced in that upper room. Mr. Pollard's eyes were as lively as a squirrel's, and how they lit up one day when he confided to me that the only thing he needed to complete the happiness of his life was a gold ring. This remark sounded very natural to me. It gave me the feeling that I might be listening to Little Claus, in the fairy-tale. He had an afflicted son, deaf, dumb, and deficient in wit, whose name, like mine, was Jack. We two Jacks would communicate with each other by various grimaces. He was a wonderfully good boy, considering what his life was and what his highest hopes had to be.

I used to devote an hour to walking into Hove on my lecturing days. It was the best part of four miles; but it was totally against my nature to take the train or the bus. Thus I must have always arrived at my classes hot, untidy, dusty, and very tired. The road as I have already hinted, skirting Portslade and a little place called Fishersgate, ran through melancholy open spaces and desolate building-plots—I expect there are trim villas there to-day—and was separated from the sea by acres of dinginess and, if I recall correctly, a few gas-tanks. The particular road I finally selected to traverse was newly made and totally unfrequented, so that I had already snatched for myself out of the lap of the fates one of my chief life-exigencies, the possibility of walking where I could meet few of my fellow-men, when destiny brought it about that a mad woman who also preferred a lonely road chose the very days and the very hours of my peregrinations to take the same way. She was wont to carry a heavy basket and whether I had the decency to help her with this object I cannot recall but I used to enter into conversation with her.

Solitary women carrying baskets have played a sort of symbolic part in my life. If I were to add a card to the mystic tarot pack, I would add, between "the Hanged Man" and "the Man with Three Staves," "the Woman with the Basket." This particular basket-carrier, who is now linked for me, as long as I live, with that stretch of desolation between Southwick and Portslade, explained to me the precise terms of a very close and singular relationship that existed between herself and the sun. I cannot recall all the details, but the influence of the sun made her very happy and very unhappy, according to some secret reciprocity between them. My readings in Greek poetry had been very limited up to that moment, though I still possess the little Oxford edition of the *Iliad* with "Powys Ma., care of W. B. Wildman, Sherborne, Dorset, England, Europe," written in its flyleaf, which Mr. Young, that head master who was so bullied by the school conservatives and who wrote *Olim fuit monachorum*, made use of when he taught the Sixth Form; but I am now in a position to see that my "Woman with a Basket" resembled the unfortunate Cassandra who was at once loved and hated by Apollo. She had a large head, and an enormous figure with a bare throat; and she used, at intervals in our conversation, to point to this bare throat, which was of a livid ashen-grey, explaining the feelings in her nature which her relations with the sun excited.

All this I took absolutely for gospel truth, and in the light of the instinctive attitude towards the cosmos which to-day has become a kind of revelation in my bones I was completely justified. What I blindly felt then, and what I still blindly feel, is that what is called dead matter, or inorganic matter, or inanimate matter, is in reality *the organic body of some sort of living being*; and it is this refusal to believe that there is any fragment of matter which is not part of the body of something or that there is any "body" of anything without its corresponding "soul," which has given me my grand clue to the essential truth of all the ancient mythologies. Personally I have a shrewd inkling that this instinct of mine could be justified—if I were a cleverer thinker than I am—by a subtle train of reasoning; but I am content to assume it without bothering about proving it.

I got comfort, too, from talking to this "Woman with the Basket," because of the satisfaction it gave to my man-to-man sense, or my man-to-woman sense, of the equality of all souls, a feeling that might be described as the inverse side of the emotion at the back of communism.

I used to lecture at one school in the morning and another in the afternoon and I used to have my lunch, which always consisted of tea and bread and butter and boiled eggs and some kind of jam, in a little bakery upon Church Road near the Hove Town Hall. Here I tried my Rousseauish, equality-of-all-souls feeling upon a youth of my own age—that is to say twenty-one —who also used to have his tea-lunch in that little pastry-shop. I would probably amuse you a great deal if I could recall what we talked about, when once in my propitiatory manner I had broken the ice, but, as usual, all I can remember of this youth is the physical impression I got from him which was unappealing and unattractive to a degree that was distressing to me. What, I wonder, was his corresponding physical reaction to me? Possibly much the same! He was very pale, very long, and very boneless and soft, and he had a narrow bird-like head; whereas I was very ruddy, very gaunt and very angular, and had a "cat-head." I know one thing! We did not reveal to each other—no, not by one smallest hint—whence we came or what our job was. We probably hovered gingerly round politics and alluded cautiously to the danger of a war with the Boers.

We were the extreme opposite of Prince Myskuin and Rogozhin, talking in their railway carriage in Russia. I did not like the way he ate, I did not want him to be there at all. How annoying that I should see him still so clearly, when I have forgotten the hundreds and hundreds of beautiful girls I taught, and the hundreds and hundreds of beautiful girls I stared at as they bathed in the sea or as they lay prone for my delight upon the beach!

I very soon became queerer than ever in my diet. I used to persuade the Pollards to provide me with great bowls of bread and milk. For some reason these tasted less of the grocery shop than anything else; and indeed they excited the desire of Cousin Ralph, when he came to stay with me and found nothing but groceries placed before him.

"May I, cousin, *might* I, cousin," he begged, in his most Hymettian tones, while his Saxon-Thane eyes gleamed like those of Harold Godwinson, "have some bread and milk too?"

What were these years at Southwick, and my subsequent years at Court House near Lewes, most remarkable for in my growing consciousness? My years at Dorchester, before I went to the Prep., were remarkable for the untrammelled expression of every side of my nature. My years at the Prep. were years of alternate happiness and misery. My years at Wildman's were riddled, as if by rifle-shot, by the accursed presence of that torturer in the dormitory below mine. My years at Corpus were remarkable for unmitigated idealism, free of all vice, and for the complete disappearance of every form of erotic excitement. Well, these years I am now beginning to describe, years which included my marriage, and my first lecture-tours, years that lasted till I moved to Burpham in West Sussex; are the years in the whole course of my life up to this moment when I came nearest to insanity. I had *played* at insanity to escape that Tiberius in the dormitory below mine—would that I had struck at least one blow on behalf of his victim!—but in these nine years of my life, and *that* is, when you think of it, a long epoch in a person's days, I gave complete rein to so many manias and aberrations that those who knew me best must often have wondered how far in the direction of a really unbalanced mind I was destined to go.

At Cambridge I had been eccentric; but my eccentricities had taken forms that have been consecrated, so to speak, by the ages, as noble and worthy peculiarities; whereas now, living by myself first at Southwick, and then at Court House before my marriage—I became a tiny bit better *after* that, but very little—I gave myself up to neurotic aberrations which must constantly have wavered and toppled on the verge of madness. My nervous *power*, however, and the vitality of my constitution were so terrific that I never had the remotest danger of what is called a nervous breakdown. I have always been the kind of person whose spirit is so defiant, whose will so obstinate, whose pulse so steady, that he can *go on carrying*, as a camel carries its load, a vast orb of neurotic manias without any of them being able to break the rational balance of his brain. If anyone asked me whether I had ever been mad I would answer as Natalia did in *Wilhelm Meister* when asked if she had ever loved: "Never or always!"

It was not till some while after my marriage that I discovered what pleasure I could get from lying down on Brighton Beach beside some prostrate young woman, and either exchanging erotic glances with her, or gloating like a satyr, fevered

with the heady juices of Cyprian berries, upon any aspects of
her legs or knees or ankles that the felicity of chance, or the
auspiciousness of the occasion, caused to be revealed.

Eventually I came to be familiar with every portion of this
vast pebbled beach, up which the Channel waves roll with a
large primeval heave of deep-sea waters, unbroken by any
obstruction; for Brighton, as Londoners know so well, has a
more elemental exposure than any other seaside resort. I came
to know its pier-piles, its stone groins, its shelters, its sea-walls.
I came to know each spot along its colossal front, where
between beach and parade, the sweet-sellers, the cockles-
mussels-and winkles-sellers, the minstrels with blackened faces,
the Punch-and-Judy shows, the comic-singers, the preachers,
the toy-vendors, the fish-dealers, the photographers, the fruits-
and-nuts pedlars, the toy-balloon men, the "captains" of
the yachts *Skylark*, the fishermen, the pleasure-boat men, were
all wont to be found. In and out of these motley scenes I would
follow my maniacal quest for provocative feminine forms
basking in that blazing sunshine and amid the smells of seaweed and fish and tar and sweat and sandwiches and rope and
paint and cheap perfumes and foam-drenched petticoats and
bilge-water and beer. I ultimately became aware of certain other
men—and their eyes, eyes that had almost lost all human
expression, shocked me and terrified me—who had evidently
reached a point of obsession far beyond my own. No heartless
seducers of women, no neurotic perverts, that I have ever
encountered have had such a look of being hopelessly *damned*
as these elderly gentlemen betrayed in their curiously high-
coloured faces, as if they lived on the hearts' blood of women,
as they hunted and stared and eternally stared and hunted! Did
the people they stared at ever grow conscious of the eyes of
these spiritual hyænas? I doubt it! My own impression is that
few women have the remotest idea of the insane impersonality
of masculine lust when it runs amok at these deadly and sterile
tangents!

The question arises would a love affair have saved me at
that epoch? *Hardly!* I was at that very time on the point of
being happily married, and this maniacal pursuit of the sen-

Q

sations of impersonal lust increased rather than diminished after my marriage. If I had become a Turk of the old regime, and had been given a harem of Houris, would this mad desire to stare and stare at women, at the way the gods have moulded them, so differently from men, have come to an end? I doubt it. The curse laid upon lust is not only its maniacal craving for novelty. There is something else. I fancy that even Solomon "in all his glory," must frequently have left his harem of hundreds to prowl in disguise about the environs of Jerusalem where another generation of forbidden Bathshebas might be glimpsed through cedar-trees and casements and lattices.

A cynic might enquire of me: "What is all this fuss about? Where lies the evil in what you are describing?" The only answer to this question is Shakespeare's at the end of *Lear*. Regan and Goneril must have had *that look* as they hunted for eternally new "Edmunds"; and yet Cordelia, with her very different expression, came to the same end. But the mind that cries "the same!" because of this same end, turns from the whole tragedy, the whole mystery, the whole exultation. Without this difference—granting that same end!—futility scrawls her name from zenith to nadir.

Yes, I was neurotic to the extreme limit in those days; and yet in the interims and interludes of my obsessions I found myself sensitive in a most transparent manner to certain impressions. For instance—strange as it may seem—I have never felt the poignant magic of the spring more exultingly than I did when I lived over Mr. Pollard's grocery and confronted that forlorn backwater and those littered boat-building yards. I remember the emotion, just like a tremulous breath quivering through my stomach and heart and bowels, that the first buds and the first shoots of emerald green produced in me. It was in those places that I first had that feeling that young girls seem to have, of *smelling violets* under the dead leaves. This is no mere phrase. I remember in my wretched back bedroom, and in my bow-window looking out on little else but salt water, receiving an impression many a time as if there were green banks of cowslips and violets in the sailing clouds.

I can clearly remember after all these forty years how as I walked those four miles into Hove rather than be condemned to take train or bus, I used to repeat to myself certain passages from the poets, using them, as a nun might use the syllables of her breviary as a key to the kiss of the Spouse. Clearly can I recall particular places and not picturesque places either, where especial lines enthralled me. I link up for instance that unequalled couplet: "Mid hushed cool-rooted flowers, fragrant-eyed, blue, silver-white, and budded Tyrian" with the reek of a chemical factory, with ashes smelling of horse-piss, with palings creaking in their desolation, and with dust-heaps sighing to dust-heaps. And I link up the lament for Fidele: "Fear no more the heat o' the sun, nor the furious winter's rages," with a certain arid and empty enclosure, just behind the Hove railway station, near which—it is forty years ago, reader!—used to stand a most melancholy little ginger-pop booth in which I used to refresh myself. When I say I had an ecstasy in the entrance of this forlorn shanty at the back of Hove Station as I told over, like holy beads, this Fidele dirge, I am not exaggerating. I can recall the little volume in which I found it; for sometimes, in spite of all that the cultured say, you get more of a thrill out of a casual quotation than out of the original in its proper setting. The volume was Dodd's *Beauties of Shakespeare* and I got almost equal pleasure from "Come away, come away, Death," and from "How shall I your true love know from another one? By his cockle-hat and staff, and his sandal-shoon!"

I have told you how deep the instinct of acting goes with me, and how I always feel towards the spiritual gestures it calls upon me to make as if they were religious *acts of grace*, and how I justify it by identifying it with the grandiose rôles played by the people of Homer, and how I feel as if it were the abandonment of this dramatic heightening of one's personal life-illusion that has produced the widespread sense of futility in our time. Well! I had, during these crazy years, another thrilling experience, when an ecstasy of happiness came over me so intoxicating that it was as if I trod upon air. This happened when I was walking somewhere beyond Old

Shoreham and Lancing and was following a path across some
fields that seemed to be leading—and did eventually lead—to
one of the most picturesque of East Sussex villages. The path
passed the gate of a tiny cottage with a rambling garden where
a girl was gathering sweet-peas. I wish I could recall what this
girl said to this half-mad Bachelor of Arts trying to forget the
fatal loveliness of her sex's legs, as he used his own to walk on
and on and on into the sunset; but I can clearly remember the
issue of our encounter, which is where the point lies. She gave
me a bunch of flowers; not sweet-peas, for what she gave me
had very long stalks and very large blossoms. Could they have
been lilies? Are there any kinds of lilies that bloom while
sweet-peas are out? I can't recall! But this I do know: these
long-stalked flowers, whatever they were, filled me with a most
singular rapture. Was I experiencing, in honest-to-God reality,
that fantastical frenzy over a beautiful object that Oscar Wilde
—poor devil, he was on the edge of the precipice in that year!
—was wont to make such to-do about? Not a bit of it. If I
know anything of myself what gave me that ecstasy was partly
the kindness of the donor, partly a sort of ritualistic feeling,
as if I were a priest carrying the pyx, and partly the purged and
proud sensation of feeling myself an erect biped—anthropos
something-or-other—trudging over the surface of the earth,
holding by their cool, fresh stalks a handful of its loveliest
children. I had already acquired my lifelong mania against
picking flowers; and the fact that I was thus compelled to enjoy
the breaking of this law by somebody else added no doubt to
the uniqueness of my pleasure.

What in fact I enjoyed was the performance of an act that
seemed at once symbolic and pious, pious in the old heathen
sense. And, while I am speaking of this, I can well recall a
similar thrill of curious satisfaction that suffused my whole
being, when once, after my marriage, when I was living at
Court House, I had to go to a near-by gamekeeper's cottage
with a wicker basket to get some fresh eggs. These episodes
may seem ridiculously trivial; but my concern just now is simply
with the history of my strongest feelings, not with a defence of
the adequacy of what called them forth. Just as I had not

heard of Walter Pater before I left Corpus, my rustic ignorance was so great that it was only in this year that I learnt of the existence of Oscar Wilde; learnt of it just at the moment when everyone in England was on the verge of hearing of his catastrophic downfall.

How was it that with my eccentric mania for imaginary sylphs, so much less substantial than any real feminine persons, I would tire myself out searching public gardens, public beaches, public parks and village greens to catch those glimpses of real women that thrilled me so? The answer to this is that I made a fetish of the limbs and ankles of women, to the complete neglect of their other charms. When their knees and ankles pleased me I found no difficulty in assimilating the rest of their persons to the particular form of ethereal loveliness I craved.

So completely cerebral was the whole thing with me, that I remember once on the Brighton front coming to the austere conclusion that it was a purer, higher and nobler thing to make a cult of the beauty of young men rather than that of young women. Vividly can I recall the complete desolation that fell at that moment upon land and sea! The light went out; the air grew chill; and I realized that though no real girls equalled the pictures of them in my mind, life became as grey and sinister and weird, as if under an eclipse of the sun, when the feminine principle was expurgated.

It was while I lived over Mr. Pollard's grocery that a friend presented me with a beautiful high-bred bitch retriever. I kept her with me by night and day and took her for walks over the downs. But trouble soon followed. After long meditation I named her "Thora." This I did because in my intense and self-tormenting fastidiousness I wanted to find a name that only certain races could pronounce. But it was not long ere the companionship of Thora made me sick and faint with a very strange revulsion. My Corpus idealism hàd now turned into a thousand frantic and misery-causing manias. I was for ever struggling to make my real life correspond to a mental and sensual fastidiousness that was an appalling tyranny. My chief suffering came from the accursed way one set of images—

beautiful ones—kept linking themselves up with other images that were comic, grotesque, or revolting. I had in one portion of my being a diabolical sense of savage and even brutal humour. This sense, constantly suppressed, would sometimes revolt and cause me severe mental shocks! For instance I used to cross with a peculiar and romantic satisfaction a low bridge that crossed the backwater near the Southwick Harbour. I liked to think that I had at my disposal, near my room, so symbolic and sympathetic an edifice as a bridge.

But one day, for these little necessities of nature, just because I desired to imagine a life entirely free from them and was for ever trying to *think them away*, were always impinging irrelevantly upon me, I had occasion—for the place was an unfrequented one—to urinate as I paused upon this structure. That simple occurrence made the whole view from my window accursed. I had wished to name this bridge and what must the suppressed demon in me do but insist that instead of some name like "Thora," which only certain ancient races could pronounce, I should call it, in gross Saxon speech, the "P——g Bridge!"

But what happened to me over Thora was much worse. I had occasion ere long, as may be believed, to realize that the companion of my walks belonged to the feminine sex, that fatal sex with whose existence, when I tried under the influence of Plato to obliterate it, the sun and the moon had gone out, and the realization that until this dog's death all my walks upon the surface of the grain-bearing earth were to be, so to speak, "feminized" caused me an epoch of extraordinary suffering! A gulf of femininity opened beneath my feet. It made me shudder with a singular revulsion. Everything I looked at in Nature—well can I remember one particular walk when this happened—presented itself to me as a repetition of the feminineness of Thora! I could no longer enjoy the singing of the birds. They might be feminine birds! I loathed the thought that so many of the trees and the flowers possessed feminine organs. The thing went so far with me that I became panic-stricken lest I myself should develop feminine breasts, breasts with nipples, resembling the dugs of Thora. It was unpleasant to me even to encounter the harmless little hedge-flower that my father would never fail to remind me was named"Nipple-Wort." For several years—and, mark, you, this continued for a long while after my marriage—I used to be at the most careful pains to arrange my knife and fork on my plate so *that they should not point at my breast.* Having come with such imaginative intensity to visualize my provocative sylphs as beings who yielded so completely to my embraces that there was no solidity left in them, I began to feel as if there were no longer any real solidity left in Nature, as if, whichever way I turned, the firm substance of the earth would "go in."

Another worry I had at this time was the constant necessity I felt under of forever washing my hands. I became a perambulating Pilate. I would stand outside doors calling to people to open them for me lest by contact with the handle I should make my hands dirty. And much worse than this, as far as the actual effect it had upon me was concerned, was my steadily growing aversion to certain fabrics. Things made of cotton were my bane. I couldn't touch a tablecloth, *or eat off* a tablecloth. It was hateful to me—for in my ignorance I confused linen with cotton—to touch a sheet. Handkerchiefs were my abomination, unless they were made of silk. To see a woman hold a handkerchief in her hand was intolerable to me.

But what was worst of all to me was the idea of the reproductive sexual processes. No one has ever lived who more devoutly wished that children were born from trees, or, like the warriors of Cadmus, out of dragon's teeth sown in the earth. I made friends with a gipsy-man who kept an old curiosity shop in a remote part of Brighton and I can recall how when I was with him once in Brighton Station and he made some casual allusion to the seed out of which our race is engendered, I became so staggering sick that he had to lead me into the refreshment bar where I could recover myself by swallowing brandy.

It was while I was at Southwick that Ralph Shirley, through Rider and Company, Limited, published my first book of verse. Very conventional these were, and very imitative; but you can imagine the emotion with which I surveyed my first "galley-sheets" when I got the proof! I carried these "galley-sheets" into Hove; and I remember reading them seated on the beach by the side of one of the great stone groins that they've built there to break the force of the waves. One of these verses was addressed to W. B. Yeats, who wrote me a lengthy and most exciting letter in acknowledgment, a far more interesting letter than the contents of the volume justified. I have unluckily lost this letter but I remember how he told me that I was lucky to be still in the stage of "free imagination" before " the mill of character" ground me down to a particular shape. I am afraid it has been only too easy for me to fight shy of *that* menace. I dare say my old friend Thomas Henry would say I am still in the stage of "free imagination!"

My discovery of the poems of W. B. Yeats was a notable event in my life. It was in North's Book-shop on what I think was called the Western Road that I found the volume and I think it must have been the first collected edition. It was an ornamental, yellowish work, with some striking symbolic figure on its ivory-coloured cover and the purchase of it and the possession of it enchanted me. I read it with passionate delight, from beginning to end. I especially liked: "There was a man whom Sorrow named his friend; and he, of his high comrade Sorrow dreaming, went walking with slow steps along the gleaming and humming sands, where windy surges wend." It was I fancy, after Wordsworth, the very first volume of poetry I had ever bought! I carried it about with me. I came to know many of its poems by heart. It satisfied a certain aspect of my nature down to the ground. I liked: "Tossing their milk-white arms in the air; shaking their milk-white feet in a ring; for they hear the winds laugh and murmur and sing of a land where even the old are fair . . . and I heard a reed of Killarney say——" I can even recall the figure of Mr. North himself, who sold it to me, a lean, reserved little man with a coal-black beard.

It was in Hove too, that I got my first volume of Thomas Hardy. Little did I realize what a stone circle of monoliths and trilithons, grey with the lichen of centuries of English tradition, I was entering, when I chanced on this volume; or

what a memorable influence, calm, austere, noble—just the
influence needed by a coward who loved colour more than
form—I was submitting to when I got hold of this book. It
was "Far From the Madding Crowd." It was a small, plain,
brown volume in a very simple binding. I recollect reading
nearly half of it in one single walk; and, as with all the books
I have loved best, its actual substance cardboard, paper, print,
and the words "by Thomas Hardy," passed and repassed into
the gates against which I leaned, into the tree roots under which
I sat, into the pond willows on whose branches I laid my
hand, into the road-dust that blew up in my face as I moved
forward step by step, turning pages that seemed to me—so
full of ironies and pities were they—not pages of a book at
all, but wind-shaken oak-leaves in some oracular grove of
Dodona!

When I got the "galley-proofs" of my copy-cat verses—
"Odes and Other Poems" was its proud title—I certainly felt a
wonderful delight. But I was not deceived. I knew them—who
if not I?—for what they were! Had not a certain little girl, not
long laid in the cold ground, given me "The Poetical Works of
John Keats"? Yes, I knew I was a mere imitating copy-cat,
repeating, repeating, repeating the rhythms of men of genius. But
though there was nothing in "Odes and Other Poems" to justify
it, and though "Odes and Other Poems" might have remained
even unto this day my sole printed claim to originality, I knew then,
just as I knew twenty years later, when I had not published
anything else, that I *was*, in some way impossible to prove, a
great and for all my cringings and propitiations a terrifyingly
formidable genius!

On what did I base this opinion, or conceit, if your prefer?
On nothing. I mean on nothing outside the silence of my own
thoughts and feelings. I had been secretly conscious, ever since
in that lane at Shirley I pretended to be "The Lord of Hosts,"
that I had the power of tapping some deep reservoir of magnetism that could be used—when I was driven to the wall—to
blow the wall up, to lay it flat, like the walls of Jericho. The
issue has always been a perfectly simple one. I regard myself
as a voice crying in the wilderness, an individual with a devilish

shrewd inkling as to the hidden tricks of the creative and destructive forces of the cosmos, and with something more than an inkling as to the craftiest, foxiest, and wisest way of seeking happiness for myself and of giving happiness to the entities I encounter.

Powys Ma., alias Moony, "claims," in fact, as our cynical Americans say of every human statement, that he is in possession of a "Way" of life, to which the instinct of self-preservation in the human race must ere long bring a great many people, whether they be Communists or Fascists or simply Englishmen. But this "claim" of mine is naturally regarded by my enemies as one of the most megalomaniacal follies that have ever obsessed the barber-college brain of a bowing and scraping dancing-master in a young ladies' academy and by my enemy-friends as a lovable weakness in a windy oracle, whom yet one cannot help liking.

Finding the real satisfaction of my pride therefore in a secret sense of power that did not *need* to prove itself to the world by any overt evidence, feeling myself, in plain words, to be—in spite of all evidence—a great magician, it was nothing to me that "Odes and Other Poems" was so thin a thing. I lived then, as I live now, *entirely in the present*. I had no ambition. I did not make—I have never made—one single move to forward my career. Stop though! *Once* I did make such a move, and quite recently too. This occurred indeed only five years ago, when in great eagerness to get "Wolf Solent" accepted by Simon and Schuster, I carried the opening pages of this story out to Sea Cliff on Long Island and there read them to the extremely sympathetic ears of Mr. Schuster's mother.

Glancing at "Odes and Other Poems" now in its gold and apple-green binding I do think I am dimly aware, though it may be an illusion, of a certain faint feeling of the spring that emanates from it. It may well do so, even after the lapse of forty years; for I have never responded with my whole nature so thrillingly as in those days to the miracle of the rising of the sap. When the snow melts in these New York State hills I still feel on the air something that goes back, not so much to the cowslips of Derbyshire, or to the primroses of Wessex, as to those barren, littered, ramshackle rows of little stucco houses with grass-patches by the side of bill-boardings among which I would stand, and where I would feel, stealing over the tree-less downs like a supernatural presence, drifting along the sea-margins like a divine breath, stirring in the grass between the whitewashed stones like the scent of hidden violets, the eternal recurrence of the birth of life.

"O Daughter of Demeter," murmured then, with a pathetic sincerity of emotion behind the prim phraseology, my poor muse's thin scrannel-pipe, "O Daughter of Demeter, yet once more I touch my lute to hymn those virgin tears, shed while the wailing of thy sweet compeers proclaimed thee born to Pluto's sullen shore——"

It is curious how my nature has always—I dare say it is some far-drawn Welsh strain—found its sincerest inspiration in the contrasts of exile. Here was I, so far removed from the "verdurous glooms and winding mossy ways" of my father's West Country, here was I, lodged over Mr. Pollard's shop, between the roof of a dissenting chapel and a salt-bitten back-water, yet feeling the spring, as I tried to tell in my formal precise manner, imitating the imitators, more rapturously than I have ever felt it before or since!

It was during my vacation at Montacute that I received a post card from the great Thomas Hardy himself, thanking me for the poem I had addressed to him in this apple-green volume and inviting me to pay him a visit. It was a moment of moments for me when I obeyed this summons and set off, passing through Yeovil and Yetminster and Evershot and Maiden Newton and Grimstone and Frampton, to the familiar Roman town. It is likely enough, though I had often been through it to Weymouth, that I had never got out at that well-known Great Western Station, in the waiting-room of which my father had once described to me the Martyrdom of Archbishop Latimer, since those days, a dozen years ago now, when we lived at Rothesay House. Did I think, as I made my way down the old South Walk, of my persecuted "Spanish maiden" or of that other little maid, with long straight fair hair, whom I teased so rudely? I don't remember. But I do remember, as if it were yesterday, every sensation I had as I walked along the path by the railings of Fordington Great Field, thus approaching the famous "Max Gate" for the first time!

I gathered up my spirit within me and resolved to be worthy of the summons I was now obeying. Nothing could have been kinder than Hardy's reception of me. He took me into his study, the chief glory of which was, though it was yet unfinished, the great new *Oxford Dictionary*. He showed me the manuscript of *Tess*. He presented me with a paper edition of the same book. He gave me tea on his lawn. I remember telling him how I detected in his work that same portentous and solemn power of dealing with those abstract-concrete phenomena, such as dawn, and noon, and twilight, and midnight, that Wordsworth displayed in his poetry. He accepted the comparison, I remember, as a just one, but he proceeded to animadvert in no measured terms upon Wordsworth's pious optimism. He called my attention to Edgar Alan Poe's "Ulalume" as a powerful and extraordinary poem. In those days I had never read this sinister masterpiece, but following up Hardy's hint I soon drew from it a formidable influence in the direction of the romantically bizarre. I invited Mr. and Mrs. Hardy to visit us at Montacute, an invitation which, to my delighted surprise, they accepted; and I enjoyed a second red-letter day in taking him to our church and to the Abbey Farm; though it was left to the son and heir of the squire himself to show these notable visitors over Montacute House.

It was on this occasion that Hardy explained to me how the ancient builders of our church had deliberately left the chancel a little askew in order to represent the manner in which the Redeemer's head sank upon one side as he gave up the ghost; but I well recall how, as we issued forth from these symbolic meditations amid the tombs of Mr. Phelip's ancestors, and I pointed out to our visitors the house where the most beautiful girl in our village lived, he gave a curious little start.

"We get back to humanity, back, back to humanity, Powys!" he chuckled.

It happened that there were imperceptible frost-marks that

day in the road, making those odd little creases and criss-cross wrinkles in the mud that my father always loved to see, and these minute tokens of the processes *he* knew so well, were not missed, though I had missed them, by the hawk's eye of this other Dorset-born noticer of such things.

The longer I fix my mind upon this far-off day the more vividly it all comes back to me. That morning I remember announcing to my father and to all the family that the greatest writer *then living on this earth* was coming to visit us! All the while my father was praying, in that noble deliberate way he had, using naturally, easily, and quite *extempore*, the very language and accent of the old Tudor founders of our Church, the very tone and style of that "human, too human" Archbishop Latimer, whose heroic and yet passionately-shirked death he had described to me in the waiting-room at Dorchester, I was saying to myself: "He is coming! He, *He* is coming!" just as though I were Homenas talking to Pantagruel about the great one, the unique one, the Pope-God. All the while my father, with the whole-wheat brown loaves from Stoke-sub-Ham and the great pat of yellow butter from Mr. Cole's dairy before him, was filling the nine mouths left to him—one of his progeny no longer needing earthly food, and Littleton and Theodore away—I was thinking to myself with beating heart: "He will be here at our next meal, *He* will be here!"

And when in its slow, smooth, majestic manner the train belonging to the Great Western—monarch surely of all railways—finally drew up, and he, with the first Mrs. Hardy at his side stepped out, what did I not feel! Do you think I have forgotten even what he wore that great day? Oh most carefully was he dressed, consonant, in his Dorset-bred mind, with a formal visit to a Somerset vicar. He wore a light tweed suit, with knickerbockers to match, and he had thin black stockings on, almost like those in which I had seen his friend, William Barnes, walking so stately down South Walk. Llewelyn, after his fashion, and in a manner that even I—John, the arch-imitator—cannot copy, has told how, when we took him down to the Robbers' Castle under the high garden-wall, and called upon him to write his name in the band's archives, he wrote, in that clear classic hand I had seen in the manuscript of *Tess*, "Thomas Hardy, *a Wayfarer*."

I was already worrying in those days about the slaughter of animals for human food; and I remember, when I laid my scruples before him, how he said that in his opinion only very big animals ought to be killed, as in this way the flesh upon their bones would go farther.

Frail as an elf Mr. Hardy was, but his hands were the hands of a master-craftsman and his great greenish-black eyes, dark as those of Leo XIII, gleamed forth like the eyes of a ger-falcon over his hooked nose and military moustache. Such were the impressions, such was the "contact," as they say in America, that I received as my reward for my first published book!

When I was not taking Thora—that poor beast whose dugs took away the very solidity of the earth from under my feet and made me feel as if anything I touched *went in*—for walks over the bare downs behind Southwick, and when I was not hunting for some sylph-like figure recumbent on Brighton beach, at whose knees and ankles I could glare like a mad ogre, while I forgot that there were such things as breasts in the world at all, I got into the habit of frequenting the old curiosity shops. These I would scour through in a sort of frenzy looking for one treasure only—a print representing some great man! "Great men" took the place in my disordered mind that they take in those ridiculous little children's books, written by old-fashioned ladies, and entitled *Boyhood of Great Men*. By degrees I collected a terrific number of these prints representing "great men"—poor devils, they looked, many of them, as if they suffered from manias and megalomanias as badly as I did!—of whose names I had at least heard mention. What a lot of French "great men" there seem to have been in history, and how fond they were—these particular ones—of dressing up like the ancient Romans! I cannot say I received much personal inspiration from contemplating the formal countenances of Vauvenargue and La Rochefoucauld, of Marmontel and Fontenelle; but I derived unspeakable satisfaction from filling every empty space on every wall of Mr.

Pollard's upper room with these be-wigged and be-laureled heads.

All the antique shops I entered in this quest were not run by such kind shopmen as my gipsy friend. The ones in Hove were not nearly as friendly as the ones in Brighton. In one place—and I blush recalling my humiliation still—a rude smart devil, when I went out, after turning over at least a dozen portfolios without even finding a print of Boileau or an engraving of Bossuet, and murmured wistfully, "I'll come back again soon," replied to me with a sneer: "Oh, we'll send for you, *when we want you.*" As I write these lines the peculiar smell of those old portraits of classical worthies comes upon me, and the peculiar yellow look of their ornamental margins with iron-mould stains and little worm-holes.

If I only had contented myself with a few cheap, normal, simple stage-appurtenances for my exciting rôle as a kindred spirit of Calderon and Manzoni and Lope de Vega and Novalis, these solemn spectres whose resounding names were my only knowledge of them, all would have been well. But what must I do but get into my half-crazy head that I ought to "study" the ancient Norse Sagas. This was no doubt the influence of *Theodoric the Icelander* coming back! It was also those perpetual allusions to "sagas" in Sir Walter Scott. If I had seen in the book-catalogues *Fragments from the Runes* recited by Norna of the Fitful Head, or advertisements of the *Enchantments* used by Michael Scott, or *Selections from Hermes Trismegistus* or the *Prophetic Books of Prester John*, I should at once have ordered them. It was my first experience of that easy fatality with which young men, with their names on the university books can run up bills at Cambridge.

My "Sagas" arrived and I found myself turning their pages with a chill dismay. It came over me then, as if for the first time, that Providence had not endowed me with what people call "A Gift for Languages." I had dallied with Hebrew and I was to dally with Welsh; but at the language of the Norsemen I only gave one hopeless glance. But this one glance meant that I cut many valuable pages too roughly; and there was no sending them back. I think it was eventually as much as my year's allowance that my father had to pay for my interest in Norse mythology.

I held in my impatient fingers *Marius the Epicurean* during this time, but the devil a word of it could I grasp. It was not as bad as the "Sagas"; but the loveliness of it went completely over my head. I suppose I expected an exciting story; not quite in the style of *Quo Vadis* perhaps, but full of refined scenes of heathen wantonness. No one at Cambridge—neither Koelle nor Gooch and least of all Dr. Perowne—had helped me to understand what beauty of style meant. I came to this secret at last—I presume in the course of my own voracious readings in the "Great Writers" Series and the "English Men of Letters" Series—but I can tell you when I *had* enlightened myself, I took a passionate care that the young Llewelyn, at that time still at Sherborne, should not grow up in my ignorance. He certainly did not! When *was* there a time when this young rogue of a born master didn't know what the words "a noble style" convey to the responsive intelligence?

And now I come to one of the most extraordinary episodes in my life—an episode that must have lasted nearly ten years—my intimate friendship with the poet Alfred de ——— I owe this high privilege, one of the happiest chances of my life, to none other than my enterprising host. Mr. Pollard must have had an eye for the exceptional in human nature, as he had for gold in a ring.

"There's a man you would admire, Mr. Powys," he remarked one day, glancing respectfully at my portrait gallery, "who lives at Portslade. I am going to take the liberty of introducing you two gentlemen to each other."

It did not at the moment present itself to me as likely that Portslade, a place I passed through daily, could produce, after the fashion of Mantua or Cockermouth, the kind of "great man" I admired, but I gave Mr. Pollard the benefit of the doubt and expressed my willingness to meet Mr. de ———. It did not take more than one encounter to link me and my womanish hero-worship with hoops of steel to the astonishing personality who soon presented himself. Alfred de ——— must have been over seventy when I first met him and I remained his devoted henchman for nearly ten years. It was only his final retirement to London under the care of his son who was always kind to him that separated us at last. I never learnt the circumstances of his death nor do I know where he was buried. I served him well, and the last time I saw him he declared in such thundering tones, in the big restaurant at Victoria Station, that my son was like a Greek God, that he covered the child with confusion.

He was very tall and very thin. His mouth and chin were covered with scanty grey hairs; his deep-set handsome eyes never needed glasses; his wrinkled forehead resembled that of Schopenhauer. His clothes were always as ragged, and to confess the truth as ancient and disregarded, as those in which Ulysses disguised him as a beggar. His stomach—very different from that of his devoted Boswell—must have had a lining of cast-iron. He could live—and did actually live at a pinch—on crusts and scrapings, but he also had the greatest power of swallowing raw spirits that I have met in anyone before or since. I would, after my fashion, treat him to tea in our numerous excursions along those Sussex highways but no tea I could procure, or make, was ever strong enough for him. In the middle of our conversations he would suddenly stretch out his lean hand and long bare wrist—he seemed to wear no underclothes at all—and snatching up the slop-basin would pour its contents at a gulp down his iron throat. His lean Don Quixote legs would always be displayed in their nakedness when he crossed his knees, and his boots seldom had laces. In spite of all this Mr. de —— was unmistakably the great gentleman. He came of a noble family. He was himself by rights, I believe, a baron; and I can assure you that under certain conditions his manner and tone were more than baronial. But he prided himself—such was his humour—upon being a shrewd manipulator of human weakness in high places.

"Powys," he would say, with a flickering smile and shrug of his thin shoulders, "Powys we must propitiate Magnates."

I never myself beheld in him much of this propitiation of "Magnates." It fell to me, as a matter of fact, to do the propitiating, when I eventually made my grand efforts to get him

R

the public recognition which he deserved. I have never put myself out so much in all my days as I did for Mr. de ——. I was his disciple, his faithful lieutenant, his equerry, his man-at-arms, the bearer of his shield, the purveyor of his cap of maintenance. I tried for long to conceal from him the fact that I ever wrote poetry myself. I even suppressed *Odes and Other Poems* as if it were some obscene or indecent publication. My friend's confidence in me was sublime. When I took to giving public lectures it was incredible to him that anyone but himself should be their subject. I did, as a matter of fact, and indeed do still, think highly of a certain sombre and simple power that his verses possessed. Let me try to remember some of them.

> "I seek the Deity. I wrestle most,
> I who sit scorned outside the Temple-gate.
> In vigils of the night I keep my post.
> Others are sure. I only watch and wait.
> I supplicate. Who answereth my prayer?
> He doth—in murmuring waves, or not at all!
> In clouds He is transfigured in the air:
> Thro' the dense forest echoes His footfall.
> The amazing stars—each is a heavenly sphere:
> The ineffable surrounds each mountain height.
> In the vast universe, or far or near,
> Throbs the great Heart of all, by day and night!"

We used to meet and talk, both of us in very loud voices, in every kind of queer place. All the shabbier and more out-of-the-way taverns between Shoreham and Brighton knew us, and we would extend our pilgrimages in a great many directions beyond that coastline.

Mr. de —— had composed a poem called "A Walk to Poynings" before I knew him; and he and I shared ruminative, almost mystical "walks" of this old-fashioned Sterne's *Sentimental Journey* kind along all sorts of side-tracks and bypaths of that district. He was acquainted with many picturesque Sussex villages, lying in their secluded beech-groves in the folds of the bare downs, and he behaved in all these sea-coast hamlets as if he were some infidel Don Quixote expounding in sombre rhetoric, among these homely Christian monuments, stern

Lucretian doctrines about a desolate God-forsaken cosmos. He and I were very much alike in our complete lack of any sense of social nuance or historic proportion. Our excited voices, the voices of an aquiline-nosed lean old man and an aquiline-nosed lean young man rose and fell as we stood among the patient tombs and under the echoing porches of these quiet purlieus of rural piety, denouncing the consolatory assuagements of the faith of our fathers and prophesying planetary catastrophies and universal overthrows.

Sometimes with an ineffably sweet smile illuminating his wrinkled face Mr. de —— would recite to me his favourite lines from the older poets, lines that *smelt*, if I may say so, like those old pieces of furniture in Penn House ante-room.

"On her white breast," he would quote, "a sparkling cross she wore, that Jews might kiss and infidels adore!" And then he would suddenly burst out—taking not the least notice of the astonished passers-by on some Brighton pavement, or of the bewildered landlord in some Shoreham inn—"Old as I am, for ladies' love unfit, the power of beauty I remember yet; which once inflamed my heart—and still inspires my wit!"

But he would deal in matters sometimes that were nearer home.

"Powys," he would say, "you cannot live with a woman for forty years without loving her!"

And then he would narrate to me astonishing episodes from his early life, how he suffered from a sunstroke once when a young officer in the service of the Old East Indian Company in the days before Disraeli made the Queen an Empress, and how his father was an ambassador of some European country, at the Court of Lisbon.

As we wandered along some darkening road between the downs and the sea with the sun setting in the west and the moon rising in the east, the old man would compose such lines as these.

> "O Moon, O Sun, ye dual agents, say
> What is this world between ye that ye share,
> Adam and Eve of fearful Night and Day,
> Ah! why so speechless in the trembling air?"

The very day we first met under the auspices of the lively Mr. Pollard he recited to me a singular set of verses he had composed long ago when he had his sunstroke in India, and as I write the words I can hear his reverberating voice and see his formidable gesticulations, like some aged actor in the days when a London town-crier might be calling out in the clattering streets. "The great poet, Mr. John Dryden, lies a-dying in his lodgings in Soho!"

I often repeat to myself these vigorous exhortations to the Inanimate:

> "Rocks, stony Rocks, that lie around in silence,
> Brooding thro' ages, solemn and sublime,
> Let us emerge from lethargy with violence!
> Let us adore the Author of all Time!"

I have never given to any work of my own the indomitable labour I lavished, day in and day out, on the polishing and revising of Mr. de —— poems. Two separate volumes of them I actually managed to get published before I had done. I journeyed to the country house of Mr. Fisher Unwin. I even carried Mr. de —— himself up to London and in the studio of Mortimer Menpes, full of chat about Whistler, I compelled two countesses and I don't know how many baronesses to acknowledge his genius. One of these grand ladies whispered to another on this occasion that I resembled a gladiator. I certainly felt like Pursuivant with a brazen trumpet. The first of Mr. de ——'s books we called *Ultima Verba*; and since it was impossible to go *further* than that, when it came to the second one I named it, with the help of my old *School Dictionary*, *Noctis Susurri, Sighs of the Night*.

Implacable atheist as my old friend was in his public harangues—how his voice used to resound along the dusty walls of the old waiting-rooms in the Brighton Station!—I used, in the dead watches of the night, as I lay in some adjoining chamber, to hear him praying earnestly and passionately, and almost as loudly as when in the daylight he denounced such paltry superstitions! I feel a certain shame about telling this, as if I were betraying my master, but his career—the career of a man between seventy and eighty—and the name of some ancient love of his, used to be referred to again and again in this secret colloquy with the First Cause.

All this time I was hunting about for a house wherein to settle when the day, now not far off, of my marriage came. Houses have always had a peculiar and quite special fascination for me—houses of a certain kind! I was indeed as particular about my houses as I was about my girls and in precisely the same way. That is to say it was an ideal house I hunted for —not a house "Not made with hands, eternal in the heavens" —but the Platonic idea of a house, the Entelecheia, or pre-ordained blossoming-forth, of this primordial necessity.

It will become clearer, as I try to articulate what I felt, why it is that I have taken, during all my days, not the remotest interest in my career. Mr. de —— at least during his midnight hours— took more interest in this thing, in one's success, in one's future, in one's prestige, than I did. In fact I have some-times been guilty of a certain deliberate *malice* in this direction. It is as though I nourished some weird Saturnian contempt for the judgments of men, and appealed to some higher court against the verdict of the inhabitants of this planet. I took quite seriously those words in *Lycidas*: "Fame is no plant that grows on mortal soil, or in the glistering foil set-off to the world or in broad rumour lies."

It is most important in writing the tale of one's days not to try to give them the unity they possess for oneself in later life. A human story, to bear any resemblance to the truth, must advance and retreat erratically, must flicker and flutter here and there, must debouch at a thousand tangents. But it is quite clear, and borne out in a thousand cases and incidents, that I lived so completely in the present all along that what is called ambition had no room or time to sprout. Ambitious people are forced—as one learns from reading their lives—to cut down rigidly upon their contemplative tendencies, to harden themselves *against* their momentary sensations. I *lived* for sensations; and have always, in my deepest heart regarded such a life as the only adequate return we can make to Nature for giving us birth!

Human sensations are Nature's self-expression. They are the earth's awareness of herself. They are like the blossoming of flowers—the only way in which the rooted life of the organism can realize itself and *be* itself. Besides, as long as I had enough to eat and drink, enough to purchase a certain measure of privacy, enough to buy tobacco and cigarettes, enough to take me where I could turn upon the ankles of women my idolatrous and ravished stare, enough to save me from working in a school or an office or a barber's shop or a factory or a farm or a mine or on ship-board, enough in plain words to dodge, avoid, shirk, run away from, sneak out of that *manual labour* upon which—and don't you suppose I didn't always know it!—we other men are privileged and petted parasites, what on earth did I want a career for? You will say —putting one's duty to humanity aside—"for the sake of winning reputation, approval, respect, honour, renown!" But, my good friend, you are forgetting "the rock whence I was hewn and the pit whence I was digged." You are forgetting my father! I inherited from him, and was strengthened and fortified in, by watching him and listening to him, an abysmal personal pride that was sufficient to itself under all conceivable conditions.

When that Hove tradesman was so rude to me, in a way that a Brighton tradesman would never have been, it humiliated me where I was most sensitive of all; that is to say in my dignity *as man to man*. I then learnt what it was that led my father to prefer the company of the most disreputable and drunken members of his parish to the company of smart, clever, new-fangled persons. Such persons were always ready to mock and to sneer at his old-fashioned ways and indulge in those debased forms of facetiousness which made my father feel a fool, just as they make me feel a fool; whereas the village atheists and drunkards he met, or old Nancy Cooper the witch-wife, or the circus-men when they came with their whirligigs, or some tattooed ex-sailor-tramp on the Yeovil Road, would make my father go off in a spasm of well-being, rubbing his hands, protruding his upper lip, and full of the feeling that he had conducted himself as *his* father would have conducted himself, in a manner worthy of a countryman and a gentleman.

You will say that it is easy for a man in a long black coat and with an account at Stuckey's Bank to come off triumphantly from an encounter with Nancy Cooper, or a tipsy mole-catcher, or a foul-tongued hawker of rabbit-skins. I am not so sure. It is not quite as simple as all that. There are moments, when the human eye meets the human eye, that it recognizes a certain basic reciprocity, and there are moments when it does not! At least it is very certain that the average worldly person would not have felt transported with pride at having acquitted himself so well. He would not have given the thing a second thought. It was in his simple and majestic rapture over such occurrences that my father was so great.

Great or not, I learnt from him to ground my pride upon a certain basic human dignity that had nothing to do with success in the world, and that a tramp could have as much as a clergyman, and a poacher as much as a grave-digger. And I learnt moreover—and here I went beyond my father, who had at least an eye to what the weather would be on the morrow, and to what the Afghans or the Zulus, or the Boers might take into their heads to do—to live each day, as the old evangelical hymns say, *as if it were my last.*

But "all the same for that," I got extraordinary satisfaction at this epoch in looking for a house to settle down in. And Mr. Pollard—putting both Danish schooners and gold rings out of his head—was all "alive-o" to assist me in this search. And so one day I fetched the little man from his counter and led him off to give me his opinion about a house I had found in Southwick itself. Never shall I forget, no! not if I forgot Mr. Pollard and the backwater and the bridge and the ships with Scandinavian flags, the impression this house made upon me! It was very near the railway-line. You could see it from the train as you left Southwick. It had large airy rooms with tall French windows opening upon a leafy garden. I have an obscure notion that it must have been a French-looking house; and a French-looking garden too. I can only tell you that the emerald-green lawn winding in and out of its tall trees, was greener, softer, more enchanted, and yet more dim and enclosed, than any grassy expanse I have ever seen. With Mr. Pollard at my elbow I paced this magical enclosure. It was hidden from all the rest of the world, but revealed to the railway passengers who travelled, and there were not few of them, between Worthing and Brighton. But the very nearness of these passing trains seemed to make the grass greener and the tree-trunks more rooted and still.

The place satisfied a desire in me that had a curious resemblance to what I felt when after striding up and down the whole length of Brighton beach with eyes like the eyes of a ger-falcon I settled down at last by some soft, receptive feminine form whose ankles I could at least pretend belonged to a sylph-like body. I always used to fancy I could get the same indescribable feeling from the way the gods have moulded a woman's body if I were alone with her in a bedroom, but I never could! I slept at different times with three sisters of the same family, and I did experience some queer romantic emotions then; and intermittent feelings, too, of a tremulous tenderness as far as one of the three was concerned, whom in a room in a disreputable back-alley I used to watch strumming on a cracked piano, while the old workhouse-man, employed as a doorkeeper, would replenish our pair of guttering candles. For long afterwards whenever I was left alone in any room with a miserable piano I would try to reproduce that particular wistful little tune. It was to the accompaniment of that tune that I had sought something from women, which I knew well only the strange, inhuman chastity of street-girls could ever come near satisfying.

You must not suppose that these wanderings of mine were unattended by risks and dangers. I remember on the ground-floor of a Brighton house being spied upon once by an indignant cabman, who ceased not from his troublesome activities till my landlady turned out my companion and myself into the street. A scandalous person, and yet with a certain Mrs. Quickly turn of humour was the mother of my particular Doll Tearsheet. The saying that was most often upon her lips—and remembering my inauspicious cabman I rather appreciated such a sentiment—was: "I never do and never did like on-lookers."

But though I derived plenty of romantic and sentimental overtones from being with these street-girls I got hardly any erotic pleasure. My desire, directly I became friendly with the girl herself, changed into a sort of ideal attachment. It was as if I were "in love," as they call it, with each one of these sweet baggages. My feeling had all the romantic respect, all the exaggerated deference, all the ideal tenderness, that are supposed to be the sign of a normal love-affair. I was an extremely young man then but I behaved with these wenches like an aged, infatuated dotard. I would buy my favourite one clothes; but being very poor and not being able to send *these* bills—as I had done over the "Sagas"—to my father, and, moreover, having not the remotest idea of what clothes were suitable for these ladies' particular profession, I made sad mistakes. I recollect buying my friend one costume, that I saw in a shop window and admired extremely, which she indignantly declared would have suited a postman! No doubt it had stiff braid, or shiny buttons, or something that didn't harmonize with the softness of feminine taste. I probably thought it looked like the attire of one of those enchanting boy-girls, or girl-boys, in Shakespeare's comedies.

I suppose there never has been anyone less of a Don Juan than I was. But that has always been my difficulty with respectable women. Respectable women *want* Don Juans, not fantastic-brained idealists who have perverse manias for people's ankles; whereas these Brighton wenches had minds very much like my own, and nerves very much like my own. What is called "passion" had no existence for them, or for me. They were permeated with manias and riddled with superstitions, and so was I. They were profoundly coarse, but withal excessively fastidious, and such, I have a shrewd notion, is my own character.

One of them used to tell me that what she disliked most was to sleep with a man with a wooden leg; an experience which she described in detail exactly as I would have described it, whereas her ideal in men, an ideal she hesitated not to picture to me very often and very eloquently, was, point by point, a masculine counterpart of my own imaginary sylph. I was obviously not her ideal, any more than she was mine; but we had pleasant times together. Lust and lasciviousness had nothing at all to do with my feeling for these kind girls; not, at any rate, after the initial impulse that led me to pursue them. My attitude towards them was an ideal one. It was the worship of the eternal feminine in the only form I could worship it *where my manias made no difference*. It gradually became apparent to me that if I wished to satisfy my impersonal lust it was no good going into shabby bedrooms with girls for whom I felt nothing but a romantic tenderness. I soon decided it was wiser for me to stay in the open and indulge my obsession by staring at what I considered desirable forms, as they lay prone or supine on the pebbles of the beach.

I discovered, however, at that time a new manner of satisfying my frenzied eye-lust. There were theatres at the ends of all the bigger Brighton piers and in the winters there would be given certain small travelling pantomimes in these places. At one of these—I forget on which pier it was—I beheld at last, actually in the flesh, a real, living incarnation of my ideal sylph. It is impossible for me to describe to you the loveliness of this figure. She was an extremely quiet girl, grave and self-possessed, and of a very dark complexion. She had præter-naturally long legs, very long slender thighs, narrow boyish hips, upright, rather square shoulders, and ankles of a ravishing perfection. I suppose she was a sort of supernumerary ornament, like a lovely figure on a Grecian urn, for she did nothing during the whole performance but simply stand there. She did not even turn round: so I had no way of telling whether her flanks were as divinely moulded as the rest of her body. But of course they must have been. They must, they must! For she was the sylph of all my long, straining, yearning, desperate desires, and I could see that she was perfect.

I had so well learnt my lesson under those guttering candles of my old workhouse-doorkeeper that you can believe I made no attempt to speak to her or to approach nearer to her. I did not even catch her eye. I expect she never guessed that such an idolatrous, abandoned, sacramental worship ·of her body could ever possibly occur. She was just an awkward supernumerary and would always remain so. Probably she supported a tipsy father and an invalid mother. Or she may have lived in Brighton, and just hired herself out, to stand in the wings of Christmas pantomimes, in order to earn money to buy presents for her younger brothers and sisters.

I walked in from Southwick to every single performance while her pantomime was being played, and sank down into my seat each time with a deep-drawn sigh, to give myself up to an ecstasy that never failed me. Finally I came one day to find this heavenly entertainment flown away and some wretched earthly melodrama being solemnly played in its stead. I used to think in those days, and for many, many years afterwards, when with trembling eagerness I bought my ticket at various box-offices,, or made my way between the recumbent figures at various seaside resorts, how miserable, how dull, how wretched, how pitiable, how drab, how tedious, how dreary, how intolerable, and how totally without interest, must the lives be of people who were not engaged, as I was, in this delirious and enthralling hunt after eternally anonymous human limbs. Yes, it was evidently only at pantomimes or where I could find young ladies lying on soft grass, or on warm pebble-stones, or on pleasant sand, that I could enjoy my real fetish-worship, my intense religious idolatry, of those aspects of the feminine shape—I could never admire it all in all— which so enraptured me.

But in this house and garden under that high railway-bank at Southwick it seemed to me that I found a parallel in the realm of the non-human for the sort of ecstasy I got from my desperate anonymous quest. I thought of myself as worshipping the sun and the moon from this enclosed garden. I thought of myself as going in and out in summer bringing with me the feeling of leaves and grass and earth-mould, and of sitting in winter over the fire, reading—in translations however—the stories of Norse Mythology. But none of these *definite* thoughts touched the real heart of what I felt! As I paced that lawn, and kept going in and out of that French window, I felt that my real soul, below all these outward movements, was experiencing some extraordinary pleasure, a pleasure that was sexual and yet not sexual, that had to do with women, and yet had not the faintest connection with women. What I kept reverting to was the thought of *how long* I would live in this house, and how I would know the way every wind blew there, and where exactly the suns and moons in their seasons would appear and disappear there.

Mr. Pollard said that he thought he could share this house with me when I was married, keeping his grocery shop as it was, but paying me, if I were the one to deal with the rent, for the garden produce. He felt, just as I did, that it was a shame that such a place should remain untenanted a moment longer.

I cannot quite tell how it happened, possibly during a visit from cousin Ralph or from Littleton, but the idea of taking this house by the railway—whether in collaboration with Mr. Pollard or not—melted into the air as rapidly as it had risen out of the air. I suddenly decided that even if my father did raise my allowance from sixty pounds to a hundred pounds, as he said he would do, I ought to put myself in the way of making more money before I married. Money, rather than enchanted gardens, ought I decided just now to be my objective.

So I journeyed to Eastbourne; and indefatigably dragging myself round that elegant resort, in less than a couple of exhausting days I had called upon nearly a score of girls' schools. Of these—for I must have had nothing less than a miraculous power with these excellent ladies—I actually obtained five wherein to lecture and at least double the price that I was earning in Hove! I got five Eastbourne girls' schools; and from each, for an hour's lesson I received a pound.

After this I used to travel to Eastbourne regularly once a week, and on no more nourishment than a cup of tea and an oatmeal biscuit, and intermittently scraped and harrowed and scoured and raked out and bent double with the ulcers in my stomach, I used to give all the whole five lectures and earn *in that one day* what I considered—with my other sources of income—enough to marry on.

I felt however—now that I had found out that the number of sylphs educated in schools was very limited—that I would enjoy lecturing on a larger scale; giving in fact public lectures. It had been my destiny every day to pass the entrance to Hove Town Hall and it was now my destiny every day to pass the entrance to Eastbourne Town Hall. I decided to hire both these edifices. And this project turned out to be easy. Not "all of them," as Mr. Blanch would have jested, but a very large hall in both of them I had no difficulty in obtaining; and for less, I believe, certainly not for more, than a pound a-piece.

Mr. de —— took a great interest in these proceedings even though the topic of my first public lecture, which was in the Hove Town Hall, was not entirely confined to him and his work. It spread out in fact, I think, over three or four centuries of English literature. Mr. Pollard too took an interest in the project, and indeed turned out an indispensable aid; for he got, if I remember right, my bills printed for me, and was on the spot to collect, if I am not mistaken, the box-office receipts with his own hands. These, all in all, amounted to three shillings and sixpence. For my audience consisted of three women and one child; the child being let in for the sixpence. I can see Mr. de ——'s quixotic figure now seated in the front row, nodding a little when I spoke of the prefaces of Wordsworth but sitting up very straight, and assuming the expression of a stern but not unpersuadable connoisseur, when I quoted from the unpublished pages of *Ultima Verba*.

You can believe how thrilling it was to me when Littleton came to visit me at Mr. Pollard's. Here was that old story coming true that we had told each other on the road to Milborne Port, that he would stay with me when I should be earning my living where there was water to fish in! The water at Southwick was the deep salt sea, and the fishing was not in Littleton's style; but we were together, and my happiness, at any rate, was complete. We used to walk far over the downs; Thora with us, her femininity, *pro tem.* happily forgotten. I never talked to Littleton about my vices—I do not do *that* to-day—but you need not think we lacked topics of conversation. He was reading Catullus then for pure pleasure and without a "crib," for he was always a scholar, and lying on the thymy turf of those chalk hills—for I had no desire to disturb his passivity when he was in his Catullus mood—I would watch, as he read, the "meadow browns" and the "clouded yellows" and the "azure blues" and the "gate-keepers" and the "painted-ladies" just as if we were back again in the old Dorchester times and were prone at the bottom of one of the trenches of Maiden Castle. Ah! to the end of my days when I think of Catullus, I shall hear Littleton's voice, lingering out the rhythmic sounds, as if they were circles on water when a fish has risen, and ever and anon lifting his ruddy face and turning his grey eyes upon me to make sure I miss nothing of it, just as he used to do when he first learnt the trick of making perfect rings of tobacco-smoke!

We had one startling experience which I confess did not show us up very heroically. We were drifting composedly along the summit of the hills, observing the darting white rumps of one kind of down-bird and the rosy marks upon the feathers of another, when suddenly we were confronted by a thin wire fence on the other side of which a pack of ferocious bloodhounds, or were they mastiffs, rose on their hind legs, and with open jaws and terrifying leaps tried desperately to get at us. Theodore would, I fancy, have chuckled not a little could he have witnessed his two elder brothers beating a hurried and not very dignified retreat. It is seldom in this world that it is permitted to human beings to preserve a mood of unruffled sentiment for very long. Had that fence been a few feet lower I don't like to think what might have happened. Or would the presence of Thora have preserved us alive?

Having decided against that house under the railway-line I set out one day with Littleton for a very extended search for what I wanted. I was a vegetarian then, and I think I astonished my athletic companion by my capacity for walking. As we started along the Brighton front—full of memories for me that I dare say Catullus would have comprehended more readily than his translator—I remember discoursing to Littleton upon my method of lecturing. I told him I had invented a new art, the art of "Dithyrambic Analysis." We skirted the very portion of the town where the inventor of "Dithyrambic Analysis" had found his perverse desires so often turned—as if by sorcery—into ideal sentiment, and striking inland, straight across the Downs, came down into the valley of the Sussex Ouse, within a mile or two of the town of Lewes. Here we explored the little village of Rodmell—I think that was its name—where there was a farmhouse to let. We returned however without my having committed myself to anything; but I had received a very favourable impression of the environs of Lewes as a landscape wherein to bide; and after Littleton had left me I made other explorations in this direction.

I think it was the couple of miles' walk from Lewes to that farm by the banks of the Ouse that deterred me from settling there; but it had got lodged in my mind now that a farmhouse, if I could only discover one not too far from a railway, would suit me better than anything else as a permanent abode. With my five new schools at Eastbourne, as well as my allowance of a hundred pounds a year, I felt myself to be a man of substance. Perhaps a small but very ancient Castle might present itself.

Such was my mood, when, at last, after a few more excursions, I found what suited me. It was not a Castle, not even a little one; nor was it an Abbey, nor a Priory, nor a moated Grange. But it *was* a farmhouse; and I got it for the modest sum of forty pounds a year. It was however a sufficiently romantic place and possessed an historical name; for it was called "Court House," and it went back—not the actual building, but some earlier edifice—to the days of Henry III, and was reputed to be the spot where the King held his Court after the Battle of Lewes. It was on the outskirts of the hamlet of Offham, near the spacious eighteenth-century dwelling of Sir George Shiffner, Bart., a sturdy, ruddy-cheeked old gentleman, who was both the squire and parson. It lay in a fold of the high Downs, behind which the sun vanished early in the winter days, the hill just above it being called Mount Harry, after the father of Edward Longshanks, and the Downs beyond it rising to a height of nearly a thousand feet at an eminence called Ditchling Beacon. Court House was only about half a mile from the little station of Cooksbridge, on the line between Lewes and Hayward's Heath; and I recollect how when I emerged from the train at Cooksbridge I was considerably bothered in my idealistic mind by what I felt to be the commonness, even the *lowness* of this name! I had inherited from my father a proud contempt—like that of some old rice-eating Samurai—for all culinary excesses, and it irked me to think of settling down near a place dedicated to cooks. You must remember that I had not yet idealized this noble profession by reading the Chitterling chapter in Rabelais.

Consoling myself as well as I could over this frying-pan name, I made my way along a pleasant avenue of trees towards my destination. How well did I come to know this avenue in later days! It was under these goodly trees that I had to pass every time I visited the little Offham Post Office, where an ex-butler of Sir George Shiffner acted as postmaster.

"Sir George has asked me," this worthy man was destined soon to remark, "about the new tenant at Court House. Sir George wanted to know if you had brought your servants with you."

But it was more in connection with my own inner life that this leafy avenue became lodged in my mind than with anything that Sir George said or thought. It was the tops of these branches that I gazed at one day presently as they made a delicate tracery against the sky and derived from the sight one of those strange mysterious ecstasies to which I was subject. It was after turning the illustrated pages of an history of Early Italian painting that this vision—if so it can be called— transported me; and what it really amounted to was a sudden revelation of the magical loveliness of twigs and leaves when they make a sharply-cut filigree, an intricately delicate pattern, against a grey sky.

It was here too that I was destined to be tormented by that Demon within me that took a fiendish pleasure in calling up revolting images. I lived, just then, under such a terrific strain of poetical idealism—using my will to obliterate unpleasant things and to concentrate upon lovely things—that this very strain gave a deadly aid to this filthy-minded Devil. It was, by some fatality, in connection with the poetry of Cowper that I came to be most plaguily tormented at that time. As I have already hinted it has taken me something like forty years— wretched magician as I am!—to deal adequately with this Devil's tricks; that is to say to sprinkle the Holy Water of Lethe over objects that he has tried to spoil for me by plastering them with his Devil's dung.

It was not long now before the filthy rogue would never let me so much as summon up in my mind the idea of poor Cowper without strewing the road before me—this road that I had thought was exactly the sort of thing that would have pleased this poet—with what do you suppose? With bullock's blood and black snails! If any reader of this passage—for *all* readers cannot be sound and sane—recognizes a mental affliction of his own in what I am narrating, let him take comfort.

I have—and without the aid of any psychiatrist either— found out various mental tricks wherewith to *wash* my thoughts. The will to forget! Have faith that your will *can* get the trick of forgetting and in the end it will be all right. We are all in secret fighting for our sanity. The great thing is to have more than one string to our bow.

It was along this road too when Littleton came to stay with me at Court House that I once—I blush to relate such doings—insisted that he should walk all the way to Offham a few paces behind me. I explained that I *wanted to think* and that his breathing got on my nerves. *"Let us think!"* I would cry out in those days to anyone walking by my side. It was here, too, that Littleton and I had a fierce quarrel about Home Rule for Ireland. I was in favour of it. He was doubtful of its wisdom. It was the *tone* in which he was doubtful that annoyed me, however, not the doubt itself; and taking him by surprise I rushed at him like a madman and flung him into the ditch. Here we continued to struggle, much to the consternation of some worthy stranger who was coming blamelessly along at that moment. It was when we grew aware, from the depths of our ditch, that this good man had climbed over the opposite hedge in terror, that our fury abated, and clambering back into the road we loudly hummed a reassuring tune, lest the runaway, now half across the field, should summon Sir George's game-keeper.

On this, the first occasion of my seeing Court House, I stopped at a labourer's cottage nearby to ask for the keys. There was no one there but the woman of the cottage who willingly enough came along with me. As we went up the drive, with outhouses on one side and stables on the other, my companion laid her hand on my arm. "The other way, the other way, the other way!" she cried, and made a bolt for some bushes that grew behind the house. I followed her without difficulty for she was a heavy woman. But it did strike me as singular that she should find it necessary to make her way through these bushes on all-fours. She expressed herself, however, as anxious that my first view of Court House should be from the hillside behind it. She was right. Its brick-and-flint walls and yellow lichened tiled roof *did* look more pictur-esque from the back; for its façade had been cemented.

But the woman told me her story, before she unlocked the door, and it was not a pretty one. She explained to me quite frankly, using the plain words, that in a day or two she intended to retire to the County Lunatic Asylum. Thus did the inventor of the art of "Dithyrambic Analysis" enter his first Sussex home.

Chapter Seven

Court House

IT was the Pollards who helped me to settle into Court House; but whom do you suppose I succeeded in getting as my housekeeper till I should be married? No other than Mrs. Curme, whose husband had been my father's gardener at Rothesay House! Yes, Mrs. Curme herself—*née* Bellamy— the widow of that aged man, bent nearly double, with a coun- tenance like Sir Joshua Reynold's picture of St. Joseph, for whom I dug such craftily-concealed pits in that new Dorchester garden! Mrs. Curme was an old woman then; but she remained extremely handsome, and her manners were those rather of a lady-in-waiting than a servant. She was just the person for me at that juncture, when in my crazy folly I was carrying half the milder aberrations, mentioned in "Kraft-Ebbing," on my obstinate shoulders. In those days I would not have any meat in the house, no! not so much as a rasher of bacon; but Mrs. Curme consoled herself by drinking hot beer, beer heated on the kitchen-stove. This, with the unpalatable carrots and turnips provided by the husband of the woman who had first shown me over Court House, was the poor lady's sole diet, all the while she looked after me.

The handsome old woman was lonely at first—when I was away lecturing in Brighton and Eastbourne—but she very quickly made friends with the daughter of Sir George's game-keeper who used frequently to drop in, of an after- noon, to keep her company. At such times Mrs. Curme's spirits rose to a high pitch; and as she moved about so stately in her spotless apron and big lace cap adorned with purple ribbons she would suddenly be seized by a mood of daring revelry.

"Dash my cap and whiskers!" she would then sing out. "Katie, my dear, let's have a cup of tea!"

I took all my meals in the kitchen, waited on by Mrs. Curme; and I can well remember one evening, as we sat together over the fire, talking, as we almost always did—for in her youth she had served the family of our austere Governor of St. Helena—about Napoleon, how I said to her:

"Wouldn't you like me to read a little poetry to you, Mrs. Curme?"

I must have said this in exactly the tone in which my father, when some bedridden old woman wanted to go on telling him about her ailments, would say:

" Wouldn't you like me *to read a few words?*"

And without waiting for an answer I hurried off to my "study" and came back with the works of Swinburne, from which I read—in thundering tones, more adapted to the Hove Town Hall than a peaceful kitchen—such resounding infidel rhetoric as:

"Thou hast conquered, O pale Galilean, the world has grown grey with thy breath!"

After some twenty minutes of such reverberating rhodo-montade I laid the book down and enquired how my hearer liked it.

"Mr. John," said Mrs. Curme gravely; "I do thank 'ee, Mr. John, from my poor heart. It does me good to hear the dear Lord's name mentioned so frequent!"

It was Mrs. Curme's way, part of the courtly manners that were a second nature with her, never to turn her back to me. On leaving my study—for I had a study at Court House—she would always walk a few steps backward, making as she did so not exactly a curtsy, but a sort of obeisance of her whole aged frame. But she would not even present herself before me—this refined old lady upon whom I ought to have been waiting hand and foot—without knocking first and asking for permission to address me. This ritual would regularly occur every night. I would be reading Colonel Sinnett's *Esoteric Buddhism* or Mrs. Besant's *Seven Principles of Man*, when there would come her knock on the door.

"May I come in, Master John?"

"Yes, Mrs. Curme."

And when she had carefully shut the door behind her, and was standing there, so old and so handsome, before me:

"May I," she would enquire, "say good night, Master John?"

"Yes, Mrs. Curme."

"*Good* night, Master John!"

And with that she would walk backwards to the door and let herself out.

One of my manias was for changing my shirt and all my underclothes *every day*; and Mrs. Curme fooled me beautifully over this. She would remove my clothes at night, and having just simply *ironed* them on the kitchen-table, bring them up again next morning with my can of hot water. On these occasions she would just knock on the door and hurry downstairs again without a word. Experience had taught her that men, young or old, are often in a touchy frame of mind when they first wake up.

The husband of the lady who took refuge in the lunatic asylum after introducing me to Court House was the most typical South Saxon labourer I have ever seen. A long silky grey beard he had, and cold steely blue eyes. Since it was clear that his wife intended to remain in the asylum this blue-eyed Gurth got a person to look after him, out of the Lewes workhouse.

This "grave housewife," as Homer would have called her, was what Rabelais would have named an "old trot." Her most casual observations were rich in philosophical plaintiveness. Her favourite saying was: "We be all born; but we bain't all dead yet," an observation that might have been a translation of an aphorism of Sophocles. This singular person went by the name of "Aunt Stone" and her dearest crony was an aged tramp called "Happy Mary."

Happy Mary was a round-faced woman of incredible age whose visage was tanned by weather into a rich mahogany and who lived on the road all the year round; having an especial clientele of back-doors and her favourite set of workhouses.

I am glad to be able to record that for several years after my marriage Happy Mary used to keep Christmas in Court House kitchen; and here she and Aunt Stone would celebrate a kind of Witches' Sabbath, the most startling feature of which was a performance that these lively old beldames were wont to describe as "The Candlestick Dance." This dance must have been a very ancient one, and certainly was of a heathen character; more adapted in fact to the rites of Hecate than the birth of our Saviour. In the course of it this pair of old wives hitched up their "cutty-sarks" and proceeded to skip, in abandoned eldritch glee, over an array of candles disposed at convenient distances along our kitchen floor.

Under Mrs. Curme's regime, however, there were no greater revels than the sipping of Lewes ale, kept warm upon the stove, and readings from the Dionysian poet who makes "Galilean" rhyme with "Lethean" and "God" with "rod."

It was at this time, my father having presented me with two hundred pounds for the furnishing of Court House, that I stopped buying prints of great men and began to buy their works. These I especially delighted to purchase when they took the shape of leather-bound quartos and worm-eaten folios. Such bookish treasures were unbelievably cheap at the end of the last century.

There was an amazing second-hand shop for instance in those days in the very heart of Brighton, within a few hundred yards of the Regent's famous Pavilion. It was kept by a dignified little man called "Mr. Smith," whose chief assistant was a huge black-bearded fellow, resembling the ogres in fairy-tales but with one of the mildest and most Early-Christian countenances I have ever seen. Here I purchased a folio of Sir Thomas Browne, two folios of Dryden's Plays, a folio of Beaumont and Fletcher—the very one that Lamb describes buying and "collating," late one night, with sister's help—Baskerville's Catullus, Tibullus, and Propertius, bound in plum-coloured morocco, Fuller's *Holy State*, Bentley's famous edition of *Paradise Lost*, in quarto, with a lovely *youthful* picture of the author on the title-page, and the vast illustrated first edition of Dryden's *Vergil* with pictures of all the contemporary magnates

—as Mr. de —— would have called them—who subscribed
for its printing.

There was another second-hand bookshop, in those days,
not far from the back-alley retreat where I learnt—or *should*
have learnt—that bedrooms hired at eighteen pence "for a short
time" had a sedative rather than a provocative effect upon my
amorous propensities. Here—in the bookshop I mean—there
used to sit upon a high stool, which always made me think of
the seat Eli the Prophet used, a sort of venerable image of a
book-collector, of apoplectic proportions, and with a heavy
hydrocephalic head. The type of books *he* kept were both more
expensive and more recondite than those in the "Smith" shop.
They were indeed totally beyond my means and absolutely
beyond my book knowledge. But the white-faced idol on the
high stool was an incorrigible controversialist and full of the
most erudite heresies. Argument he placed above cash; and
with him I would argue by the hour upon the "Baconian
Theory," he defending it, I attacking it; till one day in the heat
of discussion I roundly warned my gentleman that persons who
"moved the bones," even in a spiritual sense, of the Man of
Stratford, were in danger of falling under the curse of that
great known Unknown. My heated words, as chance would
have it, were grimly fulfilled; for, a few days after this particular
argument, on reaching my friend's shop I found the shutters
closed, and a little card affixed to the entrance announcing
the death of the proprietor.

No prophetic voice came, however, to my own ears just
then, warning me that young men who frequented bookshops
to gather fuel for their lascivious thoughts are in danger of
bolts from heaven. As youthful opinions go, I was orthodox
enough in those days both about God and about Shakespeare.
It was only after I had lectured in Germany, and made friends
with German professors, that serious divergencies from
received human opinions began to sprout up in my rustic
mind. Meanwhile, as has happened before in human psychology,
correct opinions continued to run parallel with secret vices.

I found a small bookshop in Eastbourne, whose proprietor
—almost as youthful as myself and by no means confined to a

high stool—dealt in a sort of private lending library of fantastical "erotica." The chief peculiarity of this young man—
who by the way must have saved many perverse persons from
putting thoughts into actions—was the muted whispers in
which it was his custom to speak. He gave me the impression
of being a priest—a somewhat ambiguous young Ion—of the
worship of the mother of Eros. Never once did I hear his voice
raised above this sacrosanct murmur. From him I procured
much dubious printed matter, which with trembling hands and
shaking knees—for "wicked" books, have always seduced me
far more than "wicked" persons—I would carry back by train
to Cooksbridge and carefully conceal when Mrs. Curme came
to say good night.

It was, however, from the Brighton shop that I bought in
French the *Memoirs of Casanova*, and I may say at once that it
was more for the sake of my vice than for the sake of my
culture that I learnt this "language of civilization" as they call it.

I was indeed torn in two directions as far as books were
concerned. I soon acquired a mania for reading Guy de Maupassant. This was not, I can assure you, due to any love for his
"art"; for I held then, as I hold now, that that kind of tricky
brevity is the very lowest form of literature. Nor was it due
to any respect for his ideas; for the materialism of this Norman
sportsman, whom Nietzsche so guilelessly calls "that great
Latin" never had the least appeal for me. I was one who on the
one hand remained an obstinate idealist, and on the other hand
remained a desperate pursuer of cerebral lusts. But this cult
for Guy de Maupassant's works most fatally conflicted with
my passion for old quartos and folios.

I actually went so far as to carry in my arms—it was as
heavy as half a sack of flour—that colossal first edition of
Dryden's *Vergil*. I carried it over the Downs to the train at
Lewes, scrambling up Mount Harry like a maniac, glowering
down like a demon at Sir George's umbrageous domain,
hurrying past the racecourse, and not resting till I had exchanged
my burden for I know not how many paper-backed volumes
of the French Realist. But no sooner had I scrambled through
these books—and I devoured them day and night—than all I

wanted in the world was to get back my *Vergil*! This, by means
of drawing still deeper on my domestic exchequer, I eventually
did; and though I doubt if my dear son will ever want, any
more than I ever wanted, to *read Vergil* in that un-Vergilian
translation, he will, I hope, be pleased to see this stately tome
ornamenting his shelf for many a long year. It will at any rate
be a "cloudy trophy" of the intermittent character of his
progenitor's aberrations.

No member of my extremely inartistic family has less of an
artist's feelings than I. My father has managed, in his majestic
and silent way, to instil into me the feeling that it is undignified,
affected, effeminate, and even fashionable, to take the least
interest in bric-à-brac, or what they call "objects of art." Thus
I can well recall—and I am to-day thoroughly ashamed of this,
for my father would never have done such a thing—habitually
tearing out the fly-leaves of my books to use as "spills" to light
my pipe. I was a destructive idiot in this; but it was a different
thing from when once as a child I beat off the heads of a
quantity of daisies with a stick, because two girls were insisting
on amusing themselves with each other and ignoring me—
I can remember the furious life-hatred—it was in a meadow
at Upwey near the Wishing-Well—that filled my heart as I
murdered those daisies.

And yet parallel with this boorish brutality I would carry
my insane fastidiousness so far as never to allow my masculine
guests to touch a book on my shelves after visiting my privy
until they had washed their hands. I can remember once when
Theodore came from his Suffolk farm to stay with me at Court
House being rebuked by him for this lapse from gentlemanly
behaviour in terms so extreme that I never erred in *that*
manner again! But I erred in much worse ways.

That is the curse upon anyone who has once got the gad-fly
grubs of neurosis under the skin. These devils have no sooner
been driven from sucking blood out of one part of you, than
behold! they are trying it again at another. All I can say is—
for the comfort of any kindred sufferers who may read these
lines—that it *is* possible, by the crafty use of certain habitual
mental tricks, without having to retire whither my poor guide

to Court House retired, to go on living in the world and having moments too of thrilling enjoyment, while you remain perfectly aware that you are *not wholly sane*. Let me indeed breathe this in your ears. There is a deep and subtle pleasure, that only we madmen know, in outwitting these psychiatrists by never being driven to the point of having to undergo their treatment, or if you *have* to undergo it, in making them believe you are cured, when you know perfectly well you are *not* cured! And let me add, that, just as I saved myself from my worst suffering at Sherborne by pretending to be mad, it is possible to save yourself, *the other way round*, by pretending to be sane!

Well, to continue my story. It was about this epoch that I suddenly became obsessed by a terror of being killed in a railway accident! This fear I overcame in the most shameful way; a way which I kept secret from everyone. Littleton, Llewelyn, my *other* Littleton—they are all now hearing of this, with the rest of my readers, for the first time! *I secretly always travelled first-class*. I now can remember the queer sense of shame—feeling my father's majestic eye upon me in unspeakable reproach—with which, at the little aperture in that Cooksbridge station I used to receive my *white ticket*. "First-class return to Eastbourne, if you please," I would murmur, in as natural a voice as I could assume; and there was the white ticket, handed out to me quite simply, as if I had been Sir George himself. That bit of cardboard used to burn in my pocket as if it had been the "yellow ticket" that poor Sonia had to get in *Crime and Punishment*; and once how covered with confusion was I, when an easy-going acquaintance of mine, passing along the platform at Lewes, perceived, crouching in that padded interior behind the carefully curtained window and those cushiony supports for languid wrists, the familiar hooked-nosed profile and protruding upper-lip of his crony, the tenant of Court House! I got the notion, you see, that first-class passengers did not appear so frequently in the lists of the dead in railway accidents as did those who travelled third-class; and I suspect I was not far wrong in that conjecture.

It must not be supposed that because, with my stomach

seething with acids struck from the rock of my nerves by the rod of my vice, I would give my five Eastbourne lectures upon a glass of milk and an oaten biscuit, that I had outgrown that greediness which transformed Powys Major into a demon, who at Tuffin's pastry-shop would gorge itself on apricot paté, and at Wildman's tea-table would devour plateful after plateful of stickily-new bread and butter, using its front teeth like a famished rodent.

I had my mania for bread and milk all the while I lived at Court House, and I found a bakery in Brighton where they sold a particular kind of whole-wheat bread, very sweet and very thick and fragrant, which, melting in the milk, formed a gruel as "thick and slab" as an ogreish heart could wish. The same Lewes acquaintance who caught me in that first-class carriage caught me once running breathlessly up the hill from the Brighton front to the Brighton station, with my arms full, not of classical folios, but of naked loaves of bread, which according to my notion of what was poetical, I would insist on hugging to my breast without any paper covering.

My conscience was just as active, however, as my vices; and though the gastric acids induced by my activities used to pour out over my ulcers like sea-water over sea-anemones nothing could induce me to relinquish my exhausting editorship of *Ultima Verba* and *Noctis Susurri*, or my eternal assignations with Mr. de ——. Towards this old gentleman indeed I acted more like a devoted young woman than like a fellow-poet.

But a great event came into my life at this time, namely my first encounter with Bernard Price O'Neill, my best and life-long friend. I owe my friendship with Dr. O'Neill entirely to my marriage. Without my marriage I should never have known this man of unique genius. A double-dyed Celt, born of a mingling of Irish and Welsh blood, Bernie O'Neill has been not only my best friend but the best friend our family as a whole has ever had, or is ever likely to have. It has been his custom for years—and long may it remain so!—to visit every one of my father's offspring in faithful sequence during his summer vacation from his London practice. We all tickle his comprehensive humour in one way or another; and without betraying a single confidence—for his discretion is as deep as his comprehension is wide—he has acquired a particular and separate understanding with each one of us. How it has come about that such comprehensive sympathy is possible—for all of us *feel* as if we were divided from one another by fathomless gulfs—it is impossible for me to say.

Though Bernie is an admirable physician, I cannot think that his comprehensive human instincts are scientific. I think they are what Spengler, speaking of Goethe's mental processes, calls physiognomic. They betray an æsthetic as well as a mystical relish for the fact that people's characters are as fabulous as they are. They penetrate and enjoy, these instincts of his, as if everyone he met were a precious plum-coloured morocco-bound volume, printed by Baskerville.

What have we not, we Neanderthal-skulled Powyses, learnt from this soft-voiced humorist, this whimsical connoisseur of the Daedalean Palimpsest! His very expressions have been dipped again and again in the dyeing vats of each of our separate styles of living, of thinking, of speaking, of writing. He had, he *has*, the hall-mark of the true humorist, that trick of using the same imaginative tag, like the refrain of an old magic song, again and again, applying its point, its tang, its prosperity, to the contrasting chances of the moment. His goodness is the goodness of Nature herself, something easy, inevitable, spontaneous, non-moral, beyond the ordinary distinctions of right and wrong. His quaint aphorisms, no! not aphorisms, his fantastic oracles, no! not oracles, his rare commentaries, all these had a mellowness and a lustre from mere repetition that thickened out for us our lives, so that when we came together we quoted him without quoting him, and felt over again, in a kind of secular transubstantiation, the rich strangeness of his unique reactions! He supplied our Powysian life-cult—so rustic, so earth-bound—with overtones and undertones drawn from the erudition we suspected, the popular slang we avoided, the art we despised. He secretly fed his own fantastical imagination with revelations from the circus, the vaudeville, the argot of the market-place, the broadsheets of the whole mad Beggar's Opera of the great city. He was an adept in the extremist pages of all the Cagliostros of modern literature. He knew every drawing of Beardsley, every quip of Whistler, every paradox of Wilde. But below these, while he seemed for ever rolling upon his tongue some Shandean extravagance, it was Rabelais who garnished his most characteristic accents with the full body of their idiomatic savour.

What had Bernie done, felt, thought, said; how had Bernie behaved, reacted, *looked*, under the maddest conjunction of surprising circumstances—thus we were always reporting to each other.

Slight but plump; frail but solid, daring but retiring, wayward as an Aegripan in the train of Silenus, yet meticulous as an illuminator of ancient missals, Bernie was then, and is still, one of those unequalled personalities who appear sometimes upon the earth as if to put what are called "creative artists" to complete shame. For his unrivalled genius must e'en perish with the memory of us who know him as he is; unless, which is possible, he is destined to survive us all! For Dr. O'Neill can never grow old. Like an elfin being, drawing nourishment from some celestial fountain of youth, "age cannot wither him, nor custom stale."

His nose is thin, his lips full, his brow spacious, his eyes shining with a mixture of animal furtiveness and divine intelligence. His clothes seem always to hang heavily upon him, as if in his unobtrusive personality some court physician of field-mice, marmosets, and wombats had assumed human attire. An impassioned virtuoso under his lamp and among his books, his prints, and his thousand whim-whams of recondite inspiration, he is yet even more himself when running hastily forward, his pinched nose, grey moustache, shining eyes, perspiring forehead, protruding, like his arms, from his bundled attire, until falling down on his knees before the object that has excited his attention, some fairy-ring, some caterpillar, some fungus, some flower, some beetle, some moth, some slow-worm, some feather, some gossamer-seed, some bit of moss or lichen, some queerly-marked leaf, or oak-apple, or rose-blight, or cuckoo-spit-grub, he examines his treasure with the ardour of an obsessed naturalist.

Heaven forbid I should annoy him, as Coleridge annoyed Lamb, by the over-unctuous tone of my words. I would fain describe my friend as Suetonius would describe a Cæsar. But certainly to see him advancing along the middle of a country lane in his woolly vestments, peeping, peering, pondering, pillaging and for ever making little violent rushes, like a Pantagruelian humming-bird, from hedge to hedge, is to see a human being for whom no single leaf's tracery, no single butterfly's wing, no scratch, no mole, no stain, no scurf, no wrinkle, no blot, no dye, no freckle, upon the smallest spore of organic life, lacks or is without the occult signature of the Absolute. And the same intense microscopic interest in life, half-scientific, half-mystical, that gives Bernie such a radiant look as he turns the pages of his drawings from the old Masters, and causes him to run so eagerly into fens and bogs and swamps and spinneys and forest-glades, hunting for white violets, or snakes' skins, or silver-washed fritillaries, or hawks' feathers, or fairy-cups, or golden-eyed toads, gives to his intercourse with all feminine persons, young and old, pretty and plain, a mysterious enchantment that is hypnotic. In spite of a congenital deafness that prevents him hearing everything that these "sweet-natured wenches"—for such all women seem to him and probably *are* under his clairvoyant comprehension—murmur in his ear, he behaves to them in a manner as gentle as Chiron the Centaur when he carried Argive Helen across the flood.

Indescribably happy were the days—always too short and too rare—that I was permitted to spend with Dr. O'Neill. We used to make spasmodic excursions together in many directions, although it was left to Theodore to have the crowning interest of accompanying this Celtic Rondibilis to the shrine of the Holy Bottle in Chinon on the Vienne. But I have stayed with him in one of those historic narrow streets near the British Museum, for it was in a bookshop there that we bought together the three volumes of Schopenhauer's *The World as Will and Idea* translated by Haldane; and I have stayed with him in Brighton, for I have been in his company when I was meeting the young woman who scolded me so for trying to dress her up like a postman.

But it was at Weymouth—Weymouth, always the centre of the circumference of my mortal life—that the disordered fandangos of my obsessions received their most memorable "imprimatur" from this Physician of the Bona Robas of Hammersmith. Do you recall, my dear friend, how we once stayed at the Gloucester Hotel and talked so late into the night on that moonlit balcony looking out over the glittering sands and the statue of George III? I dare say I have often, in my cat-head manner, missed some delicate irony of your invention, but I have an impression that it was at once the oracular gravity and the undeniable wisdom of some moonlit talk between Goethe and Jacobi that was the theme of your fancy that particular night. And have you forgotten all that I said to you about some anonymous daughter of Nereus, who may have been Glauce, or Thaleia, or Cymodoce, or Thoe, or ox-eyed Halie, or Limnoreia, or Lacra, or Doto, or Proto, or Callianeira, or glorious Galatea, or Orithyia, or fair-tressed Amatheia, and whose loveliness I courted, after my cerebral fashion, while you were resting for a while, out of the burning sun? It was on that visit to Weymouth that we used to dodge the grand tables of the royal hostelry where we slept and have all our meals in a little tea-shop where the eggs used to be poached with an especial delicacy and laid upon the buttered toast with a peculiar daintiness by a young woman who was far gone in her pregnancy.

It was in a tea-shop like this, perhaps in this very one, that Hardy once told me he had caught a vision of the original of his Tess, long after he had told her story; and it was of Tess that Bernie and I thought as that friendly girl waited upon us.

Theodore—who had by this time got rid of his Suffolk farm, and was staying at Studland in Dorset, not far from where he finally settled down—came on a steamer to meet us during that visit, and spent several days with us in the rooms of a Mrs. Fancy near the old backwater. I shall not easily forget the striking impression I got of this strange brother of mine as he waved to us from that incoming steamer as we stood on the pier-end. His visage could look sometimes as stern as an ancient stone circle; but at other times it would crumple up into a fathomless chuckle of amusement, when, under his heavy moustache, for he wore a moustache in those days, and often against his will, his mouth would twitch, in tune with the flickering droop of his tragic eyelids. I can well recall on one occasion during this *à trois* visit to Weymouth, how Theodore and I—drawn together by some funny ineradicable feeling for that tract of salt-marshes known as Lodmoor, by crossing which any child of my father must of necessity feel the bony fingers of the dead past grope at his vitals—left Bernie on the pebbles beyond the sea-wall, to watch whether a net, being then pulled in, had a mermaid in it, and made our way across this singular expanse, going even as far—led on by that indescribable bond, or covenant, or understanding between us—as a rather desolate copse of sea-bitten, wind-shrivelled trees, where once, *long ago*, at least so it seemed to us then, we had exchanged various romantic secrets, secrets in which certain occult symbols, such as "The Dagger and the Primrose," kept repeating themselves; secrets that were, I can assure you, far too ambiguous and bizarre to be more than hinted at to Littleton.

Theodore's attitude to Lodmoor, as well as to that thick ever-green hedge between the Public Gardens and Preston Road, along the dusty length of which we used to trail, so wearily very often, on our way home, as well as to that great stone house, which I used to think must be the biggest house in the world, as well as to that stucco house with a tower, where Dr. Smith used to live, under whose jurisdiction Penn House survived so long to be our family-refuge, Theodore's attitude, I say, to all these things, must have been very much the same as mine; full of queer, odd, not always pleasant or always pretty flotsam-tags of memory, funny feelings, that seem to be at once as sacred as those fantastical objects the Israelites kept in the Ark of the Covenant, and as negligible as the falling snowflakes upon the drive at Montacute, that Rogers used to sweep away even while they were falling.

To me all these re-visitings of Weymouth were attended

with thoughts that, as Wordsworth says of the weight of custom, were "heavy as frost, and deep, almost, as life." There were certain moments when those pebbles opposite Brunswick Terrace seemed to contain a mystery that pressed upon my brain, they and the deep greenish-grey volume of inrolling waves that were so deep just there until I felt as though they belonged *to a life within life*. Hard round wet pebbles and transparent depths of water—what was the secret they held; and what was it that made their conjunction just there so peculiarly significant? And the smell there used to be between the *outer* door of Penn House and the *inner* door—a smell that had sand in it, and faint, just discernible fish-scales in it, and riband-seaweed in it, and wet linen in it—why did that particular smell, full of sensations totally distinct from any I was feeling at this later time, always come stealing over me again?

It was the same when, with Bernie and Theodore, I crossed the ferry over the Weymouth Harbour, from the stone wharf near the entrance to the pier to the slippery stone steps at the foot of the old turf-covered Nothe. As I dipped my hand in the flowing tide and watched the short easy strokes of the boatmen, those strokes where the oar was scarcely ever turned in the "feathering" twist of the wrist which my father always used so conscientiously, my mind would be struggling to bring together three quite different strata of emotion. I wanted to give myself up to the soft, faint half-sad feeling of my escaping past. I wanted to savour to the full the rich fantastical humours of my two original companions, humours which always grew more and more divergent, as the accidents of wayfaring and the bizarre shocks of chance encounters roused them into life. And finally—and this third urge of mine was fatally disturbing to the ease of mind required for the other two —I would be all strung up with the expectation of some chance of satisfying my absorbing desire to gaze undisturbed at those feminine charms, *teretesque suras*, that at this epoch could make the world a paradise to me.

I could always confide quite freely in Bernie about such matters. He was invariably sympathetic with the most convoluted turns and twists of my perversities, and would often

T

willingly, at a word, separate himself from me when I desired for my wicked purposes to be free and alone. But how often when our excursions were over and I had lavished long precious unreturning hours on my exhausting and barren quest did I curse myself as an insane fool for preferring such a sterile search to the divine glow of his companionship! Of course on the rare occasions when my fastidious eroticism was satisfied I did not regret it; but much more often did it happen that I sacrificed my invaluable hours with Bernie and at the same time was cheated of any reward for this treachery.

Bernie and his family were accustomed, after my marriage, to stay near us at Court House; either hard-by, or in the outskirts of the village of Plumpton which lay in the direction of Ditchling Beacon. And it happened that there came, before long, to stay with Bernie, at Plumpton, just as my old friend Harry Lyon would come to stay with me, a new and most resplendent invader of my life. This was Louis Umfraville Wilkinson, in whose parents' school in Suffolk Theodore always says he was treated as boys *should* be treated at school. It was in their boyhood that Theodore made friends with Louis Wilkinson; but it was at this time, when he came to stay with Bernie at Plumpton, that I first met him. And what a resplendent personage he was! A good deal over six feet, of a frame at once powerful and soft, his locks bronzy-gold, his nose masterful, his mouth formidable, his cheeks quick to blush a bewitching carmine, Louis, fresh from Oxford, full of an irresponsible and heathen zest for adventure, was certainly a startling apparition on the twilit stage of my furtive and gingerly-stepped *pas seul* round the maypole of life.

Theodore had, in his own curious manner, prepared me for this resplendent apparition. He had, after his fashion, named Louis Wilkinson "the Archangel," and having once established this awe-inspiring appellation he would treat the word in as familiar and homely manner as if he had called his friend Golden-Locks. He would say: "This Archangel likes his meat under-done"; or he would say: "This Archangel is afraid of cows"; or he would say: "This Archangel wears a belly-band round his waist." Once when he remarked: "This Archangel is a good-looking dog," his interlocutor indignantly burst out: "Good-looking, say you? He is beautiful in mind and beautiful in body!"

Below all his exterior imposingness, however, and for all his Oxonian intransigence, our handsome Louis had many innocent and charming characteristics. He had a way of blushing scarlet, like a tall girl, at any word that put him to shame, till the blush, suffusing his manly cheeks, went burning down his soft neck till you felt that it reached his very bosom. Under the surface of his antinomian humours he was—what am I saying? he *is*—of a solid sweet-natured un-malicious disposition. He is even, under the surface, profoundly domestic, if not monogamistic, and his real essential egoism—for egoistic he certainly is—is rather that of the Mid-Victorian era than of our present disconcerting epoch. With his deep-rolling resonant voice he was born to be an orator just as I was born to be a comic actor, and I am proud to recall that I was the one who first persuaded him to stalk forth, like Mark Antony in an Oxford gown, upon the University Extension platform.

It has been one of the most revealing things in my life, the peculiar nature of my friendship with Louis. He was always, and with touching fidelity, one of Theodore's staunchest friends. He liked, admired, and respected Theodore much more than he ever has done me. With Llewelyn, however, he was the most at ease; and many a time have I listened to one irrepressible laughing-fit after another, as if from a couple of Prep-boys, while these two healthy-minded lovers of Helios Hyperion were together. I will not go so far as to say that Louis's attitude to me came to resemble the downright attitude of D. H. Lawrence to the sophisticated Middleton Murry, for Louis has absolutely nothing in common with the author of *The Rainbow*; but all those ambiguous margins and fluctuating windrows of my nature—to which even Llewelyn has referred ere now as "John's spiritual insincerity"—were to Louis unmitigated vexation. When they seemed to him authentic he found them morbid; but as a rule they struck him as riddled through and through with a perverse and sickly falsity that revolted him.

As for me I felt sometimes affectionate to him, sometimes jealous of him, but always so completely different from him that I would soon lose interest in any attempt to justify myself. The more strongly did he express his opinion of my mental and spiritual trickery, pointing out that I was betraying all the hardly-won values of the life of reason, the more my masochistic and malicious humility would lead him on to misunderstand me and lambast me further and further. At such times he resembled a great healthy-natured male unicorn, in the midst of a garden of fragrant white roses, who suddenly shows by his tossings and tramplings and rearings that a serpent has got through the picket-fence.

When we were both lecturing in America he expressed most beautifully his mixed feelings towards me in that admirable story, *The Buffoon*; and from this book the discerning reader can see how genuinely fond of me he was, but, at the same time—aye! how hurt and irritated!

The last time we met, and years ago *that* seems to me now, Louis discoursed to me, with extraordinary eloquence, on his ideas about the art of Satire, a form of literature which he insisted upon rating extremely high; in fact as high as any. The truth is that Louis, at his best, belongs to the school of Aristophanes, while I, at *my* best, try to combine the somewhat contradictory characteristics of Socrates and Euripides! I merely mention this, the latest of our many dissensions, to indicate the fascinating intellectual gulf that divided us. For of course to my mind—save for the accursed art of the short story—satire is about as abhorrent as anything I can think of! It is true I enjoy, in my convoluted masochism, being the *subject* of satire; but the satiric element in my favourite classics, in Rabelais, for instance, or in Don Quixote, I treat just as I used to treat as a child the sophisticated fooling in *Alice in Wonderland*. I take it gravely and literally! I pretend to myself by one of those lying tricks that my friend takes exception to, that it is *pure fantastic narrative*. Louis, I suppose, could catch me out over Swift, for it is hard to see how you could take *The Tale of a Tub* in this premeditatedly literal manner, but it is true I have always preferred to read *about* Swift than to read Swift;

though I have, all the same, a shrewd inkling that the particular kind of madness revealed in his terrible and revolting verses is a morbidity more familiar to me than to "this Archangel."

In those Court House days, Bernie and Louis were extremely intimate not only with me but also with Harry Lyon. There was a time when Bernie lived under the same roof with Harry Lyon, just as there was a time when he took part in the publishing business with Ralph Shirley; but these epochs were transitory. Between such a double-dyed Celt as Bernie and my formidable Saxon-Thane cousin there could not be any permanent intimacy; and, as for Harry, it only needed the conversion of this excitable Norman to the Christian religion to fling down a reverberating bomb-shell in our midst.

It was after a voyage he made to Australia that Thomas Henry actually became a practising Anglo-Catholic, and this event brought down on his devoted Bayeux Tapestry skull, not only the satiric wit of "this Archangel" but a great outburst of sheer schoolboy ribaldry from all of us except myself.

Another new friend who, as women say, "came into my life" at that epoch was, just then, steadily, year by year, leading me towards the Church of Rome; and thus, though my arguments with Harry went on with redoubled fury I was hardly in a position to make fun of him. Our earnest high-pitched ringing tones used to rise night after night from that lonely little farmhouse. I can well remember once seeing the form of a very large fox outlined against the sky on the hill above. Perhaps the strident tones of theological argument have an attraction for foxes. At any rate I remember how the beast— and it looked like a wolf—lifted up its head and barked. I let Thora out to deal with it. But Thora was reluctant to ascend such a steep redoubt in the face of the enemy.

Llewelyn was still a schoolboy at that time; but he soon went to Corpus and soon after that made friends with Louis; and then it was brought about that Suffolk country-ways— "I'll larn 'ee to be a twoad!"—and Dorset country-ways joined hands, if I may say so, in the rude heathen dance that was danced round the passionate convertite that Harry had now become. These honeysuckle rogues even composed a ditty of derision about him which they would chant in unison together, like a pair of young cannibals at a blood-feast. You might have supposed that this youthful extravagance at the expense of my ancient bosom crony would have roused me to his defence, especially as I was myself hovering round the idea of becoming a Roman Catholic; but not at all! I had suffered so much from this hard-hitting proselyte's sardonic sense of humour that I took an evil pleasure in seeing him baited. Nor will the observant reader forget the occasion at the Prep when I peeped out from my ambush by the latrine wall to see a small boy beaten by my minion. To derive a secret and malicious delight from such vicarious sport came only too easily into the circle of my deep-rooted vice.

The religious emotion is an emotion very closely connected with sex; and the feeling it excites very quickly gathers that dangerous quiver in the tone of its expression that implies some stimulated sex-nerve. Miss Weston, in her book *From Ritual to Romance*, has shown how the images of the spear and the grail in the ancient cults were a sexual symbolism converted into a religious and romantic one.

Pondering on all this now I have a notion that my platonic Idealism, running parallel with my cerebral perversity, was secretly more annoying to Harry Lyon—as heresy is always more annoying than infidelity—than all the downright pagan naughtiness of Louis and Llewelyn.

My brother Bertie formally entered at this time, as my own son did, a score of years later, his remarkable architectural office which was then in High Street, Kensington. Here the unwearied Harry Lyon would revolve, like a human searchlight, in his velvet jacket and his elegant shoes round his great table of drawings, biting furiously at the stem of his pipe, as if it were the mazzard of an enemy, and ever and anon flashing forth, from his quivering Cardinal Newman lineaments, sword-thrust after sword-thrust at those who refused to bow down before Jesus. Assuredly out of this young man's commanding mouth "there went forth," as the Scripture says, "a sharp two-edged sword!"

It was an extraordinary moment in my life when I brought

pressure to bear on my father to allow Bertie to enter Harry Lyon's office. Deep down, in the pit of my stomach, below every argument I was using, there kept tugging, as if my father's long fingers had laid hold of my navel-string, that same deep proud exclusive old Welsh prejudice against this familiarity with the papistical "House of Rimmon," which he himself was feeling! It was my father in me that all along had reserved a scoriated "Terre Gastée" at the bottom of my heart, where no lively camerado could cultivate a civilized garden.

"Up to a certain point, up to a certain point, John!" he kept repeating, when I asked him whether we ought not to have confidence in our fellow-creatures.

I can remember, too, the actual spot, at Burpham in Sussex, a few years later—at the foot of Wepham hill it was—where Harry Lyon said indignantly to me "I would like to talk to your father, *man to man*."

Ah! Thomas Henry, I am afraid you are not the only human being who would have liked to talk "man to man" with the Vicar of Montacute! No, no! Why should there not be one solitary, individual left in this lively world who is reserved with all mortal persons, "beyond a certain point, John"?

What an unfair advantage the eloquent has over the inarticulate if the inarticulate does not sometimes keep, as they say in Dorset, "his wone self *to* his wone self"!

Bernie, on the contrary, never found my father's proud reserve in the least annoying. It was the chain-armoured crusader in Thomas Henry, I think, that felt so sure that Christian humility should *be carried by force* into the remotest fastnesses of heathen pride. Bernie, being even more Celtic than my father, understood perfectly these basic withdrawings. Bernie himself is unfathomably reserved. Here are we . . . three writers . . . Llewelyn, Theodore and John; and the devil a one of us has Bernie ever taken into his confidence as to what he thinks of our writings! He, from whom I first heard of Dostoievsky, Theodore of Nietzsche, Llewelyn of Montaigne, has never, no! not once through all these years, betrayed by a single word how our books strike him! The truth is, the more I think of Bernie, the more I come to recognize that the gift of expression, whether in speech, or in writing, or in any art at all, is totally and entirely inferior to a certain indescribable genius for life.

My own genius for life in those days was shockingly crude. It is extraordinary what violent contrasts of selfishness and unselfishness there were in my habits. I would leave everybody, leave everything, leave my duties, my responsibilities, my affections, my own mental interests, in order to rush off to my weird and not very human pleasures at Brighton! Certainly my peculiar vice did—for good or for evil—help to de-humanize me, even beyond my natural and, so to say, my congenital inhumanity. To get to Brighton, by hook or by crook, became for me what his particular drug is to some hopeless drug addict. I would have gone there from a bedside, from a death-bed. I *did* go there from one death-bed. With this mania dragging at my accursed imagination I would make any tricky excuse to any mortal person. I acquired that sinister cunning that corpses sometimes look as if they were endowed with, and that madmen—with much more extreme forms of madness than mine—so often reveal!

While I was on my way to Brighton I trod upon air, I smelt stocks and pinks and lilies-of-the-valley. I resembled a magician's puppet come to life. I ran down the slopes of the hills. I imagined myself on the way to some incredible paradise of sylphs. All this was not—you may be sure—for the sake of any real sylph, any more than Don Quixote's feelings for his imaginary Dulcinea were a real lover's feelings. It was for the sake of *anonymous ankles*, that I rushed over those miles and miles of downs, ankles whose accompanying human personalities I could not have put up with for half a day!

All this while my gastric ulcers used periodically to seize upon me and make me press myself upon railings and lean over gates and jab my knuckles in desperation into the pit of my stomach. My nervous excitements used to cause the most deadly acids to pour forth within me, and trickle, like drops of some fermenting devil's brew, upon the raw places they constantly aggravated. I used to tell myself as a sort of comfort—

and I still hold it to be the truth—that I was lucky to have these sufferings in a portion of my body so far removed from my brain. What I always regarded—and still do—as the worst kind of suffering is pain in the head, pain caused by neuralgia or by earache or toothache. My ulcers were often intensified by spasms of villainous dyspepsia, and they would wake me up at night, and I would roll from side to side, in sharp distress. These nightly attacks were always what I dreaded most. In the daytime—though I used to twist about on the floor sometimes, as Llewelyn noted later, like an injured wasp—I always seemed able to keep up my high spirits. I frequently felt happy and strong within my soul even while I was writhing like a wounded slow-worm.

Following the example of my father, I used at that time to bathe in the sea with a grim and stoical joy. I never did this at Brighton, for I grudged the waste of precious minutes that could be more excitingly spent, but I always bathed at Weymouth whenever a chance offered. I had never won more than my "Reds" at Sherborne, which meant that I could not swim very far; and I wonder now to think of the courage with which —coward as I was—I would swim out into the sea beyond my depth and then turn and swim back. When I turned to go back I had to concentrate my whole nature upon my intention to get into my depth again. These occasions when I swam, even a short distance, out of my depth, often come back to me now! I used to get a thrilling pleasure when with my head elongated above the waves, and feeling as primeval as an ichthyosaurus, I would stare at that noble line of cliffs, Redcliff and White Nose and the rest, stretching away towards St. Alban's Head!

By the way I always think of that monumental promontory under the name of St. Alban's Head, though they now tell me it should be "St. Aldhelm's" after the Saxon saint who founded Sherborne School. But my father thought nothing of St. Aldhelm. He had a childish difficulty in pronouncing certain words; and when this difficulty arose he either *made them his own* by mispronouncing them, or he relegated them to a limbo of artistic and fashionable affectations.

My own malicious hostility to both fashionable and affected

people finds a deep and I dare say a misanthropic satisfaction
in saying "St. Albans" when I know it is "St. Aldhelms"; and
I fancy this obstinacy of mine is an illuminating psychological
illustration of the amount of malice and black bile that is so
often mixed in with the poetical and romantic element in all
Conservatism. The truth is I am a born *reactionary*; and so I
think is the Devil. It is God who enjoys stirring things up
and forcing the past to lose itself in the future. The Devil has
a romantic passion for the past; and when you carry the past
far enough back it becomes the chaos out of which our
energetic and lively world scrambled into being. But, mark
ye, I am not so conceited as to think that life would be toler-
able or even possible if left to the Devil. It is at some compromise with God and his evolutionary methods that we ought
to aim.

But to return to these occasions when I stared at St.
Alban's Head as I was swimming, with considerable trepidation,
out of my depth. It has now become a kind of religious rite
with me, like muttering a Latin Psalm, to revive the feelings
with which I swam out of my depth. I turn it into a mood in
which, with the pride of the devil, I defy the world! I am at
bottom a sort of three-in-one, like a Welsh Triad! I am a
Punchinello, a Proteus, and an extremely fussy old woman.
And this Punchinello-Proteus, old-Miss-Betsy soul of mine
can change its triadic skin like a snake. And it can work the
most curious conjuring tricks. It can for example derive
extraordinary pleasure from feeling itself to be *a young girl*.
This girlish metempsychosis is the one that I enjoy toying with
in my imagination most of all. And this is exactly—if you are a
real psychological critic—what you would expect a Wordsworthian like me to feel. Of course I often enjoy feeling myself
to be an extremely old Punchinello-Puppet, but when I change
from this into the part of a young girl, in the complicated
cosmic play of which I am the protagonist—aye! but what a
thrill I get! It has always been a singular satisfaction to me to
indulge in this curious imagination. I derive a quaint sort of
genuine erotic pleasure from turning my withered elderly
shanks into girlish limbs.

Indeed my own view of all this pathological theorizing that Freud has started—my own sympathies are very much in favour of Jung—is that our present psycho-analytical dogmas break down when they deal with a person who, like me, has both an abnormally powerful imagination and an abnormally strong will. For myself I disagree with this whole modern tendency to disparage the will and the imagination in favour of *letting yourself go*. My theory is that it is with the reason that we attain the irrational, with the will that we change our character, and with the imagination that we re-create the world!

If for instance I were to announce to an orthodox psychiatrist that I derive extraordinary pleasure from imagining myself a young girl, especially with a young girl in love with another young girl, his stupidly rigid pigeon-holes of thought compel him to think of me as—well! you know the sort of jargon he would use in the effort to turn me into some fixed, definite, finally-labelled victon of abnormal eroticism. Not at all! A person can be childish without having infantile fixation. A person can be influenced by his father without having the opposite of the Œdipean Complex. What I would say of myself is that I have a morbid fastidiousness, a super-refined, almost *maidenly* detestation of the grosser aspects of normal sexuality. It seems quite simple to me. In my non-human cult for impossibly slender sylphs I resolve myself—like all true contemplative ecstatics—*into the element I contemplate*.

When I write my essay about my great master Wordsworth I shall show how his cerebral mystical passion for young women is intimately bound up with his abnormally sensual sensitiveness to the elements. *He wanted his girl to be an Elemental*. And in his poetry—where people betray their deepest souls—he loved, above all, to *imagine himself a girl*. I myself idolize the particular type of a girl I call a sylph to such a tune that I want to destroy everything that is not sylph-hood. But I still want to make love to what attracts me! And so, refining upon flesh-and-blood and winnowing flesh-and-blood, till it becomes purified if not beyond Nature certainly beyond normal *human* nature, I contemplate my sylph as if I were another sylph, or, if you prefer it, as if I were a salamander contemplating the ravishing limbs of an undine. It is extraordinary to me, considering the abnormal strength of my constitution and the demonic force of my will, how brittle, how fragile, how attenuated, how purged, thinned-out and transparent, how like a quivering candle-flame, all my intensest responses to life are. When I am peaceful and content or when I am struggling with obstacles I feel perfectly solid and opaque; but the minute a thrilling wave of happiness transports me, I feel as if I turned into air, into fire, into water! I actually experience the physical sensations of floating, of flaming, of flowing. Who knows if a certain kind of happiness does not dehumanize me and restore me to my natural birthright of Elementalism?

It was certainly towards the non-human condition of floatingness and flowingness that I struggled, when, by swimming out beyond my depth, I felt as if I resolved myself into air and sky and sea! One of the most daring things I ever did—and Dr. O'Neill can bear witness to it, for I was with him when I did it—was to swim out into the deep sea from Chesil Beach! I had heard my father speak of doing this, and so I must needs do it too, although Bernie himself, a very good swimmer, refused to swim so far. Indeed I have never in my life seen any mortal person bathing off Chesil Beach.

And now I must turn to quite a different matter. I have always had a very strong, an almost hurtingly strong sympathy with tramps. I would identify myself, in a sort of imaginative projection of my spirit, with these strange wayfarers. There is an awareness that has been the accompaniment of all my days; namely an intense realization of the privilege of having a roof over my head, a blanket over my bed, dry boots on my feet, a good fire to warm my shins, and a dish of bread and milk in front of me! Never have I taken for granted the inestimable privilege of being assured of the necessities of life. It is the one point where I drop my touchy individualism and grow humanly and most humbly thankful. I feel grateful not only to Chance, but to the actual human race, whose "collective" activities in this great twenty-five thousand years "Plan" of theirs, have given me protection from these elements I am always praising so! I remember well picking up a drunken tramp once, near that ditch where I fought with Littleton when he sneered at the Irish Party in Parliament, and helping this troublesome companion along the road so that he might sleep in my empty stable; and I was astonished at the haughty distaste with which my old friend, Mr. de ——, advised me to let the fellow alone.

"He belongs to the rabble, Powys," he kept muttering as the tramp lurched against us. "He is devoid of intelligence." And then irritably avoiding the man's staggerings, Mr. de —— would continue quoting Lucretius to me, and demonstrating from the Milky Way above our heads, the absurdity of yielding *our* intelligence to the superstitions of the vulgar herd.

As I say, I owe the friendship of Bernie entirely to my marriage, which was a singularly happy one; and I owe to my marriage too my chance of developing and deepening another intimate friendship I made at this time. I refer to my relations with John William Williams. J.W.W. was the first real *Papist* —that race of beings regarded by my father as in some especially close conspiracy with the Devil—whom I had ever spoken to in my whole life; and I was simply spell-bound by a *wisdom* that seemed like a deep rich earth full of divine nourishment where grow the multitudinous roots of the things—so many of them!—that I had come obscurely, and in my own fumbling and clumsy and rustic way, to value.

My nature at that time simply craved this kind of nourishment—something with a real tradition behind it, where the myths I loved, and the ballad-poetry I loved, went down deep into the soil of history. I was a born clown, a born zany, with senses porous to the mysterious magnetism of the Cosmos, and with the rooted gravity of a dedicated Simple Simon. That passage in Matthew Arnold's poetry that uses the extravagant phrase: "And through his lovely mien let pierce the magic of the Universe!" would at that time have applied to me, if, in place of "lovely mien" you used my old appellation at school. "And through his ugly mug let pierce the magic of the Universe!" The intermittent hurting, from my gastric ulcers, did a great deal to keep me in a state of nervous jumpiness and touchiness; and at the same time this sharp distress, in the very centre of my magnetic vitality, seemed to increase the devouring intensity of my peculiar vice. The sharpness of the discomfort caused by my ulcers seemed to have the power of transforming itself into lust. Out of these recurrent spasms of vicious hurting a sensitized and electrified *fluid* seemed generated, that was always forcing its way up from the depths of my being! And this devil's fluid in my occulted midriff seemed to be a "conducting" rather than a "non-conducting" element, and through it, as through an intensifying medium, certain thrilling waves of magnetic vitality, coming from what seemed like some underlying planetary reservoir, kept pouring, keeping my spirits up in spite of my physical suffering. This suffering, you must understand was not a perpetual accompaniment of my days. Sometimes for weeks I would be free from it; and then it would return. It was recurrent and intermittent; and I dealt with it as I had done since it first attacked me at school, where it was intensified by those heavy sodden masses of new bread and butter that I hungrily swallowed twice a day, and by my orgies at Tuffins' pastry-shop. At the Prep the butter had been—to my taste—so unpleasant, that, just as Llewelyn used to do at home, where the butter was perfect, I would make a "sop" of it in endless cups of strong sweet tea. Now, in place of this, I had bowls of bread and milk. These I used to prepare with a great ritual for myself. I would crumble up the new loaves of whole-wheat bread that I carried home from Brighton, hugging them, as if they were girls, in their pristine nakedness, against my throbbing stomach, and then greedily devour them the minute I had got back to Court House and had washed my hands and put my head into a basin of water. On the day of lecturing at Eastbourne, where I gave five lectures in about seven hours, I never had anything but a glass of milk. Aye! how well do I recall the sensation of pressing my knuckles into my stomach while I spat forth drops of burning acid upon pavements, upon station-floors, upon railway-carriage-floors, and even on the steps of the grand houses where my lectures were given!

This hurting in my stomach went on steadily, getting

worse rather than better, for some ten years after my marriage. What I remember most vividly, out of all my years of travelling about England, for I am now approaching the beginning of my "University Extension" epoch, are of course in the first place the shifts I was put to, the miserable, exhausting, pitiful shifts—rewarded by oh! such rare oases of satisfaction—to fulfil my maniacal erotic quest on these journeys, but in the second place the sickening moments of dead-sea desolation that came to me from my ulcerated stomach. I can remember now exactly, when walking in the twilight, for I have always been thrifty about taking cabs, and like my father have always preferred to walk where it was humanly possible—"I like to be *independent*, John, my boy!"—when walking, I say, through the darkening streets of some Midland factory-town, on my way from the railway station to where my host lived, how it felt to be driven to put down my bag on the kerbstone, and, thrusting my fingers down my throat in sublime disregard of the passers-by, to struggle to retch up some of the cruel burningness in my vitals. I can recall how once when I was doing this, certain artificial teeth, what nowadays they call a "plate," fell out into the gutter, and how I groped for them in the obscurity and how gratefully I pressed them back, all muddied, into my mouth and taking up my bag hurried forward once more.

Louis Wilkinson, when we were together in America, slyly observing "his old College pal"—such was his own jest, a jest that summed up one of the most complicated relationships that ever existed between two men—emerging from his train and waving the porters off, was wont in his humorous manner to observe that my expression at those times resembled the expression of a person who was "taking up" not his *grip*—for into this savage-sounding object my travelling-bag was by this time transformed—but his cross! It was, I remember, as my train was coming into Rochdale one afternoon, that the man sitting opposite me in my third-class carriage, for I can promise you that that first-class grandeur of mine did not last long, remarked, in concern at my irrepressible gyrations: "Do th' a feel *teerible* sick, young fellow?"

By the time that I met John William Williams whose ancestors were far more Welsh than mine—and he was a friend I owe entirely to my Eastbourne lectures—what I craved to enjoy in the nature of sylphhood had become cruelly limited. So seldom, oh, so seldom, did I find what I wanted, and I only wanted to look and look, that the upshot of it was that my chief interest consisted in seeing how much I could make of the smallest cantle of "sylphishness" in young ladies. I doted on women's limbs and on their ankles, and on their necks and on the backs of their heads, but I could only enjoy what I adored when I purged—so to speak—their femininity of all those attributes that were not only irrelevant, from my point of view, but actually forbidding. There was, for me, in the regions of possibility a ravishing feminine loveliness that I desired with a lust that absorbed my whole being. But apart from this I shrank away from them. Apart from this they filled me with a singular distaste.

By degrees, however, I came to discover that I could dally with the minds of women with extraordinary advantage to my insight into life. I came to find almost all women possessed of absorbing mental interest for me. They seemed, all of them, with the single exception of *society women*, whom I loathed from the very bottom of my heart and whom I regarded as poisoners, perverters, spoilers, degraders, ruiners, destroyers, of all the dignity and poetry of human life, to be far more interested in the sort of generalizations about the universe that interested me than men *ever* were! Indeed I am ready to confess, for all my shrinking from certain aspects of femininity and my blind fury when I found directed towards myself the least movement, the least stirring, of most kinds of feminine love, I used to find the conversation of the average men I knew a heavy effort—exciting in a way, but oh, such an effort!—after the conversation of my women-friends.

But returning to "The Catholic," for so I got into the habit of calling him, I wish I could describe to you, as these mortal adjuncts and appendages of this divine spirit struck my attention, how my friend's soft black-brown hair, how his nobly rounded forehead, how his deep hazel eyes, eyes that had the peculiarity of turning black, yes! of shooting forth *black fire*, when he got excited, made such a characteristic "ensemble" with his proudly compressed yet sensual underlip, his prominent and frequently unshaven chin, his thin classical nose, his frail body. "The Catholic" had been trained to be a priest and though he had never taken the final orders, it was an instinct with him to wear the dark clothes and assume many of the external manifestations of a man set apart to ponder day and night upon God and Immortality.

On the one memorable occasion when my old Sherborne friend W. E. Lutyens, the great mile-runner, met "The Catholic" he was horrified by the greenish tinge, as of certain kinds of cavern-mosses, that had come in the passing of time, to adhere to some of these pseudo-priestly garments. Lutyens —bless his mile-runner's heart!—even went so far as to use the expression "shabby-genteel" with regard to my friend. But then our Lutyens has a shrewd smack of Teutonic blood; and it seems difficult for that great and well-drilled branch of the Undying Aryan to detect the aristocratic quality in certain types of shocking attire! Lutyens was engaged at that time in composing a poem on the Children's Crusade into which he threw all the childlike purity of his nature; but it took more than a childlike Monk of God with the feet of an Achilles to pluck the heart out of J. W. W.'s mystery!

As for Littleton, when *he* met "The Catholic," all he would say, when commenting upon the occasion, was, "Poor little man!" repeated in the peculiarly tender, and yet faintly patronizing tone that the good-natured Giant in a Country Fair might use for the irascible Dwarf.

But Bernie appreciated "The Catholic," though with less humorous unction, I think, than he displayed in the case of Mr. de ———. But with what subtle prelatical relish did "The Catholic" himself report to me his first interview with Bernie. It was in a wayside tavern, on some road out of Eastbourne, that he talked to me about him. Here this great scholiast loved to philosophize, by the hour, while the little barmaid of the place watched his extraordinary profile with as much kindness and wonder as the good Maritornes used sometimes to show,

U

in *her* hostelry, when erudite matters were under discussion. "He told me he was an Individualist," the Theologian remarked, sipping his port wine and answering the barmaid's warm gaze with the glowing courtesy of a seraphic doctor, "but I think he felt that it was very important for him to make his position clear to me at the start."

J. W. W. was at the time I knew him writing that convoluted piece of sophisticated argument which was later published under the title: "Pascal, Newman, Loisy, and the Catholic Church." How it all comes back to me, his meticulously small handwriting in the manuscript of this book and the intense passionate eloquence of his complicated reasoning! His favourite word—long before Einstein—for you must remember I am describing events that took place ere the nineteenth century was over—was the word "Relative." By the help of this magic word J. W. W. would evoke a body of rich and subtle thought that served as a sort of covered bridge between conservative orthodoxy and the most rebellious modernism.

I am not perfectly sure to this day how far I advanced with my pragmatical, pluralistical, mythological mind, in understanding his system. A system it was, however; and it was as carefully worked out as the Hegelian System itself. I think what it really did was to project a defence—anticipating some of the subtlest tendencies in Neo-Thomism—for the traditional scholastic position which cut the ground under the feet of the very cleverest modernists; not so much by "stealing their thunder," as by proving that in the circle of orthodoxy itself every basic doubt they proclaimed had already, in some profound Hegelian way, had taken up, included, subsumed, accounted for. I cannot tell you what happiness I derived from listening to "The Catholic's" expositions. His mind had an astonishingly comprehensive, as well as an extremely picturesque and dramatic scope. All my old passion for the great gnostic heresies—which have always been to me, and are still, far more exciting than any modern science—were revived as I listened to him. Here was a living Marcion, but of course, really, he was a living Athanasius, who gave me the same thaumaturgic thrill that I used to get from Robertson's *History of the Church*, as I read it in that monastic library at Sherborne, in the intervals between gazing at slender-ankled girls in the margins of old editions of *Punch*. Although the various barmaid-friends of my erudite teacher can scarcely be said to have caused me the lively feelings of those dainty ballet-dancers in *Punch*, they did, along with the port and the sherry my friend drank, give me a lovely sensation of being at last in a world where the intellect and the senses could fulfil themselves together and by their contact enhance each other.

There were moments when our two natures—this great scholastic thinker's and my own—fused themselves together in an exquisite and even rapturous flame of excitement. This generally happened in regard to certain single lines in Shakespeare, in Homer, in Dante, in Milton. I have never met anyone—no! not even Cousin Ralph, though his knowledge of poetry was more comprehensive and his enjoyment of it more continuous—who caught the full imaginative "body," so to say, of a great inspired line in the way my friend caught it. And in prose it was the same, only here "The Catholic" had fewer rivals; for before meeting him, I had never met anyone who had an imaginative passion for Pascal or a subtle and humorous appreciation of Bolingbroke. What black lambent light used to flash from my friend's eyes as he lifted his wineglass from the little round tables of a score of Saracen's Heads and King's Arms, and Lord Nelsons, and Red Lions and Antelopes, and White Harts and George and Dragons to share with me the magical effluence—indescribable, unutterable!—transporting us both and quivering through us as if with the sweet pangs of Love himself, as we exchanged quotations from Milton! The drastically suppressed but never *quite* extinguished tendency to proselytize in "The Catholic" enhanced and intensified both the original raciness and the scholarly nicety of his critical appreciations; and indeed the mere fact that he was for ever trying to include all the rich workings of the unfathomable Cosmos within the rational-irrational circle of the Church's doctrines gave a constant excitement, like the excitement of the Quest of the Holy Grail to our discussions of our favourite authors from Rabelais down to Dickens.

I would meet "The Catholic" regularly on the days I lectured at Eastbourne, and he would come for prolonged periods to stay at Court House, where he soon became as much of a *persona grata* as Bernie himself.

There was always a certain tendency to a deep temperamental clash between Harry Lyon and "The Catholic," due to the fact that the Norman's debouchings into the sanctuary were at once more arbitrary and more emotional than the Welshman's. I well recall in the Station Inn at Cooksbridge once, making the remark, when "The Catholic" was qualifying, with rather over-elaborate caution, some wild Swift-like outburst of Thomas Henry's, that it was like Machiavelli taking upon himself to tutor Cæsar Borgia.

It was from Court House that I set off one summer to give my first trial lecture at Oxford before the University Extension authorities. Incidentally I had to speak before a considerable audience; but this audience had no idea that the speaker was on his trial, and this ignorance made everything easier. By some occult destiny, resembling the kind of destiny that Spengler gropes after in the events of history, I was called upon by Mr. Marriott, then the head of the Oxford Extension Society to lecture upon the Arthurian Legend. For this lecture it was only necessary for me to buy *one book*, namely the work on the subject published by the Professor of Celtic Literature, the Welshman, Sir John Rhys. Rhys's book, however, did not *then* give me the extraordinary mystical pleasure, I might almost say the sacerdotal excitement, that I derived from it thirty years later, when I read it over and over again on ship-board and even learnt passages out of it by heart; but it was, even at that time, a significant though a very obscure and rather puzzling book. I had already read Lady Charlotte Guest's *Mabinogion*, and I think we possessed in our own shelves, or at least our relations did in theirs, the green-covered "Globe Edition" of Malory's *Morte D'Arthur*; while *The Idylls of the King*, almost as familiar to me as Longfellow's *Hiawatha*, stood always in the Montacute drawing-room, on that old rosewood chiffonier from Penn House where they had to submit for more than a quarter of a century to the glittering effrontery of our gilded school prizes.

I cannot remember one single original point that I made in this, my first "Extension" lecture, but although ignorant then, as indeed the subtlest of our existing scholars were, of those deep erotic mysteries subsequently discovered in the *Grail Tradition* by the great Miss Weston, I must have known enough, from the *Mabinogion* and from Malory to clear away a vast amount of Tennysonian moralizing from what Spengler would call the dew-wet roots of our Faustian "culture." Anyway, Mr. Marriott, for so this energetic parliamentarian called himself in those days, accepted me very soon into the inner circle of "Extension" lecturers, and it was not long before I was travelling all over England, giving, for both Oxford and Cambridge and even sometimes for the University of London, the particular type of "Extension" lectures that were to prove so acceptable to the average intelligent public, and so contemptible to all conservative academicians.

I well recollect in the unsympathetic reviews of Hardy's tragic tale, *Jude the Obscure*, how poor little Sue's attitude to intellectual matters, and even Jude's own, were held up to scorn as branded with the unscholarly brand of "University Extension." Personally I have always been prepared to arise fiercely in defence of this sort of popular culture. You will, I believe, find on its side such great imaginative spirits as Pythagoras, Socrates, Plotinus, the Gnostic Heretics, the Scholastic Heretics, Montaigne, Goethe, Ruskin, Matthew Arnold, Walter Pater, William James; whereas, from Aristotle to Scaliger, and from Scaliger to the classical Paul Valéry, this sort of loose, irresponsible, careless, imaginative handling of philosophy has been regarded with contempt.

I had no sooner begun my life of peripatetic philosophizing than the cry "Charlatan! Charlatan!" went up. This is the particular type of abusive word, as when women call a man a *cad*, calculated, and indeed *intended*, to hurt some deep *amour propre* in the masculine bosom. But these people caught a Tartar when they called me as they have always done, and do still, by this opprobrious name; for instead of trying to ward off this unpleasant appellation, I accept it and glory in it! I am indeed, with regard to "charlatanism," what Nietzsche became in regard to morality. The persons who use this term against me are exactly the type of persons who all the way down history have been the enemies of everything I value most in life. They hate, distrust, and despise imagination. Like Charles Lamb's typical Scotchman, they have no notion what the word irony means, and their only conception of humour is the sneering facetiousness of worldly common sense. Above all they distrust, out of their respectable and pompous prudence, what is a second nature to me, the dramatic gestures of a born actor! My most spontaneous and childlike feelings, feelings that spring straight from my blood, my nerves, my soul, seem to these sagacious worldlings, with their eye on the sense of proportion of our established habits of thought, a set of fantastical poses and uncalled-for outbursts of naïve idolatry.

When they cry "Charlatan!" what they really mean is: "How dare this fellow talk about Dostoievsky's Christ, and about Plato's Eros, and about Goethe's 'Mothers,' and about Wordsworth's *Intimations of Immortality*, and about the 'art' of Henry James, and about the 'critical values' of Walter Pater, and about the 'cosmic emotion' of Walt Whitman, as if these recondite subjects, complicated enough to fill the whole span of several real scholars' life-work, could possibly be lugged into an address to working-men and tradesmen's assistants!" These natural enemies of mine, these "Philistines" of Culture, as Nietzsche calls them, *dare not*, for the life of them, bring Christ and the Mothers and the Grail and the Over-Soul and the secret of Jesus and eternal recurrence and being-and-not-being and the monochronos hedoné of Aristippus and the pleasure-which-there-is-in-life-itself of Wordsworth and the absolute of Spinoza and the mystery of the Tao and Fechner's planetary spirits and the mythical elements of Empedocles and the natural magic of Shakespeare's poetry into an interpretation of the Sleeping Beauty or of the Castle of Carbonek. These are very special products of evolutionary thought, they would argue; they are questions for the erudition of scholars. They have to be studied in connection with the study of history and of sociology.

To parade such topics before an unacademic audience is to give yourself away as no better than a vulgar conjurer. Thus would speak my father's ancient enemy, the scientific professor; and I, with my father's good flannel shirt round my loins and a strip of my father's Stalbridge blanket serving me for a scarf, am still prepared not only to call St. Aldhelm's Head St. Alban's Head but to regard the magic of the *Mabinogion* as a nearer approach to the secret of Nature than anything you could learn by vivisecting dogs.

Does my agitation seem to you not only extravagant but extremely affected? Well! if it *is* affected it cannot be an interesting case of paronoia, megalomania, and maniac elation! Or do you want to regard me as both a humbug and a madman? Personally for myself, I would define this vein of "charlatanism" in me which you are so afraid of as the clown-element, or the comic-actor element, *in the essence of all psychic truth.* Without this element—which is the perilous drop of the aboriginal berry-juice of old Saturn's blood—the pursuit of truth would resemble something between a four hours' speech by Mr. Gladstone and a four weeks' visit to some scientific retreat, where they investigate dogs' saliva through slits in their necks. In plain words truth would be, as it is to these haters of "charlatans," something at once portentously pontifical and shamelessly cruel.

According to the admirable system of University Extension the lecturer was always entertained in private houses; and thus it came to be my destiny to become exceptionally familiar, not only with all parts of England, but with all manner of types of English family-life. I have a shrewd suspicion that this perpetual living among strangers, this perpetual talking to strangers, helped to deepen my congenital ego-centric isolation, just as I fancy it did in the case of Matthew Arnold for whom I have so many instinctive sympathies. He, it is true, was not a University Extension lecturer; but his labours as an Inspector of Nonconformist schools must have brought him into contact with very much the same strata of English life as that

amid which I spent this long decade of my existence. Such a
life sent the fastidious Matthew Arnold racing off to Celtic
myths and Homeric poetry, to get the taste of all that gregarious
facetiousness out of his mouth; and it must have been the
tediousness of so much of this human back-chat, even at
Oxford, that made Walter Pater flee to the country, flee to
London, flee to Ancient Rome, flee to the Cloister, flee to
the Urbs Beata of his imagination.

What is left to me now at this distance, beyond my angry
revolt against so much of it, of all those ten years of travelling
from one end of England to the other? That last sentence
expresses nothing less than the literal truth. There was one
weekly or fortnightly round among these lectures that caused
me to leave Newcastle-on-Tyne before six in the morning
when I used to see the sun rise over the bleak Northumberland
hills, lecture in Lewes, after I had seen the sun set over the
South Downs, and get to my home in West Sussex that same
night. But what do I remember of all this? What did all this
add to my own secret mental and æsthetic development? I will
answer you in a sentence. As in the case of my three years at
college, these years of travelling about England stored my
mind with a heterogeneous chaotic mass of fragmentary
impressions; impressions, not of people, for they, with a very
few exceptions, have passed almost entirely out of my mind,
but of various aspects of the Inanimate. These are the sunken
treasures, heaved up from the deep-sea bottom of my incon-
stant memory, by a thousand little daily chances, that I owe
to my ten or fifteen years, whatever it may have been, wandering about my native land! Yes, they come into my head these
fleeting pictures by what seems pure chance. I am crossing,
shall we suppose the great "flat lot" here, for in "up-state"
New York they call what *we* call fields "lots", and I will
suddenly feel myself leaning over a grey river-bridge at
Tewkesbury, or sitting under a hedge near the outskirts of
Stafford, reading Henry James, or making my way along a
pastoral field-path, between the town of Huntingdon and some
little village in those parts, where certain Swiss relatives of
my father, from Rousseau's Geneva, used to live, or entering,

in my brother Bertie's affectionate and quizzical company, some quaint little town on the river Trent where he was mending the church steeple, or finally, shall I say, walking by the river at York. York—*old* York—has so many occult and mysterious memories for me that it is no wonder that in my exile I have settled in New York.

I acquired a queer fondness for that city. I like its rambling un-antiquarian ancient walls. I liked the way you could get so quickly out of the place and into such lovely and romantic country. I liked the narrow streets and the second-hand bookshops. I liked the painted glass windows in the cathedral. There was one spot near the river at York where I once experienced a very extraordinary sensation. This was that sort of sensation that seems, when you first feel it, to be an absolute proof of the doctrine of pre- and re-incarnation; but which later strikes you as being something even subtler and more significant than that. In fact what it really comes to be is a feeling as if all such similar experiences in the lives of your ancestors were linked with yours and as if there were innumerable separate living souls within, so to speak, the consciousness of our earth, that kept on brooding for ever upon the miraculous wonder of inanimate things being like *what they are like* when you come upon them with a meditative, contemplative mind!

This experience must have taken place when I was in my early thirties; but again in my early forties, during the War, I was in York with Bertie. He was then in uniform, and at night those narrow streets had to be made pitch-dark, for York is uncomfortably close to the North Sea; but the walk I took with him this time, teasingly interrupted, though it was, by the perpetual salutes he was always returning, and though it was in a quite different direction, conveys to my mind at this distance the impression of a weir, and of an ancient dam and of a footpath through deep green grass, and of *some* kind—I am not clear about *what* kind—of tall flowers in a muddy ditch. These may very easily have been specimens of that curious plant known as "Comfrey." If so, I am sure that John the Lecturer, preparing for America, and Lieutenant

A. R. P. preparing for France, exchanged a word about their progenitor; for my father never passed a ditch without—and proud was he to be able to do it—naming Comfrey Comfrey, Water-Veronica Water-Veronica, and Meadow-Sweet Meadow-Sweet!

Gloucester too was a city I got especially familiar with; and to this day I think of it as fulfilling some deep craving in my nature, a craving that I would be hard put to it to define. Something about those particular ancient streets, those ancient bridges, those ancient cloisters, those old inn-yards, those romantic up-raised stone footpaths under Gothic masonry, used to give me again and again as I returned from my afternoon walks a certain vague obscure delicious feeling, quite impossible to put into words, but of extraordinary value in my secret life. How can I so much as approach a definition of it? It was clearly not directly concerned with any æsthetic loveliness; for when I call up now, after all these years, what pleased me most in those walks it is not of the precincts of the cathedral that I think. I think of a somewhat dilapidated entrance to this old city, a lingering twilight-darkened highway, leading up from certain vague, misty wide-stretching water-meadows. This highway, I remember, as it approached the region where in old days the city walls must have been, crossed an ancient stone bridge. Beyond this bridge, in that obscure evening light in which I always see it, the road trailed upward, *itself lingering*, so I almost feel now, as if it were loth to leave the river-mists and to face the traffic, till it led me into the heart of the town. And there was an intermediate region, between the bridge and the town, where this entrance into Gloucester seemed really, in some obscure way, enchanted. Between straw-smelling stables the road went, where, amid darkened shapes of great wagons, lanterns seemed to be moving of their own volition. Under rain-washed sign-boards and weather-stained roof-eaves it led me on; and it seemed to be always passing cavernous warehouses and mediæval-looking shops in the dark interiors of which there seemed to be flickering candles.

Was it that the thrills of mysterious delight that always

ran quivering through me as I came up at nightfall from those chilly water-meadows were the resuscitation of far-away pre-natal memories, or even, further-drawn still, memories that descended to me from my ancestors? If this latter were the explanation it was natural enough that this most purely Celtic of all our English cities, this place of enchantments, co-aeval with Caerleon and Camelot, should have stirred up these sensations in me! But in my secret heart I think my emotions went yet further back and yet wider afield. What I think did actually arise in me at such times, and arises still when those visions recur, was a re-birth of the more vague, the more intangible, the less ponderable feelings of the human race itself; not merely of certain Welsh ancestors, not merely of *my* ancestors, but of *all* our ancestors; roused up in me just at this moment by some predetermined reciprocity between my personal nerves and this coming up into the warm Gloucester streets from the chilly river-mists!

It must not be supposed that these delicious memory-vignettes snatched from out the abysm of time from my ten years of travelling about England, and coming upon me now with such indescribable enchantment, were confined to what I saw on my travels. Many of them revert directly to Sussex itself.

As I have already explained, Court House was an isolated farmhouse on the north side of the high downs, just under Mount Harry, and not far from Ditchling Beacon. On this inland side of these steep downs there lies that lovely track of wooded and pastoral country known as the Weald. Here, not very far from the Ditchling Road, were several dedicated haunts for anyone who like myself resembled a wandering wild-duck in his mania for lonely rushy meres and the solitary pond-waters of moated granges!

But I had not to go as far as these romantic spots to find a place where I could enjoy my misanthropic solitude. Just below Court House, on the outskirts of the Weald, there was a wonderful wood, of oaks and hazels and elms and beeches, called by the Walter-de-la-Mare name of "Waringore." To this wood I would almost daily repair, and penetrating into the centre of it walk up and down a narrow mossy path, strewn with rubble and fallen twigs and old dead leaves, and sprinkled in autumn by crimson toadstools and in spring by white violets. Perhaps the most ideal of all daily walks to my taste would be a narrow path through a hazel wood *on perfectly flat ground* that went on and on for three or four miles! I remember perfectly well thinking to myself as I trod this path through Waringore, that, whatever was happening to me in life, just to be able to stare at this green moss, at these fallen twigs, at these blood-stained funguses, was sufficient reward for having been born upon this cruelty-blasted planet!

But, as I say, within a few miles of us, were even more romantic spots than Waringore Wood. Of course when I make an effort to conjure up all these spirit-memories what I get back are simply certain imaginative and visual impressions. I completely forget names! There was one extraordinary old place—half manor-house, half ancient mill—that we used often to visit, quite near the Ditchling Road but I rather think on the other side of Plumpton, whose name totally escapes me. There was an ancient church, too, with an enormous yew-tree, that always had an unusual number of red fairy yew-berries on it, somewhere, it seems to me by the side of a large pond in the middle of wide-stretching woods.

Before we left Court House we made several very exciting expeditions into various neighbouring villages—anywhere within a radius of five or six miles—with a vague idea of changing our abode; for it was an unsatisfactory sensation, you must understand, never to set eyes on the orb of the sun, no! not in the height of the summer, after two o'clock in the afternoon! Some of the most vivid of all my mysterious, floating, drifting, suddenly-appearing, suddenly-vanishing islands of memory come back to me from these wayfarings. Aerial fragments of scenery, they are, *landscape-revenants*, materialized for a second, and then withdrawn whence they came! Images they are of half-seen roadways, parcels of woodland, portions of wagon-rutted lanes descending between primrose banks, isolated patches of village-greens, with muddy duck-ponds, angry geese, croaking frogs. . . . All

these visions come floating along the airways of my mind in
clear distinctness, not like aquarelles or pastels, not like ancient
oil-paintings. Nor are their margins blurred, nor are their roots,
in those mental air-spaces, left trailing, nor are their edges vague
or their shapes ruffled; and yet all their horizons are so dark, so
dark, that when they vanish, they vanish without leaving a
trace behind!

It was to my marriage I owed my first trip abroad. This
was nothing less than an excursion to Rome! I had never left
Great Britain before; and you can imagine my excited response
to the blue-smocked porters at Dieppe and the strange ivory-
tinted foreign houses along the quay. We left from Newhaven
and there was a terrible storm in the Channel that day; so that
the first thing I saw when I struggled to reach the deck from
amid the crowds of seasick people were the masts of a ship
that had just been sunk outside Dieppe harbour! We had
brought the first two volumes of Gibbon with us, as a prelude
to seeing Rome, and one of these volumes was lost for ever
in the dizzy confusion of that unfortunate crossing. So
exhausted were we indeed, after those long hours of relentless
tossing, that we remained for that night unambitiously in
Dieppe. The next night, however, we were safe in Paris, and
for several days we stayed at a little hotel called the Hotel
Louis-le-Grand, Rue Louis-le-Grand, quite close to the Opera,
a place that I afterwards found referred to in some story of
Balzac.

My cerebral inhumanity displayed itself in unnatural and
spasmodic debouchings into solitude during this trip. How
my companions and my relations ever tolerated my erratic
and wayward humours in those days is more than I can
understand. I wonder now that with one accord they didn't
dismiss me in disgust from their over-strained indulgence and
send me to the devil, to live, if I wanted to, for ever and a
day, in some dingy lodging near my alluring, lust-drugging
erotic bookshops.

Willy O'Neill, Bernie's younger brother, was with us on
this occasion, a scholarly reserved man, with hollow eye-
sockets, out of which looked a pair of the most melancholy

grey eyes I have ever seen, and it was under his hyper-æsthetic and rather sardonic guidance that we turned our innocent rural gaze upon such things as the Mona Lisa and the Venus of Milo.

My attitude to the historic works of art presented to me then was composed in equal parts of an indiscriminate idealism, derived entirely from books, for my artistic appreciation was small and my artistic knowledge nil, and a fantastical life-illusion of myself as a sort of Derbyshire-born Goethe. Goethe's *Travels* I carried with me, at least their translation in the Bohn Library Edition, and every now and then I would scribble in my note-book certain verses of my own composition, verses that gave me a curious pleasure to write, not because they expressed one single thing that I really felt, but because, while I wrote them, I felt that I was acting out my ideal of myself, as *John Powys visiting the Fountains of Rome.*

What I was really doing all this while was groping after a double fulfilment of my erotic desires and my intellectual desires. And yet this is not altogether true; for I moved blindly, desperately, and with a certain abandoned reckless-ness, along my obscure "Gloucester Road" of lonely personal sensations. How do I justify such behaviour? How do I justify —do you mean—my being "the soulless monster of selfish-ness" that some have called me? Indirectly, my friend, I do this, indirectly, indirectly; for I am too wise an antediluvian monster to argue with you in *your* language. But the truth is the transports of thrilling delight that these indescribable sensations of mine give me, these feelings that I would describe as the *marginal sensations* of the human race itself, seem to me so valuable a thing to come to consciousness in this world at all, that I—as this thing's "medium," or hollow reed—am entirely justified in being as I am.

It was, as I say, owing to my marriage that this miracle of my father's eldest son being in Rome came about; but I must confess I often acted badly and ungratefully during this noble adventure. I did however eke out our funds a little by giving lectures in one of the Roman hotels to an exhausted group of young ladies from Eastbourne. Willy O'Neill's patience came to an end once, when I insisted upon giving I know not what number of cigarettes to one of those boy-flower-sellers, dressed in what comes back to me now as moss-green velvet, who at that time haunted the steps of the Piazza del Spagna. We did not quite come to fisticuffs on that occasion but to something very near it; and I remember using the excuse of our altercation to absent myself for several solitary hours.

So rusticated was I, for all my lecture-journeys, that it was in Rome that I first saw that mode of popular conveyance by electricity called in England a "tram" and in America a "trolley"; and to this day I never hear the curious tinkle of these crowded vehicles without smelling that unique smell of sun-baked horse-dung and garlic which mingled so indissolubly with my Roman impressions. It was the look of those astonishing classical viaducts, as our train drew near the city in the twilight, that gave me my first real thrill; but this selfish and indeed unkind mania of mine for seeing things alone woke me up early that first morning in our little Pension and drove me out, hurrying down the street, hunting desperately for I knew not what. What I *did*, by some chance light upon, and it was my first monument of antiquity, was the Victory Column of none other than that arch-despiser of victory, Marcus Aurelius. By this time I *had* learnt to appreciate Pater's "Marius," and it was with those magical periods of the great Sophist, periods like the eloquence of his own Apuleius rolling through my head, with all their rich philosophic fancies and all their honeyed semi-erotic affectations—"like painted flowers, Marius thought"—that I stood entranced before this pictured column, rather than with any desire to become a Stoic. I am sure I don't know by what philosophic name to name the supreme ecstasy that I had in Rome. It came to me half-way up those stately steps from the Piazza del Spagna to the Pincian Hill—I think our Pension must have been hard-by that spot—and just about opposite the house where Keats died. I remember distinctly the emotion I had at that moment; and it was one that I have never had since, from that day to this. I do not think its implication of the presence, in this blasted and blighted globe, of "a stream of tendency" to something so magically beautiful as to be a kind of Eternal Thing could be called an epicurean idea or a stoic idea. Perhaps it is an idea to be found in the old Welsh Triads!

The warm sun, the golden dust, those broad *short* steps, that seemed to us constructed so that these proud Romans should go up and down without a movement that was inelegant or undignified, the thought of the unapproachable genius of young Keats, dying but living for ever, those little boys in their moss-green velvet, the stones of Rome themselves, soft yet perdurable, like everlasting Time, the zephyr-stirred trees of the Pincian Hill, the murmur of the great smouldering city below, the far-off Dome of St. Peter's "semper eadem . . . securus judicat orbis terrarum," all these things at any rate struck my Celtic mind, just as their architypes must, ages ago, have struck the invading Gauls, as if here indeed was the Urbs Beata, the Urbs Calipolis, the imperishable Stone Circle, the undying Navel, of our poor Gothridden Corpus Mundi, Corpus Delicti! And within the straw-stuffed interior of the jerky Puppet-Idealist that I was, there formed the words of a strangely impassioned prayer: "May all this go on just as it is!" I prayed. "Let me pass, let me and my crazy obsessions pass— but let Rome abide for ever!"

Perhaps it was immediately after my silly burst of fury with Willy O'Neill that I rushed off by myself into a flower-shop and bought a laurel wreath so enormous that I was much put to it, even with the voluble driver's help, to get it into the vehicle. Clinging to the rim of this Olympian offering I was driven in triumph to Keats' grave where I proudly placed it— and more than a whole year later a traveller assured me that its remnants, embronzed leaves and twisted wire, were still to be seen.

I think the most harmonious and the most perfectly felicitous of our united experiences in Rome was once when from our hiding-place in a deliciously sunny and secluded spot on the Palatine, safely removed from the sinister ruins of the imperial palaces and close to the altar of that gentle unknown god— perhaps, for all divinities sooner or later came to Rome, an altar to Ceridwen, the Cymric Demeter—we implored our sardonic and disillusioned friend to fetch us a bottle of wine. Never have I—no! not in any land—tasted such flower-fragrant and honey-sweet wine as that with which our melancholy epicurean ally returned! In what treasure-cave of the "deep-delvèd earth" he discovered it I cannot tell; but its effect was beyond the effect of mortal grapes. It was like that Nepenthe, given to Argive Helen in Egypt, wherewith she caused both yellow-haired Menelaus and young Telemachus to forget their griefs, as they sat ensorcerized beside her, watching the purple woollen threads pass to and fro, to and fro, across the lap wherein the head of Paris had lain!

How rarely out of a person's life do moments return to the mind that are like that royal death-robe of Jesus, woven of one seam, flawless, absolute, without a single knot or wrinkle or crease to destroy its smooth perfection! Well! such was this radiant hour on the Palatine Hill; and it was with a combined gesture of deep religious feeling that we emptied that bottle's last drops to our tutelary neighbour, that gentle unknown god! It is a curious and significant thing—for before very long these lively vandals within my iron frame, my cursed ulcers, succeeded in making both wine and cake totally impossible for me—that just as in Rome Willy O'Neill fetched us that divine bottle so on our way back, before he left us at Marseilles, he conjured up an extremely aged and decrepit Frenchman, who in the middle of the night, when we were faint from want of food, offered us large slices, light, crumbly, honey-tasting, of the most miraculous home-made cake I shall ever know again. The scent of damask roses was mingled with the sharp salt airs that came in to us from the darkness outside; and as we ate that cake, rushing through the night along the shores of the Mediterranean, it seemed to me that having drunk the blood, I was now permitted to devour the flesh, of some anonymous "Numen inest," some "unknown god" of my remote Cymric ancestors, that I might—and again might not—call upon at a crisis. Or does it happen that at certain particularly sacramental moments in your life you are permitted to enter into some mysterious conscious relation with the spirit of the earth itself?

x

I used almost always to walk the four miles to Lewes when I made my professional starts in the mornings, and I generally went by the road through Offham rather than over the downs. This I did because I had my gown to carry and my elusive sylphids' essays, as well as the books, sometimes heavy ones that I had to quote from. Luckily I was not bothered with note-books, for as was the case with the old biblical teachers, the Lord, the God of my Father, always put it into my head what I was to speak. It came to pass however that after that miraculous trip to Rome which my undeservedly fortunate marriage brought me I used to suffer extreme pangs of gloomy rebellion from the sight of the quiet and harmless tradesmen's villas at Lewes, and at the sight of the quiet and harmless tradesmen themselves, blamelessly pursuing their lawful avocations. It was one of my crusading friend Harry Lyon's foibles to denounce in round terms what he called "the lower middle-classes." *We*, I suppose, were to be regarded as belonging to the upper middle-class, if not, God help us! to a niche that was higher still; but all the stupidities, meannesses, and moral hypocrisies of our land were attributed—and I listened to it all without a murmur of protest—to these unfortunate trading-classes. Looking back now upon the whole thing with a mind schooled by listening to Americans and to Communists I am amazed that I didn't speak up for these small clerks and shopkeepers and factory managers and commercial travellers and pawnbrokers and office-assistants; for after all this is the whimsical and idiosyncratic class from whose ranks our great imaginative novelists have filled the ideal world with their unequalled creations.

But my mind was really occupied with other matters; and so I submitted without protest. But looking back now on those days I am afraid any Communist, not to speak of any Middle-Western American, would have regarded the life then led by myself and by Bernie and by Louis Wilkinson and by "The Catholic"—all of us with a small unearned income—as the real cause of our gravest faults and our most serious neuroses. Bernie knew this, with an infallible instinct.

I remember well the austere glee with which Harry Lyon

who always kept his own nerves in order by desperately hard work, told me that our friend had announced: "What Jack needs is *a good sound flogging every morning!*" Well! I have learnt since then the art of inflicting this flogging on myself every morning; and Doctor Rondibilis was perfectly right.

But it seems extraordinary to me now why, when thus carrying my gown in what the late T. Oatley Bennett used to call my "ferret-bag," and hugging against my stomach all those books and papers, I didn't feel a glow of warm, secure, Charles-Lamb-like peace, and humorous life-unction, from making my way into this old country-town. In place of this I felt constant waves of angry revolt! I had at that time a mania for Hazlitt, whose peculiar kind of self-conscious egoism I can see now was an important landmark in my intellectual development; "but," I thought to myself, "Hazlitt was a sort of scholar-gipsy, wandering about the world as he pleased, and completely selfish in all the ordinary human relations. Why am I forced to live a virtuous and settled life?" And then I would quote to myself some of Hazlitt's most ego-eccentric and sentimental passages with an inward glow of admiration and envy. I tried to get hold of his *Liber Amoris* for I always fancied that I should find in that book something parallel to my own maniacal preoccupation with anonymous femininity. But of course Hazlitt's girl was anything but anonymous! I can see now, so clearly, the olive-green cover of my *Selections from William Hazlitt*, though subsequently I bought all his essays in certain separate little books that had paper covers. But with the exception of Wordsworth and Walt Whitman, I got a deeper psychic-sensuous thrill from the mere look of that Hazlitt cover than I have got *from any other book*. Peace be to his ashes! I am glad that great Nature ordained that the last words of this ragamuffin egoist, whose defiant radicalism nobody could "square," were the surprising ones "Well! I've had a happy life!"

But certain essays of Hazlitt—certain passages in certain essays—I would in those years read over and over again. They became as it were *incantations* to me, incantations summoning up my soul to be true to its inmost destiny! And what was this inmost destiny that I had the wit to recognize, though so obscurely, and, like a faint submarine light detected through fathoms of deep greenish-coloured water, the grace to follow after throughout my days? Well, I would define it as the pursuit of a certain particular type and sort and kind—it is necessary to winnow it down, through all the three dimensions, to something very quintessential—of *purged sensation*, the sort, the kind, and the type of sensation that is at once very sensual and very psychic! You see it was really something that pointed me towards this non-human road, where a self-centred egoist chews the cud of universal human experiences that I found in the touchy and cantankerous Hazlitt. Oh, how I used to repeat the lines—and I can see them now as they looked on the actual page, and the way the margin looked, and the way the capital T looked!—"Wave on, wave on, ye woods of Tudderley! Wave your tall tops!" and so forth: and it was from these sentimental-selfish ramblings, combined with the fact that the testy, dark-browed rogue was always on the side of the angels and had a mania for metaphysics, that led me to be interested in *his* ideal author—the author he evidently treated exactly as I treated him—Jean Jacques Rousseau.

How well I remember watching out the turn of the centuries —the nineteenth becoming the twentieth—in the little dining-room at Court House, a room decorated in the particular neo-William-Morris style which at that epoch was affected by Harry Lyon. I can remember absolutely nothing about my feelings at this momentous historic hour, except that I was conscious that Something much bigger than a year was dying, Something that, compared with a year, was like a sturgeon compared with a stickleback.

My son, who was born in the new century, will, I suppose, hardly live long enough—though, of course, he *could!*—to see the figures 2000 written on the newspapers, the London "Izvestias" and "Pravdas," of those days; and it is strange to me to think that before his birth, and before the birth of so many personable young men who are now my dear friends, I was watching in the pitch-black midnight under Mount Harry, the dying of this monster of time. "Wave on, wave on, ye woods of Tudderley!" It has been of interest to my son to pay a visit to Court House of late; and I do not wonder. From what shore of Limbo was he waving his arms to me then?

It was during the Boer War while we were still at Court House that I obtained the exciting job of giving a set of English lectures, under the official ægis of the Free City of Hamburg. I hurried to Hamburg, by way of Rotterdam and Amsterdam; but I had no Willy O'Neill to help me to understand the genius of Rembrandt and Ruysdael and Hobbima as I had learnt to appreciate Watteau and Fragonard. But I clearly remember feeling vividly that an Englishman was by no means a *persona grata* in Holland during the Boer War. I doubt very much that if I had even explained to those "lower-middle-class" Dutchmen, as Harry Lyon would have called them, that I shared the opinions of my fellow-Welshman, Lloyd George, and was entirely hostile to that imperial Trinity, Rhodes, Chamberlain, Kipling, it would have made any difference.

I had hit upon an unfortunate moment for my visit. But aye! what pleasure I have slowly, very, very slowly, come to derive from painting! It is the only art, outside literature, that will ever *deeply* appeal to me; and even this within rather narrow limits. But I have needed no Willy O'Neill to initiate me into my instinctive preferences among painters. My deepest favourites I discovered for myself and I am very proud of it. Domenico Theotocopolos, El Greco, I discovered for myself. Nicolas Poussin I discovered for myself. Ruysdael and Hobbema and the landscapes of Gainsborough I discovered for myself. For Giorgione and Watteau, though, I learnt to appreciate them through Walter Pater I soon found I had, if I may say so without boasting, a certain measure of natural affinity.

Angels and ministers of grace! but what an escape, what a divine escape, certain wonderful—though pseudo-classic and pseudo-artificial!—landscapes have been to me in different epochs of my life! I must hasten to confess to a "penchant" for the disparaged creations of Salvator Rosa. I like wind-torn jagged tree-branches, and I like ancient mossy tree-stumps, and I like roads winding under colossal viaducts with goats and sheep and herdsmen resting in the shade and cavalcades advancing along far-away ridges towards remote rock-built castles! I sometimes am even tempted to dally with the notion that I—the son of Charles Francis Powys—have in me some of the instincts of a landscape painter! Landscape pictures have certainly played a part in my life that I sometimes think goes down to the very bottom of my soul. *Old* landscape pictures I mean! These are the only ones that have affected my secret life, though my friends can give me their clues to the modern ones, in occasional flashes. But I need no one, I *want* no one, to teach me the magical enchantment of old faded landscape paintings! This is the purged and winnowed world of humanized Nature that my non-human passion for certain essences of human life is so deep in love with! This is the world of old bridges, old tree-stumps, old walls, old terraces, old avenues, old turrets, old rivers, old causeways, old roads, winding over historic hills towards more historic seas! This is in fact the world of that ideal "Road to Gloucester" that in the secret depths of my being I am seeking for for ever, seeking for *sans cesse*, for in it, and in it alone, is the Inanimate—an Inanimate rendered holy and fetish-like by its contact with humanity—disentangled from the vulgarity of the passing moment.

Yes, while I looked at those Rembrandts in Amsterdam the world had reached that particular sequence of months when the Dutchmen in South Africa were making it extremely uncomfortable for our Empire, and I was reminded of these public events by the immense satisfaction with which the waiters in the hotels where I stayed used to lay beside my plate at every meal newspaper headlines that grew daily more and more derogatory to the dignity of an English traveller.

Fortunately Providence has withheld from me, as it had withheld from my father any gift for foreign languages, and until I got to Hamburg and was confronted by the only too obvious, and indeed gross humour of "Simplicissimus," depicting my Sovereign, and that in the last month of her long life, in anything but a dignified position, I only realized by the gestures of derision and distaste which I underwent how intensely we were hated on the Continent of Europe.

Very distinct to this day remain my impressions of Hamburg. Those verdigris-green roofs of sombre Lutheran churches, those dark deep canals bordered by huge over-toppling sombre warehouses, that sense of something at once monstrous and fairy-story-like, that feeling as though certain kinds of commerce and trade—trade especially in such commodities as coffee and molasses and cinnamon and nutmeg and rare lumber and extravagant wines and precious perfumes and spices—had gone on in these places for a thousand years, that feeling ·that there had been great plagues in these tall Gothic houses, and that all these black-stained piles against which this sombre phantasmal canal water gurgled and lapped, were brushed night by night by the passing to and fro, to and fro, of grave black-gowned, grey-bearded ghosts, all these things made an indelible impression on one who was now sucking the dugs of the round world very much as he had sucked apricot paté in the yard of the Prep.

But I was not to escape without having a vision of loathsomeness and sickening disgust. The especial Demon, in the lunatic asylum which I kept locked up in my cat-head, whose pleasure to vex me with disgusting imaginations was so lively and obstinate, the same Demon, who had strewn the avenue to Court House with bullock's blood and black snails, now bestirred himself to attack my peace and to sap my energy.

It was in Hamburg amid all those great sloping roofs and those massive warehouses and those dark canal wharves covered with snow that I had one of my miserablest occasions of wanting desperately to find a close-stool and not finding one. So deep an impression did this devilish experience make on me that even to-day, when I see snow on the ground, I am liable to feel a twitching in my nether gut as if I were holding back the excrement of weeks. But unforgettable though this experience was—and I have noticed that priests and ministers and clergymen, and doubtless their sons too, have more difficulty with their natural evacuations than other men—my mind was more ruffled, although my whole personality was not so paralysed, by a certain coloured picture that appeared in a popular, possibly a *comic* German paper.

It was a picture that had a woman's breasts in it and in some way connected with these breasts a great deal of blood. But this blood, at least to my morbid imagination, was not ordinary blood. It was very pale, but it was also very vivid. Indeed it must have been due to a triumph of art in the colour-printing of that prosperous epoch that even from across the road this blood was visible. It seemed to have the power of leaping from the page and of splashing over my face; yes! even into my mouth and down my throat. Nor did this blood-stained Milky Way stop at my throat. It sank into me until it reached some deep-buried "loathing-nerve" that licked it up with frenzy; licked it up as fast as those centuries-blackened wharf piles licked up the plague-spotted waters of those canals! In regard to physical impressions *of a certain kind* I have, I am sure, nothing less than the Devil's own imagination. I *know* I am not being silly or conceited when I say that in certain directions I have as powerful an imagination as Swift.

In certain directions too—and with regard to certain unpleasant impressions—I am as one who goes to and fro *without a skin*. This morbid and indeed almost monstrous sensibility is something that you pay a heavy price for; nor, if you express it in writing, do you always, as Mr. de —— would say, "win favour with magnates." Magnates tend as a rule to feel as if you were saying to them: "Go, go; you're bit!" like Swift when he damns our cruelties and stupidities. Nor does a person with a terrible imagination get much pity. I know well what I am talking about; for my vitality is so terrific, my constitution so adamantine, my will so strong, that it is difficult for people to believe that so galvanized a Jack-in-the-Box, making such lively gesticulations should be completely skinless and raw under its motley jacket. Yes! I was followed about by those breasts and that blood. I used to go down to those black canals and those cinnamon-scented warehouses with hurried and eager steps, trying, as I trudged through the discoloured snow to avoid, if possible, all the innumerable shops, and book-stands and paper-stalls which made me feel as if from the paps of the whole round world issued forth milk and blood!

I was lecturing at Bremen—in English, you must understand, always in English—when our great Queen died. "We will not let ourselves," so I was told she had said, "be killed by Mr. Kruger." But she had been forced—that most arbitrary and most womanly of all great Queens—to "let herself be killed" by *something*, and dead she lay. Wept for bitterly she was by all those "lower middle-classes" denounced by Harry Lyon, and with her went the age of Dickens and Tennyson and Matthew Arnold and Darwin and Carlyle and Ruskin and Disraeli; and with the crowning of her son came in the age of Mr. Wells and Mr. Bennett and Mr. Galsworthy and Mr. Kipling. I was, as it chanced, lecturing on Byron in some old Bremen edifice when Victoria died and having broken short my exposition of the art of "dithyrambic analysis," I was taken to the historic wine-cellar. Here the rule was that if you entered before midnight—an admirable rule for such a place—you could stay as long as you liked. Was it of Byron that I thought as my student friends entertained me with their praise of the latest deterministic philosophers, or was it of the dead Queen?

Alack! It was of neither of these! 'Twas of Heine I thought, and of those strange verses of his composed in this very place, and of his weird love-affair with the executioner's daughter, and of his curious "penchant" for puppets and puppet-shows. I can well remember how, in my hotel bedroom, that next day, the windows of which opened on the buttresses and pinnacles of some mediæval-looking building, as I composed one of "Jack's descriptive letters" to be read aloud at Montacute to my father, I was seized with a real flood of inspiration. This event made a terrific impression on my mind; for it was really the first time in my life that I had known what literary inspiration meant, or had felt its peculiar and recondite thrill. It was all lavished upon one of "Jack's descriptive letters," and I am certain that my father fidgeted and even groaned before it came to end, longing to go out into the garden and stretch his legs in the terrace-walk before his morning's work in his study.

It is quaint that all I can recall of it now is a single phrase, in a long reverberating sentence, a little in the style of De Quincey. The words that come to me now are: "painted signboards swinging," but I have a vague sense that it represented a secret special delight that I took in thinking of the way an old historic town like Bremen could fade off on all sides, without the mediation of suburbs, into fields and lanes and moors and forests. I imagined the old barns and the old inns and the old churches, and the old burying-places, and the old village-shops, and how different they looked, according to whether you were entering or were leaving the walled-in city! Thoughts such as these, bringing to my mind what Matthew Arnold calls "the murmur of a thousand years" were always the ultimate winnowings of my happiest moments.

Nothing gave me a greater thrill than when my personal sensations—especially of this rich-charged romantic tinge, as of the entering or the leaving of an ancient city—lost the narrowness of their merely personal quality and became the anonymous deposit of all the generations of my race, yes! of all the men and women, who went in and went out, in the diurnal ritual of their days!

I have all my life been very well treated by Jews; and have always, as I think is generally the case with Englishmen, found all my lodgements within the tents of Israel extremely lucky for me. In Hamburg I received a great deal of hospitality from Jews. They all spoke English, and were indeed people of a most mellow and erudite culture. I recollect well coming as near, in one inspired conversation with some rabbinical Talmudish Johann Cohen, to an explanation of the mystery of fate and free will, as I have ever come to in my life. In some very deep sense these wise and courtly refugees seemed congruous with the historic atmosphere of Hamburg. Perhaps all this trading by sea in these coffees and teas and rare lumber and rarer spices, gave to the transactions of commerce something romantic, something "rich and strange," which garnished the character as well as the purses of those who took part in them.

The truth was, I got from my visit to Hamburg—but oh, how I longed for the day of my return home!—a sort of accentuation of my secret life-cult, which made me, after this experience, more deeply aware of what I was doing and where I was going. There was, in the house where I stayed, a shrill-voiced canary; and whenever I think of the place this canary's full-throated long-drawn twitterings come to me with a nostalgic pang for home and the feeling of black canals, white snow, verdigris-covered roofs and a stream of blood from a woman's livid breasts.

Back once more at Court House I began the twentieth century, just as I had ended the nineteenth, by the concentrated search as I travelled these long distances up and down the country, for the two master-sensations of my life, the sensation of enjoying protracted ecstasies of saurian lust, as if I had been a cerebral "voyeur" among ichthyosauruses, from gloating over the anonymous and if possible the *unconscious* bodies of feminine representatives of my race, and the sensation of enjoying, from the wanderings of stray gusts of evening-wind, from the glimpses of stray columns of dawn-smoke, from the motionlessness of old barges beside old weirs, from the flowing of grey waters under gothic bridges, from the groaning of demon-branches by desolate cross-roads, a purged and yet an universalized essence of all those marginal experiences that fill the poetry-books and the ballad-books.

Those were the days when in my travels about England I greatly enjoyed two other things—the pleasure of eating enormous quantities of raw sweet chocolate, instead of anything more varied, for my daily lunches, and the pleasure of reading insatiably volume after volume, all the novels I could lay hold of, of Dickens and Thomas Hardy. I used religiously to force myself to ponder, as I travelled, upon some confounded, never to be written romance of my own; and aye! the sweet, the voluptuous relief, when, after these accursed attempts to fix my mind upon imaginary scenes and persons, I used to sink down in my third-class seat, with my back to the engine, while through the window came the varying scents of half the countrysides of England, and luxuriously turn the pages of these enchanting books. I can recall sitting on a bench in the autumn, in some public park at Southampton, absolutely absorbed in a trance of delight in "*Little Dorrit*," and all the while voraciously devouring "plain chocolate," much in the same way I used to nibble chocolate creams at Westbury House, while lost in the excitement of *Twenty Thousand Leagues under the Sea*! And just as even to-day I rarely see the sun going down without recalling how Captain Nemo from the deck of the *Nautilus* uttered the words: "Descend thou radiant Orb!" so it is hard to see a dwindling hill-road without thinking of Hardy or a grotesque chimney-pot against a lowering sky without thinking of Dickens. For myself it is a certain picturesque expanse near some wharf steps with all manner of congested barges and other small craft in the very heart of Bristol that I mingle now most clearly with my memories of these chocolate feasts. How I used to be "divided, this way and that, in the swift mind," between swallowing all, all, *all* of what I purchased, and handing a scrap, a morsel, a moiety, to some youthful passer-by!

There was one large and sombre house in Arnold Bennett's *Five Towns* where I used to stay, that had a curious and convoluted interest for me and not a few temptations. At a later date, when Llewelyn was thinking of coming to America with me we came together to this house. Indeed we journeyed together round the whole fortnight's circle of my far distant lecture-places, beginning, and I think ending, with Manchester. He conjured up however in his whimsies, his flights, his penetrations, and his final judgments, such scandalous names for my various hosts and hostesses, that for fear any of them or of their offspring should ever glance at these pages I dare not reveal them! While he amused himself in this manner I was trying to force him to read *The Prelude* as a way of preparing himself for crossing the Atlantic, but in the stir and the back-chat and the human encounters of those days he did not read very far.

It was in one of the most characteristic of these Arnold Bennett *Five Towns*—a place where I even went so far, when I was in one of my "divine," as I was wont to say, rather than one of my "devilish" moods, as to design a Pantagruelian amphora for my son, now soon to be born, upon which I caused to be engraved the words: "bon espoir y gist au fond" —that this old large dark house was, where the devil used to whisper in my ear as I went in and out. But my nights always ended innocently in this place; for I would retire at an early hour and find a noble great fire blazing on my hearth; and for hours and hours I would sit up reading *The Return of the Native* or *Far from the Madding Crowd* or *The Woodlanders* or *Jude the Obscure*, while all the while voluptuously and luxuriously, more after the manner of a young woman than a young man, I would take piece after piece of chocolate out of my bag and nibble it in my absorption; till by degrees as I listened to the wind in the chimney the genius of Hardy would drive my demon away and some formidable Spirit from Stonehenge would come rushing out of the Magic West into this dark house and my whole inner being would change. Then I would sit with my bony knees close to the red coals and feel myself to be as formidable and as powerful as that south-west wind itself! I would feel myself to be what the great Magician Merlin was before he met his "Belle Dame Sans Merci."

I was still living at Court House when, leaving "The Catholic"—even as one would leave one's Father Confessor— to guard my castle in my absence I set out alone with Bernie, to spend a fortnight in Paris. "The Catholic" told me afterwards that he was singularly tickled by the extreme naïveté of my letters home, extracts from which were daily read to him. I would, it seems, always close my oratorical account of some famous picture in the Louvre by such quaintly blunt words as: "The colours are red, pink, green, and a peculiar purple. The shadows are dark-red, dark-pink, dark-green, dark-purple, and in some cases nearly black. There are some curious blue and silvery spaces in this picture."

The pathetic thing about my pursuit of my erotic vices at this time was my ignorance of the various devices by which Nature—even with a fastidious maniac like me—could have side-tracked it into satisfaction. As it was, this desperate, exhausting quest of mine, instead of leading me to any satisfying "Grail," whether Christian or Pagan, led me, like the restless Sir Pellenore, into a hunt after a quarry that was itself a "Questing Beast." And oh, how nauseated and sickened and disillusioned and seized with a deep loathing I was, during that visit to Paris! Bernie, like all wise, humorous imaginative persons dealing with a fanatical idiot, often went his own way, leaving me—for he had his own affairs to attend to—to shift for myself. I went therefore—just as any simple-minded East-Anglian on Theodore's Suffolk farm would have been led to go, had he been in Paris; though on my life I think any bellringer at Montacute would have known better—to one of those gala-night places adapted to the grossest Anglo-Saxon taste.

How different from one another are the wandering erotic desires of mortal men! I suppose there may have been a certain number among the boys in Wildman's House, whose "amorous propensities," as Dr. Johnson would say, might have been excited by this particular resort. Perhaps it would have appealed to the blue-eyed old gentleman whom "Aunt Stone" looked after when his wife retired into obscurity. But to see a person and a fairly good-looking person, belonging, or apparently belonging, to the same sex as the most ravishing of my sylphids, tossing up a flurry of petticoats and displaying a flurry of under-garments and then drumming on her rump with her fist, while she screamed: "Bon face! Bon face! Bon face!" in the very tone that Punch, on the donkey-stand at Weymouth, used to cry "Toby! Toby! Toby!" was a spectacle, as far as I was concerned, calculated to freeze into Arctic ice every lecherous impulse in the human frame. In the end I set out alone for Rouen in order that I might enjoy—while I struggled to get that obscene cry, "Bon face! Bon face! Bon face!" out of my head—Ruskin's favourite façade of St. Ouen. It's a wonder, however, that I didn't behold, poised above those flamboyant buttresses and battlements and pinnacles, some colossal Gargamellian rump, pedestalled on that heaven-aspiring pile!

But what did come upon me in Rouen—making me forget both the puritan eloquence of Ruskin and the civilized amusements of Paris—was a diabolical attack of my gastric ulceration. Oh, how I twisted and writhed on my bed in that little Rouen hotel; and how I cursed, from the very bottom of my nauseated heart those pestilent French cooks before whom the epicurean Heine, after visiting London, fell on his knees in religious adoration. To confess the truth French cooking had the same vertiginous effect upon me as the antics of French harlots.

I am anxious however to revert to the characters of my four chief *male* friends of that epoch. I knew very few girls who were acquainted with all four of them; but it certainly would have revealed their subtlest peculiarities most beautifully, and in a manner worthy—if such a paradox may be hazarded—at once of Henry James and Dostoievsky, if one of my girl-friends *had* encountered, freely and without restraint, these four remarkable persons. I can visualize, like a map, the situation that would then inevitably have ensued! Harry Lyon would have talked to the girl, while she was with him, with the utmost tenderness and consideration. He would have entered into many of her most feminine problems with the gravity and astuteness of a family lawyer or a family physician. She would have felt that here was a practical-minded elder brother upon whom she could entirely rely; a brother who, quite naturally, was immune to her charms, but who "liked her," as girls say, "for herself, and *not for that*." So the incident would have passed, and Thomas Henry's Cardinal Newman profile, with its Voltairian grimace, would have received an unqualified benediction from the angel who records such things, had it not been that the very moment the rustle of petticoats had died away a torrent of furious Swift-like invective upon all the historic frailties of womanhood would almost certainly have burst from his lips.

Our radiant Louis, on the other hand, "this Archangel," would have, without beating about the bush, taken time by the forelock, her friends by surprise, the wench by storm, the recording angel nodding, and Heaven itself, one might almost think, in a complaisant, relaxed, Mohammedan mood!

And what of Bernie? I trow well, at the bottom of her

heart, the maid I speak of would have preferred Bernie's attitude to that of all the rest. For without—indeed very much to the contrary!—taking a fraternal tone, Bernie would have hastened to point out to her some red-veined fungus, some green-veined moth, some blue-veined kingfisher's feather, some fanciful flake of pellucid pollen dust on the corolla-cradle of an infinitesimal water-buttercup, and all with such tremulously whimsical, such humorously intense concentration upon herself, that the girl would have imagined that in some subtle way she was as responsible for the fungus-vein, the moth-vein, the feather-vein, the corolla-vein, as she was—or as she must have felt she was—for the blue-veins in her own soft skin!

And what of "The Catholic"? Here I can answer with a more absolute assurance and from a more direct observation and experience even than in Bernie's case. "The Catholic," if it were summer-time, would suggest to the girl that they should both take off their shoes and stockings, and walk side by side over the thymy turf of the downs. Meanwhile he would alternately quote to her the poetry of William Blake and explain to her various recondite points in the doctrines of St. Thomas. If it were winter-time, however, he would sit on the sofa by her side as she sewed, or stand by her side at the sink as she washed up, and with wave after wave of the most formidable magnetism pouring forth from the dark-gleaming pupils of his green-black eyes, he would explain to her the paradisal emotions she would feel, the thrilling revelations she would win, the self-control and yet the delicious self-release she would attain, if she could only "relatively"—for the greatest philosophers could do no more—approach the System of Things along the lines that the exigencies of our universal human nature had proved to be, for us at any rate, in a certain sense infallible.

Although it seems a curious thing to do, to aim at the devoted sensibility of one young person all the intensest characteristics of my Pantagruelian cronies, it is in accordance with my deepest understanding of that mysterious Grail, whose first acquaintance I made, in a literary sense, when I lectured

at Oxford, that I should cajole my valued companions to
reveal what the *Mabinogion* calls their "peculiarities" from
contact with a friendly girl. If you were to press me, in my
turn, to indicate how I would behave in this particular case,
I would answer: "in exactly the opposite way from Harry
Lyon!" It is true I would disregard her beauty as much as he,
but in place of giving her any wise and practical counsel I
would pick her brains; and when she was gone I would say to
myself that I had never thought of *that* before, or of that or of
that, or of that!

It was at Court House that I got published, with the
combined aid of my father and of Cousin Ralph, a second
little book of imitative poems, all covered over, like the first,
with golden fleur-de-lys. Perhaps the neatest poem in this
gilded Book of Imitation, will at least indicate to a discerning
reader that I had already begun to follow Theodore in acquiring
a taste for Nietzsche's writings.

> "A parrot to an eagle came,
>   And boasted that he knew
> The language and the ways of men,
>   And things both old and new.
> The eagle looked him up and down
>   With eyes of burning coal:
> 'Fly with me then towards the sun
>   And hear the thunders roll!'
> 'I am afraid,' the parrot said.
>   The eagle laughed full high:
> 'That is a word I have not read
>   In earth, or sea, or sky.
> Back to your perch! These lonely heights
>   Were not for parrots made.
> I would not leave my eagle flights
>   To learn to be afraid!' "

But perhaps the least conventional poem in this small
collection is one addressed to the throbbing of my gastric
ulcers, a poem beginning with the words, "O Pain" and
expressing the hope that in the Resurrection there would be

Y

no revival of the Spirit of Pain, whatever else might rise from the dead.

It is not to Harry nor to Bernie, nor to Louis, nor to Ralph, nor to any of my brothers, that I owe my first definite encouragement to write the sort of mystic-humorous, Pantagruelian, Shandean, Quixotic Romance that is now the chief ambition of my three score years. This encouragement I owe entirely to "The Catholic." It was my pleasure and my fantasy, while I lived at Court House, in this most reprehensible and irresponsible epoch of my life, to compose an interminable and totally unpublishable story, a story in which I let myself go to the extreme limit. The two chief protagonists of this crazy rigmarole of imaginative monstrosities were "The Catholic" himself and Mr. de ——. Mr. de —— unwilling to cast upon his noble European relatives the faintest disrepute by his many desolate eccentricities, chose about this time to change his historic name to that of "Carlyle." Heaven knows what put it into my old friend's head to select "Carlyle" but that is what he did. I am sure he knew less about Carlyle than about Pope or Dryden, but for some reason the sound of the syllables hit his fancy.

In my unpublishable Work without a Name I called Mr. de —— Mr. de Woztnak, and "The Catholic" Cousin Taxater. John William Williams pondered over this crazy book with the utmost seriousness. As oblivious to its profanity and its obscenity as he was to the manias of its author, he had a Goethean power of making all human aberrations venial, and all human intentions divine. For J. W. W. the Devil had had his claws so pared and his tail so clipped that he was a pitiful rather than an opprobrious object. Good, to this profound thinker, was the grand "Absolute," Evil the grand "Relative." Alas! this is a doctrine that my own knowledge of the workings of my own heart makes very hard of acceptance! But my friend's taking so seriously this Bedlam composition gave me the utmost delight. I went on writing it for him alone. I sometimes think I could write huge folios for One Person alone, if it were the right person.

I began to bring all my friends into this book, inventing a

gesticulating procession of these disreputable puppets and trailing them up and down that Limbo-Strand of my wildest abortions of fantasy, the Esplanade at Brighton! I eased my heart, and more than my heart, in this debauched bundle of shreds and patches that I would unpack for "The Catholic" wherever we could find a fire and a table and an incurious barmaid.

Meanwhile, of course, time was passing; and I was entering my thirtieth year. And absolutely nothing had been accomplished! Think how few there are among the writers of our time who at thirty have done nothing! At twenty-nine I had neither written a book, nor begotten a son. I had done nothing, except to get Mr. de ———'s poems published. There must have been many who considered that I was wasting my life and would never come to anything and deserved never to come to anything.

But all this while in my own secret heart I knew there was one person who did not think I was wasting my life, one person who was as totally devoid of ambition for me as he was devoid of ambition for himself, one person who considered that if you earned an honest living and could enjoy your walks and coming home to your tea, all was well, all was as God intended. This was my father! It was in complete harmony with my father's ways—though he would have been angry at what I was writing—to throw my energy into a composition that was as remote from any chance of "propitiating magnates" as it was from forwarding any conceivable career. And so I wrote on and on, about Cousin Taxater and Mr. de Woztnak, for the benefit of "The Catholic" alone. It appeared as if I were destined to be as ego-centric in my writings as I was abnormal in my eroticism and diseased in my conscience.

And yet, for all that, if I had died at the end of my Court House time, I would certainly have cried out, in the manner of my admired Hazlitt: *"Well, I've had a happy five years!"*

Chapter Eight

Burpham

IT was Harry Lyon, with the help of the Reverend S., who was at that time the Curate-in-charge of our new home, who helped us to leave Court House—where the downs separated us so much from the sunshine—and settle at Burpham near Arundel in West Sussex. We had often admired from the train as we travelled from Brighton to Portsmouth, "en route" for Salisbury and Wessex, this particular tract of country and I think I must secretly have "willed" that I should settle here. My father, however, had evidently some deep obscure prejudice against it. At any rate, in a manner rather unusual for him, he refused me any financial help.

It fell therefore to the destiny of Mr. S., our benevolent parish-priest, to produce the necessary loan; and for the expenditure of five hundred pounds I found myself the sole owner, for nine hundred and ninety-nine years of the little walled-in cottage and garden known at that time as "Bankside" and later as "Warre House." Thus I became the third one of my father's family, since before the days of my great-grandfather, to own in fee-simple, or whatever it is called, a parcel of England, from the surface of the chalky soil to the unknown, and possibly fiery centre of our terrestrial globe.

And at once—for however far removed from quarrels over land and houses a person's dominant impulses may be this business of owning property carries its troubles—I found myself in the midst of bickerings and contentions. When Harry Lyon first brought us to visit his friend, Mr. S., I looked with sympathetic interest at the village boys and girls playing catch-as-catch-can along the top of the great pre-historic embankment that enclosed one side of our small garden. This Arcadian scene cast such a tender light upon the whole spot that as we proceeded along the little path leading to the chalk-carved, flint-embattled church I was suddenly transported by a burst of indecorous excitement, and in the excess of my feeling I flung my stick, the successor of "Sacred," against the wall of the school-mistress' thatched cottage. Harry Lyon severely rebuked me for this childish behaviour, indicating that for a man of thirty entering upon a new phase of his career, such boisterous manifestations were unseemly.

I soon found that they were not only unseemly but somewhat premature; for to be looked down upon by a number of children as I paced my trim lawn was an aspect of affairs I had not counted on. Like my ambiguous Brighton friend I did not appreciate "on-lookers." Thus, as time went on, being resolved at all costs to have the privacy of my small retreat kept intact, I caused a gigantic board, inscribed "Trespassers will be Prosecuted," to be erected on the top of our fortification. The village of Burpham awoke one morning therefore to find its historic rampart transformed overnight into the private property of an impecunious lecturer. The indignant natives acted at once. Certain among their bolder spirits, leaving their beer-mugs at the "George and Dragon," which was conveniently hard-by, transferred my board to a neighbouring ditch, where its threats of prosecution could be innocuously addressed to snails and slugs and field-mice. Once more was it replaced; only to be once more removed to the ditch.

Thus matters went, till one day I remarked a Personage standing on this debateable eminence, who was clearly not of the village. He was dressed in a dark suit, rather in the manner of my friend "The Catholic," and there was something about his heavy-browed, tragically-lined, dark-bearded countenance that made me think at once of a Titian portrait of a Renaissance despot. He remained there for some while, apparently surveying with ironic curiosity my Trespassers' Board, and then, without a word or a gesture, climbed slowly down the bank and strode off across the field. It was not till he was well out of sight that I learned his identity. He was the owner of the quarrelled-over embankment! He was in fact our Sovereign's hereditary Grand Marshal, the first in rank of all the peers of England, Henry Howard, Duke of Norfolk.

Most of that part of the country, except for isolated little patches like this one that I had just purchased belonged to the Duke of Norfolk, and on the other side of the tidal river there stretched away for miles, with its sweeping uplands, its beech clumps, its wild deer, its bracken, its rare beds of Atropa Belladonna, his famous Arundel Park. No English castle, except perhaps Windsor itself, looks as impressive from a distance as Arundel Castle. You see it standing on the edge of its park, above its river, with the silvery gleam of the Channel a few miles behind it, and you feel that Sussex can boast her "melancholy seignorial woods" as well as any chateau on the Loire.

The downs above Burpham—and here, you must understand, we were south of their high range—sloped up very gradually to their highest summit from amid cornfields and clover. On their north, where Amberley Castle was, the downs sank into the valley as precipitously as they had done at Court House, but on the seaward-looking side, they sloped up so gently as to be under cultivation till they almost reached the top.

The Duke of Norfolk owned, as I say, the bulk of all the land you could see from these chalk hills, but he rented it out to large tenant-farmers, who had enormous tracts under their control. The two big tenant-farmers in Burpham were Mr. Collyer of Peppering, and Mr. Graburn of Wepham, both of them "magnates" as old de —— would say, and both of them blest with lively and charming families. Nothing could have been kinder, nothing could have been more hospitable than were these amiable families to us. We even stayed at Peppering while our cottage was being made ready for our reception; and, though beyond the fact that we were anxious to settle in the place and were vouched for, as it were, by Mr. S., we had no claim of any sort on these people, they accepted us in the heartiest old-world style.

The man I became personally most intimate with in the village, apart from Mr. S., was a retiring but not unsuccessful writer. He had already written one or two books when I first met him, and while we lived in the village he wrote several more. This was Mr. Ticknor Edwardes. In those early days Mr. Edwardes lived in what was called the Red Cottage, a house on the main street of our village, though he had a retreat for his literary work in a smaller cottage nearby. Not only used he to compose nature sketches for the London periodicals, but he used to write with professional authority on the subject of bees. He kept bees himself, and being exceptionally skilful with his hands could, if my memory fails me not, make his own hives. It was soon after the War, I think, that he decided to take Holy Orders. At any rate the last time I saw him he was not only a clergyman but had recently been appointed Vicar of Burpham. Mr. Edwardes was a man of meticulous nicety in his literary art. I recollect being confounded by the elaborate craftsmanship with which he laboured; pondering on words, taking words up, as it were, and laying them down, just as he did with the materials of his hives! May his ministerial utterances, under that ancient Norman arch, carved in chalk at the top of the little aisle, be as full of the sweetness of the Word as his carefully constructed hives were full of honey!

I always liked Mr. Edwardes uncommonly well. I liked the tough-wood texture of his bodily presence! The truth is I have always had a tendency to select my particular friends on purely physical grounds. This tendency jumps with my whole inner nature, with my peculiar talents, with my gift for "dithyrambic analysis." It is the way I always go to work in literary criticism, and it gives me the power, I will not say of *becoming* the personality I am dealing with, but at least of diffusing my identity through its identity and of realizing myself through the medium of its sensibility. The thing in its essence is a kind of spiritual eroticism and in my case it is intimately connected with my vice as a *voyeur*. Does not all literary penetration spring from some subtle sublimation of our deepest vice? From a *voyeur* I become a *clair-voyeur*. What I really do is to plunge down, below the external "bricks" that my friend, or my author, "drops," below his lapses, his "heavy weather," his superficial egotisms and vanities and irritablenesses. I flow like a magnetic current through the substance of his nature, penetrating with my spirit the stuff out of which his flesh is made, following the vibrations of his nerves, tracking his being's effluence as this volatile breath rises up like steam from the thawing ice of his identity.

Yes, at bottom the thing is physical. My literary likes and dislikes are physical, quite as much as my personal ones. And this applies to the dead equally with the living. I like and can understand, for example, the physical quality of Wordsworth's flesh and blood, while I instinctively shrink from that of— Browning, let us say! Now Mr. Edwardes' physical presence had an appeal for me beyond the wisest remark the honest man might make. His long nose, his opaque, ivory-parchment skin, his tree-root neck, his shy, nervous, wild-animal brown eyes, all these manifestations of his personality were revelations to me of the essential goodness and soundness of his solitary soul. He possessed that grave, solid, imperturbable reserve, that stiff pride, mixed with disarming spasms of humility, that have characterized so many of the old-fashioned interpreters of English piety. Can I put it better than to say that Mr. Edwardes represented for me that soothing and quiet sense of "protected" well-being which emanates from certain of the Collects in our Book of Common Prayer? Take the Collect, for instance, for the Twenty-First Sunday after Trinity. Could anything give a person a better sense of security in a chaotic world than these words? "Grant, we beseech thee, merciful Lord, to thy faithful people pardon and peace, that they may be cleansed from all their sins and serve thee with a quiet mind." Such a tone, such a calm assumption, may be as different from the mystical ecstasies of other interpretations of the faith as our downs are different from the desert; and the words may be only, if you must have it so, translations of the piety of Christendom; but they are translations sealed with the stamp of our English nature. It was in the strength of this "quiet mind" and this "pardon and peace" that my father was enabled to control the dangerous cataclysms of his Cymric inheritance.

And what characters there were in those days in our village
for Mr. Edwardes to contemplate with his patient and reverent
observation! Some of them live still. Others are dead; dead,
and buried between the sloping roof of the old church and the
field-path leading up to the downs. What a man was Mr. Budd
the blacksmith, Mr. Goodyear the carpenter, George West the
landlord of the "George and Dragon"!

I feel ashamed that I did not get to know more intimately
our actual farm-labourers. But they were reserved South
Saxons, I suspect, not at all inclined to wear their hearts on
their sleeves, for philosophic daws to peck at. One old man,
however, I did get to know pretty well—I think he must have
been the grandfather of a beautiful little invalid boy I used to
see standing in a garden where our tidal river washed the
ruins of a very ancient malt-house. Round and ruddy-gold as
the full moon when it first rises, was this aged man's countenance; but the long seasons of tilling the fields had so constricted
his lower limbs that, as he stumbled about, the space between
his legs resembled the curve of an ogival Gothic arch.

But it was the same at Montacute, and the same at Court
House! I have been much less able to make friends with real
men of the soil than my father was; far less than my brothers
have been. Why is this? I think it is because my maniacal
pursuit, of what seems to flee from me in ever-narrowing
perspective, causes me to turn a lack-lustre and not *deeply-
involved* eye upon these Hesiodic figures, the poetry of whose
life gives me such ideal pleasure. Theodore can get what he
requires in a glance, in a pause, in a silence; for the wandering
airs of his disturbing inspiration have fed upon the atmosphere
of these lives. Llewelyn can do it by his gift for exciting
confidence and by his swift genius for grasping earth-bound
essentials. Our youngest brother, Willy, who became, while
I was still at Burpham, a Somerset farmer himself and learnt
to speak the dialect, could make friends with any carter, any
ditcher, any shepherd, as naturally and easily as I could make
friends with a priest.

But I could not do it. The thing made me nervous, made
me as cowardly and obsequious, as if I were dealing with so

many Dukes of Norfolk! And yet I *feel* as if I were behaving to every labouring man I meet in a perfectly direct man-to-man way. It would outrage my life-illusion to the very roots, *not* to feel this. And the queer thing is that in my encounters with working men I tend to put myself out much more than Llewelyn ever does. I will stand "on one leg," as they say, nodding and wagging my head in the presence of some old fellow's ramblings, while Llewelyn, having maintained both his own integrity and the man's would bid him "God-den, Mr. Tup!" and bugger off.

No, I don't believe I excite a quarter of the confidence that Llewelyn does. Human beings—even the simplest—are quick to catch these nuances of character. People know that my nervous flatteries and lively propitiations cover up a touchy wild-animal yearning to be off and away. In a certain sense it might be said that it is the ridiculous impulsiveness and the transparent abandonment of my manner with people that accounts for this curious lack in my life of friendships with men of the soil. I puzzle them, I agitate them, I embarrass them, just as certain kinds of highly-strung women disconcert me.

Llewelyn in his dealings with them never for a second tries to slough off the country gentleman's tone, the tone of an honest, earth-loving, warm-hearted squire, talking to a shepherd, a gamekeeper, a carter, a stone-breaker. But I have so de-classed myself in my own mind that in place of this dignified, decorous tone, that shows decent respect both to my interlocutor and myself, I throw all sense of proportion to the winds and proceed to talk to Thomas Tup, as I might talk—save for a more quickly beating pulse—to Thomas Hardy. And this sort of thing does not please people. The only people I have ever known it to please are old family servants who understand it as ducks understand water and *tramps* who regard it as revealing a kindred divergence from the tone of established position in this world.

I must add to this brief list two more human types and with them the roll of those who like my method is complete. Negroes understand it, and all priests understand it, and these latter inclusions alone make me reluctant to give it up. With priests I am always entirely at my ease. I understand them as I do *not* understand a shepherd, a fisherman, a ploughman, a mason, a plumber, a miner. And they understand me. Nuns, monks, and friars, priests, hedge-priests, half-priests, all understand me and seem to like me! By the Roman Church I have always been treated with the most miraculous clairvoyance. She seems to know, this ancient nurse of wayward humanity, that my constant mutterings about "angels" and "devils" and about "Divine" moods and "Devilish" moods, is anything but a pose or an affectation. She knows by instinct that it is the revelation of a soul that has somehow blundered into a consciousness of something outside the astronomical universe.

I have often wondered how I would get on in Soviet Russia to which I feel as much attracted as I do to the Catholic Church. I am so simple in my tastes, and so unambitious, that as long as I had the smallest room to myself and enough kopecks to keep me in bread and tea and cigarettes, and as long as I had a road, or even a path across a common, where I could walk alone, I believe I could be happy there. Only I should be always wanting to share the contents of my samovar with some mystical Father Zosima. I fully agree that I ought to be forced by a Communistic State to share the burden of manual labour. But, when I've done my share, I want to be free *to turn from the State altogether*, and from all tedious mundane concerns, free to discuss God and Freedom and Immortality with learned and pious men! Yes, I agree altogether with my Communistic friends that I ought to be forced to do some sort of manual labour. But I do not agree with them that it is a waste of time to discuss God. It is not that I myself ever want to go to church. I never feel the remotest desire to do so; and when I pray, as I weary myself with doing, I pray to idols and fetishes and images, to sticks and stones, to the Sun and the Moon and the Earth.

Sometimes I pray to a saint, like St. Thérèse, and sometimes to Jesus; but never to His Mother and never to God. Nor is it that I am scared to pray to God for fear of having to give up my erotic sensuality, or having only to smoke ten cigarettes a day; for I know perfectly well that my conscience as the voice of my secret life-illusion is as much of a worry now as it would be if I regarded it as the voice of God. It is the sufferings, the atrocities in the world, that have made me come to feel hostile to God, just as that terrible picture of the pain of Christ, referred to in *The Idiot*, tempted Rogozhin, if not the Prince himself, to plunge into atheism, so as to be revenged on a First Cause that allows such things.

If the downs at Court House prevented the sunshine reaching us till the afternoon, all day long at Burpham there poured in upon us with the full flood of sunshine the voices of children, the bleating of sheep, the lowing of oxen, the ringing of bells, the stamping of horses, the tinkling of anvils, the sawing of timber, together with the most cheerful voices from the George and Dragon. We had so much sunshine in fact and such lively sounds in every direction that it seems strange that my proud and vicious loneliness was not melted, humanized, precipitated, made into a sweet savour of humility. Watching me like a Hawk of God, as I turned this way and that way in this blaze of sunshine and friendliness, for I must have appeared to him like a polar bear in a zoo of cheerful christian beasts, Harry Lyon would try, try sometimes with bitter tears, to break the proud spirit of my isolation. I can see his ascetic countenance now between the jasmine flowers outside my study window, contorted, as was the countenance of the poet Dante, when in that boat in the livid swamp, under the crimson battlements of Dis, he saw his enemy "well soused" by the demons. I can hear now his prophetic voice warning me that if I refused to be human and humble or to change, like Pharaoh, my hard heart, I would suffer the earthly hell, at any rate, of having to smile and smile and smile while my wolfish heart devoured itself amid the sunshine and the sheep.

Looking back on it all now I can see that much in my evasive and tricky character deserved such reprobation; but on the other hand the instinct in me that revolted against feeling myself dragged like a submissive Paynim, by this hard-hitting Knight of the Red Cross, to a compulsory baptism in the waters of humility, seems still a justifiable one. "The Catholic" always used to uphold the doctrine that it was very wrong to attack *the essential nature* of a person, his inmost temper, his life-illusion about himself. This to J.W.W.'s Thomistic mind was the sin against the Holy Ghost. "The Catholic" himself always followed the Goethean method of assuming that a person's character *was already* what the reformer wished it to be, and what he wished it to be was ever in accordance with the person's temperamental fatality. *My* St. Thomas on the contrary was wont to tilt armed cap-a-pie, hell-for-leather, straight into the inmost fortress of a person's temperamental fate. And yet what a noble figure he was, like some chain-armour Brother of the Templars or of the Hospitallers of St. John, as he flashed out so devilishly on the side of the angels! He certainly never bowed down in the House of Rimmon, and I fancy his bitterest and most sardonic outbursts only burst into flame when the live coal in his heart spat and hissed under the impact of my hyperboreal ways.

My misanthropic avoidance of my fellow-creatures was not, all the same, nor is it now, entirely due to inhumanity. It is partly due to the extreme opposite of this; to an unhealthy consciousness of the formidableness, the overpoweringness, of human personality. How I used to sneak out of that little enclosed garden, between the George and Dragon and the carpenter's shop, and thread my way furtively among the graves of the churchyard, in order to reach the downs without having to salute anyone or to speak to anyone! It was almost impossible to do this; and everyone I did meet was so nice that it was hard to pass by with just a nod. I was like a Pelican of the Wilderness lodged in the most picturesque of murmuring dove-cotes! As my indignant Knight Templar never ceased from warning me, my refusal to grow humble and loving threatened to make me eat out my heart in motiveless malignity. How I used to dread meeting those charming and innocent people! I did sometimes summon up enough courage to converse with the plough-boys and shepherd-boys; but they showed signs of being as afraid of me as I was of them; and of the older farm-hands I was as shy as Theodore used to be of the people on his own farm. And yet I reverenced each one of them from the bottom of my heart!

In *that* point not the most austere Communist could find any fault in me. As I have hinted before, every human being of the class of "workers and peasants," has always filled me with exactly the same sort of disturbing awe that I feel in the presence of great lords. To tell you the truth apart from priests and tramps and old family servants, I fancy the class of persons I felt most at my ease with was that very class of clerks and small tradesmen so austerely animadverted upon by Harry Lyon.

Everyone at Burpham, who could afford it, had a boat on the river, which ran at the foot of the hill on which the village stands. It was a tidal river and the boats were fastened to high stakes in such a way as to enable them to rise and fall with the tides. The difference between low tide and high tide was astonishing, fifteen feet at least I should think, and at low tide the mud was an ugly spectacle save under certain effects of light. At high tide, however, the surface of the river, brimming and smooth, became surprisingly beautiful. I soon bought a strong sea-boat at the river-mouth, which was at Littlehampton, a few miles south of Arundel; and it became a passion to me to row this boat, sometimes towards Arundel and Littlehampton, sometimes towards the little villages of South Stoke and North Stoke where the river ran deep and dangerous under the stately wooded slopes of the enormous park. Once, when Bernie was with me, and once when my brother Bertie was with me, both sturdy oarsmen, I got as far down-stream as Amberley, where another castle rose straight out of the water meadows. I remember bathing by starlight in this river with Bertie once; and, on another occasion, when Bertie was in a mood for fooling, I remember sinking with him for so long under the swift tide that our companions grew anxious.

This River Arun, especially an estuary of it, called the Old River, along which there ran a secluded tow-path and where the tide was obstructed by immensely tall reeds full of the harsh cries of invisible reed-warblers, made a deep impression on my mind. When my passion for rowing began to wane, I got into the habit—and this custom lasted for several years —of pacing up and down this secluded tow-path by the edge of the Old River. Quantities of *yellow* loosestrife—many varieties of which it amazes me to find here in New York State, on the banks of the Agawamuk—grew by this hidden tow-path, not to speak of the better-known purple variety, "that our rude shepherds call a grosser name, but our cold maids do dead men's fingers call them," together with meadow-sweet and willow-herb and hemp-agrimony.

But the River Arun, take it all in all, never made a wholly satisfactory impression on my mind. The truth is I do not like tidal rivers. To me they are always a little sinister. In their strange double nature they resemble some monstrous offspring of an unnatural mating! Sea-fish mingled with river-fish in the waters of the Arun, but this only made me long for the glittering fresh-water dace of the Norfolk Wissey. What shocked me most to see were floating bits of ancient seaweed, carried for ever backwards and forwards, forwards and backwards, as the recurrent tides rose and fell. There was something infinitely sorrowful to my nature about this incessant ebb and flow. These irreversible tides took to themselves the character of some ghastly Eternal Recurrence, and there came to be for me a singular desolation about those doomed pieces of seaweed.

During my earlier years at Burpham, when I was always rowing myself up and down that river and feeling so proud to take my friends with me, I decided to stop writing my huge unprintable book, and begin upon a proper, a normal—or as normal as I could make it—Romance. Well, do I recall certain passages from this work, which never was finished, and, as far as I remember never read to anyone. One was about a priest—how my mind ran on priests!—who was pictured by me as sitting at a window of a certain old inn I used to frequent with "The Catholic," whose walls rose directly out of the water, close to the bridge into the main street of the town. Another was concerned with the river under the little chalk-cliff at Burpham; and in this passage I remember describing, luridly and vividly, the gurglings, the suckings, the moanings, the lappings, the grumblings of the tidal water as it sank back into the phosphorescent mud.

Burpham certainly offered several quite startling varieties of landscape. The one that appeals to my son the most, in this birthplace of his, is the wilder portion of the downs. Northeast of the village a very ancient chalk-path—probably mediæval, for it is called the Leper's Path and there is a Leper's Window in the church—leads over the bare open hills to a little remote hamlet, lying away from all the world, called Lee Farm. The people of this place, by reason of their isolation from the influences of modern life, possess a poetical naturalness rare in Sussex, though common enough in Wessex. This is the landscape that my son loves best of all, and I used to love it too and frequently visit it while he was still an infant. But what I used to love myself even better, for it was still more lonely, was the heart of what were called "the Gibbet Woods." Here they hanged a man once who robbed the Royal Mail, and this unfortunate young man's indignant spirit seemed to keep people away from the spot! Never in all the years that Burpham was my home did I meet a living soul in those Gibbet Woods. I used to love the margin too—I have always been one for margins, for edges, borders and thresholds—between woodland and downland where the Gibbet Woods mingled with the open downs. This, even more than that hidden tow-path by the Old River, was my favourite walk for a decade. I must have come here a hundred times a year for about ten years, which must mean that I have skirted that margin between woods and downs no less than a thousand times! It was a lovely place, a place exactly adapted to my nature.

It was here one summer that I encountered a great number of White Admiral butterflies, and it was here that I murdered, for the benefit of my son's "collection," a perfect specimen of the rare butterfly called a Hairstreak.

But between the edge of the Gibbet Woods and the hill above the Leper's Path was an eminence on the top of the downs from which the sea, some half a dozen miles away, was clearly visible. This particular eminence was of extraordinary interest to me. It was called by the surprising name of "Friday's Church," and what it really was, was the site of an ancient Norse shrine belonging to the goddess Freya. There existed on that spot in my day—I think it is all gone now—the relics of a lightning-struck thorn-tree. A fragment of this tree's blackened root I profanely and sacrilegiously tore up—avenge it if you must, great nordic goddess!—and placed on the top of my bookcase.

It was within a few months' time after our arrival at Burpham—and indeed we had only just got ourselves snugly settled in when the event occurred—that my son was born. Like Goethe he was born in August—the month of the favoured of men—but unlike Goethe he had a heathen god-father to his christening! Mr. S. performed the ceremony; but Littleton Alfred's sponsor and representative in the historic religion of his race was none other than my atheistical old friend, Mr. de ———! It was a pretty sight to see this aged Lucretius clasping in his shaky fingers, the wrong side upper-most, a neat version of the Book of Common Prayer as he stood at our Burpham font; and it was a charming poem you may be sure, in the old-fashioned courtly style, that he composed to celebrate that day.

Littlehampton was not so far, not nearly so far, from Burpham, as Brighton had been from Court House; but although the birth of my son did not, for all my happiness in it, transform the magnetic current of my vice, I never had the same incentive to rush to Littlehampton as I had in the other case. But all the same I did, and that not unfrequently, make my way to this seaside town; and when I did so it was, accord-ing to my wont, on foot rather than by train. I derived con-siderable pleasure from the sea at Littlehampton, quite apart from my eternally disappointed quest, and the long walk itself was always a delight to me. The centre portion of my way lay across wide-stretching meadows; and at one point, near a very ancient church in the open fields, I had to pass a curious pond where was a great bed of watercress.

This pond was of immemorial antiquity; and in ancient days it was reported to be the abode of a fabulous monster known as an "Avanc." I did not give much thought to this Avanc, but there was something about that field-path, and even about the desolate little stucco houses that I passed as I drew near to Littlehampton, which stirred in me all those strange feelings, feelings that seem to reach me from similar human experiences undergone centuries ago, that certain wayside gates and palings and barns and hedges and old walls and old tree-stumps have the power of evoking. What always gave me a special thrill at Littlehampton itself was a particular kind of emerald-green seaweed that covered the older pier-posts there; but in all the visits I paid to those far-stretching, glimmering sea-sands and that swirling river-mouth I never once, to the best of my recollection, was vouchsafed a glimpse of any of the embodiments of immortal loveliness that my fancy used to conjure up as I passed that watercress bed of the Avanc.

"The Catholic" used frequently to visit us at Burpham, and so near to the Roman Church had his convoluted metaphysic brought me, that once, when at Littlehampton in his company, I actually left him reading Pascal in an out-of-the-way tavern, while I took the drastic and apparently fatal step of calling upon the local priest! I can remember now the uncomfortable sensation that seized me, as if I were an actor who had suddenly discovered that his imaginary rôle was turning into formidable reality, as I waited outside that priest's door. But the man was out; and I took his absence as a deciding omen. Theodore's laconic commentary upon this action of mine was a characteristic one.

"Of course," he wrote, "we know you do it to annoy your father."

I am always prepared to allow for the presence of some drop of black bile, some "dram of eale" behind my most plausible doings; but if it were my father that I had wanted to "annoy" by these antics I certainly was worsted at my own game. For my crafty begetter, doubtless knowing his first-born's weaknesses through and through, assumed, like any wise old Dorset shepherd dealing with a tricky black ram, a gesture even more dramatic than my own.

"How," he said to me, as we hugged our bony knees side by side over the drawing-room fire, while from the Holy Ikon brought from Russia by Uncle Cowper two pairs of almond-shaped Byzantine eyes watched our Welsh ways, "how can you give me a blow like this, John, in my old age?"

This was enough for me. I capitulated at once, glad enough I dare say of the excuse for doing so, but when my father went on and said: "You will write to Mr. Williams at once then?" I bade him good night.

As a matter of fact in the profound psychic intelligence of "The Catholic" the truth had already grown clear; namely that, after that unpropitious call on the Littlehampton priest, though I might be led to the water, I would always dodge the drinking. I think he realized too that what my nature craved in the Roman Church *was* precisely what my father suspected, a metaphysical justification for my inherent and irrational mania for fetish-worship? What I wanted was to be allowed to worship a magical Christ without having to take up my cross and follow Jesus, to be allowed to worship sticks and stones and idols and images and the sun and the moon and the earth and the morning-star. I wanted, in fact to do exactly the very thing that my father suspected I wanted to do: "to bow and scrape," as he would always phrase it, lifting, like a war-horse among the trumpets, his proud "Ha! ha!" in answer to the tinkling of the Mass bell.

But if my father got the better of me over the affair of my becoming a Roman Catholic I got the better of him over the affair of his making Littleton, in place of his eldest son, the executor of his Will. At least I thought I did! In his heart of hearts my father was divided in his attitude to me. He was at once tender and protective towards me, but always—and not altogether without reason—distrustful of me. I had so often wilfully and wickedly teased him, baiting him, as Bertie always maintains, though I cannot quite credit this part of his story, as I used to bait the *bulls* in our vicinity, and I think, though he was much more worried, as indeed, everyone seems to be more worried, by Llewelyn's disapproval than by mine— "Why are you looking so grave at me?" he once demanded of that fifth son of his when he was in a bad mood—he was always a little nervous as to what his first-born might *say* to him. Upon Littleton, on the contrary he tended to lean, just as I did myself, and in him—and he had good reason—he felt complete confidence.

We were walking together through "Stoke Wood" at Montacute, the scene of so many dramatic crises in all our lives, when he fell into my hands over this matter of his Will. His Will must have been a problem of deep concern to him; for his distrust of lawyers resembled the distrust that old Pippard, his aged sexton, had of "they Members of Parliament." Whenever he had an interview with a lawyer he would take the precaution of *sitting down* upon the most important document in question, lest it should be spirited away or changed into something else beneath his very nose. With the main issue snug and safe under his lean hindquarters he felt prepared to cope with matters. But he was nervous now, as we walked together side by side through Stoke Wood, for it was not a case of sitting upon his Will but of justifying his will.

"I have been making my Will, John, my boy," he said, "and I have decided to make——"

Here he paused as Littleton himself used to pause before he jumped over Preston Brook—"to make *Littleton*," he emphasized the name, and that was *his* jump across that brook I always shirked, "my executor!"

I think it was an entirely unexpected thing to my father when I did not receive this news with my usual equanimity. I grumbled and hummed-and-hawed disconcertingly as we passed the tall beech-trunk inscribed with so many love-knots and sweetheart's initials, and this so disturbed my father that he uttered an astonishing remark as a commentary upon my lack of urbanity.

"No one, John," he said, "likes to be thwarted!"

I boasted just now that I got the better of my father over this matter; but really I am not at all sure that I did. What on earth did he mean by using that word "thwarted"? I might have been some subtle conspiring younger son, some crafty Jacob, who for years had been plotting to steal Littleton's birthright, and had now been found out at my tricks! As a matter of fact I believe the truth was that my father used the word "thwart," just as he did so many other words, in a peculiar sense of his own. What he really meant to say was: "Of course, John, I can understand you don't like this. No one *likes* it when another is preferred above him."

I can so well remember announcing the first news of my son's birth to Bertie and Llewelyn—both of them then in Wilson's House—as I walked with them along the Yeovil Road, that road along which Littleton and I used to run home from Wildman's. Following the example of my father I always made important communications in the open air and if possible during a walk. I have always felt safer, like the Titan Antaeus, when I can draw on the magnetism of the earth. It is not that I necessarily become more honest. I become a more successful diplomatist. I avoid betraying myself by the use of such a word as "thwart"! Well do I recall an earlier epoch than this, when staying with old Littleton at his first assistant-mastership at Bruton, I woke up one morning in "Plox House" where he lodged and listened to "the sweet of the morning."

I was reading *Sense and Sensibility* then, and like all our family I read Jane Austen purely for the *romance* of the tale; that very thing that the mature young wit was always scoffing at; and, as the scents of Somerset, the breath of damp moss and of faint primroses, came in through the window, together with the thought of celandines, still lustrous amid their shining leaves, the idea of that leather-bound old volume I was half-way through mingled with the thrilling sense that Littleton and I were going to walk that Sunday all the way to King Arthur's Camelot, there to meet the young Llewelyn and the yet younger Willy, hurrying at top speed from Sherborne.

How well I recall seeing those two little boys in their Eton jackets, their white collars, and their tall rather battered silk hats. Aye! in spite of all I endured at Sherborne the thought of silk hats and white collars always brings primroses and celandines and pink campions and dog-violets back to my mind. But, oh dear! I can see now the very field-gate below Corton Down where we had to announce to them the catastrophic news—so peculiarly shocking to us all—that the Squire was beginning to cut down the trees on the top of Montacute Hill.

It must not be supposed, though I was a University Extension Lecturer now and had given up my schools, that I never went to Brighton from Burpham. I did still go to that Paradise of imaginary sylphs, but I used to get out at Angmering station on my way back and walk the five miles to Burpham through the heart of those Gibbet Woods. With all my fussy conscientiousness in so many matters, this was an epoch in my life, between thirty and thirty-five, when I never experienced one single prick of remorse over my secretive vicious pursuits! Did my cerebral sensuality conflict with the far-drawn imponderable ecstasies that came to me—oh, from what obscure horizons!—as I made my way through those hazel woods? Not for a moment! As I hurried along those narrow mossy paths I would dig the end of "Sacred's" successor deeply into the yielding mud, and glory in the *double good* of my tortuous life. I was like a drug-addict, I suppose; who can live a happy and decent existence, as long as he is not altogether forbidden his "one thing needful." But I did not deceive myself or act the hypocrite to myself. I would have always admitted that compared with the healthy paganism of Llewelyn my peculiar saurian lust, so insatiable and so impersonal, was more like a mad specialized craving than like the natural bubbling-over of the great amorous instinct that makes the world go round.

It was in those earlier Burpham days, after my son was born, thirty years later than my own birth and sixty years later than my father's, that I suddenly acquired a passion for everything Welsh. I bought Welsh grammars, Welsh dictionaries, Welsh modern poetry. I bought an elaborate Welsh Genealogy, called "Powys-Fadoc," and mightily chagrined was I when I found no mention of my father's ancestors in it! I bought everything I could lay hands on that had to do with Wales and with the Welsh people. Alas! I had not learnt yet, in spite of my folly over those unlucky Sagas, that Providence had deprived me of the least tincture of philology. I soon gave up trying to learn Welsh. But the *idea* of Wales and the *idea* of Welsh mythology went drumming on like an incantation through my tantalized soul. I had no vision so far—*that* was still to come—of myself as a restorer of the hidden planetary secrets of these mystical introverts of the world, but the gods having made me, instead of a conscientious scholar, an imaginative charlatan, I resolved to realize with my whole spiritual force what it meant to be descended—to the devil with "Powys-Fadoc"—from those ancient Druidic chieftains!

Hovering one sultry August afternoon after my fashion, like a famished ger-falcon, up and down Brighton front, and I recall to this day the peculiar smell of cockles and mussels mixed with great heaps of dead seaweed that tasted at that moment so salt-sick to my palate, I wondered whether I had the gall to give up "Warre House," to *sell it*, why not, to the good-natured Mr. S., and wander off with my family and my folios to some remote hiding-place in Mid-Wales! But the older my son grew the more impossible of realization became this wild scheme.

And yet it may be that I was doing, in some deep sense, for all my dislike of leaving Brighton, a wrong to the romantic basis of my nature, in not following this craving! Perhaps I *should* have managed to learn Welsh; perhaps the mysterious Invisible Presences of that land of enchantment would have helped me to renew and transform my being, like Taliessin, in that immortality-giving Cauldron of Ceridwen, not so much purging me of my vice as fulfilling and satisfying my vice, so that my cerebral quest might be brought to an end, not by suppression or self-denial, but by "subsuming" it in some "Monochronos Hedoné," in a sylphishness, shall I say, that should no longer be selfishness! But in this matter of Welsh mythology I became besotted! There is one portion of my puppet-show personality that might be said to resemble a puppet Don Quixote. Quite in the manner of Don Quixote I kept telling myself stories of how all the friends I ever quarrelled with, or had serious differences with, or imaginary grievances against, would be totally "confounded," as the National Anthem says, in all their "politics and knavish tricks." by my retreat to Wales.

Two battle cries, so to speak, kept sounding on in the

background of my misanthropic heart. One was: "I have a son, a son, a *son*, who, as he grows up, will take my side against the world." The other was: "I have Wales, Wales, *Wales*, to take refuge in, where I can send my enemies to the Devil and possess my soul in peace."

And all the while, as was the case with Don Quixote I had no real enemies at all! Samson Carrasco was a friend in disguise; so was the worthy barber, so was the curate, so were the bewildered women-folk. But I was in an agitating quandary. My ghost of a human soul hammered, like a goblin with a drum, upon my ghost of a human heart. Should I, or should I not, leave Sussex and go to Wales? The salt-sick, bilge-water smell of that particular spot where I stood on that sweltering August day to commune with my heart, my feet upon the stones of a sort of fish-market, slippery with scales and blood, how it comes back to me now, mixed with the poignance of that difficult dilemma! It is curious to think of such a thing, but I verily believe those broken claymores and those heroic gestures of the clansmen in Aytoun's Lays rose up from amid fish-scales and sweat and dust and blood and seaweed and menaced my craven hesitation! But those broken claymores pointed in vain to the land of my fathers. I never did take refuge in Wales.

It was at that time that I had an amusing encounter with the new Corpus authorities, who no longer, like Mr. Moule and Mr. Fanshawe and Dr. Perowne, fled from the undergraduates into their studies. I took upon myself to deliver a discourse, in Louis Wilkinson's room in John's, upon what has always interested me more than any other subject, the relation between sex sensuality, in all its confused aberrations, and religious ritual. Louis' room was crowded with the more independent spirits of the Cambridge æsthetic circles. I commenced in the highest feather, and the art of "dithyrambic Analysis" became so extravagant as I went on, largely due to the whimsical encouragement of a Chinaman, who had a seat just below where Louis had made me stand, that a moment arrived when another foreign undergraduate became so upset that he wrote little notes to Louis to have me stopped.

Louis had friends of every complexion in those days and of every extravagance of opinion. In his imperturbable East-Anglian sang-froid he was less frightened of fantastical human masks and of monstrous antinomian gestures than any person, man or woman, I have ever known. Had he been present when Ivan Karamazov entertained Satan, Louis would have serenely joined in, tasted the infernal haschish, brought elaborate logical strictures to bear upon Ivan's spiritual ambiguities, and finally indicated in no half-terms to the equivocal Devil that the world is *much less complicated* than he and his tricky Russian friend were trying to make out.

It was an East-Indian who was so particularly upset by those words of mine that made the Chinaman clap his hands; but I can assure you there was someone else there who was even more upset than the student from the Ganges! This was, for these were days you must remember before the appearance of Miss Weston's *From Ritual to Romance*, a trembling emissary from the Corpus High Table, the very Table, by the way, in all *its* ritual, where I had myself been a guest that same night, drinking that famous wine—little did I understand about wines!—before shogging off to the precincts of John's. In my subsequent trouble over this Pythagorean speech, in which I displayed my "golden thigh," it was against the better judgment of "The Catholic" that I answered the authorities in the manner in which I did.

"The Catholic" who had himself been at Corpus, and indeed was converted to the Roman Church while there, though subsequently he had to flee to Oxford, was indignant with me for the way I answered, and I do not wonder. For I replied to this official warning from the College of my father and grandfather in a strain of masochistic humiliation. My reply was indeed either a revelation of ironical malice or was a shocking exhibition of panic-terror, or was a most singular example of Christian forbearance. Let my reader decide for himself which of these impulses was my dominant motive. I declared to my correspondent that I had behaved in a most ungentlemanly way. I said nothing about the despatching of a sheep in wolf's clothing to the rooms of my friend. I swore that it was unpardonable in me to drink that sacred Corpus wine at the High Table and incontinently to rush off to discourse to Chinamen and Hindus in a vein more resembling that of Lucius Apuleius than of a graduate in an English Foundation. I added that it was my full intention to explain, in a less excitable and more seemly tone, the real gist of my views upon the erotic element in religion, in a public lecture in Cambridge, entirely open—if they cared to come—not only to frightened emissaries from High Tables, but to Deans, Masters, Fellows and Tutors.

It was in vain that "The Catholic" demonstrated to me, with arguments drawn from both the "Realists" and the "Nominalists" of the Mediæval Schools, that whatever *my* sins were I had a perfect right to indicate in what particular points my accusers fell short of the Thomist ideal of perfection. It was "The Catholic" himself who had encouraged me to study the psychology of sanctity and he must have felt at that moment as if he had converted a gesticulating Punchinello who, having got into his wooden pate that a "saint" never defended himself, derived an exquisite sensual pleasure from falling flat on his face and letting people walk over him.

My own view now is, looking back from the standpoint of sixty at my character at thirty, that this cringing before the reproach I received, although it may have had something of masochism, something of ironical malice, something of cowardice, was in essence the expression—though I doubt if I shall get many readers to believe this—of a naïve and, without boasting, an embryo-saintly desire, to return blessing for cursing. I was in fact coy about using weapons in my defence, and I am so still, that might make my antagonist uncomfortable; for at the very bottom of my soul, below all my dramatic gestures and below all my protean metempsychoses, there lies a vein of abysmally simple childish goodwill, reluctant to hurt the feelings of man or beast.

Odd though it may sound, I really do think I come nearer to "loving" my enemies—though I confess it is rather a fussy anxiety that their quaint life-illusions should not be hurt than

any warmth towards them—than anyone I have known,
except "The Catholic" himself. In plain words—say what you
please—I *know* that in certain subterranean motions of my
spirit I am much more like the "Idiot" of Dostoievsky than
I am like Cagliostro! I daresay I have a touch of Ivan Karamazov in me too; that I do not deny; but in this particular
case I am pretty sure that mingled with my masochism and my
ironical malice and my pure cowardice there was also, quite
distinct and definite, a well-meaning wish that these worthy
authorities, who so totally misunderstood me, should continue
in their feeling that they were on the side of the angels!
Down at the bottom of my nature I seem to discern the
presence of a quite special and curious "goodwill towards
men." I really believe that it is the presence of this unusual
kind of "goodwill" that is the cause of the most fantastical
misunderstandings in regard to my character.

I am afraid you could not call this "goodwill" by the name
of love; certainly not love in the ordinary human sense, implying warmth, sympathy, affection. And yet when I read the
famous list of attributes, given by St. Paul—with whose personality I have many points of extreme sympathy—to that
mysterious *Agape* he makes so much of, I find that this funny
species of "goodwill" in me does seem to worm its profane
way into very theological company! It has, in fact, always
fascinated me to wonder into what precise psychological
elements this mystical "love of the saints," of which one hears
so much, actually resolves itself.

Let me for a moment be blasphemous enough to steal
St. Paul's *Agape*, and call it "charity" once more as our proper
old version has it. The truth is these conceited modernists,
with their broad-church stupidity, totally lack the imaginative
subtlety of the great old translators. Damn them, they ought
never to have been allowed to cheapen the subtle Christian
religion, that only idiots and poets and saints and angels and
devils understand, to their own level of commonplace morality.
Every fool, but a modernistic explainer-away of the magical
power of old words, knows perfectly well that "charity" in
this particular place means something different from bestowing

alms on the poor. Those old writers knew by instinct how the word "love" would be sentimentalized and prostituted, exactly as it has been.

However! Whatever sort of a mysterious feeling it was that this singular word implied, I would greatly like now to bring the whole question into the free and clear arena of imaginative discussion. My own secret feeling is that D. H. Lawrence, in his admirable attacks upon "spiritual love," has lacked the serpentine penetration to discover the true psychic mystery concealed under the syllables "*Agape*." Whatever occult, Magian, thaumaturgic meaning this *Agape* may have had it would seem at any rate to be something completely different from Dante's terrible inferno-creating "Amore."

Let me return, however, to the bottom of my own soul where I am on safer ground! I do admit, for I am not anxious to fall too deeply into Jean Jacques Rousseau's way of justifying himself, that the amber-tinted drop of "good-will" I am talking about is not a warm, glowing, affectionate attraction. But, such as it is, it is *exactly the same* when it is directed towards people as when it is directed towards animals. It is in fact an amber-coloured bubble-drop composed of the very stuff of my bowels of compassion! Do I bewilder you, reader, with all this rigmarole? Let me make it clear. When I rescue a fly drowning in a pool with the end of my stick I am obeying exactly the same impulse that made me—against "The Catholic's" opinion—prostrate myself flat on my stomach before the Corpus authorities. I wanted them to feel that they were in the right! Of course I do not deny that I was rewarded for this gesture towards these authorities by a delicious surging wave of masochistic emotion! But what *is* any subtle virtue if not something that rewards everybody concerned? Llewelyn, had he been old enough then to play the rôle he played later in my life, would have roundly denounced my behaviour. But he would have denounced it on more direct grounds than "The Catholic." He would have plainly said that I was in the right and the authorities were in the wrong; and that in a world like this when people act contrary to the "sweet reasonableness" of attic wisdom they ought to be *stood up to*. Thus would

Llewelyn have defended honesty and sincerity in this blown bubble of a world irridescent with illusion!

Yes, even if my amber-tinted drop of "good-will" so child-like in its incorrigible naïveté and resembling what Dostoievsky's "Idiot" displayed when he was least inspired, has no connection with the mystery of the "love of the saints," it certainly exists independently of the less equivocal human virtues! It never for a second occurred to me, as I thus cringed and cringed in the presence of what was obscure, that "I owed it to myself" to get the truth threshed out. "By Gis and by St. Charity," the minds of sensible men are not devised, formed, adapted, adjusted, constructed, or even intended, to jump at one leap into a thing as subtle as this psychic-sensuous Tao, or "way," to the brink of which, on the strength of that Corpus Christi wine, I had unthinkingly blundered.

No wonder the Chinaman enjoyed the spectacle of my "spirit-led" inspiration, and no wonder the East-Indian was so agitated! What, in my childishness, in my cerebral vicious-ness, in my Punchinello gesticulations, in my naïveté, I had stumbled on, was a Tremendum Mysterium of the first water. Like Peredur, in the Welsh myth, my Simple Simon foolish-ness had led me on to the very edge of catching a glimpse of that Marriage of Psyche and Eros towards which so many mystics have groped. I have always been one for borderlands and no-man's lands and what children call Tom Tiddler's grounds; but I had no rational notion, no notion at all, at that time, where I was going. But you can see, all the same, that having been understood by no one except a Chinaman in my roundabout approach to the Tao, it was appropriate enough that I should reply to the magnates of my father's College, in a sort of Chinese.

But they accepted my equivocal "apologia" in a friendly spirit and I *did* give that public lecture in Cambridge. I made the occasion of giving it, in fact, an opportunity for an exciting meeting of all my most intimate friends. Llewelyn had just come up to Corpus; and he and Louis found lodgings for them all. Bernie was there and "The Catholic" and Cousin Ralph. It was a wonder that I did not "realize" a scene out of my

unprintable work and bring Mr. de —— too! I recollect how
we all had lunch at an inn not far from the old Trumpington
Mill. But the lecture fell flat. The Chinaman came, but was
grievously disappointed! I had bowed down in the House of
Rimmon. My vision had departed.

It amuses me now to recall the fact that many years after
this failure at Cambridge I gave my final lecture at Oxford under
similar conditions. Here again I collected my friends together
for one of these dramatic "symposia" for which I had such a
passion. At Oxford, however, it was upon Rabelais I lectured
and though my new friend Tom Jones, was there, and my
brother Bertie, and both Bernie and Louis, "The Catholic"
could not be persuaded to come. The Oxford he had known
had been that of Ernest Dowson and Lionel Johnson, and I
expect he felt he could not endure to see the new generation.
But my lecture was as much of a failure as my public one at
Cambridge had been. It was not outspoken enough for my
friends, and it was too outspoken for the authorities!

The last of these grown-up "Volentiā Teas," at which I
played both the wilful magician and the romantic master of
ceremonies, took place in London, at a small hostelry on the
river near Billingsgate. This time Bertie, for a very sufficient
reason, was the important guest, but Bernie was there too, and
I got "The Catholic" to come by going myself to fetch him
from where he was then living at Reigate. "The Catholic" had
always a deep burning passion—I can call it no less—for
Spain. It is indeed one of the tragic things, in a life that always
moved on the edge of tragedy, that this man was destined to
die without once seeing the country he loved. He made it a
kind of desperate secret cult to "prepare" himself for seeing
Spain. He was reluctant to go till he felt himself "ready."
But he never went. He died in France. Spain, however, was in
my mind as I saw him sitting there, drinking what I fear must
have been the very poor wines I had provided, and in my
blundering puppet-showman way I compelled them all, as we
looked down on the sunlit tide of Spenser's river, "to drink
to Spain."

I was in a wild and extravagant mood. Yes, I was in a very

high-pitched temper that day, for I had with me—and they all
accepted her most graciously—a little street-girl called Lily,
with whom I had made friends, and in whose company I had
just gone on a "Sentimental Journey" to the grave of Dan
Leno, the famous clown. What with the influence of this dead
Yorrick, and Lily's presence, I seemed unable to restrain my
high spirits. Well do I remember the first night I spent with
Lily. She became suddenly frightened of the view from the
battlemented window of the room we had taken which looked
out over the river near Waterloo Bridge, for it was near the
wharfs on the southern side of the Thames. In my naïve manner
I confided in Mr. de —— about her nervousness and I was
astonished at the tone, like that of some rakish eighteenth-
century Lord Mohun, of the aged poet's comment.

"What an engaging situation, Powys!" he exclaimed; and
then smiled and sighed wistfully.

This girl, Lily, created in me, or I suppose I should say
my life-illusion encountering *her* life-illusion created in me, a
most delicate and complicated happiness. Of course she fooled
me a good deal. I fancy she had a "beau" of some sort—what
in that particular profession is known as a "bully"—who
probably kept himself in liquor and cigarettes by my periodic
"presents"; but what was always striking me most about her
was innate respectability. She was the most respectable girl
I have ever known; and this in spite of the fact that she shocked
me when she first took off her clothes by the way she padded
herself, especially round her emaciated little hips, in order to
look plumper than she was. As had happened with my Brighton
girl, I had hardly known her a week before every vicious
feeling I had towards her sublimated itself into pity and
tenderness, into a romantic ideal sentiment that gave me
delicious transports.

Being under "The Catholic's" influence at that time my
whole nature was stirred to its depths by the magical richness,
palimpsest upon palimpsest, as it seemed to me then, and
indeed does still, of the poetic religiousness of the generations,
that was revealed in the cadences of the Roman liturgy. My
brothers and I—it was what we all had in common—had

acquired, out of our readings from earliest childhood a deep earthy response to the Authorized Version of the Bible. But this mediæval Latin, this liturgical Latin, endowed those well-known images and metaphors with a strange and novel glamour. The fact that it was all ritual too, and in a profound sense all *acting*, satisfied my dramatic nature as nothing had ever done before. The occult mysteriousness of these holy syllables, the way in which the passion of the Psalms and the sensuous beauty of the "Song of Songs" were forever repeating themselves, caused me to go about in a sort of drugged beatitude.

> "Vadam ad montem myrrhae, et ad collem thuris.
> Dilectus meus candidus, et rubicundus, comae
> Capitis ejus sicut purpura Regis vincta
> canalibus. Quo abiit dilectus tuus ,O pulcherrima
> mulierum? Quo dilectus tuus declinavit?
> Fasciculus myrrhae dilectus meus mihi, inter
> ubera mea commorabitur. Fulcite me floribus,
> stipate me malis, quia amore langueo."

What I realized at that time was indeed nothing less than the very thing I had so delighted that Chinaman, as I fumbled towards it, drunk with Corpus wine, by *just* touching—the mystic marriage of Psyche and Eros!

Tough-minded clever people would have gazed with humorous disgust at my antics under the combined spell of Lily and the Roman liturgy. "Hypocritical loathsome sentimentality!" they would have thought. But I am prepared now, after thirty years, to defend my raptures to the uttermost! You can't sponge a powerful emotion such as I had then off the slate by repeating "disgusting sentimentality." The fragrance from the personality of Lily—though the cheap scents she used were worse than the pieces of felt with which she padded her little body—cast a glamour round whole districts of London for me! It was in "the Borough" I used generally to meet her. How well I came to know all those streets that led southward, past the old Elephant and Castle! I used sometimes to cross London Bridge to reach this district, and sometimes Waterloo Bridge. The words "The New Cut" come drifting back to me in connection with those happy days. But though the names grow faint that belong to the great City, her spirit does not, nor her divine courage, nor her infinite relish for life, nor her subtleties in enjoying it! Country-born and country-bred as I was, my quest for the magic that women alone can work endeared London for ever to me! In Paris I found pornography enough, enough to satisfy the trembling knees and the shaking fingers, but in London, always, always, I found poetry and romance! If I did not quite reach the point of crying with Elia: "O City abounding in whores, for thee may Rainbarrow and Bullbarrow, Pilsden and Polden, Alfred's Tower and Shaston Camp go hang!" it is certain that the girlish magic which emanated from the consumptive chest, padded hips, and false jewellery of Lily gave to London, especially on *Shakespeare's side* of the Thames, a deep rich intoxicating glory, like one of those quivering sketches of Turner, where the thick smoke clings about funnels and masts and bridges and warehouses, like the desire of a lover about the limbs of his mistress!

It was in some dark, sombre warehouse-shop, just the sort of place that Dickens, after Scott and Hardy always my favourite novelist, would turn into a circus-tent of angels and demons, that I bought a little leather-bound Roman Psalmody. Do you think I refrained from making Lily write her name— "With love from Lily"—in the title-page of this book? I can well remember the very spot where I made her do this in a street near Kennington but she scolded me, like the ultra-conventional girl she was, for "attracting attention" by writing in a book in a place "where it might make anyone wonder."

I am sure I am not deceiving myself when I say that Lily never had any particular affection for me. I was continually shocking her respectable susceptibilities; nor was her attitude, when this happened, always as "engaging" as her alarm at that high window. Her extreme propriety and, for all *I* could see, her rigid chastity, encouraged me in the end to begin introducing her to my more respectable friends. But, old-maidish as this street-girl was, she was either too faithful to her "beau" or too habituated to the routine of her profession, which has its conventions as well as another, to lend herself

AA

to that sort of moralistic aid which we of the upper-middle class, when we are not exploiting them, tend to extend to women of her type. Bernie was the one I think who caught the final glimpse that any of us had of Lily, and his bulletin was that the young woman had grown plump. So perhaps her escape had been very complete; and she had got rid of her "beau," her admirer, and her saviours, all at one fling.

But the epoch of my life I have now arrived at, when I was about thirty-two or thirty-three, is an epoch memorable to me for ever as representing the real beginning of my lifelong intimacy—for it was closer than ordinary friendship—with my brother Llewelyn. Llewelyn is twelve years younger than I am, so that it was during his vacations while he was at Corpus and during his holidays, while he was an usher and a tutor, that we used to go about together. Our happiest times were at Montacute. Day after day we would start off in the morning and walk north, south, east and west. Day after day we would start off in the afternoon and walk, God knows how far, again. We went to Tintinhull and Ilchester, to Odcombe and Yeovil, to Ham Hill and Ilminster, to Norton and One Tree Hill. There were few lanes, few cattle droves, few sheep tracks, I might almost say few foxes' paths, that we did not know.

I can remember so well how once after what might be described as a "Command" tennis game at Montacute House, we set off in the radiant high spirits of an escape from good behaviour, across Tintinhull Great Field into the Fosse Way, across the Ilchester flats, into Ilchester, where we actually got a boat at the inn and rowed upon the river there; as we rowed we quoted poetry to each other without end, or limit, or pause, *read* poetry to each other, felt so much in harmony with each other that our souls within us broke in waves of happiness; each soul against the soul of the other. Our intimacy seemed to imply that what we felt, we felt not as two entities but as one entity.

We used to love to linger at the village of Tintinhull. This was, I think, our favourite place of all, where the old stocks stood yet under the trees, and where Llewelyn liked to pretend, to enhance the blessedness of being alive, like Montaigne causing himself to be waked up in the night the better to enjoy the pleasure of repose, that his brother John, lay stiff and stark, with what he himself often declared was natural to him, *the cunning of a corpse*, in the "morningless and unawakening sleep," between church and tavern.

It was while we were entering Tintinhull one day that we met a tramp who after staring for a long time in a trance of admiration at the beauty of Llewelyn, who smiled back at him like an angel, cried aloud in his rude excitement:

"O Woman's Mouth! O Woman's Mouth!"

Did I, as we went on in the glimmering August haze, quote the beginning of the great Shakespearean sonnet:

"A woman's face with Nature's own hand painted
Hast thou, the master-mistress of my passion."

Indeed I might well have done so, considering the bond and the sacred covenant between us. And I might have concluded too with the final lines:

"But since she prick'd thee out for women's pleasure,
Mine be thy love, and thy love's use their treasure."

Llewelyn was certainly, during those years he was at Cambridge, more full of the abounding magnetism of life than any human being I have ever known. He literally radiated the sun-born exultation that mounted up with immortal exuberance within him. Everything he touched turned to imaginative gold. His humour, his high spirits, seemed inexhaustible. He drank of Life till he reeled into the morning-mists of Creation. He became one of those Sons of the Morning that William Blake imagined. Alas! it was only a few years of this super-human radiance that the Powers allowed him. Mortal men—even such as are born in August—are forbidden to become as gods, knowing good and evil. Too soon the thunderbolt fell that doomed him to a prolonged struggle with tuberculosis. But, as all who know him are aware, even this crippling of his strength, even this sapping of his vitality, left his sturdy zest for earthly existence—existence on any terms—unimpaired, and his "natural force" unabated. He "steered right onward" with his flag mast-high, even though his top-gallant sail swung in tatters and his rigging was lying over the side.

Llewelyn's compassionate regard for me will remain, until I die, one of those things in the world to be set up against life's abominations. He has always seemed just as pleased over any success of mine as over his own. And in the profoundest sense of the word, for all his whimsical Narcissism, he has a humility that often makes me jump.

We are just the opposite in *this*. He has the humility of a real artist, whereas I am too proud to take my work seriously, save where it gives me some particular thrilling sensation. As a writer I am even more abandoned to sensations than I am in real life. But how often have I heard Llewelyn cry out, when his writings have brought him some especial triumph:

"You see, John, I am not a dizzard after all!"

No, he certainly is not a dizzard; but in a purely *academic* sense, though more cautious than I am, he can be almost as childish.

Theodore's genius, for all the simplicity and purity of his style, is much more disillusioned, in a sense much more sophisticated, than anything possible to us. But Llewelyn is in reality something different from just a writer. He belongs to that rare company of Englishmen who—after our great poets and our great humorists—remain the peculiar and special glory of our race. He is a man of action; but a man of action of a very special type, the type *who act in order to feel*, not the type who lose themselves in action. His real peers are such rare formidable personages as Doughty and Clifford and Cunninghame Graham; and like Doughty he naturally and instinctively expresses himself in poetical archaisms. In his notions about politics and public affairs he tends to resemble Wilfrid Scawen Blunt. His favourite books remain always the same, the old wily, shrewd, quaint writers, full of mellow wisdom and wanton whimsies, like Thomas Burton and

Montaigne, but I think, beyond prose-writers of any kind, what has the greatest effect upon his inveterate habits of feeling is the ancient ballad poetry of England and Scotland.

I have had the privilege of watching his growth from the beginning into that rich *idiosyncrasy* which now distinguishes him; and I confess that in my conceit of my superior cleverness I was stupidly slow, much slower than I was with Theodore, to recognize where he was a better writer than I. He too was slow to recognize this; and he has always tended to overrate my intellectual influence upon him. This has seldom been more than what a fast-moving restless theoretical intelligence can exert over a banked-up, earth-bound nature. What I really did for him was what Mr. Blake, Mr. Wildman, Mr. King, old Koelle, G. P. Gooch, and, as far as "art" is concerned, Thomas Henry Lyon, did, if you roll all these very different persons into one, for me. He listened to me, watched me reverently, wondered at me critically, took warning by me, and went his own way.

As a little boy his idol was Littleton, who returned his love with a warmth of which my "cold planetary heart" was incapable. Faithful and infinitely tender to Theodore he has always been, and I noticed that when, grown to man's estate, he became Theodore's companion. Theodore would relax, unbend, utter quips and jibes, chuckle and feel happy, nay! be impishly merry with him, in a way he never felt able to be with Littleton or with me; no! not since those early days at Sherborne, when in his Prep. straw-hat and his Eton jacket he would await us at the top of the hill for our Sunday afternoon walk till we came hurrying out of Wildman's yard.

If I suffered when I first went to school what must Theodore, so much more predisposed to suffering, have gone through? It comes back to me now what a relief it was when he went to Louis Wilkinson's people at Aldeburgh where I could tell from his letters how much happier he was. When I think of those mournful grey eyes, under that straw hat, that used to turn to us as we came hurrying up that hill, when I think of the same forlorn gaze fixed so hopelessly on the weary stretch of the road to Saxmundham market, it does my heart good to envisage the formidable grey head that now nods over the fire, chuckling at Llewelyn's stories.

Had my father stopped begetting children before his fifth son was born a certain relaxed and untrammelled humour in Theodore might never have enjoyed itself, nor certain sardonic comments aimed at life found their responsive billet. I am myself, I fancy, at once too impulsively innocent and too wickedly self-absorbed to be the perfect companion for him that Llewelyn is. In earlier days, before certain funny ways and funnier fancies we both indulged in had been beaten smooth by life, it was quite different. But how quaint it is to think that my youngest brother Willy is the only one of whom I have ever been seriously jealous as far as Llewelyn is concerned! I never was jealous of his intimate link with Bertie. But I did—and I can recall my emotion with precise vividness —burst out savagely once over Willy. It was when we were all together one afternoon, seated in the terrace-walk at Montacute, that this, to me, soul-shaking event occurred. Llewelyn was always something of a tease—he has a faint touch of my own sadistic tendency, but *so* faint that he can afford, as he can with every other perversity, for he is the least suppressed person ever born, to give it entire vent—and on this sunny afternoon he set himself to tease me. This would have been perfectly all right if he had not brought Willy into it, for he had teased me quite remorselessly many times before, as for example when he described with terrifying gusto the manner in which an old gentleman we knew had gone raving mad and become what Llewelyn called a "Ramper," and as when he described a half-slaughtered sheep, its wool grown scarlet with its own blood, as when he described in detail the contents of a pornographical book of the sort most kindling to my vicious imagination; but his bringing Willy into it set me off. Willy, powerful and silent as he was, and singularly well-pleased to be alone, was always one for certain irrepressible giggling fits when any pompousness, or priggishness, or unnecessary spasm of nerves, presented itself in an elder brother.

But to be the subject of a humorous attack from Llewelyn,

accompanied by spurts of suppressed amusement from Willy, was too much for me. I got up trembling and shaking from head to foot, extended my arm to its full length, and my long index-finger to *its* full length, and cried in a shrill high-pitched voice, like the voice of old Meg Merrilies or Norna of the Fitful Head:

"*Young man*, I'll never forgive you for this!"

I have often been furiously angry with Littleton, but never without plunging at once into a physical contest, which, even when I got the worst of it, mightily relieved my feelings. But this anger was a very different thing! This was the sort of wrath, with that dangerous pit-of-the-stomach quiver in it, that as a rule only women have the power of exciting in me. This event took place on that terrace-walk at Montacute which has become to us like the Rialto at Venice, or like the Forum at Rome, a place dedicated to oracular and memorable remarks. It was on the terrace-walk that I confided in Llewelyn and Louis about the Fear that needed so much skill, and so many wiles and devices, to keep in subjection and reduce to oblivion. I was even then far too crafty a ruler of my unruly mind to confide in them the nature of the existing "avatar" of this Demon of many Incarnations; and if you force me, reader, to tell you the precise truth, I was astonished at the cool way these two young blades received this hint of my underlying insanity.

But the heart alone knoweth its own aberrations. It was in the terrace-walk too, and in the presence of Llewelyn and Bertie, that I cried out once: "Oh, for something really startling to happen!" And you may believe I remembered that dangerous speech a little later, when the War came bolt upon us. It was in the terrace-walk that Theodore, when he had an unusual mood of felicitous well-being, heaved a great sigh and exclaimed to our surprise: "I feel like Southey in Portugal!"

It is extraordinary how united in our life Llewelyn and I became, considering the enormous gulf between our temperaments. We have been friends in the old Homeric sense. I only hope I did not bring down his consumption on him when I stretched out my bony finger towards his chest in that threatening manner. As a matter of fact, looking back at my life from the foot of this wooded hill in New York State, I am struck by the fact that, for some reason or other, I have seldom laid a curse on anyone—and for this reason I have come of late to restrain my maledictions—but some crushing catastrophe, very often death itself, has fallen on the person. I could give you instance after instance, and Littleton can bear me out in the earlier cases, of persons who have insulted, ill-used, mal-treated, attacked, disparaged, maligned me, meeting with some overwhelming if not some fatal disaster! Is it possible, I ask myself, is it conceivable, that I who from that far-off afternoon in the lane at Shirley when I played at being the "Lord of Hosts," have been always imagining myself a magician should really be possessed of a certain fatal power over my enemies? The *coincidence*, anyway, if such it be, has happened so often that I have given up allowing myself to indulge in feelings of hatred.

Llewelyn will lift his eyebrows when he comes to this passage. His assurance is certainly definite enough that the visible world is made up of a checkable verifiable palpable material substance that will go on its way for ever, through what, to me, is an unthinkable void of Not-Being, even though all minds, including that of the Demiurge, were to dissolve into air; but I note in him a curious indulgence to many of my superstitions! The truth is, he'll be indulgent to any of them and even go half-way, as long as they remain honestly and primitively *heathen*, but the second they approach Christianity, as a system of Truth, they stink in his nostrils, and he casts them from him with angry contempt.

I think the vast difference between Llewelyn and myself can be best realized in our attitude to ourselves. I am far more elusive, far less solid, far more trickily neurotic than he in my attitude to myself. I use myself for the sensations I can get out of myself, but I never cast a tender eye upon myself. But you can see at a glance how Llewelyn's attitude to himself perforates his flesh and blood; how it flows outward like an immortal stain or dye, how it characterizes his accent, his gestures, the least lifting of his eyebrows, the least clouding of his forehead.

For all *my* propitiations and for all *his* sun-born sweetness I doubt if either of us really ever forget a deep outrage to our life-illusion. How far we *forgive*—I really do not quite know! I think I am more likely to go out of my way to be nice to persons of whose character and tone and temper I disapprove than he is. Llewelyn says I am a spreader of carpets. He says I spread carpet after carpet before people, leading them on and on and on, till finally they discover they have crossed a kind of pit—like those pits I dug for old Curme in the potato-garden—and at *that* point, when they can't step back, I fall upon them, bursting out in one of my quivering rages and denouncing them for things which *at the time they did them* I passed off with the utmost affability.

But if I am what might be called an extreme type of anti-narcissism, Theodore, in the convolutions of his terrifying originality, goes further still. Let us take, since I am now talking of grown-up men, our characteristic ways of dealing with our beards! One of my dominating manias is a dislike of the thought of dipping a hirsute face into a cup or bowl or flagon; and it sets my teeth terribly on edge even to think of wiping my mouth with a napkin, a thing I always do with the back of my hand. My hatred of handkerchiefs is so great that I invariably turn my eyes away when my interlocutor is using one; and how people can use their handkerchiefs, while they keep their eyes fixed upon you, is a wonder to me. The almost universal human trick of looking into your handkerchief after you have blown your nose, seems to my finicking punctilio a reversion to the ways of dogs. The more than complaisance, in fact, with which so many persons regard their excretions is a mystery to me. I get pleasure from doing what, in imitation of our good Squire, I will call "pumping-ship"; but I take no pleasure in beholding what I have done. I am certainly no *voyeur* there! I am a Manichean, the son of a Manichean, and it is in my fastidiousness as much as anything else that I resemble my father.

"This egg is so messy!" he would indignantly declare,

looking hopelessly at our preoccupied faces, till once more, his long spatulate fingers holding the tiny silver spoon, he fell to struggling with that tricky protoplasm.

But to return to our beards. How queer it is to think of our smooth boy-faces, as we passed up our plates for more of Mr. Cole's butter, or of that unequalled brown bread that came from a baker in Stoke, and cajoled our father into telling us for the thousandth time how he was wont to use "climbing-irons," when he hunted for hawks' eggs, wearing beards at all! Littleton has, I believe, a football champion's objection to growing a beard. Llewelyn, I know, always grows a great defiant buccaneer beard when his illness makes a special effort to compel him to "cave in," and I think it gives him a mighty comfort at such times to feel like a Dutch sea-captain. Bertie has grown a beard of late and has trimmed it and pointed it. Its effect with him, I think, is to intensify a certain quizzical air he has that always makes me feel as if I were an appealing Liliputian in the presence of an affectionate Gulliver. I felt this once, I remember, in the London Tube; and I seemed to be growing so rapidly smaller and smaller and smaller under his affectionate gaze that my voice sounded in my own ears like the voice of Alice in Wonderland. Bertie is like my father's Giant Grumble. Dr. O'Neill once remarked that every member of our particular offshoot of the Powys family was like a separate branch of one single tree-trunk. If this *is* the case, the branch represented by the initials *A. R. P.* is the one most conscious of this unity! Without question Bertie does, of all of us, most closely resemble my father, and, like my father, his undemonstrative feelings have roots that go straight down, like the deep-burrowing root of a dock-plant.

But I have not yet referred to the beard that Theodore at one time wore. He was wearing it I think when he wrote his *Soliloquy of a Hermit.* I am sure it got on Theodore's nerves to feel himself one of a clamorous, boisterous, self-complacent, optimistic crowd, as I am afraid we sometimes must have seemed to him when we gathered round him at his remote retreat, drawn by the magnet of his personality. I have often noticed—and I think I understand his feeling—that when we moved about around him, in our awkward innocence, he would shrink into himself, and grow physically frailer and slighter, and even move and speak in an indrawn muted manner, as if he were only disguised for the nonce in our Powysian flesh and blood and would very willingly put it off. At such times, as he withdrew himself into himself, an expression of stricken, smitten, *terrible* melancholy would rise up, like an ice-cold film from the silt at the bottom of the sea and diffuse itself over his grey eyes. His eyes at such times would grow very much larger, and in some alarming way closer together, and would curiously darken.

But the Demon that tormented him never allowed him to betray its great buggerly horns at such times, but would force him to brood over some wretched little nuisance or some teasing little worry. He was like a tragic Prometheus whom the vulture that gnawed his liver forced to complain to the sympathetic Io about the cold snail-slime upon that promontory, or to the pitying Oceanides about the gnats in the wild currant-bushes up there.

Of course in a sense all we mortal men are the same in this matter. The First Cause has got his lasso round the "funny bone" of each of us, and loves to give it a twitch now and again, to show who's the master, while what we *tell* one another is that our porridge is cold, or that our door lets in the draught, or that "something's bitten us." Yes, in his inspired directness, over the little realistic details that pinch and prod and tickle and scratch us all, Theodore has, for all his eccentricity, a stark universality that resembles that of Dürer. Certain scenes in his books seem to me unsurpassed in their humour, though I confess there *are* passages here and there that I invariably skip, just as I have skipped, since I was in the Prep., Dickens' description of the murdering of Nancy. If this is a weakness in me from an æsthetic point of view, I can only declare, like an obstinate old woman, that while there are many unspeakable things done and endured in this ghastly world it is painful to me when one of my favourite writers refuses to leave to God his monopoly in holy terror.

As I say, I think I can understand something, though no

doubt not all, of the withdrawing-mood that made Theodore tread so gingerly where we were apt to go ramping and rough-shod. I can even follow afar off the feeling in him that always led him to speak of our begetter, not, as I am doing in this book, as *my* father, but as "*your* father." Thus in an unmistakable manner he removed himself by at least one remove from all tincture of sentimental clannishness.

When I call myself an *anti-narcissist* I mean that I have a morbid dislike of thinking of my physical appearance. The only portions of myself that I ever dwell upon with any complacency are my knees and my hands. But if I am an anti-narcissist, what, I ask you, was Theodore when on an occasion when it was imperative for him to refer to his beard, instead of speaking of it as "my beard" he spoke of it as "*this* beard"? Had he been a Mohammedan his version of the oath, "By the Beard of the Prophet," would have been, "By *that* Beard of *your* Prophet." It was in a similar mood that he would detach himself even from his favourite writers, always referring to Nietzsche, for instance, as "*that* German."

Nothing could be farther from Theodore's ways than my own convoluted habit, when people are vexing me, of luring them on to do it more and more and more, as if just to see how far they will go, my tendency in fact of revenging myself on them by encouraging them to victimize me. Even when my dog annoys me, by prolonged and head-splitting barking, never a finger will I lift, never a word will I breathe to stop him. I hate a barking dog too much for that! And my cat I will let sit on my chest, as I lie on my back writing, while its tail jerks my pen. In this passivity my motives are two-fold. I really do hate to destroy even a moment's pleasure in any living organism; but I also feel too furiously indignant with the beast to push her away!

Do I ever burst out, where Theodore is concerned, in those fits of blind rage that I have displayed at times towards Littleton and Llewelyn? *Me genoito!* Never, never! And why is that? I think it is because I have seen a degree of suffering in Theodore's face that I have never seen in either of theirs. How can I burst out, though no one knows better than he how

to catch a person "on the hop," when I see him wearing those
fearful scars of thunder? You can't be wicked towards someone, however his *bon mots* may hit the weak spot in your
armour, upon whom the First Cause sends his "urchins" to
"exercise."

By slow degrees during these first five years at Burpham,
after my son's birth, I did begin to get better control over my
nerves. Did my approach to Roman Catholicism help me in
this? I cannot tell; but I think the sense of my son's being in
the world did something. On the other hand I had deep moods
of rebellion against all responsibility, against everything that
interfered with my being a free-booter, like William of
Deloraine, with my stick—the successor of "Sacred"—as my
spear, and with those third-class carriages, whirling me all
over England, as my "dapple-grey steed." I well recall a visit
we paid with my son to Norwich, to the kindest relatives that
a man ever possessed. Looking back on that visit now what
would I not give to enjoy that drawing-room—all the wonderful Northwold pictures and furniture, the gilded Louis
Quatorze chairs, the portrait of William Cowper, yes, even
that very picture of Venice which used to hang where those
blossoms of the magnolia grew outside, all, all, all gathered in
that old house in the Close—and to drink to the dregs the
delicious cup of remembrance, remembrance of those days
when I was so happy by the banks of the Wissey and with
Littleton!

But the terribly deep urge in my restless nature for a
satisfaction of that double exigency within me, desire for a
certain kind of erotic thrill and desire to be a magician, drove
a villainous and heartless wedge between my triumph in my
son, my happiness in taking him to the edge of that Norwich
river, and all those passionate memories of Northwold. I
wandered about the old castle grounds, like a lost soul, hunting
for any kind of fleeting satisfaction for that queer vice that
obsessed me; and, in the enforced intervals of this, I pondered a monstrous epic poem, to be entitled "The Death of
God." Of this poem I *did* write no less than six little exercise
books full. I must have written from five hundred to a thousand

lines! I remember one extravagant passage towards the end—
or rather towards where I broke off and left it—that introduced
in some wild scene "out of space, out of time," a distorted
phantom of St. Paul, and I remember winning a rare word of
commendation from Louis Wilkinson himself, when I read
this passage to him, one day on the terrace-walk!

It is curious how late any sort of moral sense within me
with regard to my vice came into being. There was no trace
of such a thing in those days! Nor did I realize in the least the
difficulties, the obstacles, the practical hindrances that make
it so hard even for the most detached person to find complete
satisfaction for his erotic cravings in this world. It was not
till I had visited America and found there, in so many deliberately provocative performances on the burlesque stage, a
satisfaction that I have never found before, that my conscience
—so active in other directions—began to bestir itself. This
new disturbance was partly due I believe to my fastidious
reactions against these burlesque shows. At any rate when I
came back from America it became a by-word in my little
circle, the way I would refer to my "divine" mood and my
"devilish" mood. Indeed I used to make frantic struggles at
that later date, when I was about thirty-five, to shake off this
erotic obsession altogether; but as far as I can recall now, in
those earlier years at Burpham, I was impregnable to the
stirrings of conscience where my *voyeur* mania was concerned.
To be the nympholept, or "sylpholept" I then was, seemed to
me so absolutely inevitable that it never crossed the threshold
of my consciousness—not even when I approached the
Roman Church—that I could struggle against it. The mere
sound of the syllable "girl," as I have already hinted, whether
you rhymed it with "pearl" or not, opened such a Paradise to
me that everything else in life became negligible. I seriously
think it is very likely that since those vision-tormented Monks
of the Thebaid no mortal brain has realized the magical desirableness of girls to the extent I did!

My epic poem, "The Death of God," was modelled on the
blank verse of Milton, Keats, and Tennyson. It was an extremely
imitative poem, but since it was after all, a narration, I was

compelled to be more original in it than I had ever been before in my verses. There are, in fact, several passages in it—I possess my long-hand fair-copy still—that really *have* a certain inventive, and even a flickering poetic, merit.

And what did I feel, instinctively, intuitively, and with what Matthew Arnold calls "the Imaginative Reason," about the secret of the cosmos at that time? I will tell you. I felt exactly as I have felt all my life! My father's faith in Evangelical Christianity was the single thing about him that never affected me one jot. Harry Lyon's Anglican conversion did not affect me; and, as you have seen, the least touch of my father's crafty *argumentum ad hominem* was enough to blow "The Catholic's" influence off the chess-board. Harry Lyon's final conclusion, "Jack has no soul," does not, however, *inevitably* follow from my refusal to accept the Anglo-Catholic faith, or even the Roman Catholic faith. It certainly does not follow from my inability to accept my father's evangelical faith.

On the other hand I have never been able to feel assured, as Llewelyn does, in the rooted solidity of this visible world, and the poppycock-insubstantiality of everything else. The game I played in that lane at Shirley when I felt myself to be the Demiurge, the game I played at Dorchester when I became a magician calling up Escrawaldons and Dromonds from the abyss, the game I played at Sherborne, when I hid in the oak-tree below the Honeycomb Woods, the game I played at Cambridge when I refused to be converted to Science by Sidney Roland, remained the same game that I played at Burpham, as, suffering from my ulcers, I watched from my deck-chair my son climb up and down the laburnum to that high bank. The background of my game was the certainty— not a rational theory, mind you, but a certainty grasped with that "illative sense" of which Cardinal Newman speaks—that this astronomical world apprehended by our senses is only one mental bubble, real as far as it goes, but only one little drop, among endless other cosmic bubbles of similar *mental stuff*, bubbles of solution and dissolution, from the innumerable centres to the innumerable circumferences of which move the thoughts that create and destroy them.

I have always believed that the imagination and the will have a creative power. What a person wills and what a person imagines become a mysterious part of *what is*. It is madness to spend your days trying to eliminate what your own will and spirit and imagination are perpetually adding to the mystery of life. I have always known—ever since my father brought it about, as we walked to Preston Brook at Weymouth, or across the fields to the Ashbourne Road at Shirley, or home, with our watering-pots full of minnows, from the Stinsford Brooks at Dorchester, that his giant and his fairy should over-come *The Professor*—that the most vain and treacherous of all pursuits was the pursuit of truth. Socrates is right. What we need is more wisdom. We have got enough knowledge! The greatest word ever uttered on earth about truth was when Jesus said: "I am the truth." However wrong His ideas may have been about God and Sin and Judgment, He was surely right in His main point, namely that the ultimate "truth" in this world of mental bubbles is a living organism.

These electric forces are only real, just as the old "matter" was only real, when they are considered as portions of a living Being. I assure you I cannot remember the time when I did not feel the universe to be *a congeries of living organisms*. Some of these are visible, some are invisible, but when Llewelyn talks to me of a checked-up, verifyable, solid-block monistic universe, I cannot take him seriously enough even to get angry. Good God! Why the wildest fancies of a madman have more of *the real reality*, the creative reality of life in them, than the whole of this tricky objective mirage that people nowadays call "space-time." What I had *not* realized in those days and indeed have only realized during this last decade is that it is possible to use all these old theological conceptions, covered by such expressions as Morality, God, Immortality, the Free-dom of the Will, Prayer, Redemption, and so forth, to serve your own private secret purpose, while you drop their super-ficial ordinary meaning.

Why should we allow the old-fashioned religious people to have such an advantage over us? They certainly *do* have an advantage over us in many important ways. Why not steal their crafty devices and use them for secular ends? For example, according to religious people you ought at every moment to make mental efforts to be loving and humble. Very good! I agree entirely with this method; I agree with these constant efforts! But since lovingness and humility are not what I am most in need of just now I feel completely justified in substituting a *different effort*, an equally sturdy one I hope, but a *different* one. Thus I steal the psychological devices of my father and my grandfather and use them to my own ends.

Carlyle was so delighted to discover that ancient monkish saying: *laborare est orare*, "to work is to pray." What I have been led to substitute for this aphorism, according to my "Philosophy of Representation," is a motto that would run: "To endure is to pray"; or to go a step further: "To endure joyfully is to see God." What I mean is that our modern pseudo-science and pseudo-realism tend to corrupt the up-mounting spring of life-acceptance in us, which keeps us going in spite the "urchins" of the First Cause. The old religious faith gave our forefathers the stoical habit of drawing their life-energy not from external conditions but from within. That they called this power, welling up from inside themselves by the name of "God" had an historical justification which is lacking to-day. But *that* is no reason for deserting the living well-spring of mysterious magic within us. Never mind the name! The point is that we *have* the power of re-creating the universe from the depths of ourselves. In doing so we share the creative force that started the whole process. It is personality, the out-rushing energy of living organisms, that underlies all the criss-cross currents of the world. Every time a living being gathers itself grimly together, and draws on its inmost vitality to be happy *in spite of all*, it is doing what our sturdy ancestors called "praying."

By degrees I got very attached to certain among the Burpham inhabitants. The generous-hearted Mr. S. married and moved away, but with Mr. Edwardes I continued to enjoy a pleasant literary friendship and never failed to admire the quiet gravity of his character.

The great event of the year at Burpham was the sheep-

washing which took place in a narrow estuary of the river.
Early in the morning a vast continuous stream of woolly sheep
would pour down the lane past our house, filling the whole
space between the walls, and making a peculiar sound unlike
anything else. Mr. Edwardes in his rôle as a writer of nature
sketches was always on the scene. So was the handsome
bearded blacksmith, Mr. Budd, leaving his formidable sons
to work at the anvil. So was Mr. Goodyear the brown-eyed
genial carpenter, and George West, the shy, gentlemanly inn-
keeper, whose father had had the George and Dragon
before him. Mr. Goodyear was always a good friend of mine,
though I vaguely mixed up his name with a terrifying passage
in *King Lear*. I astonished him, when first we met, by my quick
recognition of the magnetic quality in his jovial countenance.

Nor was there missing at that sheep-washing the youthful
shop-keeper of our village, George Roadnight. The respect
we had for this incomparable young man remains with me
still as a most happy memory. With a smooth high forehead
and a large ruddy clean-shaven face, with a choice and even
meticulous manner of speech, George Roadnight played the
part of a benevolent Home Secretary to our small hamlet.
A Liberal in politics he seemed to stand as the mediating focus-
point between all the clashing and contradictory forces of our
little community. We all came to him; we all leaned on him;
we all trusted him. I have never known in my life any human
being so dedicated to take the right path in troubled waters!
The side upon which George Roadnight was was always the
right side; and Mr. Mais, the vicar, who resembled a saintly
sea-captain, had the sagacity to support him.

Contrary to what often happens in energetic families, the
sons of Mr. Collyer and Mr. Graburn, our two squire-farmers,
for the Duke of Norfolk obliterated all ordinary distinctions,
stuck to their parents' homes, and finally took their parents'
places. They were youths of good parts and of charming
presence but they were almost as shy of me as I was of them.

All these persons used to meet by the river's edge during
that sheep-washing time. But personally I only went once,
and then only for five minutes; for I am frightened of even the

nicest people when they are together in a crowd. I can remember coming bolt up against the whole band of Mr. Graburn's men, eating their meal in the harvest-field, and I was so terrified that in dead silence I shuffled past them as if I had been a deaf-mute.

It was during my northerly travels, in those earlier Burpham days, that I first met another important addition to my inner circle of friends. Louis Wilkinson used to laugh at me for the way I insisted on calling it a "circle," as if we were I know not what kind of a group on the left bank of the Seine. But it *was* a circle; and contrasted with it my group of intimate American friends, Mr. Dreiser, Mr. Masters, Colonel C. E. S. Wood, Mr. A. D. Ficke, Mr. Robert Bright, certainly do not make a circle! Mr. Bright, my oldest American friend of all, does not even know these others that I have mentioned! This final addition to the inner circle of the people of my life—for it is hard to make intimate and familiar friendships after forty—was Tom Jones. Like "The Catholic," though his departure from this world was a much sadder one, Tom Jones has been dead for several years.

Before he died—some half a dozen or more years ago—he wrote me a five-page letter, in his well-known clerkly hand, relating the wretched misfortunes of the final years of his life. He was a super-skilled clerk in an old Anglo-American House of cotton importers, and in the service of this firm, in the Cotton Exchange at Liverpool, he lavished his life's energy and his extraordinary mathematical gifts. It was the War and the subsequent Depression that produced the events that ended in Tom Jones's death. He had lived in lodging-houses all his life on one bank or the other of the Mersey and he died in a lodging-house in Birkenhead. I cannot say that our English world treated this noble, passionate and secretive Welshman as his brain, or his spirit, or his heart, deserved. Woeful was his end. He came to London to spend, as was his wont, his Christmas with Bernie, but his departure was a forlorn one, and as he got into the familiar train, to take his solitary way back to Birkenhead they tell me he remarked to Louis who saw him off, that he had had enough of his life on the terms offered him then by destiny. A few days after that visit his landlady found him dead in his bed. With a single exception the death of Tom Jones affected me more than any death I have as yet known.

How often have I slept with him in those Mersey lodging-houses! Curiously enough he was, except for Llewelyn and Bernie, the only grown man I have ever slept with. On my soul I cannot even imagine myself sleeping with any other man. I loved Tom Jones. Louis used to maintain that I only loved him because of the incalculable advantages I got out of him; out of staying with him in his various places, out of being treated by him to endless teas and coffees in those sumptuous Kardomah cafés, and, above everything else, out of enjoying the privilege of knowing his innumerable girl-friends. My exultation and my rapturous happiness during my visits to Tom Jones in Liverpool were indeed unparalleled. Louis is right there. But I can swear across my heart that I loved the man *for himself*, as girls say, apart from the aura, the radiation, the delicious glamour, that of necessity hung about him! Those periodic visits to Liverpool certainly remain among the happiest times of my whole life. And why? Because, for once I lived in a classic atmosphere of complete freedom as far as sex is concerned! It has never happened to me again.

I have had love affairs at other epochs. I have had romantic infatuations at other epochs. These Liverpool experiences were neither love affairs nor infatuations. They were, purely and simply, friendly erotic encounters between men and women. They were enjoyed with no afterthoughts of emotional agitation, no complicated responsibilities, no tragic jealousies. They were experiences of perfectly simple, honourable, delicious pleasure on both sides. They were Arcadias of idyllic felicity. They were an eternal recurrence of the Golden Age. I had never met such girls before. I have never met such girls since. They were mostly, I fancy, women of that "lower middle-class," so denounced by Harry Lyon. But I dare say if even Harry Lyon, for such monkish knights are not always unkind to the ungodly, could have followed Tom Jones and myself through one of our long adventurous days on those

Mersey banks he would have moderated his opinion. For Harry Lyon, as I trust I have already indicated, in my turgid struggles to delineate his unique character, has nothing of the snob in him.

Possibly he would have tried to prove that "Tom Jones's girls," as I used to call these sweet-natured women, belonged to the proletariate. They certainly were different from the Bohemians of New York. I have never properly mixed with the livelier denizens of Greenwich village; but must not the intellectual and æsthetic jealousies of young people who are setting out to do what in America is called "creative work," militate considerably against the pure enjoyment of men and women in each other? But perhaps they *were* proletarians, these wonderful Liverpool girls. Perhaps they were what all our women-folk will become in a few hundred years! Or perhaps the real explanation is that they were Welsh, like Tom himself. I do vaguely feel that I have read somewhere in Sir John Rhys's writings, of a charming Welsh custom called "bundling," according to which young men and young women could indulge in all the dalliance they liked, short of the final consummation. Yes, I suspect they *were* Welsh; for after all Liverpool is our biggest city in the immediate neighbourhood of Wales. It is very doubtful, I fear, if any of you lovely daughters of the Mersey get a chance of reading these lines. But if you do, discreet elderly persons as ye must be now in your Cheshire homes, please try and remember me! *Can't* you recall that funny-looking friend of Tom Jones who was always reciting Milton?

Those Liverpool visits were so exciting to me that I cannot remember so much as one single time in that city when I suffered from the hurting of my ulcers. Life in Liverpool, with Tom and his friends, seemed to have a magic power of curing ulcers.

Oh, how intensely it all comes back to me! One girl, the daughter of a seafaring family, had limbs that were so slippery-smooth as to be hardly human. This pleased me well; for the Undine type has always had a maddeningly provocative effect upon me. But with one of the most charming and beguiling of all these people I had an experience similar to the one that so shocked my Brighton friend; but I was not shocked a bit. I doubt if I should have been shocked if she had been changed into a wooden image. Another among them made things more piquant for herself by constantly talking about Hell. Of course I knew that if considerations of that kind were to come up, I was the natural candidate for the flames. For there I was, using all the advantages I had from my sacred Corpus Christi education to win favour with these honest people; playing Cagliostro in fact! But who knows? Putting fears of Hell aside, I dare say the exchange was fair enough! They were certainly thrilled when Tom made me recite "Lycidas" or the "Ode to a Grecian Urn" or that poem of Landor's which begins:

> "Artimadora, Gods invisible,
>   Whilst thou wast lying faint along the couch,
>   Have tied the sandals to thy veined feet,
>   And stand beside thee, ready to convey
>   Thy weary steps where other rivers flow——"

And if they got pleasure from my recitations, a pleasure which proves how the simplest women can be brought to respond to real poetry, it can be believed how I was transported when they let me take them on my lap and caress them. As for Tom Jones, that descendant of Welsh Bards, it was a wonder to see how he would watch us, glowing and chuckling with satisfaction, just as if he had been the master of a successful puppet-show.

How different certain situations in life are, between the way you know them to be yourself, and the way they might appear to an unsympathetic onlooker! To most sophisticated people, I suppose, these encounters of ours would have appeared at once rather childish and rather maudlin, lacking in all elements of the picturesque and the piquant; yet to me they were of an intoxicating charm! Aye, but how I would like to cajole my readers to see, hear, feel, touch, taste the full physical and psychic situations of these events; so that even if they cannot restrain their dislike of the protagonist, at least they must say to themselves:

"This clown is a fine excuser of his rascalities; but the rogue is such a *naturalist* that we now hold the documents in our own hands, and can judge him as he deserves!"

Many a time I used to sit at eleven o'clock in the morning —for those Liverpool firms seemed to allow intervals for coffee at that hour, as well as for lunch at one, and for tea at four— at the "Kardomah Café," discussing with Tom his ideas of Nietzsche, for he possessed all "That German's" works, and listening to his own philosophy, which to my constant surprise seemed entirely drawn from the poetry of Keats. I can remember when he first told me, quite calmly and rationally, that in his opinion the deepest and subtlest philosophy of life that we could attain existed in poetry, and especially in that of Keats. By degrees however I came to see what he meant, and it was a striking enough conclusion for a man to have arrived at, whose whole life had been spent in office-work in a city like Liverpool. But I can tell you I made use of Tom's ideas a little later, when I wrote, for Methuen, an exhaustive work on Keats. This work was never published, because, in my absurd pride, I refused to change its more patent extravagances, but its composition forced me to clear up many problems in my own mind.

It was in this "Kardomah Café," enjoying the only palatable coffee I have ever tasted in Europe, I heard for the first time the strains of Sousa's "Stars and Stripes." Aye! but how those exultant, reckless, cynical, devil-may-care strains delighted me. I derived from them a notion of the character of the American spirit which still seems to me, after all these years, no unworthy interpretation!

When evening came we would always return to Tom's lodging—for he was meticulously careful to be a regular and considerate lodger—to partake of the usual tea-supper with the family. Oh, how impatient I used to grow, as I listened to my friend's sagacious propitiations of these various home-circles, for he changed his abode many times, and how I would tremble with excitement when very quietly and deliberately and in the most matter-of-fact way, he put off his slippers and put on his boots—all his landladies seemed to let him make these changes by their parlour hearth—and announced casually that it was time for us to be going out! It often occupied my mind—but I kept my thoughts to myself—*where* it was that these worthy family-circles supposed that their discreet lodger was taking his friend from the South. Did they think that we went to the theatre *every* night? And what excuse did Tom make—that was another problem to me; but it seemed a deep part of my friend's life-illusion to arrange these important matters without talking about it—when from some particular house we frequented he would come back alone.

I humoured this peculiarity of his to the full. I remained completely docile and passive in his hands; but it can be believed how my heart would beat, when, as sometimes happened, I found myself waiting in dead silence in some completely strange and darkened "front-room," till certain formalities had been gone through, or until certain respectable and unsuspecting persons had "gone upstairs," and the coast—the coast to my "Embarkation for Cythera"—was clear.

I have no doubt that in the intervals of my reciting "Lycidas," or "Intimations of Immortality," or "Tintern Abbey," Tom Jones found time to whisper his laconic reassurances into fair ears as to the harmlessness, as far as "getting people into trouble" went, of his eloquent guest; for in the curious "milieu," at once eminently respectable and sublimely non-moral, in which he moved, I had to beat only one really ignominious retreat. And even *that* was due to a fit of ill-timed drunkenness on the part of someone, rendering my recitation of "Intimations of Immortality" less opportune than it usually seemed.

When I consider my rôle of poetry-reciter in those quaint places, alternating with my more formal art of "dithyrambic analysis," I see myself more and more distinctly as a sort of vagabond play-actor wandering through the world with a Jew's harp under my Master of Arts gown and acting like one of those gipsy-tinkers at a fair who hangs behind with the rustic wives.

Tom Jones was really a remarkable-looking person. He suffered, all the while I knew him, and it seems to have grown worse before he died, from some cruel injury to one of his feet, the ligaments of which had been clumsily operated on, causing him much discomfort and making him limp. This lame foot must often have hurt him abominably. He would frequently fall silent as we walked together; and well I knew what that meant! He was a small man, but much more powerful than he appeared. At a crisis he was very formidable. Many a time he extricated himself from some appalling predicament by the air of a desperate and dangerous duellist. His countenance was singularly like some of the statue-busts of Julius Cæsar; though his mouth, at once morbidly sensitive and morbidly mobile, betrayed his Cymric origin. It will always be on my conscience that I didn't get him over to America at the last. He would have made a wonderful accountant. Forgive me, forgive me, Tom! Thus, at this late day I talk, I who have not taken one single step to find out even where they have laid my friend's bones. No wonder Theodore used to say of me, quoting Blake, "My brother John, the evil one, in a black cloud making his moan!"

When we woke up side by side, Tom and I, in those various lodging-house bedrooms, he would always scramble out of bed, limp to the window, pull the muslin curtain aside, and then, in his old-fashioned long white night-shirt, his Cæsarian nose snuffing up the promise of the day, light a Gold Flake cigarette. His fingers were yellow with cigarette smoking. It was his Balm of Gilead as he dealt in "markets" and "futures," his Mandragora under the blows of fate. Did he wake up at dawn that day when the woman of the house found him, while some pale window in Wallasey grew "a glimmering square"? What were his last conscious thoughts? To which of his girls did his spirit turn? He told me in that long letter that he "saw nobody any more." He asked me about his chances of getting on in America. Why didn't I wire him the means to sail at once? If I hadn't the cash I could surely have borrowed it. He must in his time have spent double the cost of such a voyage on me. No! I put down plenty of sympathetic words—little black marks on white paper signed "Jack"—but I did not wire him his passage money.

He often used to leave his slippers downstairs, as well as his boots, when his foot hurt him—"Mr. Jones's slippers" moved carefully aside when some little "Marchioness" cleaned the shining fender—and limp upstairs in his socks. I can feel so clearly the warmth of his body, as we would turn round, after saying good night, to go to sleep with our spines touching, two middle-aged, masculine skeletons, back to back, and curved as children are in the womb! He does not have any friendly spine to warm him in his sleep now, in that chilly Birkenhead cemetery.

"Tom's a' cold" now, till the end of the world.

Though my ulcers were hypnotized into complete nonexistence the second I got out of that familiar London and North-Western station at Liverpool and saw Tom's long nose and blue eyes under his bowler-hat, or heard him give his faint embarrassed whistle—he always uttered this plaintive little sound, like a starving bird, when he felt uncomfortable—it was on my way to Liverpool that I had the first of my queer fits of unconsciousness, when I would suddenly fall like a log. The Devil, or, if you like, God, must have meant me to fall on the track in front of the train at the junction in Gloucestershire were I collapsed. But my tutelary angel caused me to fall on the edge of the platform instead. As these fits repeated themselves—but, all in all, I don't fancy I've had more than four of them—they acquired the power of obliterating my memory for as long as half an hour, and sometimes for more, both *before* and *after* I fell.

Thus at Burpham, during one of my holidays, I remember standing on that fortress-bank underneath our Notice, whose threats to trespassers were by that time signed, "Estate Office, Arundel," and picking some white roses that had gone trailing and trespassing there from our south wall, when, like a bolt from the blue, darkness covered my eyes; nor did I regain my consciousness till I found myself lying in my bed. To this refuge I had it seemed *unconsciously* walked!

The same thing, save that my unconsciousness lasted much longer, happened to me at Sneedon's Landing, New York, opposite Dobb's Ferry. I was alone at the time, and had walked some distance, at least a mile and a half, along the lonely Alpine road, and had plunged into those thickly-grown woods which border it on both sides. I can just remember leaving the road, when the bolt of blackness fell; and when, so to speak, I woke up, and I must have walked at least a mile and a half in total unconsciousness, I found myself in that house by the river from which I had started. And I awoke to consciousness to discover myself caked in mud from head to foot, as if I had been rolling in a ditch, while I was dismayed to discover that the worst part of the mud was my own excrement. It was then that I came near ruining Llewelyn's beautiful new overcoat which he had lent me, wherein to make a fair showing when I came to New York. That was the epoch when my Western and Eastern lecture-managers, due to a hasty Jack-in-the-Box antic of my own, were having a lively tug-of-war over me, and I fancy the agitation of this may have had something to do with my seizure.

The last of these curious collapses occurred about eight years ago in New York City itself. It was in fact from a spot in Hudson Street that my soul paid a temporary visit to the "powerless heads of the dead." Since then, with the attainment of a more peaceful life, my fits of unconsciousness have been confined, thank the Lord, to my pillow. In those days, however, my ulcers grew steadily worse and worse; and there at last came a crisis, when having stopped in pretty wretched suffering at Malvern and being off again I forget whither, I threw up the sponge at Worcester, and, causing myself to be driven to a hotel, took a room, sent for a doctor, drank the poppied syrup he brought me, and fell into a wondrous trance of irresponsible peace.

Who should come hurrying to my aid at this juncture but my touchy old crony, Harry Lyon! Leaving his blue pencil drawings in his Kensington office, taking the Great Western express from Paddington, lo! here he was, by the bedside of his Punchinello brother-in-law, in whose sawdust interior some important, and, as far as we knew, some vital spring had been broken at last. For several days T. H. L. was with me in Worcester, where he scolded me roundly—in his irrational angry affection—for being such an unsympathetic companion! The truth was that as the opiate which the doctor gave me wore off I was singularly reluctant to return to the hard struggle of life. I was in the mood of Tom Brown in the old school-story when he had been half-killed by the bully Flashman; or to use a more poetical comparison I felt like those comrades of Odysseus who had tasted the Lotus.

But Harry Lyon had tasted of no Lotus; and, like the Greek hero, his ears were filled with wax so that he could hear no siren-songs. He enthusiastically informed me that in the cathedral in this busy town he had stumbled upon the grave of none other than King John, "poisoned ill-fare, forsook, cast-off," poor caitiff-brother of Cœur de Lion. How well I remember Thomas Henry's indignant remonstrance, because in my lotus-drugged state, I didn't display an active enough sympathy with his burning interest in Worcester Cathedral. But I was as quiescent, and docile as a lamb in his hands, and not exactly ungrateful either, but with a spirit that longed only to drink "a deep and liquid rest, forgetful of all ill."

On arriving at Paddington we drove to the London specialist whom the Worcester doctor had recommended. He barely looked at me—my Punchinello countenance must have been a repulsive ashen-grey—before giving me a card of admission to the London Hospital. I think he thought I was done for. However, after a week or two in the London Hospital, I recovered my interest in life. I read—thinking of Tom Jones and his philosophy—the Letters of John Keats. And I watched the death of a young man whose bed was close to mine. What is there so peculiarly shocking about those "screens" they put round the dying in hospitals and through which only the relations and the nurses and the priest are allowed to pass? It was the custom in that place for those patients who were able to get out of bed to help a little in looking after the others. This was a new experience for me; but before I got well enough to get up I used to lie on my back and pray. I prayed in accordance with an original device I invented at that time, and which I still practise, though with certain small differences. I have always been a believer in *some* magic power possessed by prayer though I have never been particular in what name, or to what power, I uttered my invocations.

In the London Hospital, where, in my large public ward, there were many sufferers, I invented the trick of concentrating my mind on *variously coloured angels*. I directed the attention of one set of coloured angels, purple ones let us say, to one sufferer, and those of another, vermeil-tinctured ones perhaps, to another sufferer. In this way, as I lay in this great White Ship of Suffering, I felt I was not altogether wasting my time.

The person destined to come and take me out of the hospital when I was well enough to leave was my father's chosen executor. How striking did Littleton look in his tweed suit as his athletic form appeared in that ward! We went by train to Burpham, and I can now remember the greedy relish with which I partook, the second I got home, of a mighty bowl— much larger than was advisable—of my favourite bread and milk.

I soon found that I was not a bit better for my three weeks in the London Hospital. A relative of Harry Lyon's came to nurse me; and I used to lie out all day, for it was summer-time then, in that small garden under the great fortress bank. I was peaceful and happy, but by no means recovering. In fact the exit from my stomach into my bowels had become infinitesimal by reason of the growth of my ulcers. Finally one evening, to my own immense relief, but to the dismay of my attendant, I began to vomit. It seems to me now inconceivable how I had survived so long with what at that time came from my unlucky stomach! I must have vomited a whole bucketful—forgive me, reader!—of the foulest excremental stuff possible to be conceived. It must have been accumulating there for years. "An ounce of civet, good apothecary!" It was of a dusky sepia tint, a colour I had not so far hit upon for any of my tutelary angels.

The spectacle of that bucket, which was duly kept for his inspection, decided our doctor, a tall Irish friend of ours called D'Olier, to pack me off, in all haste, back to London. Here I entered a nursing-home near Harley Street and was very speedily operated on—being an incredible number of hours on the table. For some reason, however, the surgeon hesitated to go so far as "gasterenterostomy," and confined himself to various local cuttings and temporary graftings. The anæsthetic art at that epoch had not reached its present acme of perfection; and I cannot express to you the Dead Sea of revolting nausea to which I awoke that evening. They soon gave me a cup of pretty strong tea, however, according to the excellent custom in English nursing-homes, and I quickly recovered from the worst. But for what seemed whole days after that I was allowed no water; and I can remember begging my nurse to let me have within my vision a glass of water, so that I could practise my *voyeur* aptitude upon this pure element.

Llewelyn came to visit me in that nursing-home; and I was profoundly struck by his look of concern. How well I have come to know that disturbance in his rugged and sensitive countenance, contorting its features, even as a sweet water-spring disarranges the rubble of a mountain rock! Over his own illness—when it fell upon him—his face would cloud and grow grave; but it never *contracted* with quite the same spasm of concern as over this collapse of mine. Llewelyn's attachment to me remains a source of continued wonder to my mind. Littleton's I understand, for it is like mine for him; but Llewelyn's has something else in it, like a trouble in the Sun at some chasm appearing in the rondure of the Moon.

I had acquired a mania for Walt Whitman in those days; and I used to lie at dawn, for I woke early in that place, looking out over the roofs of London, and trying to cope with the impressions of life in the way he did. But I soon found that it was impossible for me to "accept" the cosmos—all these loathsome abominations, all these shifting Masks of Fear—in Walt Whitman's *tout ensemble* style. For a long time the clue to any master-word for myself was obscure; but as the years passed I finally discovered this magic sign, this thaumaturgic gesture, in the word "forget." Perhaps Walt Whitman really *was* the one man in the world who actually could envisage all and accept all. But I was different. Or did I see more than he saw? *Were things worse than he knew?* These are questions no man can answer! The nerves of the tortured alone know the torment. But I found by degrees that for me the clue lay in having faith in my power of "forgetting" what I could *not* accept. Thus below all my energy and ebullience of spirit and Pangloss-like insistence on the best rather than the worst, at bottom I am a pessimist. How can I be anything else as long as there are entities in the world—human or sub-human—who are doomed to endure such unendurable things? I have enough imagination to *become*, although in a faint indirect half-and-half way, these children of perdition, these little ones "offended" by the First Cause, these lynched negroes, these victims of cancer, these animals in traps, these vivisected dogs.

But I am no saint. My primal affair is the difficult one of keeping "Number One" happy. Have I told you yet, by the way, that one of the words my father found it impossible to pronounce was the word "difficult"? He always pronounced it, even in his sermons, "*difficut*," leaving out completely the letter "l." But though I am no saint, and though I fight in my own devious fashion for my own hand, I refuse to be "squared" by any tricks of the First Cause. I won't say I am not grateful to *something*—for gratitude is a strong impulse with me—that I am not the victim of American policemen, or of Chinese bandits, or of an Alabama mob, that I am not a Jew in the hands of Hitler, or a dog in the hands of a vivisector, or a foundling in one of our old-fashioned English workhouses, but I tend to lavish this gratitude upon some special guardian angel rather than upon Providence. To thank God for sparing you, when He so delights in tormenting others, has always seemed to me a questionable proceeding.

I don't mind being "archaic," as the Russians say, with regard to other feelings, but when it comes to this one I confess I am a modern of the moderns. It seems odd that the son, grandson, and great-grandson of a clergyman, not to speak of the father of one, or of a priest, as *he* would prefer me to say, should presume to change the names of the two Greatest Commandments. But I cannot do less than plead guilty to this impertinence. In place of: "Thou shalt love the Lord thy God," I would substitute: "Thou shalt force thyself to be happy in thine own soul"; and in place of: "Thou shalt love thy neighbour as thyself," I would substitute: "Thou shalt be merciful and pitiful and considerate *to all living organisms.*"

For what, in the name of Jesus does this biblical "love" mean? That's what puzzles me! I can understand D. H. Lawrence's "dark gods," which are simply erotic attractions and repulsions; and I can understand perfectly the Chinese reverence for parents. And I can understand tenderness and pity and wonder and awe in the presence of *any* human being. It is this business of "lovingness" that puzzles me, and, to speak quite plainly does not altogether please me. I have seen, now and again, a look in the eyes of this "love" that gives me a very queasy feeling. Nietzsche and D. H. Lawrence are undoubtedly right. There *is* something "funny" about this Christian "love." At any rate it needs a thorough heathen analysis. Dostoievsky who understood it to its fathomless depths was himself doubtful about it. And it is not as if I hadn't in my own nerves a devilishly meticulous conscience. But my conscience has *never*, not in all my life, commanded me to "love." Perhaps this is not anyway the business of your conscience. But I don't think I exactly "love" *myself*, though I exploit my sensibilities to get the particular sensations my nature requires. No! the character I admire is a character that is a rod of iron to itself and a well-spring of tenderness and pity for others; a character that forces itself to be happy in itself, blames no one but itself, and compels itself to clear away obstacles from the path to happiness for every organism it encounters.

While I was in the nursing-home I had a stomach pump administered to me. I shall never forget my feelings as I was compelled to open my mouth—like the mouth of a tragic mask imitating a little bird—while my nurse held towards me a capacious rubber tube, and waggled the end of it, indicating that it was my rôle to swallow it. What we poor mortals do go through! But I think I would prefer to have the stomach pump again rather than to have that delicate little instrument whose name begins with a "C" thrust into my bladder by the narrow path of what the poet calls a man's "brutish sting." This mechanical relief was one of my chief trials when I finally

submitted to "gasterenterostomy" in New York; but except
for having my "enemas" given me by an "orderly" in place of
a nurse, a refinement no doubt due to trans-Atlantic respect
for womanhood, I suffered much less in the Post-Graduate
Hospital under Dr. Erdmann, than in that London nursing-
home.

Soon after my operation I was taken, in company with my
little son, to Bognor. Here I enjoyed a lengthy convalescence;
and Nietzsche is absolutely right about convalescence being
the most purged, the most sensitized, the most rapturous condition into which a human personality, at any rate when it is
not "at Liverpool," can possibly fall. I was pretty weak then,
and I shuffled about leaning on a stick; but aye! I did enjoy
such rare and winnowed sensations! All my satyrishness
vanished *pro tem.* I never went down to the beach save as the
invalid protector of a little boy. But I used to drift off on some
heavenly rambles by myself in that curious flat country, formerly the bottom of the sea, across which you can now catch
sight of the spire of Chichester Cathedral. I visited William
Blake's Felpham and walked like a sentinel round the actual
cottage, heavily thatched and close to the sea's edge, where he
saw some of his most poetical visions and where his fight with
that arrogant soldier got him before a Chichester Judge. Blake
resembled Nietzsche in the way he turned any grotesque episode
of his real life into a mystic symbol of the whole trend of his
intellectual destiny. This is the function of the creative imagination that it can find a marriage of Heaven and Hell in the most
grotesque, humiliating, sordid, and apparently trivial event.

But the feelings that came to me as I shuffled feebly about
these rural environs of Bognor, were more precious, more
evasive, more universal than anything I got from Blake's cottage! They hovered about me, they beckoned me, they led me
on, while I was reading in our pleasant lodging a work less
conducive to delicate and spiritual thoughts than any book I
can think of. This was not my *Memoirs of Casanova*; for *that* I
had already sold, for thirty shillings, to the very East-Indian
who had tried to stop my discourse on "Religion and Sensuality"; and with this sum, obtained by selling vicarious lechery,

we had bought an arm-chair, worthy of an abbot, in which my son still sits. No, it was John Morley's life of Gladstone; and for the lack of everything that makes human character exciting and human history interesting, those two typical English statesmen, thus harnessed up together, were at once the epitome and the apogee.

I certainly should not have remembered this book, and I might not even have remembered Blake's cottage, if it had not been that those solitary invalidish walks round Bognor were filled with some of the most entrancing over-tones and undertones, wafted on the most arbitrary of winds, that I have ever known in my life.

I can recall a greater number of the mysterious feelings that are for me the very essence of existence in connection with this little seaside place than in connection with any other town I know except Weymouth. And they were not particularly remarkable, these lanes, these hedges, these ditches near Bognor. They were the reverse of remarkable! But they were unfamiliar to me. That accounted for part of what I felt. They were like those scenes you look at out of a train window. They were like the backgrounds in those pictures of landscapes that you glance at and pass by in a gallery. I saw them for a moment, these roadside tree-stumps, these grey fragments of old walls, these little spinneys at cross-roads, these ragged thorn-bushes with hollows underneath them scooped out by rabbits and dogs and children and suggesting long, hot, idle Sunday afternoons and the far-off twilight songs of blackbirds. I saw most of these field-paths, these wayside heaps of stones, these hawthorn stumps, these wind-blown tamarisk-bushes, these dung-heaps by old cattle-barns, these cart-ruts going down to the sea, once only, for I was always exploring in new directions, but for that very reason, in my sensitized state, they became more than just hedges and ditches round the town of Bognor!

Not that they were transformed, not that they became picturesque or "artistic." But I saw them as they had entered, and as they had left, the consciousness of men and women, going about their affairs, seeing them without seeing them, as they followed their purposes and their desires. But I saw them as they were—no! as they were when they had passed through the half-conscious consciousness of all these human minds. I saw them as you see the designs round the illuminated letters in old breviaries. From being "minute particulars" they became "universals," each one an enchanted "gleichnis," or symbol, of that secret burden of unspoken knowledge under which all those inanimate things that are the background of our life, droop, stiffen, or hold their breath when you catch them off-guard.

As I look back on these successive epochs, in my long-drawn-out days, I find it hard to follow the spiral curves of the hidden continuity. But this I *do* know that before I met Tom Jones, or learnt from him to diffuse my impersonal craving over the thousand and one little *accompaniments* of erotic desire, I went through many desperate and rather ghastly experiences. There were times during my travels, especially when I visited the great factory towns of my native Midlands, when my "nympholeptism," if that is the word for it, became so famished that I would walk for miles through the most wretched and sordid streets hunting for little squalid news-paper-shops, that sometimes contained provocative, if not pornographical pictures in their windows. These desperate lust-starved walks may have been good exercise. They certainly resulted in many abominable moments of exhausted, arid, ashen disappointment. I was always being offered the obscene, when what I wanted was a drop—oh, only one little drop!— of the contents of the mystic Heathen Grail!

I can well remember an experience I had in one desolate factory town and it interested me, now that I have grown acquainted with the doctrines of Communism, to visualize myself simply as an historic psychological illustration walking like a restless demon through these wretched streets, not with the idea of changing the evils of capitalism, but solely with the idea of finding some miserable picture in a miserable window of a girl's long legs. This particular town, I fancy, was in my native Midlands. I had entered a theatre of some kind in the desperate hope—I was always so pitifully hopeful

—that I *might* stumble on a pantomime such as I had seen on that Brighton Pier and perhaps even behold again that Sylph of Sylphs whose limbs I shall idolize till I die!

In place of a pantomime, however, I was confronted when I settled myself in a front seat, by an intolerably tedious acrobatic performance. The stony unmoved stare with which I regarded the only performers of this desolate spectacle— a middle-aged man and his wife—evoked such an access of professional indignation in their hard-worked breasts that they actually whispered together and glared at me like a couple of assassins. So deadly indeed was the hatred I excited in these two poor mimes, for except for me all the front rows were empty, and indeed there was only a handful of people in the whole place, that a point came when the tension grew frightening. I felt as if the whole thing were becoming some monstrous and insubstantial evocation of my own perverse desire, mocking me in a ghastly mirage that smelt of "poisonous brass and metal sick." I felt as if I had lost my sanity. I staggered out I remember, dazed, frightened, shocked, sickened, my lust turned into cold cinders; and as I squeezed my way between the dusty evil-smelling seats to get out of the place I can recall experiencing a sharp stab in my side, so sharp that for the moment I thought I had been stabbed by some unseen steel instrument! The whole incident always came back to me as having something really queer about it, something taking place on that perilous edge between spirit and matter where we have to gather up all our forces not to feel dizzy and sick.

That tearing stab I felt, as I squeezed myself between those evil-smelling seats in that empty Theatre of the Damned, did it come from one single focussed, concentrated, *supernatural* vibration of hatred from those two acrobats? If it did, you will no doubt consider that I heartily deserved it! But you must remember, reader, that I had been lecturing *sans cesse* for months, tearing at my very vitals in my crazy inspirations, spending all my free hours, walking, walking through interminable and desolate streets: and when, for once, I had found a theatre open, open in an hour when I was free, was it any wonder that I turned a stony stare upon these luckless performers?

But, oh dear! You may be right that I deserved this thrust of a poisoned bodkin for my brazen inhumanity. The truth is that those outraged performers, in their silvery bangles and tights, whose savage curse caused this queer spasm to arrest their stony-eyed scarecrow auditor as he took his way between those mephitic cushions had no idea that they were putting their evil wish upon one who was already half-mad.

But you will say to me, were there no brothels I could go to? Brothels! I had not the remotest notion as to how to go about it to find such places. As a matter of fact to this day I have never entered a brothel; and I think it is pretty certain that I shall die without having known that almost universal masculine privilege. But what, you will say, of harlots who have their own private rooms? Could I not, as I had done at Brighton, as I had done in the case of Lily, make friends with someone of *that* type, in Manchester, in Derby, in Coventry, in Leeds, in Birmingham, in Halifax, in Sheffield, whom I could intermittently meet, as my pilgrimage of dithyrambic culture circled upon itself? Well! I did try that once; but oh! it was such a desolate failure.

It was in Birmingham I tried it. For a wonder, while I was staying in that town, I put up not in a private house, but at a hotel, and after my lecture I roamed the streets of that stronghold of Joseph Chamberlain, like a "stygian soul" groaning and gibbering "for waftage." At last the event I had been hoping for really happened. Very late at night I was accosted by a friendly young woman. She was evidently of the very poorest class of street-girls; but she had a friendly look, and something about her reassured and pleased me. I had not read a word of Dostoievsky in those days or I am sure she would have reminded me at once of Sonia. I dared not give her a liberal sum of money, for I was at the beginning of my "round"; and though no doubt a young lecturer in Periclean times could have charged to his "School" at Athens such an expense under the general head of "entertainment,"

I did not, at the beginning of the twentieth century, feel like appealing to the authorities at Oxford.

Well, we bargained, that young woman and I, in the deserted midnight street in the completest affability, and she consented to take what I could afford to give her. She took me to her house which was a very poor one. In the downstairs room there were several children asleep; and a man, my Sonia's father, only he was less loquacious than that precious rascal, sat by the fire cleaning harness, a great pile of which, as if for more than one horse, lay heaped upon the floor. The fellow greeted me with a nod, made some casual reference to the weather, and I followed the girl up a flight of narrow attic-steps to a room above. There were only two rooms there; and I was led to the inner one, which was evidently the girl's own bed-chamber. This room was clean but extremely bare. My companion closed the door, put down the flickering candle which she held, and immediately, without speaking a word— and it was clear that the man downstairs would have heard any word she *did* speak—and without taking off a shred of clothing or even unlacing her muddy shoes, lay down on the bed.

I had made, before she had time to do this, a feeble little motion in the direction of a timid caress, and I would willingly have sat down on the only chair I could see and taken her on my lap; but this automatic rush of hers to the bed, as if we were a pair of wound-up manikins, forced to go through a set of mechanical gestures, filled me with dismay. Were her other clients—and I don't know whether to hope or not that these weren't very numerous—habituated to go through this mystery of mysteries, this ritual of rituals, in such an auto-matic manner?

The girl on the bed looked at me and then looked at the flickering candle and then shut her eyes. A long silence ensued, during which the man below must have continued patiently polishing his harness. At length she opened her eyes and we stared nervously and rather reproachfully at each other. Mean-while our silence was unbroken, not only because the man could hear every word; but because our talk might awaken those children. Finally she scrambled to her feet and gave her skirts a vigorous shake. The moment was an extremely uncomfortable one to me; and she, I think, felt a little scared as well as more than a little cross. To ease the awkwardness of our mutual embarrassment, I hurriedly produced the money upon which we had agreed.

Then, still in unbroken silence, she picked up her candle, opened the door of the room and led me downstairs. Was she deeply hurt in her *amour propre* I wondered. Had my perverse ways roused the same indignation in her as they had roused in those two acrobats? Or was she, after all, rather relieved to be let off in this way, and without the loss of a penny? I have no idea! Women *are* very conservative in erotic matters, and a girl who was eking out the family livelihood in this particular way felt she had a right, I have no doubt, not to be bothered with psychological niceties.

"You pay me for a definite thing," I suppose she would have said to me, "and why should I trouble myself any further? You buy and I sell, but this wretched money of yours which my poverty accepts cannot purchase from me one jot of interest in your personal peculiarities."

The man in the room below bade me good night without lifting his eyes.

From what I have been trying to make clear of my perverse cravings and of their famished desolation as I trailed across England on my voluble mission it can easily be understood what an oasis of paradisic happiness "Tom Jones's girls" brought to me. It was not that they really changed my attitude to these things. But my impersonal desire diffused itself, under the influence of Tom, over the charming receptivity and friendly understanding of these honest girls. I have never encountered again such a group, or such a "stratum," I might almost put it, of feminine possibility. How was it they should *all* have been so nice? It must have been the genius of Tom! He must have combed the highways and byways of Liverpool for sweet-natured, imaginative femininity.

In my convalescence at Bognor I became as free from all these obsessions as I had been during my idealistic years at

Corpus; and, as had happened in that case, what I enjoyed in my escape from both my sadistic thoughts and my crazy nympholeptism was no "intellectual love of God" but a quiet animistic waiting; a waiting, as I shuffled about between those low sea-banks and those wide ploughed fields, till first one intermittent rumour and then another, blown lightly upon wandering sea-airs, came to me from the withheld secret, that secret which can never reach us save momently, faintly, fitfully; and then only when we are detached from the worries of the world.

Chapter Nine

Europe

M Y ulcers soon began to plague me again, aggravated, as before, by those devilish acids whose ferocious activity is denoted by the guileless word "dyspepsia." It was Louis Wilkinson, during one of those pleasant visits he used to pay to us in the holidays at Montacute, who boldly and daringly put it into my head to ask my father to give me the money to visit Italy. I can remember leaving Louis on the landing, between the nursery and my father's dressing-room, while with beating heart I knocked at the study door. I can remember the almost too exciting emotion with which I came flying upstairs to communicate to him and to Llewelyn that my father had agreed to produce this money! None of us would have dared even to *think* of asking for money to visit Italy with no better excuse than ill-health; but such was the pragmatic influence of Louis' golden-good-looks, combined with his gusto for perilous encounters, that I not only carried the "study" by storm but won my amazing request.

Behold me, therefore, established in a small lodging-house in Florence, along with the best possible of companions, and with money enough to stay there for several weeks. And what effect did Florence have on me? I am not enough of a traveller to be certain about such things, but in those days I used to say that there was something in my nature that adapted itself to life in Italy more easily than to life in France. This may, of course, have had to do with the food; for Italian food certainly does suit me a lot better than French food; better even than German food. Spanish food, when finally I reached "The Catholic's" ideal land, prostrated me with spasms of withering dyspepsia. But in Italy I enjoyed all I got to eat. I enjoyed the goats' milk: I seemed always able to procure fresh eggs and decent tea; and as for spaghetti, my lacerated stomach yielded to that national dish and adapted itself to it as if I were a native.

And the moral influence of Florence seemed as good for my manias—if you call it "good" to be lulled to sleep—as Bognor had been, and as, in earlier days, Corpus had been. With my fair companion I really did "study"; most painstakingly, the pictures in those palatial galleries. In sculpture and architecture I took much less interest, to confess the real truth, hardly any; but the feeling of the rose-scented, garlic-scented, grape-skin-scented, dust-scented sunshine, as I sat down on any sun-warmed stone or on any fragment of marble, and leant my back against a pillar or a porch, filtered through me like some precious unguent, fragrant as balsam, and of the colour—for it seemed to me to possess a colour—of ancient, mellow, gold-brown sherry wine, and made the whole of human life seem in some mystic way *redeemed*; I will not say redeemed of evil, but certainly of the dark, morbid, hyperborean evil, by which *my* nature was threatened. Thus my life in that cheap Florentine lodging turned to the sun, turned like that classic plant that Milton talks about, the plant Moly, that could produce a golden flower, *but not in this soil.*

The only book I can remember reading during all the weeks I was in Florence was Nietzsche's *Ecce Homo*. High in the hills above Settignano, if my memory does not fail me, the sun-warmed slope lay, where I gave myself up to this nobly-maniacal book and pretended to myself that I too, in my day and hour, would be a proclaimer of planetary secrets. While I toyed with these imaginings and felt stirring within me my old magical power, my companion made a rough bird's eye sketch of the outlines of Florence—the Duomo, the Tower, and all the rest—as these storied shapes smouldered and quivered beneath us in the hot afternoon sun.

Dull though I was, dull as a sun-drugged lizard in the crevices of a Fiesole convent, to the intellectual and æsthetic values of architecture, I had the power of plunging my very soul into the sun-baked marbles and stones of Florence as long as I could feel them and enjoy them simply as so much inanimate substance in the ancient habitation of the human spirit. It is this power of being thrilled through and through by the simpler, vaguer, more generalized aspects of a famous object that has so often brought the charge of charlatanism against me. It is an old charge. I had even a relative who called me by this opprobrious name before I left college. But I hope I shall always be proud of this charge!

Charlatanism, at least the brand I cultivate of this disreputable commodity, consists in being so transported by the large, general, simple aspects of something exciting in life, or nature, or books, or history, or psychology, that *without waiting to get the details correct*, or the passage verified by exact scholarship, you just rely on your private taste, prejudice, imagination, inspiration, and abandon your whole being to the delight of brooding over what you see and feel. The impulsive communication of your feelings in this matter to others is the gesture which brings down on your head this term of abuse. Judged by the standard of the professional persons who dare not even *feel* a reaction to anything wonderful and magical in Nature or Art without being sure of all the evidence and without congratulating themselves on their credentials as adepts and on their documents as experts, why! some of the most illuminating writers in the world would have to be labelled by this disparaging word.

But I—thank the Lord!—am not only a "charlatan" in regard to *others*. My most secret, personal, and intimate moments of happiness are of this kind. I suppose the greatest literary pleasure I enjoy now, second to thinking and talking about Dostoievsky, is the thrill I get from reading Homer, in the "Loeb Classics" edition, with the Greek on one side of the page and the English on the other. The "Loeb Classics" are indeed my charlatan's Bible. I can brood over a couple of lines in any of these four wonderful volumes with incredible pleasure. Personally I prefer a great deal Professor A. T. Murray's translation of the Iliad and Odyssey to the more popular ones of Lang, Butcher, Myers and Leaf. I love to do with my scanty scholarship in Homer what Whitman did with his primitive and simple objects in nature, I remain at the starting-point. I "loaf and invite my soul" in the presence of the baldest and briefest passages.

Take, for instance the line about Achilles and his immortal horses, Zanthus and Balius. After he has declared to Zanthus, the one who astounded him by predicting his approaching death, that he knew his fate perfectly well, after he has uttered his proud "alla kai empes," "but all the same for that," he plunges, without a word more, into the mêlée. This plunge of a man who *knows his fate* is expressed by the poet in a line that gathers our nerves together, tuned and taut, as if they were the very reins seized by Antomedon, the hero's charioteer! Over the surging rush of the final line I cannot dwell long enough. I know the line by heart. Many a time it has steadied me in some "alla kai empes" situation of my own. And yet—hunt through the pages of my Homeric Lexicon as I may—I've never been able to discover the meaning of the two short words, one consisting of a single unaspirated long "e," and the other of an aspirated "r" and an "a," with which this line, the last of Book Nineteen, ends!

What I call my "charlatanism," and in it lies the secret, not only of whatever inspiration I may have as a writer and speaker, but of my deepest personal happiness, is the fact that I can repeat this line to myself, *and to others*, with exactly the same thrill, without knowing what two of its words mean, as if I knew their meaning with the completeness of a philologist as scholarly and thorough as the author of *Ecce Homo* himself! The extreme slowness of my development as a writer no doubt came from this peculiarity in me; for in speaking you can conceal your ignorances more deftly than in writing. Besides, this very habit of mine of obstinately beating time with what I might call my "imaginatized sensations" militates against the labour required to communicate these feelings to other minds. I had for so long to satisfy my pride, which for all my superficial humility is fathomless, by my own secret knowledge, or —if you quarrel with that as too bold a brag—with my own secret idea, of the value and depth of my imaginative perception.

But when I recall those weeks in Florence, and all I drank

in of the magic of life in such a place, I feel wretchedly ashamed
of the silly tempers I would fly into over any small mishap or
misadventure. I feel bitterly remorseful for instance when I
recall how once we set out to go to a theatre and arriving at
the box-office discovered that in our rustic caution we had
forgotten to remove our common purse from under some loose
board or matting in our room, where—just as my father would
have done—we had secreted it from thieves. I was so ill-bred,
I remember, in my foolish petulance with my companion, who
was of course no more responsible than I was for our blunder,
that not a word would I utter, as we walked back, when a sudden unexpected vision of Giotto's Tower evoked from the
person at my side an impulsive cry of delight. As far as pictures
are concerned it was not Giotto, with his fresh and spring-
like grace, but the more Byzantine Cimabue that made the
greater impression on my mind. How well do I recall going to
that particular church at the end of what now comes back to
me as some long dusty street in the direction of the railway
station, where that immense non-human almond-eyed apparition from the age of ikons stares forth from the eternal immo-
bility of her sacred Not-Being into the transitory confusion of
our unholy Being.

It was somewhere on the street leading to this Santa Maria
of Eternalized Symbolism that we used to go every afternoon
to get our tea. My heroic companion would convey on my
behalf to this humble retreat, for I can assure you it was no
"Kardomah Café," a bottle of the salutary pick-me-up known
as "Sanatogen"; and I can vividly recall the sensual satisfaction
with which resting my hawk-beaked "cat-head," like an Egyp-
tian idol, against the frescoed wall of the cheapest tea-shop in
Florence, I sipped this beverage and devoured one after another,
just as I can imagine that bird-beast idol doing, certain delicious
little buns that the place provided. My companion gave my
private preoccupations a fine jolt one day as we sat in that dark
retreat watching the golden atmosphere outside settle down,
like a veritable Danaae shower, on the faded oleanders and
dusty laurels, by nudging my elbow and pointing out to me a
young madman who sat at a near-by table. Subsequently we

came to speak of this startling figure as "the Dostoievsky-man." Whether he was actually an insane person we never discovered; but as with intense gravity he played draughts with himself and every now and then glanced furtively round and muttered some furious malediction, he seemed to bring into that place a psychic aura that was even more alien to Italy than our own. He too, just as ourselves did, lacked that indescribable wholesomeness of sun-burnt classic blood, a wholesomeness that while it evidently flourishes on garlic and spaghetti evokes the feeling that it draws its strength from contact with hot dusty marbles and crumbling masonry perforated with sunshine.

I forget how many weeks we stayed in Florence; but long enough for me to yearn to escape, even from the Uffizi and the Pitti, and get away into the "country"! This accordingly we tried to do. But my father's dislike, nay! malignant hatred, of trams and buses, influencing us even in this far-off country we set out on foot. And misery, nothing short of forlorn misery, was our reward. For in place of struggling boldly up the hills above the city what must we do but take a road into the level Tuscan plain; and this road we pursued till devastation overwhelmed us. Never have I seen so many vineyards—all inaccessible! Never have I seen such beautiful gardens—all fortified by impenetrable railings! Never has the effluvia from human excrement found so congenial an abiding-place as between those interminable walls. In my companion's case a sort of miasmic fever was the result of this "getting into the country," while in my own I became the victim, as I always did when I was on the Continent, of the most villainous constipation. Oh, the cruel discomfort of this most evil, and, when you think of it realistically, perfectly disgusting complaint! It got worse in Venice. I put it down to the sour wines, among which, in agreement with Mr. Ford Madox Ford, I feel especially suspicious of the *white* variety.

But if you ask me what I got out of Florence towards the intensification of my identity, or towards the acquisition of cunning craftiness in my wrestling with life I think I would say, "a certain way of absorbing the actual substance of weather-stained marbles and stones, and a certain way of absorbing the sun-scented road-dust on the steps of old churches, old monasteries, old bridges, so that I could feel the eternal solace of a rich antiquity without bothering my head about the niceties of æsthetic distinctions or teasing my wits about the accuracies of historic conclusions."

As a matter of fact I was singularly lucky in my companion, who was a rapid worker at her art; so that when we finally went on to the Adriatic, there were no long hours of fidgety revisions of unfinished sketches, and she moved boldly forward to the capture of the Venetian spectacle. But we were both pathetically rustic and simple-minded in our patient obedience to what the books said—not only Baedeker but the more literary authorities.

Fatally bookish I was in those days as far as art was concerned. I could enjoy a delicious sense of well-being from ancient buildings, especially, if I may say so, from certain particular materials in the fabric of these buildings, as long as I stayed in the open air; but once inside one of these historic edifices, though in indiscriminate devotion not the most un-Sitwellian tourist could possibly have surpassed me, my bookish predilections made it hard for me to try to find out what it was that I really and truly felt. What I did enjoy, or tried to enjoy, was always the literary atmosphere thrown over things by my favourite writers. And this worked negatively as well as positively. Because at that time I was growing weary of Ruskin I forced myself to dislike his admired Tintoretto. Because at that time I was reading D'Annunzio I hunted everywhere for specimens of the work of Paolo Veronese. Finally, by reason of that incomparable essay of Walter Pater's, the genius of Giorgione ran, like the sound of water along marble steps, through all my reactions to the palatial doorways and the opalescent flights of steps as the sky brightened or darkened, and the canals grew green and blue and black.

Our limited funds made it necessary to husband every penny of our resources. We discovered very humble lodgings by the aid of a waiter we made friends with, but our room looked out on a little canal and I can now remember the rich

colours of a picture my companion made of a gondola just
under our very window, that glowed in the hot noon-sun
under a piled-up load of fruit.

Contrary to most human experience that engraving above
the bed at Northwold where Littleton and I used to sleep, that
engraving we used to swing as we discussed our fishing
exploits till it made holes in the ceiling, had not indicated half
of the wonder of these fairy-story palaces that rose about me
now "like exhalations" out of the lapping water. But all the
while, between my real sharp, shameless, unequivocal impressions of this unique place, this place that alone of all mortal
places answers to the vision that precedes realization, the
thickly-charged atmosphere of the coiners of phrases, the
atmosphere projected by the scribblers on paper, kept forming
and re-forming, like those yellow-tinged vapours of drifting
cloud that come between the moon and the eyes that regard her.

Venice to me, however, has always been much more the
Venice of the equivocal Henry James than of the lusty Byron.
It is a shame that my wretched physical state, during those
precious weeks, should have made, but such is the truth, a
deeper impression on my mind than the pink feet of the
pigeons of St. Mark or the tables of that hospitable café past
which all the idlers of Europe drift. St. Marks might waver
before me like a temple built by the children of Nereus out of
the iridescent half-lights of the shifting sea. In vain! In vain!
My mind was perpetually revolving the problem—for I could
get no help in any shop—as to whether I dared attempt an
entrance into a hospital, solely for the benefit of a clyster.

Our funds would have come to an end long before this,
and we would have been forced to return, if it had not been
that Llewelyn, then helping Littleton, who by this time stood
in Mr. Blake's shoes as headmaster of the Sherborne Prep,
sent us money to keep us where we were. But this proved to
be the last sum of money that Llewelyn could fling away for
many a year; for when we finally reached Paris, on our way
back, we learnt that he had been attacked by tuberculosis and
was prostrate on his back in one of those small houses between
the cricket field and the football field, in the very place where

the sad little figure of Theodore used to await us as we came
hurrying up the hill from Wildman's.

I recall it now as a singularly good example of the total
lack of proportion, restraint, tact, balance, decency, dignity,
that my mind sometimes displayed, that after visiting Llewelyn
at Richmond Villa and arranging to accompany him to Switzer-
land as soon as he could travel, I despatched a letter-card to
him in the familiar Yeovil Post Office—I can smell the peculiar
smell of the place now as I moistened the edges of this pale-
blue missive that was itself its own envelope—in which I
quoted those lines in Marlowe's *Faust*.

"See where Christ's blood streams in the firmament!"

Llewelyn's hæmorrhages had stopped before I saw him;
and his undiminished humour was shamelessly heathen; but it
was one of my peculiarities to link up the emotional feelings
I had for the men and the women I liked best with some
desperate dramatic passage or some resplendent historic
gesture. My emotion doubled itself in this curious way. It was
as though I was so inhuman that the tears only rushed to the
back of my eyes—and that was as far as they ever came except
by reason of a woman's kindness or cruelty—when some tragic
aspect of a friend's life could be linked with the death of Cæsar
or Socrates or Christ, or when some proud imperiousness in a
friend's endurance could be linked with Napoleon at St. Helena,
with William Blake at Felpham, or with Swift in Dublin. My
emotional response, in fact, to the poetic and dramatic in human
history is so deep and intense that I have only to make, in
casual conversation, a passing generalization about the Homeric
Greeks or about the Spaniards or about the Russians or about
the ancient Welsh, and lo! at the back of my eye-sockets there
gather excited tears. The same is true when I recite, or when I
comment upon certain magical single lines in poetry. But it is
odd that *more* than a single line, taken in one dose, has no
tendency to make me cry. It *has* to be that ineffable touch of
genius which in the nature of things cannot be kept up.
Certainly in the line: "See where Christ's blood streams in the
firmament!" that I wrote in my boldest and most violent handwriting inside that little bit of blue paper whose fastening up

DD

with spittle made the tips of my fingers twitch, there is an extraordinary dramatic power as well as beauty.

I dare say the boy from my father's dentist and the girl from the cashïer at his bank, entering at that moment to despatch telegrams to their clients and fumbling with the sharp pencils at the end of long strings that the Yeovil postmaster supplies, wondered what was making this hook-nosed ruddy-faced man, while he licked his fingers so meticulously and jabbed down the edges of his letter-card so thoroughly, stare at nothing, as if he "saw more devils than vast hell could hold."

But Llewelyn never minded these large grandiose inaccurate gestures of mine. "John in his translunar mood," or "John in his planetary mood," he would say to himself, reverencing me in his hero-worship; when really it was "Sawney John," the King's jester, at his familiar antics, paying himself with the tinkle of his own gold, and feeding himself with the smell of his own goose.

But what a journey it was when I finally set out with Llewelyn! We stayed one night at Newhaven because of the bad weather, and I know we went to Paris first. From Paris we took a train that passed through Laon; and in this fairy-tale Gothic city, for so it seemed to our fevered eyes, we spent one of the most curious nights of my life. Llewelyn could walk, but he walked bent over, stooping forward like an extremely aged man, and as he walked he clutched with his fingers the bosom of his waistcoat just above his heart. He did this so constantly that by degrees his waistcoat came to resemble one of those tattered military flags that hang from the roofs of churches. But his passion for travel, for experience, for the bivouac shocks of adventure, was so insatiable, and my own delight at being with him, for he turned everything we encountered into grist for his mill, was so reckless that we neither of us could resist the temptation of plucking out the heart of Laon's mystery.

The inn where we stopped was a most romantic one and filled me with memories of Sir Walter Scott's novels, while the room they gave us had an ancient fireplace, where a huge wood-fire was burning. Here a bottle of native wine was brought to us, called for by the younger "Monsieur," and after drinking it, we made our way, Llewelyn bending low as he walked, almost as low as old Mr. Curme used to bend, and never ceasing to clutch at that fatal spot in his waistcoat, through narrow cobble-stoned streets, till we arrived at the Cathedral.

The next day we went on; and if I didn't knock a hole in our carriage window to let in the air, I certainly came near doing it before we reached Basle. Here once more we broke our journey, and I remember well how in my thoughts of this being the place where Nietzsche taught Greek I displayed so much indifference to an accident that Llewelyn had to one of his teeth—losing it in fact as we stared at the river—that we had quite an angry quarrel. But we reached the little Swiss town of Clavadel at last, not very far from Davos-Platz; and Llewelyn was put to bed. His cure proved a slow and ticklish one, its worse set-back being the result of a mad walk which he under-took—for his guardian angel has been put to it all his days to save him from the upshot of such doings—over some famous mountain-pass.

But I went to see him again before he left that place, and in my own secret life this second visit to the Swiss mountains was a momentous one. My head was as full of the hyperborean breath of Nietzsche's imaginations as that "nipping and eager air" was full of frost. I was busy with my unpublished *Life of Keats*; and I well remember my exultation as I trod that glitter-ing snow under those dark pines and allowed my spirit to dally with the notion that it would be my destiny one day to give to the world a philosophy as startling and new as that of the author of *Ecce Homo*.

How well I recall my arrival at Clavadel on that occasion! I had stopped in Paris on my way through, and had nourished my worst fancies—not my sylphid ones, but *the others*—by the perusal of certain unspeakable books. I found Llewelyn's corrugated head buzzing with what he called, in his serious but smiling way, his "social preoccupations." These seemed indeed extremely thick upon him up there; for from what he told me the affairs of the heart, or shall I say of the exasperated nerves,

of these stricken people, were not less than astounding. He told
me that one of them had just shot himself "for love"; but the
disease he suffered from having *moved his heart* he was on the
road to recover from this peevish gesture. I had to submit,
the moment I arrived, to being attired in evening dress, but
even this was not enough; for with his own hands my young
Lord must needs wash, comb, and brush his bewildered elder
brother into an appearance befitting "a relation from home."
It was all surprisingly like Thomas Mann's *Magic Mountain*;
but I can now see Llewelyn's look of shame and disgust as he
snatched from me one of my abominable books and flung it
into a mountain stream.

It was during this epoch of my life—the reader must forgive my wretched memory for exact dates—that I was invited,
in my rôle of Oxford Extension Lecturer, to give a set of talks
on English and American literature at Dresden. Never shall I
forget my protracted visits, for I went more than once, to this
beautiful eighteenth-century capital of Saxony. Here too, I was
meditating my *Life of Keats*, the undercurrents of which had
been furnished me by Tom Jones, but here again I was tormented by a damnable recrudescence of my worst vice. In fact
my Dresden experience was one in which all the contending
elements of my tumultuous inner nature seemed to rise up
from the depths and contend for mastery.

In my romantic way I began by rejecting the obvious
English Pension and landed myself in a weird room, looking
down on the tops of red-flowering chestnuts in the older part
of the city. My landlady resembled the witch of the Brocken
in Faust. Storks might have built in her chimney and there
was a smell of something repulsively like mortality itself, in
the place where I slept. That smell was really an awe-
inspiring thing. It came up from the boards. It was as if I had
to retire every night not only to a mausoleum but to the
hideous embrace of Dissolution, the thought of which so
terrified little Juliet in the play. Moreover it was impossible to
reach the quarter of the house to which American refinement
has given the appellation of "toilet," without passing a
suspicious and very surly dog, a dog of small proportions but

of pronounced Anglophobe views, whose agitation was terrific every time I gingerly stole down that passage. This domestic obstacle did not, as you may surmise, conduce to the normal working of my bowels, and it soon turned out that my life in Germany was no easier in that intimate sense than had been my life in Italy. Week after week this accursed constipation acted like a blight upon my days. Finally, after eking out a little external comfort by borrowing a tin bath, so that I could at least appear before the Royal Highnesses who listened to my lectures outwardly clean, I sacrificed my idealism and fled to the *English Pension* where I ought to have gone at first.

But that chamber of mine looking out on the flowering chestnuts and reeking of dead men's bones served me well as a satanic sanctuary in the seclusion of which I could devour those frightful books, which I still kept shamefully buying. My great trouble lay in disposing of the wretched things when I had hurled myself through them, which I always did with beating heart, fevered pulses, and trembling knees. Once I left a pile of them behind me, as if I had been some monstrous Stygian bird whose excrement was the literature of Hell, in a public lavatory. Another time I hurried for miles along the further bank of that noble Dresden river, into which in the end I flung one particular volume that I had found too obscene for my taste. For you must remember, reader, that I retained my fastidiousness even in my worst vice. It was only the most purged and winnowed allusions to sex that I could endure, and the least reference to normal sex functions turned my stomach. Savagery and blood I could not tolerate for a moment. It was the *idea* of sadism, an idea that had to flit and float and hover, like those tenuous heat-waves that you watch sometimes above the surface of a field, that alone excited me. I was the very opposite of the type I have heard described as "the human panther." Yes, in the very torrent and tempest of my trembling wickedness I could only really enjoy a book— strange though this may sound—that "ended happily."

In that Northwold rose-garden, with its lily-pond in the centre, where, when Littleton was fishing in the "big" pond in the shrubbery, and I had to keep calling to him to get the reassuring sound of his voice in answer, for it frightened me to think of *coming suddenly* upon him, I remember once catching a frog and thinking of using him as that cold-blooded wretch, Izaak Walton, teaches you to do, as a bait for fish; but do you think I could bring myself to put a hook into him? *Jamais de la vie!* As I say, I only *practised* sadism about three times in all my days; on those worms in the Northwold summer-house, on those newly-hatched little birds in the Sherborne quarry— and even of *that* incident I am doubtful—and on those beetles I once killed at Rothesay House with scalding water. Never has any cerebral vice been as exacting, as exclusive, as limited in its scope, as mine. The merest approach to normal sex behaviour quelled my excited desire like blocks of ice, froze it dead, like that cold water that my nurse used to throw over me at Shirley, when in my innocence I tried to tell her about my feelings. But those epochs I spent in Germany in those two successive years were crucial times for me in every respect. All my most indigenous feelings whirled up to the surface during those months and there struggled with one another for the mastery.

I remember writing to Louis Wilkinson, who was burgeoning and basking, like some great Theodoric the Ostro-Goth, between sun and sea at Sorrento, how my imagination was more deeply satisfied by the massive castles, the Brocken Heights, the fairy forests of the hyperborean North than by all his olives and citrons and marbles and roses of the South.

One of my Shirley cousins, as dear to me as Ralph himself, and who, like Ralph always "believed in Cousin Jack" suddenly appeared at Dresden, and though immensely amused at the spectacle of my harangues before Prince Johann George, carried me off for a holiday to Weimar. Never, I fancy, has Goethe received such adoration from an introverted Celt as I offered to him then; and by my cousin's influence I actually was invited by Frau Foster Nietzsche to take tea with her in Nietzsche's own house. Imagine what I felt when this devoted lady showed me the dead man's books, his editions of those "Great Latins" he so ridiculously overrated, De Maupassant,

Merimée and so forth! There was, I remember, a certain
modern French idealist among these books, an author I had
never heard of; but against some eloquent passage of his, in
praise of "the resolute pursuit of the higher truth," Nietzsche
had written in pencil in the margin, several times over, the
words: "in vain" . . . "in vain" . . . "in vain."

The Saxon Professors whose rôle it was to arrange these
lectures were the most charming of learned men. They gave me
delicious beer-soup in their own homes, they took me for
endless excursions into the mountains; once as far as the
Bohemian border, where I proudly sent postcards home to
Montacute with the imperial Austrian stamps on them. They
took me to the Opera to hear *Carmen*, to the theatre where a
Shakespearean company arranged its plays to fit in with the
lectures I was giving, and finally, before I went away, they
allowed me to choose, in the great warehouse-rooms of the
Meissen China factory, whatever piece of china I liked the best!
I chose an amazingly beautiful table-centre, composed of a
score of shepherds and shepherdesses and standing about three
feet high. I shall never forget the pride with which I unpacked
this royal donation, on the little lawn at Burpham, with the
crossed swords of Meisen china on the outside of the case,
and wisps of the softest mountain-moss spread round the
delicate figurines within!

I never left Germany in a hurry after my lectures were
over, for I found I got on splendidly with Germans wherever
I went. I walked through the foothills of the Black Forest.
I went to Heidelberg. I stayed at Nuremberg. I visited a friend
in Mannheim. But do not think as I rattle off these grand
names that I am not aware of a floating crowd of half-forgotten
wayside "eidola" of German country-life that are far more precious to me and far more *germane* to the matter, than any
wooden Madonnas or any crag-built castles on the Rhine.
Yes, amid those other dominant passions of my nature which
the occult and mystical sympathy I felt for that country stirred
up in me, my supreme mania—the only one that rivals my
"sylpholeptism" and my winnowed sadism—for wandering
along narrow roads and deserted cattle-tracks, past barns and

sheds and windmills and water-mills, past church yards and ancient inns, over time-worn bridges, by the edge of old canals, through ancestral parks and along the borders of lakes, up forest-paths among fern-grown rocks and across smooth levels of pine-needles, down by the margins of reedy swamps and the dusty outskirts of market-towns; my mania, I say, for wandering among scenes such as these, scenes that come with a fresh shock to me when I think of them now and that I shall probably never see again, was satisfied in Germany as it has seldom been satisfied anywhere else in the world! Often and often since then, "amid the din of towns and cities I have owed to them, in hours of weariness, sensations sweet, felt in the blood and felt along the heart, and passing even——" but since you, reader, are neither Tom Jones, nor one of "Tom Jones' girls," I will quote no further.

It was after one of these spiritual and cerebral debauches in this land for which I felt such mystic attraction that on returning to Burpham I found that in the exigencies of domestic purgations, as Mr. Micawber might express it, in other words in "Spring Cleaning," a full-length plaster figure of the Venus of Milo and a full-size bust of the Apollo Belvedere, objects, that in my crazy idealism I had cherished since the earliest Court House days but which had descended, in worse and worse decrepitude, from study to tool-house, from tool-house to out-house, steadily receding, as *my artistic taste improved*, till they crumbled away to nothing, had been carried off by the dustman. This event would have been more of a shock to me than it was if it had not been that at that time I was in the throes of one of those feverish obsessions I had come to call my "devilish moods," but, as it was, I had very unpleasant qualms. I am more, or worse if you will, than a sentimentalist, when it comes to the Inanimate, especially to any inanimate object that could possibly, by the furthest reach of the imagination, be regarded as an idol, or totem, or fetish or sacred stick or stone.

As Llewelyn loves to hint, with my pre-historic "cat-head," my Horus beak, my mouth like that of an Aztec idol, I resemble some archaic doll-demon, out of whose gargoylian lips water might eternally pour, or into whose equine nostrils incense might eternally rise! Thus it is always with an instinctive *fellow*-feeling that I am, as I say, a good deal worse then sentimental about inanimate things. Something breathed the breath of life into Powys Major's "ugly mug," and why should Powys Major not have the power of breathing the breath of life into a plaster statue of the Venus of Milo? Suffer as I have done, and am doing, and doubtless *shall* do from this fatal "animism," that forces me to walk as delicately as Agag all the days of my life, and believing in this idolatry of mine, amid the clash of chances and possibilities, only to the tune of about one to ninety-nine, I feel that it is essential that *someone* should lift up his voice in these days, when the head of Science is as swollen with arrogance as the head of Nero, and timidly and faintly, but still obstinately, suggest that the magical view of life has as much right to "rise again" as the Lord Himself.

As soon as my lectures began to be successful on the other side of the Atlantic and I had some pocket-money I began to treat my younger brothers to various excursions. I remember there was quite a council of state held over me in our ancient forum, the terrace-walk, when Louis Wilkinson brought back word how extravagant I had become in my tips to waiters and porters! It was severely pointed out to me on this occasion that it was a disgrace to "throw away money" purely for my own self-indulgence, when "honest cods" of my own flesh and blood had to live deprived of so many things. It only needed this hint, for I can assure you the verdict was as emphatic as it was unanimous, for me to begin reforming in this matter. I treated Bertie to a visit to Rome, and Llewelyn—alas! still with uncured lungs—to a trip to Venice.

Aye! but I got, as they say, "my own back" with double and treble interest in both these instances! Shall I ever forget the heart-beating excitement of the early morning in Rome, for I had got there first from another direction, when I met Bertie's train. Nobody but A. R. P. would have had the wit to discover that he arrived at dawn, or the still greater wit to communicate with me by telegram to that effect. But there he was; and if I did not show off my Roman knowledge by

taking him into the "Term Museum" straight from his train—
for it was but a step—it was only because I wanted to show off
my discovery of something even more desirable to Bertie, just
then, than lovely marbles in a garden of roses, namely a real
Roman Bath with shining classical tiles! But after breakfast,
and I can remember it all as if it were yesterday, my childish
excitement kept mounting and mounting. How could it else
when I felt like the Chief of the "Volentia Army," introducing
the bravest of my robber band to the unequalled treasure I had
discovered? I wanted Bertie to set his eyes first in Rome upon
something that would be much more symbolic for him and
much more charged with his proper destiny, than was my own
first view of that singular "Victory Column" of Marcus
Aurelius. So I took him by a roundabout approach, circling
through various narrow streets, but always getting nearer and
nearer to my objective which was nothing less than the
Pantheon.

I knew that next to organic, massive, soil-suggested buildings, what the heart of this fourth son of my father loved the
best was red wine, especially when he could drink it straight
from where it had been "cooled a long age in the deep-delvèd
earth." I had previously noted a small underground warehouse
devoted to local vintages just out of sight of the entrance to
the Pantheon, and in front of this place, seated on a bench in
the sunshine, I watched with delight, like a woman watching
her warrior—for with A. R. P. I always felt weak and frail
and feminine—my companion's Roman profile grow genial, if
not jovial. Then, and not till then, did I lead him round the
intervening buildings and we came bolt up against the famous
portico. There it was—the temple to all the gods in the City
of all the gods!

"Agrippa. Cos. Fecit," we read; and the responsive gravity
of my laconic brother contented me to the bottom of my heart.
His silence was as expressive, in this first decade of the twentieth century, as was that of the historian Gibbon in *his* moment
of time, as he stood at gaze on that spot. And how like an
ancient Roman A. R. P. looked, when, a little later, I saw him
take possession of the Baths of Caracalla as if he pondered how

they might be restored to a proper use. I was well rewarded for plotting this occasion.

What might be called the structural inevitabilities of architecture, the. austere pleasure to be derived from the fatality of materials in this pragmatic art, was never more deeply revealed to me than when I watched the way his interest gathered, intensified, or ebbed. But there it is! In spite of all Harry Lyon's attempts to make an art-lover of me, to the bottom of my soul *I am no artist.* "In vain, in vain, in vain!" as Nietzsche wrote in the margin of that French sermon. My way of taking life is poetic, imaginative, sentimental, *never* æsthetic! That is why I felt so ashamed and so sad when my great plaster Aphrodite went to the limbo of broken dolls. I loved her as a poetic symbol! What did I care if she were a botched and bungled toy? The truth is that all the authentic emotions I got in Rome were poetic, and, in my own childish sense, philosophical. They were profoundly un-æsthetic. Even my fondness for Goethe's travel-diaries failed to enable me to get any solid gain for the real life of my soul from Michael Angelo or Raphael or the famous fragments of Greek sculpture. Up and down those galleries I wandered, as I had done on that earlier occasion, and as I was to do again, but never once was I really arrested, ensorcerized, carried out of myself. Pathetically did I stare into those bulging, lidless eyes of the equestrian statue of Marcus Aurelius on the Capitol Hill. "In vain, in vain, in vain!" the imperial disillusionist seemed to say to me.

"You are what you are; and your escape from the Transitory into the Eternal will never be through the plastic arts."

How quaint and humiliating is the real truth about these curious matters, in the changes and chances of a person's life, when he actually dares to blurt it out! My whole life can be divided in two halves; the first up to the time I was forty; and the second *after* the time I was forty. During the first half I struggled desperately to evoke and to arrange my feelings according to what I admired in my favourite books; but during the second half I struggled to find out what my real feelings were and to refine upon them and to balance them and to harmonize them, according to no one's method but my own.

But it does remain lamentable how little I got from the world-city. Think what Rome holds of the accumulated art, in statuary and painting, of all our western world! Think of the famous Greek statues that are in the Vatican Museum alone, from that amazing torso of a man's back near the entrance, over which they tell us Michael Angelo would mutter and grope, fumbling with his fingers after the Vulcanian tricks of the demiurge, to the stately "Diadunemos" at the end of the long corridor. Think of that Sistine Chapel, under the dizzy ceiling of which the middle-aged Goethe, like a great blue-bottle fly, managed to clamber. I used to glance at that exalted foothold, among those gigantic pictured shapes, and feel absolutely sick at the thought of being up there.

But if you ask me from what, in these visits to Rome, I remember deriving any real, natural, and purely personal pleasure, among all these wonders, I would answer from the grey-blue hills and the thin, tall cypresses, rising in some of the backgrounds of the paintings of Pintoricchio. Such at least is my impression to-day; but I may easily be confusing Pintoricchio with some other painter.

The truth is, though it seems a queer thing for the person to say who once overheard himself, at the trial of the *Little Review* in New York for publishing *Ulysses*, described by one spectator to another as "The English degenerate, John Powys," I have always been of the opinion that certain simple nobilities in personal character are serious rivals, merely as planetary phenomena, to the greatest work of art in the world. I confess I hesitate a little when it comes to literature; for I feel as if *King Lear* and *The Idiot* and *The Possessed* and *The Brothers Karamazov* resembled, in a closer way than these other arts can ever do, the heroic grandeur possible to a real human person.

Well! it was to Llewelyn that I went now, in whose character, little as he knows it, exist these particular heroic qualities that however much you may detract from the freedom of the will seem to me as great as any possible work of art. Yes, to Llewelyn I went now, when I was about thirty-six or thirty-seven, and carried him off to Venice. It was at this time, owing to the success of my lectures, that I told my father he could stop giving me the allowance of a hundred pounds a year which it was his principle to give his sons when they married. As often happens, however, in gestures of this sort, I was not totally pleased at the ease and promptness with which this hint was acted on!

Oh, how well I remember Llewelyn's excitement when I announced to him that I was going to take him to Venice. It was in the potato garden, near the crumbling wall of Ham Hill Stone across which lay Cole's orchard where we used to shoot at cole-tits and marsh-tits with our catapults, and he was lying in his deck-chair amid the tangle of nettles and ground-ivy and stone-crop, listening to a thrush breaking a snail's armour upon a stone; and when I told him he positively cried aloud with joy, so that Willy, hidden in the laurel-bushes, came out to learn the news. He had grown weary of his long sickness, and the idea of this daring excursion thrilled him through and through.

But I received a very stern letter from A. R. P. on this occasion which brought down by several pegs the pitch of our high spirits. I intended to travel to Venice by that express from Paris that the hero of Proust's book must have taken on the occasion when he felt that famous unevenness in the paving-stones of St. Mark's, which, like that mouthful of the Madeleine dipt in camomile-tea, gave him one of his immortality-proving ecstasies; but we were going to meet a very spirited and beautiful girl in Venice and we were also to meet there that resplendent habitué of historic Europe, our brilliant friend Louis. It was the fact that I was smuggling Llewelyn off to encounter such provocative persons in such a provocative place that troubled Bertie. He accused me of acting "as I always did"; of sacrificing others with reckless unscrupulousness to my lust for dramatic excitement.

His psychological if not his moral insight proved, I regret to say, completely justified. John *was* at his old dramatic tricks again. John *was* at his old trade of a cerebral Pandarus. Well! on this occasion John was fairly "caught on the hop."

At Milan, on our way home, Llewelyn fell seriously ill, and we had to remain for weeks and weeks in a hotel in this city till he could move on again. But this was afterwards. This was when we had supped full on the forbidden fruit. For that Venetian visit was a unique experience in both our lives. If Llewelyn paid for it at Milan with hæmorrhages and kidney stones he enjoyed it at the time hardly less than I did. It was lucky we had Louis with us, for he, as he always did, kept his head whereas Llewelyn and I worked ourselves up to such a pitch in our jealous contest for the favours of the beautiful girl who was with us that *our* heads were completely turned. She insisted on dressing up as a boy; and we would accompany her in her gondola in this attire to the remotest possible spots where gondolas could be propelled! If Louis had not kept intact his East-Anglian sang-froid heaven knows into what wild events Llewelyn and I, in our mounting rivalry might have been led.

What I call my heart was hit as it has not been often hit. Though this organ does not change its physical position like that one at Clavadel it is by no means what you would call a passionate heart. But whatever kind of a heart it may be it was certainly pierced through and through by one of the arrows in *that* quiver! It was in fact in a state of such wild imaginative elation that all my insanest mystical impulses whirled up to the surface while all my passion for dramatic gestures responded with kindred motions. The feelings that this beautiful girl in boy's clothes excited in me rose like flames that were as many-coloured in their flashing sword-points as those angels I had prayed to in the London Hospital.

There was some small kind of a war going on at that epoch between Italy and some other country; and I dare say our appearance when we escorted this girl about Venice was odd and striking. At any rate we were disembarking from our gondola one day not far from the Bridge of Sighs when we found ourselves surrounded by an imposing band of officials. It was explained to us that we were under arrest. "This," they said, indicating our friend, "is a feminine one; yes? no?"

Llewelyn whispered to me that it was just as if they had caught a hatfull of trespassing butterflies and discovered among them, by the markings under her wings, a fine female specimen.

This is the only occasion so far in my life when I have been in the hands of the police; and really when we were all led into some upper-chamber, and made to stand in a row before a grave personage at a table, I felt as if the chief of the "Volentia Army" were being treated as he had so often treated our little nurse from Berkshire, in that robber's roof-attic at Rothesay House!

Our Venetian address was carefully taken down—an hotel on the Lido—and then came the question of our home address. Not one of us had a "card" except Llewelyn, and he had, by some chance, one of my father's. Never had those familiar words: "Rev. C. F. Powys, Montacute Vicarage, Somerset" sounded so out of place; but the Venetian official chuckled a good deal and handed the card to one of his subordinates. We caught the word "padre" exchanged between them accompanied by what no doubt was a sly commentary on the progenitive capacity of priests in England. An official at once hurried off to the Lido to verify our story, and once again Llewelyn saved us; for, after his fashion, he had so courted, cajoled, caressed, and generally bewitched our landlady, that the woman led the emissary to think that our social position at home, in spite of the padre's card, was a tremendous one, and that we were only behaving in our accustomed manner, like so many Milords Byron.

But my excitement during those wild Venetian days rose to a pitch that I have never known before or since. I remember going alone to Verona one day and being so elated by the thought of Juliet in her tomb, by the vast stone Amphitheatre, and by that gondola-loving boy-girl, that like Faust I could have cried out to the moment, even if it brought the Judgment Day with it "O stay! Thou art so fair!" There were clouds without water sweeping across the Verona sky; and their ominous appearance, together with an extraordinary revelation of lightning without thunder, had driven everybody out of the Amphitheatre. And as I sat in that vast semi-cirque—but what was its vulgar Roman antiquity really, compared with the mystic stone-circles of my own land?—my whole nature seemed transformed. I cannot recall now whether or not that boy-girl was actually seated by my side. She was certainly enthroned in my insane imagination; but sometimes it comes back to me that she *was* with me under that lightning without thunder, and sometimes that I was alone that day.

Undoubtedly there do come occasions in a person's life when the underlying fatality of his identity gathers itself together and rises up from the fluctuating waves of his nature like a crested sea-serpent from the bottomless silt. At such moments, whatever stains are on his conscience a person feels able to shriek out, like Macbeth: "Though Birnam Wood *be* come to Dunsinane; and *thou* opposed, being of no woman born; *yet* I will try the last!"

Alone in that Roman circle, under those clouds from which no drop of rain fell, the thaumaturgic element in my nature rose to such a pitch that I felt, as I have only done once or twice since, that I really *was* endowed with some sort of supernatural power. To what end had the gods thus dedicated me? Merely to indulge in "dithyrambic analysis" before bewildered, puzzled, derisive audiences? I refused to believe it! I refuse to believe it still. What I felt at that moment in the Verona Amphitheatre was the very thing I had been obscurely fumbling my way towards through all my lusts and my obsessions. I felt it again, only five years ago, when I visited Stonehenge with Littleton on our way from Sherborne to Northwold. The feeling that comes over me at such times is one of most formidable power. It makes me conscious that below all the maudlin silliness of my gaping countenance—and I willingly confess that, even more accurately than the word "zany" or "punchinello," the word "maudlin" exactly describes the wool-gathering, absent-minded foolishness in my face—I conceal a demonic formidableness of my own, of which my enemies were well advised to beware! As I have hinted before, no amount of "manic elation," or "paranoia," or "megalomania," can explain the fact that I am the most unlucky person in the world to insult or malign. The evidence of this—of my being able, I mean, and quite unconsciously too, to exercise some kind of "evil eye," on people who have injured me—has so piled up upon me all my life that it has become a habit with

me to pray to my gods anxiously and hurriedly for each new
enemy!

But it is not only at great moments like this one at Verona,
when all the symbolic figures of my unbalanced fancy, the
good and the evil ones together, a whole invisible galaxy of
Christs, Merlins, Pythagorases, Laotzes, Goethes, Blakes and
Nietzsches whirl up about me, that this monstrous and almost
non-human sense of power possesses me. I have had this same
feeling quite recently when walking alone over these free hills
in "up-state" New York where the most romantic thing I can
hope to see is a stone wall without mortar, surmounted by a
wooden fence without nails.

At these times I am aware of my skeleton going to and fro
over the surface of this round earth; but, accompanying my
perambulatory skeleton, I feel the presence of a spiritual power
emanating from my bones, and dominating my bones, that
moves with me as I move "like a pillar of cloud by day and a
pillar of fire by night." My friends and neighbours, I willingly
confess can hardly be expected to see any evidence of this.
What is apparent is an excessively polite, indeed a fawningly
friendly person, with a face of foolish intensity, and a perfect
passion for "drawing people out."

It is curious too how little this supernatural power of mine,
that I was so conscious of in connection with our boy-girl of
the Venetian canals, does me any good in the direction of
making me rich or famous. It saves me—I do think it has done
as much as that—from worrying about the lack of money. But
in its formidable simplicity it is linked to a veritable serpent
of convoluted maliciousness which rejoices in behaving
absurdly as long as it can disconcert the children of this world.
This serpent of malice, of which no one would guess the
existence from observing my maudlin expression of foolish
eagerness, is weighing and judging my various interlocutors all
the time and encouraging my imagination to rove and stray in
the most bizarre, monstrous, and to confess the truth *shocking*
directions. I will, for instance, be listening with flattering
attention to some pretty society woman, when at that very
moment, I am imagining a monstrous and hideous *tail* un-

twining itself from under her, or a revolting and unthinkable *horn* growing up between her shoulder blades! Or I will be listening to some potentate of this world—one of Mr. de ——'s "magnates"—while he explains to me the way to handle my life, and behold! I will see this good, easy man's figure stark naked, and not only naked, but as if he were upon a dissecting-table, where his "viscera"—of which my scientific knowledge is, I confess, somewhat shaky—as well as what Rabelais calls his "bum-gut," assume a prominence altogether dispropor-tionate to his human cranium.

But this convoluted malice turns itself most willingly upon my own reputation for gravity and respectability. No sooner do I detect the remotest sign that some honest man regards me as an arch-humbug, than I dance my best malice-dance, for his benefit, and trick myself up, for I am a veritable Proteus among Punchinellos, in my most extreme Cagliostro cloak.

A very teasing mental weakness of mine caused me acute distress during these Venetian days. There must be a veritable Demon of Auto-Sadism dwelling within me; for the more thrilled I became with the ambiguous beauty of our boy-girl companion the more rigorously did this Demon within me set himself to spoil my pleasure. Do you know what this Demon used to compel me to do in my perverted mind? And it was clearly a mental proceeding that could only be regarded as sadistic *towards myself*. He used to compel me to smear her beautiful form from head to foot with some grotesque sticky substance, such as marmalade or treacle! Analyse this trick of the poor human brain for me, reader, if you need a problem in psychiatry! My triumphant delight in this beautiful boy-girl no doubt seemed to her own proud intelligence to be doing her secret original identity only a very dubious kind of honour. It was as if she had succeeded in turning the head of some super-puppet, some Quixotic man-doll, who had been taught to say "Christ," and "El Greco," and "Dostoievsky," during the epochs when he was the companion of these magicians, but who now could only repeat *her* name. It was even as if, in his erotic delirium, he was forever mixing her up with all the other thaumaturgistic figures who had made him dance and gesticulate and utter his cries, all the way down the ages! But if I did "sing such a song," as Llewelyn would say, I was without any doubt as completely enslaved by this boy-girl's beauty as far as my peculiar type of heart, the heart of a cerebral idolator, *could* be enslaved by a human woman. I was so enslaved that in my jealous desire not to break one link of this enchanted spell—and no doubt our white-admiral's flutterings, now in the direction of Llewelyn, and now in that of Louis, helped to bind it the faster—that I completely lost, on one curious occasion, my usual affable politeness.

Somewhere down by the Rialto, in a very crowded and very narrow canal, we encountered, as we were propelled through the water, a floating equipage that resembled the barge of Cleopatra, or perhaps I ought rather to say that ship, so often delineated in Greek vast paintings, that carried the great god Dionysus on his triumphant voyage. This other gondola, whose high ornamental poop collided with our own, was actually covered with the most wonderful skins of leopards and lynxes and it was handled by a Being who might very well have passed for the Faun of Praxiteles. In the stern, lying on a leopard's skin, was a personage who, as I learnt later, was one of the most whimsical writers and one of the most beguiling men of the great world.

Blinded by the spell I was under and furious at this contact with fashionable society, I lifted my voice, the moment I heard the Baron—for it was none other than the famous Baron Corvo—begin enquiring whether we were engaged for the rest of that week, and in a shriek more worthy of Lancelot Gobbo than of Signior Antonio I screamed ferociously: "Up to the hilt! Up to the hilt! Up to the hilt!" It was much more as if I were ordering some hired assassin to plunge a dagger into the Baron's heart than as if I were answering an invitation to a Venetian palace and I am afraid the gentleman missed nothing of its stridency. He looked appealingly at Louis as much as to say: "Protect me from this savage."

Llewelyn's collapse at Milan did not endear that place to me. Indeed it was hard for me to link up this active city, with the glittering pinnacles of its grandiose church with Leonardo and his "girl-boy" pupils. I use that expression purposely, for *our* boy-girl of Venice was for ever murmuring broken and incoherent praise of this mysterious artist of whom I knew nothing except those sentences in Pater about his passion for the flowing of many waters and for the inscrutable smiling of one particular woman. Evidently in some sharp and intimate sense, totally beyond the comprehension of my unscientific mind, this girl had caught the artist-enchanter in the very act of performing one of his strange other-side-of-the-moon conjuring tricks with Nature. And Goethe, it seemed, agreed with this girl in the matter of Leonardo.

But just as I had attempted in vain to follow the simple-subtle utterances of my great master among the marbles and pictures of Rome; just as I had stood at the Lido on the very spot where he had for the first time seen the sea and seen nothing but a tiny little sea-horse that Llewelyn found, so it was in vain that I tried to capture the thrill he got from Leonardo's "Last Supper." I could not do it! It still remains that the only artists I have ever really appropriated to my authentic inner life—and Goethe himself says that if you don't do *that* it is of no avail that you rush through these treasure-houses—are El Greco, Nicolas Poussin, and certain particular and rather conventional landscape-painters, like Ruysdael, Gainsborough, and Ruskin's *bête noir*, Salvator Rosa. As for those marble pinnacles of the cathedral in Milan I viewed them with positive distaste. What could I, who had so often seen the majestic earth-bastioned towers of Ely rise up out of the fens, get for my spirit from this fantasia of civic elegance?

The truth is that what alone among these things really satisfies me, what alone I can rest upon and contemplate in a gallery for any length of time, is a landscape painting. I forget names so shamefully; but I know that Gainsborough and Ruysdael are only two among a number of painters any smallest specimen of whose work it would be a sensual delight to me to possess. And the kind of landscape I love so deeply and understand so well is the commonest kind of all in any old picture-gallery. Of modern pictures I am maliciously ignorant. I cannot describe to you the haste with which I hurry past them to reach one of these old, mellow, time-worn canvases of poetized and conventionalized scenery such as my soul loveth. The older and more famous works of art I have been clever enough with the help of books, to grasp intellectually, up to a certain point, but there is a type of conventional, poetical, *romantic* landscape, usually somewhat dusky and mellow and blurred with age, a type of picture that, I fancy, must belong to the late seventeenth and early eighteenth centuries, that I need no Harry Lyon, no Brother Bertie, no boy-girl authority on Leonardo, to interpret for me.

As I write now, lying at my American window, watching the chickadees in the frozen snow steal the crumbs from my favourite flock of starlings, I can call up a vivid "imago" of the sort of picture I always look for in these galleries, and to tell the truth seldom experience any difficulty in finding! It will have a ragged tree-trunk in the foreground with a good space of rough ground round it containing moss, lichen, twigs, straw, loose stones, and a few anonymous weeds. It will have a few unobtrusive figures tending cattle, and beyond these an old stone bridge with a man or a woman driving sheep across it, the animals following one another with that curious sense of something that goes on for ever, something lifted out of time into eternity, such as Keats suggests as belonging to the figures on a "Grecian Urn." And my picture will show in its further perspective some huge fragment of crumbling masonry, a portion perhaps of a fallen temple or the remains of some gigantic aqueduct. Delicate grasses and the trailing tendrils of wild plants will be seen growing between the stones of this ruin and the mere existence of our doubt as to its original nature will enhance the value of what might be called the *abstract idea* of ancient masonry, making it a symbol of the work of the generations, sinking slowly down into the earth from which it arose. And then beyond this majestic fragment would be seen the wide-stretching branch of a great tree, dusky and dim and of a brownish-green colour, like one of those branches that stretch forth in so monumental a way in the "Fête Champetre" of Giorgione. Behind this branch will be seen long lines of dark rolling clouds, alternating with a receding distance of pale green ether. But the massive ruin to which I have referred will be broken at one particular point; and there the eye will catch a vague uncertain glimpse of distant water; a river perhaps, or a river-mouth, widening into the sea. At any rate there will be faint silvery gleams upon that distant water, gleams that will lead the mind on and on and on, till it loses itself in the boundless.

My Venetian boy-girl whose feelings towards Leonardo must have closely resembled those of Luini or Beltrafio, though I dare say they anticipated many of the now famous opinions of Paul Valéry, could not, for all her passionate scorn, destroy my love of these old, mellow, conventional eighteenth-century landscapes.

"What do you *exactly see* when you look at these conventional pictures?" she would indignantly ask, in the true Paul Valéry manner of trying fiercely to reach the unappeasable objective of perception, tearing away the subjective as if it were some sort of clinging bindweed.

"I see what pleases me in Nature," I would reply, "only *more* of it; and with the rest left out."

"But what do you *feel*?" my boy-girl would insist.

"I'll tell you in two words, my dear." I would answer. "I feel *sensual lust*. My contemplation of these old tree-stumps, of these bits of broken wall, of that ancient bridge, with the sheep crossing it for ever and for ever, of that far-away silvery gleam on the distant sea, gives me the same sensation that I get when I contemplate you yourself; at least when I contemplate you when you are in a placid mood or, better still, fast asleep! Yes, what I feel when I gaze in such deep satisfaction at these eighteenth-century landscapes, is a definite psychic sensuality. It is much more than the physical sensation of eating and drinking. It is exactly like what I feel, when you, my beautiful one, allow me to hold you on my lap!"

After endless discussions between Llewelyn and me, excitedly conducted at his bedside, in the intervals of his bodily anguish over the pain of a kidney-stone and his mental tension over the state of his lungs, it was arranged that our Venetian boy-girl should be with us at Genoa, from which

harbour it was decided we should take a Dutch ship to Southampton. As if it were a picture from a life in some different
age I can remember a particular scene on a high balcony, at
early dawn, overlooking the harbour at Genoa. Red geraniums,
endless red geraniums, come back to my mind in connection
with it, and the particular way the ripples of a calm sea catch
the white light of dawn as Dante has noted in the beginning
of the Purgatorio. And I can see Llewelyn's troubled forehead
and that "woman's mouth," that so stirred the Tintinhull
tramp, as he leans forward, still in that kind of old-fashioned
white night-shirt that used to be so carefully inscribed "Ll.
Powys" in indelible marking-ink for the benefit of his Sherborne
or Cambridge washer-woman, supporting himself against a
marble pillar on this Genoese balcony, tantalized by the cruelty
of the handicap of his illness.

The Dutch ship on which we sailed for home strikes me in
retrospect as a sort of "Flying Dutchman"; for she came, I
believe, from Java, and she stopped at every port, so it seems
to me now, from one end of the Mediterranean to the other.
At the Lisbon harbour, where we finally touched, I bought for
myself an immense Spanish cloak which for a long while was
the passionate envy of every woman I knew. *Some* particular
woman got hold of it in the end; for like the seamless garment
of the Lord it could not be divided. But those Arab cities of
the North African coast, on the brink of the authentic desert,
went into my feverish head and out of it again as if they had been
pictures on a screen. I *was* faintly jerked into an awareness of
Algiers by being forced to ride a beast of some kind—I know
it was not a camel; and I can scarcely believe it was a horse;
probably it was an ass—and I was thrilled to see "dark faces
with white silken turbans wreathed," and to take off my boots
in a mosque, and to watch water-sellers carrying water in
skins, and to see loaves of bread exactly identical with those
I had just seen in Leonardo's picture, touched by Christ's own
fingers.

I have never been hated in any company to the tune in
which I was hated by officers, crew, and fellow-passengers, on
board that ship from Java! Llewelyn's consumption seemed the

last straw in the account they held against me. He *looked* by this time, you see, as ill as he really was; a thing which seldom happens with him, and I can recall one of these officers shaking his fist in my face and crying out in broken English: "Don't you dare ever again to bring that brother of yours on a Dutch ship!"

My next foreign excursion was to Spain. I saw "The Catholic" before I set off to the land of his heart's desire. I suppose that Council on the terrace-walk which had a tendency to regulate my money matters would have strongly protested against my taking "The Catholic" with me! He was settled at Reigate at that time, and there I went to his house, and stayed alone with him. Up and down the streets of Reigate I walked with "The Catholic." It was, I think, the town of his birth; so that he not only knew every picturesque old hostelry in the place but every stick and stone in the environs. Well do I recall being grievously irked by the firmness with which "The Catholic" carried me, one afternoon, out of the public gardens, where I would fain have lingered indefinitely. But we had only had a week together, and after all he *was* half a priest; so I suppose it was natural enough that he relucted to take himself off, as Bernie would have done, leaving me to glare, like the Head of Medusa, at some solitary young woman who sat with crossed legs upon a bench.

It was of Bolingbroke's writings that my friend talked as we drank our port and sherry in those Reigate taverns; for always, with what was probably the instinctive impulse of a monk or a holy man, "The Catholic" fled from whatever secular house, even if it was his own, he might have been dwelling in, and hurried off to the erudite anonymity of a friendly tavern. He always said he thought better as well as wrote better in some inn-parlour. That singular book of his, that book which anticipated, as well as refuted some of the subtlest reasonings of Modernism, *Pascal, Newman, Loisy and the Catholic Church*, was no doubt largely written in inn-parlours. I can boast the honour of having decoyed him to write a *little* of it at Burpham; but that may have been because his friend Father Tyrrel, the famous Jesuit, was actually borrowing from me—during his final unhappy controversy with the Vatican—certain works of Newman that he could not find at Storrington just across our downs, where he lived till his death.

Of Pascal "The Catholic" never failed to talk to me. He talked passionately, even wildly and with a gathered-up intensity of feeling that amounted to the sort of heroic desperation which so often appears in Miguel Unamuno. Unamuno was, I think, one of J. W. W.'s religious correspondents, as was certainly Père Brèmond in France, and the Baron Von Hügel in Germany; but I know this: that none of the Neo-Thomists of a later day, not even the learned and eloquent Maritain, catch that tragic, mystic exultation, with a flash in it like the point of Balin's fatal spear, with which my friend used to utter his convoluted "apologia," both for himself and for his hero, Pascal.

It is when I think of the intensity of emotion, and of tragic emotion too, not mere sentimental feeling, with which "The Catholic" used to defend the Religion of the Saints, that I find it difficult to refrain from being a little puzzled when I contemplate such formidable-brooding foreheads as Darrow's in America and my own Llewelyn's in England, setting themselves so indignantly against these things. But I suspect, as often happens in other spheres, that the intense feelings at both ends of the scale are really nearer each other than the *laissez-faire* attitude of those who are "neither for God nor for His enemies" is near to either of them.

I snatched the opportunity—how disgusted with me would "The Catholic" have been had he known!—of remaining a day or two in Paris in order to rush, like the madman I was, through an orgy of my forbidden books. But I must relate in this connection a very queer psychopathic phenomenon, namely the fact that after racing through a collection of these evil books, I found myself, at the end of a magical spring afternoon, with the horizontal sun falling on these unspeakable volumes tossed about on the floor of my hotel bedroom and the balmy Paris air full of the scent of lilacs and lilies of the valley and horses' dung—for the *fiacre* had not yet given way to the "taxi"—floating in through my window, with my erotic desire still wholly unsatisfied and all exciting power gone from these works. So carrying my books, some of which I had barely skimmed to the nearest square that had a dustbin where I could get rid of them—for I was not so scrupulous in Paris as in Dresden—I set out to some sort of a vaudeville performance the advertisements of which attracted me.

But there is something about the French stage with its artistic provocations and extravagant indecencies that seems always to freeze my wicked thoughts into a chastity as cold as death; so I was left to that old miserable condition from which only Tom and "Tom's girls" had ever saved me, the condition of burning with the desire of a *voyeur* but finding all I looked at turn to dust and ashes. I was reduced to that bitter knowledge that my frantic eroticism will I suppose learn "in vain, in vain," throughout eternity, that since the real essence of all desirableness exists in the activity of the imagination, it is better to force yourself to be thrilled by what you have got—for to the imagination, *as to God*, all is possible, and reality and unreality *are the same thing*—than to hunt through half the dustbins of Paris, to try to find what you have thrown away.

Well, I finally took the train for the South; and you may believe that my excitement to get a glimpse of Touraine, the land of Balzac and Rabelais, and possibly even a sight of those "melancholy seignorial woods of Blois," described by Pater in *Gaston*, soon made me forget those Paris dustbins.

How long and luscious and green the meadow-grass was along the banks of the Loire! I have seen green grass in my time; seen it in the Shirley meadows, in the Stinsford meadows near Dorchester, in the dairy-fields at Montacute; but on my soul I've never seen pastures as green as these were that that southern express rushed through. All too soon for me was the landscape swallowed up by darkness; but in the morning I forgot there were such things in the world as green fields. All was yellow and brown and golden and burnt umber.

I was in Spain. You can believe how the figure of "The Catholic" and his tragic and terrific resolve "to hold," as he always used to say, "religion by the hair" rose up and stood by my side as I got out of the train at Madrid. I had been mocked ere I clambered into my berth for the night by a group of fashionable young Frenchmen and I can tell you it was with relief I saw these young sparks enter a grander hotel than I could afford.

It is most remarkable how I excite either strong feelings of derisive hatred as I go about or strong feelings of exaggerated respect. And this is especially true of young men. I've got on wonderfully well with young Americans, young Germans, young Jews, and young Englishmen—never with a young Frenchman! This I think is due to the fact that my type of imagination, my type of humour—if you can call it humour, and, after all, there *are* precedents for it—and my type of intelligence, are all exactly opposite to the dominant French types of these things. One Frenchman alone, my honourable and dear friend, Monsieur D'Aoust, has put himself out to be gracious to me; and the delicious savour of his appreciation has been so penetrating that it makes the fact that it *is* such an exception all the more emphatic.

But to be alone in Madrid was a pleasure far beyond anything I had anticipated! Walking up and down that sun-baked little garden at the entrance to the blood-tinted Prado, gazing at the royal Palace through iron bars, desperately trying to appropriate to my imagination the scoriac backgrounds of Spanish pictures with their tawny dust, their abject vegetation, their desolate crags, their leafless demon-twisted branches, walking along narrow stone terraces poised above echoing thoroughfares, drinking cup after cup of a coffee that seemed to me less agreeable than any liquid I had ever poured down my throat, I had that delicious sensation that I am always struggling to feel, of being a real stranger to the whole of our planet—a stranger from Saturn, say!—wandering up and down the earth, and observing without hatred, without curiosity, without envy, without love, without disgust, the customs of the tribes of men as if they were the ways of fish in an aquarium.

But one of the most exciting events of my whole life was now to take place. I had prepared myself, you must understand, for this pilgrimage to Spain, though not as scrupulously as "The Catholic" would have done. But I had practised reading Spanish till I could read easy novels—not *Don Quixote*, but books like those of Blasco Ibanez—and among other works of this voluminous author I had read with thrilling delight the one about the cathedral at Toledo. This book pleased me even more than Hugo's *Notre Dame* and it is in any case a *genre* for which I have a strong predilection, just as I have for books about certain legendary places where in the very soil there linger vestiges of the old local magic, books, I mean like that little masterpiece by Maurice Barrès, called the *Sacred Hill*.

I had been stumbling through these Spanish stories, guessing and skipping grossly, but getting enough out of them to keep me going, for at least a year, so that I was not totally in the dark about Spain, not, that is, from any ordinary point of view; but I *was* totally in the dark about her, a mere epicurean literary amateur, like Barrès himself, from the point of view of Unamuno, or of "The Catholic," or of the ghost of that wry-faced king of all tragical puppets who had certainly come either on Rosinante, or in the head of his creator, to this part of Castile.

Well, anyway, I started for Toledo, that city of cities, leaving Madrid as early as I could in the morning. The train I went by stopped at every little station; and indeed I might say at every little hamlet. It was, in a most literal sense, what Americans call *an accommodation train*. Once it stopped where there was a group of gipsies travelling to Toledo who had lost an amazingly coloured cockatoo which had flown into a tree where from the windows of the train we could all observe it, bowing its great beak and flaming crest up and down, as if in worship of some super-parrot in that burning sky. Whether the engine driver, or the guard, of this "accommodation" train was the one destined in the end to bring the bird down from its tree of prayer I cannot tell, nor can I remember that the gipsies showed any particular emotion, of either pleasure or vexation, when, with resounding gasps of steam, our benevolent locomotive resumed its journey.

I can remember every detail of my stay in Toledo as if it

were no more than a year ago. Following my father's habitual custom—"I always like to be independent, John, my boy"—I walked from the station to the town. I was astonished to see what looked to me like the granite boulders of some wild tract in Dartmoor, bordering the outer bank of the river, which rolled, yellow as a lion's skin, at the bottom of a precipitous gorge. I seem to remember the ancient bridge, which I crossed to get into the city, as an extraordinarily narrow one; and unless during all these years, I have beguiled myself with curious inventions I remember seeing the words, "in this city it is forbidden to beg or to blaspheme," inscribed on the bridge-head. But it was the narrowest of bridges and it spanned the wildest of streams; and if I think of it in connection with that desperate Eel-Bridge that had to be crossed in the Grail legend before you reached the Castle of Carbonek, you must remember that to be entering Toledo entirely alone, save for the phantasmal figure of "The Catholic" at my side, was one of those occasions in a person's life when the most insignificant "omens of the way" became charged with unutterable mysteries.

For so long had I watched my friend's dark, desperate, passionate, *tragic* attempt to clutch Religion by the hair of her head that to be now in the heart of that very Spain to enter which he still regarded himself as unworthy, seemed an incredible, almost a sacrilegious thing; at any rate seemed a thing that it would be a sin against the Holy Ghost to treat casually, lightly, and in an "artistic" manner. I really had managed to pick up enough Spanish to read Blasco Ibanez's *Cathedral* with some idea of what was going on in that picturesque tale; and now when, under the guidance of a lad who resembled a Nicolas Poussin shepherd-boy, I visited the enormous edifice it was with an extraordinary satisfaction that I clung to the iron rails of that strange central altar. Toledo seemed full of iron bars, iron bars that *had* to be clung to, as some old magic law in Malory might have insisted, before you could even get a glimpse of these thaumaturgic successors of El Greco's ecstatics!

My Nicolas Poussin shepherd-boy led me at one point to

one of the most sombre houses in one of the most stony streets in the whole town, and there we waited outside a postern that might have led into Count Orguz's burying-place, until a man in a black cassock opened an iron gate, a man to whom providence had given the most unsmiling, un-humorous, devilish face I have ever beheld, to lead us into the little church where the El Greco's picture of the Interrment of Count Orguz was to be seen. "Seen," do I say? Approached on your knees rather; peered at, while your forehead—and your soul too—was pressed against iron bars!

If the huge and cavernous interior of Toledo cathedral with its vast incrustations of labyrinthine complexity satisfied me with that curious satisfaction that I felt among the roots and rabbit-holes of those high banks above "Lover's Lane" at Sherborne and that I felt in the lath-and-plaster "under-roof" at Rothesay House, and that I must have felt *when I came back* from my first infantile exposure to the dangerous out-of-doors world at Shirley, it was scarcely less of a satisfaction to my whole nature when my boy took me—I was thankful to escape from that other terrifying *psycho-pompos*, or guide of the damned—into what they call "The House" of El Greco. I am in the habit of declaring, when I dare say it would be better to hold my tongue, that I am not only ignorant in matters of art but maliciously hostile to the "artistic" point of view. This is true. But I suspect it comes from my old furious battles with Harry Lyon, to whose superior knowledge I had to bow, while my deepest vitals pulsed with the desire to confute and confound him.

But in the matter of El Greco—whose peculiar genius I found out entirely for myself, and then lived long enough to watch him grow into a cult among the very æsthetes I so wrangled with—it was just as it was when I first got hold of Dostoievsky. Indeed I think there is something in common between El Greco and Dostoievsky. When, for instance, I recall the figure of my own namesake John, though it is John the Evangelist and not John the Baptist, I can remember now how it seemed to me as if the great mystical colours of the soul, the noble Pantagruelian colours, blue and white, were projected through its flesh and blood, along with the flame of the sun and the greenness of the grass, until the very stuff of its human consistence seemed to become porous to the creative breath, not only in regard to its form but in regard to that even deeper mystery that underlies what we know as "colour." I had always instinctively revolted against that saying of Blake's, that "The Catholic" used to quote with such approval, "He who does not prefer form to colour is a coward," but my ignorance of the technique of the arts prevented me from justifying this obscure protest. But here in this flame-colour and in this grass-colour, *piercing* the flesh of St. John from the very soul, you might say, of the First Cause, was an energy not a wit less spiritual than that manifested in the Blake-like power of El Greco's drawing.

It was a shame that I could not stay longer by myself in Toledo. It was my accursed gastric trouble that soon blighted my Spanish adventure. I could cope all right with their cigarettes; and, fool though I am at foreign languages, I got further with Spanish than I had ever done with Welsh; but their food and their coffee destroyed me. I can remember now drinking cup after cup of Spanish coffee in a gloomy eating-house of some kind looking out on a sort of market-square near the inn where Cervantes, or Don Quixote, for it was hard for me to separate the movements of the two, was wont to put up. And though my stomach was seething with this cursed coffee—and in my recklessness I imbibed *white wine*, always the worst of poisons to me, on the top of the coffee—my incorrigible romanticism, heedless of scientific accuracy, so long as I got the thrill I wanted, discovered in certain Castilian peasants just come in for marketing an overwhelming resemblance to the grave, dry-humoured, taciturn north-countrymen, described in the Waverley novels!

How indeed did I—for a man's secret psychology is better revealed when he is travelling alone than in any other situation —compare, as I went about Toledo, with the kind of figure that most young, bookish, academic Englishmen, sons of parents of the upper-middle class, would have presented in my situation? I think I was different from most of these by having begun to learn even then the tremendous secret, the great Homeric secret, of having the courage of my limitations! Candour with yourself, save when you are deliberately forcing yourself to forget the thoughts wherewith you torment yourself, is the one thing needful; and after that, to be unashamed of your ignorance and childishness. My whole intellectual history could be summed up as a struggle to harness my magnetic vitality, which is so terrific, to the plough, not of my cleverness, but of my simplicity. And my guardian angels have helped me in this by saving me from all shame over the matter of inconsistency. This acceptance of inconsistency—a most essential thing in anyone's experience—has been made easy for me because of my habit of living out my life from the basis of what might be called a *pluralistic world*, like the world of Homer, where everything around you, air, water, earth, fire, is the living body of a living spirit.

As I went about Toledo, therefore, I was totally shameless in my rustic English ways, and recklessly shameless in my rapturous delight at all the Spanish ways which were so different from everything I knew at home. It has always been a characteristic of mine to take a malicious pleasure in displaying all my ignorances and simplicities in the presence of the type of people who are proud of their knowledge of the world. This I am especially addicted to in the presence of sophisticated persons who indulge in that particular *savoir-faire* tone, or "know-all" tone, which travellers of all countries tend to assume. From persons of this breed I used to turn with relief to the thought of my friend "The Catholic," whose religious and imaginative life went so deep, and who was, for all his intellectual subtlety, so passionately simple in all the great emotional issues.

But this *spiritual malice* of mine is one of the dominant elements of my life and it is all the deeper and more formidable because in my dealings with people I invariably conceal it. I am revealing this secret now under the inspiration of my memories of Spain, but it is so little understood by my friends that "The Archangel" cannot resist giving way, when he deals with my character, and even with my facial expression, to that

particular kind of irritation which we all feel in the presence
of what strikes us as affectation, while another old friend, but
she has not suffered from my weaknesses as deeply as "The
Archangel," declares that this "malice" of mine, to which
I am always making dark and lurid allusions, is a pure invention! But it is *not* invention, any more than my excessive and
shameless expression of what I feel is an affectation.

I am a born actor; but my "acting" takes place in a dimension of life beyond the level of the theatrical, a dimension of
life where even to half-believe, or, if you will to half *make*
believe, is to share in the creative secrets of that eternal blower
of magic bubbles, Nature herself.

This "malice" that I am trying to analyse, as I recall the
shameless simplicity of my feelings as a traveller, is, as I have
hinted, a deeply misanthropic thing. In the depths of my being
I feel simple, natural, childish, direct. In the presence of things
and people that I dislike I feel transparently hostile, but my
impulse is either to escape by running away, or to escape by
turning my inmost identity into an untouchable pebble-stone.
I have a strong vein of the belligerent in me; but this I instinctively suppress till the occasion that excited it has passed away.
I have acquired, in this particular, a self-control that acts so
spontaneously and so automatically that it has become almost
impossible for me to fly into a rage. So hard indeed has it
become for me to show anger in the presence of people who
are injuring me, that sometimes, to produce a desirable effect,
I have to *pretend* to feel, on the surface, the emotion which I
really *do* feel in the depths, but which, in the middle-stratum,
so to say, of my nature, I have already automatically suppressed!

But towards things and people who attract me my feelings
resemble those of an enthusiastic young girl. I am often
secretly amused, in my analytical mind, by observing the kind
of person I become at such times; for I become so eager and
impulsive, so transparently and whole-heartedly elated and
excited, that my whole being, all my flesh and blood, all my
nerves, all my muscles and fibres, suddenly feel as if they were
porous and transparent. My soul gets so excited that it feels as
if it were pouring itself, like water or air, through my body,

and taking my body up into itself, and perforating my body with its emotion. I feel, at these times, light as air; and the greater my exultation the more frail, slight, weak, brittle becomes my body! Yes, it is a strange and curious thing that the more transported with happiness I am in the presence of a person or a thing, the more do I feel as if I were a young girl. When my bones melt with delight in the presence of an expression, a look, a glance, a word, a gesture, in a person I like, or in the presence of *some single line* out of the poetry of Milton, or Dante, or Homer, or Keats, or Shakespeare, for the sensation of tears which arises then at the back of my eye-sockets never comes from suffering but always from happiness, I have an extreme awareness of feminine fragility, feminine eagerness, and what might even be called feminine abandonment, towards the person or object in question!

I am not a homo sexualist—I would shamelessly confess it to you, reader, if I were!—and I am the extreme opposite of a narcissist or exhibitionist, but when I am attracted to something rugged, massive, primordial in men, men like my father, or my youngest brother Will, or Theodore Dreiser, I feel as if my emotion were exactly like that of a young girl, tremulous with hero-worship. The quaint and grotesque thing is that even while this girlish feeling dominates me my own *appearance* remains almost as rugged and formidable—in some cases *more* rugged and formidable—than the person whose primeval simplicity I am idealizing!

You will perhaps wonder how it is possible that any sadistic tendency can co-exist with this impulsive girlish abandonment; but the curious thing about my sadism is that it is the sadism in almost every particular of a woman. Deep, deep in my nature lies the vice of a sadistic woman, and that, no doubt, is the reason why I abhor all forms of cruel sport, and shrink instinctively from all bloodshed and brutality. It destroys my pleasure when, in a sadistic book, in fact I skip page after page with shrinking disgust, bloodshed is described.

But to return to my "malice." What I feel so deeply is that —as "The Catholic" used to say—no one has a right to force his æsthetic and moral values upon the spirit of another. A person's life-illusion ought to be as sacred as his skin. Thus while I struggle to be unworldly and unambitious and unfashionable and unclever, as I have a perfect right to do, just as religious people have a perfect right to try to be *good*, it fills me with an indescribable maliciousness when I meet people who in their insensitiveness to the subtleties and ironies and diabolical complexities of human character feel a crude contempt for the childish and eccentric. I do not feel malice towards people like "this Archangel," who get indignant with me as "affected," or towards devoted friends, like her who thinks that my "maliciousness" is a fantastic invention. The people I feel malicious towards are the worldly, fashionable, rich, society people, or the clever sophisticated academic people, who are not merely annoyed, like "the Archangel," by what they consider my affectation, but who conceal their discomfiture at my insight into their essential stupidity by abusing me as a sensualist. But in both cases, in the case of "the Archangel" as well as in the case of these others I shall always carry my peculiarities in their presence to the extreme limit. I suppose to many people, quite different from those I have mentioned, the idea that a grown-up person who has lived in this world for more than half a century of completely conscious life can deliberately struggle to make himself as simple, as natural, as childish as he can, and as eagerly and impulsively spontaneous as he can, is a repulsive idea, and has even something *indecent* about it.

I, therefore, who, if I know myself at all, am the extreme opposite of a "narcissist" and the extreme opposite of an "exhibitionist," am driven on by my malice to become more and more innocent, naïve, artless, childish and even foolish! Yes, few things give me a greater thrill, a thrill that *is* actually sensual, a delight that might easily be accompanied—though I do not say it is!—by feelings of erotic excitement, than making a fool of myself in the presence of people who cannot endure to see the decorous surface of life ruffled in any way.

Strange though it may sound in your ears, reader, after all my scandalous confessions, I am perfectly certain that there exists, twisted in with other threads in the fabric of my nature, a curious moral sensitivity that has been found ere now in the "foolishness" of saints! My malice, however, can hardly, I fear, be regarded as a saintly characteristic, and this element in me tends to grow especially erotic and sensual, though never sadistic, when I encounter people—and in these days there are so many of them—who are clever without being original, smart without being subtle, intelligent without being intellectual, and who, above all, are always talking about these thrice-tedious "complexes." Have they *no* intellect, *no* philosophy, *no* insight? Can't they see that all chatter about "complexes" is destined to pass away in a few years and be superseded by a completely new set of clue-words?

The truth is that down at the very bottom my malice is not only misanthropic; it is also philosophical! What makes me feel more malicious than anything else is this cock-sure conceit of the importance of modern science. I have gained something like everybody else, from modern machinery, modern inventions, modern philosophical ideas. But it remains that in my opinion the two greatest utterances in the world are Pilate's question: "What *is* Truth?" and Jesus' unscientific and superpersonal saying: "*I* am the Truth." These two remarks together cover the whole field. In fact there is in reality no such thing as scientific *truth*. There are scientific methods, scientific hypotheses, scientific guesses, and scientific inventions; but "truth" is something that in its inherent nature—simply because it is alive—for ever must baffle science. Science can torture and kill the possessors of truth, but truth itself will always escape; and it will escape because it is never totally without consciousness, never totally without free-will, never totally without the god-like power of destruction and creation.

Another human type that excites this sensual malice in me is the expert-type, the virtuoso-type, the type whose professional *savoir-faire*—is made stupid by pure conceit. I have been attacked and derided by this teasing type all my life. I am a standing annoyance and a standing threat to these professional mandarins. When I am in their company I cannot describe to you the voluptuous pleasure I derive from struggling to be a greater fool than Nature has made me! What it really is that makes these people so angry is that my deliberate simplicity and artlessness drags down their ambition, makes futile their pretensions, and reduces to nothing their whole life-illusion. For them the purpose of life lies in competition; for me in contemplation. For them the urge of life is towards being successful and being heard of. For me the urge of life is towards enjoying the mystery of the elements and the magic of erotic sensuality.

My whole philosophy is based upon my father's monumental simplicity; and towards this I strive as Christians strive towards Jesus. Fortunately, though my nature is subtle as the devil in certain serpentine directions, it is also almost morbidly childish; and so it has not been difficult for me, though hampered by the derision of both friends and enemies, to get pretty far in this life-long struggle to simplify my routine of living.

It is possible that I should have remained longer in Toledo if I had not imbibed the disagreeable notion that the inn where I stayed had been built above its own cesspool. So I went back to Madrid and the next day took the train for Seville. "The Catholic" was perfectly right in making his passionate protest against the average sophisticated traveller. I remember a book on Toledo by Barrès which bore upon its cover a picture of himself, of this clever, cultivated Alsatian, looking down on El Greco's city from a neighbouring eminence, as he might have looked down on a fantastic Spanish play from the balcony of his French theatre.

In the feeling that I was representing my passionate friend —the friend of Unamuno, but hardly of fortune—by treating this country he would never see in a mood different from mere literary appreciation, I did my utmost to miss nothing of the qualities of the place, when I did finally reach Seville. Here I met Louis and a lady we both knew well, and I can remember how the obstinate way in which I pursued my various superstitious cults proved a bit too much for these two friends of mine. Indeed it is very seldom that I meet anyone prepared to put up with *all* my various manias.

Llewelyn is indulgent to most of them; though even he does not like waiting at pillar-boxes while I thrust my fingers down the orifice to make certain my letters do not stick. Differences of temperament leap up, however, with extreme violence when you are with your friends in an alien land. I told you how Lulu himself got angry with me in Basle, on our way to Clavadel, because, in the fuss I was making about Nietzsche's having taught Greek there, I was unsympathetic when one of his teeth fell out. With Bertie in Rome I had an angry dispute, but A. R. P.'s quizzical dogmatism would make a saint lose his self-control, about the wording of a certain telegram to Paris. Bertie wanted to make it laconic and cheap; I insisted on its being voluble and expensive. "Is it not sad," as the philosopher Kwang always says when dealing with the pathetic stupidity of mortal men, that I can't think of Rome without thinking of this row with Bertie; nor of Seville without thinking how I annoyed the "Archangel." I can see the scene now, as if it were only a month ago; see myself climbing down a long flight of steps to the banks of the Guadalquivir in order that I might baptize the handle of the hickory stick, which was "Sacred's" successor then, in those Andalusian waters. This was a fixed habit of mine, this dipping my stick in all the historic streams I encountered. I did the same thing five years ago, in the river Test at Horsebridge; but on that occasion my stick was plucked out of my hand by a great mill-wheel, and actually carried round with it, so that when it was finally picked up out of the river it was several hundreds of yards down-stream and I felt as if a miracle had been performed.

But sentimental antics of this sort always disgusted Louis Wilkinson, who was one for keeping a sound mind in a sound body when on his travels: while our lady-friend, who despised us both as fussy egoists, came to the conclusion that my kind of selfishness was more troublesome than his. Perhaps she was right. You must not forget, reader, that even our wise Dr. O'Neill exclaimed once that what "Jack's manias" needed was a sound flogging every morning. I expect the sight of "Signore Jack," as they had called me in Italy, throwing all decency to the winds as he bent over that river made my friends feel a spasm of positive hatred for me. Not the same kind of hatred:

for the girl must have seen how authentic my morbidity was, while Louis must have felt that I was deliberately trying to pretend I was some kind of mystical mediæval pilgrim, bent on "acquiring merit." Anyway the upshot was that when I came up out of the Guadalquivir, for this stick-baptizing could not be done hugger-mugger, it had to be done ritualistically, I could see the distinguished figures of my indignant friends receding into the remote distance.

But as day followed day and Louis tried to make me get some notion of the quality of Moorish civilization, my mania for everything connected with Nietzsche came upon me and drove me to admire the walls of the tobacco-factory more than either Moorish towers or Moorish gardens. For it was this tobacco-factory that plays such an important rôle in the opera *Carmen*; and it had not escaped me that Nietzsche, to revenge himself on Wagner for *Parsifal*, had gone fifteen times to listen to Bizet's music. I have no doubt that my turning the wall of the Seville tobacco-factory into a symbol of the clash of such vast immemorial ideals, as those represented by *Siegfried* on the one hand and *Parsifal* on the other, was one of the most deeply authentic, deeply felt, and fully realized gestures of my life. If I had approached that wall to touch it with the handle of my stick, though it might not have struck my companions as quite as tiresome as my conduct on the banks of the river, I expect our girl-friend would have said to herself: "If Signore Jack had the spirit to throw himself into the Bull-Ring it *would* be something," while "The Archangel" would have thought: "Does the old idiot suppose that these damned 'Ideas' of his fight like spitting pussy-cats?"

But I am prepared even now to enter into a lively defence of my dramatic awareness of the clash of human ideas, which I maintain *do* fight, not like pussy-cats, but like angels and devils. What really I did see as I stared at those factory-walls, was the *Apollonian* cult of Goethe and Nietzsche, struggling not so much against Wagner, who was the inspired medium, as against my own Cymric Imagination, which was the real Dionysus, and of whom Wagner's *Parsifal* was merely the Holy Bacchanal.

When I think of the subtle and tremulous intensity of our Welsh legends, all this Nietzschean laudation of hot, violent, Southern Toreador-passion, rouses me to a tense pitch of contrariety. It is just here that I would quarrel with all my æsthetic friends. They say they find the beauty of the world so poignant that they can't bother with mystical Gladiator-Shows. But to me the difference between the ideas of Nietzsche and those, say, of Dostoievsky, has the same sort of vibrant magic in it as the difference between sunlight and moonlight. My mind is too restless and too impatient to give itself up for days on end to analysing the effect of Moorish art upon Gothic art.

Did not "The Catholic" himself glory in the dramatic excitement of metaphysical conflict? Why! I remember his telling me that once in a Papal College at Rome the only thing he could think about was Martin Luther! What I like about Germans is that they *take ideas seriously,* and regard the conflict of ideas as the most deeply stirring drama upon this planet, as in my opinion it most certainly is; and though the æsthetic type of traveller who takes nothing seriously but certain recondite "auras" and "atmospheres," and who hates everything that belongs to the mental drama of the human spirit, looks upon these *romanticists of ideas* with weary disdain, it seems to me that the pleasure of indulging in half-poetic, half-philosophic generalizations about the history of human ideas, such as was so dear to Goethe and Nietzsche, is one of the most entrancing delights there is, and one that carries with it an intoxication second only to the intoxication of erotic ecstasy.

It is the fidgety, uneasy awe with which so many people regard every theory advanced by modern science that takes the heart out of the real drama and the real romance of great ideas. Most people are not sceptical enough. If you are sceptical enough about all human hypotheses, clear down to the very bottom of the abyss, then, and then only, and not till then, are you in a position to enjoy the significance, not merely of the spiritual atmosphere of the countries through which you travel, but of the great romantic drama of races, cults, religions and philosophies concerning which almost every stone in these historic places has its own particular palimpsest.

But if my friends got annoyed with me for my manias, in Seville, they were very tender to me over my gastric trouble, which now most evilly invaded me if it did not altogether engulf me. They shared my shrinking from the bull-ring; at least the girl did, and I *think* Louis did too. But we went to a cinema of a bull-fight, where a toreador was badly wounded, if not killed. But how many of the horses in this performance were disembowelled I cannot say, for, as though I had been the "Archangel's" young daughter rather than a man ten years his senior, I kept my eyes tight shut all the time. I confess I was amazed during our time in Seville at my friend's power of dealing with people and with events and with our enemies.

He was, and is—witness *his* autobiography—a lover of fighting for fighting's sake. I have never in my life seen anyone who stood up to officials better than Louis. I can see his tall form and his golden hair and his flushed cheeks now, as he bandied words with these—to me—absolutely terrifying persons. He packed us all into some kind of private conveyance, and proceeded to guide us—after much study of road-maps— from Seville to that ferry from the mainland that crosses over to Gibraltar. I was in high spirits during this trip. I recollect how once when we had left our conveyance in order to explore an enchanted path under some gloomy pine-trees, we came upon a host of tall blue irises. Another time I remember astonishing my companions by a vein of bragging bravura. It was no doubt the presence of the lady that led to this cock-crowing. But at one point I flatly refused to leave our conveyance when to our consternation the driver insisted on crossing a bridge that seemed suspended by a filament over a whirling stream.

We caught some ship or other at Gibraltar, and left "The Catholic's" sacred country without seeing Granada, and I have never again set foot on Spanish soil.

Is it, do you suppose, a deadly and treacherous betrayal of a person's character, the sort of details he recalls from his pleasure-trips of long ago? Well! I take it that a great many considerations enter into this, but I can certainly say with truth that the details which evidently bit the deepest into me were connected with three particular aspects of my life: with my vice, in regard to the buying of those wicked books; with my stomach and bowels in regard to my ulcers and my constipation; and finally with those rare indescribable ecstasies that came to me from old fragments of masonry mingled with certain aspects of Nature. These usually occurred when there was suddenly conveyed to me from the outside of some old building—any building that blent itself with the elements— a magical sense *of having been there before*, of having felt these feelings *hundreds of years before*. And it was when this sensation used to go thrilling through me that I tasted an unforgettable psychic taste in my mouth. Yes it was at those times that an immortal taste on the palate of my spirit used to transport me; a taste which, I suppose, issuing forth from some little transitory impression, becomes the under-sea essence behind all our great mystical words, behind "immortality," behind "eternity," behind "destiny," behind the very "elements" in the worship of Christ.

It was about this time in my life—I cannot get these events in perfect chronological sequence—that I treated my youngest brother Willy to a few days in Paris. Our "dear companion" on that occasion was the same painter with whom I lived those long happy weeks in Italy; but neither she nor I was the sort of person to overpower a young lad with sophisticated matters. We all three in fact were as naïve in our enjoyment as if we were at the circus in Ilchester. But we had a devastating time in finding adequate lodgings. Without the belligerent "Archangel" to act as cicerone, and with a knowledge of French so infantile that we were sore put to it to discover anything we wanted, our pleasure in the adventure was qualified by interludes of villainous discomfort. Our perpetual *Voulez-vous* and *Avez-vous* must have sounded like the voices of the rooks on Montacute Hill for all the effect they had. The first lodging we secured turned out to be an especial kind of a bawdy-house; while in the second, which was situated on the island near Notre Dame, we were incommoded by an agitation far more disturbing than illicit loves. For our lavatory was flooded, both by day and by night, an inch deep in water. For all I know this may have been caused by some incursion of the Seine, which certainly flowed hard-by; or it may have been a French custom; but whatever its cause it proved a distracting worry to the visitors from Montacute Vicarage. To "do our business" we had to wade ankle-deep in an eddying stream, a situation which was anything but calculated to soothe and flatter a person's touchy interiors.

But we finally took refuge in a heavenly retreat, in a very different region, a beautifully clean little hotel, called "Hotel des Grands Hommes," which I heartily trust still flourishes. This was situated quite close to the Pantheon and was largely occupied by university students, and here we were almost as much at ease as if we had been at the "Three Choughs" at Yeovil.

But I remember how, when wandering with Willy in the neighbourhood of Les Halles, down in some narrow streets among tall, ancient, very Gothic-looking houses, houses that had that dim, rich, massive, *intricate* appearance, which, of all things in an old historic city fascinates me the most, we both looked up, just as a couple of Pantagruelians, and caught sight of a lovely sylph-like figure looking down upon us with intense interest from a mediæval casement high up above our heads. This vision, I recollect, was as disturbing to William as it was to John, but whether it was John or William who made the gesture that caused the figure to disappear I cannot tell. Its vanishing was clearly not followed by any descent to the street-door; and, though we could not help lingering there a while, she never came back to that high mediæval window. Even now, as I think of this incident, an indescribable sensation, like that of some old romance of a thousand years ago, steals over me. If you cannot follow me, reader, in this, I have no more to say: but I am certain that my own secretest happiness, as I go about the world, comes from certain revelations of this kind to which I am porous, and to which I am continually struggling to make myself more porous.

These revelations have to do with precisely such recurrent human situations as the one in this case, of two men watching from the pavement of a street a solitary girl in a high window.

You may laugh at me, as I am accustomed to being laughed at, but I cannot tell you how strongly I feel that the kind of imagination which the gods have given me is *more* than imagination! In fact almost all the power we *call* "imagination" may come from an actual tapping of some great reservoir of planetary, if not of cosmic, experience. As I write about this episode now, the whole thing comes over me as if from the touch of a magic wand! It is because of these revelations of the eternally recurrent moments of human life, moments which, like this one of two men looking at a girl in a window, must have repeated themselves for thousands of years, that I feel such a nostalgic preference for ancient buildings over modern ones.

To get this sense of "eternal recurrence" which is to my mind the secret of the most significant poetry of our race and a feeling far more important than any scientific "law," you must have *something* old in the background. Nature is always old, and therefore Nature can always serve this purpose; but, if you are flung into the midst of a city, what you *must* have is the presence somewhere or other of buildings old enough to give you this sense of the continuity of the generations. To the modern æsthete all that I am saying now will sound literary, sentimental, *affected*. But it is these moderns themselves, not I, who are the "affected" ones. *They are shutting off the magnetic current* between themselves and the accumulated poetic feeling of our race's long history.

No, this emotion of mine, which always returns to me when I think of that figure at the high Gothic window, amid a dim intricacy of balconied masonry, must have, whatever its secret may be, a mysterious connection with the organic link that binds together the human generations. We inherit other things from our remote ancestors; *why should we not inherit particular memories?* Why should we not inherit, buried fathom-deep in the soul, certain intensely vivid moments of awareness, moments that were experienced by the men of old time hundreds, even thousands of years, before we were born? But even if what we inherit is only the capacity for response, or the groove of response, to such heightened moments, it is certain that, just as we add something of our own experience to the great familiar works of art, like *Hamlet* or *Faust*, so we are all of us allowed to re-experience in our own lives emotions and gestures that have recurred again and again down the ages. A girl at a high battlemented window in the midst of a dim confusion of balconies and roofs, is, I admit, a simple enough image and no unusual one, but by having recurred through so many ages and by having gathered to itself the feelings of so many generations, it comes to be something symbolic and mysterious. This actual girl may have been a silly little good-for-nothing, a wanton hussy, a selfish baggage; but that is only what she was *superficially*. In essentials—though she were the most frivolous girl in the town—she answered to the gathered-up poetic emotion of thousands and thousands of years!

But whatever may have been the nature of my feelings, when Willy and I looked up at this tall house in the neighbourhood of *Les Halles*, it is certain that this was the one solitary occasion in all my passings through this city—for I have never stayed there longer than a fortnight—that I experienced what you might call a *romantic* sensation.

Out of this same epoch of my past too, as I think of the Paris I explored in those days—though on this occasion I was with the friend who will be the hero of my next chapter—there floats in upon me the agitating episode of my buying Sarah. I have always been interested in parrots. It has taken half a century to conquer the parrot-tricks in myself; and under the influence of this always fantastic new friend of mine—who soon became, and remains still, a sort of adopted younger brother to me—I sneaked into a bird-shop before I left him in Paris and bought, not only Sarah herself, but her gigantic cage. Never shall I forget my crossing alone from Dieppe to Newhaven with this voluble, but to me entirely incomprehensible, companion. My ignorance of French, as it is spoken by both parrot-sellers and parrots, was so extreme, that the personal refreshments that I shared with my prisoner must have been extremely tentative.

But the tenacity with which I embraced that enormous cage knew not a minute's lapse. Wherever I went, between Paris and

Burpham, Sarah went too. Had all the beguiling forms that tempted St. Anthony come dancing round me, I still would have hugged that cage. To journey with Sarah was like journeying with an Abbess. Straight home I went in spite of the fact that we had to change at Brighton. Sarah and her great cage would have kept Casanova in the path of virtue. When we finally arrived at Burpham her language found better interpretation. But it seemed to *my* ears that all she did was to repeat over and over and over again: "Oh dear! Oh dear! Oh dear!"

Chapter Ten

America

I AM so bad at dates that I forget the exact year in which I first "set sail," as we say, for America; but it was in the winter—*that* I do know—and it was on board the old Cunard vessel, the *Ivernia*, that was later lost in the War.

Tom Jones saw me off from Liverpool, and you can believe how the strains of that gay and reckless "Stars and Stripes" of Sousa's, heard through the coffee-fumes of the Kardomah drummed in my head.

"They will be a daring and cynical lot over there," I thought, "if that wild tune does really hit them off."

And when old Tom, with his long nose, tormented mouth, and blue eyes, all under the familiar bowler hat, had gone off to his office, and I was left waiting for the second-class gangway to descend, you can believe with what nervous feelings, for this was my first deep-sea voyage, I peered into the countenances of my fellow-travellers.

Very soon, indeed as soon as "we"—that significant "we" of a chance-flung group of strangers—had got into the Irish Channel, I began to feel, mounting up from the deepest gulfs of my nature, an emotion that was to seize upon me intermittently during the whole voyage. This was an emotion—you must forgive me reader, but I *must* confess my moments of pride equally with my moments of humiliation—of the queerest and the most grandiose kind. As I stood by the rail of the second-class lower deck, which must have extended further than in many ships, and watched the foam-flecked, marble-streaked mass of water move—for so it appeared to me to do—in one vast flowing volume towards the land I was leaving, the notion came to me that I was bound on some occult mysterious errand, an errand of tremendous importance in the spiritual history of this planet. How *can* I describe exactly what I felt as again and again, by day and by night, when I found myself alone, I gazed at that flowing water and at those floating patterns of white foam? The feeling I speak of, though deep and intense, was not very articulate. But what it amounted to, I suppose, was a vague sense of some portentous inspiration, coming, if I may put it so, from immortal presences, and to be delivered, as if I were a mouthpiece of Camelot and Carbonek and Stonehenge and Paladour, to the people on the further side of the ocean.

The odd thing was that, when I cast about in my mind to discover the nature of this oracle that I, like Taliessin in some new incarnation was destined to reveal to America, I could not think of so much as a single opinion or idea! As Harry Lyon used to predict would surely happen to me as a punishment for my lack of principle, I was as devoid of any conviction in religion, morality, politics, æsthetics and all philosophical problems, as my old friend, Aunt Stone.

"We be all born; but we bain't all dead yet." Aunt Stone used to say, and such really seemed, when I sounded my brain on this matter, about all that I could reveal to these far-off hordes of "articulate-speaking" Americans.

But destiny had decreed that however I might leave what I had to say to the inspiration of the gods, I was to be supplied, as far as Fate could supply such a thing, with the most perfect stage-manager that I could have invented in my wildest fancies. This was no other than G. Arnold Shaw, who, after a year at Oxford, had been sent by destiny to seek his fortune in Canada. But the "sealed orders" of Arnold's stars were more powerful than any horoscopic intention, and it was not till a quarter of a century later that my friend paid his first visit to Canada.

And now I will reveal to you a curious psychological fact. I can remember, after this lapse of twenty-five years, about half a dozen of my fellow-travellers on the *Ivernia*, while between that first voyage and my last, that is to say out of a total of some fifty crossings, for I used at first to go home twice a year,

I can with difficulty recall the personalities of two or three. It is just the same in other connections. The boys in the Prep. and the boys at Wildman's I can remember by the score! I can see their faces now, exactly as they were, the little angels and the little devils. But of the men at Corpus I can only recall one or two; and out of two decades of lecturing in America it is deplorable how thin a procession of remembered figures passes across my mental stage.

What does this imply? I think it implies that when you are plunged into something not only new and strange but of a restricted scope and without offering much chance of escape, human personalities double the piercingness of their pressure. But Americans had such a huge background that personalities lost themselves in it. If I end up in prison or in a lunatic asylum, I shall have round my death-bed a set of even more vivid images of my fellow-creatures than I saw when I disembarked from the *Ivernia*.

There was a young man from New Orleans, who had a French name beginning with "G". This young man had a thin long face of calm and classical dignity. He wore, in place of a collar, a black silk scarf, which enhanced his resemblance to those French "Great Men"—those Fontenelles and Rochefoucaulds and Vauvenargues—with whose portraits, in Roman guise, I used to awe Mr. Pollard. I frequented the society of young Mr. G. more assiduously than that of anyone else on the ship. As I have already hinted, my childish, or perhaps I should say my young-girlish passion for the romance of history, a passion which has lent itself to the most fantastic idealizations, leapt up like a flame at the idea of New Orleans and *the Creoles*. I don't suppose for a moment that Mr. G. was a Creole; but I had read about such people in some book of Charles Kingsley's, and the word was magic in my ears. Mr. G. certainly did come from New Orleans and I felt that my voyage to America gathered to itself an additional glory from being able to talk, as freely as I might have talked to a man from Littlehampton, to a personage from such a place.

It was Mr. G.'s portentous silence that chiefly impressed me. He was the ideal companion to lean over the side with,

watching for whales or dolphins or flying fish or sea-serpents.
I could gaze for hours at the blue-black water, which certainly
did not rush by below me at any terrific speed, for we took,
if I am not mistaken, a whole fortnight to cross, and then,
should any touch of nostalgia disturb me I could soothe myself
by staring at this young man's classic profile. But once, I
remember, after we had walked up and down that deck in
deep silence and for an interminable time—for it appeared
that Mr. G. and I resembled each other in our reluctance to
spend a dollar upon a deck-chair—pausing to lean against our
favourite rail the man from New Orleans surveyed the horizon.
Suddenly I became conscious that his perfectly modelled
lips were making those tentative quiverings that very silent
people sometimes make before they can bring themselves to
utter words. Would the remark about to fall from those
beautiful and melancholy lips, as the young man's eyes fixed
themselves upon that infinity of sea convey to me some omen,
some clue, some augury of what awaited me over there?

"Cats," he began. "Cats, Mr. Powys," he repeated—and the
curious thing was that nothing had led up to this announcement—"are afraid of dogs. They *are!* Cats are afraid of dogs."

I have never known such a voyage, as that first one of
mine, for the unadulterated simplicity of a small group of
English, Irish and Americans. Do *all* voyagers, on all liners,
tend to become distressingly simple? I fancy they do. I fancy
the explanation is that men and women in their domestic
homes are persecuted by one another to such a tune that a
thousand simple sillinesses and innocent follies to which they
would love to give way are cruelly suppressed. This is much
more the case I believe with women than with men. Men let
off the steam of their silliness in their "pubs," their "saloons,"
their "clubs." In any case a man's silliness takes as a rule a
more sober form than a woman's. I am speaking of older
people; for I do think when it comes to boys and girls that the
silliness of boys has a certain maudlin brutality in it that is far
more unpleasant than the giggling and showing off of girls.

But I think on the whole that women really do behave in a
more silly way on board a big liner than men do. Cards and

drink keep so many men occupied, not to speak of their interminable bragging conversations. But women on shipboard, if they are not sick, get queerly restless, get seized with a feverish longing for distraction. Sometimes I have even felt, as I watched the exuberant spirits and the lively gamboling of all these worthy ladies, as if men must still be the grave killjoys in every gay harem. But I dare say it's their houses as much as their men, perhaps even in some cases their children, that hold them in this gloomy subjection. But whatever it is, it has struck me again and again in my trips across the ocean as a singularly touching and pathetic thing, to see all these middle-aged women worked up to such a fever of giggling and tom-foolery. I have come to the conclusion that voyaging matrons were really much more like children than young girls; for there is as a rule a seriousness about young girls even when they are most deeply thrilled, and a shyness and reticence, that restrain them from becoming the mænads of a voyage.

Aye! but how well I at last came to know what might be called "the psychology of the second-class saloon." Here indeed were human traits that repeated themselves *ad infinitum* and *ad nauseam*. For instance I always remarked that there were two or three young men on every ship who seemed *born* to be second-class passengers on a liner just as some of us are born to be poets, or baseball players, or acrobats.

On a second-class deck these young men really *lived*. Here they burgeoned, here they flourished, here they radiated shining auras of high spirits. I suspect—if the truth were known—that these young men were all unsuccessful at their jobs, all unsuccessful with women, all liable to be fooled by their friends, all liable to be pitched into by their enemies. They all possessed that particular kind of glittering eye and wiry frame that generally go with prominent veins in lean necks and heads that recede at the back. I knew them infallibly on the very first day when we trooped in procession into the dining-room to be allotted our seats. I knew them by their eye. Out of their eye gleamed an unholy energy; and I noticed that every woman and girl on board always shared my own uneasiness and distaste in the presence of this energy. For it was the very reverse of a sensual energy. It was the sap of life gone into the cords of the neck, and into the muscles of the arms and the legs, rather than into the brain or the senses or the imagination.

I used to call them to myself the "Shuffle-Board Boys"; for it was always an impassioned joy to them to cause those round wooden counters to shoot forward over the smooth deck till they stopped at some particular chalked number. Wet or fine, rough or calm, windy or still, in cloud or in sunshine, these "shuffle-board boys" would disport themselves. Their energy—this life-force gone into the cords of the neck and into the muscles of legs and arms—gave them and gave everyone near them no rest. They never sat still. They could not resign themselves to the real rhythm of the ship, moving through this vast mass of water. They opposed themselves to this elemental rhythm all the while with muscular contortions of arms and legs. When they weren't pushing those round objects about, they were walking round and round and round the deck. On these occasions they would pick up some young woman, whom they delighted to propel as if she were one of their favourite discs. She was generally some young athletic woman proud of not being seasick and anxious to show off how fast she could go. But once released by her shuffle-boy all her feminine instincts forced her to sheer off. She saw that the gleam in those shining eyes was not the gleam of response to the ruffled feathers of a fluttering mate, but the gleam of a demented muscularity.

And among the shuffle-board players I noticed that on every ship there was a particular predestined youth, who in addition to being a "deck walker" had been endowed by Providence with a passion for executive work; and no one on the ship, no! not even the poor escaped house-wives, get such satisfaction out of a voyage as this young man. Sometimes there was a pair of them but not often, for such super-activity is not born every day. But oh! with what sinking in my heart, as, hidden away in the smoking-room or on one of those stationary top-deck benches—for I was always miserly about deck-chairs, though I used to steal a rest in one now and again—I would observe advancing towards me, with his double-shuffle eye and his executive step, this organizer of concerts, this promoter of sports, this arranger of sweepstakes!

I have a notion that the typical second-class set of trans-Atlantic passengers is far more gregarious than either the steerage, where difference of language keeps the races apart or the first class where the chilly presence of a few prodigious celebrities keeps these human-too-human traits from breaking out. Well! Well! If I could escape from the shufflers and steer clear of the sports, and subscribe to the concert without having to attend it, in brief if I could be the Loch Ness monster that I was, there were many aspects of these innumerable crossings that I enjoyed hugely.

I enjoyed the idea of the captain reading divine service on Sundays. I enjoyed the exciting catacomb way, as if it really were a *tremendum mysterium* causing a crack to yawn in the laws of cause and effect, in which any Roman Catholic priest who might chance to be on board celebrated Mass. I enjoyed watching for the spouting of whales and I never leaned on any ship's rail but I imagined the sea-serpent rising up out there before me, incredible, mountainous, with the hoary slime of the unthinkable gulfs trickling from his blind-worm's beard!

The *Mauretania* was, and will always be, my favourite liner. I derived extraordinary satisfaction from going forward once, to the extremest prow of this splendid ship, and watching the way it cut the water like a horizontal guillotine.

The only time I was badly seasick was when Llewelyn crossed over with me. We both were miserable on that occasion and remained long in our cabin, he in the lower berth and I in the upper one. It was on this trip, which must have been about my tenth crossing, that I made my first acquaintance with Dostoievsky. I can see now that old tattered second-hand edition of Vizetelly's translation of *Crime and Punishment* that I was reading while Llewelyn kept murmuring in his misery the word "ginger-pop." Under the title of the book the publisher had added the descriptive words, "a realistic novel," presumably to give the reader an idea of something out of the ordinary. But it was not for its "realism" that *I knew my Master* the moment I got into this work. It was for the extreme opposite of "realism." It was for the overpowering intimation that you do not have to go outside the mind in order to find God and the Devil.

But to return to the *Ivernia*. It was on this ship, and on this voyage, that I met for the first time, met as a complete stranger, my life-long friend and bosom-crony, Mr. G. Arnold Shaw. Arnold Shaw has had a greater effect upon my life than almost any other person. He remains, for I am thankful to say when I recently visited him on Staten Island he was just the same, the most unmalicious, unvindictive, and, in many ways, *unselfish* character I have ever known. But I must be careful what I say; for the bed-rock of his character resembles my own. That is to say in the depths of his being he is sceptical about everything that exists, or subsists, or that is *said* to exist or subsist. Yes, at the deepest bottom of his heart he is sceptical. He is indeed—just as I am—a natural-born disciple of the greatest of all philosophers. I refer of course to the philosopher, Pyrrho, who when asked, at the end, whether he was alive or dead, replied, "I do not know."

But now I am going to initiate you, reader, into an important psychological secret, which, like all the deepest secrets of our contradictory human nature, sounds at first like a paradox. As Heraclitus long ago taught—and the indestructible *livingness*, as even Goethe was forced to allow, of certain aspects of the Christian faith bears out his teaching—the magnetic energy of the system of things is dualistic, and depends upon the coming together of opposites and of contraries. Arnold was, and no doubt is still, a born doubter; and as for myself there is much I cannot believe. But, and here lies the paradox, so far from this profound scepticism in Arnold and myself lending itself to the bad sides of our character, we have invariably found that the more we indulged it the nearer did certain aspects of our eccentricity approach to what—queer fish though we were—belonged to the realm of Simon-pure sanctity.

Of all attitudes of the pure intellect the most utter scepticism is the one—out of some paradox in the occult nature of the cosmos—that lends itself, when you come really to consider it, to the life and to the condition of being a saint. I am, as I tell you, both an anti-narcissist and an anti-exhibitionist. I would blush, as Rabelais says, "like any black dog," to catch myself approaching the verge of these aberrations. But I cannot help often recalling a certain family-group picture that shows me as such a hopeless Ninny, as such an imbecile-idealist, that I always summon it up before me when I desire, for purposes of my own, to identify myself with extreme foolishness.

To believe in nothing, to be a Pyrrhonian sceptic down to the very bottom of your nature, and yet to put into practice— if not actually to feel—many of the most subtle emotions which have been from time immemorial linked up with the idea of a saint, does not that strike your mind, reader, as having in it not only something for which *irony*, with all its nuances, is only a rough-and-tumble synonym, but something which marks a real step forward in that planetary *casuistry* with the difficulties of which all higher intelligences are forever struggling?

And what I was in my pantomimic clown-manner, my friend Arnold was in his humorous Yorkshire manner. We were in fact—lecturer and manager—what people call "a fair pair." I was the clown of our circus, and Arnold was the ring-master, the fellow with the smooth forehead, the bland smile, and the long whip. How roguishly he would crack this whip when his poor Cagliostro was despatched on a tour half across the Continent!

"A *mean jump* for you, John!" he would say with a chuckle.

But how sweet he was to me, how unbelievably unselfish and disinterested and ungrasping and considerate, in private life! We never went a step but he used to look after me as if I had been a china doll rather than the toughest member of the toughest family in England. I can even remember once—and it was a beautiful saying and Arnold little realized *how* beautiful—his suddenly remarking, when I was harassed by all sorts of nervous and emotional worries:

"*Put it all on me, John.*"

Never has there been any one at once so childishly honest and so shamelessly contemptuous of the grave pose of respectful honesty as Arnold was. O how well we suited each other! We were both more than a little anti-human, more than a little malicious to the solemnities and respectabilities of the academic and even of the pseudo-academic world. Arnold never had one ounce more worldly wisdom, or one ounce more worldly ambition, than I had. In fact when he first became my manager I only gave him *twenty per cent.*, which, considering the usual relations between manager and lecturer, was a good deal too little. Our attitude to the art of lecturing was identical. We both regarded it as a public entertainment, and we both relucted at the idea of its being turned into a "cultural stunt." Our attitude to our audiences was the attitude of Catholic priests, not that of Protestant ministers. We rebuked the mighty and exalted the leper.

For all our Pyrrhonian scepticism we had very strong prejudices and antipathies. We both favoured the Flesh and the Devil; but were full of malicious hatred of the world. Even more than moral pomposity we disliked a certain type of patronizing intellectualism. Our grand advertisement always was:

"If our circus is not *enthralling*—to the Devil with it!"

Now it was not very long before the eccentricities in our show began to have various disconcerting effects. We came to be heartily suspected, feared, disliked, detested, by the usual type of ethical person, male or the reverse, who by natural proficiency and suitability for such a rôle, was the type who organized our various provincial lectures. Our career therefore was constantly being exploded by violent altercations; not with the people in the audience for these would turn up in their biggest crowds just after the worst kind of misunderstanding, but with those whose business it was to get the people together and to pay the bill. These persons, preoccupied with the idea of helping the cultural interests of the community, used sometimes to *smell a fox*; in other words to get a faint whiff of the humorous detachment with which this mountebank and his manager regarded the whole business of lecturing. To both of us I was, I fancy, a mixture of a comic Dan Leno and a prophetic Savonarola.

Arnold himself was almost equally delighted by my inspired "grotesqueries" and my wild prophetic incantations. Like Owen Glendower I "called up spirits"; and the more devilish and startling these denizens of the "vasty deep" were, the more Arnold chuckled. He would always sacrifice "the box-office end of it" to God knows what Aristophanic and Swift-like contortions.

It was the daring and always belligerent "Archangel" who first got Arnold to start lecture-managing; and I myself only sneaked into the benefit of it when all was in working order. As Louis most justly observes in *Swans' Milk*—his own auto-biography in his own "genre"—he was in certain respects a better lecturer than I was. This is true. Louis had it in him to become, with certain quite conscious improvements that he acquired by practise, one of the best of all possible lecturers. I never was that. I indulged in constant violences to good taste. I yielded to outbursts of intoxicated malice and infernal spleen. I worked myself up into such ecstasies of anger against the whole well-constituted and well-ordered half of society, that I babbled, burbled, bubbled, blurted my very soul out, in spasms and spouts of bloody foam. I was as one possessed.

It was really *a great new art*. By getting rid of all "high-brow" solemnity, of all academic "correctness" and "docu-mentation," under the Rabelaisian encouragement of my unique circus-manager, I succeeded eventually in *hollowing myself out*, like an elder-stalk with the sap removed, so that my whole personality, every least movement I made, and every least sound I made, and every flicker, wrinkle, and quiver of my face, became expressive of the particular subject I was interpreting. I was "the Reed shaken by the Wind" that the people *did* go forth into the desert to see; but the fact that Arnold and I had the same schoolboy contempt for every species of pretentiousness made me in the end a sort of deboshed John the Baptist. I became in fact the kind of Jokanaan that a Salome might really have loved before she cut off his head.

My "dithyrambic analysis" began, under Arnold's sympathetic management, to change into something that I seriously consider—now that I have given it up—to have been an extraordinary phenomenon in the world. In the calmest and coldest blood I would like seriously to say, as I look back at it from this distance, that I regard what was called my "lecturing" as a thing in the history of the platform—if not of the stage—that will not soon occur again.

Although despised, or only very condescendingly patronized by the Gentile intelligentzia of New York, I found profoundly appreciative audiences among the Jews and the Communists. The Roman Catholics, too, invariably supported me through thick and thin. Did these profound psychologists recognize by instinct how passionately devoted I was to the idea of the saints? Did they recognize me as a mad but infatuated Jongleur de Notre Dame? Certainly of all my audiences throughout my twenty-five years of lecturing in America, and Arnold would bear me out in this, those who liked me best were Jews, Communists and Catholics. Of course I must confess that the presence of rich people, especially of rich *society people*, in my audience, always had the effect of making me say wild, reckless, and sometimes unpardonable things.

When I lectured, as I often did, in a Catholic convent, or in a Jewish synagogue, my romantic sense of the historic significance of these ancient religions was so great that I felt a proud awe at being allowed to speak at all in such places. But not all of the writers of America treated my performances with the studied contempt of the clever megalopolitans.

Both Dreiser and Masters appreciated me at the very start. Masters, I know, was derided for his interest in me. It was treated as a sign of some pastoral lack of sophistication in him that he could tolerate such a charlatan. I am sure I don't know whether people laughed at Clarence Darrow for it, but he too had a decided "penchant" for my oratorical Punch-and-Judy show. As for the poet A. D. Ficke, a much younger man, he composed, long before we became the close friends we are to-day, a most humorous and really imaginative poem about my lecturing.

In California I had the honour to become a protégé, and a friend too, of that noble old Poseidon of the Pacific, Charles Erskine Scott Wood, while the poet George Sterling always went out of his way to be nice to me. I can see now, so clearly, that amazing profile of George Sterling's, sometimes like Hermes Argeiphontes, and sometimes like a cameo portrait of Sigismondo Pandolfo Malatesta, Lord of Rimini! He certainly struck me as having all the characteristics of all the poets I had ever read of; yes, down even to his trick of carrying his works on his person, and being prepared to recite them at any second, proudly and humbly, to king or beggar. He used, in the gentlest kindness of his heart, to take me to his club, and I pray to God I had the wit, as I am sure I had the decency, to conceal from him the venom of my attitude to all social groups except those among rustics and proletarians. And cannot I see too, and shall I not always see, the white-bearded, Walt-Whitman-like figure of Colonel Wood, as he made his way, stepping nimbly as a young man, with his arms full of queer parcels, from Chinatown, past Santa Maria of Guadaloupe and up to the top of Russian Hill?

It was at the colonel's house on Russian Hill that I had my only encounter with that great American poet, Vachel Lindsay, in whose interpretation of religion I always detected something that reminded me of William Blake. I felt very friendly to him and he must have been quick to catch my feeling, for he asked me to go down to the station with him and see him off to Los Angeles. This I felt I ought not to do just then, as it was the colonel's birthday, and I fancied he wanted me to stay. But it was my one sole chance of making friends with this remarkable man and I have been uneasy about it since on the grounds that I might have made things nicer for him by going with him; for I can be as wise as a woman with a poet that I venerate as much as I did Lindsay.

As for Edwin Arlington Robinson, I met *him* very early in my American life and nothing could have exceeded his courtesy to me or my respect for him. It was the clever Megalo-politans of New York who got it lodged in their heads that I was at once a tiresome poseur, full of silly affectations, and a long-winded, tedious rhapsodist, interminably praising the ancient classics.

The truth is I am at once too much of a demented satyr and too much of a fanatical saint to deal adequately with this problem of enemies. When I observe myself, while I shave, I am often startled by the look I have of positively maudlin unworldliness! Not a line, not a wrinkle, not a curve in my countenance expresses that worldly shrewdness, that look of being a slick one in a crafty pack, that practically every normal human being possesses.

But it is not only my satyrishness and my mediæval tricks as a novice in mystical sanctity that prevent my getting angry with people or advancing my career at the expense of people. I have a vein of malice in me of a very curious kind. This malice makes me lead people on to misunderstand and to disparage me. It belongs to the very depths of my nature. It belongs to an instinct in me that always wants to confess the very worst, *so that I shall not be found out*. It is the same instinct that, in the garden at Northwold, used to make me shout to Littleton, so that I should hear his answer and *not come upon him suddenly* in the way.

I can analyse every pathological move in my own nerves in this queer chess-game of the soul. Something or other has hurt me and jarred my nerves. Aggravated by this vibration I turn upon life and madly mock and jibe at it, with blood spurting out of my private hurt, as if from the neck of a decapitated fowl. I seem to get a sensual satisfaction from jerking my headless neck-stump up and down at life. Thus when I have been totally misunderstood, the hurt I feel at being misunderstood drives me on to be worse understood! And the curious thing is that at these times when my nerves are twanging their devil's tune, and I am deliberately exaggerating my foolishness, I suddenly grow aware of a definite sexual excitement. Like the unlucky young man in one of Dostoievsky's shorter stories I have lashed myself up into such a frenzy of zanyism that I feel as if I were making love to some eternal zanyishness in the heart of the cosmos. It is a very odd thing that it should give a person sensual pleasure to go on and

on and on exaggerating some peculiarity that has led to some
monstrous misunderstanding! But such certainly is the case
with me. And against what object, I ask you, is this malice-jig
of my decapitated pride, directing its frenzy?

Not entirely against myself: not entirely against my
enemies: against the first cause, the first cause! Yes! it is
wonderful to chant a litany of gibberish in the face of the
Emperor of the Universe! Dante knew as much as that, and
no poet has ever indentified himself so completely with the
cat-calls of the damned.

I certainly am a funny one in my dislike of competition.
But there is no danger that others will follow me here. I do
not see the least sign that any of my enemies will be tempted
to imitate this peculiarity. In fact the more I hold back from
playing leap-frog with them the more they play leap-frog with
me! When I make it a point of secret honour with myself to
lose in arguments, in discussions, in controversies, my rivals
in the world's colosseum, simply think that they have won.
But, mark you, *I* never feel I am in the wrong! I cannot exag-
gerate to you my rooted conviction, on the contrary, that I
am in the right! And yet I yield, and yield, and yield, and yield;
and I do so with a kind of sensual ecstasy.

The truth is that the roots of Hell and Heaven are very
close; but shall I agree with Blake that the prismatic bubbles
of truth which rise the most beautifully, and float on the air
the lightest, come from the consummation of the marriage of
these antipodes? *I am not sure.* The oldest part of my mental
belfry is always ringing with a tintinnabulation of silver bells,
and "I am not sure!" "I am not sure!" "I am not sure," is
what they say. But what I am going to confess to you now is
really very curious; but I get the same pleasure from yielding
up my egotism with people as I get from the malice with which
I play the zany! Everybody I meet seems to want to assert
their ego. "I! I! I!" they cry. No one seems to get the depraved
pleasure I get from turning my "I" into thin air and helping
my friend's "I" to swell and swell till it's a regular balloon.

My progress and track through life can be easily followed
by all the wonderful balloons that go sailing up to the sky;

balloons that formerly were little miserable soap-bubbles! No one—not even my intimate friends—can possibly realize the shifts, the subterfuges, the evasions, the devices, the serpentine coilings, the mole-like burrowings, to which I am always resorting, purely and solely to ward off some hurt to their pride, some blow to their life-illusion, some loss to their self-esteem —and this with practically every person I meet! It is interesting that I should have thus been inspired to discover a way of "acquiring merit" unknown to any Christian cult. Perhaps it is really some trick, derived—if there were by remote chance *anything* in my pretence that I am a re-incarnation of Taliessin —from the ancient Druids.

But it really is curious why I should have come to have such a deep superstitious mania for trying to make every living entity I encounter think more highly of itself. That is what I do! I flatter the life-illusion of birds, fishes, beasts—especially dogs and cats, to whom, without any "love" for animals, I quickly become a slave—and of every man, woman and child I meet. And I carry this mania into my very prayers, for I am always praying to *some* idol or angel or daimon, to the absurd and crazy length of praying five or six times a day for someone whose felicity I envy, and for someone else whose physical nature is antipathetic to me. I used to regularly pray for one of my worst enemies—no, not at all that he should see the error of ways!—simply and solely that he should be happy and prosperous.

Of course I am Pharisaic to boast of these matters to this tune; but I can't help that. If I am a Pharisee, I *am* a Pharisee! And even under the gaze of the Great Magician who cursed them I suppose I should continue boasting after their fashion. "I fast twice a day. I give alms of all that I possess . . ." etc., etc., etc. The truth is I have, I think, really a more religious than mystical nature; and though I get a humorous and even malicious delight when my favourite Kwang-Tze attacks Confucius and jeers at his "Benevolence and Righteousness" I am sure I would have made a receptive disciple to that fussy ritualist.

But I expect my unscrupulous mania for causing momen-

tary happiness—at whatever cost to the discipline of their
character!—to every entity within my reach, would have been
condemned by both Laotze and Confucius; and I am sure it
would have been denounced by Jesus. But in this matter I am
incorrigible, whether I got it from the Druids, or from African
negroes. With the exception of the Southern Americans who
try to justify the lynching of these negroes from whom I
derive so much of my spiritual culture, I always feel that
people are *as they are*, and were born *as they are* and that the
best I can do for them is to flatter their vanity and "jolly them
along"! Yes, I must make the utmost of my "Pharisaism";
for it is clear that that is what at bottom, if you can be a
superficial thing at "bottom," I am. What I really feel is a
sickening pity for every sentient thing, victimized, as we all
are, by the great sadist who created the world.

Certainly this fussy anxiety of mine about making human
beings, along with wasps and wood-lice and little fishes, as
happy as I can make them by flatteries and lies, whatever kind
of Druidic cult it may be, must certainly be an un-Christian
line to take, for I don't find many English, or Americans either,
who share this unscrupulous peculiarity.

Once or twice after contemplating my own malicious
attacks on my own worldly career I have wondered what it
would feel like for such a hybrid as I am between a saint and
something worse than a satyr to be conveyed to platforms in
Vienna or Paris or Madrid or Moscow or Prague or Berlin,
there to dance my world-zany's dance? The feeling of power
and glory I would have thus obtained would no doubt have
pleased me well. But I should have needed to be as Shakespearian as Charlie Chaplin, and much more saintly than Gandhi,
to carry out such a programme and keep my soul intact.

But short of that kind of arbitrary and wilful glory I worked
—under my friend Arnold—in exactly the way that suited me
best, and that was the best for the development of my peculiar
inspiration. Roman Catholics, Communists and Jews! How
deeply have all these appreciated me! Why should that be so,
do you suppose? I will tell you why! Because all these three are
in essence *intensely religious*, for even the doctrinal atheism and

official materialism of Communist theory have most strangely to do with the controlling religious nerve. All these three are "international" too, in the way a Welshman can understand that word. When however I hear certain unpoetic and un-romantic people use the word "international" it fills me with such weariness and with such a sense of all the life-sap being taken out of human history that I begin to think about the maddest undertakings, such as starting a movement for an autonomous Wales; but when I see a Catholic or a Communist defying some despotic state for the sake of Christ or the pro-letariat, my blood surges up in sympathy.

Yes, it was because such deep layers of sacred mythological passion were stirred up in me whenever I referred to the Jews or to Communism or the Roman Catholic Church, that these three supported me so fiercely against all my enemies during my twenty-five years of life in America. And it was just because my best audiences were proletarian that I was encouraged to despise more and more all the ordinary conventions of lectur-ing. To these people I tore my heart to pieces. For these people I gouged out my most sensitive nerves with my own finger-nails and wrote with them in blood upon the throbbing air.

My performances before my East-side audiences ceased to have any connection with ordinary lectures. With these subtly intellectual and extremely nervous Jews it was no longer necessary for me to restrain myself. And I gave up restraining myself. I let myself go to the extreme limit! I became a sort of lacerated and yet mystically-sensual Dionysus—a Dionysus of East Fourteenth Street. And not only of Fourteenth Street. For under Arnold's encouragement, and often guided by an enterprising personage called Mr. Gould, I was conducted to such remote little radical halls that it took hours of exhausting wayfaring to reach them.

But whenever I *did* reach them I poured out my whole soul to these responsive and sympathetic children of Israel. You can well understand, reader, what I felt when as a champion of Jews, Communists, Catholics and Negroes I used to hear of the activities of certain patriotic Americans who without daring to let you see their faces were wont to waylay and torture precisely such an Englishman as I was! I certainly do hold that the noblest death a self-respecting person could die would be to be killed trying to rescue a negro from these miscreants; and as I travelled in the South—though when the point came I expect I would have funked it—I used to tell myself stories of how when I finally reached the side of their victim and was lynched with him I would die giving this base rabble "a piece of my mind."

In all these lectures, that were so much more than lectures, I worked myself up to such a pitch that I *became* the figure I was analysing. Such was my young-girl-like receptivity that just as Wordsworth's young women give themselves up to the elements so I gave myself up to the spirit of my particular man of genius. And it was with almost an erotic emotion, as if I were indulging myself in some kind of perverted love affair, that I entered the nerves of Dickens or Paul Verlaine or Henry James or Dostoievsky or Keats or Blake! I well remember, in one East-side hall, while an acrobat friend of mine sold my books how I ceased to interpret my author, who was Gorki that day, by words at all, but interpreted him, like Thaumast in Rabelais by physical movements. You see my whole idea of *criticism* was different from the academic idea. What I aimed at was a sort of transmigration of my soul, till, like a demon possessing a person, I serpentined myself into the skeleton of my author, and expounded his most eccentric reactions to life from the actual nerve-centres where these reactions originated.

There is no use trying to conceal the fact that Nature from the start had made me an actor. My brother Littleton could bear me out in this. Oh, how he has suffered from my acting! In my extreme infancy at Shirley I acted the part of my father in the pulpit, although I cannot remember ever seeing him in that Shirley pulpit. And on these occasions Littleton had to represent not only the whole of the congregation, but the clerk repeating the responses. In those happy years at Dorchester before I went to school I acted two parts, that of the general of the "Volentiā Army" and that of the scholar magician—a sort of Michael Scott—who invented a mythology and a language which were to be forced upon the unfortunate "Escrawaldons." At Wildman's I acted—to escape that fiendish bully in the dormitory below—the easiest of all rôles for me, that of a madman. At Corpus I acted the part of a guileless Wilhelm Meister, a Boswellian disciple, insatiable of great sages and their recondite idealisms; and it was an intrinsic part of this acting to make old Koelle, and the terrifyingly learned G. P. Gooch, into what the Buddhists call my "Gurus." They were quaint enough "Gurus," in all conscience, this pair; but Harry Lyon was too "artistic," besides I knew him too well, to serve in that rôle, and my strongest imagination could not see Mr. Fanshawe or Dr. Perowne or even the ironic Mr. Pollock in the light of a "Guru."

I had found it a little difficult to hit upon any appropriate mask wherein to trick out my protean life-illusion while I lived at Burpham. I was, was in every sense of that word, too *exposed* there. Between the Knoll and the Gables, between the inn and the saw-pit, between the school and the Duke of Norfolk's fortress-bank, I found it difficult to be anything but the rather absurd, rather suspicious, extremely good-natured *Mr. Powys*. Probably the wisest thing I did during that long decade of my life was to buy for my son, at a shop in Arundel, the human bear called "William," who subsequently met with such extraordinary favour in my household that he was supplied with a special "governante," in the person of a certain "Miss Welsh," whose more limited intellect, but better-balanced character, he was wont to startle by his daring speculations.

But for myself it was not clear to me in those days in what direction my restless life-illusion *could* enlarge and expand. My enemies will probably lean to the view that I was getting what I deserved; in other words that I was a paranoiac fox, fairly run to earth. My son preferred watching moles and mice on our debatable bank to going for exhausting walks over the downs. Thora, in her old age, I had myself destroyed with chloroform. My statue of the Venus of Milo was broken and lost. Methuen and Co. found my *Life of Keats* too eccentric. I myself found my *Death of God* too conventional. I remember very well how as I used to survey these tremendous sheep-washings, where the bearded Mr. Budd, the brown-eyed Mr. Goodyear, the courtly Mr. West were all so busy helping Mr. Collyer's or Graburn's shepherds, while George Roadnight would be taking photographs to be turned into picture-post-cards, I would feel as though I were neither fish, nor flesh, nor fowl. I would grow nervous and jumpy. I would feel as if I were some fantastical idol, dug up in that old fort. I would feel as if everybody present at that sheep-washing when I appeared on the scene must be saying to themselves: "God! I'd like to give that crazy ninny a good healthy ducking, along with these 'ere ewes!"

And even in my Oxford extension tours I had been forced "to mind my P's and Q's," forced to remember that many of my audience wrote essays for me and received university certificates. Why, on one occasion the Oxford authorities actually decided that I must never lecture on any historical subject again, because the examiner of my students reported that the only notion these poor people had of the Roman emperors was the "personal equation"—I had never heard that expression before and it greatly alarmed me, as though inadvertently I had been guilty of something that was at once indecent and mathematical—derived from the scandalous gossip of the mischievous Suetonius.

Nothing could have been a better index of my inherent "charlatanism" than this perverse substitution of the most morbid details about the Cæsars for an adequate study of the great historians. But I was in America now, America the ideal country for mystagogues, demagogues, thaumaturgic preachers, theosophic illuminants, occultists, conjurers, table-turners, mediums, Chatauqua-culturists, Utopians, Shakers, Mormons, Second Adventists, East Indian Yogists, Red Indian "Controls," worshippers of Quetzacoatle, worshippers of Mumbo Jumbo, new-thoughtists, psychists, psycho-analysts, psychiatrists, psycho-careerists, not to speak of teleportists, telepathists and televisionists. And not only was I in the land where only the maddest of egoists scrambled to shore after the submerging of the Lost Atlantis, but as I quickly discovered, I was in the land—just as Sousa's music had predicted to me in that Liverpool café—of the most cynical and sardonic irresponsibility that the human race has ever evoked! In other words I was in a land exactly suited to my medicine-man character. As my dear Louis laments, in a distressed and almost querulous tone, I "loved it."

And the beauty of the paradox—which alone is sufficient proof of what terrific misunderstandings go about the world and become the historic truth of a deluded posterity—is that precisely what I "loved" in America was *the escape from humbug*. "This Archangel"—as others ere now have done—got hold of the stick by the wrong end.

Quixote puppet as I am, prophetic scarecrow as I am, draggle-tailed hermit-whore as I am, it had seemed to me that a certain type of mock-virile, mock-downright, mock-simple, mock-honest, mock-humorous, mock-modest psychological element in England was far more dangerous to what Aristotle or someone calls the "Good Life" than the most double-dyed hypocrisy that there has ever been in the world. This particular attitude seemed all the worse because with "honest, honest" Iago, it concealed its hostility to the "Good Life" under the guise of a bluff "cheerio, carry-on" manner.

And what did my charlatanism, and the charlatanism of my friend Arnold, really amount to, as he composed, and I accomplished, all these "mean jumps"? Bah! it didn't go more than skin-deep; whereas my academic enemies—on both sides of the Atlantic—are not honest enough *to be* charlatans; for their pretentiousness is so propped-up and buttressed-up by layers of conventionality, by fold upon fold and crease upon crease of false values, that nothing could induce it to make a fool of itself *lest it should lose all!* That is where the essential honesty of my charlatanism and Arnold's lay. *We* could make fools of ourselves to the uttermost, we could be zanys and mountebanks, to the extreme limit, and yet keep our essential integrity; whereas one single lapse from their worldly caution, in these sly magnates, one little stumble in the direction of looking an ass, and there is a ghastly possibility of a complete unmasking.

And the point is that the bravado and boasting and business-slickness of Americans does not invade their souls to the extent that conventional traditions and all their worldly pompous humbug invade the souls of certain types of Englishmen. Honest Englishmen have the advantage over honest Americans by reason of their richer sensuous nature; but of the two types of humbug the American type is less hurtful because it is more superficial. And what a comfort it was to me, what a breath of fresh air, to escape the complicated system of English snobbishness! As a matter of fact in a *social* sense—which is of course the only important one—America is a real and most authentic democracy. Socially it is hardly less democratic than Soviet Russia; and as the Russians have clearly seen, for they "love it" in just the way I do, the mass of Americans, whatever bourgeois ideas they may have, work with their hands, for pay, for love, for necessity, just as if they were proletarians.

We English judge Americans by the "travelling rich" who are the repulsive fungoid excrescences, parallel with our own worst vulgarities, of their free, unexclusive, chaotic democracy.

It is quaint that I can remember absolutely nothing of my first impression of the New York skyscrapers! Perhaps this was because I was so full of the idea that I had come to America, like some wand-bearing Argiephontes, with a message from the gods, that I was too absentminded to see them! Like that vision of Charles Lamb's of the Lake Country *without its mountains*, I looked at New York City, and the skyscrapers were gone.

I was met, however, by Mr. Miles, the President of the Philadelphia Lecture Society, and he was incredibly kind to me. Conducted by him to Philadelphia I was handed over to the directorship of Mr. Charles Atkins, now the head of the enormous Brooklyn Institute, who was not less friendly, and who remains a person for whom I have retained, for nearly thirty years, quite an especial respect and affection. Mr. Charles Atkins, in spite of his responsible position, is a man who long ago took Dr. Johnson's advice and "cleared *his mind* of cant." Austere and competent steward as he is of this terrific institution there is a look in his eye, and in these matters I have the infallible penetration of an psychological adept, that reveals a man who does not deceive himself.

I know it must have been the winter—though of what year I have no idea—when I arrived in New York along with Arnold Shaw on the *Ivernia*, for Mr. Miles met me at the docks with a hired sledge with tinkling bells and took me straight off —he was a spirited little old man who was always smoking enormous cigars—for a ride through Central Park.

My first American lecture was, I think, addressed to the Ladies' Club of Madison, New Jersey, my second, I know, was delivered before that great, unique, proletarian audience, by far the most exciting audience in America, which comes together on so many nights in the week in the huge Rotunda of *Cooper Union*. On this Cooper Union platform, the site of my second lecture in this country, I think I indicated pretty clearly that I was no mere Pierrot of Culture, but had in me "something dangerous." My subject was "The Republic of the Future" and I well remember that I predicted the coming into being of a state of things not all unlike what has happened in Russia.

Before very long I found that I could summon up in my lectures something that resembled that Druidic *hypnotism of speech* which in my *Glastonbury Romance* I have attributed to Mr. Geard. And what, when you really come down to it, *was* the nature of this magic message, from the gods of the old world to the market-places of the new, that had exulted within me as I played "Twirly-whirly-twill" and "hunt the slipper" with my companions on the *Ivernia?* Something it was, from those far-off "sacred hills," from Glastonbury Tor, from Cadbury Camp, from Shaston, from that peak of Snowden, where, quarrelling with Littleton and Theodore, I had written *Love Never Dies*, that I found I could call upon, so as to make the proletarian sages of Cooper Union "sit up." I remember so well how my conclusion that the republic of the future would be state socialism was criticized by the Anarchists present. As I had just sworn on landing that I was neither an Anarchist nor Polygamist I was surprised by the eloquence with which I was now instructed in Anarchist doctrines.

When thinking my thoughts, while the man from New Orleans told me about cats being afraid of dogs, I had not included these daring and congenial notions in what I had expected of America. The bold thoughts of my audience at Cooper Union must have found kindred soil in my Celtic nature for I remember a little later in Chicago refusing at the last moment to address an audience whose authorities had cancelled a lecture by some famous anarchist.

But in spite of my temperamental sympathy with anarchists I stuck steadily to what was really more like Bolshevism than anything else in my calmer moments. Some kind of state socialism was the stain or dye, if I may say so, of the perpetually unrolling scroll that came out of my mouth! Such a scroll—as you see them, in old mediæval illuminations, issuing from the mouth of an angel or demon—was in my case, as I howled and whimpered and chanted and burbled and danced like a dervish, inscribed with the insignia and heraldry of State Socialism.

What I was always indicating was the brutality, the vulgarity even, of the sort of optimism that has never recognized the monstrous grotesqueries and appalling cruelties of life. It was not that I ever denied that we all had, somehow or other, to forget these unspeakable things, to forget the pain that conscious sentiencies were enduring every second by reason of the basic world-arrangements of the First Cause, but the hieroglyphs inscribed on the mediæval scroll that unrolled itself from my demonic mouth pleaded and jeered and wept and shrieked against the sort of bastard comfort which so many eloquent but unimaginative preachers in America were always advocating.

What happiness from life we can attain, what revelations about life we can reach, what beauty in life we can respond to, must always have as their background—so, in my desperation I argued—an awareness of the terrible necessity of forgetting the unthinkable things which the cruelty of the First Cause has prepared both for those who accept Him and those who reject Him. What I endeavoured to indicate was that though we all had to forget so much, there was no reason why we should pretend there was nothing to forget, or nothing beyond what a sturdy nature was able to face.

It was, I think, this realization of the appalling cruelty of life and the unspeakable depths of wickedness in human beings, that made my lectures more acceptable to Catholics and Communists and Jews than to any others. The mediæval universe, as we know from Dante, had as its very foundation those eternal sufferings for which *Divino Amore* has created a cosmic "locale" from the beginning, and in the Catholic liturgy we pray—just as Unamuno and my friend J. W. Williams were always praying—"O deliver us from Eternal Death! O deliver us from Eternal Death!"

There was always a sort of under-tide in my lectures indicating that however much moralists tried to put the onus of the unspeakable abominations in the world, and of all the sufferings of animals and children in the world, upon our power of free will, it still remains, as St. Paul says, that "the whole creation groaneth and travaileth in pain together"; and I must have felt as I tried to make this clear that the terrible *lacrimae rerum* in the System of Things was *allowed for* more thoroughly in the Catholic temper than in the more boisterous "aura" of Protestant ministers or ethical preachers. It was allowed for—so it seemed to me—at every point in the Catholic cult, not only in the idea of the Inferno, but in the Wounds of Christ, in the Sword that pierces His Mother's heart, and in all the wild desperate ritual-cries that are so full of that planetary "groaning and travailing." Then again the mere Cult of the Mother of God seems to hint at a certain element of irrational pity behind the universe, to which those of us who suffer from its judicial cruelty can turn for relief.

It was natural enough, coming as I did from such places in the old world that I should find it inevitable to lay stress on the magical element in life. My idea of the relief and the release to be got from religion has always been quite as magical as it has been poetical, and as far as my secret personal life was concerned the particular kind of self-control I aimed at, and the particular kind of mental concentration I aimed at, had more of the stain and tincture of mediæval sanctity, or, if you like, of Tibetan sanctity, than of any natural heathen goodness.

And meanwhile my whole instinctive reaction was always in favour of believing—if I had to believe—the impossible in preference to the improbable. I think it was Oscar Wilde who said something about this; but anyway Tertullian's cry, "I believe *because* it's impossible," has always aroused a kind of savage sympathy in me.

"And why," I asked myself, "should I not be what I was born to be in my deep heart?"

Was it not the whole secret of personal life to find out what your innate nervous and mental fatality was, and then to drag it into your sorcerer's cell and work magic on it, and make of it your peculiar apparatus for testing your "truth" among all the "truths" of which the universe is crowded? Born as I was to be a pluralist, a totemist, a fetishist, a mythologist, a polytheist, and even a "chaoticist," with a conscience about which there was always something fussy, fanatic, casuistic, Pharisaic, I am sure if I did ever acquire any scraps of mediæval or Taoistic wisdom or advanced any distance along what they call in Tibet "the short path" it must have come about by reason of the power and self-control I attained by forcing myself every day to go through an unbelievable number of exhausting ritualistic performances! I had my own secret road to Camelot; but I always had a sneaking fondness for the common highway thither, full of a scaramouch company of judicial astrologers, Tarot-card diviners, Cabbalists and Thaumaturgists, together with a procession of catch-penny sorcerers and all the helter-skelter tag-rag of pitiful invokers of idols! Indeed, though I prefer to protect my hiding-place from such scatterbrains, and have a mania of my own *against knowing the future*, I can see no reason why we should not at least investigate the dangers with which our own character threatens us by the use of any one of those occult divinations, which Her Trippa, with a tamarisk-branch in his hand, recommends so eloquently; such as Geomancy, Chiromancy and Ceromancy, not to speak of Tephromancy, Sicomancy and Icthiomancy.

Indeed I soon began to perceive, as I went about America, even without the aid of Chiromancy or Sicomancy, what tendencies in my nature were likely to be dominant, when once I was released from the traditions and conventions of my native land! I perceived from the alms that I felt compelled to distribute to beggars, just as at school I was compelled to give Littleton the whole of our hamper and hand over my week's allowance to the astonished young woman at Longburton, as well as from the way I would force myself to pick up leaves and sprays of vegetation out of the city gutters or from under people's feet on the hot pavements, that I had at least a few of the hallmarks of a candidate for sanctity.

But I had yet another and a far more subtle way of "acquiring merit" and that was the manner in which I refrained from any attempt to change the characters of the new friends I made or to bully them into the values that I held. Some deep instinct put it into my head to believe that all sentient living things can have a right to their own personal identity and their own personal pleasures. I had come to recognize that in conversation with people it is silly to try to force them to embrace *your* values, *your* disgust, *your* excitements, and that it is a *splendide mendax*, a meritorious treachery, to flatter them into self-complacency and well-being. I felt with all my imagination, as I have already hinted, that every organism in the world ought to be fed, comforted and "jollied along," and that as long as you could give their poor forlorn nerves a few thrills of ecstasy in this bitter and unfeeling world, any number of "lies" were lawful.

Thus, down at the very bottom of my nature, I had pity for every sentient organism, and not even content with this I was always endowing *inanimate things* with feeling too, and putting myself to the most irksome detours and debouchings in order to increase the well-being of these children of Limbo. What in fact had begun to get itself lodged in my mind was the idea that I ought to feel as if no living being, except myself, could help itself from acting and feeling exactly as it *did* act and feel, and that therefore to be angry with it for its ways and peculiarities was unthinkable.

Most tough rogues and shrewd rascals, and even many healthy-minded "honest cods" regarded such feelings of mine as the worst kind of priggishness. But it was not priggishness. I was so hustled and rattled and distracted by my own manias that these mediæval and mystical intimations came much more nearly to resemble insanity than any airs of unctuous self-righteousness. Even when I was aware at the bottom of my heart of a deep, cold, malicious condemnation of the ways of my acquaintances I always concealed this feeling, and never displayed anything but an eager, vibrant, and almost gushing appreciation of their good qualities.

But it was not only in such "saintly," or, if you *must* have it so, such priggish directions—though I assure you that no one who had undergone what I had at school could possibly be priggish—that my nature began putting forth curious and startling shoots.

In regard to my vicious under-life, America gave me as lively an encouragement with her burlesque shows as Paris had done with her wicked books. If some pleasure-hating, Mephistophelean ecclesiastic, searching about for a weapon with which to persecute that sweet, natural, lovable sensuality of normal clippings and claspings under haystacks and hedges and "where not, why not," advocated so eloquently in the works of Llewelyn Powys, I greatly fear he could derive only too plausible arguments from this confession of Brother John. Too many of the erotic emotions that have overwhelmed and transported me, with that sort of obsession that renders *nothing else in the world important*, are of so abnormal a character that Llewelyn would find it hard to be indulgent to them.

Yes, my ecclesiastical Torquemada would, I fear, be encouraged by my revelations, to argue that such picturesque and beautiful light-o'-loves imply a sweet-natured and healthy normality that is as rare as genius itself. Life being as perverse as it is, the great god Eros, when reflected in the mirrors of our monstrous aberrations, no longer retains that darling appearance whose "sweet usage" little Psyche so grievously lamented, but assumes a Baal-like, Dagon-like, or Baphomet-like aspect. Once give *carte blanche* to the "brutish sting" in you and you may find yourself, before you're done, confronted with temptations that would sicken Tiberius. Once heave up the sluice-gates of lust to the limit, such an ecclesiastic might argue, and you will find that Ivan Karamazov knows more about this job than any poet save Cousin Swift. To enjoy as much sensuality as we can without causing grief to anyone is certainly the safest rule, but where you least expect it Demogorgon will leap up and you'll find yourself projecting thought-eidola such as you hesitate to confess to a living soul. The truth is, to make sure that the seed of our race doesn't dry up, the First Cause has taken measures far more dangerous than was necessary.

Very soon after I reached America and had found my headquarters in Philadelphia I had to make long journeys about the country. On these travels I soon began hunting desperately for means of satisfying my Voyeur's vice. I well remember lecturing at New Haven where Yale University is; not however under the auspices of that university. I have never been invited by the real authorities of any of the big American universities to speak under their auspices, except the University of California; and even there the personage who introduced me was in such a sour temper that he apologized to my audience for not being able to say anything reliable about me because my name was not in the British *Who's Who*.

But the contempt with which I have been treated—I who have been such an unwearied peripatetic philosopher to the American people for so long—by the big fashionable universities has been more than made up for by the way I have been welcomed by the small colleges and the remoter state colleges. The pathetic thing is that these excellent little places never realized what a complete free-lance I was! They supposed they were hiring "a typical Englishman from Oxford." They always were deceived in the gown I used to wear and took it for an Oxford gown; and it tickled my fancy and made me think how it would have tickled old Fanshawe's fancy when I was asked whether Cambridge "was not a private school for Oxford."

But it would be absurd in me to let my vanity grow really touchy when I think how all my passionate discourses on

Homer and Dante and Goethe and Dostoievsky went for nothing at Harvard and Yale. They went for almost nothing at Oxford and Cambridge. The real truth is that to have had any dealings with any of these exclusive places would have terrified me and awed me to a point of misery. I was at ease and happy with my girl schools and normal schools and far-away state colleges. I was not at all alarmed by women's clubs. I was thrilled by lecturing to nuns and novices. Most of all I was entirely and freely myself in synagogues. The sight of those great words about "the unity of God" always excited me and called up the romance and the grandeur of the long history of Israel to my imagination. No matter if I were myself a fairy-tale Welshman. I liked to make my bow, now and again, to the God of Abraham, Isaac and Jacob.

It was at New Haven, as I hunted about for fuel for my smouldering flame, that I remember once finding some wretched little provocative periodical that gave a miserable and forlorn caress to my woebegone craving. At that time I did not know a single American woman to speak to; though it would have made little difference *if I had* unless she had been a very queer sort of woman, for the last thing I wanted was a solid, living-and-loving jealous bedfellow. What I wanted were naughty puppets, incarnations of response to lust and *nothing else*; delicate, heartless, subhuman beings, such as those maddeningly-teasing Undines and Salamanders, created out of the elements by the old philosophers. Alack the day! I dare say many of these old philosophers were, in their time as frightened of the professors of Salamanca and Padua as I was by the professors of Harvard and Yale. But as a matter of fact not a living American woman did I know till after I had tapped many other desperate resources of the hunted and demon-ridden human soul!

One great discovery of mine was nothing less than those sordid-looking penny-in-the-slot machines that used to stand in rows, if you knew where to find them, in the New York of thirty years ago. They used to stand on either side of certain narrow hall-ways; hall-ways that always had a ghastly, sepulchral, and quite special kind of daylight in them, as if the cold codfish-eye of all the *two o'clocks* that have ever taken the heart out of a living day had been recaptured and imprisoned there. By turning the handles of these desolate machines and peering through a little spy-hole—when I had disposed of a nickle—I was privileged to play Peeping-Tom while certain extremely unsylph-like ladies, of plump and matronly aspect, gravely, and with no sign of coyness, removed their outer garments. Here were peep-holes indeed, just as if they had been invented for the special benefit of a rusty-minded cerebralist in a foreign land!

But, alas, my taste in these matters had been so refined upon by all those slender figures in pantomime costume that I used to enjoy in the pages of *Ally Sloper*, that I cannot recall that these machine-manikinesses of New York ever gave me *one single second* of real satisfaction. The *idea* of them, however—and I remained a true Platonist, even in the matter of penny-in-slot machines—kept my hopes on the *qui vive*, I "never *was*, but always *to be* blest."

I had heard wild tales on the *Ivernia* of exciting scenes to be witnessed in the Bowery; and thus it was not long, as I passed through New York on various "mean jumps" from Philadelphia, before I found my way—always on foot, like my father at Shirley, but not, like him, looking for hedge-sparrow's eggs—into this dare-devil quarter. Here indeed were a great many of these Caves of Venus-Mechanistica; and I shudder still to recall—for what we poor mortals are ready to go through when the Devil drives is past belief—the peculiar *smell*, quite literally "a savour of poisonous brass and metal sick" which assailed my nostrils in these places.

It certainly must be allowed that though America did eventually satisfy my ambiguous cravings more completely than they have been satisfied anywhere else, save by the reading of those wicked French books, she also, if you can call such a continent a "she," shocked and outraged the finicking refinement of my vice almost as grossly as Paris had done.

Alas! when my brother keeps on linking together this cult of the terrible goddess with cowslips and cornfields I laugh the devil's own laugh, like a hideous hobgoblin, thinking of the sort of things to which, so far removed from cowslips and cuckoo-flowers, *my* "primrose-path" led. Lucky, yea! thrice lucky, are those whose æsthetic taste, whether cultivated by Pater or by Proust, can look with complacence on the predicaments into which their lechery leads them!

Many people will think that it shows a monstrous lack of a sense of proportion in me to write of picture-machines in the Bowery as an important aspect of my life in America. But what on earth would be the use of my writing my life at all if I did not try to get to the heart of the matter? But there *were* other things that interested me beside this pathetic quest. I well recall, for instance, a most exciting party, of all the American poets that could be collected at a moment's notice, to meet this "Oxford lecturer," this lecturer who had never lectured to an undergraduate in his life except when he was drunk, a party at which I clung desperately to Edwin Arlington Robinson, whose personality has always attracted me as much as his singular genius. He took me later to his room up-town, and I remember what a gleam of real Apollonian radiance illuminated that simple retreat, when, after his fashion, he spoke with a proud and noble reticence of his poetic purposes. I pleased him by my obviously honest pleasure in those poems about odd, quaint, derelict men meeting in the basement of the Brevoort Hotel; and I delighted him by my enjoyment of the phrase: "Come out, you laelaps and inhale the night; and so he went away with Clavering!" I told him about seeing a picture of a laelaps—which is in Homer a storm-wave but in later ages a monster like the one they have found recently on the French coast—in a book shown us as children by Mr. Knipe, my father's rector, and the poet was pleased by my unsophisticated enthusiasm. I expect he thought to himself: "Can all Oxford lecturers be as artless as this excellent young man?"

The worst of all these *Musées*—and some of them really were "Hell Museums" in the first years of this century—was one I got into somehow in a low-down district in Chicago. Here the poet might indeed have cried to me,

"Come out, you laelaps, and inhale the night!"

Some kind of a *danse d'enfer* was announced to be going to take place later on, and you must remember, reader, that what was forever alluring me and leading me into these places, places that in themselves always filled me with pure fright and cold repulsion, was the Platonic idea of slender sylphid forms, forms with little oval heads, and hips like those of delicate boys, and with ankles as fragile as wild anemones, such as I used to pore over in prolonged ecstasy—and I can recall the feel of those window-seats now—in the old school library at Sherborne.

I waited and waited in this indescribable place, and the fact that it was below the level of the road brought all the Balzacian tales of Chicago's underworld into my childish mind. What I really was was a well-meaning bookworm with an indescribable craving to stare for hours, without let or hindrance, at the limbs of boyish girls who would smile back at me. This laudable and legitimate longing had so far been denied me, whether by destiny or chance or the wisdom of my guardian angel; but as on this occasion, every time I saw an announcement of any performance of this sort, all the Houris of Mohammed's paradise floated before me! On this occasion I was completely alone in this place save for a man in a cage and a monkey at liberty. The man returned me no answer when I timidly asked him about the performance; and, as time went on I came to the conclusion—not very willingly, for I had murmured at intervals to him some of my most propitiatory remarks—that he was made of wax. The monkey, however, was made as I was made, and as I watched him an obscure unease began to grow upon me, the elements of which, at this distance of time, I cannot distinctly summon back.

Did there arise some really rather ghastly and sub-human reciprocity between the agitated nerves of a sex-starved he-ape and of an abnormally excited lecturer, both of them waiting, waiting, waiting, till this procession of Houris that we saw advertised before us should actually enter? But in vain did that monkey and I, like the disguised knight in *The Talisman* and the hermit of Engeddi, wait for the appearance of the

impossible. In *The Talisman* the girls did at least *appear*, and
they even sprinkled roses, though it was a cave in the midst
of the desert; but in this Chicago basement no girls appeared,
and the waxwork man, and the monkey and the "Oxford
lecturer" grew less and less satisfied with one another's looks.
But still we waited on, we three entities, two existent and one
subsistent, waited, as all the world waits, for some mirage
of its heart's desire, and all the while *my* heart kept pounding
its devil's tattoo, not only from erotic anticipation, but from
nervous alarm, for I had been told in Philadelphia that two
mysterious Demiurges, called respectively "Bath-House John"
and "Hinky-Dink" had power, like the dread Baphomet in
Cabalistical Magic, to bind and unbind all who descended
below the level of the lake in that city to which Walt Whitman
raised "the perpendicular hand" and saluted as "Chicago, the
great city"!

But I had to return to Philadelphia. And there—even in
Philadelphia itself—it came to pass that I found something
that really did—at least in idea—cause my satyr's heart to leap
up. As with the quest after Lilith, the demon-angel, whom you
hunt for in far-off countries, while all the while she is—to
quote Walt Whitman again—"installed amid the kitchen
ware," it was in the Quaker City that I found my miraculous
discovery. I found a place in fact where there was a penny-in-
the-slot machine containing real, not merely pictured, ladies!
I only visited this machine once; so it is clear that the aura of
the spot could not have been very seductive; but I thought of
it long afterwards when I was in England, and—such is my
extraordinary disposition—this *and this alone*, this penny-in-
the-slot with the human ladies, decided me to resume my
lecture-work in America, at a moment when, for the sake of
my ulcers, which were devilishly bad just then, Llewelyn was
trying to make me give up lecturing altogether!

My slot-machine ladies who, I presume, could see nothing
of their admirer except a pair of frantic eyes, responded, it
must be confessed, very casually and indifferently to the tinkle
of my silver pieces falling at their feet. They were two middle-
aged women, seated in a not uncomfortable little tent, and in

II

spite of that furious pair of scoriac eyes that saw "Helen's beauty in a brow of Egypt" they continued calmly conversing with each other about their children and what they would cook for supper, and what was the price of certain hats they had seen for sale on Market Street. Of the eyes that were straining at them through those brazen apertures they thought no more than they thought about the eyes of their Creator.

I was quite a long time in America before I discovered this country's grand vent and outlet for the repressions of a puritanical public opinion. I refer to the burlesque shows. For the benefit of such of my fellow-countrymen as are unacquainted with this stage performance I must tell you that the burlesque show—at least this was the case thirty years ago—was attended almost entirely by men. They were extraordinary performances—at least so it seemed to me—and it was almost unbelievable to me that such heavenly sights could be permitted to be seen at all in a world like ours, "rigged in the eclipse and built with curses dark." There was very little plot in the burlesque show in my day and what plot there was was concerned with the knock-about adventures of a couple of clowns, one generally masquerading as a Jew and the other as an Irishman. Very often, no doubt, they *were* a Jew and an Irishman; but whatever they were, the brutality of their words and of their jests and gestures was simply astounding to me. Compared with these burlesque jokers, Charlie Chaplin was as refined as Charles Dickens; and as for my old friend Dan Leno, he was like a fool from Shakespeare!

I remember what struck me as especially shocking was the sardonic and savage derision of tramps and hobos. I suppose the bulk of these audiences were travelling salesmen, what in England we call "commercial travellers." Anyway most of them, I take it, belonged to what Harry Lyon used to call the "lower middle class"; and I suppose it did not jar on their nerves, as I am sure it would have jarred on the nerves of almost any aristocracy, to see tramps and beggars and cripples and imbeciles—all the derelicts, in fact, in the great struggle "to make good"—held up to ferocious mockery. But to my mind—with sympathies fed by Sterne and Lamb and Scott and Dickens in whose works these innocents are treated as almost sacrosanct—to behold rags and crutches and the gibberings of idiocy *made sport of* was extremely startling. I suddenly seemed to envisage millions and millions of terrifyingly competent, smartly dressed young men, indulging in paroxysms of laughter, while they pointed their well-manicured index-fingers in vibrant derision, both at myself and at all those great and imaginative intellects I had loved best in life, such as Mr. de —— and "the Catholic"—yes, and Dostoievsky himself. What I beheld in these places was, in fact, all the basic instincts of the bourgeois nature allowed, for once in the history of the human race, unfettered expression. In the old civilizations it has been either the aristocracy, brought up upon Greek and Latin, where beggars are often of course *gods in disguise* and where the step from your king to your tramp is very small, or it is the mob, whose blood-lust must have bull-baiting, cock-fighting, and gladiatorial butchery, who have given the dominant tone to public entertainments. But, seated in these places, I was permitted to perceive what kind of amusement best tickled the senses of Harry Lyon's "Lower Middle Class."

And I discovered that apart from the burlesque portion of it and the making sport of tramps, this bourgeois entertainment pleased me uncommonly well! Did it carry back my æsthetic taste to a certain ancestor of mine who was a tanner? I certainly have never derived from any theatrical entertainment the intoxicating pleasure I got from these shows. I detest the movies. I care very little for plays. Indeed, except for English pantomimes and a certain queer Russian-Jewish play called *The Dybbuk*, I have never received one single thrill, either in mind or soul or senses, from anything on the stage except these queer entertainments. I don't go so far as to say that I despise *all* acted plays, or that my loathing of the movies is without a *single* exception, for I sometimes have felt myself, when I was lecturing, to be acting like Sir Henry Irving, and I have an almost religious idolatry for Charlie Chaplin, but, speaking roughly, it is certainly true that the American burlesque represents the only art of the stage, if it *be* an art, from which I have got thrilling delight.

But if I am justified in regarding these entertainments as providing something that satisfied all those ribald, Rabelaisian humours, gross and fantastical and brutal, such as the refinement of their women-folk was wont to suppress in American men, you would suppose I must have resembled them! Was it, in fact, the tanner coming out? By that good man's memory I am sorely tempted to swear black and blue to you, reader, that I enjoyed these comedians intensely. For the truth is I am shrewd enough to know intellectually, and with that "artistic taste" which Harry Lyon bludgeoned into me, that these comic portions of American burlesque *are* a humorous art of exceptionally high order. There are aspects of them that rival Joyce's *Ulysses*. There is a lot in them that resembles the "Satyricon" of Petronius. I can very well imagine the morbidly fastidious Nietzsche *forcing himself* to like this sort of farce, and calling it "brave Aristophanic truth."

But alas! what I am occupied with here is a picture of myself as I really do feel myself to be, not as it would be so wonderful if I were. And the lamentable truth is that I did not enjoy this Aristophanic comedy at all! I suffered from it. I tried not to see it. Had I dared I would have shut my eyes while it went on! Unfortunately I remembered too well that pair of avenging acrobats in the Midlands; and besides, *sometimes*, if I kept a sharp look-out, I could see some ravishing form in the wings. I certainly shut my eyes, and my ears, too, *mentally*; and just waited, like a sulky dog in church, till this Aristophanic shower of inspired patter, if that is what it was, was over. But some things I couldn't help seeing. For instance it was characteristic of a certain basic brutality in this humour —like the brutality of Panurge to Ding-Dong—that when some smart young springald wished to show his contempt for a cripple or a tramp or an idiot, what he did was to press his hand palm outwards against the wastrel's naked face, forcing it against his nose, eyes, mouth, lips, chin, with a certain *bed-rock indecency of outrage* to all that is most sacred and touchy in a human person which I did eventually come as a psychologist to recognize as one of the least pleasant aspects of American humour. Humour of this kind—but of course, like other national traits, American humour has many different facets—is in reality the first phase of the lynching process. When you have stimulated your aversion to a person who dresses like a scarecrow, and is in all probability a "degenerate," by pressing your fingers against his mouth and lips and cheeks and forehead and nose and eyes, the natural sequence of your line of approach, if you are a clean, bright, upstanding lad, with the intelligence of a "high-pressure salesman," will be to "treat him rough"; in other words to put a rope round his neck.

No, although I was not unaware of the "Aristophanic" power, gross though it might be, of the clowning in these burlesques, it was not that which so enthralled me. Once having accepted my peculiar life-long vice, once having allowed for the indestructible nympholeptism of my nature, it will surely not be surprising to you, reader, that, save when these feminine choruses were entirely composed of persons of my own age, my head used to be completely turned by what I saw. But oh, how brief, how cruelly brief, seemed to me those heavenly interludes! And often they danced so thick and fast that I was unable to take my delight in any single one of them. Once, however, I recollect observing one girl, in some interlude when their rapid movement had a breathing-space, quietly take a comb from her hair and proceed to comb her tresses as nonchalantly as if she had been alone before a mirror! It was this kind of little natural gesture that, in moments of memory, would always return to melt my bones. I would say to myself, at such times:

"How *can* this be sinister and dark and wicked, when the thrill I get is so full of an enchanting, irresistible sweetness?"

For in connection with these burlesque shows I have now to confess a very peculiar phenomenon. For the first time in my life this craving of mine for contemplating the limbs of women began to appear to my conscience as wicked. How this came about, or why it came about, I cannot tell. Perhaps it was the presence of these almost entirely masculine audiences that affected me so. Or was it that my growing tendency to the *ascetic*, my growing tendency to try to mould my life—you must not laugh, at me—upon the lives of the mediæval saints, made *all* sensual pleasure seem an evil thing?

But perhaps you, reader, are a person of intellectual interests and you are prepared to say that you don't give a damn what I felt under these conditions. You are impatiently waiting for me to tell you what my attitude was to the philosophical movements of the beginning of this century, such as Pragmatism, Neo-Realism, Determinism, Vitalism. Or you are wondering how I was reacting to the socialistic propaganda that was always crossing my path. Well, the truth is I *was* reading at this time many philosophical books that arrested me profoundly but only a few of these were recent ones. Hegel, though I found him very difficult and obscure, always fascinated me. I can recall at this very epoch—in a holiday at Burpham, for in those days I used to return to England twice a year—reading Wallace's translation of *The Logic* of Hegel in what was called "War Field," the great meadow so often waving with Mr. Collyer's wheat and sprinkled not only with scarlet poppies, but with rose-coloured fumitory, tiny wild pansies and the curious parasite called broom-rape, and I can recall the intoxicating and in some queer way almost voluptuous feeling, deep and obscure and mystical that seized on me on that particular occasion. I had a mania—and I have it still—for every sort of metaphysical system. My Protean nature, so singularly fluid, seemed able to wind itself, like a vaporous serpent, through the intricacies of any philosophy that was bold enough to recreate the malleable and receptive world for me. I had what was undoubtedly a strong erotic desire to embrace the magical loveliness of the world, just as if that vast mysterious Presence were a feminine being. I will not boast that I fully comprehended what I read; but I comprehended a good deal, as is proved—or seemed to *me* to be proved—by my power of embodying and contrasting these great systems as if they were contending persons in a high tragic drama. But my nature was always flinging itself into these systems as if with the intensity of a physical love affair. It was indeed because I demanded certain real, concrete, almost sensual feelings from a system of metaphysics that I got so much more pleasure from Hegel and Schopenhauer than from Kant.

What they really were to me, these systems, was so many burlesque shows. I skipped the mathematics just as I shut my eyes and ears to the patter, and I enjoyed the spacious curves of cosmic truth as I enjoyed the noble flanks of these friendly women. But the pleasure of metaphysic was not only like the pleasure of looking at dancing-girls, it was also like what I felt for those artificial romanticized landscapes which appealed so strongly to my nature. What I found in the fragmentary "logoi" of the old Greek thinkers, for instance, a sort of poetic and dramatic mysticism, I found diffused, like a penetrating incense through Hegel and Schopenhauer. Bergson, though people soon explained to me his main ideas and I appropriated them craftily enough, for they suited my most casuistical moods, *I could never read*. He was too wire-spun, too French, too—what shall I say?—too *elegant* for my taste.

But aye! how I used to sink into Hegel's thaumaturgic convolutions! How I used to swallow, with this old sea-serpent of thought, the shining pebbles of all the rims and margins and windrows in the world. I remember reading a book on Hegel by an American called Harris in the train between Philadelphia and Lancaster, and getting an ecstasy of sensual satisfaction as I mixed up in my mind Harris and Hegel and the little green shoots of wheat—if it was wheat—coming up in those rich arable lands!

But William James was a startling delight to me, too, for all his roguish jibes at Hegel. I responded with a lively Cymric reciprocity to his Pluralistic ideas, which, in my fluid and incorrigibly sceptical mind, seemed quite as *conceivable* a vision of things as any self-evolving, self-dividing, self-reconciling absolute. I can recall one occasion, when I was heading for Trenton where I was to give a lecture, being so absorbed in William James's *Varieties of Religious Experience* that I permitted my train to stop at the station and to leave the station in complete oblivion of my purpose.

What I am aiming at in this book is a living portrait of

myself, both as I was, and as I gradually became, and for this reason you must not grow impatient, reader, as I limn my picture, line upon line, and tint upon tint, by what you may regard as an over-emphasis upon the erotic aspects of existence. If it has happened, by the will of fate, that in *your* life the erotic element has not played the dominant part that it has played in mine, you are at once luckier than I have been and less lucky! You have escaped a great deal of grotesque tragic-comedy, but you have been deprived of many thrilling and rapturous expectations and perhaps also a few paradisic fulfil-ments. As I have pointed out, the tremulous and thrilling ecstasy, sometimes of an intensity that made the passing moment seem to touch the Eternal, that I got from the con-templation of these girls' limbs in these burlesque shows was of a sweetness that, as I look back upon it now, I certainly find it hard to regard as evil or blameworthy. Indeed from my present point of view I heartily commend it.

What I do *not* commend now—and I need not tell you how I loathed it *then!*—is precisely the so-called "man-of-the-world" tone, the tone that refers so grossly, coarsely, obscenely, and again so flippantly and facetiously, to the spectacle of women displaying what the old writers used to call their "charms." These "charms" were objects of such ensorcerized worship to me that to say that I did not feel "reverence for womanhood" as I gazed at them, with my soul shooting forth lambent fire from my eye-sockets, would be ridiculous.

That old lecherous wretch, Father Karamazov, was mur-dered and damned *not* because he found something idolatrously exciting about the body of every woman he came near, but because he was heartlessly cruel to Alyosha's mother. And is not this a curious thing—I have never got anything but the austerest discomfort from bare legs on the stage. I agree with Dr. Johnson when he told his friend Garrick that it was the *silk stockings* of his actresses that excited his amorous propen-sities. I was always seized with a certain shy aversion when these women appeared with bare legs; and as for the presence of women completely undressed, such as is a favourite amusement with the French, I would be ashamed—out of my devotion to their provocative sweetness when they've *got their stockings on*—to confess the extreme distaste I would feel. I would feel exactly like a fastidious old spinster. Why, the mere bringing together of the word "woman" and the word "naked" a conjunction which is apparently a temptation to many, always fills me with a cold and sickening aversion.

And I am prepared to defend this feeling of mine as natural. It is Nature herself who puts these arts and caprices and whimsies and reticencies, these "sweet reluctant amorous delays" into human sensibility. The charm, the magic, the loveliness of women are increased a thousand-fold when they put at least some clothes on. Can it be that the reason why I feel so malignantly hostile to the French stage and am so completely seduced by American burlesque is that in Puritan countries you have been so accustomed to getting your pleasure in small, sideways, imaginative trespassings, and from making *a great deal of a very little*, that what you have actually come to think of as the Platonic essence of womanhood and its overpowering sweetness is an evasive and delicate nuance entirely composed of imaginative suggestion and liable to be destroyed in a moment by the bare truth?

It is at any rate fully in harmony with my own philosophical *subjectivism*, fully in harmony with my fierce determination to live all my days in the power of the imagination that I felt as I did in this matter. I have always selected from reality rather than worshipped reality. I have spent my life enjoying the margins and horizons and windrows of life rather than its grosser bulk. Is it not natural, then, that I should get a thrilling pleasure when my idols wore stockings but shrink away in dismay when they wore none? And is it not above all characteristic of my preference for faces in mirrors, suns in mists, and moons behind clouds, that I should have derived such tantalized transports from the way these provocative beings danced in and out in the intervals of the clowns' patter?

The key to my whole character, not only to its difference from the bulk of the men who crowded to these shows but to its difference from the cynical minority who were sprinkled among them, could have been detected in a moment, I am sure, by anyone who looked at my expression. I must have had a look that was, in regard to the lower part of my face, like that of a guileless idiot, an idiot whose one idea of heaven was to stare at women forever, but that was, in regard to the upper part of my face, its smouldering concentration, its hooded forehead, its sparrow-hawk beak, like the look of some ambushed Neanderthal watching the gambols of a group of Cro-Magnon girls. It would have been seen from both my formidable glare and my gibbering mouth that I was completely devoid, I will not say of humour, but of that particular sense of the ludicrous that accompanies a society-conscious or custom-conscious intelligence. It would have been clear from my face at those times that while I was hopelessly abandoned to some kind of desperate feeling I had too much in common with an Inanimate Puppet to be likely to do any harm to the sweet beings I glared at.

But, as I have hinted, for reasons which are not very hard to understand I was cruelly persecuted from the time I was forty to the time I was fifty by a steadily increasing asceticism. The truth is I had now begun, for the first time in my life, to get it into my head *that erotic delight was evil*. Now it is easy to see how it was that this blasphemous error entered my brain. Erotic delight for me has always meant lust, and lust alone; and it was simply because of the extraordinary part played by this impersonal, anonymous lust in my own life that I conceived the notion of its being evil.

I myself had noted in the case of my brother Llewelyn, that champion of natural joy, how horrified he was when he saw those unspeakable volumes in the French language that I brought to Clavadel. The only rule I seem able to reach about it all is that *when no one is hurt by it*, any sort of lust is permissible. But so deep is my superstitious notion that erotic feeling *in itself* is evil, that it will only be by a considerable effort of the will that I shall ever allow myself to read again —if ever I *do* allow myself—those sadistic books that melt the marrow in my bones! I have, moreover, been often troubled by the occult East-Indian fancy that to call up sadistic images, whether by reading or by thinking, is a dangerous and wicked thing, on the ground that it projects certain *eidola* upon the air, which, by working on the brains of passers-by might drive a half-crazy person into abominable crime.

Pittsburgh is one place that has burnt itself in upon my mind. I used to go continually to lecture in Pittsburgh, sometimes at the ladies' club there, where for long I was a great *persona grata* and sometimes at the Carnegie Museum, where the Diplodocus impressed me more than I have ever impressed any audience. The Diplodocus indeed made the deepest impression on my mind of any entity, not in human shape, that I have ever seen; and I think of it still as a curious symbol of that epoch of my life. It was, as I say, at Pittsburgh that I went through my most dramatic struggles with my ascetic, and, to confess the truth, my morbidly rampant conscience.

It was a Catholic audience who used to come drifting past the Diplodocus to hear me in this singular spot. How faithful to me, how profoundly comprehending the Roman Catholics of the United States have always been! The aged Mother Superior of "Notre Dame" at Baltimore prayed religiously for me, and sent me some holy magic talisman too, when I suffered the operation they call "gasterenterostomy"; so that even that awful-sounding piece of surgery proved harmless. Indeed, though the greatest of living surgeons, Dr. John Erdmann, knew nothing of the prayers of Sister Meletia it had something to do with these as well as with the great man's skill that my pulse remained absolutely normal throughout this experience. Harry Lyon, who was in America at that time, sardonically commented on what the nurses told him when he came to see me in that Post-Graduate Hospital. He said he found them murmuring among themselves in regard to this Welsh Rasputin under their care:

"This is no man: this is some god or devil!"

The truth is there undoubtedly does exist, in the case of every great religion, what you might describe as a fore-ordained temperament. And this predestination of taste is a chemical, a physical, a material tendency, working as negatively in anyone's *dislikes* as it works positively in anyone's *likes*.

This Catholic audience, under the very nose, as you might say, of the dragon, came instinctively, and as if drawn by a magnet, to hear the modern Cagliostro, as he disparaged Robert Browning and exalted Dante.

But certainly to the end of my days I shall remember the terrific moral struggles I underwent in the "down-town section" of Pittsburgh. Except for Philadelphia and New York I know Pittsburgh better than any other city in America. Every street in Pittsburgh, every bridge across her rivers—for she is, as you are aware, almost an island, an island of iron, such as might have been built by Hephaestus—has had the Inferno-Purgatorio-Paradiso scoriatings, brandings, embalmings of the divine farce of an arch-puppet's battle with himself inscribed in bloody tokens all over its pavements and over all the lintels of its doors. You see I used to stay at the old Fort Pitt, an hotel to which I became very attached; and from this retreat it was but a short distance to the nearest burlesque show. Every inch of the pavements between these two places was inscribed with the bloodstains of those "divine" and "devilish" moods which seemed such preposterous folly to the well-balanced mind of Louis Wilkinson. I used sometimes, when the limbs of the chorus were too plump for my fancy, or when too many beggars and cripples were "treated rough" by smart young men, to rush out of the theatre long before the performance was over—for, as I have told you, the clowns' Aristophanic patter, though from an æsthetic point of view the best fooling in the world, could not mitigate my fever—and walk up and down one or the other of those terrific iron bridges; where as I watched the blocks of ice, or the red and green barge-lights in the water, I would vow desperately to myself, by various solemn oaths, by the sun and the moon and the earth and the styx, that from this particular afternoon November 15th, 1912, let us say, to the end of my life, I would never go to a burlesque show again!

You do not turn the key to the final turret of my nature, reader, until you realize the immense weight of the anti-social maliciousness, inherited from my father, with which—not less then than now—I confront the conventional and vulgar facetiousness of the crowd-conscious mind. What always thrills me so much about the minds of women is that they never indulge in these gross jibes of *bawdy conventionality*. But men of the world, as they love to think of themselves, take these magical occasions, that to an excitable nature—and to an intellectual nature, too, by God! for I am not going to allow that these sneering catchpoles pierce deeper into the mystery of life than Homer and Dante and Plato and Dostoievsky—are beautiful and tragic and purgatorial and paradisic, as flippantly as they take the comic page in their daily paper! It is in fact perfectly amazing to me to watch these worldly-minded proppers-up of social custom, who obviously are using the crowd's most conventional humour, which is the extreme opposite of real humour, trying to drag down the heavenly delights that less perverted people know. Yes, pardie! It is these facetious worldlings who with their shallow jokes are the real perverts; and they are perverts too, if I may use such an expression, *against the Holy Ghost*.

But they never have been able, at least not for very long, to disconcert or discountenance a son of *my* Father; a son of that man in whom so gigantic a childlikeness was balanced by so gigantic a pride! And so I continued to stare at the lines and curves of the forms of these burlesque show women—when, at least, they were not *all* proportioned like Gargamelle—with an emotion in which, as I look back to it now, I cannot detect the least touch of evil. The only way I *can* now see a possible loophole for evil would have been if, in my thoughts, I had pretended that these women were ashamed at my staring at them! But I am sure they were not. And if they *had* been, I was far too ravished by the simple contemplation of their anonymous "charms" to have been aware of it. I would however deeply like to know, now, exactly what these women *do* feel. I wonder if they feel what men dancers would feel if *their* forms were being gazed at in rapture by an audience of women?

But I must implore you, reader, to try to realize what it meant to me that these exquisite beings, beings capable of giving a poor wayfaring wretch such raptures of delight, could actually be persuaded to put on these boys' clothes and dance in and out in the midst of such clowning. Just consider what a thing it was, that without any danger of being beaten, or abused, or sneered at, or jibed at, or hooted at, or flogged into insensibility by moral gangsters or ethical assassins, it was possible for a morbidly timid person like myself to share the delight of the immortal gods when they first stumbled upon the idea of a woman's form!

I suppose, calm reader, it is impossible for you to imagine the emotions that quivered through me, every time, seated as near the orchestra as I could, I heard the deafening overtures to these entertainments? The actual music was of course nothing and less than nothing to me. I tell you if the musicians had been the greatest in the world I would still have waited in trembling impatience till their preluding was over. These burlesque show people little guessed what a hermit they were converting. I cared nothing for drama, nothing for vaudeville, nothing for the opera, nothing for the circus. I was in New York the whole time the Russian Ballet was there and I never went once to it. I was occupied with something more planetary, more poetical, more magical, more satisfying, than music or dancing or the arts of design!

Why, if I only went to a sufficient number of these burlesque shows I might find myself staring at a woman, at a girl, at a sylph, like that one I saw on the pier at Brighton, saw for seven days of heaven, and lost forever and ever! One thing was quite certain. I should not see that Brighton girl, or anyone even remotely resembling her, if I went to the Russian Ballet at the Metropolitan Opera every single night for the whole season. And doesn't the mere word "season" when considered in connection with the sullen Neanderthal malice that it used to rouse in me, reveal the insane anti-social lengths to which my nature could go when it allowed itself the full swing of its monstrous prehistoric simplicity? No! This solitary, anti-social, romantic, *poetic lechery* of mine as it enjoyed some single unknown feminine form, was supported by such a weight of pride that it took upon itself in its huge arrogance to despise the whole of the Balzacian tittle-tattle and glittering fashionable "réclame" that rose and fell, like the ripples of an enchanted sea, round the bizarre performances of the famous ballet.

It would not be correct to use the word "desire," and it would certainly be totally misleading to use the expression "lust after" for what I felt on the rare occasions when I could concentrate my contemplation on a form that really satisfied me. This form then became to me the whole secret of the pleasure of life. I wanted nothing beyond what I had already. I cried to the moment, like Faust:

"Oh, stay! Thou art so fair!"

The truth is I had inherited from my father an anti-social, anti-fashionable malevolence that knew no bounds. I had only to hear current talk—and you know how art circles do talk! —to revert with malicious fury to the life of a Thebaid anchorite. I *was* an anchorite, surrounded by all the sweet feminine forms of an anchorite's cell! But in my relations with all the actual people I encountered I was an angel of consideration. I set myself to acquire, by constantly training my will, a terrific self-control and a punctilious courtesy that was super-human. Between forty and forty-five, when I was tearing my soul to pieces for American audiences, I approached everyone I met with a tender deference and subtle flattery that you would have supposed would have bewildered them. But it did not bewilder them. Sub-consciously they must have recognized that I really had an intense desire to give them a thrill of happiness.

"We all," as my brother Theodore says, "like to be praised"; and I would add that most of us like to be extravagantly praised. Well! Why should I not have been appointed by Providence the "praising medicine-man" to the much-enduring human race? I have always been one for considering people's feelings, one for trying desperately to give them a glow of self-satisfaction; and though, I confess, there have been cases when I have gone too far, take it all in all my intense, eager, appreciative way of listening and agreeing has, I believe, perceptibly increased the happiness of my small world-circle. Just as my own idea of Paradise would be an eternal burlesque show, from which all burlesque had been eliminated, so my idea of making people happy was to create for them an atmosphere from which all criticism was eliminated.

I got more and more attached to Arnold Shaw as my lecture-scope widened. He had then—and indeed has still—the most unwrinkled forehead, the clearest blue eyes, the most childlike mouth, of any man I have ever known. He was one of the most original and—to me at least—one of the most enchanting of men. He had no intimate friends. "John the Fizzle," was all the friends he wanted; and even with me he was a queer mixture of Rabelaisian openness and tactful reserve. Like myself he never went to theatres, or to movies, or to concerts, or indeed to any entertainments, other than those given by his own lecturers. Unlike me he was never a vegetarian. But I am tolerant in such things. His childish delight in a good dinner was as a matter of fact an irresistible sight. I have never seen in my life anyone eat steak and onions with greater gusto. Arnold had a Gargantuan laugh. He would throw back his head and open his mouth as he laughed, until he looked exactly like one of Doré's pictures of Carpalim or Epistemon.

From his constant reading of Rabelais he acquired the habit of always using the word "paunch" in place of stomach or belly. Indeed he used this word as a kind of magic formula wherewith to exorcize the gloomy demons of puritanism. By fits and starts he was a brilliant lecture-manager. New and always very imaginative schemes were forever emerging from his fertile brain. He was not a great reader; but, when at last he really read Rabelais, he took to it like a beetle to dung, a cat to milk, a duck to water, a moth to a candle, a dog to carrion, a malt-worm to beer, and a Yorkshire child to its mother's breast. After this epoch-making reading his conversation was always garnished with Rabelaisian tags. Released by the genius of the Curé of Meudon a kindred genius leapt up from the magnanimous and unworldly "paunch" of this guileless man.

Together we treated the whole business of a lecturer's profession in the most irreverent, wanton, fantastical, and cavalier manner. When things went from bad to worse in any

of our less lucky epochs—for though in our good days I used
to make, under Arnold, as much as a thousand pounds a year,
at other times my income would sink alarmingly low—
Arnold and I would sit opposite each other at "The Village
Kitchen" on Greenwich Avenue, or at "The Two Steps Down"
on Eighth Street, or at "Child's" at Fourteenth Street, or at
the old French Pastry Shop, now "The Rochambeau," or at
Halloran's on Sixth Avenue, and the Rabelaisian-manager
would turn upon the charlatan-lecturer a countenance of such
childlike despair that I used to wonder to myself what would
actually happen when I had not one single audience left. For
I had no trade, no strength to dig, no knowledge of business.
I was totally ignorant of mathematics. I couldn't work a typewriter. I couldn't wait at table. I couldn't drive a car. I had
no notion how to deal with cows or horses. I had already tried
taking Littleton's lower form at the Prep., and I couldn't
keep order for three consecutive minutes! My only possible
refuge, I suppose, would have been to get myself, by hook or
by crook, into a theological college and there aimed at being
ordained, as my father, grandfather, and great-grandfather had
been ordained before me.

It was only our incorrigible and childlike hopefulness that
kept up our hearts in these bad days. There were times, you
must understand, when I had only two lectures a week, on one
of which Arnold was supporting *his* family, and on the other
I was supporting *mine*. At such times our fees became very low.
We jumped at anything, Cagliostro and his circus-manager
had to live. But there was infinite "give" and "yield" between
us; and always fathomless reserves of generosity, buoyancy,
and good-nature on Arnold's side. Once when I only had one
lecture a week for a whole season in New York—a lecture at a
girls' school at Greenwich for which I received thirty dollars
—Arnold found for the nonce some other way of supporting
his family, and allowed me to divide the whole of that thirty
dollars between myself and *my* family.

Under the kindly and dominant influence of Colonel
C. E. S. Wood, the author of *The Poet in the Desert*, I did on
one occasion betray my friendship for Arnold by signing a

K K

contract to lecture indefinitely under another management on the Pacific; but no sooner was I back in New York than I became as eager as Arnold was to compromise things with the Pacific and renew our ancient alliance. I am afraid my erratic nature was by no means a soothing influence for my friend; for our life together ended sadly enough, ended indeed in Arnold's suffering a complete nervous collapse and a serious illness. On his recovery from this illness he was forced to take a less nerve-shaking job than the management of John the Fizzle; but no external separation has altered in the least our lifelong affection for each other and I still believe I am the only man in the world who understands Arnold's unique character or does full justice to his unusual gifts.

That he has flashes of genius in business, and not only in the lecture-business, must be clear to many; but I believe I am not boasting when I say that I alone realize the endurances and magnanimities of his inner nature. My brother Llewelyn did not always do full justice to Arnold and he has confessed to me that he would listen with blank amazement when, after some indiscretion of mine that made it hard to find me any engagements, Arnold would smile blandly at him and remark cheerfully:

"*John's a Fizzle.*"

In Louis Wilkinson's curious book about himself entitled *Swan's Milk* he misses a fine opportunity for bringing to bear his satiric pen upon the figures of Arnold and myself in our relation to each other. The truth is that Arnold had a way, I will not say of bullying Louis, for that was not an easy thing to do, but of treating him without that consideration for an Archangel's radiant life-illusion which he always displayed in connection with my convoluted *amour propre.* "Our Doc" he used to call him; and Louis' European aplomb would sometimes emerge with its beautiful mallard-feathers not a little ruffled and awry out of that singular office in the Grand Central where Arnold concocted his lecturers' "mean jumps."

Louis was indeed the stately and nostalgic Harlequin of our little circus in which the deboshed Welsh Clown had wormed his way into some mysterious "rapport" with the Man with the Cracking Whip. It has always been a bewilderment to me

that Llewelyn should regard Louis' frankly expressed satire
at my expense as unkind. I think it is, on the contrary, one of
the tenderest and most affectionate compliments I have ever
received. He wrote the "Buffoon" about our relations and a
gay and entertaining book it was, but I am sure no one reading
it would accuse him of any malicious intent. You might as well
say that Arnold himself, while eagerly basting, like one of those
merry human maggots engendered by the Curé's god-like
and cheese-like brain, his goose upon his spit, was malicious
when he used his favourite schoolboy words to describe the
calamities that threatened the head of his friend.

You can see how quickly, reader, I am tempted to transform
what I have to say about America into a minute description of
my personal friendship with another Englishman. The queer
thing is—and I fancy that both Dreiser and Masters will agree
with me in this—American men are not adepts at the delicate
art of friendship. I am not talking about homosexual relations.
These exist here of course as everywhere else. But I am talking
now about friendship, as Montaigne describes it, in that
passionate passage referring to his own friendship with
Etienne. The number of friendships between men that I have
seen going on in America are extraordinarily few, considering
that I have spent over a quarter of a century in this country.

Nor is it that men are more intimate with their women than
Europeans are with theirs. Indeed I think that fewer love-
affairs, fewer marriages, in America, develop into intimate and
intellectual friendships between the sexes than in England.
Men and women are divided from each other in America as
they are among what we call the working classes in the old
world. Women have their own work at home, their own jobs
in office, or factory, or store; and they have their own circle
of friends, too, just as the man has his circle of Dicks, Charleys,
Teds and Freds, that he greets so familiarly. I do not think that
American men confide in their wives, though there are exceptions to this of course, as completely as Englishmen do. The
truth is they do not confide—in the deep sense of the word—in
anybody! These Dicks and Charleys *talk* freely enough of their
personal affairs to one another; and as a seasoned traveller in

this country I can assure you that they talk freely about themselves, their wives and children, their parents, their job, their church, their pastimes, to any stranger who will listen to them.

But their real soul, their inmost soul, *they keep entirely to themselves.* And I do not think it is from reserve or reticence that they do this. They do it for the same reason that they would find it impossible to refer to their secret sexual life. They are unaware of so much as the existence of this inner Being of theirs, this Eternal Being who has such strange raptures! Yes, I know I am on the right track here. The spiritual life, the erotic life, the intellectual life, the life of the awareness of our subtler senses, is simply non-existent to most American men. Mind ye, I don't say it is not there. It *must* be there. But they are innocently unconscious of it. How they find anything to talk about with one another is a mystery to me. They are fond of bawdy stories and humorous anecdotes but when these come to an end unless you plunge into the technique of machinery or the management of your business it is hard to keep things from falling flat.

American women on the other hand are as sensitive to the mystical-sensual aspects of life as women in the old world, and in mental restlessness and general intellectual acquisitiveness I think they have a passionate curiosity beyond that of the old world.

But American men are most assuredly a race by themselves among all the men on the face of the earth. There are no men like them. I know *where I am* with a Negro, with a Chinaman, with a Mohammedan, with a Spaniard, with a Russian, with a New Zealander, with a Hungarian, with a German, with a Turk. But I don't know where I am with an American. I do not say that he embarrasses me or makes me feel shy, or that I lack gratitude to him for his benevolence; but I cannot relax in his presence, or let myself go, or speak my mind. He is frank where I would be secretive; and again he is reserved where I chatter like a magpie. It would be difficult to be in the company of an Englishman of my own class for five minutes without giving myself away in a manner that would make all but my oldest American friends think I had gone off my head.

I don't necessarily mean give myself away in erotic things. I mean in whimsies, caprices, fantasies, manias, humours, oddities, idiosyncracies, apathies, antipathies, sympathies, prejudices, the whole paraphernalia of that pyschic-sensuous margin of life which is the most precious thing in the world. No, I don't mean obvious erotic things, or obvious obscene things! These I *have* heard talked about in America, either when men were alone or when men and women of the intelligentsia were getting drunk together. I am not referring to things that are shocking or outrageous or scandalous. I am referring to things that are evasive and subtle, things of atmosphere, things of religion, things belonging to those floating, drifting mysterious over-tones and under-tones of life which are in reality overtaking us all the time, but of which if I spoke to an American man he would look as uncomfortable as if I had turned before his very eyes into what they call a "fairy" or into what they call a "cake-eater."

As Henry James said, that master of atmosphere, when he was fleeing from the sensuous sterility of his fellow-countrymen,

"American women are the aristocracy of America!"

It is an almost terrifying thing, this impenetrable spiritual reserve of American men, I have dallied with the idea that it comes from the soil and the climate and was a characteristic of the Red Indians. But this may be a pure fantasy. Certainly it is hard for the simpler type of American man to "get the idea" of what you mean by enjoying intellectual pleasures as if they were of sensual pleasures. I think it is the imaginative element in intellectual pleasure that they find most difficult to appreciate. It is when the imaginative reason begins to play upon life that such teasing distinctions as the characteristic American one between "highbrow" and "lowbrow" begins to grow blurred; and a slow, ignorant, imaginative person is felt to be of a higher intellectual type than a clever, lively, smart one.

Some Europeans have quarrelled with the kindness of Americans. Far off from me be such ingratitude! I here and now protest to all the recording angels in the occult universe that I have received more unalloyed and disinterested kindness in one year in America than in ten in my own country! What are the dominant American virtues? *Kindness and humility!* No unchristian virtues these, eh? as Mr. Pecksniff might opine. But it is true; and these two holy cardinal virtues form the largest components of that simple heathen goodness which Sir Walter Scott with his last breath told his son-in-law "was all that mattered."

American men are tragic without knowing that they are tragic. They are tragic, by reason of the desolate thinness and forlorn narrowness of their sensual and mystical contacts. Mysticism and sensuality are the things that most of all redeem life. Let the workers march to triumph, singing the International. But when you *have* marched, when you *have* reorganized society when you *have* given the people bread and the circus, the question comes, *what next?* It is then that we want to commune with angels and demons; it is then that we want to worship the elements; it is then that we want to return to the imaginative and poetic life that Science has for so long been destroying.

Let the cause of the workers come first; but while the workers are overcoming their enemies, there is no reason why their friends should not tap this old planetary rock to draw forth new psychic and sensual nourishment. Man is *an enjoyer* as well as a destroyer and a creator; and these are days when, more than ever before, humanity needs to sink back into contemplation. Not all the heroic appeals of the noblest cause in the world can turn the unconquerable Faustian "I," the old Homeric and Biblical "I," into a permanent cog in an impersonal machine. This impersonalization, this thinning down of the life-pulses, the life-nerves, the life-senses, the life-imagination of human beings has been achieved in America without the least restriction upon unbounded capitalism. The phrase "rugged individualism" has grown to be the catch phrase to describe the life-destroying condition of this old state of affairs. Individuals became "rugged"—though such "ruggedness" looked repulsively *sleek* to the naked eye—by hardening their hearts against all the things in life that can be described as poetical or philosophical. Our unfortunate human nature has never been subjected to conditions quite so anti-pathetic to all the most interesting stimuli to poetic human feeling since the beginning of the world, as it has been subjected to in America. One can only hope now that the great Mr. Roosevelt, by some inspired conjuring-trick, may be able to change the actual tempo of human psychology in this amazing country in at least *some* important ways.

And yet I know well how greatly I shall miss, when I leave America, certain free and noble aspects of life there. When I think of our English social distinctions, and of our deep-rooted snobbishness, that evil vice from which we all, without exception suffer, when I think how afraid of each other we all are, how abominably self-conscious about these wretched little differences, how nervously patronizing to those "below," how nervously obsequious to those "above," when I think how many levels and sub-levels of social life we possess, to be struggled into, or dropped out of, when I think of all the conventional bird-lime there is to be washed off, before we can de-class ourselves out of "upper class" or "middle-class" or "working-class," *into intelligent and indulgent humanity*, I can make a shrewd guess at what I shall miss.

There *is* real democracy in America; and in spite of all the wicked power of money you feel it all the time. A man is a man in America, and a woman a woman, though the former *may* be called a "guy" and the latter be ever so "emancipated" and "highbrow." That he is a de-personalized man, pathetically anxious to conform to type, heart breakingly averse to developing anything idiosyncratic or original, does not un-man him; or that she feels towards him a double charge of feminine contempt for the male's lack of subtlety does not divest *her* of her womanhood.

Vaguely conscious of the psychic and sensual sterility of his native air the American's attitude to Old World values is shown in his troubled, half humorous, half bewildered restlessness. Seeking he knows not what, he rushes about in ever-improving automobiles, drugging himself, distracting himself, exhausting himself, in a blind sub-conscious struggle to find that psychic-sensuous Absolute of human satisfaction which the basic conditions of his life deny him. As long as he can be a pioneer, all is well! Any primeval wrestling with Nature solaces him while it numbs and atrophies him. But the tragedy of an American begins when his pioneer-psychology has no further outlet. Desperately then does he hunt the wind, recklessly then does he rake the dust! To say he worships the dollar is a preposterous lie. It is we who worship *me money*, as Sexton Truggins puts it in Theodore's book. What the American worships is not even power. It is some will-o'-the-wisp *idea* of power, bringing with it the prestige, the reputation, the glow the glory of being the one who has "huffed" the other, in the great cosmic game. What the American cannot grasp, and what gives him a vertiginous and ghastly sense of a yawning gulf, is the planetary law of Nature that all human action is only a means to contemplation.

But how often, if I leave this country, will the wild, free, boundless *chaos* of it all come back to my mind! For a certain kind of cosmic picturesqueness, at once shocking and liberateing, as if among the engines and the machines and the well-appointed "homes" you kept stumbling upon rock-ribs of scoriac lava, this vast continent has no parallel. The bleak prehistoric bones of the aboriginal planet, as it was before man appeared on it at all, seem always ready to stick out amid this hurry-scurry of "modern improvements." And *that look*, the look of a *homo sapiens* perpetually confronted by cosmogonic insecurity, by the presence of catastrophic and cataclysmic matter—the original elements of a world prior to man's world —such as we see in the faces of the grim aboriginals of this land, is constantly to be caught on the most spry, the most clever, the most modernized of American men's countenances.

If I have learnt anything from my life in America it is a certain lonely and perhaps rather desperate stoicism, a certain stark endurance of one's fate in the presence of air and water and fire and the basic rock-structures of this earth. You must remember that every American man is a Jack of all Trades. In the midst of his towering cities, in the forlorn and woefully standardized "residential-sections" he has built for himself, you find this cheerful, nervous, restless, humble-minded person, without mental recreations, without æsthetic interests, without spiritual or sensuous contemplation, hammering, sawing, chopping, brushing, cleaning, polishing, improving, pulling down, building up, like a competent, shrewd, cynical, kindly, but quite mad, super-artisan. He may be a manipulator of half the railroads of the country, or he may be a furnace-stoker in a flimsy apartment-house, put him on his back underneath a broken motor-car, and you will see a man who can be happy—and perhaps only entirely happy—when he is tinkering at the bolts and screws and pistons that he, or others like him, have caused to take shape from the bowels of a gouged-out planet! It is this competent grasp of the essentials of machinery, of tools and engines, of inventions and the art of running inventions, this restless concentration on the industrial exploitation of Nature, combined with an absence of all aristocratic airs, that creates the yearning and wistful admiration with which our Russian friends—since their upheaval—tend to regard Americans.

It is hard to worship Demeter in America. I cannot conceive of any expression less appropriate in this country than the expression "our Mother, the Earth." The Earth is *not* a mother to an American. She is a tool-shed, a smithy, a tank, a malevolent but sublime volcano, out of which so much horse-power calculated in terms of so many dynamos or kilowatts is forced to erupt.

It is curious the way a person can adapt himself to a life apparently completely alien to that for which he was born! This whole long epoch of my life, from the time when I was forty till the time when I was fifty-five, I spent almost entirely in trains and hotels. It was a queer existence. Anyone would have supposed that it would have so scraped and combed and twitched and raked and harrowed and rattled and jarred the little cells of my brain and the nerves that connect them with the vital centres of my being that I would have soon become a victim of some disease like St. Vitus's dance. But it did not work out like this. In the first place I have a constitution, if not a frame, of iron. In the second place I have acquired some mystical, perhaps even Tibetan trick, of sinking back upon the

Cosmos or upon the Mystery of the Tao behind the Cosmos, which I can always make use of at a pinch. However cynical and materialistic you are, my good calm reader, you cannot very well, if you are anything of a psychologist, deny that my spiritual attitude to myself as, I won't say a re-incarnated Taliessin, but as a formidable Argeiphontes, or messenger of the gods, was an attitude calculated to have a very vital effect on my fund of nervous strength. I acquired the power—indeed it came very naturally to me—of giving myself up completely to the little sensuous pleasures of the passing moment.

My nature is so extravagantly simple and childlike—this is why crafty worldly people cannot understand me and take me for an arch-poseur—and I defend this simplicity with so much malicious hatred of the clever sophistries of the world, that I was in a very strong position for enjoying—in despite of my more worldly fellow-travellers—every single one of the little pleasures afforded by the conditions of travelling. I enjoyed all these little things with spasms of delicious happiness, just as a child—especially a young girl—enjoys herself, when she feels the simple delight of skipping down a road on a fine day, or of kicking up the leaves in the gutter on a gloomy day. The expression *enjoys herself* exactly expresses the simple subtlety of what I am trying to say.

It was always a pleasure to me to lie in my lower berth, when I had a long morning of travelling before me, and there was nobody in the upper berth, and listen to the milk-cans rattle on the platforms of the smaller stations, and to all the vague village sounds that were penetrating enough to reach the interior of the train. And how I enjoyed it when I had, as often happened, the wash-room entirely to myself! And how satisfactory it was when "The Diner"—that all-hallowed word to travellers—was the very next car to where I slept! How well I can recall feeling about in the darkness behind those heavy green curtains for the book I was reading—some new volume of Conrad, perhaps, which I had propped up on the rack—and then carrying it in my hand with a sense of ritualistic well-being, just to have it as a companion, for I rarely read at meals, where I sat down by some window in "The Diner" to enjoy a leisurely breakfast!

Although I always felt a little nervous about the effect of coffee, I often used to have it, and it always acted upon me like some miraculous haschish. To sip my third cup, for when I *did* allow myself this luxury I went to the limit, and, with my thumb in the page where Dona Rita pursued by that stone-throwing cousin is saved by "Monsieur George," and with my eye on the shack-littered banks of the Mississippi or the "Blood of Christ" mountains of New Mexico, or the Osage hedges of Kansas, or the huge red barns with their stately silo-towers of Wisconsin, while my cigarette smoke ascended in blue spirals and some sweet-natured African, whose cosmic benevolence surrounded me like a golden mist, bowed low over the silver on the tray, to think to myself, "Will Llewelyn be able to meet me at the station when at last I get back to New York?" were experiences that must have sunk down into the deepest levels of my consciousness. Those were certainly exciting times when Llewelyn really was with me in America.

Mr. Atkins thought it appropriate that we should wear our tall silk hats, bought either at Damon's in Yeovil or at Lemon's in Sherborne, as we went about Philadelphia, and I can recall one occasion when we were hooted if not pelted by a gang of boys, as we pursued our blameless way—Powys Major and Powys Quintus in their Sunday attire—to try to find the zoo in the public park. It was on that very occasion—and doubled up with "Jack's pain" I remember I was just then—that I first discovered El Greco; for there was an astonishing picture of his in a gallery out there representing Our Lord's Passion and with what looked like a background of livid icebergs behind His wrestlings with the First Cause.

It was in that first visit of his to America that Llewelyn got his consumption. He was only twenty-five then, who is fifty to-day; but I wish I could hold myself entirely free from the responsibility of his life having been accompanied so wickedly by the Danse Macabre of those little white bacilli. For the truth is I did not look after my younger brother or take care of him on that first visit as I ought to have done. I am sure it was in some awful place in New York City that he caught the germ of the thing, when he was being hunted, harassed, and bullied by certain unsympathetic audiences that were very different from my East-Side Jews.

But to return to my own affairs at a much later date I began to grow aware as I went about this continent that I was really performing a definite rôle in America, a rôle where I had no rival. I mean I was attracting to myself like a magnet all the neurotic unhappy ones, all the lonely ones, all the *misfits*, in the whole country. I became the acknowledged enemy, and I hope I shall always remain so, of all the well-constituted and success-ful, as these opposed themselves to the failures and the abjects and the ill-adjusted. Thinking of the words on the arch in Washington Square, "Let us raise a Standard to which the wise may repair; the Event is in the hands of God," I feel tempted to say, "Let *me* raise a Standard—*Vexilla Regis pro-deunt Inferni!*—to which the 'morons' and degenerates and imbeciles and poets and idiots may repair: the event is in the hands of Chance."

For just as you are able to find in the vast stretches of prairie-grass in Oklahoma and Texas little delicate flowers of a beauty almost incredible, so, in the appalling stretches of the dusty moral normality of this country you come, here and there upon characters of the most unbelievable originality and brittle charm! And the point is that living where they did these unfor-tunates had never had one drop of encouragement or one breath of sympathy—not one!—until I, the Quixotic champion of the immoral against the moral, of the religious against the conventional, of the poetical against the worldly, of happiness against success, came trailing and drifting past, ironically "bowing and scraping" to their intolerable magnates, but tipping them themselves the sign, the token, the password, of the freemasonry of all intellectual souls! What I really did was to bring to these victims of the unbelievable "Wasteland" the healing sense that all the noble spirits of antiquity and the Middle Ages, all the subtle and penetrating intellects of the human race, were *on their side* and lifting their voices to them, all the way through the centuries; assuring them that they might bow down as low as they pleased in the House of Rimmon, as long as in secret they served the true God!

Yes, my twenty-five years of lecturing in America cannot have been wasted. Incessantly, never varying, by irony, by rhetoric, by sardonic malice, by diabolic bitterness, by Dickensian humour, by passionate poetry, by all the "natural magic" of my Welsh ancestors, I made myself a Voice crying in the Wilderness, *Ego phonè boontos en te eremo!*" Gravely, quietly, gently, and in a tone far too serious to be boastful, I am prepared to say that while I was lecturing between these two American oceans thousands and thousands of imaginative and sensitive men and women who had no other hope—the megalopolitan Smart Alecs can always take care of themselves—were never without a passionate interpreter.

"And what," as my American chairmen always used to say, "was my message?"

Well, I am inclined to think that that old well-known Goethean tag, that I dare say my erudite "Guru" at Cambridge, Mr. G. P. Gooch, was the first to repeat to me, would best express the quintessence of what I shrieked and danced and yelled and roared and whispered and wept for the sake of all these lonely ones and funny ones:

"Im Ganzen, Guten, Schonen, resolut zu leben!" "Resolve to live in the Whole, in the Good, and in the Beautiful!"

With how quaint, old-fashioned and almost pathetic a sound must those proud Teutonic words strike the ears of the young swashbucklering disillusionists of our time! And I dare say I myself have long seemed to these same sturdy realists even as Stepan Trophimovitch in *The Possessed* seemed to his son Peter Stepanovitch, not much better than a doddering windbag. Windbag as I may be, no one will ever know the strangeness of the singular incidents, of the miraculous chances, that occurred to me as I went on these journeys. But I myself shall remember these things for ever in England or in France; and while I hear the peevish whistlings of *our* trains, the great booming mastodon-bellow of the locomotives of America will drift over me and bring it all back.

I shall see the face of an old negro whose shanty I came

upon in a country walk in the heart of Georgia, and who, when I told him I was a lecturer, refused to believe such a thing of so dusty, so untidy a person, and a person so obviously *not* "a Southern Gentleman," until he had despatched Sarah his wife for a copy of Cæsar's *Gallic Wars*. And so terribly severe a Latinist the old man turned out to be that when I left him, after my stumblings through a paragraph or two, and went my way, he seemed still unconvinced as to my business in life. We parted good friends however; for I had remembered enough of my lessons in the Prep., to make it clear that I did full justice to the old gentleman's own scholarship, even though I did not share it.

And I shall see again that extraordinary scene at the end of a very exciting lecture on some philosophical subject at the Hebrew Institute in St. Louis, when a tall, majestic, wild-looking man suddenly got up at the back of the hall and in a clear authoritative voice demanded if the lecturer could tell him "whether King Arthur would ever really come back to his people"? I shook hands with this man afterwards; and he was even more remarkable-looking near at hand that at a distance. His name was Rhys. Doubtless he was of the blood of the Princes of South Wales. I never got his address and I never saw him again.

And I shall see the coffin of my kind and courteous friend, the translator of Cicero's *De Senectute* in the Loeb classics. It was at the State University of Arkansas at Fayetteville that I met this wise, gentle, retiring, and learned man. He was so courteous and kind to me! I went several times to this little town, in such lovely pastoral country, not so far from the unfrequented Ozark Mountains. Arkansas is one of my favourite states. The poorer people here, like those near Joplin, Missouri, and Galena, Kansas, are in a sense my *ideal Americans*. This district of this vast country—this South-Western portion of the Middle-West—seems quite different from the rest. The weather is warm and relaxed here, though subject to wild typhoons and to great winds coming across Texas from the Gulf, and it is easy to pick up a casual, scanty, careless, squatter's livelihood, varied, on the border of Oklahoma, by fabulous strokes of luck, when the poorest person *strikes oil* on his scrap of land. All men are equal here, in the deepest sense of that word, all are carefree, all are worshippers of the great goddess Chance! No one in this Arcadian land feels any respect for rich men, or for thrifty men, or for great commercial magnates. Oil or zinc can be obtained by the poorest in the easiest way, and may, at the turn of a wrist, make such a person rich as Little Claus in the fairy-tale! Poor though so many people are, and ramshackle though their dwellings may be, there is a sense of easy, relaxed contentment in this district, totally different from the hard struggle "to make good" in other portions of the United States.

I am not the only Englishman who has discovered the "beauties" of Arkansas. I had not long been ensconced in a perfectly charming little hotel on the edge of the town, a place from which I could wander out into what seemed an infinitely undulating and umbrageous park stretching to the horizon, when I was called down to see a visitor. I was amazed to find in the hotel parlour a stocky, powerfully-built, ruddy-faced compatriot, looking like an ex-sea captain straight from his ship off the Bristol Channel! This friendly fellow-countryman led me to his house, situated, as it seemed, in the midst of a noble park-land, over which, to my nostalgic joy, floated an enormous Union Jack. Here his good lady prepared for our refreshment a stately fish, so admirably cooked upon a wooden platter that I was fain to put aside for that day my vegetarian principles. Have you guessed, reader, who my friend was? None other than the famous Mr. Finger, full of exciting stories of the not less famous Mr. Cunninghame Graham!

But Judge Falconer was no less good to me than Mr. Finger, and I soon discovered that his admirable translation of Cicero had been originally made to comfort, in extreme old age, a near relative of his own. You can therefore imagine what I felt when on my next visit to Fayetteville, after preparing as classical a discourse on "The Art of True Culture" as I could think up in the train, I found, in the vestibule of the hall where I was to speak, nothing less than the actual coffin of my Arkansas Cicero. Dead and cold he lay; nor could the best-turned of my periods, so carefully composed to please him, reach that quiet head. Were the sad words of Catullus the only requiem for this fine scholar:

"Soles occidere et redire possunt;
Nobis, cum semel occidit brevis lux,
Nox est perpetua una dormienda!"

or when I said to myself:

"I *know*—beyond all reason—that we share a life outside this whole astronomical spectacle!" was I but a false oracle over the body of this translator of *De Divinatione*"?

But my recognition *had* pleased this elderly scholar; and there were thousands of other Americans, old and young, scattered about this country to whom—and it is no vain brag—my scarecrow apparition and wild and whirling words must have been as rain to transplanted roots! For the megalopolitans might mock me as they pleased as a bastard Chautauqua-chatterer, and I did really speak once at the original Chautauqua in a great open-air tent on the "Idylls of the King" and made that touching crowd listen to, "So all day long the noise of battle rolled, among the mountains by the winter sea," and they might mock my friend Masters for thinking that there was anything to get from such a windbag, but the truth is that below all my mountebank-malice, below all my naughty passion for tearing my own repute to tatters, I always treated these audiences of grave, simple men and women *on equal terms.* I thought aloud in their presence, thus doing them the greatest courtesy that one man can do to other men! I reverenced from my heart—and they knew it and saw it—this wistful craving for real culture that these damned megalopolitans mocked at.

My Oxford gown, which was really a Cambridge gown, "got it over" with the sleek magnates who were paying for these Sops to Cerberus, and it was not till I had skipped off and was well on my road to fresh fields that these sly rogues, who thought they were turning the people away from dangerous thoughts, discovered the spiritual dynamite I had scattered!

What I really was doing for this quarter of a century was undermining the clever fashionable Herods of America and like that other John—so impervious to Salome—"preparing the way of the Lord." In other words I was holding my Ciceronian brief, up and down this land, for an essential Renaissance of Life, as against the jangling and the jargoning, and all the tricky obscurantisms, of the passing hour. I can only pray that *now*—when I have nothing but my pen wherewith to carry on the fight—I am reaching these same lost misfits, these "morons" as they are called, who like myself, but without my Legions of Devils, are being constantly oppressed. But the new President—that man after my own heart—has his eye on all this, as on much else in this land, and my belief is that the change he is occupied in bringing about is a much deeper, a much more psychic one, than most people realize. For nearly thirty years I have been praying that such a man might dominate this great country. More power to him!

It would be a gross misunderstanding of my attitude to America if any European person supposed I under-rated all the good I've got from my life over here. It infuriates me to listen to ignorant, irresponsible "summer-butterflies" traducing America! They know as little about the platonic "essences" of this extraordinary land as they do about Russia, *with which it has so much in common.*

I would like to record here and now, on the eve of my return—if the gods are propitious—to my native land, that at least one European, if an Englishman *is* a European, feels that he owes more, in the matter of his inmost spiritual growth, to America, than to all the cathedrals and all the castles, and all the writers too—except Homer and Dostoievsky—of the historic Old World.

During all this travelling I suffered at intervals, not constantly, but at pretty frequent intervals, from my accursed ulcers and from that evil acid dyspepsia which stirred them up. I never touched meat—for I was a vegetarian on principle now—but for the bulk of these fifteen travelling years I did not by any means always eat vegetables. This I think was partly for the sake of economy; for I was so extravagant in my tips to waiters and so fastidious about the hotels I went to, that I should certainly have wasted my substance *en route* if I had not

L L.

been extremely parsimonious over my diet. My gastric trouble, or so I conceived, dictated this economy, while a vein of almost rustic miserliness, encouraged it; but, in addition to these motives, this simplicity in diet *suited my taste*. At one time when my ulcers were at the worst I lived entirely on "hominy," which is a species of cereal, on ice-cream, on raw eggs, and on milk. But as a rule for every meal I would have the same things, tea, dry toast, fried eggs, and guava jelly. Mr. Blake, when at the Prep. he had us in to dessert, used to give us guava jelly.

I was still very greedy over what I liked; and just as I had devoured apricot-paté bought at "Tuffins" and new, brown bread-and-butter at Wildman's, eagerly masticating these things, as a water-rat does, with my front teeth, so now I rolled against my palate three times a day what were called "individual" jars of guava jelly. If this greediness of mine makes your gorge rise, reader, I must hasten to swear to you, across my heart, that *for the last five years*, since I have lived upon milk in these New York hills, I have lost completely all trace of this furious vice. I get a faint satisfaction from taking *thin* bread-and-butter to my tea; and I enjoy the feeling of drinking milk. But that is all! If I could outgrow my other vices as I have outgrown this one, I would yet approach, before I died, that mediæval, or, if you prefer it, Tibetan ideal of life, which all my days has beckoned me and allured me.

My beautiful but critical friend Louis quarrels with me for liking America. "He *loves* it!" he cries in dismay, just as if to "love" America were enough in itself to prove a person's degradation. Well, I must plead guilty to this charge. I must indeed pile up my guilt; for I have not only loved *America*; I have greatly, and most faithfully, and for more than twenty years, loved American *women*.

But listen, Louis; listen, you supercilious Archangel: let me give you some practical, material, physical, pragmatic reasons for this weakness of mine. In the first place it would not have been possible "to keep Burpham going," and to give my son the education, at Sherborne and Corpus, that my great-grandfather had given my grandfather, and yet to leave a little over for my personal pleasures—such as visiting Venice in company with yourself—had I confined my services to the Extension work at home. In the second place my life in trains and hotels—though you may have once caught *that look* on my face—was a grand escape from all those worries in English social life to which—being, as you so naughtily tease me with being, such a sensitive—I was peculiarly alive. My temperament is at once so fussily, superstitiously, maniacally *altruistic*, and at the same time so fluidly and sinuously *egoistic* that my best chance for living that life of psychic-sensuousness which I have deliberately selected for myself is to flee as far as I possibly can from all human responsibilities. And not only from responsibilities—from possessions too! For I have in me a vein of unbalanced miserliness. I have in fact an almost crazy possessive instinct. How I hugged that absurd football my father gave me at the Prep.! I would have hid it *inside my ribs* if I could have saved it from desecration. How I cherished— beyond all rational proportion—my ridiculous umbrella at Wildman's; for which I was so savagely derided by C. Minor and D. Major! How intoxicated with the lust of a landowner I was when Mr. S. lent me the money to buy that tiny freehold overlooked by the Duke of Norfolk's bank!

And think, my dear Louis, what my freedom was during these fifteen years of travelling about America. I had no cares or responsibilities. *I had no work*; for my lectures themselves were the most pure "inspiration" that has ever flowed, *through a human reed*, from the gods "who hold broad heaven." All I had to do was to sit in Pullman cars, gaze out at the passing scenery and read romantic fiction. It was the ideal life for a sentimental servant-girl; and I have a good deal of such a girl in me.

But I have not yet touched upon the most important blessing in this nomadic life of mine. I had escaped from Englishmen altogether. I had *almost* escaped from American men; for you can believe how I avoided the smoking-rooms and smoked my own cigarettes only when they were empty. And now, in place of English and Americans, I found myself in contact with a race of human beings who are as superior to the rest of humanity, in all the qualities that I, as a philosopher, have come most to admire, as moss is superior to lichen. I refer of course to the American negro.

Slavery, with its appalling slave-ships navigated by so many sea-dogs of English birth, has at least, this worst crime of our race, resulted in the emergence of a divine and incomparable breed of men and women. The cruelty of the Southerners—and by no means only of what are called White Trash —to this noble race, I must leave to the Jesus Christ of Michael Angelo's Judgment, that Jesus whose coming these Africans themselves await with such passionate and perhaps not ineffective faith. I always think of that Christ with His hand raised to smite as being the Judge—and a Jewish one too!— before whom these cruel devils will one day have to stand. Meanwhile these Americanized Africans, the only imaginative Christians left on earth, except for a few far scattered Catholics, "go *inching along*, like the pore inch-worm, waiting for Jesus to come!"

He will come, my friends. *He will come.* I found *that* out during those fifteen years of travelling in American trains and staying in American hotels. Jesus Christ will come, King Arthur will come. And it will not be a day of rejoicing *for all.* When He said "they know not what they do," He was speaking of what such persons were doing to Himself, not to what they would soon be doing to His sheep.

Yes, the American negroes, regarded by White Trash—and not only by White Trash—as an inferior race, are in all the qualities that, as a peripatetic philosopher, I have come to admire most, one of the greatest races of the world. It certainly does make a person's heart sick to see how our superior cleverness and our superior machinery put a race of this sort so completely at our mercy. How this black race did redeem humanity for me as I moved about their adopted home! I found them on all sides. I found them while I was lecturing in New York, Chicago, Philadelphia, Detroit, Cleveland, St. Louis, Boston, Baltimore, Pittsburgh, Los Angeles, Buffalo, San Francisco, Milwaukee, Washington, Newark, Cincinnati, New Orleans, Minneapolis, Kansas City, Indianapolis, Jersey City, Rochester, Portland, Denver, Toledo, Providence,

Columbus, Louisville, St. Paul, Oakland, Atlanta, Omaha, Worcester, Birmingham, Syracuse, Richmond, New Haven, Memphis, Dallas, Dayton, Bridgeport, Hartford, Scranton, Grand Rapids, Paterson, Youngstown, Springfield, Des Moines, New Bedford, Fall River, Trenton, Nashville, Camden, Norfolk, Albany, Lowel, Wilmington, Cambridge, Reading, Yonkers, Duluth, Elizabeth, Lawrence, Utica, Waterbury, Oklahoma City, Schenectady, Fort Wayne, Evansville, St. Joseph, Knoxville, Bayonne, Peoria, Harrisburg, San Diego, Wilkes Barre, Allentown, Wichita, Troy, Hoboken, and in hundreds of little out-of-the-way places whose names escape me now; and I came to look forward to every "Diner" because of its African waiter and to every night-coach because of its African porter. The mere sound of these people's voices—musical with a music that springs from a soul at once mellow and childlike—was enough to heal all the wounds and all the outrages that owing to being such a "sensitive" and owing to having such old-fashioned ideas I was bound to suffer among the lively populations of these busy cities.

The religion of the American negro is the most poetical, and therefore the most *religious* religion to be found in the United States. Is it any wonder that I felt so drawn to this noble persecuted race, with their Roses-of-Shiraz voices, their sacred endurance, their infinite childishness, their "Numen in est" sense of the holiness of all that lives?

Every kind of religion touches me to the heart except those modernistic forms of it where ethics take the place of angels and where the First Cause takes the place of Christ. I am as susceptible to religion as I am to the beautiful limbs of women. Communism appeals to me just because it excites the religious emotion. Catholicism appeals to me for the same reason; and for the same reason do all the traditional Hebraizings of the Hebrew race.

The average American is essentially moral, *but essentially irreligious*. And I think this is largely due to his lack of poetic imagination.

Not only did I escape all human responsibility, all work, all serious contact with people, all anxiety, all care, by spending my life for fifteen years in trains; but I could afford to give my son that feeling for the gods of a particular spot, that feeling for the old customs together with the old walls, old plants, old trees, old hedges, old brooks, old spinneys, old lanes of a particular spot, that is perhaps the most important thing that a parent can give to a child. It is wicked to whirl children about the world and to lodge them in hotels and transitory hostelries. Do you know what you become when you do that? You become a *god-killer*, you sprinkle the poison-gas of your vulgar novelty-hunting on the heads of all those little gods that are children's best guardian-angels. And you atrophy for life their power of imaginative play; you murder their power of vegetative contemplation, while at the same time you exhaust and tire out for life that precociously-developed reason which you so much admire.

Thus while I escaped from the world in railway trains, a mode of travelling for which I have a particular penchant, I enabled my son—as he watched his cat "Barney" catch moles and his dog "Whisker" catch rats—to sink his soul into those folded hills, till it hid itself like an otter by the "Old River," till it came forth like the Thyme by the Lepers' Path, till it hovered like a kestrel in the infinite blue air.

Of course I had, during all these long years, times when my nerves moved a peg or two in the wrong direction. I can well recall one such occasion in the Middle-West. I was in the Claypool Hotel at Indianapolis; and I can now see the leather chairs of the old writing-room there and the deep capacious inkpots on the long tables at which the unwearied drummers wrote to their buyers, their employers, and their girls. I was reading at that time a volume by Andreyev, published I think by Knopf; for those were the days, in the early part of this century, when translations from the Russian, more than any other books, were influencing the unperverted taste of the American public. Sologub's *Little Demon* and *The Breaking Point* by Artzibasheff, I particularly remember, for I depended very much upon fiction in those days and was wont to read romance after romance. I recall well how when I had exhausted these Russians and had read the Polish *Homo Sapiens* and the

German *Song of Songs*, both, I fancy, published by Huebsch, there was nothing else in any of the bookshops or any of the railway-counters of the least interest. I used to wander desolately between the book tables of these shops, and never find anything I cared to read! I well recall to what profane lengths I was driven in Chicago by sheer miserable necessity.

Then, all of a sudden, came a great influx of semi-autobiographical novels out of England. *Of Human Bondage* appeared and *Sinister Street* and *Carnival*, and *Jacob Stahl*, and *Clayhanger*, and the *Stucco House* and *Fortitude*, and *The Man of Property*, and *Demetrius Road*. And very soon after this—miracle of miracles!—the yearly appearance began of one or other of Conrad's romances. But it was the Russians more than anything else—more I think than even Mr. Mencken or Mr. Cabell—for Dreiser had a long while yet to wait for *his* mighty influence to begin its march—who really broke up the rural simplicity of American taste at the turn of the century.

The recondite art, sublime in its devoted remoteness from the vulgar, of Henry James, never seemed to reach the bookshops at all! I recollect searching steadily once, in the first decade of the present century, and this, you must remember, was *after* the publication of *The Wings of the Dove* and *The Ambassadors*, through every single bookshop in the city of Baltimore, *and all in vain*. The finest quintessence of Henry James's genius appeared, I always think, in that you might call his *middle* style, that is in the five years *before* 1900 and in the five years *after* that date; but if these volumes were not to be found in Baltimore they were hardly likely to be picked up in Omaha, or Iowa City, or Denver, or Fargo, or Needles, or Joplin, or San Antonio.

But to return to the Claypool Hotel. This was an occasion when other nerves than those in my duodenum began to twitch. On this occasion I can well recall how all the grey madness of decomposition moaning to itself as it washed to and fro and "floated the measureless float," surged up around me and left me numb and inert. I didn't need the spasmodic Andreyev to throw me into cold sweats, but I do remember feeling that his tale about Judas Iscariot was not the right food for a person on the verge of some weird nervous collapse. A queer paralysis took possession of me. The air was full of nameless dread, but I could see no escape, nor could I lift a finger. I still felt this devilish quiescence, as if the life-force were draining away from my veins, when I reached Chicago, where I used always to stop at the old Stratford on Michigan Avenue.

Louis was somewhere in the city at that time, but I had not the spirit to call him up. Like an Incubus embracing a Succubus, Inert Misery and I sat cheek by jowl on the unmade bed of our room in the Hotel Stratford. Loving moments did we spend, lacing up and unlacing our boots, flattening our hooked noses against the window, staring at the grey horizon of the lake, reading the word "Gideon" upon the cover of the Black Bible, and looking at the word "Principessa" on my ancient bag, bought long ago in Verona for ten lira, which the bell-hop with sportive tact had chosen to place close to the spitoon.

But these bad moments were very rare. And would Louis have been justified, I wonder, in taking exception to one aspect of my life in these places, which certainly did make me "love it"? I refer to the fact that not only did I escape all real contact with my fellow-creatures, except in the case of a few young ladies, whose kindness may the Mother of God reward, but whenever I did come into contact with the human race it was always as *my audience* or as *my attendants!* The fact is that though for ever in trains and hotels I was really for many years largely alone, never uttering a single word except when in the company of some kind girl, or tearing my soul to bits in my "paper-chase" lectures.

In my first American visits I always used to stay with my most hospitable American friend, Mr. Robert S. Bright, the eloquent Philadelphian lawyer. Mr. Bright is a Virginian and a strong Jeffersonian; so that I imbibed from him, at a very early date, a pretty shrewd notion of how far America had seceded from her original democracy. Later, however, I lived, along with an ideal companion of my own blood, in very tall but very tiny rooms, looking out across the grassy lawn of the First Presbyterian Church, upon the lower portion of Fifth Avenue. Then there came a time when I had no fixed abode anywhere, not even in New York, and I began to "feel," as they say, "the draught"; but this was ended when I found myself established, along with two other children of my father, in rooms looking out on the Theological College in what is called the Chelsea district of the city.

I have often lived in the district known as "Greenwich Village" but I never really—any more than Llewelyn did— shared the Bohemian life of that Latin Quarter of New York. Where I lived what really *was* a Bohemian life was in Chicago. Chicago became my headquarters for some four or five months in certain successive years; and here I had rooms alongside of my famous compatriot, Maurice Browne, and the bulk of his Little Theatre company. This was a very happy and a very exciting epoch in my life. I was constantly travelling to Kansas City and other places—Davenport, Iowa, among them—but I spent long enough in Chicago to become the only privileged outsider in this remarkable Little Theatre group. Maurice Browne became my intimate friend, and my Impressario too, for he used to trick out his Little Theatre in the Fine Art Building with consummate skill for my orations *and according to my subject*, and as he himself chose these subjects, they were sufficiently startling; and here, for the one and only time in my life, I was destined to play the Intellectual Pierrot against an appropriate *Yellow-Book* background. And I enjoyed all this. I felt, under Maurice's influence, like a gravely comic character in Wilhelm Meister! I felt as if I had become a privileged Initiate in some heavenly Alsatia, some Thelemic Cloister of Art, where the ritualistic and symbolic elements in my performances, that had hitherto only been recognized by the devoted instinct of Nuns and Communists met with a subtle æsthetic response. I've never been more like an inspired Pantaloon, in a setting designed by Aubrey Beardsley, and a Libretto composed by Ernest Dowson, than I was then; and here, while against some background put up by Raymond Jonson I interpreted such writers as Wilde and Verlaine and Heine and Blake and Walter Pater, I danced my dance before dancers, and played my acts before actors.

How well I can now see Maurice's expressive physiognomy

quivering with vibrant reciprocity as it responded to my sallies, until, like a holy stag in a mediæval tapestry when the wind shakes the arras, he would toss his Mephistophelean baton into the air and dissolve the enchantment he had called up.

But think what an oasis it was in my lecturing life—and with no shred of responsibility either, for poor Maurice had to do all the worrying—when I could sit for hours at their rehearsals in this secluded place, like a centaur drunk with berry-juice in a fairy-ring, looking, and you may believe I did not weary of these vigils, at the lithe and lissom figures of Maurice Browne's young ladies, as they practised the chorus of some unending play, perhaps of Euripides, perhaps of Yeats, perhaps of Maurice himself. How these devoted young women used to work! And how Maurice Browne, his vivid features convulsed with æsthetic passion, would skip up to the stage in a frenzy of excitement and then rush back again to his seat, where he would sit crouching, sphinx-like and glowering, with an expression like that of Kubla Khan, when, between "sunny dome" and "caves of ice," he heard the "ancestral voices."

Most of the young ladies of the Chicago Little Theatre married—for you can believe how pretty they were!—and ceased to be nymphs and fairies and Trojan women; but, as I followed their lives and the lives of others like them, it was borne in upon me that the particular and special charm of American woman—this aristocracy of America—springs from the fact that they *create themselves*. Yes, these young people choose, select, design, plan, sketch, execute, and finally clothe, in this bewitching flesh and blood of their own invention, some private and quite original idea of what it would be exciting for a girl to be.

All Maurice had to do to supply his Little Theatre with novices was to go out "into the by-ways and hedges"; in plain words into the buses and trolley-cars. All American girls are potential actresses. They can "make themselves up" for any mortal rôle on earth, from that of a Grand Duchess to that of a strolling gipsy. They actually decide upon what kind of accent and intonation they fancy will suit them best; and having decided on one that matches, let us say, their eyes and their hair, or the droop of their head, or the slenderness of their waist, or the warm depth of their bosom, they just *invent it* and then practise it till they are perfect in it. And this really is what they do with their whole character, their tastes, their tricks of manner, their ways of behaviour. All American women are, in fact, *made and not born.*

But since the essential being of women and their inmost nature cannot be altogether made over, cannot be made *not to be feminine,* a most charming and piquant situation arises, which is—or at any rate has proved to be to me—peculiarly provocative. The delicate arrest we get when women dress up like boys, a transformation that has always been singularly appealing, undergoes in this case a kind of spiritual sublimation. American women, in other words, "dress up like boys" in their souls! Thus while they carry by necessity their feminine nature about with them, the contrast between it and the brave mental bravura, the "doublet and hose" of their self-creation, has a disarming awkwardness far more appealing than any possible masquerade of ordinary women.

Women of other countries let their womanliness alone. They refuse to meddle with it. But American women are meddling with it all the time; and though they cannot, as I say, make it *not to be feminine,* they are for ever putting it into situations where its own feeling of strangeness gives it a special appeal. It is not so much that American women carry the harem with them while they play their open-air boy's rôle, or their intellectual student rôle, though I *have* heard them accused of just that. It is much more as if they were constantly saying to their lovers:

"It's amusing, isn't it, what we women are like? But it's much nicer being a woman than you guess!"

But American women were my luxury, my holiday, my rarely enjoyed oasis. As I have hinted, my real message was to the oddities and queer ones and half-mad ones with whom I was always making friends. These were my inevitable cronies, my natural camerados, my instinctive affinities among the tribes of men. The deepest emotion I have is my malice against the well-constituted as compared with the ill-constituted. Dwarfs, morons, idiots, imbeciles, hunchbacks, degenerates, perverts, paranoiacs, neurasthenics, every type of individual upon whom the world looked down, I loved, respected, admired, reverenced, *and imitated*.

I expect I still think of that well-constituted torturer, in the dormitory below ours at Wildman's, and of his ill-constituted victim. That bully was a strong, handsome, brave fellow, "a fine, clean, up-standing youth," his victim was weak, timid, and anything but striking in appearance; and every night we used to hear it going on. Do you think I'll ever cease to pray that somehow, somewhere, there may be a punishment for such things? I tell you if they "know not what they do" it only makes their crime the worse.

Well, at any rate my own particular kind of pity has turned, because of long suppression, and because I have never exercised my formidable fingers on a fellow of this type, into what undoubtedly is the noblest emotion I possess, a prophetic anger against all scientists who vivisect dogs, all Southerners who lynch negroes, and all men and women who ill-use children. And I think I am a more dangerous enemy than is usually realized. As I tell you, without my *consciously* doing anything about it, there's not a bully-boy who has ever crossed my path who has not come to serious grief!

And I have a curious power too of identifying myself with those morons, these idiots, these imbeciles, these degenerates, against whose bare faces, as I used to observe in my favourite shows, the well-constituted pressed their hands; so that it may be that as I go through the world I really do possess a curious "evil eye" for those who torment these "little ones." I sometimes think that, as in Dostoievsky's case, a sublimated sadistic tendency is an organ of insight of which the oppressor may well beware! O ye cohorts of queer ones, of "half-born" and "funny" ones, ye whose secret endurances I alone know, I shall not soon forget you! There are so many of you in America; and you suffer all the worse because there are no groups, no classes, no barriers to protect you from the brutality of the normal. But if I have had ere now any occult potency in the avenging of my own wrongs may I have the same, and much more, in the avenging of yours!

It can easily be believed in my wanderings through America that I took good care to have time to go for a walk of some sort every day. Yes, I have "gone for walks" in every state in the Union except those of South Dakota, Arizona, Nevada, Wyoming, Washington and Utah! I lived for half a year in Hollywood, not I can assure you, in connection with the Movies, but because I was lecturing in Los Angeles and wanted to live in the country. The hills near Hollywood exactly suited me for walking; and I found an incredibly cheap hotel there, and an excellent little teashop. I also had tea in the famous studio, while he was directing and rehearsing "The Pilgrim," with none other than Charlie Chaplin himself.

Most eloquently did this great genius describe to me a certain ideal performance, at once profoundly humorous and profoundly tragic, that at intervals kept teasing his imagination. He was dressed, when we had this conversation, in his most characteristic make-up, and I noted how unbelievably beautiful his hands were! After I had listened to him for a while, his brother went out and came back with a tea-tray; and, except in one solitary case, I can tell you this was the only really *thin* bread-and-butter I ever had in America.

My hotels, of course, were often in the very centre of their cities, and so I was frequently pretty exhausted—for I never would take trolleys—by the time I returned from these walks. But such was my power of enjoying the most delapidated specimens of grass, or moss, or plants, or trees, or shrubs, or old walls, or vistas of roadway, or bridges over rivers, or wharf-sides, or tow-paths, or cobble-stones, or stables, or chimneys with smoke coming out of them, that I often used, after my fashion, to be really quite happy as I explored the most unpromising environs. I was, of course, laying up for myself a rich treasury of sharply cut sensuous images, fragmentary vignettes of the inanimate, essences of the past, that would grow the more rich and the more magical, the longer they lay in the sepulchre of my mind, till the time came for their resurrection.

As you can imagine I had my favourite cities, my favourite hotels, and my favourite walks. Of all the towns I visited it is, I think, Springfield, Ohio that comes back to me with the kindest aura of memory, though I went to no show there, and made love to no woman there. But I went to the cemetery by that pleasant river and made love to its dead; and I let my soul drift off, far off, till of those peaceful Ohio pastures I built an airy causeway of suggestion, across which I could call up my memories and intimations, so that the tow-paths and hazel spinneys and cattle sheds and toll-pikes of my own land mingled with white-washed houses and sun-bathed damask roses and huge red barns of these Ohio farms. It was at the Bancroft Hotel that I used to stay when I was in Springfield and I can recall every step of the road I used to follow to get out into the fields. Fargo, North Dakota, was another place where I enjoyed myself and where I was able very quickly to escape from the town.

And then how vividly I remember my long visits to the two chief college towns of Oklahoma! They treated me in both these places with peculiar consideration and I came to know extraordinarily well the cries of those plaintive birds called "kill-deer," and the heavenly green of the rustling cotton-trees that grew along the yellow streams with their blood-red banks. Lancaster, Pennsylvania, too I shall never, never forget. I feel a curious tenderness whenever I think of the Women's Club there, a club called "The Iris Club," where they allowed me to lecture on Hegel and Spinoza and Schopenhauer, in spite of the fact that they were nearly all the wives and the mothers of professors in a learned College. Nor did those kind "Iris Club" women ever protest, though my lectures always went on for an hour and a half.

I often found it *impossible to stop.* That was my worst fault as a lecturer. I used to *try* to stop; and even begin my peroration; but something, some delicate nuance, some metaphysical nicety, would come sliding into my brain, and I would go whirling on again in my spiral dance, like that mad storm god in Hiawatha. There were even times when I would lecture without a pause and in a constant mounting crescendo for no

less than two hours! Cagliostro as I was, it seemed beyond
even my juggler's art to bowl Hegel out in the wretched
sixty minutes usually allotted to lecturers.

As far as the architecture of American towns went I had a
particular fondness for that in New York State. Not the faintest
intimation did I have that a time would come when I should
settle down for five quiet years in New York State, for I took
it for granted that my destiny was to go on lecturing till I
died. But I got to know Utica and Troy and Syracuse and
Albany so especially well. I was calmly and quietly happy in
these gracious Dutch places. I derived a sensuous satisfaction,
difficult to describe, from the very unevenness, brought about
no doubt by the mellowing influences of time, of the bricks
in those old pavements. Mellow brick paths seemed to be
perpetually leading up and down hills but always above them
hung enormous branches of historic trees, looking even older
than the bricks, branches that, as they rested upon that sunlit
air, seemed for ever waiting for the return of their proud Van
Rensaeller "Patroons," and meanwhile lying back, as those
dignified old Dutchmen did, upon grave and statesman-like
speculations!

I lectured many times in New Orleans and used to walk,
till I was worn out, up and down those unique old streets, with
their fairy-story courtyards, wrought-iron trellis work,
romantic balconies, and Spanish-looking casements. I got an
entrance somehow into one real Creole garden—the only
really "enclosed" garden I have ever seen—and you can
believe how it satisfied my craving for continuity in this
dynamic land when the elegant old ladies who lived there
gravely and discreetly encouraged me to "bow and scrape,"
as my father would have called it, before the holy images among
their fantastic flower-beds, and finally confided in me that they
had never, in the whole of their long lives, crossed the broad
street that separates old New Orleans from the modern town.
It would sound more appropriate in this chronicle of my life
if I could assure you that I always left New Orleans with reluctance. But the truth is I always left it with alacrity and relief!
Why was this? Well! I will tell you. To me to whom the worst

devils that dwell in mortal nerves are not unknown it was enough to hear one single story of *what was possible* where the institution of slavery was unchallenged, to make me feel I were better in Kansas City, in Denver, in Des Moines, in Omaha, than in this lovely hot-house of ambiguous legends.

My roguish manager Arnold would be always announcing to me, "John, I've got a mean jump for you *now!*" and one of the very worst of these jaunty trips was when he acquired the habit of sending me into Canada. I forget where it was, but I can vividly recall a certain wayside junction where, from midnight till two or three, I used every week to lie stretched out on a bench. Canada and the Canadians puzzled me. I do not yet understand them. They are certainly very different from Americans. Perhaps they *are* "more English than the English." If so, I can understand my difficulty in "getting," as Americans say, "their number"; for what might be called *extremely English* persons have always puzzled me. I feel no hostility towards them. I don't think I feel rebellion against them. I am only superficially afraid of them. But there it is! They remain baffling and mysterious to me.

I certainly have derived immense satisfaction from prowling round the walls of the convents in Montreal. What queer feelings of attraction, pity, dismay, I used to experience towards these harmless dedicated persons! The fact is I have a mania for nuns. It is true that I instinctively revere all priests—for I always feel a romantic and superstitious tremor of credulity in the presence of what, after all, *may* be a definite creative magnetism, evoked by the anonymous intention of generations of human faith. But towards any nun I feel an emotion that combines superstitious reverence with something else. This "something else" is not, as my clever psycho-analytical friends will at once jump to the conclusion it is, a tremor of convoluted sadism. I believe it is connected very intimately with what the ancients felt for Demeter and Persephone.

Just as the mystery of femininity is carried by most American women with a certain charming awkwardness as if they were girls, dressed up as boys, so, in the case of nuns, while they remain women in one sense, they are women who have passed through such a desperate ordeal that their nature has undergone some subtle change. No, it does not excite any sadistic feeling in me. It excites awe and terror. I would think it my duty to exert all the influence I had to stop a daughter of mine from becoming a nun. And yet I have an odd feeling that I should very quickly, if I saw much of any nun, kneel on the ground before her, put my horny forehead against her knees, and howl like a hypnotized wolf!

And what would have been my feelings in those days, if, by some mad chance, I *had*, really and truly, sobbed my heart out at the knees of a Montreal nun! I think this woman would have become for me—I speak with all reverence—exactly as if she had been Demeter herself sitting by the wayside. I mean that here would have been a woman, a woman who *could* have borne children, but whose unborn Persephone has become instead an embodiment of the Mystery of Death. She has gone through, this woman, such a tragic ordeal, that no normal birth-pangs are anything to what she has endured.

Well! there it is. As William Blake say, "*Bless* relaxes; *Damn* braces"; and it probably would do me no harm at all to have a friend like Louis Wilkinson always hidden in the bushes when I am at the knees of Demeter. My love of truth however compels me to set this down that something desperate in both their fates, something rendered chaste by a terrifying ordeal full of what Unamuno calls "The tragic sense of life," brings close together for me the fate of a woman who belongs to all men and the fate of one who belongs to God alone. But I am not only a devotee—though afar off—of nuns and harlots.

There is yet another class of childless woman to whom I feel unbounded reverence and attraction. I refer to those rare and sensitive Beings usually called Old Maids. I could very happily spend my days, and nights too, with an Old Maid. I understand them through and through and they understand me through and through! Old maids always confide in me and trust me; and although I do not wholly and in a literal sense tell them *everything*, I tell them much more than my friend Louis would regard as conceivable, or, if conceivable, as either "indicated" or discreet.

M M

I am not indulging in any spasm of vanity nor am I deluded by any fixed idea of conceit, when I say that there has never been before and never will be again any self-revelation as passionate and dramatic as my lectures up and down America soon became under the encouragement of Arnold Shaw. I gave vent to all my feelings, all my prejudices, all my instincts, intuitions, clairvoyances, adorations and loathings. Optimists of every sort came in for my subtlest and most serpentine disparagements! I have myself become something of a battered Pangloss since that time; but it is a Pangloss *who has seen what he has seen*, and has only acquired in his old age the trick of "cultivating his garden."

My intermittent stabs at the abominable wickedness of vivisection were, let us hope, not less effective for their spasmodic delivery or from the fact that I always listen politely to the talk—diplomatically adopted to laymen—that these crafty torturers indulge in about anæsthetics. In the same way I trust that my contempt for the shallowness of moralists was not rendered futile by my distrust of psychoanalytical psychiatry. My whole art of self-expression in lecturing was as a matter of fact based upon a certain kind of mental independence, an independence which I was always desperately trying to convey to others, for I regarded it—and do still regard it—as one of the most important elements in human happiness and by no means exclusive of the devotion of a scholar to the Past.

This cosmic pride of mine—you can call it "comic" if you like, but mine will be the last laugh in our altercation—implied a mental process by which I thought of my "ego," the inmost "self" within me, as independent of the accident of being born a man, or of being born a man upon this earth! To look at human life with the eyes of a stranger, as if I had suddenly been projected out of space—as indeed in a sense I had—into this particular society, was the attitude which I sought to assume as my final spiritual refuge; for this and this only could offer me a real escape from all the teasing frets and fevers, all the worrying envies and jealousies and competitions and comparisons, of the ambitions of the world.

The curious thing was that I derived renewed strength,

vitality, magnetism, electric force, and even some kind of mysterious planetary energy, by giving a lecture. Instead of being vampirized by my audience, I vampirized *them*. I was always in my highest spirits after a lecture, especially after one before a *mixed audience*, for in this way I renewed my life-sap by drinking the blood, and I do not speak altogether figuratively, of older men and women as well as of young men and young women!

Just as if I had been one of Mr. Charles Fort's disconcerting cosmic visitors, what really paid me for lecturing was not the fees I shared with Arnold, but the actual *sensation* I got from it and the life-energy I imbibed from it. Such sucking up of crowd-magnetism I found to be one of the most marvellous of human restoratives. When I stopped, after lecturing for an hour and a half, or even sometimes for two hours, I felt light, airy, frivolous, gay and butterfly-like; whereas my audience were so wilted, so drooping, so exhausted, so wrung-out, that they were like people who had spent a night of the extremest form of erotic debauch! As a matter of fact I used sometimes to come to the lecture-hall absolutely exhausted. I had been, let us say, for one of my long walks into the environs of the town, hunting for those natural objects whose society I generally preferred to that of my own race, and I had probably stopped *pro tem.* the hurting of my ulcers with tea and toast and guava jelly. At such times I used to squat down on anything that was available behind the stage and proceed with deliberate Tibetan craft to make my mind a blank. This I generally had no difficulty in doing, and with my mind in this condition I could sink and sink into I know not what fathomless depths of sub-Being. Then, when the appearance of my chairman broke in on my repose, I would implore the good man to make a long speech.

But American chairmen, from my experience of twenty years, are the most laconic of all chairmen. An airy allusion to some story about a negro, an even airier allusion to a similar story about an Irishman, a list of the lecturer's works, in the compilation of which a daughter's book-learning had clearly been called upon, and the good man, as a general rule, made haste to hurry down from the platform. But in pleading whispers I would beg him to prolong his speech, not out of any wish to be praised, not in order that I should have time to observe the audience, though I did, I confess, sometimes glance hurriedly over it, in search of some exciting young man or young woman, not, least of all, to think about my subject, for *that* I always left till the Lord should tell me what I should say, but solely that I might go on practising, even on the platform itself, my restorative trick of sinking to the bottom of the world.

If the chairman was unselfish—and he often was—I could return from Nonentity, or from the condition of the Inanimate, in good time to stretch myself out and lick my lips like a cat at the milkman's knock, and feel a thrill of sensual satisfaction in the presence of the great reservoir of human magnetism into which I was now going to dip my ladle!

This sounds as if, in the detachment of my misanthropy, I really was becoming a monster, a kind of were-wolf; but to counter this sinister impression you must remember that not a day passed but—as a boy-scout vows to do—I used to put myself out to try to enhance the well-being of *some* poor sentient devil. The happier I was in my erotic vice the more burdens of this sort I laid on myself. Lucky, yea! thrice lucky, were all the beggars who encountered this obsessed philanthropist, as he hurried along, far too agitated to care what he had for lunch, on his way from his hotel to the burlesque show!

I was reading Dostoievsky in these days; and with the exception of Dorothy Richardson I feel that I owe a greater debt to Constance Garnett than to any other woman writer of our time. Her translations of Dostoievsky are superb, just what I feel translations from the Russian should be; that is to say they do *not* attempt the silly and vain task of substituting *our* ways of speech for that of the extraordinary people of these books; but they allow the English words to retain, hovering about them, something that is strange and stiff and queer and *foreign*, so that, even in their English disguise, you can still smell the original Russian. I need hardly say that I regard Dostoievsky as being as much greater than *all* other novelists as Shakespeare is greater than all other dramatists. This extraordinary man's passionate sounding of all the neurotic abysses of the human heart not only goes infinitely deeper than that of the cleverest psychiatrists of our day, but as an imaginative artist he seems to me to surpass all the rest.

Whenever I got the chance I felt it was "laid upon me" to lecture on Dostoievsky; though, of course, in doing so I had to make of my spirit a sort of desperate goose-quill wherewith to write on the bodiless air. But often, as you can guess, I would be enormously relieved when some particular audience asked to have a discourse on Tennyson, or Carlyle, or Ruskin, or Emerson! If they *let me choose* I felt it was only due to the "funny ones" in my audience to choose Dostoievsky; but I never deviated from what the audience chose, even if it were an author not as yet on my printed list. Nor must you assume that my audience *always* sat patient and passive while I played my tricks upon them! There were very often persons present who smelt the fox, or, if you like, the wolf from another planet, and became bristly and snarling. I think it has always been "one up for me," in my method of lecturing, that I managed to divide my audiences into two opposite camps, one of agitated lovers, and one of implacable enemies.

I was at Youngstown once when I was lecturing on Dostoievsky and I stirred up a fine row. Never again was I invited there.

You have already understood, I expect, that from the start I was sympathetic to the Bolsheviki? I recall lecturing at Clinton, in Massachusetts, at the very moment when the Bolsheviki were struggling for supreme power, with their cry, "The Soviets!" and I soon felt that I was dividing *that* audience into two beautifully hostile camps. This arousing of conflicting currents of psychic chemistry in my silent "reservoirs of magnetism" was never, as you may suppose, displeasing to my misanthropic guile. But I did, quite seriously, sympathize with the Bolsheviki, sympathize instinctively and honestly with them; and so, when I gratified my Jacobin instincts, by annoying instead of propitiating the "magnates," my attitude was an honest one though it did incidentally gratify my personal spleen.

But I suppose my temperament is really that of a Jacobin, a Jacobin influenced by Jean Jacques Rousseau, and with not a few anarchistic leanings, rather than that of an orthodox Marxist. All the same I certainly do feel that all we artists and poets and novelists and philosophers and play-actors are crafty parasites, just as the bankers are, upon those who work with their hands, and that *only those who do work with their hands* can possibly hope to have a perfectly clear conscience in this bitter world.

But it was an exciting night, that night at Youngstown. What upset these good people was not any revolutionary attitude in me, but my obstinate persistence—even in Youngstown —in trying to be a mediæval saint! Dostoievsky that night worked like a firebrand upon all the dangerous explosive in my nature. The black flame in Dostoievsky's dead and buried eyes burst out, demonic and angelic, between the furnaces of Youngstown, and blew this poor audience sky-high.

Feeling from head to foot a curious trembling, and making little movements with my shoulders just as my father used to do, I began to tell these people that most characteristic of all his shorter tales, the one that in the French translation is entitled *L'Esprit Souterrain*. It is about a young man who with terrible eloquence changes the heart of a prostitute, and then turns wickedly upon her, only to call her back at the last when she leaves him in disgust, not however calling after her as loudly as he *could* have done. In no story of equal brevity does Dostoievsky sound so tragically the perversity at the bottom of our troubled hearts. I think it was the first time that these busy employers of foreign labour and their hard-working wives had ever had the lid taken off from the terrors of our human soul, and that this should have been done to them in a "worth-while programme" as they must have regarded this discourse of the man in the "Oxford gown," made them feel betrayed. In place of the "worth-while," behold! they were being pushed towards a cranny in the floor out of which came sulphur and brimstone!

There was a tremendous hullaballoo. The lady who was responsible for the coming to town of this wolf in sheep's clothing burst into indignant tears. I have found in America that while you can jeer at Omnipotence with perfect impunity, it is very dangerous even so much as to make use of the word "prostitute." One of the prominent local clergymen there, I think he was a Presbyterian, rose from his seat in the front row and austerely withdrew, not however without banging the door behind him as an aggrieved child might have done.

If I have any psychic power at all it is a power of melting God and the Devil into One person, and then of letting this person loose and making Him run amok among moralists. As I have already hinted, the protean fluidity of my nature is such that I could give myself up so completely to the author I was analysing that I *became that author*. This was agreeable to my audience when the author was Ruskin or Tennyson; but it was disagreeable when it was Swift or James Joyce.

I think myself that my best lectures were on the Tragedies of Shakespeare; for in these I could indulge to the limit my actor's vein *and yet* be dealing with what Nietzsche calls "first and last things." I fancy I often caught, in my emphasis upon the tragic gibberish that Shakespeare loves so well something of that emotional-sardonic rattling of the tin cans of the world's rubbish-heap that you get in T. S. Eliot's *Wasteland*. The truth is the lecture-platform to me was always a return to my real essential self after tiresome practical debouchings and after hypocritical encounters with acquaintances and friends. One day I hope to lecture "for love," every Sunday, in some available barn or chapel, to which misfits and "funny ones," persecuted by normal civilization, can make their cockle-shell pilgrimage over hill and dale.

My respectful awe in the presence of Communism is due to two quite personal things: first to my conviction that I am a parasite upon those who labour with their hands, and second to the miserable incompetence I display whenever I try to use my hands myself! Yes, the platform has been everything to me. It has been the bed of my erotic joys. It has been the battlefield of my fiercest struggles. It has been the gibbet of my execution. It has been the post of my scourging. It has been my throne. It has been my close-stool. It has been my grave. It has been my resurrection. On the platform I have expressed by a whisper, by a silence, by a gesture, by a bow, by a leer, by a leap, by a skip, by the howl of a wolf, by the scream of a woman in travail, certain inspirations concerning the secrets of life that, without any vain boasting, I do not think have been expressed very often in this world.

My enemies, and those worse than enemies, my patronizing admirers, who are even now skimming this excitable work, will doubtless affix many semi-scientific labels to my aberrations, have indeed probably already rushed to their psychopathic text-books to find out what I can possibly be up to, when I refer to my power of experiencing the emotions of women and girls. But the more I soak myself in the work of Shakespeare and Dostoievsky the more I recognize that both these men have the magic power of *becoming women*. *That* is the point. *That* is where the intelligencies of our modern critics are so dull. They do not understand what the meaning of the word "Imagination" is.

But it was not only into women I could transform myself when the old Druidic spirit, the spirit of Taliessin of the many incarnations, took possession of me! I could become inanimate objects. I could feel myself into the lonely identity of a pier-post, of a tree-stump, of a monolith in a stone-circle; and when I did this I *looked* like this post, this stump, this stone.

My "lecturing" really was—only there were so few who heard me that had the wit to grasp such subtleties—a sort of focussing, through one single twisting, leaping, shuffling, skipping, bowing and scraping human figure, of some special comic-tragic vein in the planetary consciousness. But when I say there were few who caught the importance of what I did, these few, I am proud to say, were personalities to conjure with. Both Dreiser and Masters always recognized me for what I was. From those great men, each after his own peculiar fashion, I drank up all the glory I needed. Isadora Duncan too "got my number," even as I most assuredly got hers! Maurice Browne was like a cousin to me. We knew each other just as cousins know each other, understanding each other in many cases only too well; but always finding it a little difficult to get the exact focus about each other or to see each other in that proper and perfect proportion in which we shall both appear one day before the Judgment Seat of God.

Between Colonel C. E. S. Wood and myself there was something of the same mixture of solid affection mingled with temperamental reservations as might have existed between a touchy nephew and a formidable uncle, only in the case of this remarkable old man our relations were complicated by the fact that he was so much more in a position to help me than I was in a position to do anything for him. We were, as I have often told him, like Zarathrustra's eagle and serpent—I of course being the latter. He used to dominate me, for my good, by his formidable blue eye; and then, when I dodged and wavered and hummed-and-hawed and evaded and turned into vapour, he would suddenly say:

"John, what *is* it? What *is* the matter with you?"

But of course "the matter" simply was that I was feeling as Proteus felt when he was clutched tight, through all his transformations, by yellow-haired Menalaus. The truth is I didn't like being influenced, no! not by the noblest and dearest. No, I have never liked being held, not even by the wisest and most affectionate of human hands. I am like the wind. I have to blow *where I list*. Perhaps this is one of my feminine characteristics. Or is it the devil in me and pure misanthropic malice? I don't know what it is; but at a hint of being held down to *any* course of action—off I sheer, with a cry like the cry of the cuckoo.

Colonel Wood and Llewelyn between them got me to decide to try a new and a feminine manager on the Pacific Coast and to give Arnold the go-by. Maurice Browne was "on the Coast" at that time and he had authority of some sort and in connection with my new manager over an enormous theatre. I was full of eagerness to write a play for this theatre, since it was entirely in the control of my personal friends, and I did compose a tragic and rather Strindberg-like play about Chesil Beach which I entitled *Paddock Calls*. This play was actually advertised as "soon to appear" but it was never even rehearsed; and since then I have sheered away more than ever from the stage. It was not long, as you may believe, in those Pacific days, before I began to pine for Arnold Shaw. I longed to be back

again on my own private "stages," namely the familiar platforms of Cooper Union and Labour Temple. But I am anticipating; for it was war-time now and when *Poetry* accepted
a poem of mine—and I herewith beg Miss Monroe's leave to
quote a little of it—it appeared among sorrowful requiems to
dead soldiers. It will show you, reader, that I had not changed
my imagery very much, or the instinctive bias of my supernatural cogitations, since I wrote about that Demon of Corfe
Castle when I was ten years old.

> "The hope I hold
>   The leering demon-days
>   Deride, and reason plays,
>   Snug as a raven on a gallows tree
>   Its ancient game with me,
>   Flapping its wings and lewdly gibbering
>   'Life is a humorous thing!'
>   But on I fare, clutching——
>   It is not gold,
>   The hope I hold.
>
> "The hope I hold
>   Nature herself with glee
>   Derides. And destiny
>   With evil goblin laughter indicates
>   The adamantine gates,
>   And with a maniac-chuckle rallies me,
>   'That way is closed, you see!'
>   But I fare on, clutching——
>   It is not gold,
>   The hope I hold.
>
> "O hope, whose face in madness I have kissed,
>   O hope, that art a mirage and a mist,
>   Shall I destroy thee now, and laugh thereat?——
>   It is too late for that."

Before I got away, however, from this alien Pacific, back to
my more familiar Atlantic, I chanced to give, in this same
monstrous theatre—and really it was of prodigious size—a
morning lecture on Strindberg which turned out, totally

against my wish, to be the best lecture I have ever given in my whole life. There were, I think, ten to fifteen persons present; while a couple of theatrical retainers whose echoing footsteps sounded like those of aged pew-openers in an empty cathedral creaked about in the rear of the vast enclosure.

But the mere fact that I was "up against it," the mere fact that I was reacting in my heart against "the Coast," the mere fact that I was secretly pining, in this grand foreign edifice, for the dear, delapidated "John's-a-Fizzle" circus, stirred up within me that formidable daimon which, as I have hinted to you before, *can* be reached somewhere in my nature, and which when it *is* reached has the Devil's own force. Absent-mindedly I looked at those ten devoted society women sitting alone in the stalls and at the immeasurable space above their heads, rising and rising tier above tier, gallery above gallery and I became aware, more vividly aware than I had ever been, that the secret of life consists in sharing the madness of God. By sharing the madness of God I mean the power of rousing a peculiar exultation in yourself as you confront the Inanimate, an exultation which is really a cosmic eroticism, however much the Prince of this World may deride it, for it means the finding of "the eternal feminine" in Matter itself.

But whatever effect it may have been that this vast empty theatre had upon me, I was allowed by my daimon to become Strindberg as completely as any critic has ever become any author. And for some reason it seemed to suit this resuscitated Strindberg to tower up there above those ten society women like a gigantic Loki. Perhaps he was prophesying a crack in the System of Things and the emergence, as we swept forward towards the constellation of Hercules, of new dragon-slayers as well as of new sea-serpents.

It is quaint to think how impossible it was for me actually to make friends with one of the chorus-girls in those burlesque shows. But if it had *not* been so, if I had been a little less of a helpless bookworm in such matters, how I would have liked to hear from the lips of such an one exactly what it really felt like to be gazed at as I used to gaze at these delicious beings. It is a curious thing to say, but I have a shrewd idea that such a girl would understand far better than any man—except perhaps a village idiot if he could speak—what a mysterious Grail, though I suppose I must say a *heathen* Grail, her unequalled form was, as it rested for a moment in her dancing and suffered my soul to swirl and eddy about it, like the sea-tide about a marble column.

Well, I had had many happy days with Llewelyn on the Pacific, and it was by the side of this far-off ocean that he finally gathered his forces together in a drastic decision to earn his living as a writer in New York. No one who does not know him as I know him can have the remotest notion of the nobility and unconquerable charm of Llewelyn's personality. Most of us are made up of so many conflicting and widely separated passions that we are often a distressing and displeasing spectacle as these forces obsess us. It is not only my own violent anti-narcissism that makes the contemplation of my life often so extremely disagreeable to me. It is the fact that my life *has* been, over and over again, though redeemed by its crazy draggle-tailed intensity, decidedly un-æsthetic. But Llewelyn's life has been sound throughout, clean to the kernel, like a good hazel-nut. When he sways in the wind, he sways altogether! You can sharpen your teeth upon him *and no harm done*. You can taste him, and he is firm and sweet to the core. We all seem to have some maggot in the head except Llewelyn! But it looks as if the little white gentlemen in his lungs have brooked no psychic, no pathological rivals. No worm i' the bud from a spiritual or nervous ambush has been able to make its "bed of crimson joy" in the heart of this fifth son of my father.

And, what is more, he has the power to throw his genius into his life, into his least word! Theodore can do this too. I look at them both with wonder. All that I, "brother John the evil one," seem capable of is an alternate response, like a reed shaken by the wind, to obsessions by good and evil spirits. Theodore and Llewelyn seem made of solid wood, one of blackthorn, one of hawthorn, whereas I feel as if the invisible powers had squeezed all the pith out of me—the bitter elder-pith—so that they might be able to blow long eldritch calls to one another from Deep to Deep. And when they're *not* doing that—welll you have seen the weak, brittle, trampled, hedge-gap appearance of a torn elder-bough!

You must remember, that between the age of forty and of fifty-five, as I went about America, it was incumbent upon me to reconcile myself as best I might to the fact that Llewelyn stood, as a writer, as much higher than I did, with competent judges in America, as Theodore stood with competent judges in England. They were both recognized authors while I was still "John, the Talker." How well I recall the puzzled and commiserating expression upon my brother Littleton's face as we spoke of this once in those Angmering Woods at Burpham when the bluebells were out. He looked frowningly at the blue-bells, frowningly at the pink campions, frowningly at the wood-orchids. He allowed a chiff-chaff to repeat its name unheeded. He let what might have been a wood-argus flutter by. "But ——" he murmured; and in that "but" were all those old study-days at school when he did my Greek verses for me at Wildman's! The truth is it had been not a little difficult for Littleton to get into his head how inferior to what Theodore and Llewelyn could show of real originality and striking style my windy "art of dithyrambic analysis" was, *when it was written down!*

It was lucky for me perhaps during those years, when Theodore and Llewelyn, the one in England and the other in America, had left me so far behind, that certain very personal considerations would have made it a monstrous thing if I had let myself suffer jealousy. One consideration was Theodore's self-laceration, which in itself, even if I hadn't been disarmed by his genius, would have nipt such feelings in the bud, and the other was that Llewelyn's personality was conveyed so completely to his writing that if you had enjoyed the one it was impossible to feel envious of the other. As Goethe puts it:

"Love alone overcomes our jealousy of what surpasses us."

But I don't want to make myself out *too* perfect! I well remember once hearing in a town in Iowa about a very philosophical, very gentlemanly, and very learned recluse, whose favourite writer was "Powys." I wonder if Theodore and Llewelyn have the same odd sensation when they hear or see the word "Powys," and learn that it does not refer to themselves? I think members of very few writing families feel so rarely "funny feelings" in the pits of their stomachs over the successes of the other members, as we do; but on *this* occasion, not so much that Theodore was put so high, but that, as Theodore would himself say, this fellow "turned his thumbs down so low" on me, I certainly did feel something not very nice! And my informant saw quickly enough that he had aroused my interest, for he hurriedly went on:

"He says *you* are only a milk-and-water writer. It's Theodore he likes. It's Theodore who knows what life is."

I would certainly have supposed I was enough of an admirer of my brother's genius, to accept this verdict with equanimity—but not at all! Sometimes the devil loves to cause a self-respecting philosopher to hop like a flea. There were plenty of occasions when I really was able to conquer every flicker of jealousy over the recognition, in so many revered quarters, of Theodore's genius. It would have been a sorry thing if this had not been so; for hadn't I known for years the unique value of what had lain so long stored up behind those tragic grey eyes? I had not done all I might have done; I had left undone so much—we all had—in the clearing away of obstacles from his road. It had been left to a young wayfarer from Oxford to seek him out; it had been left to the Garnet family, those fearless explorers of the Terræ Incognitæ of Genius, to make straight his path. But I had responded—as who has not among those who read?—to this new and strange vibration. "All the same for that," as Homer says, it did need no little effort on the part of my better angel to take for granted one particular triumph his gifts won over mine.

This was when I was living in Patchin Place in New York and the famous Clarence Darrow came to see me. Since Daniel Webster's, no human skull can have appeared on this continent with such "deep scars of thunder entrenched" as this singular man's. From very early days Darrow had supported me, just as Masters and Dreiser have done, though I have never been as intimate with him as with these others, his rivals, though not quite his contemporaries, for he is several years older, in the wonder and awe of my own generation of great Americans.

On several occasions he expressed himself as willing to debate with me—he and I were both pretty deadly debaters—not so much for the interest of it, as out of his desire to give a friendly lift to my back-sliding career—but neither of us felt any strong urge to the encounter; and so in the end, like Glaucus and Diomed in the Iliad, we left the religious Trojans and the sceptical Greek to the other's respective spears. This business of debating bulked often quite large in my life.

The only time I ever met Bertrand Russell was when he convinced a thousand and ten people, at a hall in New York, that the institution of Marriage had passed its zenith, as against the nine hundred and ninety who responded to my mediæval defence of the *raison d'être* of this "tragic tension." It was Will Durant though with whom I really *enjoyed* debating, true and noble philosopher as he is, and I enjoyed it just as a mischievous sharp-tongued woman, free to hit at her sweet pleasure *below the belt*, would enjoy having a tussle with the much-enduring Socrates. I have spoken of my freedom from jealous bitterness in all these clashes between rival intelligencies, but I was nothing to Durant! I have never seen, and never shall see, as long as I live, such sublime patience, or an irony so unfailingly sweet-tempered.

But to return to Darrow and Patchin Place. I naturally regarded the visit of this great Lawyer for the Defence, this smouldering and inspired Devil's Advocate, this champion of all Dogs with a Bad Name, as a high compliment, and mingled with my Boswellian respect for the man was, I have no doubt, an element of pride that I was the person thus honoured. Theodore certainly would have noted this element in the nervous agitation of his elder brother. But, after a while, not being one for what they call light conversation, Darrow asked if I wouldn't "read him something." I was on the point of explaining that my works were out of print and that just then I possessed none of them worthy of his notice, when—not exactly with a blush but with a certain burning sensation in my cheek-bones—I came to understand that it was not from *my* works that the great man wanted me to read. Indeed it soon appeared as I threw myself—heart-whole now—into my reading from *Mr. Weston's Good Wine* that this savage enemy of illusions regarded both Llewelyn and me as simply not in the running with Theodore. Here too, as in Iowa, I heard those words:

"*It's Theodore* who knows what life is!"

But on this Iowa occasion no awe for a great Advocate was there to keep my pride in its place. I expect I had been so often called by the young journalists of New York what they considered—though as a philosopher I differed from them there—as the most contemptible thing, second to a conjurer, that anyone could be, a "lecturer to ladies," that this connoisseur's milk-and-water struck a bruised spot in my secret pride. Anyway what must I do, in the middle of my lecture that night, but suddenly burst out, *à propos* of nothing,

"*Some* people call other people 'milk-and-water.' They don't realize that this is the highest praise! The Milky Way itself spouted from the breasts of Juno; and water poured forth from the side of Jesus!"

People who think that Llewelyn has nothing but praise for my ways know little about either him or me. The most merciless criticisms I have ever had have come from Llewelyn. "You are spiritually insincere," he told me once. The truth is that what he finds most difficult to tolerate in me is my trick of *living up* to my poetical mythology. By this I mean my way of behaving as if the imaginations of the ancient poets concealed more than mere subjective fancies.

A characteristic example of this difference between us has occurred only to-day when I open a letter from him, written from his Dorsetshire sick-bed and with his hurt eyesight, telling me of his impressions of my seaside tale as Alyse Gregory reads that book to him. My poor Magnus "havering" over the image of his beautiful Curly evidently strikes this bedridden Odysseus as beyond contempt: but he turns from this to animadvert in disgust at the way in *Glastonbury* I make my John kneel down at Stonehenge *and pray to the Stone*, uttering as he does so, the words:

"Please make Mary Crow happy."

The use of the word "Please" in this invocation seems

especially to annoy Llewelyn and he roundly lambasts my incorrigible John for it, calling him "a Prize Ninny." Now I am especially anxious to publish these strictures of Llewelyn's, because of the totally mistaken notion, that some of his girl-friends have spread about, that he suffers from a maudlin devotion, amounting to a "complex" for his eldest brother. *He suffers from nothing of the kind.* He loves me, but, like the Lord, he chastises the most where he loves the most. At the same time I will neither yield one jot, nor abate one tittle, of this vein of "Ninny-ism."

In the first place what is the deepest, secretest purpose of my life? I can answer categorically: "To enjoy the sensations that I like enjoying, when I am most entirely and shamelessly myself." Now I *know*, not only from looking in the looking-glass when I shave, but from certain realistic photographs, that there is an unmistakable ninny-look or zany-look in my face. This look answers to what I feel, and to what I let myself feel, and to what I maliciously encourage myself to feel! *And why not?* Why should I devote myself to feeling and expressing only noble, monumental and dignified sentiments? It is natural to Llewelyn to be dignified. It is *not* natural to me. I can be formid-able as the Devil at a pinch, and, as Louis deplores so sadly, a certain scoriated and long-suffering expression, resembling that of an actor playing Christ, often appears spontaneously on my countenance when I am alone. But why need I have laid upon my shifty, Protean, unfrocked hedge-priest shoulders the neces-sity of being dignified? You will remember how St. Paul refers to the sensuality of heathen? "It is a shame even to speak of what they do in secret." Well this, I take it, implies that certain vicious doings are not altogether dignified. But "let the galled jade wince; my withers are unwrung." Being as you know, not one for the normal rites of love, and being totally unashamed of this peculiarity, there is really hardly any aspect of my secret life that I would hesitate about revealing to the exacting Apostle.

"I too," I would tell him, "am a Pharisee and the son of a Pharisee; but if I enjoy the voluptuous sensation of making a ninny of myself, *why not?* You are not the only one, Oh great Magian, who can skip before Dionysus! Did you never read in

Euripides, a psychopath like yourself, about the soothsayer, Teiresias? And Teiresias, even among the dead, was still a prophet! You tend to put your thumb down on the Church, Llewelyn, and you think as little of Dostoievsky as of St. Paul. But I swear to you, my friend, that there were elements of the Christian madness, of this "pernicious" Christian superstition thousands and thousands and thousands of years before the historic Jesus. And deep, deep among the psychopathic elements of this wild madness lie the intoxicating sweetnesses of ninny-ism and zany-ism.

A ninny I fancy is a person who feels and looks like an undignified fool, while a zany is one who carries this peculiar cult into his *behaviour* and even makes an art of it. Cannot you see that there is a deep and subtle *irony* in all this, and a perfect awareness as to how it strikes the "daughters of Saul," when I gird up my loins and dance before the Ark, like David or Dan Leno? Cannot you see it is the profoundest of all religious gestures, and far the oldest? None of your conventional Archdeacons would dare to give themselves away to this tune, and it would horrify them to see me do it, as some have been scandalized to see the priests play ball in the cathedral of Seville. What would some quiet George Herbert, even, feel if he came upon me tapping the altar-stone of Stonehenge with my head?

But on the contrary if one of those pre-historic skulls that are named from the places where they dig them up, could rise from the dead I am sure you would behold *it* joining me in my prostrations, and using without a blush as many "pleases" as it could mutter! Don't you see there is a malicious *sub-irony* in the very use of this baby-word, breathed between my horny Neanderthal pate and the hard surface of such a stone! For God's sake let these poor Archdeacons go! Nature will right herself. *She* knows that these worthy men have to earn their living as everybody else; and she knows that you and I don't work with our hands any more than they do! Separate in your mind this wild, mad, "Christian" neurosis—which sees so deeply into certain particular secrets of life—from the transitory and conventional morals of to-day.

This ninny-ism of mine is not quite as unintelligently sentimental as it appears. As a matter of fact it is a bubble from the very abyss. It is at once an arraignment of the unsympathetic First Cause, a propitiation of the mysterious magnetic entities concealed under the mask of what we call Matter, and a malicious challenge to the parrot-like cynicism of all this pseudo-science of the modern world. It is moreover an act of the kind of "faith" which springs from a scepticism far more devastating than that of any cocksure materialism. It is the "I believe in the Incomprehensible" of the one Creed, that, in its historic continuity, links the religion of the cave-man with the religion of the philosopher. In my ninny-ism the swamp-dragon of the beginning of things protests against the shallow rationality of the hour and "swindges the scaly horrour of its foulded tail" in defence of the inexplicable. In my ninny-ism the madness of the mystics of all ages rises up, and goes "inching along like the pore inch-worm" of the Jesus-crazy negro, muttering about "still small voices" from the East and "small rain downraining" from the West.

When you get really down to the bottom of this, Llewelyn, all that I am asking is the liberty to feel what I like to feel and to express it as best I can. Is this allowed in your pagan kingdom or is it not allowed? *Not* allowed! Very well. Where then does your kingdom differ from this kingdom of this world? In being more beautiful, you say. So be it. Yours is an æsthetic tyranny, theirs a moral one; but the sweet bitch, "Fay que ce Vouldray" —if I get the old Rabelaisian French correctly—must to kennel under both your whips! The upshot of it is—here stands Powys Major, trying to give to his fellow-men, what has been attempted so often without much success, a real honest self-portrait; and if this ninny-arch of my hurriedly sketched eyebrows displeases you, and you feel you could hit it off more to the life with a Mephistophelean down-slant, so be it.

"We know what we are; but we know not what we may be."

Pondering so often upon their experiment in Russia, I often find myself playing with all sorts of conjectures as to how I should get on in that amazing country. Like that unfortunate man in *The Possessed*, who was persuaded to shoot himself to prove that his will was beyond the difference life and death, I should certainly be always drinking tea. There seems a tendency there, too, just now to do the very thing that for nearly thirty years I have been calling on Americans to do—to read the Classics. So maybe I should be allowed to lecture on Homer; and even if I persisted in saying "Please! Please!" to stone-circles in Novgorod and "I want! I want!" to the crescent of the moon in Kief, they would only think of me as "archaic"; not as deserving of punishment, not as a candidate for an asylum, but as one who, which indeed is the case, does more harm to himself than to anyone else by his grotesque superstitions.

You see this lecturing life of mine encouraged my tendency to live entirely in my own self-created world, a world composed of my response to books and my reactions against an energetic capitalistic society. And it made me profoundly subtle too in what I might call the art of "indirect reaction"; as for example when I would convert my malicious hatred of the commercial hurly-burly around me into a passionate eulogy of the saints and mystics of the past. This kind of thing I was always doing. Some accidental concatenation of place and people, some situation where my nerves had been outraged, would pile up the black bile within me, until, safe on my platform, I would revenge myself upon every aspect of our mismanaged human life, as if I had been in reality—what they call those curious freaks in "Barnum and Bailey"—an Ambassador from Mars.

Back again in the Eastern States, I found that certain particular audiences seemed created to respond to me by some inexplicable element in the occult conditions of the spot. Thus at Rochester, New York, I was always encouraged to have my full fling, partly by the presence there of my sagacious ally, Mr. Claude Bragdon, who from his calm hieratic plane of higher dimensional insight-delighted to see me toss my bauble and rattle my bells as the court fool to Lucifer, but also, I have sometimes thought, from the "aura" left still in those regions by the spiritual magic of the Indians.

Always faithful to me, too, was my old impressario Mr. Charles Atkins, and under his auspices I had *and kept*—which was not the case with Philadelphia—an audience in Brooklyn that seemed prepared to listen to me till the day of doom. The surprising fidelity of these Brooklyn Institute people has sometimes been a puzzle to me. Finally I came to attribute it to the Germanic atmosphere there. It was a thoroughly bourgeois gathering, and, on the whole, composed of well-to-do people; but I shall always remember it as by far my best Gentile audience. I put this down to that mystical craving for "cosmic emotion" which seems so deep a thing in the German spirit.

I think I am as susceptible to the subtler emanations of race as I am to the overtones of religious tradition; and I have always found that where there was a large German element in my audience I grew less malicious, less fantastic, less wilful, finding everything in this Passing Show to be but a symbol and I myself bent resolutely to live, *im Ganzen, Guten, Schonen!*

It is not easy to sum up, even in as long a chapter as this, the abiding "essence" of life in America as I came to feel it; but I must say, here and now, that I have never gone back on the prophetic instinct I felt when, sitting by the side of Tom Jones in that "Kardomah Café" in Liverpool, I listened to Sousa's "Stars and Stripes." Such a wild, cynical, sentimental chaos! And yet, with it all, such far-drawn, infinitely wistful vibrations on the air! Further from the earth, than for us at home, was that hard, clear azure sky, brighter than with us that cruel, scorching sun, and yet, as I moved among the polyglot crowds of this strange nation, I felt always that I had escaped from something much more insidious than grey skies or drifting rain. I had escaped from the necessity of too much loving and too much hating among human personalities and human institutions.

> "Melange, my own! The seen and unseen;
> Mysterious Ocean, where the streams empty!"

Chapter Eleven

The War

THE year 1914 in America seemed the crest of a wave of passionate idealism among young people, and of passionate selfishness among middle-aged people. The idealism showed itself principally in two ways; in liberal humanitarian propaganda, and in such an outburst of poetry as no nation had seen since the Elizabethan age in England. Upon both these lovely and gracious growths the cloven hoof of the war crushed down with exterminating violence.

Both as a lover of poetry and as a Parlour Bolshevik, I took a lively share in these spiritual uprisings. I felt in both the moral and æsthetic aspects of this new creative wave a return to the spirit of Walt Whitman. And here I was at home; for something in the poetry of Walt Whitman had satisfied the cravings of my peculiar nature in a way no other poetry had ever satisfied them. What I especially responded to in him was the pluralism of his triumphant mythology.

I must confess that the extravagance of his optimism often seemed to me a little "too thick"; but I liked the bold individualism of it, and if I could have *willed* the System of Things to fall out according to my own pluralistic and polytheistic notions I would have *willed* it to be very like the imagined universe of Walt Whitman. And suppose he *was* a real oracle —a real Incarnation of some demiurgic Son of the Morning? He *may* have been! But I confess much of his hope—that "Larger Hope" that Llewelyn always laughs at—seems to me too good to be true. But *it is what I like*—that universal host of sentient entities, all possessed of immortal souls, all struggling unconquerably with the obstacles of matter, all following, not "One God," but "after the Great Companions"!

One of his executors—I cannot now recall his name—gave me those two strongly-bound volumes of that private edition of his poetry that he sold to the English for ten dollars and that was well understood by *so many* of our poets. We English are the only race in the world that put happiness before everything else—we *un-æsthetic people!*—and Walt Whitman's gigantic sense of well-being suited us from the start. We are rooted and grounded in this cult of "happiness" in a way Americans are not. Too restless are they, too nervously tense, too buoyantly brittle, too easily worn out, and too soon ready to collapse into premature old age. It must be confessed, however, that they are more spontaneously concerned about the "other person" than we are; and their whole self-love, with its wild fumblings of telepathic antennae, is in a thousand subtle ways different from our more crafty, more deeply entrenched egoism.

This became plain to me in the extraordinary kindness I received from the Paul Jordan Smiths in California. I stayed a great deal under the hospitable roof of this learned young editor of the *Anatomy of Melancholy* and his magnanimous partner; and I certainly learned there the noble lengths to which American unselfishness, so gallant and unassuming, is able to go.

It was my old crony Maurice Browne, that scoriated dragonfly of so many spiritual Colosseums, whose own egoistic weaknesses are so like my own that I find it impossible to get any perspective on them, who introduced me to one of the most interesting Americans I know. This is Mr. James Abell, in whose lineage both the violent pioneer element of the South-West, and the easy-going aristocratic element of Virginia, meet and clash, to the fascination of a fellow-philosopher, though not invariably to the happiness of their possessor. Abell is indeed always making me think of a Conrad character; and what higher praise for picturesqueness and enigmatic attractiveness, could there be than that? His actual frame—the bony structure of his body—expresses his "psyche" more than I have ever seen a human body express a human character! He seems to be entirely devoid of the important human organ which the famous passage in Rabelais declares to be the ruler of the world! Yes, Jim Abell's stomach remains pure skeleton, while the rest of his body, even to his high, spare and drooping shoulders, is decently covered.

"The Catholic," as I still call him, whether alive in life or alive in death, would have appreciated my friend Abell; for the man's brain possesses just those rare metaphysical, psychical feelers in the cloudy borderland between religion and realism which Balzac had in a worldly sense and Unamuno in an unworldly sense, and which find their rational expression in the subtleties of St. Thomas. Abell's curiously metaphysical attitude to literature for example has been of considerable value to me in the writing of my latest novels, for he has encouraged me to rebel against that Henry James rule of "straining" the whole thing through one character's consciousness.

It is by a much older friend than Abell, however, that the name "James" has been appropriated for ever in my catalogue of bosom-cronies. It is indeed a quarter of a century ago that I first met Mr. James Henderson of Germantown, Philadelphia. I had met Mr. Robert Bright himself only a short time before; met him at the same Germantown lectures; and Germantown has come to mean something very special to me in my long American life. Aye! how well I came to know every single step of that beautiful, mellow, historic Germantown Avenue! I used often to walk all the way up to Mount Airy, where Mr. Bright's house is, from Wayne Junction Railway Station, and I used to tell myself stories as I walked, tapping the old-fashioned bricks with my stick, stories such as I have told myself all over this vast continent, from San Rafael, Marin County, to Staten Island, New York, from San Diego, California, to Portland, Maine, from Joplin, Missouri, to Providence Rhode Island, stories about how wonderful it would be to live with my brother Llewelyn in a very small house of our own! The number of such small houses, from Canada to the Gulf, from the Atlantic to the Pacific, in front of which I have paused in my walks, and tapped their railings or their doorstep with my stick, thinking of this imaginary life with Llewelyn, you would hardly believe. The truth is it has been a constant pleasure, in all my debouchings to try to think out what we really *would* feel, if we lived thus together! Such imaginings have been, I suppose, one of the most efficacious among the mental restoratives by which I have warded off the various small miseries of a prolonged nomad life; and it has been rather sad to me that only very briefly on "the Coast," and still more briefly in New York, has this mirage ever solidified into reality.

I think Germantown, where James Henderson was born, and where no doubt his father and grandfather were born before him, remains in its calmness, its peacefulness, its obscure pieties, its natural sagacities, very like James Henderson himself. Here and now as I think of "James," for as "James" all the world thinks of him—not out of familiarity but out of affectionate veneration as we think of the apostles by their "first" names—and as I call up the image of his great naked portentous skull and smouldering brown eyes and imperturbable equanimity, for never in all my twenty-eight years' acquaintance have I known James to be so much as once disturbed, after that manner which we so expressively call "being rattled," by the shocks of circumstance, and as I call up those James-like purlieus of Philadelphia, so indolent, so mellow, so sagacious, so deep, and yet so involved with concrete, circumstantial *reality*, exactly as the Hegelian "idea," according to James's own favourite philosopher Croce, is so obscurely and bafflingly involved with history—I am deliberately imitating in this serpentine sentence the style of my Hegelian—Crocean—Philadelphian "calamus-root" crony—I feel compelled to try to make clear, once for all, something of the unique beauty I have found from time to time in America.

I think I have, after my fashion, and carrying a little further those Sousa strains that I heard in the "Kardomah Café" in Liverpool, really caught something of the double-edged essence of life in the United States, its brutal cynical youthfulness, its heroic reckless unselfishness. What makes so many European visitors, if they are not themselves "healthy, wealthy and wise," that is to say pretty tough, pretty complacent, and pretty prosperous, feel such unkind and bitter feelings and express such wickedly unfair opinions about America, is the dominance of youth. Young American voices are strident, young American shoulders broad, young American flanks well-fleshed, young American legs long, and we all know how the exuberance of youth seems noisy and blustering to the unsympathetic touchiness of old age. American youth often *is* insensitive and un-subtle in addition to being idealistic and gallant and candid, and of course the impact of these noisy high spirits on our shaky nerves tends to make us bitter, prejudiced, unkind, and akin to poor old Scrooge, when thrust into the presence of such riotous well-being.

What this exuberant American youthfulness wants when it is riotously rather than exquisitely happy—what it "wishes," in fact in that significant Americanism in which "want" and "wish" are identical—are strength, health, glitter, glory, bloom, splendour and dazzle. *And why not?* After all, this is what the youth of the ancient world in its day "wished"; it is what the Borgian youth in *its* day "wished"; and the sneering trepidation of neurotic and testy Modern Europeans in its presence is nothing less than that evil *resentment*, masquerading as spirituality, upon which Nietzsche animadverts so searchingly. In the old world of to-day we make it rather a point of gentility to go about in shabby or at least in well-worn clothes. But the mediæval lads must have glittered and swaggered in glimmering-new plumes and shiny feathers, until they "won their spurs"; and sometimes even after that sobering event.

Of course I was, and am still, for all my Derbyshire rusticity and Welsh "elementalism," as neurotic as D. H. Lawrence himself; and although I do my best, by perpetually reading Homer with a crib, to suppress the Sitwell sophistication and the Gertrude Stein eccentricity when these tendencies crop up in me, there have been moments in my life when an undiluted maliciousness and a morbid "resentment," in the very worst sense that Nietzsche diagnosed, have made me try to be as mincingly aristocratic in my revenge "upon the hand that fed me" as the great sluices of good middle-class blood in my veins allowed.

As a matter of fact, the only person I've ever met, except perhaps Cousin Ralph and Cousin Warwick, whose aristocratic manner seemed to me careless and charming instead of a morbid revenge upon life, was Ford Madox Ford. I had tea with him once in Patchin Place, and although he is no reader of mine and I am no reader of his, I confess I greatly "cottoned" to his noble, stately, and altogether gallant personality. I felt a curious and quite especial sympathy for him, the kind of sympathy that a penetrating woman would feel for a royal personage in disguise, out of whose battered skull all the "nonsense" has been knocked by the buffets of fate; and I could see that Ford Madox Ford had a real "penchant" for America, just as I have had myself.

No doubt there will be times in my old age when I shall remember America with melting tenderness. But it won't be of her ice-water, or of her ice-cream, or of her sanitary plumbing, that I shall think in those days; it will be of certain indescribable Sunday mornings in Patchin Place when New York lay in deep gulfs of ethereal silence. Never have I known in all my life such a heavenly silence as that was! It was a silence that seemed as if it were being gently washed by mysterious subaqueous tides at the bottom of the world. It was a silence that made you feel as if the very pulse of the Absolute had been turned to stone. And I shall doubtless think too of certain walks I took in Arkansas and Kansas and Oklahoma and Southern Missouri, that particular south-west "Middle-West" which has long been my "Ideal America," and where I found such relaxed, reckless and fairy-story fabulousness in the people and their ways that I could not feel that I was in the heart of the "New" World. Yes I shall think of that absolute stillness, that stillness of the great white bare, world-debutante actually asleep at last; and then I shall think of how in those other regions I used to follow some nut-gatherer's trail through the brushwood and tangled undergrowth in the environs of Coffeeville, or Neosha, or Carthage, where every squatter I met looked as if he possessed some secret entrance to Aladdin's Cave but was letting it go, letting it all go, from sheer whimsicality and fairy-story improvidence!

After all, the testy Europeans who say such nasty things about America have only been over there for a few months;

whereas I have been over there *for thirty years* and when I haven't been in trains or on platforms I have been walking, walking, walking, all over the continent! Sometimes I pretend to myself, that I, who have always aimed at being a "magician" beyond every other aim in life, have really learnt a few occult secrets from the spirits of the Red Indians, this most original and formidable race among all the children of men.

I still regard Longfellow's *Hiawatha* as an exciting and thrilling poem; and I differ completely from D. H. Lawrence in my choice among Indians. *My* Indians are the Red Indians of the East, not the Indians of New Mexico, or Old Mexico, or any other Mexico. It is an inconsistency in me, being the idol-worshipper that I am, but all the same when it comes to Indians I prefer heroes who worship, as my father taught me to do, a Great Spirit whose breath bloweth like the wind, to artistic tribes who worship Quetzacoatle and his feathery snake.

But as I imagine myself now wandering slowly up German-town Avenue, with the intention of visiting my friend Robert Bright or of meeting James Henderson, I want to digress a little to tell you about my encounters with Theodore Dreiser and Edgar Lee Masters. I met Dreiser first and indeed it was owing to Dreiser that I got hold of the unpublished galley-sheets of *Spoon River* for a lecture in Guthrie's Church on modern poetry. I did my best to do justice to this great poem, the most original single volume of modern poetry that it has ever been my luck to find; and that really I must have done pretty well with it was evidenced by a man in the audience remarking that he "knew personally" *a certain cow* referred to by the poet and faithfully commented on by the poet's interpreter. I am a great wor-shipper of cows, and to this Spoon River cow I devoted much eloquence.

But it was some little time after this, probably in 1915, that I first met Masters himself. This was in Chicago, where I went to see him in his law office. The poet Ridgely Torrence, whose own personality struck me as too fragile, too delicate, too highly-strung, to cope at all with the ferocious mêlée of American life, told me how he had recently visited Mr. Masters and been taken by him for several strolls about his terrifying city. He said he noted how Mr. Masters had a "mythology" of his own, into the circle of which, as if they had been more than merely ordinary men and women, every character he had known over a certain number of years was incorporated. He also commented very ably on the peculiar genius, rare among poets, that Mr. Masters has for significant names.

It was an important moment in my life when I first set eyes on the author of *Spoon River*. I had never known, save in the case of Thomas Hardy, an original poet of first-rate philosophic weight and power, and I gazed with intense respect upon this one. I felt at once, the moment I set eyes on him in that unpoetical place, that I was in the presence not merely of a formidable genius, but of a formidable man. Never I suppose has there been seen, outside the ranks of Generals of Divisions and Admirals of Fleets, such a granite *chin* as the one above which these genial and even Thackeray-like eyes gave me through their spectacles "the once over" and summed up the resources of my spirit. But I need not have been frightened. The most striking feature of Edgar Lee's character is his unwearied glow and radiant good spirits in the presence of less than normally clever men and women. If these are sympathetic people he will treat them as if they were miracles of intelligent response, and even if they are very stupid he will still talk to them as if he were talking to Shakespeare. He is the most un-snobbish great man I ever met; for instead of changing his manner of conversation when dealing with simple people I have frequently remarked that he seems in better spirits in their company and more entirely himself with them than in the case of persons of importance. I don't mean that he is brusque or unkind to the sort of people Mr. de —— would call "magnates," but the central glow of his humanity burns less brightly in their presence—unless they happen to be women!

Towards brilliant women of the world Mr. Masters does not show the malicious distaste, mingled with panic terror, that is my own attitude. He more nearly resembles Doctor Johnson; who, as you will remember, was prepared to permit the prettiest of such butterflies to sit upon his knee. But he is more of a man's man I would say than a woman's, and in this, again, he resembles one of the great coffee-house poets of the eighteenth century in England. I can see him in his wig and buckled shoes, and with his stick and his snuff-box, seated in the Ranelagh Gardens, or on my Lord Bolingbroke's Terrace, hob-nobbing with Swift or exchanging Rabelaisian jests with Gay. And yet no one, not even Dreiser, is so profoundly American as Edgar Lee Masters. His erudition in the history of his country is both comprehensive and exact, and no one has done more to dispel the sentimental humbug which the predatory miscreants who exploit the masses over here have woven like a phosphorescent cocoon around the figure of Lincoln.

Thomas Jefferson is Mr. Master's hero; and nothing has ever pleased him more than to see the great gentleman who now occupies the White House acting as he feels Jefferson would act were he brought back to cope with our imbroglio. I have compared Masters with Chaucer; but there are passages in Master's poetry, when he speaks of the basic griefs and terrible bewilderments in the simple annuals of the poor, and of the tragic recurrences of human sorrow everywhere, with its final eternal rest for all who are weary, that are much more than Chaucerian. They have something of the consolatory dignity of his own favourite Sophocles, only tuned to the more pitiful and more humble pathos of the "Terzie Potters" of our forlorn procession.

For lack of all affectation, for treating poetry as gravely and simply as the old monks treated their art of illumination, as a thing done in the simple honour of the Lord of Life, Edgar Lee Masters will not soon find his equal. His generous and whole-hearted admiration for Vachel Lindsay has always impressed me a good deal; for Mr. Masters is a born fighter, and willing enough to fall to fisticuffs with the Devil himself, and Lindsay moreover came from his own part of the country; but never once in my long friendship with him, that goes back, as I say, to 1915, have I ever heard him do anything but fiercely champion this mystical rival of his.

How clearly I recall my first introduction to Theodore Dreiser! It was when he lived on West 10th Street; where his couple of large old rooms on the ground-floor, with big open fires, receded from the front to the extreme back of the house. He was that day attired in a blue over-all smock, such as French workmen wear, and to find a desk suitable to his colossal manuscripts he had made a writing-table out of a grand piano. It was interesting to me to note how much more like Walt Whitman than like Edgar Lee Masters, Dreiser was in the matter of his feeling for clothes. Masters wants merely to pass in the crowd and to feel comfortable; otherwise *his* attitude to clothes is that of your typical scholar, un-bothered, unconscious, indifferent.

But Dreiser, ever since I first met him, which must have been in 1914 I think, struck me as a Being, as an Entity, who was as profoundly conscious of his own body, and *of what he put against his skin,* as he was conscious of the Corpus Terraqueous, and wherewithal *it* was fain to cover its cosmogonic bones. Dreiser struck me, in fact, as what you might call Matter-conscious or Chemistry-conscious, to a degree that was almost non-human. He and Masters have one thing in common, however, which strikes me as a credit to their country, I mean their lack of self-conscious "side," as we call it in England, in their dealings with the world. But this does not mean that, like Masters, Dreiser is unconscious of his body or unaware of every pulse in his body.

Masters, when he talks of Letters or writes of Letters, behaves as Dryden or Swift or Fielding would behave, smokes his pipe, shuffles about, has an occasional drink, and then forgets that he is anything but an active skull working a typewriter. But with Dreiser I feel as if I were dealing with a form of life in no way resembling that of your historic human scholar. In the first place he doesn't smoke, which in itself de-humanizes anyone. In the second place he is fantastic, queer, and as erratic in his diet, subject to alternations of wilful sensuousness with wilful abstemiousness, as he is over his clothes. Nothing with him follows any tradition. All is abnormal, sub-normal, super-normal. He is a German who admires

Russia. He is a realist who admires Mr. Charles Fort. He is a ruler of men who is happiest with women. Yet I have heard women railing fiercely at him, cursing him as more *this* and more *that*, than anyone's dainty reserve can possibly tolerate!

My own personal feelings towards these two great Americans are curiously different. Towards Masters I feel warmth, sympathy, defensive indignation, and a certain Boswellian desire to track down, to all their imaginative beginnings, the workings of his genius. With Masters I feel like a heart warming to a heart, and like a bibliophile avariciously increasing a rich collection. I never think of Master's body or what he is wearing. It is true I look with infinite satisfaction now and again *at his chin*, thinking to myself, "these damned megalopolitans will have to skip a bit, if they are going to make this old mandarin worry!"

But with Dreiser it is totally different. I want to embrace him, to pummel him, to wrestle with him, to stroke him, to cause him some physical jolt. It gave me a wicked pleasure to see him receive the shock of that extremely chilly water with his bare skin when he once bathed in our Columbia County Grotto, whereas when Masters did this my only anxiety was lest he should catch pneumonia. I always used to tempt Dreiser to play that curious schoolboy game that I used to be so formidable at with my strong wrists and fingers when I was in the Prep. Do you know the game I refer to? You stand up opposite your opponent, entwine your fingers with *his* fingers, press the palms of your hands against the palms of *his* hands; and then, as both of you clench your hands, you each struggle to force the other down on his knees! To this bout I loved to tempt Dreiser; and we used to stagger round the room with our hands upraised and our faces getting more and more distorted and pale, till our friends intervened. But neither of us ever made the other kneel!

I used to be aware—I always am aware—of surging waves of magnetic attraction between Dreiser and myself, waves which certainly are not homosexual, for neither of us have the remotest homosexual tendency, but which seem super-chemical and due to the diffusion of some mysterious occult force through the material envelopes of our physical frames. The truth is Dreiser and I are both Magicians. We are two Lamas, who, while understanding black magic and the ways of black magicians, prefer for reasons rather to be concealed than revealed, to practise white magic. We both have morbidly active consciences. Problems of right and wrong are far more important to us both than problems of æsthetics. Of course there are endless intellectual and moral fields where he leaves me far behind, such as knowledge of economics, appreciation of music, courage in standing up to personal enemies, courage in defying brutal and stupid authorities, freedom from the vice of flattery, integrity of *speech* as well as of mind. But I think the most important item, speaking as a fellow-lama or fellow-guru, where I beat Dreiser at our spiritual "game of wrists" is my power of escaping from the world. But on the other hand since my tendency to escape from the world is very largely composed of *fear of the world* and Dreiser's tendency to stay in the world is very largely mingled with a desire to fight for "the insulted and injured" of the world, I am not in a position to take much moral unction to myself concerning this advantage.

What makes Dreiser the genius he is, and the power he is, is the deep mingling of the magnetic, the psychic, the mystic, the occult, with such tremendous realism and such terrific *practical* force, things in which I am as much of a helpless outsider, as much of a timid book-worm, as if I were really the "dear Archdeacon" that Llewelyn calls me. Certainly Dreiser is a man of strange opposites and contradictions. As I explained to an admirable author of a first-rate book on his personality and his times, for all the man's cosmic feelings and planetary feelings, and for all the vein of primordial savagery in him, he can exercise, when he is moved to do so, a tenderness not only "as subtle as a woman's," but a good deal more subtle than most women I have known.

The whole of Dreiser's nature was roused to come to my aid when in 1917 I had the operation they call *gasterenterostomy* under the miraculous hands of Dr. John Erdmann. He took me himself to the Post-Graduate Hospital; and the next morning, when I had the anæsthetic, the last thing I can remember was seeing him dressed in the white overalls of a doctor, talking to the anæsthetist. He described the whole thing to me later and told me that he actually held in his hand at one moment some important portion of my guts.

All my life I shall at intervals call up the fascinating personalities of Dreiser and Masters, and bless my stars that it has been my destiny to know such men and name myself their friend. I chuckle to myself when I speak in this way, for nothing is more revealing both of the superficial "slickness" in useful publicity, and the inarticulate loneliness and reticence underlying it, of American men, that it should be a phrase you are always hearing: "Oh yes! So and so"—naming some prominent banker or promoter of companies—"*is a warm personal friend of mine.*" Well! When *I* boast, in the Red Lion at Dolgelley, of being a "warm personal friend" of the two greatest Americans of our time, may it be with my last breath!

But when you sweep aside the absence in both these men of the convoluted snobbishness of English writers, so double-charged with touchy self-consciousness, first as artists, *then* as —if that is what they are—gentlemen and scholars, Dreiser and Masters are as different from each other as two men of genius could well be. I differentiated my most intimate English friends, Bernie and "The Catholic" and Tom Jones and Louis Wilkinson and Harry Lyon by imagining their several attitudes to some strange but not necessarily pretty girl, brought suddenly into contact with them. May I be allowed to differentiate Dreiser and Masters in the same way? What Dreiser would do would be to fix a concentrated eye on this bewildered woman; and, while he hummed a mechanically tuneless tune, like a botanist examining a plant at his leisure, seek to draw out— sympathetically, you must understand, rather than unsympathetically—but yet with a kind of soul-ravishing violence, the deepest life-secrets of her essential being. Nothing that the girl might say, to this "Eye of God" fixed upon her, would pass disregarded, no affectation, no narcissism, no feminine weakness, no feminine subterfuge. All would be treated with the same intently-interested super-curiosity.

Fortunately for my imaginary lady, nothing in the world, except when a man plays the helpless baby with them, "goes down" better than this kind of passionate philosophical interest. No wonder Dreiser has been lucky! The woman in question has the wit to see—as indeed is quite literally the case—that *for the time* this formidable Being is, as we say, "wrapped up in her." Nothing exists at that moment for this mountainous personality, for his imagination, his instinct, his clutch, his intuition, his pounce, his intellect, his paws, his spirit, his infinite tenderness, his savage cannibalism, his wistful pity, his insatiable curiosity, his astonished wonder, except the inmost "little me" of this particular daughter of Eve. And, as I say, save when it's their vice to be spiritual nursing-mothers to the strong-brought-low, nothing seduces them more than this.

And now, I am going to turn my fortunate lady over to Edgar Lee Masters. What a difference! It is now, so to speak, entirely "up to" the girl herself. If I had been prompting her at these two interviews I would have told her that with Dreiser it really didn't matter what she did! She could be naughty, she could be haughty, she could be bad, she could be mad, she could be a chatterbox, she could be an alabaster box, she could be a flirt, she could be a nun, she could be a Lamia, she could be an Hypatia, she could be a blue-stocking, she could be a baggage. But prompting her with Masters I would say: "You must, above everything else, be *humorous*. Be provocative, be docile, be sweet, be intellectual, be sympathetic, but whatever you are be humorous and clairvoyantly responsive to humour." And if my lady enquired "what kind of humour"; and whether irony would do, or archness, or playfulness, or satire, I would reply: "Not only will these *not* do, but, if I know anything of Mr. Masters, they will annoy him as much as they'd annoy me! Both Mr. Masters and I want you to be sensible. We want to discover not your character, but your ideas, your opinions, your conclusions, your generalizations upon life. But at *this* point we differ a little. For I want you to remain very grave the whole time, whereas Mr. Masters wants you to be really humorous."

"But, but, but——" my lady will stammer; and then I shall come out with the whole truth.

"If you want, my dear, as a woman, to hold the attention of Edgar Lee Masters, you had better stop reading the Bible, and read Aristophanes and Rabelais."

But I have been digressing all this time, as I stroll slowly up Germantown Avenue, of all American thoroughfares the one I know best and feel most at home in. For just as women, whether "philosophical" as I like them, or "humorous" as Masters likes them, or "anyhow" as Dreiser takes them, are at home in their house and allow their minds to wander passively and at ease in a thousand careless directions, so *I am at home* on some well-known road, letting my mind wander in all directions as I glance at each familiar doorstep, or shutter, or rail, or area, or stable, or garden, or hedge, or grass-plot, or dog-kennel, or flower-pot, or muslin curtain, or fragment of stucco-wall. Oh how indescribably happy I am walking alone along any mortal street, or road, or avenue, as long as there is a brick side-walk, instead of one of these accursed pavements!

As I write these lines now, in the attic of my little "up-state" Dutch house, listening to the murmur of the flooded Agawamuk, I begin to let my mind wander amid a thousand fantastic psychological by-paths just as I would be doing if I were really at this moment drifting up, or drifting down, the slow peaceful length of that lovely old Germantown Avenue. Yes, it was in a lecture-hall opening straight upon this American "Hammersmith Road" that I first met my life-long friend, James Henderson. James is certainly one of the inmost of that "inner circle" of mine by boasting about which I used so to annoy Harry Lyon. James is one of the profoundest and certainly without exception the subtlest of all the philosophers I know. He is more obscure than my *other* James, Mr. Abell, and, I think, less interested in religion and more interested in moral casuistry; but it is with the best of philosophers, as with the nicest of women, the deeper their inspiration goes the less you need fuss about its limitations.

Putting Dreiser and Masters aside, who of course *are* famous men, I have been singularly fortunate in having for my friends both in England and America men who have been too wise to attain publicity. But I have known what I have known about them. Personally my misanthropic malice has been of enormous help in keeping in check my childish credulity about "great men" and restraining the womanish excesses of my Boswellian hero-worship. When I was young I had a mania for reading all those little lives of "Great Men," such as the "English Men of Letters" series and the "Great Writers" series, and I used to study with feverish interest the various "histories" of English literature. These works of laudation and discrimination cluttered up my hero-worshipping mind with what nowadays people call *clichés*, of every conceivable kind, moral clichés, religious clichés, irreligious clichés, æsthetic clichés, ironical clichés, disillusion clichés, cynical clichés, psychic clichés, occult clichés, grammatical clichés, verbal clichés, and even paragraphical clichés.

But by degrees I have outgrown this innocence. I now see that it is Chance, and not merit, that decides who shall be famous at any given epoch, and I have learnt not only to discount the applause of the vulgar; but also, which is a good deal harder, the intellectual and fashionable suffrages of the damned "illuminati." I have come to recognize as a basic fact in life, as indeed a sort of spiritual law, that the subtlest intellects and the rarest imaginations, in every age, are "too proud to fight," and are consequently never heard of! I have found out that merely to *be* successful, merely to *be* known, humanity being as it is, is an invariable sign, not of superiority, but of vitality. Such "glory" among men—yes! even this posthumous "fame" about which the great, deluded, innocent poets make such a to-do—requires for its attainment more energy than genius, more liveliness than sensitiveness, more brute force than imagination, and more *luck* than anything else!

But I have got, mixed in with my mystical cult of Tibetan sanctity, a vein of terribly corrosive *black bile* with which I take a wicked delight in levelling the great ones with the little ones. Thus, both as a white magician, insisting that all life is holy, and as a black magician, rejoicing in destruction, I am one who, as Our Lady sang in the Magnificat, "brings down the Mighty from their seats and exalts the humble and meek." But this spiritual malice in me is mingled with a capacity for deadly moral indignation. Sometimes when I am praying on the hill-top to the invisible powers to punish vivisectionists and lynchers, this wrath of God seizes me like a whirlwind and I spin round like a dervish in my emotion. It seizes upon me, this wrath, for all my "dear Archdeacon" ways, just as it seized upon some of the more savage Hebrew prophets, or upon the indignant Savonarola, whose voluble profile my own so closely resembles, as if it were an actual vibration of that far-travelling ice-cold magnetism, of which Dreiser has sometimes talked to me, altogether outside the *warm* magnetism of our planetary world.

I seriously have come to feel—from a thousand queer experiences—that I really have some uncanny power of laying a curse upon those whose evil behaviour has roused me, especially upon vivisectionists and lynchers; and it is perhaps for this very reason that as a rule I am so indulgent, so tolerant, I might almost say so fluid and de-personalized, with wicked people. I let them alone, I am humble and even obsequious with them; and then suddenly, when they least expect it, I call upon the Cloud-Gatherer and behold! the thunderbolt falls!

Dreiser has told me that in ordinary argument I resemble a *sack of feathers*, feathers that you can shoot at, or hit at, without making any impression! As a cloud of vapour these feathers yield, separate, accept the blow; and then, when the missile has pierced them, close up again, just as they were before. Dreiser himself is much more solid than I am, but I don't think he is much more human! I will retort on him for his "feathers" by saying that he is like a rumbling volcano, on the sides of which the goats and conies gambol and the cicada chirps—and then, all of a sudden—lo! brimstone and fire, and a torrent of smoking lava!

No! I think you can roundly assert that the majority of extremely successful men, such as the vulgar call "great," are successful because they want *just that* above everything else. Mistakes of course do happen, as when quiet mathematicians are suddenly hurled, like meteoric projectiles, into notoriety.

But as a rule it is those with energy and will and desire to be at the top who *are* at the top! But it is a very interesting psychological problem to analyse the effect of notoriety and success upon a person of literary talent. It is generally fatal! Hardy himself told me how careful he had to be not to let his megalopolitan admirers kill his genius; how he had to stick to his "home town," as they call it in America, where such dangerous glory is mitigated by the malice of neighbourhood. But it does seem to me a sorrowful commentary on human nature how snobbish, how exclusive, how supercilious any literary clique tends to become.

And this is, I think, truer of England than anywhere else. Even that convoluted spiritualizer of his own snobbishness, that sublimater of his own social prejudices, Henry James himself, makes this sort of treachery again and again a "motif" in his stories. In France, where artistic passions run so high, I doubt if there is anything like the same danger. It really is perfectly appalling in England when you get clique-snobbishness, æsthetic-snobbishness, *and* social snobbishness all mixed together in one person! But—for I am on the brink of wronging my fellow-countrymen in my Pro-Americanism—there are free spirits still in England. For instance I cannot imagine Walter De-La-Mare—to my way of thinking by far the greatest of our poets—condescending to such social niceties. And I *know*, from the long epistolary correspondence I have recently had with him, that J. D. Beresford equals even my American friends in his heroic detachment from this teasing superciliousness. I have completely lost touch with England of late but I confess when I beguiled Mr. Orage to come to tea with me in our ramshackle alley all my terrified fancies about English snobbishness seemed to melt away. This subtle critic struck me as one, who might have been wearing a friar's cord under his discreet dress.

Well, after all this is my life and not an analysis of our national weakness, but if you have any wit, reader, you will have already detected that I am myself sensitive to an unhealthy extent to every possible form of snobbishness. But I am also *bent on acquiring merit*; and so I struggle with a kind of ferocity to annihilate my snobbishness. If this only means that I am an "inverted snob," so be it. But I have always thought that this modern stunt of calling unselfishness "only a subtler form of selfishness" is a most tiresome trick. I really do think that it isn't a vain brag when I say that by perpetually struggling, in my skimble-skamble charlatan manner, using "cribs" all the time, with my classical school-books, I keep a bone-tight clutch on the tragic-comic essentials of human life. What I mean is, and I notice exactly the same thing in Mr. Masters who is always reading the Classics, and I expect this is what Bertrand Russell is driving at when he says it's a shame to let Greek drop, that by reading these old authors, you detach yourself from the itch for crowd-prestige while you enjoy the legitimate pride of a poetical self-reverence. If I—who am the most morbid of pseudo-Christian madmen and a regular demon towards my own dignity—have learnt the unction of my pride from Homer, you may take it that there is something in what I am saying!

And I find the old classic books, especially the Iliad and the Odyssey, are not only the best defence you can have against what is vulgar and garish in the present but the best help you can have in your stoical epicureanism. What I have been solacing myself with, all these long thirty years of life in trains and hotels, are the little sensuous natural pleasures to which these old poems give such a beautiful edge and such a noble heightening. Life in an American train, where the high-backed compartments create little oases of complete isolation, lends itself to epicurean tranquillity; and to novel-reading too. As I gazed out of all those thousands and thousands of train windows I generally kept my thumb in the pages of some exciting novel. How I used to look forward to my breakfast cups of strong coffee, and how I used to enjoy shaving in the empty wash-room, while I listened to the sounds of the morning tuned to the sweet-throated voices of African porters!

It is hard to acquire such philosophy; but if one only *could* become a real obsessed sensation-lover and give ambition to the devil, what a thrilling life one would have! I have an idea that while American writers are more superficially affected by success than ours are, *spiritually* they are much less affected by it. If I am correct in this, could we not surmise that it springs from the beautiful influence of chaos as against cosmos, and of chance as against destiny? Americans feel that their success must be credited, partly to chance, which, if it wanted to, could make anyone triumphant, and partly to a desperate effort of their own which others *might* have made but didn't. Whereas, on the contrary, the attitude of your successful Englishman is that there is something about his natural, passive, lying-back state, which, without his lifting a finger, has made fate love and admire him and select him as the recipient of honour.

Gertrude Stein tells us in her autobiography that Henry McBride after long warning her against public fame, is now prepared to allow her to enjoy this sweet poison in thimblefuls. I too, like Miss Stein, have the power of making a little glory go a long way; and like the same remarkable lady I am capable of getting a good deal more pleasure than anyone would guess from difficult and sophisticated writers. I have in my time, "honest as I am," got lovely satisfaction from the delicate works of Sacheverell and Osbert Sitwell and I have read with pleasure, even if I have not read with understanding, Joyce's *Work in Progress*. I like to keep, as William James did towards the Occult, an "open mind" in these matters; and though I try not to pretend, as some do, that they can follow what we know perfectly well they can't, I do take a lively pleasure in the Sitwell wilfulness and I certainly derive authentic satisfaction from reading aloud to my friends passages from *A Work in Progress*, although the meaning of these passages remains totally obscure to me. There must be some kind of sorcery in the mere sound of these fantastical paragraphs. In this matter of "glory," however, my own small dose—Mr. McBride's thimbleful—tastes—I speak with all humility—different from the Canary Sack of Charlie Chaplin, the Malmsey-wine of the Sitwells, or the Pantagruelian Argot-of-paradise of Joyce.

My small sip of glory as a lecturer, or, as I liked to think of myself, as a sort of wandering troubadour of the Classics, was *in its inherent nature* of the sort that the average connoisseur of intellectual values regards with suspicion, if not with contempt. There is a scholastical, pedantical, canonical, pontifical common-room-class-room convention, that to be a lecturer to feminine persons makes you into something midway between a woman's tailor and a woman's riding-master! Well, I have had nearly forty years of this ambiguous occupation, since I first went down to Brighton, and so far from its having injured my character or hurt my culture I have a shrewd notion that it is the exercise upon me of all this searching feminine criticism for all these years—for *they* are the ones to bring down a person's conceit and encourage his real originality—which has helped me to turn myself, I so fatally flexible and fluid, from seeking my level only in the form of water into seeking it in the form of the more dangerous elements of air and fire.

But no doubt the mere fact that for all these years I have been trailing this not very reputable, not very respectable, not always very decent Excelsior-Banner of an unscholastic culture, like a tattered Salvation Army flag, over this chaste, cruel and chaotic land, has winnowed every shred of priggishness out of me that was not already squeezed and pinched and twisted and jeered out of me at Wildman's House at Sherborne.

But I certainly have met people after my own heart as I went up and down this crazy, paradoxical land. One such—for as the discerning reader must already have detected I am struggling in this chronicle, just as if I really *were* a Tibetan monk, to confine myself to masculine examples of my genius as a discoverer—one such was my friend Dr. Walter Schott. I cannot describe to you what pleasure I have taken in Dr. Schott's society. We have been much together on the Pacific where I stayed in his house when I was terribly short of money, and once he visited me in Patchin Place on his way back from the funeral of Anatole France. On this occasion he left in my room two curious objects, resembling stage-lanterns in a Shakespearian play, which he explained had been purchased by himself from the sextons who in the dark of a Paris evening had dug Anatole France's grave. This visit of his synchronized with very drastic changes in my friend's domestic affairs; but in spite of his affliction Dr. Schott was full of amazing and bewildering speculations concerning certain very extraordinary antiquities connected with the Holy Temple in Jerusalem.

These speculations which were more curious than pious, he subsequently embodied in a privately printed work that will remain, for the bibliophiles of posterity, one of the curiosities of literature. But it was for himself rather than for any particular idea, though he had many and they were all original, that I loved him; and I loved him passing well. The man is a born genius. Some *achieve* genius—I think I have done so myself with a certain amount of help from women—but some are born geniuses, and of such is Dr. Schott. His father was German and his mother English; so that he could call at will upon the metaphysical naïveté of the former race, and the shrewd, eccentric, independent humour of the latter.

And what was this fantastical Platonist like, this gnomic comedian, whose favourite book was the Book of Job? Well! Dr. Schott has arched eyebrows. I have long ago discovered that of all aspects of a person's *native* disposition—those peculiarities given us by nature—it is our eyebrows that are the most significant of our character. Dr. Schott's eyebrows, appearing under his high sallow forehead, which itself is always surmounted by a bifurcated bush of towselled hair, are the serenely arched eyebrows of a cosmic enquirer "devoid of all guile." The great Einstein's comically innocent and bewildered countenance displays this same insignia of harmlessness. No banker, no financier, no lyncher, no vivisectionist, ever has arched eyebrows.

And Dr. Schott suited me down to the ground in another peculiarity. He combined scepticism of everything with credulity about everything; and I am convinced this is the true Shakespearean way wherewith to take life. Incidentally he was a first-rate dentist; and I would like to ask you, reader, why do many real philosophers become dentists? Dr. Schott is a dentist still, on Mission Street in San Francisco. Happy, yea! thrice happy are those who sit in *that* chair of philosophical novocaine.

It was not till after the War that I met my friend Reginald Hunter who succeeded me in my "top-floor front" in Patchin Place. Mr. Hunter, who as a matter of fact comes from New Zealand, is one of those Englishmen who always make me feel proud of my fellow-countrymen. Tall, lean, and so delicately fragile as to look sometimes almost *transparent*, Rex Hunter is one of those rare beings who, in the profoundest psychological sense, chooses once for all "the better path," and never thereafter—no! not for any worldly temptation—turns aside from it. In the midst of the most modern and "improved" city in the world he has cut his coat to suit his cloth to such a spiritual and practical nicety that he can live to himself and to his own humorous, and picturesque "vignettes," selected from all the insanities around him, without even so much as making the formal obeisance of "Naaman the Syrian" in the great brazen temple of Rimmon! I could not have borne to have as my successor anyone less harmonious than Reginald Hunter. And not only did he take over my rooms! Who else but this detached and whimsical spectator would have welcomed without displeasure or embarrassment the appearance of "Patrick" on his third-floor threshold?

Llewelyn's "companion" I think it was who first discovered Patrick, or I should say was first discovered by Patrick; but he and Llewelyn had only to meet once for it to be evident how they suited each other down to the ground. Patrick and I did not get on so well as Patrick and Llewelyn. He had a tendency I will not say to *bully* me, but to demand from me very often more propitiation, more patience, more "standing," as we say, "on one leg," than comes to me without a certain effort. But after all, he demanded no more of me than I am bestowing all the time on bustling persons who take much better care of themselves than ever Patrick did. He was and I pray to the Mother of God he *is*, a tall, thin, heavily-moustached Irishman, of the type formerly so familiar to me among the old Red-Coats in His Majesty's Forces, and he has certainly added to my vocabulary several expressions as fanciful and Celtic as I could desire. Besides all this, Patrick was wise in the most essential and important wisdom there is, the wisdom of adjusting your God-given peculiarities to your chance-given environment, with the least possible disturbance to both.

The "dear man," as old ladies say of Henry James, had one whimsy that I really did find trying, and that would have driven a touchy spinster—if that is what I had been instead of a frequenter of burlesque shows—out of her head. He had a way of using the big box for "kindling" which I kept outside the door, for I depended for warmth on an open fire, as a boot-cupboard and clothes-closet, as well as a larder. He was always mysterious as to where he slept at night; but it was clear that wherever it was it was not adapted for the preservation of private property; whereas my wood-box, usually half-empty, was admirably suited to this purpose. "I'll come for them to-morrow," he would always say when I threatened to dispose of this jackdaw-like collection.

Llewelyn and his "dear companion" were at once kinder and firmer to Patrick than I could be. They used to let him come into their room and sit by their fire. They even have been known to fry eggs for him. I was weaker as well as more selfish. I did make tea for him until he got into the habit of coming almost every day at tea-time. Then I rebelled. I decided that the particular way he used to rattle the door-handle, instead of knocking, would have worn out "the merit-acquiring" patience of the most spiritual of Lamas. Finally when I heard that noise I would take him out his cup of tea—this tea that was such a heaven to me that it seemed brutal to refuse it to Patrick—and make him sit down on his clothes-closet and drink it. In tea our tastes were identical. We both liked it, as Nietzsche says *he* did, very strong and very sweet and very hot. Our philosophy of life, though not quite as identical as our taste in tea, was almost the same, and no doubt is still, if Patrick is alive, as I hope and expect he is, except that he was a practising Catholic, and I was an unpractising one.

Our mutual philosophy amounted to a vivid Nietzschean recognition of the "pathos of difference" in the world. Both of us held the view that the rock-bottom of human wisdom is to be thankful for small mercies. I never woke up without thanking my guardian angel that I had, as my daily rigmarole runs, "clean food, clean shelter, clean bedding, and tobacco or cigarettes." My attitude to these windfalls of chance is one of never-ceasing nervous recognition; and my conscience is always prodding me to write better books so as—as I heard my friend Will Durant say once—"to fit my behaviour to my fortune."

And Patrick completely shared this attitude of mine. He was constantly congratulating himself on some "let up" in weather conditions, or in the difficulties thrown in his way before he could get hold of any liquor. This restorative he always spoke of as "refreshment." Nor did Patrick ever fail any more than did my old friend Aunt Stone to meditate with complacency on the fact that "though we be all born, we bain't all dead yet." Instead of the word "death" however he always made use of the euphemism, to *cave in*.

"There were a lot of them caved in," he would say with extraordinary satisfaction, "at the hospital last night."

Another mutual friend of Llewelyn and mine in Patchin Place, though I fancy I was a good deal more intimate with him than Llewelyn was, was Mr. Hans Kessler. Mr. Kessler is a philosopher of a very different kidney from Dr. Schott, whose encounter with him Llewelyn has so humorously described in *The Verdict of Bridlegoose*. Mr. Kessler always assumed the rôle of the sort of ferocious and savage realist who is a "holy terror," to use another of Patrick's expressions, to all affected windbags. As a matter of fact he had one of the tenderest and most affectionate hearts in the world. But his pet phrase to describe the soft-headed idealistic chatter he so held in contempt was "pretty-pretty barber-college monkey-shines"; and many a long evening have I spent in his company struggling desperately to steer clear of this opprobrium.

He was at that time in his life collecting books, and he had a very large number of every sort of historical and philosophical work piled up in his lodging. His relations with me were really quite singular and would make an absorbingly interesting psychological study. In his heart of hearts I think he shared the opinion of those cynical New Yorkers who regarded me as a pretentious ass exploiting the innocence of ladies' clubs; but he certainly did not "look forward to a Memorial Edition of my works." Indeed in a certain way he felt a protective instinct towards me and he was far too kind and tender-hearted a man to want me to find out what his real opinion of my intellectual value was. Now and then, however, he would make in my direction an alarming overture, like an unconscious hand drawn across a violin, of that executioner's "face" he was wont to assume, a terrifying grimace of condemnation without reprieve, before his lips formed the syllables "barber-college."

Hans Kessler undoubtedly has real imaginative power. His stories of his adventures were always full of striking original flights; and it was like watching a great actor to watch the fleeting expressions upon his caustic, and sometimes convulsed countenance, as he told of his experiences. But he felt it was only courteous in our rather awkward relation of a disillusioned cynic who had seen life and a lecturing idealist who admired Walter Pater, to confine the conversation to Culture. Naturally I would have greatly preferred to listen to his stories about himself, so full of picturesque touches, rather than be asked what I thought about John Stuart Mill, *his* favourite author, or about Mrs. Humphrey Ward who might easily have passed for mine. I shrewdly suspect that Mr. Kessler and I would have made a much more poignant picture, as we thus discoursed, if we could have fallen into the hands, say, of the great Gogol, than either of us in our hyperborean skulls had any idea of, for while I was propitiating a bibliophile, I was secretly admiring a traveller, and while he was propitiating a lecturer, he was secretly pitying a cake-eater.

I cannot remember whether in any of his equinoctial visits to New York, as the Literary Editor of the famous Chicago *Evening Post*, my well-loved colleague Llewelyn Jones ever met Hans Kessler. Llewelyn Jones is the only Manxman I have known, and I have discovered this; that if a Welshman wants to be defended from a formidable realist who regards his mythology as "balone" he cannot do better than appeal to a Manxman. Llewelyn Jones has the most comprehensive and the most scholarly knowledge of modern poetry of any man in America. I would never have gone on writing verse over here if it had not been for his encouragement; and I expect many another battered and way-worn troubadour would say the same. "Llewelyn Jones will settle him" would be the word, when some falsifier of poetry tried to put over a bastard coinage.

Another exponent of a culture that even Mr. Kessler could not have called "monkey-shines" had been a friend of Llewelyn when we lived together on Waverley Place and used to come faithfully to see me long after Llewelyn had gone back to Europe. This was Paul Piel, the sculptor, the inventor, and the faithful pupil of the philosopher Santayana. But it was not in any of these lights that he presented himself to me. He used to run up my stairs, two steps at a time, fresh as the morning and always *in* the morning, pass with a free, careless swing and a lightly-drummed tune, the sacred door of the poet E. E. Cummings—by which most of my visitors stole in timorous stealth, as if the Devil might burst out—and present himself before me with shining face, shining eyes, bare head, corduroy knicker-bockers, black stockings, and some torrential outburst of real, noble, Goethean, Germanic Culture! I would welcome him— it would indeed have seemed natural enough if I had embraced him—and he would sit down on my creaking bed, cross his massive legs in their black stockings, and wipe his capacious forehead.

Then I would behave to him in all serious intent, exactly as Mr. Kessler, in the ambiguity of his kind heart, used to behave to me. I would ask him questions about all those cultural matters in which he was such an eloquent authority. But between Paul Piel and me all was open, all was clear, all was above-board. Paul Piel has a child-like simplicity and a natural goodness. *I* have a child-like simplicity and a natural wickedness. We suited each other as the pendulum suits the hammer in a grandfather's clock. For Llewelyn he naturally felt the more affection. Who doesn't? As a matter of fact several of our mutual friends completely stopped visiting me when Llewelyn went away. But I suspect Paul Piel must have felt that I had more use for his theories about Greek Art than Llewelyn had. Aye! but the man was eloquent!

I was often reminded of those wonderful "conversations" of Goethe, as I played a responsive Eckermann to Paul Piel; for there was solid wisdom behind that goodly forehead, and some of his utterances had the kind of majestic clarity which makes the idea seem so much less subtle than it really is. He used to illustrate his theories by various engaging motions of his own sturdy and powerful frame, particularly of his thighs, in their tight corduroys, and of his calves, in their tight black stockings. I must have thickened out my æsthetic culture, more than I had done since the exciting Harry Lyon days, in these lively talks. Brought up—so to speak—among architects, to encounter a passionate theoretical sculptor was a new experience for me; and I dare say I embraced a good many of Paul Piel's ideas without realizing what I was doing.

It would be strange after all these years if I did not know New York far better than any other city in the world. But you must remember that I instinctively selected from this towering panorama certain quaint simple aspects which harmonized with my obstinately rustic and obstinately Gothic nature. I used to go to Washington Square from Patchin Place, either by way of Tenth Street, where I made a fetish—or even a totem—of a poplar-tree that grew by the pavement's edge, or by way of Eleventh Street, where I always stopped to talk to Rachel Phillips, who about the time I was being born at Shirley was being buried in this little Portuguese-Hebrew burying-ground, and to whose gentle bones I acquired by degrees a faithful and almost romantic attachment. Once in Washington Square I did my best not to be hypnotized by two famous inscriptions that are set up so high in that leafy enclosure, the one where Washington allows "The Event" to be in the hands of God; and the other where the University makes so much of the "usefulness"—utilitas, utilitatis—of education. Dodging both usefulness and the event, I would gaze with a curious fascination at a certain cock and sphinx which adorned the door-steps of one of those big red houses on the north side of the square, objects towards which Henry James himself must often have turned his ruminative head, pondering on the tragic ambiguity that underlies such patient inanimates.

My final objective in the square, however, was always the same, namely the path, just under the park-rails and opposite that inscription about "utility", which was the least-frequent promenade in the whole enclosure. Here I used to meet one of those emblematic, and, to my mind, with its persistent search for "omens of the way," mystical figures, messengers of the Grail you might almost call them, that all my days have at intervals crossed my path. Such was the madwoman I used to encounter by those Portslade gasworks, as I walked from Southwick to West Brighton, on my way to the first professional lectures of my life. Such was the madwoman who took me to Court House before the arrival on the scene of Mrs. Curme or of Aunt Stone. But the messenger of the Grail I used to meet in Washington Square was not mad. Nor was she an ordinary beggar. She was an Ideal Beggar. By that I mean that there hung about her that noble air of tattered distinction which you are conscious of in the Choregi of certain Greek plays. Her rags were symbolical, not a mere accompaniment of penury. They were her insignia, her scutcheon, her proud heraldic quarterings. She carried them with a certain furtive hauteur, as if they were a disguise out of which at any moment she might slip. Whenever we met, however, she fixed me with her eye as if she looked at me through her disguise.

She always walked very slowly, and, as she walked, she held in front of her a flat wooden box. I never once saw her soliciting alms. It was as if from that box she could distribute keys to the Invisible, such as the key that Mephistopheles gave to Faust when he called up Helen. Her ancient bonnet used to be gaily trimmed with artificial flowers that varied with the season, but for all that, when her lambent eyes looked at me it was like being hailed by Tisiphone, or Lachesis, or even Medusa. But I was never frightened of her. I felt that though she might be sinister in the eyes of many, she brought nothing but good luck to me. Her English was terribly broken; and it was perhaps well that this was so; for in one or two of our conversations I gathered that she really could give me a "key" from her mystic tray which would unlock—for a nice-spoken discreet gentleman—enclosed gardens that were much better left closed.

The windows of "the top-floor front" at Patchin Place looking out upon that picturesque little alley, had the boughs of an Ailanthus in front of them, that Tree of Heaven referred to by Kwang-Tze, that tree so devoid of "utilitas" and yet so perfect, that tree which the great God of Rubbish-Heaps has conjured up out of the dust to be his paramour in New York.

For ten years of my American life I had no bathroom except when I was travelling. But this was natural and familiar to me. Where was the bathroom in Shirley Vicarage? Where was the bathroom in Montacute Vicarage? Where was the bathroom even in that grand villa built for us by the Mayor of Caster-bridge? But I had plenty of fresh air and plenty of walking. I used to walk up and down for prolonged intervals that eastern side-walk of Washington Square, dodging the inquisitive dogs who with uplifted leg were perpetually keeping some elegant lady, fastened to them by a strap or a chain in humble and docile quiescence, while they voided their erotic if not ecstatic urine in places of attraction. I have noticed, since I have had a dog of my own, that these "places of attraction" can be artificially created by human attention. It has become necessary for me to avoid a particular stone or stump of which I may be enamoured lest, by noticing my absorption in it and thinking that it must be a "place of attraction" for me, my dog should incontinently make water against it.

Llewelyn and I made friends with a tiny specimen of the Dock genus, "*in* Dock, *out* Nettle," under those iron rails, and it was sad for me when after Llewelyn's departure that dock, like so many of our mutual friends, vanished away. It is a tragic thing—when considered properly—the actual destiny, in Time and Space, of a plant, of a stone, of an old glove, of a cast-off boutonnière, of a pencil, of a hairpin, of a boot-lace, of a broken walking-stick, that has played its rôle of divine interposition in some great crisis of our life and now is for ever lost.

At the entrance of Patchin Place sitting upon a crate, or leaning against the wall, was usually to be found, and I hope will long be found, the Shakespearian presence of Mr. Gilman. Mr. Gilman was a particular crony of mine; and in our time, like Ajax and Hector, we have exchanged many utensils of human use. Mr. Gilman's peculiarities and mine had much in common. We both, like the Ailanthus Tree, had a tenderness for the discarded and a predilection for limbo. We used to exchange these outcasts of the wasteland. Old chairs, old pictures, old walking-sticks were always passing between us.

One beautiful hazel-stick, the root of whose handle has a curve like the snout of a rhinoceros, came from the most romantic of all the dwellers in Patchin Place, namely the Mistress of the Cat Narcissus; but I would never have got hold of it save through the mediation of Mr. Gilman.

Even in my earlier Twelfth Street days, when with a Sorcerer of my own blood I looked out on that First Presbyterian grass-plot, I used to live chiefly on milk and eggs. I would go to the old Jefferson Market—now the Women's Prison, but I hope not the Bridewell, of New York—and come away carrying a "Grade A" quart bottle, which I refused to allow the milkman to place in the usual paper-bag. I got an æsthetic and theatrical pleasure from carrying these goodly bottles, in all their cool, slippery, life-restoring bountifulness. I used to carry them past the grave of Rachel Phillips—dead before I was born—or past that small poplar-tree, that has now got a yet smaller companion, as if I could share their life-restoring qualities, but when I had mounted the staircase of our Presbyterian retreat and found myself in our minute lodgement, I forgot both the dead woman and the pavement-growing tree, in my enjoyment of this white "refreshment."

On the strength of these Jefferson Market bottles, I often walked much further than several times round the whole of Washington Square. I used to walk down Seventh Avenue, that street which Llewelyn, in his poetic sentiment for Wessex, always called "The Fosse-Way," or down Hudson Street, often nearly to its end, or sometimes I would debouch to the river front and find some little space or gap, from which it was possible to get a restricted glimpse of the river. But that river front, for all its masts and hulls and flags and funnels, was only tantalizing to me, tantalizing and terrifying, for once or twice I met most sinister people down there and I always imagined endless weird possibilities. You see I was at once a finicking fastidious coward and a romantic sentimentalist! It suited my life-illusion to see myself wandering about dangerous sailor-frequented quarters and sitting on old dock-wharf steps watching waves over which a seagull could fly, without leaving the surface of the water, straight to the White Nose; but at the same time I was as terrified of gangsters and drunken brawls as if I had been an old lady in Salisbury close.

The youthful street-gangs used to mock me sometimes, shouting out opprobrious names after me, such as "Napoleon," or "Shakespeare." Why they did this I have no idea; for I must have looked with my old green-black ulster, my torn "sneakers," my hooked nose and preposterous walking-stick, more like a deboshed Doctor Faustus than either of those formidable great men.

The truth is that the only deviation from the norm of a bank clerk or a truck driver that was recognized by the populace of New York was that of an "artist." "He's an artist," I've heard them cry of many of my companions. But these lads showed some perspicuity. I certainly was not Napoleon; but they were right not to shout "artist" after me. It is a shame there was no Dickens going about that quarter to note what a "sight" I must have looked as I would leap back like a startled horse from the sight of a dog's turd, for for years dogs' excrement has outraged me as much as that of my own race, or from the sight of some dead horse, a very common object in those days, or from the neighbourhood of a dangerous looking dog, or from the presence of a building that gave me the idea that they practised vivisection inside it. On these occasions I would suddenly strike my stick violently into the ground, open my mouth like the mouth of a classic mask, extend the fingers of my free hand till they stuck out like the spokes of a wheel, and stride off as if a mob of lynchers was after me.

My attitude to New York City is a microcosm of my attitude to the whole of America. I regard it, just as those strains in the "Kardomah Café" prophesied I should do, as a terrifying chaos in which by the use of a certain crafty sagacity and a few magic tricks you can build a transient nest, the nest of a "Crane of Ibycus," under the iron girders of a steel bridge or against a blackening tree in a death-swamp. Even in these towering cities, the stark elements of the abyss heave up their heads. You peep out of an apartment house to behold a convulsed glacial rock or a distorted scoriac rock, and these inanimates leer back at you with a ghastly reciprocity of in-humanity. What Nature does have to put up with in America! But she can stand it; for nowhere else is she herself more *in extremis*. What is called an "amusement park" is one of the most terrifying things in this country; but this artificial Empusa-Monster is generally placed where primeval rocks or vast desolate sea-beaches are capable of putting it into its place as our European scenery would be puzzled to do. It is a wonder to see so many smart, brisk "apartments" each surrounded by its own cinders and ashes and every kind of litter, and yet confronted by Nature in her most awe-inspiring mood.

But after all I really do *know* New York better than I know any other city. Have I not had it as my headquarters for thirty years? Have I not come to feel for it that curious use-and-wont feeling, which is not the same as affection or admiration, but at the same time has a kind of cautious familiarity, a sort of reserved friendliness, which is very far removed from hatred? But if Americans with all their heroic simplicity, are sometimes devilishly cruel to eccentric and neurotic persons, and, in sudden spasms, fiendishly cruel to negroes, they do not confine such violence to these alien types. They turn on themselves! They especially turn on those mouthpieces of themselves, their own American men of genius.

America is the land of experiment, of novelty, and above all of youth, with its own especial kind of savage novelty-passion. America is a paradise for young women, a purgatory for old men—who indeed if they are to survive at all must be very tough and not very sensitive—and an inferno for imaginative American writers.

Expatriated Englishmen—and there are several of us here; some, like myself, with the recognized status of Resident Aliens —get on better than American writers of imagination. The mere fact that we *are* Englishmen helps us a lot; for though Americans have a contempt for "Wops" and "Dagos" of Mediterranean blood, they have an uneasy and sometimes rather a pathetic respect for Englishmen. When I think for instance, how much better I have been treated for these last thirty years than such native geniuses as Masters and Lindsay, the latchet

of whose shoes, as a poet anyway, I am unworthy to unloose,
it does fill me with anger against this youth-ridden, youth-
fooled, youth-besotted nation.

We English, I confess, err in the other direction. Our
island is a sort of earthly paradise for old men. In England we
wait till the reassuring tokens of dotage begin to appear, and
then with pious ardour we do more than justice to a genius that
is waning. But if Masters or Vachel Lindsay had been Englishmen, their position—when they outgrew their youth—would
have been assured, and would have increased in honour as their
vitality abated. With us Masters would have been Poet Laureate
—he certainly *ought* to be Poet Laureate of America—while
Lindsay would at least have been Sir Vachel. But it was just
the same in the earlier time. It was with us, on the other side,
that Walt Whitman, except for Emerson's brave word, got his
first deep recognition; and the contemporary neglect of
Melville's *Moby Dick* was as deep a disgrace to the perception
of Americans as was the way they treated Poe.

Clever young men and daring young women are the
honeysuckle rascals adored by the American public; and by
God! these sweet rogues know how to make hay while the
sun shines, in the Hollywood clover-fields!

Dreiser is a special case in this connection. Dreiser is one
of those formidable Men of Destiny who seem able to tap
some planetary reservoir of cosmic magnetism which renders
it of secondary importance to them what branch of mortal
activity they engage in. For once in human history the exploiters
of genius have met their match in Dreiser. He can give as good
as he takes, and a little more. But Dreiser is a much more remarkable being than you would get any idea of from his books.
Without exception he is the most astounding personality it has
been my lot—or *will* be my lot—to encounter in this mortal
pilgrimage. I regard Maxim Gorki as the greatest writer now
alive in the world; but I am convinced that, if they were put
face to face, the personality of the astonishing American
would overpower even this mighty Russian.

I would not like you to think, wise reader, that these thirty
years of American travelling have been all honey for "Mr.

Powg," as a New York firm used obstinately to name me, or for "Mr. Cow-Pat," as I was once called in the South, when I dare say they smelled out that I was a "nigger-lover." I will not say the thought, but most certainly the image, of suicide, rose up twice before me. The first time this occurred was on that confounded "Coast," as they call it; and its outward sign was a rigid paralysed staring over the side of a ferry-boat. The second time was in New York City, where its outward sign was a much briefer concentration upon those grim shining rails inside the Seventh Avenue Subway. You needn't think, either, that Comrade Fear, that Gorgonian hoverer over the background of my life, took himself off, because my other and more normal miseries made Pacific waves and New York rails want to have a word with me!

What this devilish Proteus, thus persecuting his poor brother-Proteus, would like me to do now would be to enumerate for you, well-balanced reader, every one of his metamorphoses. Nothing shall induce me to do so! Even such an autobiographist as I am cannot tell *all*. One little neglible trifling mask that he assumed however I would like to report; and this was my perfect terror of falling out of a high window. It was my crazy custom—when I could not get a room at least in the second or third storey of one of those monstrous hotels —to surround the window with all the furniture in the room before I went to bed. I made booby-traps in fact for myself *between my bed and the window* with as much serious thought as when I made pits in the potato-garden at Rothesay House for old Mr. Curme. And often, when I came home to the third-floor-front in Patchin Place, after having been as I thought contemptuously outraged—"rudely strumpeted" you might almost say, using the word for the spiritual ravishing of some as yet virginal level of my soul—by something or someone, I would mutter to myself aloud, repeating the words like a protective talisman, and oh! with what seething venom of indescribable maliciousness, some of those magical and yet in a sense *mincing* lines—and that *is* where the revenge lay—always so dear to me, from "Thyrsis" or the "Scholar Gipsy." Oh, the "miching mallecho" of calling up those "Cumnor Cowslips," those "jasmin-muffled lattices," those "white-blossomed thorn-trees," those "bluebells trembling by the forest-ways," as I made my cringing way from iron post to iron post under the resounding Sixth Avenue "El"!

The truth is that I have inherited from my Welsh ancestors a peculiar power—with something almost Jewish in it—of gathering, intellectually and imaginatively, all the beautiful *essences* of the country I am living in, while at the same time, rising up from the pit of my stomach, my "Emanation," as William Blake would say, weeps for Zion as it tries to sing the Lord's Song in a strange land.

At one epoch in my New York life Public Opinion, that wantonest of despots, decreed that on a particular day straw hats *must* be worn and on another date *must* be discarded. This led, as you can imagine, to a good deal of horse-play in the streets, and was an example of a certain crude alliance, which I have noticed cropping up now and again in America, between big business and the mob, a thing that always struck me as a peculiarly barbarous and dangerous sign, an alliance in fact between the noisy enemies and the insidious enemies of the dignity and decency of life.

Mr. Roosevelt has worked genuine psychic magic in getting rid of certain shocking phenomena in this country which are the direct result of climatic and geographical conditions. I find it difficult to imagine for instance a renewal of the activities of the Ku Klux Klan, activities which carried with them that peculiar ghastliness, that sort of *phantasmagoric* horror which is a unique accompaniment of physical brutality in America. This peculiar horror, which is really, to the imaginative nature, about the most repulsive phenomenon that the mind can conceive, found only one of its cruder manifestations in the Ku Klux Klan. I have noted it in a thousand directions, directions in which I fear, even a good president cannot quite clear the air! It comes, I believe, from the dominance of the big city over the country, and the triumph of youth over age. Average youth does not feel the appallingness of the particular horror I am talking about, the congenital American horror. But it is absurd to say there are no youthful Americans who feel it.

I expect those who feel it the most simply go mad, and that those who feel it next most commit suicide, and that those who feel it with only a moderate degree of desperation "do," as we used to say at the Prep., a "bunk"; in plainer words bugger off for Europe, as Henry James did!

For it is very hard to escape *the American horror*; and quite impossible, I suppose, to explain to those who don't see what it is that the victims of it see. The horror can be very big. But it can also be very small. Most things of this sort can be detected by their smell; and I think this particular horror is usually found—like the inside of an American coffin after the embalming process has run its course—to smell of a mixture of desolate varnish and unspeakable decomposition. The curious thing about it is that it is a horror that can only be felt by imaginative people. It is more than a mere negation of all that is mellow, lovely, harmonious, peaceful, organic, satisfying. It is not a negation at all! It is a terrifying positive. I think at its heart lies a sort of lemur-like violence of gruesome vulgarity. It certainly loves to dance a sort of "danse macabre" of frantic self-assertion. It has something that is antagonistic to the very essence of what the old cultures have been training us to for ten thousand years.

But it is, mark you, a thing of opposite extremes. *Litter*— litter for its own sake—plays a large part in it; but so also does a certain terrifying kind of soulless cleanliness! I think inanity, futility, and a certain ghastly "gimcrackism," are elements in it too. I think what is so especially shocking about it is that it is so palpable and yet so phantasmal. It is like a monstrous Guy Fawkes mask, appearing at a séance, with no human head inside it!

What are called "the Residential Sections" of the big cities reek and stink of this terrifying Presence. But you can find it too, as I have hinted, on any amusement beach, or in any amusement park. It has a wraith-like quality, it has a death-like quality, it has about it some queer ultimate desolation of emptiness, but with all this, and here lies the paradox of its shuddering horribleness, it is brand-new, spick-and-span, and strident. It is as if some hollow phantom from the last stages of human dissolution came miming and mowing up to us with a shrill concertina in its hands! It is indeed a composite Monstrum Horrendum.

Take the peculiar element in the work of Joyce that strikes our fastidious English gentility as "caddish." I don't mean the merely shocking. I mean something much more disturbing and disconcerting, something that carries a "hard-boiled" eye and a "treat-'em-rough" skin down to the very bottom of the pond. Take all this and add to it the most vividly realized spiritual desolation of T. S. Eliot's *Wasteland* and then add to *that* the tough, callous and brutal *veneer*, shiny surface over stale perspiration, of a rich "Summer Resort," and you will get *some* idea of the atmosphere I am trying to indicate, wherein all that is standardized and dispiriting groans with a rocker, flaps with an awning, sways with rusty-dusty evergreens, and gapes with a million empty garages! But, even then, you will not get all that this atmosphere means. For none of these desolations, as I pile up their physical unpleasantness, can convey a tithe of the mysterious *meaninglessness*, the absence of all that in human life is reassuring, satisfying, symbolic, that this thing presents.

I don't think that you feel "the American Horror" nearly as much among the poor as you do among the rich. I don't think you feel it at all in the real slums, though Heaven knows these places are bad enough! I *have* felt it faintly, now and again, in quarters of comfortable wage-earning people; but never anywhere as when it rushes over you, sterilizing, blighting, paralysing in these unspeakable "Residential Sections."

But to come to the War. I was in England, indeed I was at Montacute, when War was declared. I can remember hearing the trampling of the horses' feet of the local Yeomanry in the early dawn, as they passed down the road between the "Allotments" and the Vicarage hedge, and I had to be driven by Mr. Montacute, once the Squire's coachman and at that time living independently in the village, as I believe he still does, through Yeovil, and up Babylon Hill to Sherborne, where, from the Prep., I was to take my son home to Sussex. Never shall I forget my conversation with Mr. Montacute as we walked by his horse's head side by side up Babylon Hill. This kind-hearted heraldic supporter of Squire and Parson in turn spoke with courteous tact of other matters than the War as we mounted that strangely-named hill, for he knew as well as I knew with what that summer air was charged, as the preparations for the gala-day of the village gathered and gathered upon our house.

But later, that fatal summer, none other than "The Catholic" came to stay with us at the Vicarage, thus bringing it about that these two formidable spiritual influences in my life, he and my father, actually encountered each other in the flesh. It was while sitting with "The Catholic" in various neighbouring pubs, for although he hesitated not to enter the King's Arms and the Phelip's Arms in our own village I feared the wrath of my father far too much to go with him there, that fragments of that curious rumour used to reach us about the enormous Russian Army passing surreptitiously through England! The villages in our part of the country were in fact stirring with the maddest stories of Russian coins and scraps of Russian clothing left behind in the carriages of our familiar Great Western Railway.

But this book is only a history of humanity in so far as the confession of any one human soul *must* be that, and I hasten to return to my own experiences during these years. I crossed the Atlantic as usual during 1914 and 1915; but it was at this epoch that Arnold Shaw suddenly decided, "overnight," as they say, *to become a Publisher*. This decision was a momentous one for me; for just as my father always took precautions to preserve his personal self-respect and dignity from the rough-and-tumble of the world so it was essential for me to have an intimate friend like Arnold, a brother-in-arms, who shared my anti-social manias, but yet was not handicapped by them, to stand between me and the blood-and-iron mêlée. My cowardice in regard to ordinary matters of business is simply incredible. To stand up to anyone, to assert myself, in a business affair with anyone, means with me a greater moral effort than it would take to give five lectures in one day!

It is for this reason that I regarded it as nothing less than providential when Arnold one night, after a happy supper at

"Halloran's," decided to be a publisher. This bold departure in the Powys-Shaw Vaudeville was eagerly embraced by its chief clown. I was just about forty years old; I had been lecturing in America since 1905; I had not yet taken sanctuary in those rooms near the First Presbyterian church, that I subsequently sub-letted to Padraic Colum. I had only glanced into Patchin Place, where, they told me, though not exactly with bated breath and whispering humbleness, still survived the airy perch upon which the first butterfly-flight of Ezra Pound had rested its gauzy wing.

But the War, though I still went about my business, did have on me two very drastic psychological effects. It started me off at a break-neck pace writing books, for you must remember that before I turned forty the only things I had ever printed were those two little booklets of copy-cat verse that Cousin Ralph published in London. And it caused me to make a vow to give up all erotic pleasure—cerebral, voyeurish, or such as burlesque shows excited—until the War was over. This ascetic resolution did not occur at the very beginning of the War. Indeed I recall very well how once, when pacing up and down my favourite tow-path by the Arun at Burpham, I cursed the War from the bottom of my vice, because it separated me so indefinitely from those wicked French books! But back in America, and the whole business of war growing worse, this sacrifice of my vice became Powys Major's most serious offering on the slaughter-stone; the vow, namely, that I would abide as chaste as ice till the thing was over!

This turned out in a double way a greater sacrifice than I calculated on, for not only did the War make all the sylphs I knew reckless and adventurous, but it made so many new opportunities for the "Sweets of Sin." Balzac always maintained that the refraining from amorous pleasure was a great incentive to literary creation; and I expect we do make much more out of our suppressions than out of our fulfilments; but of course the real reason for my becoming an author was simply that Arnold had become a publisher.

It was in 1916, if I remember right, that with my West Twelfth Street companion I stayed in Vermont for late spring and summer, instead of going home. I felt obscurely uneasy in my mind while I was thus running away from the defence of my country; but I was considerably consoled by the fact that this was the first spring and summer I had ever spent in New England. I was indeed thrilled to make the acquaintance of Adder's Tongue, Mountain Laurel, Blood-Roots, Triliums, Spring Beauties and Arbutus.

My personal attitude to the War was a very simple and a very natural one. Perhaps it was somewhat of a feminine one too and *therefore* singularly close to Nature; though I certainly did not experience any of those ambiguous feminine emotions which seemed to delight in sending off handsome young men to the battlefield. I read Romain Rolland's *Above the Battle* and I read Russell's *Why Men Fight*; but these books had no more real effect upon me than had my habitual quotation in my lecture on Milton, from the passage in *Comus* beginning "So dear to Heaven is saintly chastity," when I had just been to a burlesque show.

With my vivid consciousness of the horror of what physical anguish could mean, with my morbidly imaginative nerves, with my mediæval conscience, I regarded the War as one single great cock-pit of suffering, to enter which was brave and noble, and to dodge which was base and ignoble. In the depths of my heart this was the view I took. All who went to the Front, or made desperate efforts to go to the Front were heroic. All who did not make desperate efforts to go to the Front were unheroic. I did not enter into the question of the absurdity and the wickedness of this War in particular, and of all war in general, for this seemed only too evident; nor did I really, at the very bottom of my heart, regard anyone responsible except the leaders of the people, and these leaders struck me as not so very different from the rest of humanity! My knife-like, masculine-feminine intelligence cut clean down through all these moral, political and rational arguments to two great prongs of the Devil's pitchfork. All war was crazy. This war, however, was not only crazy but mean and revolting, considering that it was made by cool-headed old men and cool-headed middle-aged men for the torment of hot-headed young men.

But the thing was in full blast. The young men were straining at the leash. And the mothers of men were already paying the piper. The nearer the trenches, therefore, that any middle-aged man of my age could smuggle himself, the nobler it seemed to me that middle-aged man was, quite regardless of the merits of the War. Here was a hideous cataclysm, a great burning fiery furnace. Never mind *who* started it, or *why* its victims were murdering each other! Persons of spirit hurried to get *as close to the flames* as they could. Cowardly persons hurried to get as far away from the flames as they could.

Don't "go away with the idea," gallant reader, that I didn't consider the most precious and sacred thing in the Universe to be personal life. Personal life I held then, and hold now, far more precious than any Cause, or any Faith, or any Country. Personal life and the intensifying and subtilizing of personal life is, as far as I am concerned, the only intelligible purpose of the Cosmos. Nor do I not recognize that my own personal cowardice, with its unheroic tendency to dodge the risks of war, if it could only be spread among other men, as quickly as "patriotism" and "nationalism" are spread, might result in a universal coward's strike or life-lover's strike, that might defeat the militarists. We who place our personal life above everything else, might even be worked up to defy these other men—so very like ourselves—who incite the masses to war.

But the truth is—and that is the fatal paradox—we mortals are so pathetically heroic that it will have to be made clear to us that it is more heroic to fight against fighting than to fight, before we have the guts to defy these leaders who, after all, are only ourselves turned into prime ministers and dictators. I think that the best proof offered us now of this pathetic heroism of the human race is the rise of dictatorships, whether Fascist or Communist. The situation is indeed most unfortunately clear. You can rouse men to mass-heroism when you cannot rouse them to individual heroism; for, as Voltaire said, "nothing is more unpleasant than to be *obscurely hanged.*" Like all life-and-death issues the thing is a terrible paradox. If you could only get all the artists and lovers and saints and philosophers and life-worshippers and mystics and stoics and epicureans on one side and the patriots and lynchers and vivisectionists on the other, there *would* be a war worth fighting. But, as it is, the situation is a good deal more complicated.

Personally I regard Communism with a kind of puzzled awe, and Fascism with a kind of puzzled prejudice, and of the two I am far more attracted to Communism; but it is as hard to be a coward and a Christian as to be a coward and a Communist! Communism and cowardice do not mix—at least not in these early stages of the revolution. And I am afraid my theory that a brave man would want to get as near as he could to "the burning crater" led to only lukewarm attempts to get near it myself. Even these attempts were postponed, not only till conscription in England reached well over my age, but until I had gone to the hospital to have "gasterenterostomy"; but after I was recovered from this, I did feebly bestir myself. I well recall the voice of a man in the British Propaganda Bureau in New York addressing over the telephone a man in the British Recruiting Office in the same city and declaring:

"Well! We've got a lusty recruit for you to-day!"

And how in my imagination I saw myself as I plunged into these places imploring my sergeant, on some future march, for leave to drop out to make water! *That* was my real secret terror, the difficulty of urinating and of voiding my excrement when I was in the ranks. I asked one friend of mine about this who assured me that it was "as easy as pot"; but I remembered all I had suffered at Wildman's from my neurosis over this matter, and I did not believe him. In the recruiting-room I was looked over just in the way D. H. Lawrence in *Kangaroo* so indignantly describes himself as being, but as I have almost as deep a feminine "penchant" for doctors as I have for priests I did not mind it at all!

Oddly enough I was not rejected on this occasion by reason of the fresh scar in my stomach, but by reason of some very old, and to me totally unrealized scar in one of my lungs. After this extremely feeble gesture to get nearer to the "burning crater" there happened to be a surcease of lecturing in the East, so I went once more to "the Coast." But it was not long before my conscience began to persecute me again; and presently, taking the advice of the wise old soldier, Colonel Wood, I returned incontinently to New York and sailed for England.

It was a curious experience, this voyage, for I went in a regular fleet of eleven great liners, all sailing near one another, just like the old sea-pictures of a battle-fleet; only these were steamers and had no sails. I was the only civilian on board the one I took, except for certain Y.M.C.A. officials in uniform whose muscular Christianity disgusted me, and whose discourses to the soldiers were very unpleasant to hear. A sort of sleek brutality characterized their utterances. They were a revolting parody upon all the more seductive aspects of patriotism.

The troops I was with—this must have been pretty early in 1918, when the Germans were getting ready for their final desperate attack—came mostly from Indiana, and I was always expecting them to burst out with "On the Banks of the Wabash," by Dreiser's brother Paul. But they were occupied with other matters. I well recall how one anxious lad, standing erect in his accoutrements in a boat projecting over the ship's side implored me to tell him what these things were like that he was scanning the waters so earnestly for. Being more familiar with the sea than this lad from Indianapolis I did what I could to describe the appearance of a submarine; but it must have been a very rough description; and I have no doubt it was a wonder that we two innocents, staring at those unruffled waters, escaped a more realistic knowledge.

The official medical examination for Sussex candidates under the new conscription was held, oddly enough, in the infants' school at Brighton. So here I was destined once more to visit my ancient foray-ground; once more to see "The Yacht *Skylark*" launched from that sunny beach, once more to breathe that memorially amorous air. Many a time had I passed that particular infants' school without a suspicion that a day would come when I should skip about naked as a frog within those walls while I was tested for serving my Sovereign.

Women and girls did, as a rule, in those days exercise a definitely warlike influence over their devotees; and this they did without having to carry actual "white feathers" for distribution. Colonel Wood, with his drastic-blue eagle-eye, had deemed it best for me to obey the un-ease of my conscience and hurry from "the Coast" straight to my native land. But I had written to Llewelyn in Africa, who, as a consumptive, had enabled my brother Willy to go to war by taking his place, expressing these conscientious scruples in so grandiose a manner that I blush to think of it.

Those were days when everyone who was not struggling hard to get into the firing line felt called upon to justify himself and explain in detail the importance of the various ties that interfered with his natural desire to be shot. I wrote to Llewelyn that I didn't at all like the idea of the Germans actually crossing the Channel and entering Dorset, even doing the goose-step perhaps between our Upwey Wishing Well and Maiden Castle. "Je suis gentilhomme," I wrote to him, like a tragic pierrot whistling "Malbrook s'en va t'en guerre," but what must the rogue do—and in all innocence too, for where "John" is concerned that level head grows dizzy—but yield to the quirk of showing my letter to the Elizabethan Irishman he was helping at that time, who doubtless made the devil's own face at this indecorous Pistol-like bluster.

But I was treated with extraordinary tenderness by the military examiners at that Brighton infants' school. And why *was* that? The other candidates for the trenches, who were a good deal less competent than I was, although not in any sense bullied, were not handled like brittle china. But that is precisely how I *was* handled. There were cubicles for us to undress in, I remember, each of which was designed for the accommodation of two persons.

"With whom would *you* like to undress?" the official asked me, indicating my fellow-conscripts.

I replied that it would be perfectly agreeable to me to undress "with any of these gentlemen." And so the officer selected Mr. Boom as my fellow-undresser. Mr. Boom was a very decent chap but custom had rendered it unusual for him to wash his knees. Thus ever since that day in the Brighton infants' school I have myself scrubbed my knees, whenever I've got a chance, with extreme violence, fearful lest, one of these days, I might be exposed as poor Mr. Boom was exposed. My own psychological explanation of the tenderness with which I was treated in this recruiting station is first that conscription is so alien to the English that those who employ it have a subconscious feeling of uneasy shame, and secondly that these medical officers felt that all gentlemen who were real "gentilhommes" had so long ago plunged into the "burning crater" that those who were left, along with the pacific Mr. Boom and a few half-witted tramps picked up between Brighton and London, must be so pathetically degenerate that it would be like torturing an animal to be harsh to them.

In any case I am certain that nothing is more contrary to the profoundest nature of the English race than the "military spirit," at any rate as our Continental neighbours display it and understand it. It is not from lack of endurance, but from lack of taking for granted that the military profession means bullying and being bullied, that we fail in the right temper. All our soldiership, except when the Irish come into it, is an amateur affair, a kind of sporting *tour de force*. Perhaps the sufferings we undergo at school kill the warlike spirit in us. Certainly my own experience has been that the worst bullies at school belonged, as I did myself, to the "Celtic Fringe." They were British rather than English.

So anxious were these good-tempered English that a cowardly Celtic neurotic like myself should not be sent to the War that they tracked down that ridiculous old shadow-scar in my lungs, that I had never known anything about, and sent me to a specialist in Chichester for further examination! You can believe how I thought of Keats' "Eve of St. Mark" as I wandered about the Cathedral Close after visiting this doctor. Well! The end of it was that I was exempted from service and given *carte blanche* to go back to America. I was anxious to see a little more of my relatives, however, before I left and so I decided to give lectures up and down the country for Mr. Lloyd George's especial "Bureau of War Aims."

Judging from the Versailles Treaty my "War Aims" differed in several respects from those of the Prime Minister but no one interfered with me; no one gave me any instructions; and at the Government's expense I lectured—or rather made soap-box speeches, for these addresses were always in the open air—upon my own personal ideas as to what the War was about and how it ought to end. I made a fine fool of myself in one of these rhapsodies on the future of war and peace.

This was in Wales; but I did not realize that it was in a region of Wales where the bulk of the natives, as Scott describes in *The Betrothed*, were Flemings. I encountered, of course, many Belgian refugees from modern Flanders; but this particular group was descended from the old Flemings. Ignorant of the ethnological nature of this audience, which was an extremely Teutonic-looking one and incidentally a profoundly lethargic one, I launched out on an impassioned palinode in honour of the Cymric branch of the Celts and its immemorial mythology. You can imagine what I felt when, as soon as it was over, the political agent of that district gave me a weary rebuke.

But it was a queer affair, this business of delivering "War Aims" lectures, without instructions, up and down my native land! The more I think of it, and indeed of all my experiences in England during that epoch, the more I respect my fellow-countrymen. I forget now to what particular persons I had to go, to get my credentials; but I know I went to a house actually next door to Number Ten Downing Street, and I know in the course of my wanderings I drifted through the gates of the War Office. In all these peregrinations I remember being extraordinarily impressed by the amateur, unofficial, unmilitary, unbullying air, with such an incredible amount of "yield" and "give" in it, that characterized everything I encountered!

I remember for instance how in front of the War Office, instead of generals in plumed hats I found a group of children playing marbles, and instead of mounted policemen a couple of small boys with hoops. Another example of the sort of thing that pleased me so much in England, and made me feel so proud of my fellow-countrymen, was the easy, amateur way these "War Aim" lectures were conducted. The local political agents, taken casually from both the big parties, were made responsible for all the practical arrangements; and, on my soul, these arrangements were sometimes as quaint as if we had still been in the time of Charles Dickens. One worthy gentleman, evidently disagreeing with both the Celtic Prime Minister and the Celtic Lecturer as to the value of the "spoken word" when the country was at war, made use of his trip with me to a remote portion of his county to collect eggs. In a dog-cart stuffed with eggs we sought out the particular village-green where I hoped to increase Mr. Wilson's fourteen points from fourteen to forty.

I always began my mystical discourses in the same way. "I have just come over from America," I used to shout, addressing the mothers and sisters and sweethearts of the youths that our European nationalism was slaughtering by millions, "with fifty thousand invincible young men from the Middle-West!"

At one town where I had to speak—and this curious "War Aims" tour, in which my country's authorities trusted me to such a tune, was crowded with side-lights upon the rooted individualism of our race even at such a deadly crisis—my colleagues and myself were interrupted by a meeting of Socialists which overlapped with ours. For a moment I forgot I was no longer in wartime America, and I looked nervously round for the appearance of the familiar hundred-per-cent. lynchers or the prompt emergence of Irish policemen armed with clubs, but in place of these sinister apparitions one of my colleagues, a shell-shocked soldier from the front, took out his watch.

"Powys," he said, just as if we were in a college debating society, "give these fellows five minutes on our platform, and then we'll try to answer them."

To "answer" them was indeed easier to "try" than to achieve, for true to our national characteristics, there were more allusions to the Pope and the House of Lords and the Land-Owning Dukes, than to any Marxian reasonings about capitalistic wars. I can assure you that my vow of cerebral chastity had to endure many serious and most tantalizing temptations during these tours, for many of my open-air speeches were made on sunny esplanades and beguiling sea-fronts, crowded with excitable young women made reckless by the desperation of the War.

I held to it rigidly, however; for, without bragging, I was enough of a Tibetan adept by this time to have a fairly adamantine control over what Dr. Johnson would call "my amorous propensities." I well recall how, in one inn where I stayed, this quixotic offering to the "burning crater" I was dodging had a very unexpected result in making me the favoured confidant of the prettiest barmaid I have ever seen! Nothing is more seductive to youthful womanhood than iron virtue concealing intense susceptibility; and I can now hear the groan of a disappointed rival:

"You're the one she likes, damn you; though I *did* give her a lecherous kiss!"

I must confess that there were a few "embusqués" I encountered here and there in my erratic journeys, who gave me an uncomfortable sensation. I found that my "life-illusion," as I call it, that innermost daimon, whose attitude to one's proceedings is the compass-needle of one's self-respect, while it felt perfectly at ease in the presence of men who had been and would be again, in the "burning crater," was made decidedly jumpy when I was with people more or less in my own position. I was too proud, and by nature too ferocious in self-laceration, to condescend to any "rationalizations," or to any discriminations among us "Artful Dodgers" of the Inferno. With those who were "in it" I felt weak, brittle, humble, *womanish* even; but in the company of these others, the malicious devil at the bottom of my nature kept asking:

"What are *you* doing, 'dans cette galère'?"

My young son, taking for granted that his voluble progenitor wanted to be as close to the "burning crater" as possible, suggested that I should apply for a job as a Y.M.C.A. "entertainer" at the Front, and my neighbour Sir Harry Johnston who himself had been invalided home from an excursion of this sort gave me a letter of introduction to the office that arranged such things. But, as it happened, my visit to this office was made simultaneously with a sudden intensification of activity on both the enemies' part and our own, and I was told that all permits for this kind of thing had been cancelled. Twice during this visit to England I was seized with an unholy and purely animal sense of immense relief: once when I received from Brighton my card of exemption from service and now again when I found that it was impossible for me to imitate Sir Harry Johnston and go to France as a civilian.

I finally determined, since I could not support my family on my "War Aims" discourses, to return to America. With a view to this I wrote an extraordinary letter to the authorities for whom I had been speaking, in which I announced to them that I had "decided to reside in California." At this distance of time I find it impossible to tell why I used this astonishing phrase. I don't think it was meant humorously. I don't think it was flung out in a spasm of masochistic auto-malice. But it certainly makes me blush to think of it now. It was as if, during a monstrous conflagration, when all the world was carrying buckets, I had informed the chief of the fire department that I must hand *my* bucket over to someone else, as I had to go home to take a Turkish bath!

There was a derelict from the American Army, or at any rate some unfortunate soldier who was returning to America to be punished, on the ship with me, when Tom Jones— neither of us aware that this was the last time we should meet— saw me off at Liverpool, and I used to drink tea with this forlorn wretch and promise to help him by writing letters on his behalf. But he was a singularly unappealing individual, sulky and scurvy-spirited, and when I thought of all the heroic, generous, sweet-natured young men tortured and murdered by our patriotic madness, it seemed a poor thing to be devoting my energy to the composition of letters on behalf of this one poor, sullen cross-patch, who under a normal condition could hardly have been more than a disobliging "bellhop." But there it was! The poor devil could bleed if you pricked him, and could lap up a can of ship's tea with scarcely less gusto than I myself.

In those days I used to think quite a lot about this business of Pacifism and Pacifists. The ones that were cruelly treated and badly beaten up I did feel sympathic with, but there were others that in my devilish self-knowledge I deeply suspected of using their perfectly rational principles to dodge the irrational plunge into the "burning crater." What would really have happened, I asked myself, if a nation, like this great formidable German nation—that alone was so nearly a match for the whole Orbis Terrarum—*had* found all the other races prepared to be invaded and dominated and exploited and trodden upon, because of their principles of pacifism and of philosophical spirituality? Would it have resulted in the sort of Passive Resistance that Gandhi organized, to bewilder our own Empire in India?

But I had the wit to see that if any League of Nations was to be able to suppress such an over-riding nation, the very moment it invaded another country, it would have to be a genuine International Super-State, with an irresistible army and navy that could be transported in a few weeks to the uttermost ends of the earth! And I also had the wit to see that nothing short of the sheer force of such an International Super-State could deter a newly-organized nation, waking to intense race-consciousness only to find the globe already dominated, from its natural tendency to break out.

Profoundly feminine as my intelligence is I was aware—just as all women are secretly aware—of the irresistible power of women *were they to use it*. And it often came over me that, as Aristophanes suggested in *his* burlesque show, the best solution would be for the implicit matriarchy of the human race to become an explicit matriarchy, and for "the women of all nations"—to twist a little the famous Communist Manifesto —"to unite" in one world-wide strike to put an end to this patriotic insanity.

Personally the year 1918, in spite of my anxiety over my brother Bertie's fate—for he had been taken prisoner in that last terrific German drive—was a much happier one than 1917. 1917 was the worst year of my whole life, after my years in Wildman's House at school. I put down my nervous

misery during that year to the magnetic vibrations of anguish
—like a sort of psychic "wireless"—that kept crossing the
Atlantic from Europe. My time in the hospital, when I had
that "gasterenterostomy" operation whose grand name I am
so proud of, was really a pleasant time compared with the rest
of that terrible year. I came nearer to insanity during this
epoch than I had ever done before, though of course I know,
and I dare say my reader will willingly bear me out in this,
that I am—all the while—never *wholly sane*. But I certainly had
such misery during 1917 in America that my fantastic "War
Aims" discourses, when Lloyd George's belief in the value of
"the word" let me loose on my native land, were paradisic in
comparison.

My old undying Worm of secret Fear—and how absurd to
think that by naming fear "phobia" you can diminish its
devastation?—wagged its ghastly head at me, as if the Loch
Ness Monster should be confronted by another monster—
"a bogy," to quote my old Corfe Castle poem, "that surpassed
it in height." Indeed the thing wagged its head at me as it had
never wagged it before. I was still established in that old
Presbyterian Church-House looking out on Fifth Avenue, but
when the summer grew warmer we rented or "let," as we
English say, these two little rooms, each of them so much taller
than they were wide, to Padraic Colum.

I have always loved and admired Padraic Colum, second
to few, and I have the greatest respect, and to confess the truth
a little envy, of the wise and yet artless way he copes with the
difficulties of life. Thus it was a pleasure to think of him in my
rooms. But ailinon! ailinon! how I came to regret that I had let
them go! Without those rooms I wandered about America like
a monkey in a huge garden composed entirely of those prickly
trees they call monkey-puzzlers.

I clung to Arnold and his family for a while, but Arnold
was a swimmer and a tennis-player, so that he chose somewhat
gregarious places, and my neurotic loathing of summer life in
America grew to a shrieking point. Oh, how I came to hate the
mere sight of men's bare bodies that year! I hated that bronzy
tint they were so proud of! I hated the everlasting bathing-

suits, rather than bathing-*drawers*, that they wore. I suppose what it really amounted to was this. Being the particular kind of perverse nympholept, I was, attracted to women much more as a Lesbian is attracted to them than as a man is attracted to them, and, in addition to this, deriving my greatest thrills from my *voyeur* tendencies—if that is the right word for it—than from any sense of touch, it was a perpetual aggravation to me, a sort of "adding insult to injury" in the erotic sense, to be surrounded by these tall strong lusty lively brown-skinned young men!

And these "summer-lads" of America terrified me by their morality as much as by their muscularity. Their very perspiration had a *moral smell* that made me feel desolate and lonely and homesick. They seemed to me like a different race from the human race that I knew and that I was always reading about in the classic authors. Beholding their worse than innocent nakedness at these unspeakable resorts I began to realize what extraordinary originality, what *mad* originality, American men and women, who *are* original at all, must possess, to deal with this tidal-wave of catastrophically normal humanity. Could it be, I asked myself, as I surveyed these summer-lads in their trim bathing-suits, that it was about these super-normal pillars of society that Walt Whitman wrote his lovely and passionate "Calamus" poems? It seemed unbelievable, But it only made me the more convinced that to be a genius in America is twice as difficult as elsewhere; and that when you *are* a genius, like Whitman, or Melville, or Masters, or Dreiser, or Vachel Lindsay, or Isadora Duncan, or Edna Millay, you've got to develop a sort of protective chain armour or you'll soon be driven to suicide.

Deserting my devoted friend Arnold, because of his love of bathing and playing tennis, I fled down into Virginia, and tried to hide myself there, but almost at once my terror, encouraged by all those aspects of the South that are peculiarly dreadful to me, drove me forth again. Then I fled to Cooper's Town in upper New York, thinking to myself, "Surely by the grave of Fenimore Cooper I shall find peace!" But while Fenimore Cooper's grave was all right, and I could escape beautifully there from the summer-lads and their dashing débutantes, I was not in a position quite yet to find lodgings in a churchyard.

So my blood-crony and I hired a little new unpainted shanty on the very edge of Fenimore Cooper's glittering lake. But it was perfect misery. My companion struggled gallantly for a while with my wretched nerves, but to no avail! I think my time in that appalling newly put-up wooden box by the edge of those lapping waters was almost as bad as what I suffered during the bathing-hour in that old school bath. Then a motor-boat began to frequent that portion of the lake; and to me the resounding "ticking" of a motor-boat is without exception the most unpleasant of all sounds. Twenty, nay! fifty "elevated" railways would be nothing to the ferocious malignity of this hard, unfeeling noise.

"*Tick*—damn you!—*tick!*—blast you!—*tick!*—may the devil carry you away! Tick! tick! tick!"

My kind familiar spirit, who loved hot weather and heavy foliage like a lioness, enjoyed the American summers. But to me, who for all my "cat-head" am more like a polar-bear, they have always been a complicated misery. Even here, in this cool "up-state" valley, I find the triumphant leafage of the summers more than I can endure. Too tropical, too tropical it is for my taste! Yes, even here, where in the preceding winters the temperature may have gone down to thirty below zero, these burning summers harrow my soul. In that raw and blistering shanty of ours the sun drew sticky drops out of the woodwork while the motor-boat ticked, and the lake lapped like the devil's dam. The privy was a replica of the shanty, save that its door was of such new wood that it refused to shut and the sun blazed down upon it with even more brazen publicity than upon the hovel. Finally, I used to flee inland, across the lively motor-road where the automobiles glittered in the burning sun, and hurry across the ploughed-fields till I found a cowshed. To this retreat I would carry my pen and papers.

But even from this cowshed the vibrations of anguish from the War drove me forth. I left my dark sorceress to her fate at the very moment when Rollo Peters, the loveliest and most loyal of all our younger friends, was on the point of arriving.

This alone shows what a hunted and half-crazy state I was in, for I love Rollo well; but the devil himself was tugging at my navel-string, and I fled to New York. Padraic was still occupying my room, so, in my growing derangement, I took refuge with the best of all family doctors, our unequalled Dr. Thomas, whose skill was soon to bring my beautiful nephew, Peter Grey, into the world, and the Thomases with infinite tact and kindness installed a bed for me in a neighbouring house, a big house, that was completely empty.

I cannot describe to you how *Summer in America* terrified me that awful 1917. Everything in the whole world that appealed to me seemed to have been scorched by the sun into non-existence. But what was left was not the burning lonely sands of any Arabian desert, but the growth of a luxuriant foliage, amid which, like beautifully modelled fashionable statues, super-normal, super-naked humanity disported itself with noisy chastity. The truth is I am myself so vicious that I loathe chaste nakedness as much as I loathe tropical foliage. I am just exactly like a mediæval monk who in his rocky retreat can only tolerate bare limbs when they belong to the most provocative of she-devils, against whose wiles it is his profession to struggle.

How well in that dreadful time I can recall walking round and round and round that old railed-in reservoir in the centre of Central Park! Of all parks I detest Central Park the most. I detest it as much as I love that beautiful German-designed park in Brooklyn. Central Park always seems to me far more spoiled by the selfishness of the rich than any royal or ducal park I have ever seen. If I were the Mayor of New York I would close Central Park to motor-cars; open it only in the mornings to horsemen and horsewomen, and allow every man, woman, and child, to wander about in it wherever and whenever they like, make love in it as much as they like, and sleep in it without let or hindrance.

When you are half-crazy you have the Devil's own genius of minute observation. A curiously little thing I can recall so well of that house of which the Thomases got me the key; and that was the singular effect of hot water emerging from a bath faucet in a big completely empty mansion. It felt like being inside a huge sacred tank, of which I was the solitary crocodile-god, for it was a bathroom of which it was quite unnecessary to close the door! I can now see exactly how a certain little wisp of dust-fluff looked, as it floated in this tank-bath; that bit of dust-fluff and I being alone in an aquarium that was also a Necropolis.

The Thomases *were* good to me in that awful time! They were far too sensible to do anything but quietly assume that I was *merely fretting* until I could go back to my Twelfth Street flat or until my familiar spirit returned to the city. I was not a stranger to the part of the city where the Thomases lived. In fact it was in this district, so near Central Park, that I had bought from a little umbrella-shop close to the Natural History Museum the oldest of the four walking-sticks that I now possess. It is a hickory-stick with a round handle, and I bought it from a quiet little German in that quarter, who, the very second he laid hands on it, became a ferocious huntsman of wild animals. While I was inspecting it I heard him muttering to himself. "I didn't catch," I began, "I didn't catch what you said."

"I killed her," he repeated, "with one blow."

"I beg your pardon?"

"With one blow; and I'm telling you she was no ordinary hare!"

But to return to my return from England, where the nearest I had ventured to the "burning crater" (*burning, burning, burning!*) was when I carried, at my young son's suggestion, Sir Harry's letter to the office for supplying entertainers at the Front. I did not at once—indeed I cannot remember just when I did—enter upon "my residence in California." All the events of my life in 1917 and 1918 seem to have taken place in a sort of phantasmagoric mist. I can well remember the date when America entered the War, for I was having my supper in the old Louisiana Café in New Orleans, and I recall that, in the maliciousness of my heart, instead of singing "My Country, 'tis of thee," I sang, "Confound their politics; frustrate their knavish tricks," including in my philosophic misanthropy all the nations of the world.

And I can remember the day when prohibition began, and how I bought, and this *was* on "the Coast," a colossal stone jar, like one of those jars mentioned at the Marriage at Cana in Galilee containing the only alcoholic drink I really care for, namely very strong, very cheap, very fiery, very raw whisky. I can remember too—and they come floating in upon me like pictures in a witch's crystal—the night of both the *false* Armistice day, in New York, and the *real* Armistice day. On this latter occasion I had my evening meal in the Brevoort. Now it was in the Brevoort that the great Dr. Erdmann, like Our Lord in Oscar Wilde's story, had spoken to me, after my operation, when he saw me supping there, side by side with the goldenest of golden heads, and it was indeed in the Brevoort that all the most exciting events of my American life never failed to have some kind of repercussion.

On this Armistice night, however, I must confess to feeling a fiercer and more fermenting surge of malicious hatred for my well-to-do bourgeois compeers than I have ever felt before or since. The sight of such patriots, none of whom had probably even smelt from afar the fumes of the "burning crater," was one of those sights—for I am afraid my malice is even stronger than my pity—that gave me a further jerk along the hard and narrow road that leadeth to Communism. But if my spleen at that moment turned upon my bourgeois Americans it was grossly unfair. Had I forgotten those unworthy scenes in our own London during the Boer War? But only once did I grow as ferocious in Manhattan as I did on various occasions in Boston.

Except at Ford Hall, or when encouraged by such a kindly radical as Longfellow's grandson, Dr. Dana, or by my friend Mr. Freshel, I have seemed fated to get into violent rows in Boston. Philadelphia, always my favourite city in this whole continent, preserved an attitude to my cerebral antics that was at once superciliously aloof and affectionately amused. Philadelphians are conservative and a little cynical, but they are profoundly indulgent and always on the look-out for "entertainment." But in Boston I came up against sheer hostility, hostility as bitter as my own diatribes. This atmospheric and

I might almost say astrological clash between myself and the Bostonians was modified for me by the fact that I so greatly enjoyed staying at the Tourraine Hotel, the only hotel I have ever known that possessed a comfortable library.

This amazing library always had a blazing fire and contained in its shelves all the works of Henry James. I was also mollified during my Boston visits by the pleasure I derived, which was a very intense one, from visiting my first cousin, John Hamilton Cowper Johnson, among his brother "Cowley Fathers" at the monastic church of St. John in Bowdoin Street. Cousin Hamilton and I have more things in common than I have time to enumerate here, and his astonishing knowledge of Latin has often helped to thicken out my cursory but very authentic enjoyment of Cicero and Horace. Our natures "except for these bonds," as St. Paul would say, by which I mean my own secular vices, not my cousin's priesthood, are singularly harmonious. In some things I can only say I *hope* he understands me better than I understand myself, for he will, I know, feel strongly that in this book I have made myself out at once more of a sinner and more of a fool than I really am. Well! it is not often that one's Father Confessor—though Hamilton is only this in a secular sense—regards one as a much better person than one regards oneself. Certainly if, as out of my profound scepticism of modern science I consider very possible, the Christian doctrines, *relaxed a little on the erotic side*, are representative of deep cosmic secrets, I could not wish for any more penetrating champion of my ambiguous character before the jury of the saints than this more than blood-relation.

It is queer that I should have had to come to America to get to know, putting Cousin Ralph aside, my two favourite cousins; for not only have I made a lifelong friend of Hamilton, whom, as a child at Northwold, I remember throwing into a bed of nettles, but on a lecture tour in New Mexico I discovered Warwick Powys. It is true I can only claim fifth-cousinship with Cousin Warwick, but we have twice lived very complacently together as bachelors; and have not quarrelled —which is still rarer—when in the *other* condition! Like myself, Cousin Warwick is almost superstitiously credulous about our ancestral connection with the ancient Powys-Land of Mid-Wales and I note, through all the dividing medium of Fifth-Cousinship, many curious resemblances in our emotional feelings.

But to return to my troubles in Boston. I remember speaking once before the City Club there largely composed of professional men, upon some topic connected with education, and I well recall the bitter anger I provoked when I brought out my well-worn tag about culture in America being entirely in the hands of women and carrying visibly upon it the unmistakable imprints of its maternity. I did not, as I might have done, quote the gentle lines, "My country, 'tis of thee, sweet Land of Liberty," compared with "Confound their politics, frustrate their knavish tricks" of our own most masculine invocation, but I did have something to throw out about the quaint hiatus between American culture, as it was in those days, and all that —well! all that Rabelais may be said to represent in the sphere of literary bawdiness.

But what a turn of the wheel we behold to-day! Everything is reversed. It is like a miracle. Joyce's *Ulysses*, that tragic piece of imaginative realism, has not only been "released," but has actually become a best seller, and there is no doubt that to-day America is far ahead of England in its freedom from "moral" censorship. But America has always been the favoured land of what you might call the Swinging Pendulum, and so violently has the pendulum been swinging lately that it will soon be difficult for the younger generation to even imagine the sort of attacks that a book like Dreiser's *Genius* was subject to, so brief a time ago. For myself I have such a categorical imperative, of late, against reading sadistic books, and have always shrunk so much from other sorts of realism that I find myself going back to Henry James!

But it was not only with the City Club in Boston that I became the opposite of a *persona grata*. I will now tell you how it came about that I lost my audience there of select society ladies. This was due to one of those ill-considered outbursts that so often led to a temporary "residence in California." These "residences" were sometimes merely a sign that Arnold's fertile brain was undergoing a period of exhaustion, but they were more often due to indiscretions of my own. It was in a very fashionable Boston house that I had to speak to a fashionable Boston audience. My friend Mr. Freshel—secure above all fashion—was not there to defend me and I was asked point-blank by a lady-patriot the not—as I admitted to myself—quite irrelevant question, what I, a native of England, was doing in America, while we were fighting for our life on the other side. I have so often had to blush to record my sorry lapses from dignity and decency that it is a relief to be able to put on record at least one occasion when the Lord of Hosts inspired me with my answer. I told the patriotic lady quite frankly why I had not, by hook or by crook, got to the Front. Of course if I had been *absolutely* accurate I should have said that my worst secret fear of the great bonfire had to do with my difficulty of urinating in public; but I think even my honestest critic will absolve me from mentioning urine before such ladies. So I confined my confession under this feminine "turn of the screw" to my more normal fear of German bayonets; but *that* was quite enough. Never again did the disgraced Shaw-Circus receive a Bostonian invitation.

Psychopathologists who deal in erotic matters will not be surprised to learn that although I did not celebrate the Armistice by enjoying myself at the Brevoort, I *did* celebrate it by drawing up the dam from my suppressed wickedness. I had a learned friend in America whose humour it had been for some while to make a collection of the particular books that I found so perilous and it was not long ere I came hurrying back from his library with my precious Verona "grip," bought in the Capulet-Montagu city the day of that tremendous thunderstorm without rain, literally weighed down with the brimstone of hell.

But just as always happened—and it shows how childishly short-sighted I am in such cerebral passions—a few frantic hours were enough to swing the needle of my psychic compass completely round! Off I must bolt—and I recall that particular night so well, for it was pouring with floods of tropical rain—to the nearest burlesque show. Printed provocation lost its magic so soon; whereas the real feminine form was inexhaustible. Well! Not quite inexhaustible! For from even this I have turned away, longing for a real sylph nearer than on the stage.

I am inclined to think, in fact, that the worst result of my release from my sacrifice to "the burning crater," was this same longing to find the sylph-hood I so intensely adored *closer* at hand. I was so sub-human that what I really wanted was not a woman with normal feelings, for such a woman I was dedicated to hurt, but some kind of an Undine or Elemental, entirely devoid of the natural instincts of womankind. I was indeed a fatally dangerous sort of monster, a satyr-monk, a wicked mystic; and any woman who risked getting fond of me risked a great deal. Deep in my heart I knew well that if I wanted to keep a clear conscience in the matter of women's feelings the only thing to do was to cut down at the very start upon every sort of amorous dalliance.

Yes, if I were to obey my Socratic daimon what I would have to do would be to endure the tyranny of my cerebral lust until I should discover—if such Beings *were* to be discovered— some fanciful and elemental sylphid as peculiar and perverse as myself! Luckily for me the larger number of my "fair friends," as Sir Walter would put it, were deep in love with some upstanding young springald of their own dimension; and, as you may well conceive, few rôles in life have suited me better than that of a detached but not puritanical Epicurus, discoursing in his garden, as Landor loved to imagine him, with Leontion and Ternissa.

But my maniacal desire to give a true picture of my character and my life as I really see them—and for all Father Johnson's instinct to the contrary I feel that I see them more as his God would see them than as he does himself—compels me to confess that between the ages of forty and sixty I have done as much harm as I have done good to these exquisite beings that I worship so intensely and so perversely. But, as my Crocean friend, James Henderson, says very wisely, unless remorse waters the seedlings of a real *vita nuova* it is unphilosophical to sorrow over the harm we have done. Any convoluted and even hypocritical philosophizing against the stabs of remorse I can perfectly understand and am prepared to practise; but what I cannot understand is all this tough, smart, cynical modern talk, by means of which the values that I hold, the subtleties that I discern, and the responsibility in which I believe, are reduced to the tedious level of a futile nothingness. They are *not* nothing. What *is* nothing is this or that transitory scientific theory about atoms or electrons or vibratory rays. The imaginative will of men—*that* is not nothing!

How queer it is how our dearest lovers know us not! I am perfectly aware how indignant—on my behalf—my closest friends will be over this autobiography of mine. But fortunately if "truth is to be served" I have an invaluable organ of research in myself which is more powerful than any scientific microscope. I refer to *my sacred and holy malice,* my wicked and creative-destructive joy in bringing down the dignified "John" in me and exalting the living pierrot of my soul. And what, when you really come down to it, is the use of these clever sophisticated "Memoirs" of tedious dignitaries, who never once let you see the shivering, jerking, scratching, crying, groaning, God-alone-sees-me nerve of their central "Libido"?

And you need not think that I affect my ridiculous childishness because of my curious pride in emphasizing the feminine element in my nature. Women, I know, love to excuse their naughtiness by telling you that it is "childishness." The truth is they *are* childish, but not at all where they pretend to be. Men, heaven knows, are childish enough too where they least realize it, and the more they are so, the better pleased is the deep maternal instinct in women to reduce masculine pretensions.

Now where my own spiritual sincerity comes in, is that part of my soul follows close behind my "childishness," close behind all my manias, all my superstitions, all my peculiarities, like an exultant demon-falcon, shrieking and fluttering, and deriving a voluptuous pleasure from catching myself acting like a sentimentalist or an idiot. I even think sometimes, when I consider how my deepest impulses are neither exactly sadistic nor masochistic or mystical or theatrical or quite sane or quite mad, that there ought to be coined a completely new formula for what I am; *and perhaps this is true of every separate living soul.* In fact I would modestly offer to students of abnormality the word "Cowperist" to describe what I am, a word taken from my second name. I am not a masochist, or even a zo-ophilist: I am a Cowperist. But this I do at least know of myself: I combine an extremely quick and mercurial intelligence with a lean, primordial, bony, gaunt neanderthal simplicity. My nimble wit is in fact the Ariel-like slave of my Caliban primitiveness and its deadly and thaumaturgic champion against the world.

Chapter Twelve

"There's a Mohawk in the Sky!"

THERE came a time when Arnold began a yet further extension of his activities as a lecture-manager. The late Mr. George, the well-known English novelist, had a tour under him, and the famous English preacher, Maud Royden, had a very successful visit to America under his auspices. But the strain of all this required tougher nerves than my friend possessed. The old Shaw-Powys Circus had rattled its ramshackle caravan wheels, paying "scot and lot" as it went, and taking in easy parts the ups and downs of the show business, but when it became a matter of leaving "the road," of deserting our old careless life "under canvas" and of hiring great megalopolitan halls in New York, even Arnold's Yorkshire constitution collapsed.

He had so severe an illness that on his recovery he decided to enter a completely different field of activity and to hand his ageing acrobat over to one of the professional and official firms of lecture-management. He selected the well-known "Lee Keedick Bureau" for this purpose. What largely influenced him in this choice was his personal regard—a regard which I soon came heartily to share—for Mr. Keedick's experienced subordinate, Mr. Glass, who was the one who managed the "travelling end" of this bureau's concerns.

Mr. Glass was the brother-in-law of the famous Major Pond; and Arnold always assured me that no one understood the lecture-field better than he. Mr. Glass certainly was in the old tradition of lecture-management in America. He had travelled from coast to coast with Stanley, the explorer; he had arranged lectures for the dialect-poet Whitcomb Riley; he told humorous stories about Jerome K. Jerome. He was a Scotsman;

and he had a look as if he might have been Seneschal of Glamis Castle. He was a very big man. He was the only man I have ever known who wore boots of "size twelve." It is true that I never went down on my knees to measure Mr. Glass's boots; but I came incidentally to learn their prodigious size when their owner assisted me in enlarging Patrick's intermittent wardrobe, kept in my top-floor wood-box. Mr. Glass's face was "large as that of Memphian Sphinx"; and his hands were in proportion. He was like one of those faithful, unsophisticated, whimsical old clerks in that House of Business described by Charles Lamb. His loyalty to the Bureau was touching. Not the rack itself could have induced Mr. Glass to waver for a second in his allegiance.

And his attitude to me was exactly what suited me best. He treated me as if I had been a sea-lion or a pet elephant. After my unconventional life under Arnold I could not have endured any other treatment! The kind of "ideal bluff" which some lecture-organizations indulged in would have made me sick. Such hypocrisy found no lodgement in the massive, quizzical, realistic cranium of this old-world impressario of public entertainers. But I believe in his own way Mr. Glass "got my number" very thoroughly and appreciated both my merits and my weaknesses. I know he put his hand into his pocket to help me out when I needed to be helped out; and he did what touched my heart even more than this, he spent one of the sacred anniversaries of his birthday—I expect he was a good deal older than he allowed us to guess—sitting patiently and indulgently—I can see him now!—in one of the back rows of the Labour Temple on Fourteenth Street, watching me frantically act *Macbeth* and furiously comment upon *Macbeth* for two whole hours.

Just like a true Dickens character this giant-like gentleman showman had endless anecdotes of old days, anecdotes about forgotten New York clubs, about ancient hotels, about encounters with Mark Twain; and these stories he would relate from the beginning every time he took tea with me in Patchin Place and I would know that he knew that I knew that I had heard them before! He had all sorts of wise old soothing proverbs in the front-office of his massive brain, and these he would utter as the pen fell from his gigantic fingers. These he would utter when his lecturer was quivering with agitation as he confronted some sudden journey to Colorado, or New Mexico, or Texas, or Oklahoma.

"Half the world," Mr. Glass would say with a look of genial abstraction, "doesn't know how the other half lives."

And I would find myself, when I was tempted to worry about how I was going to get down to Florida from New Orleans, or whether it was worth my while to go there at all for one single lecture, hearing him repeat the soundest of all his proverbs, a proverb that I confess I have constantly been trying, ever since Mr. Glass died, to put into practice: "Don't cross the bridge until you get to it!"

I had been working for several years under the auspices of the "Lee Keedick Bureau" when I began to realize that my gastric ulcers had moved from the pit of my stomach and pitched their tents in my "duodenum." From this new position they proceeded to carry on a series of virulent attacks on my peace and comfort. Our wise and benevolent Dr. Thomas, who had come to my rescue in 1917, came to my rescue again and sent me to the stomach-specialist Dr. Einhorn. In this learned man's serene presence I felt like a desperate St. Sebastian in a mediæval picture appealing to an unruffled angelic doctor. But this devilish hurting in my side, under my right ribs, grew worse and worse until I finally decided—since by this time I had begun to be known as a writer as well as a lecturer—to make the grand plunge, "burn my ships," as we say, and try to earn my living by my pen.

I was, however, not a little nervous of the country, in America, as opposed to the town. I knew that many of my ideas were both revolutionary and extremely reactionary; were in fact all that was most contrary to the average American spirit, and although the presence of my allies the Jews and the Communists helped me to carry this off in the big cities the fatal divergence would be only too evident when once I was dragged out of my Patchin Place Alley and "exposed" in a toll-pike cottage on a dirt road!

I had read stories in the papers, when one set of the Ku Klux Klan was quarrelling over money with another set, of such appalling cruelties committed by these people, and committed on persons who apparently were *exactly* my particular type, that I did not realize how much the prevalence of such lynchings and floggings depended upon the character of the Governor of the particular State. New York State, when I was hesitating where to settle, was governed by the present President of the United States, whose enlightened attitude to all these matters had already done incalculable good, and *had* been governed by "Al" Smith, a sympathetic Roman Catholic. I had, moreover, in many early lecture-tours, got particularly attached to Albany and Troy and Utica and Syracuse and Rochester, lovely old "Holland-Dutch" cities, whose only rivals in my affection in the whole country, were the old "Pennsylvania-Dutch" cities of Reading and York and Lancaster.

But it was neither my love of these Holland-Dutch towns, nor my admiration for the Hudson River, which I had already come to know pretty well, since my blood-crony and familiar spirit had bought with my father's money actual landed property near its banks, nor my confidence in a good Governor, that gave me the final push, or pull, that got me my "up-state" cottage. It was my long friendship with Arthur Ficke, the poet. Arthur Ficke is much more to me than what in this country is so quaintly called "a warm personal friend." He has been for years much more than "a warm personal friend" of Edna St. Vincent Millay and Eugene Boissevain. I mean he has been our friend in the European sense of sharing and exchanging sad, cheerful, whimsical, bitter, pure, impure, refined, gross, simple, sophisticated, highbrow, lowbrow, *generalizations* upon the stream of life as it flows!

The Millay-Boissevains have always been closer to Llewelyn than to me. This was inevitable. As in so many other cases, after contact with the warm sun-born, earth-rooted nature of my father's fifth son, my own "cold planetary heart" as Llewelyn loves to call it, not to speak of that devious, fluid, evasive, Taoistic element in me, that Llewelyn names my "spiritual insincerity," but which I name my magical divination, is bound to strike most high-spirited people as the falling upon them of a cold, thin, frozen, inhuman rain, drifting, drifting, drifting, in the pallid track of a fast-hurrying moon. But in spite of these chilly peculiarities I have enjoyed over and over again feelings of thrilling delight merely from watching one expression after another expression crossing the countenances of these two princely creatures. They exercise a diverse, and yet in some mysterious way a kindred enchantment; and to this enchantment I willingly yield.

But I fear they are both too sensitive not to obscurely detect in me, after basking in the radiant sun-warmth of Llewelyn's personality—and do I not detect it in myself?—the deadly non-human "Algol," or "Demon's Eye," which always coldly watches, save when it is obscured by its own emotion over some yet colder melody of Milton, the warmest and most impulsive gestures of beautiful souls in beautiful bodies!

But nothing of this embarrassment, or of this mysterious ambiguity, exists between myself and the Ficke domain. Following my rigid rule, however, which I've only broken on behalf of "Messengers of the Grail," I must confine my remarks to the male element in this felicitous partnership. I believe I understand Arthur Ficke as very few, even among his greatest admirers, understand him. If I had his own genius of painting portraits in poetry—a very charming "genre," that has died out in these modern times—I would soon hit off his baffling personality. You must remember that I used to see him in his native Iowa, fifteen or twenty years ago; so that I really *am* in a position, if only I had the talent, to limn this poet's psychic lineaments, as I have observed them taking shape, under the passage of so many years.

I have a peculiar and natural sympathy with Arthur, because he, like myself, has long been dominated by a formidable begetter, whose personality excited in his son a mixture of respect, awe, furious rebellion, and inarticulate affection. Arthur certainly possesses one of the tallest, stateliest and most elegant figures among all the poets I have known. He is in fact better-looking than poets ought to be allowed to be, and I think, take his life as a whole, his imposing beauty has done him more harm than ever the War did in giving him consumption. I think it has led—for Ficke's good looks have been made yet more dangerous to his genius by being combined with the veritablest "grand manner" in society—to his getting pleasure in the way, of all others, that a poet ought not to be allowed to get pleasure, I mean from enjoying life with fascinated and fascinating friends! Love affairs are all right for a poet, except those desperate and obsessing ones, when, like Keats with his Fanny, we cannot think, speak, talk, eat, taste, touch, hope, fear, move, breathe, without dragging in some reference to this Lamia, this Lilith, this sorceress; but enjoying yourself with your friends *is fatal.*

If Arthur Ficke wasn't such a damned fine figure of a poet his poems would include among them a majestic "Epic." This unwritten Epic I am never long with him without seeing, hanging in the air behind his magnificently poised head, looming up like a "cloudy trophy" on the drooping arras of his spirit. But to write a majestic epic you have to be ugly or distorted, you have to be blind, like Homer, or be tormented by your daughters and blind too, like Milton. Even to write a great Prose-Epic you have to spend ten years of your life with convicts, and live in exile, and see your child die of under-nourishment, like Dostoievsky, or be in perpetual danger of actual insanity like Nietzsche. It is useless to remind me how sane and well-balanced we are taught to regard Shakespeare as being. It is not true! If you rely, as I do, purely on the plays themselves it is impossible to see how these crafty moralists patched up their misleading lie at all, about this desperate spirit's equanimity.

Arthur himself may feel tempted to protest that to have been given tuberculosis by a war like this was a sufficient offering to the Far-Darter. Offering enough to make a stately sonnet-writer, a delicate refiner of infinitely tender lyrics full of sad mature wisdom, but not enough to tear out of your brooding Norse skull, as it lifts itself above your great column-like Siegfried throat, a valkyrie-inspired saga.

Why are you not thinking, my Teutonic Arthur, of nothing else in the world but of ploughing on where Mathew Arnold left off in his magical "Tristram and Iseult"? Or of driving forward where Keats himself, the idol of us all, left off in "Hyperion"? The truth is, deep in your deepest heart, my friend, you have not the courage or the noble simplicity, the heroic romance, of the shameless Germanic sentiment, which you find there, hanging like torn cathedral banners from the Gothic arches of your inmost soul! The truth is that with an appearance worthy of being compared to that of the "divine minstrel" in the halls of Alcinous, making the stranger sob so bitterly beneath his up-gathered cloak, Arthur's spontaneous river of deep Teutonic feeling has, in some subtle way been deflected, and divided, and broken into tributaries, by that most insidious of sirens the fatal culture of the Orient.

An exquisite adept, not only in Japanese Prints, of which he has written such penetrating prose and delicate poetry, but in what might be called "the art of disillusioned equilibrium," it is tragic to me to observe his self-controlled mask of courtly reserve quiver and tremble sometimes under the pressure of the old Nordic stirrings! He has in him that formidable urge towards a life of heroic action which is an element in all real poets of love and war: and, mark you, by "war," I do not mean wearing either an ancient or a modern helmet, I mean "pulling up the dam" from the basic streams of passionate love and wrath.

Naturally lacking, like all true poets, in the superficial cleverness of the nimble children of Hermes, his towering modesty has forbidden him the use of that sly, obstinate, malicious self-confidence which the earth-gods have never ceased to offer him. Without any doubt this courtly man of the world conceals, below his air of stately ceremony, the shy self-distrust of a nervous child; but it is his unhappy ability of "carrying things off" by his personal charm and his dangerous culture that prevents him, in his fatal humility, from letting the suppressed "child," in him feel defeated, sulky, angry, desperate, which is the condition out of which volcanos erupt.

But after all it is a scurvy return to my deeply-loved friend to underrate the pleasure I have had from his "occasional poems," some of the latest of which, like the one called "The Hour-Glass," have taken on, in their wistful maturity, a kind of Landorian weight. And when it comes to what might be called "social ethics," my own Stone-Age unscrupulousness has learnt much from my friend. In one thing this poet is unique, and the quality shines out nobly amid our touchy resentments. I have never known Arthur—and he is rare among Americans as a man of many deep friendships—*to give away one friend to another*. To the end of my life I've vowed to imitate him in this; for it is a noble and a classic virtue. Why, the man must be a treasure-house of State Secrets! But with the consummate art of a master-diplomatist—did he learn *this* in Cambodia?—he skates over the most dangerous "cat-ice" between his indiscreet friends and nobody would guess what a Recording Angel he really is! What I have learnt from Ficke in this difficult art of keeping one's friends in "water-tight compartments"—for it is indeed the only thing to do—has been made easier for me by my curious maliciousness. With him, however, it springs from a different source, springs indeed from the "Sacred Fount" itself; whereas I, especially in dealing with women's attitude to women, experience a purely malicious desire to prevent them from enjoying the taste of each other's blood! May my love prove a real talisman to guard Arthur Ficke from all evil.

Anyway my mania for obeying the Apostle's injunction to avoid telling tales has been mightily fortified by my friend's example. Quite apart, however, from the influence of Ficke's method in this matter, I have it in me to display a fanatical loyalty, deep, ingrown, romantic, and full of introverted malice, in the case of the posthumous wishes of the dead.

In the difficult problem of old letters I am obsessed with a superstitious loyalty. I have more than once denied myself the pleasure of reading such letters that have naturally and inevitably fallen into my hands, because I know so well how little the writer of them would wish them to be read. On this point I have had at least one angry quarrel with Llewelyn, to whose earth-rooted, sun-sweetened humour, with its passionate interest in the quirks and crochets of those who have been dear to him, such side-stepping, dark-gliding, wrong-side-of-the-moon worship seems like an evil religious vice.

Well, I must get on; for I was then, as I contemplated my farewell to the lecture-platform, nearing fifty-seven. Soon I should be sixty. As a matter of fact as I write these lines I am sixty-one, and when 1935 comes it will be exactly thirty years since, from the deck of the *Ivernia*, to the strains of Sousa's "Stars and Stripes," the notation of which I beg my musical friends to insert in the proper place, I saw disappearing from view the familiar bowler-hat of Tom Jones. My last lecture but one was in the Extension Department of Columbia University, and it was on "Faust"; and this lecture both Dreiser and Masters attended, faithful to the end. My last of all was in the Labour Temple on Fourteenth Street, and to this came, not only that ironical and secular saint, Will Durant, and my daring publishers, Max Schuster and Richard Simon, but none other than Arnold Shaw himself. The next lecture in that familiar place that had to do with the superannuated clown of the old Shaw Circus was not *by* me, but *on* me. This is the first time in my life I have been lectured upon, and perhaps it will be the last. I need hardly say, remembering my happy days in Saxony, that it was by a German. In plain words it was by Dr. Beck, Durant's original successor at the Labour Temple. Durant, in the manner of Ferney, had fed me when I was penniless. Beck, in the manner of Weimar, interpreted my legend. Durant is the wisest of the few Frenchmen I have loved. Beck is the most original of the many Germans I have loved.

It was a sad blow to me, not long after Dr. Thomas had sent me to Dr. Einhorn about my duodenal ulcer, to learn from Mr. Keedick, who misses him even more than I, of the sudden death of our friend Mr. Glass. Well, let's hope this grand old impressario for so many varied "talents," as they are named on our mortal circuit, is now explaining to the "talents" of a better Dimension than ours that it is wise "not to cross a bridge until you come to it."

As I am writing now it was at this very season a little more than four years ago that I finally settled down "up-state" in this best-governed of all American commonwealths. Even in the city I never regarded "Tammany" with the distaste which most "scholars and gentlemen" are supposed to feel. In certain ways I've always had an instinct that Tammany was more indulgent to the poor man than many conventional Governments are; but I confess I am prejudiced against the Police of New York City. This, however, is because I wholly disapprove of the American custom of allowing policemen to take upon themselves to punish offenders before they appear before a magistrate. In some ways, no doubt, there is more "yield" and "give" in an American prison than in an English one; but I cannot help feeling there is also more opportunity for individual sadism

Take it all in all my four years among these American farmers of Dutch ancestry have been very nearly the happiest of my life. In the first place, for the first time in my conscious life, for my erotic viciousness began in my early infancy, and, with the exception of those later war years when my conscience used the ointment of asceticism to soothe its prickings, continued *sans cesse* ever since, I was free from vice. Yes, with my retirement to the country of the Mohawks something that seemed to me like a veritable miracle occurred, and the Devil, like that one named "Legion," was actually exorcized! Had the great god Eros himself done this? Was it the work of an Elemental? Nature undoubtedly helped. I do not put down the change to Nature, because I have not infrequently suffered from my most desperate obsessions when in the very heart of Nature; but she undoubtedly helped. And perhaps the occupation of writing books is a better sedative for wandering lusts than the more electric, more magnetic, and much more concentrated occupation of speaking. But whatever it may have been, Eros himself, or an Elemental sent by Eros, or this incredibly beautiful "up-state" scenery, or the fact that I was earning my living for the first time in my life by writing books, or, as certain not very psychological cynics will interject, *because I was growing old*, the fact remains that these unbelievably happy four years, spent, except for a very few days, entirely in one little house by the side of the road, have been, as far as my vices are concerned, an epoch of paradisic peace.

The interesting thing is that even my sadistic tendency seems to have sunk down into some abysmal Tartarus in my soul. I am not talking, of course, of any *practice* of sadism; for, as I have already told you, since my days at school I have never hurt anything out of wicked pleasure. I am talking about sadistic thoughts. Twice, and only twice, as a matter of fact, has this most dangerous of all demons come swimming up from the depths, as Dante describes that classical devil of his Malebolge doing, on whose back Vergil and he were to dive down; and both these occasions had to do with the idea of forbidden books. The first time this happened I was walking across a bare grassy hill less than a mile from my house, and it was as if the demon-image of one of these books rushed at me like a frantic harpy, out of the air and almost carried me off to its terrible ærie. The second time the devil *did* take me off to its ærie; for it came at night when I was writing at my window with such vividness that my pulses inside my wrists *began to tick* as if I were wearing two wrist-watches.

Sappho has described the physical effects of passion, the dizziness, the fainting, the sweating, the sinking of the stomach, the knocking together of the knees; but what I experienced at that moment was the trembling of pure wickedness. If I were a gospel-preacher, like the bible-woman with whom the dying Trophimovitch fell in love at the end of *The Possessed*, I should invent the verse:

"The wicked tremble because of their delight in wickedness. Yea, they shiver and shake with the thought thereof. But when they have eaten the fruit, behold! they shake yet more; for the Lord cometh upon them."

On this particular occasion there were three noticeable stages in my struggle with Apollyon. First, half-hearted but violent resistance. Then, a sort of drunken yielding, ending in a calmly rational compromise. Finally, after several days had passed, the whole thing dropped away, leaving not even a smell of brimstone behind, leaving not even the faintest wish for the crafty compromise I had patched up previously with the Devil.

This last occurrence happened quite recently, indeed a few weeks ago; so it is a comfort to me that I do not seem destined —if things go well—to be discovered by Llewelyn reading books that make him cry out aloud:

"John, John! I would be ashamed to be caught with such stuff!"

But I am a fool to boast like this; for I know well my devil is not dead. But I really have been singularly happy during this retreat "up-state." Policemen have certainly been unlucky apparitions in my life—and I dare say there are those who share this feeling even more strongly—but ever since I was tortured for throwing that stick, as if in some ill-starred ithyphallic gesture, into the lake near Shirley, I have been absurdly afraid of these guardians of the law. Does this perhaps explain the curious sympathy, amounting to a nervous identification of myself with them, that I feel for tramps? But one singular thing has been done for me by America. The policemen over here are so fond of using their clubs in what seems to my English mind an extremely premature system of punishment and the American public is inclined to tolerate so placidly the use of torture to extract evidence, that I now feel that when I return home I shall have completely lost my fear of our own policemen.

Possibly if I were sent to Devil's Island I should never dare to lift up my eyes above the shoe-strings of any Frenchman again; but until that day arrives it is rather in the presence of Irishmen that I feel uneasy, remembering all the Irish names that I have noted in the New York City police. Perhaps, however, the worst of these illegal punishments are inflicted by what they call the "Scotch-Irish." As a Celt I hope so. But the absence of policemen in this "up-state" hiding-place of mine is not its only advantage.

The country here has the very look of the old romances that I love best. Those who love tapestry say its hills offer the same enchanted vistas as did the mediæval backgrounds to the castles of the Gothic North. It is more like England, this district of upper New York, than any landscape I have yet seen in the whole of America. It is like Shropshire. It even makes

me think of my native Derbyshire. Thus has the wheel come
full circle and I am at Shirley again! In every direction narrow
lonely "dirt roads" wind through far-away valleys and over
remote hill-tops, leaving behind them, as their perspectives
diminish, that peculiar thrill that seems to come down to us
from the generations, but which is so peculiarly hard to define.
It is an impression that has to do with horsemen journeying,
inn-lights beckoning, journeys' ends coming to lovers, to
tramps, to hunters, to camp-followers, to adventurers, to the
life-weary Dead. It is an impression that has to do with all
those mystic omens of the way that they are driven off like
hunted wild-geese by such things as "filling stations," sign-
boards, cement highways, ginger-pop stalls, and "residential
sections."

And, moreover, this vague sense of old-world romance,
which I am trying to describe, is a completely different thing
from the startling natural grandeur of virgin forests, great
prairies, vast deserts and towering mountains. It can only
appear under particular conditions in the history of any landscape and it requires a particular kind of landscape for it to
reveal itself at all. These conditions are precisely fulfilled in
the hilly regions of "up-state" New York of which I am speaking. The hills are not too high, the woods are not too continuous. Grassy slopes, park-like reaches, winding rivers,
pastoral valleys, old walls, old water-mills, old farmsteads, old
bridges, old burying-grounds give to the contemplative imagination that poetic sense of *human continuity*, of the generations
following each other in slow religious succession, which is
what the mind pines for, if it is to feel the full sense of its mortal
inheritance. Where, moreover, by an incredible piece of luck
I was allowed to settle, the actual earth-strata is peculiarly
harmonious to my exacting taste. Grey slaty boulders lie in
every direction, covered with the loveliest mosses and lichens,
and intersected where the pines and hemlocks and birches
grow by rich black earth-mould where the most delicate of
wild flowers and ferns appear in their seasons.

The rocks of this countryside too, for the region lends itself
to cattle and sheep rather than to grain-cultivation, have a

s s

peculiar and special beauty of their own, in that, along with their dark slaty masses, they present at intervals large fragments of a marble-like substance, white and glistening, where actual pieces of crystal can be detached, and where sometimes the most unimaginable green lichens spot the white surface. Nowhere, no! not in England itself, does the spring, when she comes at last, after the terrific, snow-bound, zero-frozen winters, bring with her a more fragile, a more miraculous enchantment than in this region.

I have come to know by heart, like the lovely lines of some unequalled poet, the familiar order of the appearing of these delicate tokens. First come the hepaticas, shy and dainty from within their dusky calixes, their brittle-drooping stalks covered with minute downy hairs: then the blood-roots, their white water-lily flowers protected so tenderly by their large enfolding leaves: then the orchid-leafed yellow adder-tongues: then the golden marsh-marigolds called, for some odd reason, "cowslips" in America; then the triliums, or wake-robins, purple-brimmed, like sacramental wine, and illustrating the doctrine of the Trinity before even Easter has come round: then, first of all the flowering shrubs, the white blossoms of the shadblow. The red flowers of one particular kind of maple are the earliest sign among the bigger trees: but when they have fallen on the grass there follow the yellow-green flower-tassels—washed with an indescribable "chinese-white" as you catch them against the blue of the sky—of the other maples. After the blood-roots and the adder-tongues are over it is possible to find rare patches of "bluets" in remote upland grass-swards and with the unfolding of fern-fronds on the outskirts of the woods come the airplane-shaped, vermeil-coloured polygala, a species of wild cyclamen. But I feel as if most vividly of all the flowers that Proserpina "let fall from Dis's wagon," there will return to my mind, waving in the warm wind against the grey rocks, when I am far from here, the nodding clusters of wild red columbine.

I have often told myself stories about my father visiting me in my American retreat; but——

"He is dead and gone, lady, he is dead and gone."

It was while I was hidden in a back-room in New York, a more ramshackle place than any in Patchin Place, that they buried him in the Montacute churchyard by the side of his dead. I was at the lowest ebb of my fortunes then, and was living on one single lecture given every week at a school in Greenwich. No longer could I write to him—as we all did at a pinch and never in vain—for help in my need.

> "He is gone, he is gone,
> And we cast away moan."

Yes, I could "cast away moan," quickly enough, but as long as I live I shall feel that he has not altogether died. *Non omnis mortuus est*, to twist Horace's phrase. And why should his spirit not be as indulgent now to his eldest born's weaknesses as he was that day in Mr. Phelip's park when I boasted of my grand temptations, and all he said was that it would be "a help to me, John, if you would read the lessons again next Sunday."

But how I would have been thrilled to show him these American "chickadees" that I fed every winter.

"They are a species of cole tit, John," he would say.

And then he would explain where you found their nests at Stalbridge. These little wild hepaticas would certainly have reminded him of that birthplace of his, to which he actually made his way at the last, like a dumb death-hunted animal, only to find strangers in his native covert. On the other hand how astonished he would have been to see the care that has to be bestowed in *this* little garden upon one single plant of real primroses, primroses that he saw everywhere in those Blackmore Vale hedges. And how excited he would have been to have caught sight of the magnificent "Camberwell Beauty" I saw only yesterday among these spring flowers, a butterfly that Dr. Frink, my faithfullest and almost only winter visitor, declared has been known to be seen even when snow was on the ground. And how he would have been interested in the nest of the "Chewink" that I found last year, with eggs in it, eggs marked with lovely irregular hieroglyphics, a little like our own yellow-hammer's!

Over his grave at Montacute the rooks fly, as they always have done with clamorous evening cawings; but I have come to find a singular satisfaction in the harsher, wilder, and more abrupt noises that their cousins the crows make as I carry my garbage to the skunks.

I did once, and not long ago either, write to my brother Littleton, reminding him of our passionately-conceived plan, concocted one Sunday afternoon at school, as in our tall silk hats we walked along the road to Milborne Port, about his coming to stay with me in my Curacy, which would be near a trout-stream. I reminded him of this and heartily invited him to cross the Atlantic and visit my Curacy—such as it is—on the banks of our Mohawk stream, but with the best of intentions he could not compass it. My brother Willy, however, flying from East Africa to London over the Pyramids, crossed the ocean for a couple of brief weeks to see his expatriated kith and kin. *He* did actually stay with me by this frozen river with its Indian name, and, although he got chilblains *in the face* by such tricks, insisted on making sketches after the delicate manner of Penn House and our Geneva ancestors.

I fell on his neck, like the sly Joseph on the neck of Benjamin, and a great bond sprang up between us. Twenty years! Yes it was no less than that since I had seen him last as a youth at Burpham. I had left him a simple boy, and I found him a formidable and mature man. Not only so, but I found him to combine with this massive strength an unselfishness beyond the unselfishness of women, and, along with this, that curious kind of smouldering unconscious heroism, such as distinguishes the most enigmatic and baffling characters in Conrad. How irrelevant a thing it seemed to me, as I watched him, and tried in vain to get from him any hint of the desperations that had marked his face, all my own wordy "dithyrambs" of pyschological analysis! Art? Rhetoric? Criticism? Why here before me, in the face and figure of this man of my own blood, this sixth son of my father, was actually present, realized in the flesh, all that heroic poetry I was for ever gathering up in my struggles with Homer!

By the way, speaking of Homer, I am anxious to record

again that in my view of such things the prose translation of the Iliad and Odyssey, in the Loeb Classics, by Professor A. T. Murray of Stanford University, is the best that has ever been made of this greatest of poets. It is a translation worthy to be compared with Sir Thomas Urquhart's version of Rabelais, and is far simpler and less precious in its choice of words than the famous Lang and Leaf one. My own private feeling is that these two supreme poems are the work of two quite different hands; the Odyssey being several centuries later and written, if not by a woman, at least by a poet whose sympathy with, and understanding of, women, went pretty far. As to the notion that a sequence of wandering minstrels could possibly have composed these integral works of art, such a thought seems to me on a par with the idea that a sequence of clever theologians could have concocted the Figure and the Sayings of Jesus.

But to return to these precious four years of mine, isolated from the world, in these "up-state" hills. One of the peculiarities of this region that so appealed to me is the number of old stone walls dividing the fields, walls built without mortar and bearing on the top of them sturdy beams of wood, laid cross-wise, without the use of nails. Around these ancient walls and around these tumbledown wooden fences have grown up, by the work of Nature rather than of man, tall hedges of choke-berry, thorn, and other white-blossoming bushes; and the presence of both stone walls and hedges gives this landscape, combined with the bare grassy uplands between the wooded hills, a look sometimes, especially in the autumn, that stirs up in me feelings that must revert to far-away impressions of my Salopian ancestors of the Welsh Marches.

Walking over these hills I have tried to strip myself of any pride in my lecturing and my writing. I have tried to imagine myself as an eccentric "Old Man of the Hills," called by my first name with some grotesque addition. I think it is a pity that nowadays we leave all expressive nicknames to gangsters and gunmen. It is part and parcel of the de-personalizing, de-individualizing of an unimaginative age. In my lonely walks in these hills I tried to think of myself as "Loony John" and to keep my life-illusion free of literary self-consciousness. There is a deep wisdom in the affectionate and wanton nicknames that the proletariate loves to use! It and the jesters and chroniclers of the old time have the same poetic instinct.

The worst insult you can give to a man is to turn him into a number, and this is what Society loves to do in its institutions. Even in prison if you are still Jack Straw, it is something. Nothing will come of nothing; but it would keep up a person's spirits to feel that he passed in the world as Jack o' Lantern.

The grand secret of enjoying yourself with a free heart is to get rid of ambition, rid of even the most trifling competitions with other poor devils. But we must have our pride; and we must have a very deep pride. We must have a pride in simply being ourselves outside and beyond any conceivable competition. Luckily for me I have inherited from my father a towering pride; but not a pride in anything in particular.

This is the subject I used to meditate upon more than upon anything else as I walked and walked over these saxifrage-covered hills. There is no "trespassing" here as there is with us in England. These isolated "up-state" farmers are of a mixed Holland-Dutch, German-Dutch, and English descent, but their methods, though in *some* respects they might be called "Kulaks," are singularly Communistic. They use the same machinery, taking it round from farm to farm, as in the Russian "Collectives," and they exchange a still more precious commodity; they exchange labour. And so while they own their farms and have substantial savings in the banks they are the extreme opposite of English farmers. I can walk in this region if I can overcome the physical obstacles, in any direction, all round the compass! And my neighbours don't get in the least annoyed when they see me forcing myself over or under their fences. For the first time in my life I could, starting from my door-step, walk on my two feet *wherever I pleased*. And this applies to these people's houses, paddocks, gardens, bartons, enclosures, chicken-yards, farm-yards, door-yards. Just imagine what it would have been like at Burpham if I had suddenly inaugurated the custom of walking into people's yards and across people's gardens! In America there is not only a most real "democracy," there is the latent psychology of a good many aspects of Communism. The Russians are perfectly right in making love to America.

For myself I am always thinking how I would get on in a Communistic State. It would be nothing to me to give up private property as long as I was freed from worry. Nor do I see why I could not work honestly for a Communistic State and yet live ultimately for my own secret sensations and for my own unbounded secret pride in my sensations! Oh, I have pondered on these things so much, walking about these hills! Suppose machinery *does* extend its sway, suppose science in the hands of minority-dictators *does* more and more dominate us, suppose the great battle of the future, with its own particular "good and evil," comes to be the struggle of the individual to be himself against the struggle of society to prevent him being himself, what we shall have to do will only be what the saints, lovers, artists, mystics have always done, namely *sink into ourselves and into Nature* and find our pleasure in the most simple, stripped, austere and meagre sensations.

I am entirely in favour of following Communism in getting rid of external dignities and external pomposities and external class-differences. I think that it is a weakness in me to want to be cosseted and petted and protected as "Mr. Powys, the Writer," or "Mr. Powys, the Lecturer." At the same time I could no more be an engineer or a farm-labourer or a miner, those persons upon whose labours I live, than I could turn into a horse.

What I would admire in myself would be the courage to live like a tramp, or at any rate if I *had* to have a roof over my head, like Wordsworth's leech-gatherer, or like that sly old peddlar, the hero of the "Excursion." What I have been doing in my walks for these last four years has been to imagine myself a solitary elderly man, regarded as half-crazy by his neighbours, who has escaped the workhouse, or "poor-house," as they call it in America, by means of some infinitesimal relief, or dole, upon which he can just manage to live. "Mad John of Rats' Barn" I would be then, and if I couldn't sell leeches I could at least look at newts. And at the girls too, maybe, "come Sunday," when they had their print frocks on; and who knows but now and again some Molly or Dolly or Polly would come mimsy-limsy along, when Mad John was peering over the gate. For I saw myself, while I walked over these hills, and sought to shake off and toss away every rag of exterior reputation, as at once a saintly old man and a lecherous old man; an old man who loved to warm his bones over the fire, an old man who never opened his door of a morning without tapping his head on the ground in worship of the divine ether or of Helios the Sun, and yet an old man for whom the mere fact that Providence had endowed girls with legs at all, instead of making them "all of a piece" like leeches, or with fishes' tails like mermaids, was the most blessed miracle in the world.

Independence! Independence! That is the secret of all philosophy. To be independent of the opinions of your neighbours, of your relations, of your friends; to be independent of this ridiculous itch for "being heard of"; to take the neck of your desire to compete and wring it; and then, when it becomes a question of pride, to let your pride tower up like a wavering, fluctuating, gigantic Genie from the smoke-bottle of your own magical soul!

Mind you I don't want to be "mad John of Rats' Barn" till I have written a shelf-ful of first-rate romances. But just as Montaigne who was a master life-lover is perpetually gathering himself together to cope with Death, so, though I am driven on by a terrific "libido" to write book after book, I feel uneasy and uncomfortable if I am not making constant efforts to adjust my life-illusion and my pride to a situation starker and more simplified than I have yet known. It is towards this that I have been constantly struggling during these four years of isolation. The mind—heaven help us all!—has always to be surmounting obstacles to its peace; and what I have come to feel is that since, as Heraclitus says, "all life is war" peace of mind is something that must be perpetually fought for and held with a grim clutch. I have come of late to use the phrase "premeditated ecstasy" and I would try to explain what I am aiming at in this daring expression. When our inmost self gathers up its battle-mood and *en protois iachon eche monuchos hippous!*" . . . "and into the mêlée drives with a cry its single-hooved horses," it attains an interior calm underneath the turmoil of its gesture; and this interior calm offers itself, like a clear mirror beneath confusion, to all those restorative elements, in the impinging weight of the surrounding cosmos, which are the cause of human ecstasy. In reality both the initial peace of mind and its exultant response to these elements *are creative acts of the mind itself*, of the mind using what is called "the will" and "the imagination"—whatever mysterious activities these may be—to force itself to be strong and exultant in the midst of an opposing turmoil and in the face of a catastrophic menace.

As I have hinted before—and what I say about myself applies, with a difference, to every soul in its ultimate struggle with the cosmos—these sharply-cut pathological "formulæ," such as sadist, masochist, zo-ophilist, misanthropist, extravert, introvert, homosexualist, cerebralist, heterosexualist and so forth, are too neatly scientific to cope with the mysterious impulses of a living soul. Grant life, and you have *some* form of consciousness. Grant *any* degree of consciousness, and you have an unpredictable and indeterminable element of creative will.

Just to amuse you, reader, and to arouse your analysis of your own particular mental processes, which I am convinced will escape these tedious pathological categories just as mine do, let me employ the word "Cowperism" for the particular disposition described in this book. You may not be a practising masochist, any more than I am; your sadistic tendencies may be as purely cerebral as mine are; you may loathe exhibitionism and narcissism as much as I do; and yet you may feel yourself constantly driven by what I call "sacred malice" to tear away the portentous mask of comic dignity which conceals the tragic dignity of every human soul. It is then, to the pathological activity of this "sacred malice" that I would, in my humour, give the name "Cowperism." For instance when I glory in the feminine aspects of my character, instead of slurring them over, it is this "sacred malice" that drives me on. For of course I am well aware of the vulgar pride in what is called "upstanding manliness" that such an emphasis tends to upset.

It is in fact this "sacred malice" of asserting your real

identity against the "human, too-human" mask, which, like the single eye and the single tooth of the Phorkyads, we all keep handing around, that I call being a "Cowperist," a name which, by the way, if I may give a hint to my American friends, must be pronounced "Cooperist." To a considerable extent, this book of mine, the "Autobiography" of a tatterdemalion Taliessin from his third to his sixtieth year, is the history of the "de-classing" of a bourgeois-born personality, and its fluctuating and wavering approach to the Communistic system of social justice: not however to the Communistic philosophy: for I feel that the deepest thing in life is the soul's individual struggle to reach an exultant peace in relation to more cosmic forces than *any* social system, just or unjust, can cope with or compass.

What is wrong with so many clever people to-day is the fatal distrust lodged in their minds—and lodged there by a superstitious awe in the presence of transitory scientific theories—of the power in their own souls. What we need—and the key to it lies in ourselves—is a bold return to the *magical* view of life. I don't mean to the magic of Madame Blavatsky, but to that kind of faith in the potentialities of the ego, with which all great poetry and all great philosophy has been concerned. That feeling of exultant liberation from the immediate pressure of practical life, which any "logos" from the arena of Goethe, or Spinoza, or Leonardo, or Plato, or Heraclitus, or Epictetus, or the old Chinese Taoists conveys, is what we need.

Science has not changed the human soul. Science has not changed the basic relations between the human soul and the mystery surrounding it. We are still potential magicians as long as we have faith in the power within us to create and to destroy. Social justice is one thing. The free life of the individual soul *under any system* is another thing. What we do is important; but it is less important than what we feel; for it is our feeling that alone is under the control of our will. In action we may be weak and clumsy blunderers, or on the other hand sometimes incompetent and sometimes competent. All this is largely beyond our control. What is *not* beyond our control is our *feeling* about it.

"I am a cowardly, blundering, incompetent worm."

Very good. So be it. But it is in my power to be a worm with a deep, calm, resolute cheerfulness, if not with a magical exultation.

But to return to my four years in "up-state" New York. It is certainly my opinion that a man could not—go where he might—find kinder, more considerate, more indulgent neighbours than I have found in this region. As I have made clear, I have travelled over this vast country from north to south and from east to west; but I have never found any Americans equal to these Americans. They have, in these four years, completely changed my ideas as to what the American character can be. They come of "good stock" as people say in this country; but it must be partly the climate, with its deadly winters and comparatively cool summers, and partly some curious psychic quality arising from the peculiar blending of races among them —the German with the Dutch, and the English with the Dutch, for instance—that makes them, to my thinking, so much nicer than either the thorough-going puritanical Yankees or the negro-lynching Southerners. The people of what I have hitherto styled my "Ideal America," that is to say Kansas, Arkansas, Southern Missouri and Oklahoma, have, it is true, one advantage over my friends here in being poorer, more haphazard, more happy-go-lucky, more consciously devoted to the great Goddess Chance, less conservative, less respectful towards the rich, less awed by banks and bankers.

But neither the South-West nor the nearer Middle-West can boast the old-world charm, the mellow continuity, of one generation following another in the same tradition of dignified simplicity and arduous labour, which characterizes the people I have been so intimate with, for these four important years of my life.

What a change this isolation in the country has been! No more do I meet that queer old organ-grinder whose creaked-out wistful "tavern music" used to set me thinking, as Sir Thomas Browne says such tunes did him, of "the music of the spheres," that organ-grinder who could speak no syllable of English, but who used *in sua favella*, "in *his* tongue," to moan and groan over

unintelligible wrongs, as he held my hand, like one who acted
the part of a beggared Oedipus, persecuted alike by gods and
men. No more do I see the Buddha-like face of the Jewish
ironmonger across the street, no more shuffle in my slippers
over Llewelyn's "Fosse-way," that great resounding Seventh
Avenue, till I reach the French bakery in Sheridan Square, to
buy "Croissants" and "Kitten Rolls," no more watch the
Dickens-reading fishmonger, himself a Dickens character if
ever there was one, hand over my purchase to his assistant to be
disembowelled, while he himself put my silver in his box and
gave me the best of his *l'esprit de poissonerie,* no more could I
carry my creased and dusty lecture suit down Greenwich
Avenue, past the laundry whose proprietor I had selected
because of some crazy likeness in his face to our redoubtable
Mr. Montacute of Montacute, he who drove me up Babylon
Hill, that fatal day in 1914, when I knew I was losing my home,
till I come to the little shop of the heroic Mr. A., whose son,
like the great King, was named Saul. All these forms and
shapes, together with the eternal litter of those places, and the
great steam-shovel with "Marion, Ohio," on it, that seemed
for ever scooping at the bowels of Manhattan, are now vaguely
fading away, plaintive, bodiless "eidola," gliding, like the thin
phantom of Patroclus, in and out of the gates of Hades!

But whatever familiar things of my old life were vanishing
—Rachel Philips, in her Portuguese plot, with no one to visit
her—it is certainly true that I have never, no! not since those
years when I was eight and nine at Dorchester, realized to the
full limit, my identity, my native peculiarities, my cherished
manias, my sweet superstitions. Yes, I have had, in "up-state"
New York, what is seldom allowed to mortal man upon this
earth—I have had the full unhindered swing of my personality.
I expect it is for no other reason than to get this very "swing"
that so many of us individualistic Englishmen leave the island,
whose bones are in *our* bones, and settle down in such far-off
alien spots. We carry our ways with us, our turns of speech,
our traditional routine, our rock-bound prejudices. We are all
so eccentric that penned up close together we lack space wherein to expand. And so we sail away, to have our fling among less

crowded, less furiously egoistic, less obstinate, less self-righteous, less adventurous natives!

How could I expand freely, how could I be the unmitigated, unqualified, unconscionable "Cowperist" I wanted to be, when I had all round me the class-distinctions, the class-prejudices, the back-bitings, the obsequiousnesses, the superciliousnesses, the superiorities, the perpetual psychic question, "*Is* he a gentleman? *Has* he been to a decent school?"

It must have been a considerable moment in my youthful life for instance, when hidden once behind the laurel-hedge above the road to the station we heard Mr. Phelips say to some guest at Montacute House:

"Yes, that's the Vicarage; Powys is the name; a very good family."

But here in these hills, with an "aura" around me of Mohawk chiefs, as formidable as any Owen Glendower, these hard-working descendants of old Dutch "Patroons" and old German and English settlers take me at my face value. I don't need to hide behind any un-mortar'd wall, or any criss-cross fence, to learn what my status is among such as eat bread upon the earth. *I am a man.* In the city I confess I fall below that level, and become a "guy." But here in "up-state" New York I feel I can say, even as the Lord of Hosts said to his questioner, "I am *that* I am."

Yes, I certainly have realized my identity in these New York hills. But there it is! I suppose there are always risks of one sort or another when people let themselves go to the limit in the attempt to be themselves. One of my chief risks has come from my mania for endowing every form of the Inanimate with life, and then worshipping it as some kind of a little god. This was indeed that very mania for "bowing and scraping" to idols that my father so especially reprobated. But a much worse risk than this was the trick I fell into in my solitary walks of acting God in my own person. In this extraordinary obsession I was bringing back with a vengeance my ancient past; for this is exactly what I had done in that lane at Shirley. In fact I gave myself up to an orgy of acting God during these four years.

When we philosophers are alone we naturally tend, as

Heine says, to deify ourselves; but in my obsession I went further than the innocent *auto-theocracy* that Heine so wittily repudiates. For I got into the habit, in these long lonely walks, of pretending to myself that I had trillions of trillions of "spirits from the vasty deep" at my disposal, ready to obey my indignant "white magic." These armies of "angels and ministers of grace" I thought of as *variously coloured;* and I always despatched the same squadron of them upon the same errand. I was only reverting, in this, to the method I had used in the London hospital, before my first operation, so as to feel I was of *some* use in that rocking ship of suffering; but in these hills I concentrated on sending supernatural relief to the particular victims of our damned race whose sufferings especially troubled me. I say I "pretended" to myself that I had the power to cause these entities to materialize and obey my commands. But it must have been really a little more than "pretending," or it could hardly have become the irresistible imperative it soon did become, just as if I had been a Catholic priest, who for humanity's sake and his own sake *dare not* intermit any of his miracle-working Masses.

I have in my time been foolishly prejudiced—it would take too long to explain just why—against the subtle metaphysical minds of the various Hindus I have met. I expect something in my fierce, poetical, Celtic temperament grows instinctively angry at the bland assumption of intellectual superiority which these sages adopt. I prefer the more humorous, less metaphysical Chinamen; though I confess I have had spasmodic moods of interest in Theosophy, which is I suppose based upon Hindu ideas. But the Chinese sages are the only ones who seem able to contemplate the Absolute with a sense of humour. How grave a teacher the Indian Buddha is for instance! Any allusion to Tibet however has always excited me; so has anything I could lay my hand on about the difference between White Magic and Black Magic; but something far deeper than all this is stirred in the depths of my being by stories of the Mediæval Catholic Saints. Why, the mere idea of the early Scholastic Theologians, the vivid images I have of them, the instinctive knowledge I have of the way they felt, and of their excitement in purely mystical and purely intellectual things, is something that has "thickened out," as William James would say, the possibilities of life for me.

When I contemplate the remorseless organization of our modern nations in their deliberate preparation for more frightful wars than this last one, and when I think of the blood-and-iron industrialism, which seems, whether voluntarily or involuntarily, to resemble a kind of daily war, there does seem something infinitely desirable about the passionate mystical, scholarly retirement from the world of these laborious thinkers. I feel as if I could understand much better the sort of intellectual, mystical, and imaginative life that Pelagius lived, or Marcion, or even the metaphysical Duns Scotus, than I can grasp the temperamental mentality of a modern "Behaviourist." But of course I know perfectly well that behind *every* human "formula" of life—even behind these apparently purely "scientific" attitudes—there is a will to believe.

You can't escape it! the "personal equation" follows, like an inevitable skin, every curve, every angle, of the most mathematical thinker's system. This is profoundly true of Bertrand Russell. It is true of Whitehead. It was true, as Nietzsche pointed out, of Spinoza himself. All comes back—whatever they say—to the *person* behind the thought. I do not know much about Paracelsus, who must have been half-mystic, half-thaumaturge, but one idea of his, which jumps with what I have gathered, by ambiguous hints here and there, of Tibetan adepts, has sunk deep into my mind. This is the idea that our intensely-concentrated thoughts can become "elementals," faintly-living entities, that is to say, whose dimly-vitalized shapes, once projected from the creative energy of a person's imaginative will, can go on existing and acting in some etheric dimension of that psychic plane in which all so-called "matter" floats.

It has been under the obsession of this idea during these semi-anchorite years that I have got into the habit of projecting the thought-images that I name my "angels," sending them over the face of the earth to alleviate those particular sufferings, such as the suffering caused by vivisection, lynching, trapping, the sufferings of prisoners and captives, the sufferings of "women labouring with child," the sufferings of misused children and of all victims of sadism, that have lodged themselves most deeply in my consciousness.

I have said that I was "pretending to be God"; but this does not really quite describe what I have been up to. I once read somewhere a passage from some English ex-soldier, who had dabbled in these mystical matters, in which there emerged the singular idea that what we call "God" is a magnetic, ubiquitous, vibratory force, of a sub-conscious rather than of a super-conscious character, corresponding on a very practical plane with Dr. Buck's "Cosmic Consciousness," and a force, moreover, which, in place of *praying to*, you were in a position to *command!* This queer notion of "commanding" the psychic creative force instead of invoking it arrested my deepest interest; and for these four years of retirement from the world that is what I have been trying to do.

It will not be hard for you to see, reader, if you have read this book with any penetration, that in this obsession, or superstition in the order of "white magic," I realized, in a peculiarly natural manner, though it has tended to become a most trying burden, certain very deep and far-back-rooted impulses of my identity. To tell you the truth it has needed a serious effort to my will to throw off this queer mania, thus increasingly indulged for four important years; but I *have*, and that quite recently, thrown it off, not altogether or in every respect, but very considerably and fairly suddenly. Let me, as hastily as I can, indicate to you how in these years—only leaving this place for a couple of nights twice a year—I actually arranged my days.

I would compel myself to get up any time between six-thirty and seven-thirty. This was always an effort; for I would feel extremely exhausted both in mind and body when I first got up. And at these times my whole soul seemed as it were exposed in its totality and *risen to the surface!* It was like a pool of clear hardly-flowing river water then. It was, if I may say so, *all surface*. Gradually certain thought-ripples, as I put on my clothes, appeared as if by chance, like straws or leaves or twigs —sometimes like a deadly twig—ruffling the surface of this hurtingly clear mirror. It was indeed with a kind of distressing shock, like the hurt of rape to a virgin, that, as I put on my clothes, I faced the light of the sun. The same hurtingly sensitive receptivity—just as if my soul really were a girl being ravished—would characterize my first reaction to all I chanced to see out of my window.

There is something about my soul so primordially childish, so freshly-born every day, that when it wakes it suffers a kind of birth-spasm as it issues forth from the womb of Not-Being into the jarring dissonance of Being. And so virginal is it, that it is not only hurt by the rays of the sun, or by the rocks and stones and trees or houses or walls that first strike upon it. It is hurt, *and raped*, as you might put it, by its own *accidental thoughts*. And some of these thoughts, these ripples across the diurnal virginity of my mind, are wicked, and some are good. The thought of some passage in one of my "forbidden books" will for instance ruffle my consciousness, a thought whose every ripple goes on enlarging and enlarging, as if it were off on a journey to eternity! Then the thought, the good, careful, anxious, meticulous thought, will cross my mirror, like a sudden breath of journeying wind, that I must take my net, before I do anything else this day, and make another attempt to rescue some little fish in a drying-up pool and transport them to a deeper one and one that shows signs of surviving the drought.

This matter of saving fish in my small river was constantly on my conscience all these years, and I used sometimes to have to walk as far as a mile carrying a pail of them, till I found an adequate pool for their reception. Once I was rewarded for my untiring fussiness by seeing a strange sight. I actually saw a procession of small fish working their way across a strip of bare earth from under a rock where the water had deserted them to the pool from which I was catching the others. It is not everybody who has actually seen a number of little fish crossing the dry land. It is true it was only a very short distance and it is true they were desperate for water; but you would have supposed they would have flopped aimlessly about till they perished, instead of taking this direct course.

T T

Then my troublesome impulsion to meddle with the fate of my fellow-creatures would, if it were the summer, inflict on my virginal consciousness the thought of the necessity of catching some blue-bottle fly or some common house-fly that had got into a tight place and of carrying it downstairs to let it out of my front door. Then another wicked ripple from a different "forbidden book" would cross my mind, driven by a dark evil wind, rising from nowhere.

Once dressed, the first thing I would do was to lay my finger on a little sacred talisman from the tomb of St. Thérèse of Lisieux, and to pray for Llewelyn's health. It greatly annoys Llewelyn that I should do this. But I take a malicious joy in so annoying him! If I don't mind teasing the godly by worshipping the moon why should I mind teasing the ungodly by praying to St. Therese?

Then I move to a window looking towards the North and utter prayers for, or *command* benedictions for, the people buried in a graveyard in that direction; nor do I fail to make particular mention of a certain American "Aunt Stone," a mighty maker of quilts, whose coffin I helped to lower into the grave. Then by name, image, and personality, "briefly but carefully," as Gabbitas and Thring directed me to write my applications to my first girl schools, I summon up, in a sort of providential roll-call, all the members of an extremely extensive family the roof of whose house is from that position just discernible. Then I invoke, under the name of "Ichthus" the holy fish, a particularly lovely trout which in one of my walks I found in a pool. "Ichthus, the Fish!" I chant in a sort of gabbled plain-song, "may he swim between the knees of a most beautiful lady!"

Coming down from the attic I used to be greeted by my two superb white cats—both of which I have recently caused to be assassinated by the vet—and then, while I did every mortal thing that had to be done, in the way of what Americans call "chores," both outside and inside the house, I continued my ritualistic rigmaroles. I had invented a most satisfactory way of disposing of my garbage, by conveying it to the slope of a wooded hill, where it was devoured by crows and skunks, and

like "Mr. Geard of Glastonbury" I always used to add to this
largesse a piece of fresh white bread that I cut from my loaf
and pressed to my lips as I mounted the hill, muttering to
myself,

"Christ, the living bread! Christ, the living bread!"

Then, leaving this flesh of the Saviour to the crows—but
I always placed it at a certain distance from the garbage, and a
most religious crow used to sit in a tree croaking for me to be
off—I left my garbage-pail beside an old apple-tree that I
named "Polutlas" or "the much-enduring," because it had
endured so much and yet bore fruit from its aged boughs, and
made my way towards one of the large flat stones of this region
that lay at the bottom of a thickly-wooded eminence. At the
top of this hill, which must have been about the height of
Montacute Hill, was an avenue of large heaps of heavy stones,
which I hoped were the grave-mounds of old Indian Chiefs,
Mohawk chiefs, for the Mohawks were my favourite nation;
and at certain seasons during these four years, at the two
equinoxes and at other pivotal days, I used to climb to this
wooded summit and walk up and down this "death-avenue,"
as I liked to call it, kneeling in front of each pile of stones and
invoking these dead Indians.

But every day I would go to this low-lying stone in the
grass, this grey stone spotted with lichen, and crouching before
it I would tap my head against it, uttering words "rather to be
concealed than revealed"; but incidentally calling upon the
souls of the dead Indians to cure Llewelyn of all his troubles,
whether they were of mind or body.

Before washing or shaving, for I had not touched soap and
water as yet, I now would return to the house and call my
black spaniel "Peter"—as coal-black as Faust's poodle—to
come out from under my couch and have his leash put on. I had
found it suited my duodenal ulcer to lie on my back all day as
I worked, and so, for all these four years, I wrote with a board
propped against my knees and my paper on the board; and it
was under this couch that Peter—a dog who had attained
cerebral peculiarities exactly like those of his master—hid
himself from the world. The presence of young women was in

fact as agitating to Peter as it was to me and sometimes when their clear voices reached us from far away he would tremble like a little black aspen-bush from nose to tail. Peter felt that it was incumbent upon him to warn his master when these dangerous beings approached the house. Not that he was *never* known to bark at men; but it was a perfunctory, official barking, not the bark of the ulterior danger-point, not the bark that comes from the centre of our complexes.

Peter and I understand each other through and through. He is, though of a much smaller breed—thus does History repeat itself—not unlike Thora in appearance; only Thora was a woman and Peter is a cerebralist who worships Eros with his nerves rather than by propagating his species. But his faithfulness to me is extraordinary. On certain occasions when I shut myself away from him by the whole space of two rooms and two closed doors I always find him standing sentry when I emerge. These are the only occasions, except when I am in bed, that I do separate myself from him and I do it then in order to have an enema.

For two or three years I have not had one single *natural* action of the bowels; but I have come greatly to prefer this artificial method to the natural one! For one thing it has forced me to read those great old-world books that alone have the strength, the gall, the spirit, the comprehensiveness, the heroic grossness, to *go decently* with the process of spending a whole hour at stool. In this way I have read nearly every word of the *Anatomy of Melancholy*, Tristam Shandy and Rabelais. Two volumes of Montaigne in the old French, I read too, in this way, though with some difficulty, and more than half of *Don Quixote*.

But to return to my dog. It often needed more than the sign of the Pentagon or the Hexagon to get this Mephistophelean Spaniel out from under my couch. When he was in his worst fit of agoraphobia, feeling just as I feel sometimes, it became necessary to lift up the edge of the couch. I am afraid Peter will soon forget his real name; for I generally speak of him as "The Black", and when I call to him on our walks my own private name for him is the "Very Old", because, being

now in his seventh year, he is growing perceptibly grey under
his chin. I have fallen into a peculiar kind of chant when I call
to him across these hills.

"Coom . . . along," the crows hear me intone in my particular rendering of the Dorset dialect, "Coom . . . along . . .
Very old!"

In fact when Dreiser first stayed with me out here he got
the idea, or pretended to get the idea, that the "Very Old's"
actual name was "Coom-Along".

I bought "The Black"—and I had to pay heavily for him,
for he has more ancestors in his pedigree than many of my
friends possess—at some kennels on the great Highway
between Poughkeepsie and Albany—when he was already three
years old. This fact accounts for one of his most curious
eccentricities. The singular link between us—the link between
two "Degenerates" who can name their eight grandparents—is
of a special kind. The "Very Old" knows nothing of the
tradition or convention about "master and dog." In his doting
simplicity he thinks we are just *equal friends*. I take him on the
leash along the road, because of our mutual fear of automobiles,
and only let him go when we debouch across country. As long
as we are advancing, he always stays close to me. Sometimes,
gambolling, sometimes rolling on his back, sometimes wrig-
gling on his belly, and at these times his short uplifted tail
reveals the degree of his good spirits just as, on his retirements
under my couch, his well-known receding rump, with the tail
pressed tight down, becomes a symbol of panic-stricken intro-
version. Happily and naturally does the "Very Old" caracol
round me, or shoot off on the scent of birds, for he displays
not the least interest in rabbits or woodchucks, and so it goes
till we reach the limit of our walk; but the moment I turn to
go home, this untraditional dog takes it as a sort of exciting
game to see which of us can get home first! The "Very Old",
having four legs to my two, is always the one who wins in
this game; and I perceive, from half a mile away, that small
black shape scurrying across the hills.

Such is my deep-rooted asceticism, that the mere fact of
my feeling so happy in these hills at having escaped from the

tumult of cities automatically sets me upon my heavy burden of playing at God. While "The Black" is safe at home waiting for me on the porch my own return is now delayed by prolonged pauses, during which I shut my eyes and project my various-coloured and yet invisible sprites upon their airy campaigns of rescue. It has been curious to me to discover that in these antics, during which I make spasmodic motions of my body, parallel to what the old puritans must have done when they "wrestled with the Lord in prayer", I have come to do exactly what the occult "masters" hint at as the proper method in such proceedings.

I act the Trinity in fact; for I project my waves of magnetic force from the three centres of my being; from my brain, from the pit of my stomach, and from the centre of my erotic energy. I won't weary you with a detailed description of the armies of magnetically-created spirits that I thus send forth. But I will hurriedly give you, ere I leave this subject, a laconic summary of the various victims of the cruelty of our race which these spirits are despatched, either to rescue, or, if there is no other way, to put out of their suffering.

To the victims of prison, of sadism, of vivisection, of traps, of cancer, of Americans in Georgia, in Mississippi, in Alabama, of child-ravishers in India, of child-labour all over the world, I despatched my motley-coloured and yet invisible angels. The thing was by no means a mere game to me. That it was serious was proved by the immense number of pleasant walks whose free happiness was mercilessly curtailed by these performances. And it was not that if I left out any of these rigmaroles I felt that I should *myself* suffer from it. It was in no sense an obligatory penance. What I felt was that since human beings have believed in prayer for some twenty-five thousand years who was I—on the strength of a few scientific discoveries and a few scientific theories only a few hundred years old—to intermit an immemorial custom, with which my race had mitigated, or fancied it had mitigated, the horrors of life for that vast tract of time? I had at least conceded something to science—though to a somewhat unconventional and mystical science—by turning the great wheel round, and instead of praying to

Buddha or Christ or Confucius or Zoroaster or any of *their* Gods, commanding my own private hosts of created entities, to do something to relieve these atrocious sufferings.

Of course you will say it was just a crafty trick, by means of which, without having to visit the hospitals, or the prisons, or the laboratories, without having to watch vivisection, without having to live in Georgia, I could get ease for my troubled conscience. But I cannot think that it was altogether such a trick; and I cannot think so, because, out of the abysses of my scepticism with regard to the assumptions of Science, I did seriously hold that "there might be something" in such doings. And if there was one chance in a million that my fiercely-willed waves of magnetic vibration *did* bring relief to some negro in Georgia, some prisoner in Devil's Island, some man or woman dying of cancer, some dog under the hands of vivisectors, was it not a gross and callous selfishness not to make use of any psychic power that I might possess, especially if everyone did not possess it, so as to give this one chance in a million its opportunity?

The public in America has been kept in the dark, even more than the public in England, about this matter of vivisection. There has never been upon *any* human subject so much crafty and deliberately misleading propaganda as that which the vivisectors have used to pull wool over the eyes of the world. The "sentimentality" in this matter is to be found, not in those who oppose themselves to this monstrous crime, but in the ridiculously emotional awe with which the average person, hypnotized by these crafty scientists and their sycophantic press, regards the whole problem. *Totally unnecessary cruelty* on a scale that the general public has no conception of, is going on all the while. The word "science" covers every kind of atrocity; and the issue is perfectly clear. My opposition to vivisection, particularly to the vivisection of dogs, is based upon an argument that is unanswerable. This wickedness contradicts and cancels the one single advantage that our race has got from what is called evolution, namely the development of *our sense of right and wrong*. If vivisection, as it is increasingly practised by these unscrupulous, pitiless, unphilosophical scientists, is allowed to go on unchecked—and it will go on unchecked until people feel as strongly about it as women did about women's suffrage—something that the mysterious forces of the Universe have themselves developed in us will soon have its spiritual throat cut to the bone. In other words certain forms of sickening and unthinkable cruelty that hitherto, when perpetrated by individuals, have been stopped at once, condemned by both moral opinion and law, are now—as long as we *vaguely* assume it is done for the advantage of science —tolerated as an unfortunate but inescapable necessity.

Vivisection is the new superstition, the new tyranny, the new incarnation of the powers of evil. Like all abominable wickedness that has once got into the saddle, this vivisecting science has now begun to brand as "sentimental," as "emotional," as "idealistic," as "unpractical" the deep honest realistic human instinct which it is deliberately seeking to kill. What science—using vivisection, for the obtaining of what is often entirely irrelevant knowledge, and simply because vivisection is an *interesting thing in itself*—what science, I say, is really doing, is nothing less than *suggesting to the conscience of our race*, this conscience that evolution itself has produced, that it is a sign of superior intellect to be completely devoid of natural goodness, of natural pity, and of all natural sensitiveness. And the ironical thing is that while this abominable vivisection is perpetrating worse and worse, and more and more useless cruelties, all manner of very simple and even unphilosophical people are working fantastical and unbelievable cures *by purely psychic and mental methods!*

Well, to return to these four years of country life in America, years in which I have had a greater chance to realize my identity than I have ever had before in my life; it is really extraordinary to what mad lengths my mania for invoking the psychic powers on behalf of my friends was carried. I began praying for the most remote persons! I included every single individual I knew at all well; and some most hostile to me, alien to me, and critical of me. Take Louis Wilkinson for instance. Of course Louis isn't "hostile" to me, for he has, in his way, a good deal of affection for me, but he is certainly extremely critical of me;

not so much of my writings as of my character. Well, it tickles my fancy down to the ground, and satisfies a certain particular kind of perverse humour, which is an element in me so strong that I regard it as the distillation of the very essence of my attitude to life, that I should have added "This Archangel's" name to that list of the inmost darlings of my soul for whose sake I invoke the invisible powers.

The truth is that my enemies—I am not thinking of Louis now but of those who feel suspicious of my "Cowperism" afar off—don't realize that my mania for acting the zany, together with the "sacred malice" from which it springs, contains, just as does my contradictory blending of sanctity and satyrishness, a quite definite philosophy of life, and a philosophy, moreover, that combines reaction with revolution in a way in harmony with Nature's own devious and yet magical method of going to work. But it has been a singular experience to be allowed, once in my life, what may be called a "free temperamental fling". Blake says, "Excess is the path to Wisdom"; and though I have already—now that I have decided to leave America and return to my native land—cut down drastically on the bulk of these singular performances I am doing so out of no "rational" quarrel with these super-stitions considered in themselves, but simply from a feeling that I have been lavishing so much of my magnetic energy upon them that I begin to suspect that with my advancing years I may be tapping the psychic vitality necessary for the writing of my books.

In blunter language I fancy that what within me now is rebelling against all these thaumaturgic rigmaroles is simply the life-spring of healthy selfishness. But in my ferocious auto-malice I refuse to allow this healthy selfishness to fool me into any pompous self-deception by using the old familiar argument about "my duty to my art". To the devil with "art"! I am too old a fox in the "Park Coverts" of the Cosmos to be led by the nose by any braggadocio of that kind. My writings—novels and all—are simply so much propaganda, as effective as I can make it, for my philosophy of life. It is the prophecy and poetry of an organism that feels itself in possession of certain magical secrets that it enjoys communicating. And, by the way, I certainly feel conscious of conveying much more of the cubic solidity of my vision of things in fiction than it is possible to do in any sort of non-fiction.

It is for this reason that my instinct has led me in this "Autobiography" to treat myself as if I were one of my own fictional characters, even at the risk of making myself out more of a rascal and more of a fool than my friends have supposed me to be. *Caricaturing* is the master-trick! And that is why the discreet, dignified, plausible autobiographies are so insipid and unconvincing. A touch of caricature is what we *must* have, if we are to compete, even in this analytic job, with the beautiful madness of Nature.

I wish to the devil that this book of mine would be translated into Chinese. That Chinaman, who listened to my crazy discourse, when, shrewdly stimulated by "Mr. Weston's Good Wine" at the Corpus High Table, I indicated the mystical connection between cosmic awe and the erotic urge, would be the one to get the esoteric drift of this present work! A Taoist is what I really am; but a Taoist uninfluenced by that later Buddhistic element, that indifference to pleasure and pain, which is such an un-Homeric treachery to our life's Trojan War.

I suppose one of the most exacting demands of my life-illusion is that I should feel as well as act in a *poetical* way. Thus though many of my deliberately *forced* feelings and gestures might be called "affected," though really they are no more affected than the feelings and gestures of a monk who wishes to live the saintly life, no one could say that the urge behind them, the urge that drives me to them, is anything but the deepest impulse of my nature. One of the least burdensome among these poetic obligations laid on me by my life-illusion was the concentrated piety with which I have got into the habit of praying for my dead relations. I have been as Roman in this as "Marius the Epicurean" and as Chinese as Confucius himself.

I have never passed that much-enduring apple-tree that I call "Polutlas," in my early morning disposals of my garbage, without uttering a prayer for the "rising to immortality and intense happiness" of that grandfather of mine on the distaff side whose possession of so much loose silver in his trouser-pockets impressed me as a child. And every day when I put my head in the basin—for it has entertained me from my childhood to see how long I can hold my head under water —I pray for my father's father in his grave in the Blackmore Vale.

"May old L.C.P." I burble and splutter from under the water, "rise to immortality and intense happiness!"

It amuses me not a little to notice how this "rise to immortality" prayer of mine goes so much further and is so much more daring than the quiet "May he rest in peace" of the Church. But as for my father, every morning as I stop to stare at the foaming torrent of our spring-and-autumn stream, as it swirls round the rocks within a bow-shot of this little garden, I cry aloud, to the astonishment of my friend "Sis," the unruly hornless cow, upon whose milk I live and between whom and me there is such a singular understanding, *"It's not so cold, John, my boy!"* For I envisage at these times the majestic form of my progenitor standing stark naked in this swirling stream, encouraging me to face all the Preston Brooks of the world, and finally the deep West Bay of death itself.

I have got a curious satisfaction in my wanderings about these Shopshire-looking hills from my passion for giving names to the anonymous. Wordsworth was a great one for this exciting trick of scrawling our poor human signatures, like so many lover's tokens upon the many-breasted mother of men; and I too have derived no small comfort from it. "Merlin's grave," a great mossy natural knoll, covered in the spring with the carmine flowers of the wild cyclamen, finally became so real to me that I fell into the habit of burying my face in its damp rubble and invoking the great magician, as if, while awaiting his deliverance from his mysterious "esplumeoir," he had been really present here. For this I was rewarded in a most practical way; for never have I smelt such indescribable fragrance, as if from the deep-zoned bosom of Ceridwen herself, the immortal inspirer of Taliessin, as I used to inhale from that bed of moss!

Another spot, with a wider landscape about it, I named

"Tintern Abbey," not so much because I thought of the real Tintern Abbey, as in memory of a particular hill-ridge, above a wood near Montacute, to which we used to give this name as we rested there on our way home to tea.

Here, in this New York "Tintern Abbey," there lay a gigantic floor of rock, "whose peculiarity was," as it says in the Mabinogion, the causing of an especially sharp pain to any knees that knelt upon it! It pleased my mediæval nature to see whether I could endure kneeling on this penitential rock long enough not only to pray for my son, but also for Llewelyn—whether he liked it or not!—and finally for that satirical heathen "The Archangel," who would most especially be outraged by it.

My brother Will brought me a magnificent oak-cudgel, cut by himself from an oak-tree in Hampshire and so heavy that it needs my abnormally strong wrists to walk with it at all. This stick has been one of the greatest pleasures I have had since my father cut me that laurel-wood dagger at Shirley! But it must be a Druidical cudgel, endowed with singular psychic potentialities, for as I have walked with it of late it has inspired me with the most deadly insight into my character, especially into that vein of romantic weakness which is mingled with my greatest strength. But under the influence of this stick I plunge into this weakness, joyously embracing it and yielding to it to the limit! Carrying this great stick I grow supernaturally aware of the feminine fragility, the naïve softness, the artless timidity of my nature. All my fussy old-womanishness, all my silly fears of fierce dogs and drunken men, all my meticulous anxieties and hypochondrias, seem to pulverize me as I walk past one or other of my familiar grave-yards—for I live between two of them—where I pause to "command" the joyful resurrection of these invisible bones.

But then it is that from beneath all this weakness, a weakness which grows upon me till I feel as if this great giant's club were stalking along of its own volition, dragging a nervous "Rural Dean" in tow, there suddenly rises up, from within my ribs, from a dimension, as it were, within the very marrow of my skeleton, a towering and invincible Something, that, like a terrible *Genie* from a cracked bottle of smoke, seems able to grasp this mighty stick as if it were a straw!

And now, as I prepare for my departure for my native land, it comes over me to wonder exactly what I *have* gained from my semi-anchorite life in these hills. I certainly carry with me, from my toll-pike cottage on this "up-state" dirt-road, a memory of the best neighbours that I have ever had, or ever shall have. Oh, I shall never forget them! No, not until it comes about that over my own ashes some other "affected charlatan," some other scarecrow Don Quixote with the faint heart of Sancho, pauses, as he is dragged along by his eager-snuffing dog, to gabble some rigmarole about that "immortal life" upon which the vivisectionists and behaviourists have put their final quietus, will these magnanimous neighbours of mine be forgotten!

It has been most interesting to me to note during these years, when, under the "aura" of the last of the Mohawks, I let my inmost impulses have their free swing, how my nature craves for palpable symbols, even in the most disembodied regions. For instance whenever I use my sponge I go through a most complicated mental ritual. Perhaps without being aware of it, for I know nothing about this particular occult tradition, I am really a Rosicrucian. At any rate the Comte de Gabalis himself could hardly have made more fuss as he used his sponge, as if it were I know not what kind of sacred object, than I make with mine. I find that I often repeat certain mental images until they become of *equal importance* in my litany with the original supplication; and indeed in certain cases—and I expect just this very thing occurs in the history of the human race—I would almost say they become of *more* importance than the original supplication. Every day while I hold my sponge in my hands, I become like a priest. I become a profane and secular version of what my son now is, who though still my child according to the flesh is my spiritual "father" according to the Church.

I like to think of the piety of our nature, thus binding me to my son and thus binding my father to me, as I squeeze my sponge. With the gesture of Pilate I wash my hands free

of the letter of the law, while I enjoy its fantastical spirit to
the limit. But it does so interest me to note the way in which
these mental rituals of our race originate, develop, harden,
crystallize, and finally—though in my case with one grand
fling I have flung most of it away—crumble into a poetic
memory. I imagine, as I squeeze my sponge, my father buying
The Spectator at that newspaper-stall in Weymouth Station
where I used to buy *Ally Sloper*. Then I imagine him leaving
the station with this periodical, folded in a neat roll, in his
hand. At this point in my profane Matins I always mutter the
words:

"Burdon bus rumble back to the Burdon! Gloucester bus
rumble back to the Gloucester!"

I first used the image of these two familiar horse vehicles
from the old days before motor-cars, in order to call up that
black-coated figure proceeding by the by-alleys he preferred
to the Esplanade, to make his way to Penn House. But after a
while the image of the two buses detached itself from its link
with the station or with my father leaving the station and
became an aerial equipage, "The Burdon bus" and "The
Gloucester bus," bowling along in phantom "tandem,"
through the ethereal spaces of thought.

Then I would visualize my father standing on the pebbles
outside Penn House holding *The Spectator* in a tight roll in his
hand; and I would think of *The Spectator* as containing—as
it might easily have done in those days—an essay on the
difference between Dr. Hort's view of the Second Person of
the Trinity and Bishop Westcott's. Then I would see my father
leaving *The Spectator* in the Penn House drawing-room and
emerging again with muffler and stick to walk to "The Coastguards." At this point, as I squeezed my sponge, my image
would take the shape of a certain little mother-of-pearl shell
that he used to find in the rock-pools out there. Then, making
him glance hurriedly at the clouds over Hardy's Monument,
I get him safe back to Penn House, and into his bedroom
looking out on St. John's Spire, to wash his hands. Finally my
mental image sees him seated at a solitary meal, with *The
Spectator* on the table beside him, a glimpse of "The Nothe"

accompanying every mouthful he takes, and a vision of Portland every sip of tea.

My favourite before-breakfast walk in this "up-state" home of mine was along the river by the edge of a spinney about half a mile from my house. To reach this I had to scramble along a little bank whose twisted tree-roots, emerging from the mud, reminded me of that higher bank at Sherborne above Lovers' Lane where I used to climb with Littleton. It pleased me to think that the skill I had acquired at eleven, in clinging to tree-roots on a sloping declivity, had remained with me to be used at sixty-one; but this was nothing to the pleasure I got when, walking along this river's edge, looking for trout or for the little fishes called "shiners," I suddenly thought of the Wissey and of the intense eagerness with which Littleton and I followed its windings looking for roach and dace. The sight of caddis-worms—those inch-long bundles of minute sticks animated by an invisible organism—always thrilled me with delight as I stared at this stream, and so did the reflections at its clear bottom of the long-legged water-flies. These reflections represented, like the mystical beasts in the Apocalypse, six legs, or rather four legs and two feelers, and at the end of each leg and at the end of each feeler there moved, as the creature moved, a dark moon rimmed with a silver rim.

As I shuffled along this river-path I used to listen to a little bird I privately named "Sir Witchit", for those were the exact syllables I heard this bird utter. The successor to my little house here, a man after my own heart, told me in a second what my "Sir Witchit" bird was. It was the yellow-throated Maryland warbler. It is a great handicap to me with birds, this unmusical ear of mine. I cannot fix their notes on my mind so as to recall them. Why, one afternoon when I lived at Burpham, I had no less than thirty different bird-notes interpreted to me as belonging to thirty different birds, whereas, beyond those of the blackbird and the thrush, all these sounds were just "birds in the bushes" to my ridiculous ignorance.

How do I differ from what I was twenty-nine years ago, when in 1905 I first sailed for America? Well, I think the chief difference, if I may say so, is a decided improvement in my character; not a brilliant one, not one that can be observed at the first glance, but still an improvement. Consider what I was when I contemplated with such deep astonishment the passionate absorption of Maurice Browne over the smallest æsthetic details in his presentation of *The Trojan Women*. I was more reckless, more sophisticated in those days, more dramatic and theatrical, than I am now. My Chicago Little Theatre life was indeed one continuous performance of the Actor in me. And what an exciting time it was! Everyone came to Maurice's Pedagogic Province. Floyd Dell brought Dreiser. Dreiser brought Masters, and I lectured upon them all, to them all! Arthur Ficke was always coming up from his "hometown," often bringing Witter Bynner with him, and Llewelyn Jones was constantly there. Maurice must have had a real genius for gathering people about him. But the Maurice I knew when I first met him, and perhaps the later Maurice too, but I cannot tell about that, were different from the Maurice of the Little Theatre time. The Maurice of the Little Theatre was a maniacal Messiah of theatrical art. In fact in this whole business of art—always to my rustic Arcadian nature a very ambiguous business—two persons alone have made really deep dents on my rough Derbyshire consciousness, Harry Lyon and Maurice Browne.

Both these people were fiery impassioned crusaders and both of them became, at certain epochs of my life, as far as *æsthetics* went, almost my whole world of environment and experience.

But the improvement in my character which I am now hoping to carry back to my native land has nothing to do with æsthetics. Neither the Renaissance countenance of Maurice Browne, nor the Bayeaux Tapestry countenance of Harry Lyon will gleam, I fear, with responsive ardour in the presence of the patient heraldry of my new Gonfalon. Of all men ever born into the world my father was the proudest, the most egoistic, and also the least interested in art, in literature, in philosophy! But, with all this, he was, as Hardy's Martie says of her Giles, "a good man and one who did good things."

With a nature like mine in which a magnetic fluidity, that

is neither "good" nor "bad," is forever taking new shapes under the pressure of circumstance—taking new shapes and then again, as Kwang makes Confucius complain of Laotze, "shooting up like a dragon"—it is not easy to weigh or measure any change in the core of character. All the same I *am* inclined to think that I have gained not a little by these long years of sojourn in America. I think it is to the advantage of most Englishmen to be forced out of the traditional grooves of their native life, and be compelled to cope with alien conditions in a foreign land. And in my case I think this prolonged experience has had the effect of forcing me back upon those rooted and simple elements of my father's character which made him, in spite of his obstinate egoism, a benevolent and righteous man.

But taking my life as a whole and hovering with the flight of a hawk over its variegated landscape, I believe that I detect certain quite definite "streams of tendency" in that unrolled map, moving towards the unknown future. For one thing, I fancy that the manner in which I have allowed my natural impulses towards romance and mysticism to dominate me has led to the formation of a curious gap or "lacuna," between the innate and almost savage realism, which after all *is* an element in my nature, and the imaginative, poetical cult, whereby I have romanticized and idealized my life. There *is* a vein of ferocious realism in me; into which, across the neutral No Man's Land of my suspended judgment, my soul at certain moments sinks headlong. And in this realistic mood of mine I am always grimly and starkly aware of the possibility that there is no such thing at all as this "rising to immortality and intense happiness" about which, following the cosmic instinct of Goethe, the Christian instinct of Dostoievsky, and *most of all* the secret tradition of the ancient Mysteries, I am forever muttering and gesticulating.

In this realistic mood I recognize with a grim animal acceptance that it is indeed likely enough that the "soul" perishes everlastingly with the death of the body. But what this realistic mood, into which my mind falls like a plummet through the neutral zone of its balanced doubt, never for one single beat of time can shake or disturb is my *certain knowledge,* derived from the "Complex Vision" of everything in me, that the whole astronomical universe, however illimitable, is only one part and parcel of the Mystery of Life. Of this I am *as certain as I am certain that I am I.* The astronomical universe is *not* all there is; but whether this certainty implies the survival of any portion or any degree of my own consciousness after death is a very different matter; and of this, I confess, I am *not* certain.

I derive an extraordinary satisfaction, not untouched by my curious "sacred malice"—in this case directed against the dogmatism of the Church as well as against the dogmatism of Science—from praying definitely to the Earth-Spirit under her ancient names of Demeter and Cybele. Every morning—and this I still continue, in spite of having suppressed so many of my practises—I pray to Demeter on behalf of Llewelyn, and also on behalf of all down-and-out persons in London; and I pray to Cybele on behalf of the two Littletons, and also on behalf of all down-and-out persons in New York. In this second prayer I never fail to add, thinking of Homer in connection with the negroes in Harlem, "for the sake of the blameless Ethiopians."

Now there is a path along the edge of the small stream flowing near this house where there grows an enormous and very ancient willow. To this aged tree I have given the mystic name of the "Saviour-Tree," and here and now I recommend to all harassed and worried people who can find in their neighbourhood such a tree—and it needn't necessarily be a willow—to use it as I do this one. For the peculiarity of this tree is that you can transfer by a touch to its earth-bound trunk *all* your most neurotic troubles! These troubles of yours the tree accepts, and absorbs them into its own magnetic life; so that henceforth they lose their devilish power of tormenting you. Of course we all of us only manage to live at all by means of our power of forgetting. This is Nature's supreme gift. To "live according to Nature" is to possess the power to forget. No "Saviour-Tree" can ever take the place of the precious Fountain of Lethe in ourselves; into which we can acquire the power of flinging our neurotic troubles; but, as I am hinting, a tree of this kind can at least serve as "an outward and visible sign of an inward and spiritual grace."

Another thing I have come to feel, as the result of my life-experiences in Weymouth, in Dorchester, in Sherborne, in Sussex, in America; and that is, that we must protect our imaginative individuality by every kind of cunning craftiness; and protect it too even while we are cultivating certain de-personalized primordial feelings that enable us to lose our superficial worries in what might be called the *poetic continuity* of the life of our race.

When, on that great flight of steps at Rome leading up from the Piazza del Spagna to the Pincian Hill, I suddenly got an ecstasy of mysterious exultation, in which I said to myself, "Let *me* pass and perish, as long as this magical stream of life, so noble in its heroic continuity, still goes on!" What I really did was to sink my own solitary personality in the innumerable personalities of all the men and women who for generations had gone up and down those historic steps. But this feeling has come over me, though in a less degree, in much humbler places. It has come over me in narrow lanes opening out suddenly upon the ancient peace of secluded hamlets; it has come over me as I have descended from the foothills of the Black Forest among old sloping-roofed German homesteads; it has come over me as I walked through the cobble-stone markets of Dieppe or gazed at the flying-buttresses of St. Ouen in Rouen; it has come over me as I followed the cliff-path from Brighton to Rottingdean, or the road from Cambridge to Shelford, or paused with Llewelyn by the time-worn "Stocks" under the century-polished elm-boles of Tintinhull, or followed some clover-scented cattle-track between Bognor and William Blake's Felpham.

Looking back over these fifty years, since the days when I jeered so rudely at that "Spanish Maiden" in the chestnut-walk at Dorchester, I am inclined to think that the two great electric currents of my life, the currents that have gathered and gathered their momentum beneath all the changes and chances of circumstance have been first the gradual discovering and the gradual strengthening of my inmost identity, till it can flow like water and petrify like a stone; and second the magic trick of losing myself in the continuity of the human generations. By this continuity I mean the way in which from father to son our life-sensations are handed down from the past, creating a sort of "eternal recurrence" of the poetic mystery of the *little-great* ritual, the daily acts by which we all must live.

These immemorial recurrences I have learnt how to appropriate to myself, just as if my soul had the actual trick of passing into the lives of the uncounted generations.

My father was an inarticulate man. I am an only too voluble one. My father was a man of rock. I am a worshipper of the wind. But now when from this resting-place, this ledge, this slab of stone, in the wavering Indian trail of my migrations and reversions, I look back at the path behind me and the path before me it seems as if it had taken me half a century merely to learn with what weapons, and with what surrender of weapons, *I am to begin to live my life.*

The astronomical world is *not* all there is. We are in touch with other dimensions, other levels of life. And from among the powers that spring from these *other levels* there rises up one Power, all the more terrible because it refuses to practise cruelty, a Power that is neither Capitalist, nor Communist, nor Fascist, nor Democratic, nor Nazi, a Power *not of this world at all*, but capable of inspiring the individual soul with the wisdom of the serpent and the harmlessness of the dove.

And thus it comes to pass, even while we are still in life, that when our soul loses itself in the long continuity of kindred lives, it does not lose itself in any power less gentle, less magical, less universal than itself, or less the enemy of cruelty; for what it finds is what it brings, and what it sees is what it is; and though the First Cause may be both good and evil, a Power has risen out of it against which all the evil in it and all the unthinkable atrocities it brings to pass are fighting a losing battle.

THE END

Index

Index   655